SAMS
Teach Yourself
UNIX® System Administration
in 21 Days

SAMS

A Division of Macmillan Computer Publishing
201 West 103rd St., Indianapolis, Indiana, 46290 USA

Sams Teach Yourself UNIX® System Administration in 21 Days
Copyright ©1999 by Sams Publishing

All rights reserved. No part of this book shall be reproduced, stored in a retrieval system, or transmitted by any means, electronic, mechanical, photocopying, recording, or otherwise, without written permission from the publisher.* No patent liability is assumed with respect to the use of the information contained herein. Although every precaution has been taken in the preparation of this book, the publisher and author assume no responsibility for errors or omissions. Neither is any liability assumed for damages resulting from the use of the information contained herein.

> * *Appendix F, "Useful Sample Forms," contains sample forms provided for the reader to copy and/or modify to suit his specific needs.*

International Standard Book Number: 0-672-31660-9

Library of Congress Catalog Card Number: 99-60905

Printed in the United States of America

First Printing: October 1999

01   00   99   4   3   2   1

Trademarks

All terms mentioned in this book that are known to be trademarks or service marks have been appropriately capitalized. Sams Publishing cannot attest to the accuracy of this information. Use of a term in this book should not be regarded as affecting the validity of any trademark or service mark.

UNIX® is a registered trademark of the Open Group.

Warning and Disclaimer

Every effort has been made to make this book as complete and as accurate as possible, but no warranty or fitness is implied. The information provided is on an "as is" basis. The authors and the publisher shall have neither liability or responsibility to any person or entity with respect to any loss or damages arising from the information contained in this book.

EXECUTIVE EDITOR
Dean Miller

DEVELOPMENT EDITOR
Laura Bulcher

MANAGING EDITOR
Lisa Wilson

PROJECT EDITORS
Sara Bosin
Tonya Simpson

COPY EDITOR
Kelly Talbot

INDEXER
Kevin Kent

PROOFREADER
Billy Fields

TECHNICAL EDITOR
Marijan Adam

INTERIOR DESIGN
Gary Adair

COVER DESIGNER
Aren Howell

COPY WRITER
Eric Borgert

LAYOUT TECHNICIAN
Darin Crone

Contents at a Glance

Appendixes   **597**

Table of Contents

About the Authors

JOAN RAY is a UNIX system administrator for the College of Biological Sciences at The Ohio State University. With an undergraduate degree in French from OSU, she started working on a Masters in French—but Joan got diverted somewhere along the way and, instead, is heading for the new millenium with the majority of two other degrees instead: one in Japanese and one in Geology.

Joan first started working for the College in 1990 as a secretary with a PC running DOS. Computers did not seem very interesting at that time, and she couldn't understand why her husband thought they were so much fun. Eventually, her turn for a computer upgrade in the office came, and she was introduced to the Macintosh. The computer world had changed forever! She had to get to work each day, just so that she could use her Mac. As time passed, she also began to find that many of her job duties were most easily accomplished using UNIX.

In 1997, her husband decided to leave the College's computing facility to concentrate more on his doctoral studies. To her surprise, the interview committee hired her as the replacement, and Joan began her training as a UNIX system administrator. With her husband as the trainer, it was a rather intensive training period. There was no rest, even at home.

Now, when Joan isn't writing this book or watching Babylon 5, she is busy administering a cluster of SGIs and Suns, helping users with UNIX questions, assisting users with manipulating data, and managing myriad graphics input and output hardware.

You can contact Joan via email at joray@biosci.ohio-state.edu.

WILLIAM RAY is a UNIX system administrator, programmer, and trainer. After acquiring a B.S. in Mathematics and an M.S. in Computer Science, Will spent five years getting paid to have fun—as a programmer building X Window System user interfaces. For the past six years, he has been perpetually two years away from attaining his Ph.D. in Biophysics. To maintain his sanity while arguing with test tubes and microbes, Will developed a computer-graphics center for The Ohio State University's College of Biological Sciences. Supporting an assortment of Silicon Graphics and Sun UNIX hardware, Will has been the center's system administrator, Webmaster, and acting director. He also has provided user support and UNIX training for several hundred students and faculty members who have come to use the center.

In a recent attempt to shorten the two-year graduation horizon, Will trained his wife to take over the center's administration. Although this seems to have shortened the graduation timeframe, he appears to be incapable of keeping his nose out of computer topics. So, he has been distracting himself by writing computer texts and pestering his wife about the center.

Will can be reached at ray@soyokaze.biosci.ohio-state.edu.

Dedication

To my husband, Will, for his continual support and encouragement.

Acknowledgments

Thanks to everyone who has helped with this intensive project! I would especially like to thank:

My husband, Will, for his work and enthusiasm on the project, no matter what the time of day.

John Ray, for his love of TCP/IP.

The American Library Association, for codifying a strong stance against information censorship and allowing the "Library Bill of Rights" to be reprinted in the book.

Carl M. Kadie, for researching and collecting examples of arbitrary Internet censorship and allowing the use of his "Sex, Censorship and the Internet" presentation in the book.

Marijan Adam, for being an excellent technical editor, a knowledgeable system administrator, and a sendmail guru.

Laura Bulcher and Sean Dixon, for keeping me on target and honest.

Ed Wahl, for being an IRIX guru.

Steve Romig, Mowgli Assor, and the rest of the OSU Security Group, for enlightening me on the inadequacies of the security through obscurity policy.

My brother, Ralph, for sending me email at the right time.

The cast of characters at Biological Sciences, for making every day an interesting, unique experience.

Introduction

Welcome to the world of UNIX system administration. Hang on to your hat—you're in for one heck of a ride!

UNIX system administration is hard. There's no other way to put it. For the introductory statement to a book in which I claim I'll teach you to do it in 21 days, that's probably a scary thing to read, but you're starting from the beginning, which is the right place to start. I wish I could tell you otherwise, and many books you encounter will in fact try to do so, but if I told you that system administration was easy, you'd be unprepared and discouraged when you learned the truth. Instead, start out with the premise that it's difficult and that you should consider your accomplishments as you read this book to be personal triumphs.

Why System Administration?

UNIX is a popular and quickly growing platform for both business and personal use. As a multitasking, multiuser OS, UNIX is ideal for creating network data servers, high-power computational support facilities, and multiuser cooperative environments.

Originally a cryptic and mostly text-based OS, with the advent of highly graphical user interfaces for personal computers, UNIX has also moved towards providing a user-friendly and intuitive environment.

Fortunately, if your goal is high-power computing, UNIX's "friendly face" is only a facade applied over an immensely powerful, completely configurable OS. If a computational problem is to be solved, a data source is to be served, or user facilities are to be provided, that can be done with UNIX. If you're a user, the new friendly face makes accessing all this power more convenient and pleasant.

Unfortunately, this friendly face tends to make the life of a system administrator more difficult. It does this in two ways. To some extent, this makes the job of a system administrator more difficult by burying under friendly menus and GUI dialogs the information needed to control and configure the machine, instead of keeping it in a few (perhaps cryptic, but at least centrally located) configuration files. Primarily however, it makes the job of the system administrator difficult by giving users and non-users alike the impression that UNIX is nearly as easy to operate as a personal computer.

Nothing could be further from the truth. UNIX is a vast and largely complicated environment. It takes a person with a deep understanding of the system and the ability to make decisions and modifications regarding the configuration of the system to keep the illusion of simplicity and user-friendliness alive. This person is the system administrator—the person granted complete control, and on whose shoulders complete responsibility rests, for a UNIX machine or cluster.

The unfortunate perception that this is a trivial task leads frequently to the job of system administrator being placed on the local "computer person," often with the expectation that this additional workload will not affect his primary responsibilities. It also leads to the belief that performing any given system administration task is as simple as clicking a button and corresponding misunderstandings with respect to reasonable job performance expectations.

For these reasons, there must be system administrators—people with the technical knowledge to keep everything running smoothly, a broad enough computing worldview to understand the range of effect implicit in a decision, and a thick enough skin to survive to do the job. These qualities are not universally present. It takes a special person to be able to do everything well, making good system administrators both a serious necessity and a rare commodity.

Why This Book?

System administration, when taught, instead of simply happening as a "sink or swim" proposition, is taught as a master/apprentice type profession. This training frequently lasts months, if not years, before a new and completely independent system administrator is born. Because you are reading this book, I will assume that you do not have the advantage of having a master under whom you can study or that you're looking for a leg up on the process.

In light of the fact that many new system administrators are not likely to be aware of exactly what they've gotten themselves into, I've chosen to write this book as a no-holds-barred look at the realities of system administration. This text contains anecdotes relating real-life security problems I've witnessed, metaphorical dragons I and others have fought, and windmills we have tilted at. Some are humorous, some are illustrative, and some are not pretty at all. They are all included here to give you an idea of just what you will be facing on a regular basis as a system administrator.

Many books on system administration attempt to be too many things to too many people. This book is not a compendium of every fact you could ever want to know about every possible flavor of UNIX. Nor is it a linear trek through the technical details of one particular flavor. Instead, I have tried to make the contents as generally applicable as possible, leaning towards selections that are illustrative of techniques rather than of specific details. To eliminate considerable redundancy and to make the contents as generally applicable as possible, I ha ded examples and illustrations that will lead you to the appropriate documentat your system or the appropriate online help forums that will enable you to fill in t details as they are appropriate for your local installation.

I will a you up front that certain claims that I make and some seeming facts that I stat book are actually simplifications of the truth. I've tried not to do this too fre but there are some situations that would require entire libraries (such as legal is cover with complete precision. In these cases, I've tried to give you the infor- that will most help you the most frequently. It should be sufficient to serve until e developed your own understanding to the point that you can see through my d-waving approximations.

arting the Journey

Because we don't have the luxury of having an apprenticeship relationship, I will endeav-or to give you the most important information in the 21 days that you will be spending with this book. As you begin reading, you might be surprised to find that this information is about evenly split between technical detail and philosophical discussion. As you are starting out, you might not find this choice intuitive. Technical details are probably of much more immediate concern to you than philosophy. This is the fist preconception that you must change on your journey into the world of the system administrator. Technical details are important, and I have tried to provide you with sufficient technical recipes so that you can create a functional, stable, and secure cluster of networked machines. You will, however, have a wealth of information in man pages, printed documentation, and online resources at your disposal. From these you can learn much more about any given technical detail than I could hope to cover in a book such as this. Much more important will be the administrative decisions that you make, the designs that you choose, and the reasons that you make them.

As much as I have tried to provide all the technical details you need to get started and to create a stable and secure system, I have also tried to give you a good foundation in the way that a successful system administrator thinks. Understanding and internalizing this and developing your own philosophical administrative model is your real goal in the next 21 days. For technical details, you can follow the recipes given here and accumulate more from other resources over time. In general, for technical issues, if you can make something work, it will work indefinitely. You probably won't have to worry about changing it, even if it's a less than perfect installation or configuration, for a long time. Less than well thought-out decisions about more philosophical issues, such as acceptable security requirements and personnel responsibility distribution, can come back to haunt you at the most inopportune times.

Who This Book Is For

This book is written primarily for the UNIX user who suddenly, through choice or circumstance, finds herself in the position of functioning as a system administrator. The focus is on system administration in a business or educational real-world context because this is the environment where there is the most at stake and the least room for error on the part of a system administrator.

The casual user who would like to install and administer a UNIX or Linux variant at home can benefit from this book as well. The technical recipes provided are designed to be a quick road to a system that is more stable and secure than many professionally administered systems. Additionally, although the philosophical discussion might not seem to be immediately relevant, there is a never-ending demand for skilled professional system administrators. This is largely due to the high system-administrator turnover rate caused by the rapid burn-out of administrators who were not prepared for the rigors of the job or who did not understand the importance of issues beyond the technical ones.

Given the high turnover rate and the corresponding high demand, the home-taught administrator can easily turn her skills into a potential career. The home-taught administrator who comes to the interview with an understanding of the philosophy and the corporate politics of system administration stands a much better chance of both getting and prospering in the position.

Under-level UNIX administrators, such as maintenance administrators charged only with user-account maintenance or backup handling, who are looking to expand their skill set for promotion or their own interest, can also benefit from this book. If you're in this position, be aware that your pre-existing corporate administrative policies might disagree with what I consider to be good policy. Make certain you understand your corporate administrative philosophy and read this book in the context of it. The philosophy that I cover tends towards the utopian side from the point of view of a system administrator. Sometimes the practical realities of the business world prevent the realization of this goal.

What You Need to Know

The reader of this book is expected to bring with him a reasonable understanding of UNIX, though it is quite possible for an occasional user to learn UNIX and administration in rapid succession. If you choose this approach, I highly recommend *Sams Teach Yourself UNIX in 10 Minutes*. It provides a conveniently quick introduction to UNIX essentials and the UNIX way of thinking that dovetails nicely with the contents of this book.

How to Use This Book

This book is divided into 21 one-day lessons. It's somewhat important that you attempt to read them each in order and perform the day's tasks as you encounter them. Each day's material builds on what you read and what you did in the previous lessons. The 21 lessons and activities are further roughly broken down into three intervals of one week each:

- **Week One: Days 1–7**   The first week's reading will take you through an installation of your OS and drench you in the philosophy of UNIX administration and the system administrator's way of thinking.

- **Week Two: Days 8–14**   The second week's topics will take you through several software installations and the process of securing your machines. You will also learn about real-life security horror stories, the decisions you need to make, and policies you need to enforce to avoid them yourself.

- **Week Three: Days 15–21**   By the third week, you will be adding useful functional enhancements to your machine. You finish up with a troubleshooting guide to the most common problems I've observed and get a final overview of system administrator good behavior.

Each chapter is followed by a question and answer section, detailing some of the common questions on the material covered, and by a quiz and exercises where appropriate. Where given, the exercises are entirely appropriate activities for you to be doing with your system and your time. They are things that you should, as a system administrator, be doing with your machines and your users. They have been included as suggestions of the sorts of things that you should be doing with the portion of your day that isn't occupied with following the lesson proper.

I highly recommend that you read through each lesson before starting any of the activities. I've tried to avoid including any "…but before you do that, remember to configure…" gotchas, but you never can tell. Real, live software documentation contains these more frequently than you will like, so consider it good practice to read everything before starting.

From Your Author

In many ways, I've written this book for myself. That is to say, although I learned system administration as an apprenticeship, this book contains a compendium of everything that I wish that I had known beforehand when I was just starting out. It is, therefore, very much a written record of a slice of life from a working administrator's point of view.

Having seen other new administrators struggle through exactly the issues and topics I've presented here, in order, almost as if rehearsing a script, when Sams approached me I was enthusiastic about the prospect of providing this information as a resource for other "just starting" administrators.

The techniques and recipes I lead you through in your installations and configurations are a compilation of the post-it notes that adorn most post-it–able surfaces in my office— translated, hopefully, into a form that is generally useful.

The issues and philosophy that I discuss were either given to me by my predecessor or learned through real trials in the field. Many of the points I have tried to make are things that I was told. A reasonable fraction are things that I was told, but that in my naiveté, I initially did not or would not believe.

In time, I have come to understand that there are certain things that one simply accepts as gospel when told by a veteran system administrator. The meaning or purpose might not be clear or might even seem to fly in the face of current reason, but that which initially appears to be overt paranoia, superstition, or plain old pedantic stubbornness, has proven itself time and time again to be pearls of wisdom only waiting for the right moment to shine. As it was put from one veteran system administrator to a newer administrator who was displaying slightly too much naive faith, "It's clear to everyone here except yourself that you just aren't quite smart enough yet."

I won't try to claim, in the shadow of the truly veteran administrators, that I'm smart enough yet, but I have gotten smart enough to listen.

The most important thing I have heard and the most important thing for you to take away from this book is that system administration is not a science, not a technique or a job, and not even an art form. System administration is an attitude and a way of thinking. Essentially, system administration is a respect for the power of your administrative access, an understanding and embracing of your reasons for doing the job, a large dose of paranoia regarding the consequences of mistakes, an inexhaustible enthusiasm for technical challenges, and a healthy sense of humor, all stirred into a brimming pot of ego and belief in your own resourcefulness and abilities.

If you come to the world of system administration with the right attitude or can develop it as you go, nothing can stop you, and you can pick up the technical details along the way. If you let the challenges of system administration intimidate you or the realities of dealing with your users drag you down, you are most likely doomed.

Welcome to the world of system administration. If the contents of these pages can't scare you away, in three weeks you'll have a stable and secure system that you can be proud of, and you will be well on your way to being a great system administrator.

Best of luck and best wishes,

Joan Ray

joray@biosci.ohio-state.edu

Conventions Used in This Book

This book uses the following conventions:

- Web addresses, screen input and output, commands, filenames, and information you type appears in monospace.
- Placeholders for text that you enter in code appear within <monospace>.
- The Return key is synonymous with the Enter key.

Tip

The Tip icon offers advice, teaches an easier way to do something, or explains an undocumented feature.

Note

The Note icon presents interesting tidbits of information related to the surrounding discussion.

Caution

The Caution icon helps you steer clear of disaster, alerts you to potential problems, or warns you when you should not skip a task.

WEEK 1

At a Glance

The first week explains installation of your operating system and presents a bit of the philosophy of UNIX administration and the system administrator's mode of thought.

- Day 1, "What Is System Administration?," starts you off on the right foot and gets you started thinking like a system administrator.
- Day 2, "Designing Your Cluster: From Planning to Policy," exposes you to many factors you must consider before making system administration decisions.
- Day 3, "Setting Up a Machine: From the Box to the Desktop," walks you through such things as assembling machine hardware, installing procedures, and patching operating systems.
- Day 4, "A Stroll Through Your System," gives you a break after some intense days and takes you on a tour of your machine.
- Day 5, "On Root's Best Behavior," gives you an important overview of your responsibilities as root.
- Day 6, "Deciding What Kind of Software to Install: Free Versus Commercial," looks at some of the decisions you'll need to make when choosing software to install on your system.
- Day 7, "The Most Important Accessory: The C Compiler gcc," introduces you to installing tools that you will need throughout the upcoming two weeks, and ongoing as a system administrator.

1

2

3

4

5

6

7

DAY 1

What Is System Administration?

Welcome to *Sams Teach Yourself UNIX System Administration in 21 Days*! This chapter gets you started thinking like a system administrator by introducing you to UNIX administration and some of the responsibilities of the UNIX administrator—some of which don't fall into the obvious fiddling with hardware and software as you might expect. Today you will learn the following:

- The proper relationship between the administrator and the machine—know who's the boss.

- Why system administrators exist—remember, system administration is a service position.

- All the worst things about system administration—get the not-fun stuff out of the way first!

So you've just become a system administrator (or maybe you've been nominated). What have you gotten yourself into? Just what is system administration anyway? In this chapter, you'll get an overview of what the system administrator can and should do. You'll also get what will hopefully be a slightly sobering introduction to some of the realities of being a system administrator. "Great," you're thinking, "let's just start off telling horror stories!" As negative as this might initially sound, it isn't really intended to scare you away from the task. System administration can be a stimulating and enjoyable job for the technically inclined and the puzzle-solver. It also can have its trying moments; you'll be better prepared to avoid difficult situations or to deal with them if they do occur if you go in with your eyes open.

Even if you're just going to be administrating a machine for your own use and won't have users other than yourself, with a networked UNIX machine, there is a considerable amount of responsibility. Whatever your situation, a well-planned and well-maintained system will be easier and more pleasant to use, be more stable, and if worse comes to worse, cause fewer problems than a poorly maintained one.

That being said, take a look at what you can do to make your system as good as it can be. For starters, today's lesson covers some of the problems you're likely to encounter and hopefully gives you a few things to think about that might help you minimize them. Don't be too surprised if some of these issues are ones that you haven't thought of as things to be concerned about. System administrators wear many coats, and in this book I'll be trying to at least give you an introduction to all of them. Tomorrow, you'll learn about planning your installation and about the larger issue of planning an entire facility.

General Overview: UNIX and You

Before you get into details on system administration, you will first take a brief look at UNIX and you—and how you work together.

The Flavors of UNIX

UNIX is a powerful operating system available in many "flavors" at a variety of prices. UNIX originated as a research project at AT&T Bell Labs in the late 1960s. A research group at the University of California, Berkeley followed this with its own flavor of UNIX. Since then, a multitude of hardware vendors have developed UNIX varieties for their machines, and others have developed UNIX varieties as standalone cross–hardware-platform products. These have typically been based on the AT&T or BSD flavors, with minor modifications or enhancements. Most recently, Linux has entered the arena. It was initially a student's pet project and is now maintained by a worldwide community of volunteers.

It is regularly improved upon by the UNIX community. This freely available version of UNIX seems to be gaining popularity as an alternative to some personal-computing operating system (OS) products.

As you start working with different machines and software, you will notice the different UNIX varieties: the System V (AT&T) flavors and the BSD flavors. Is one style better than the other? This question about UNIX is beyond the scope of this book (and is frequently the source of less-than-friendly discussions between proponents of different flavors). Right now, all that is really important is to be aware that these differences exist. From a practical standpoint, System V and BSD UNIX are much like different models of cars. As with cars, if you know how to drive one, you can probably figure out how to drive another. With different UNIX flavors, some files might not be where you first look, and some of the commands and/or their options might vary. The general idea, however, is the same, and with a little experience, you'll be able to find your way around almost any new UNIX you meet without adding more than a few new gray hairs.

The UNIX Philosophy

No matter what flavors of UNIX you are using, you will find that they have a lot in common. UNIX provides a powerful multiuser, multitasking environment. Key to much of this power is one of the common themes you will notice about UNIX, the concept of abstraction—abstraction of what things are, of where things are, and more. UNIX as an operating system tries to "keep things simple," and this results in such things as a single abstract model for accessing data. A user on a UNIX machine can access a file on a local disk, on a disk belonging to a machine in another room, or from a machine half the world away and never be aware of the difference. Regardless of the differences in the way that the operating system must actually deal with accessing each of these files for the user, it abstracts the user experience so that it all appears identical. As a user, you might not notice a lot of this abstraction—that's because UNIX is so good at it! But as a system administrator, it's important to keep some of it in mind.

Look at the multiuser and multitasking features of UNIX; many users can run many processes at the same time. Although only one user might actually be sitting in front of a machine, there could be many users who are connected to the machine from locations across the globe. UNIX abstracts the user experience so that to every user, the machine appears to be devoted to his use.

Files are another important concept in UNIX—everything is basically seen as a file— plain text files, programs, even hardware connected to the machine looks to the user like a file. Again, UNIX abstracts the idea of things that can be read from, stored to, or manipulated as being represented by files.

UNIX handles the arrangement of and access to these files by considering them all to be part of a hierarchical tree, with the *root* directory (/) at the top.

Note

Roots at the top? You might initially be more comfortable thinking of the root directory as being at the bottom of the tree—just like real roots on real trees. Try not to get into the habit of thinking this way. Most UNIX users and administrators will talk about root as being at the top and other directories as being under it. You're likely to confuse both yourself and any users on your system if you try to change this slightly odd custom. Just think of your trees as being upside down for now, and trust that all this will be second nature in no time.

If you were to look at the contents of the root directory (/) on a machine, you might get something like the following:

```
WAASHU joray 208 > ls -l /
    total 30655
    drwxr-xr-x    4 root       sys           35 Dec 31 09:08 1a
    drwxr-xr-x    3 root       sys           42 Feb 10 15:14 1b
    drwxr-xr-x    4 root       sys           46 Mar  2 10:37 1c
    drwxr-xr-x    2 root       sys            9 Dec 29 13:21 CDROM
    drwxr-xr-x    2 root       sys           90 Dec 29 13:21 Desktop
    lrwxr-xr-x    1 root       sys            7 Dec 29 09:57 bin -> usr/bin
    lrwxr-xr-x    1 root       sys            4 Dec 29 13:04 debug -> proc
    drwxr-xr-x   14 root       sys         4096 Feb 19 12:00 dev
    drwxr-xr-x    2 root       sys           27 Dec 29 13:21 dumpster
    drwxr-xr-x   16 root       sys        12288 Mar  2 11:44 etc
    drwxr-xr-x    2 root       sys            0 Mar  3 15:49 hw
    drwxr-xr-x    2 root       sys          109 Feb 11 11:56 lib
    drwxr-xr-x    2 root       sys           58 Feb 11 11:47 lib32
    drwxr-xr-x    2 root       sys           21 Feb 11 11:22 lib64
    drwxr-xr-x    5 root       sys           53 Feb  3 15:33 net
    drwxr-xr-x    1 root       sys           21 Feb 11 12:28 ns
    drwx------    2 root       sys            9 Jan  6 18:35 nsmail
    drwxr-xr-x    7 root       sys          512 Feb 10 16:26 old_local_share
    drwxr-xr-x    8 root       sys          101 Dec 29 11:49 opt
    drwxr-xr-x    2 root       sys          142 Dec 29 16:42 patches
    dr-xr-xr-x    2 root       sys         8880 Mar  3 15:49 proc
    drwxrwsrwx    8 bioftp     ftponly     1536 Mar  3 10:23 public
    drwxr-xr-x    2 auditor    sys            9 Dec 29 09:57 sat
    drwxr-xr-x    3 root       sys         4096 Feb 11 11:58 sbin
    drwxr-xr-x    2 root       sys           20 Feb 11 11:20 stand
    drwxrwxrwt    4 sys        sys         4096 Mar  3 15:45 tmp
    -rwxr-xr-x    1 root       sys      7826552 Feb 11 12:27 unix
    -rwxr-xr-x    1 root       sys      7820532 Feb 10 14:53 unix-old
    drwxr-xr-x   47 root       sys         4096 Mar  2 10:02 usr
    drwxr-xr-x   33 root       sys         4096 Jan 22 11:29 var
```

It all pretty much looks the same, doesn't it? The directories `/1a`, `/1b`, and `/1c` are partitions on a second drive. If you were to look at the actual device name for one of those partitions, you would learn that on this machine it is `/dev/dsk/dks1d5s0`. You'd also see that `/CDROM` is the machine's CD-ROM drive. Also, `/public` isn't even physically located on this machine; it's on a different machine in another room! Remember, UNIX abstracts things; the entries for the external drive, the CD-ROM, and `/public` are good examples of this. They're different physical devices, and one's even a drive on another machine that's being shared, but UNIX shows them all to you as files and directories.

Note

Don't worry if setting up all this abstraction sounds intimidating right now. Later chapters of this book will cover in great detail putting together just such a system. After you've done one or two installations following the lessons, you'll be able to do them in your sleep!

As a user new to administration, remember that there might be places where, due to UNIX's powers of abstraction, things might not be as they seemed when you were a normal user.

The System Administrator

Ever wondered what it would be like to have god-like powers? You, the system administrator, get pretty close. As system administrator, you can become root, the superuser. When you are logged on as root, you have supreme power over your system. You can create and remove user accounts. You can kill your users' processes. You can change your users' passwords. You can become one of your users without even knowing her password. You can fix the system when it breaks. Also, unfortunately, you can be your own worst enemy: You can accidentally wipe out your own system. Effective system administration requires a certain mindset—one that is a mix of a firm belief in your own supremacy in your domain and a healthy respect for the power and apparent capriciousness of both the machines and people with which you must interact.

Note

Both the top-level directory of the filesystem and the superuser, or system administrator, are called "root" in the UNIX world. The phrase "become root" means to log in as or change user IDs to be the superuser. The phrase "go to root" means to change directories to the top-level directory of the system.

A stern word of caution   Do not enter into the role of system administrator lightly. This statement is not meant to intimidate, but if it should intimidate you, consider whether you're really ready for the job. Remember that system administration is as much a state of mind as it is a job. The task of system administration can be highly enjoyable and stimulating because you can tweak your system to be the absolute epitome of what you want in a computer. It can also be amazingly time-consuming, frustrating, and thankless as you fight to correct seemingly untraceable problems that your users don't even know that the system has.

Remember that if you're going to be administrating a system that supports other users, you have a responsibility to them to keep the system up and stably running. Actions you will have to take will frequently not be understood by your users or will, although in their best interest, not be to their wishes. It's crucial that you're emotionally ready to deal with users who actively work against you even when you have their best interests in mind.

Be aware that if your machine is networked, you have a responsibility to others on your network to maintain your machine in a secure fashion. A security breach on your machine can compromise the security of others machines on the same network as well as that of your users. As the system administrator, you *do not* have the option of procrastinating when dealing with such things.

Basically, keep in mind that along with the god-like powers come associated responsibilities. This book provides you with lessons to train you to deal with the technical issues and to guide you through setting up a system with a high level of security and stability, but the responsibility has to come from you.

Working Together

How does the superuser tame a powerful operating system? How does a powerful operating system thwart the superuser? You will find it to be more of a symbiotic relationship. When you put in the time and effort to make your system work well, it will be stable instead of biting the hand that maintains it. If you try to take administrative shortcuts, expect that they will eventually catch up to you. Most importantly, remember who is in charge. You're root. As far as the machine is concerned, you can do anything! If there's a problem with something, don't be afraid to use that power to get in there and fix it.

Tasks of the System Administrator

What does a system administrator do? The system administrator makes it all work! To accomplish this amorphous goal, the system administrator has to perform a variety of tasks, ranging from installing software to moving furniture. Take a peek at some of what the future has in store for you:

- **Installing software**—You probably guessed this one. As your machine or facility acquires more software, it will be your job to install it, to test what can be tested, and to let your users know when it's ready for them to try. Some software packages require that you be root at installation time, whereas others explicitly do not. Of course, your users can also install software in their home directories. However, some users might not want to have software taking up some of their allotted disk space. It might be that the software would be useful to many users and would be best installed in a central location by you.

- **Adding/removing users**—As people start to hear about the wonderful software available at your facility, they will ask you if they can have an account. Assuming that they meet whatever eligibility criteria your facility has established, it is your job to create accounts for them. Conversely, as people leave, it is also your job to remove inactive accounts taking up space and creating security risks.

- **Adding/removing devices**—As you continue to add more useful software and more enthusiastic users to your system, you will eventually have to add more disk space to accommodate them. Unfortunately, the disks that your original users are on will eventually stop working, and you will also have to remove disks. Printers are probably the other most common device you will handle.

- **Dragging network cables**—Sometimes, this is a bit more like spelunking (crawling around in caves). As shown in Figure 1.1, dragging network cables around over dropped ceilings, through maintenance access crawlways, and along old asbestos-coated ductwork is one of the less pleasant physical jobs of the system administrator. On the other hand, if your building is on the older side, you're likely to be the first person who's seen some of these places since it was built. If you're the adventurous type, that might be all the inspiration you need, and you never know what sort of interesting things you might find.

Tip

Be a little careful around the lighting and electrical fixtures when you're installing network cables. You never know how well insulated the fixtures are, which can be a danger to you. Also, in some instances, you might find that some electrical systems and fluorescent lights give off enough electrical noise to cause problems if network cables are too close.

- **Adding/removing machines**—As your facility continues to grow, you will hopefully have the opportunity to add new machines. With any luck, you will also be allowed to get rid of an old one or two. Because of the limited budget granted to the facility where I work, I haven't had the opportunity to do this yet, but I imagine it to be a very pleasant experience! (Author's note: Between the time of initial writing and this book going to press, I finally got to retire one of our seven-year old SGI machines. I was right—a wonderful day!)

FIGURE 1.1

Dragging network cables around a building that wasn't designed to accommodate them is an adventure in and of itself.

- **Interior design**—As your facility grows, someone might decide (or you might have to convince someone) that the computers-in-a-closet look is no longer in vogue. When this decision is made, guess whose job it is to design the new space? Yes, it's the system administrator's! Be sure to keep graph paper, rulers, a tape measure, and colored pencils on hand; you'll need them when you're figuring out how to run your network cable and how far you can stretch that printer cable too. Hopefully, you'll have some help in moving the furniture around. The right furniture can make all the difference in the usability of your system and the pleasantness and professionalism of your facility. Figure 1.2 shows what the facility that I manage looked like before a facelift. As you can see, the work areas are cluttered, and frankly, it looks like a disaster area. In our facility, we recently shed our computers-in-a-closet look for the modular furniture and partitions shown in Figure 1.3. Even though we still have lime-green chairs, the room looks much better.

For some of you, interior design might be your first major task. You might initially think that investing the money in something like modular furniture for a computer facility is a bad idea; this much furniture could have almost bought another CPU. On the other hand, you'll find that your users really appreciate an environment that looks professional and is neatly maintained. An added benefit is that with furniture that's designed for computers, users have a lot more difficulty accidentally kicking the wiring and pulling the network or power patch-cord out.

FIGURE 1.2

Bad interior design— who would want to work here?

FIGURE 1.3

Modular furniture makes it a lot easier to run network and power wiring around the designed-in wire trays and through the wire access ports.

- **Fiddling with the guts of machines**—Hopefully, you won't have to do this too often, but you will have to open your machines once in a while. Sometimes, you might need to open the machine to add memory, which isn't as stressful as opening the machine that functions as your Web server to add memory to it. Some of the drives you might have to add or remove might be internal drives. Whatever the reason, there will come a time when you have to open the machines. Please take extra caution when you do this. Safety precautions such as grounding strips are a good idea: The likelihood of you being that 1 person in 1,000 who zaps a memory chip when handling it increases proportionally with the importance of the machine you're working on. If something goes wrong, you are not the only one who will notice. Figures 1.4, 1.5, and 1.6 give you some idea of what to expect when you open your machines to add memory. You'll notice that Figure 1.6 shows a Macintosh. Even though you are the UNIX system administrator, users know you as the "computer expert": If something breaks, you probably get to fix it.

FIGURE 1.4

Installing memory on a Sun Sparcstation IPC—the memory is identical to 30-pin 9-chip PC memory.

FIGURE 1.5

Installing memory in a Sun Sparcstation 5—the SIMMs look almost identical to the PC SIMMS shown sitting on the envelope, but they are not interchangeable.

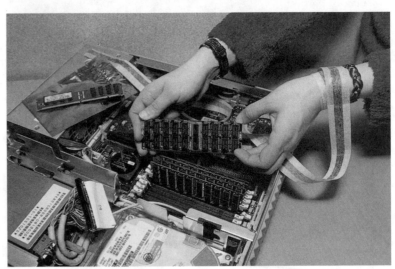

FIGURE 1.6

As system administra-
tor, you're likely to
have to explore many
types of hardware.

1

- **Monitoring the system**—Not everything you will do is as grandiose as adding or removing a machine or as stressful as tearing into the innards of one. You will also perform more basic duties, such as monitoring your system. This includes such tasks as checking the logs to make sure nothing out of the ordinary is happening and making sure you have adequate disk space available. Regularly monitoring your system enables you to catch potential problems before they become major problems.

- **Performing backups**—One of your users has just told you that the file he was using was there, and now all of a sudden it is not. Of course, he didn't do anything to cause the file's disappearance, and needless to say, it was an important file that he needs you to get back for him. Yes, performing regular backups is also part of your job. Even if you don't care about your user's important file, remember that it could be one of your files or, worse yet, that directory that you accidentally removed while trying to fix something.

- **Assisting users**—You and UNIX might have a symbiotic relationship, but there is little point to having the relationship if there aren't any users on your system. Your users' needs (presuming you're administrating a machine for other than personal use) are the reason you're there as an administrator. Users aren't going to know everything about your system without your help. Of course, your users will also come up with a variety of their own original problems—some you can help them with and others you can't. You should be able to help your user use the text editor vi to carry out her assignment to create a file with a bunch of numbers in it, but when she asks, "What do these numbers mean?" don't be troubled if you don't know.

- **Troubleshooting**—You'll be the problem-solver for everything from programs that mysteriously succumb to "bit-rot," to bugs in the operating system, to assisting users with problems they have, to the results of careless or malicious actions. Your tools include the collected knowledge of the Usenet newsgroups and the Web, which are indispensable for dealing with system and software problems, the question "What did you change?" which will frequently have to be applied to users multiple times before producing the desired effect, and more.

- **The mundane**—Remember, you do everything to make it all work. Don't want someone to walk away with your original copy of the manuals? Don't trust anyone to change the toner in the laser printer, let alone in the $10,000 photo-quality printer? Don't like discovering that you're out of DAT tapes right as you need to run that all-important backup before you have to tear down the system? Photocopying, changing toner, and ordering basic supplies are all included in the mundane tasks that you will have to perform as the system administrator.

- **The rest**—You will also have to do everything else that is not listed here but that is necessary to make it all work—"Other responsibilities as assigned," as they say.

The Responsibilities of Root

Root, the superuser, has certain responsibilities that only root can handle. You will be amazed at the number of processes that root is running—many that you as the root user did not consciously generate but that you, by turning on the machine and installing an operating system, did in fact generate.

Root has other responsibilities that you will become more familiar with, including the following:

- Rebooting/shutting down the machine
- Mounting/unmounting filesystems
- Exporting/unexporting filesystems
- Making filesystems
- Adding devices
- Configuring the machine

Root can also perform certain tasks for a user that otherwise only the user can perform, such as the following:

- Changing a user's password.
- Changing the ownership of a user's file.

- Changing the priority of a user's process. (Well, the user is privileged enough to be able to lower the priority of their own process, but only root can raise it again.)
- Accessing files that have permissions set to be otherwise accessible to the owner only.

You, as root, probably will not find much use for most of root's more user-related capabilities, except for the capability to change a user's password. Even that is not especially useful to you, but regardless of how many times you tell them to carefully memorize them, users will forget their passwords. It is your responsibility, after they have sufficiently proven that they are who they say they are, to reset their passwords so that they can again access their accounts.

Expectations as Root

Just as you have certain obligations to perform as root, if you are to do your job effectively, there are certain expectations that you should be able to have of your users and facility.

Maintaining Copies of Critical Software

A problem could develop that becomes so large that the best solution is to wipe your machine clean and reinstall everything, including the operating system. For you to successfully carry out this task, you will need to have access to an actual copy of the operating system. Don't rely on borrowed copies of site-licensed software, and don't let your boss get away with "we'll get one when we need it." When you need it, you'll have 20 users with projects that have to be done *now*, and the software you need will be checked out of the corporate library for a week.

Maintaining Copies of Documentation

Yes, the printed documentation costs money, and it's available in electronic form on your OS CD-ROM. Still, you'll have a tough time reading that CD when you system is down and you need it the most. If keeping the system up is important, then it's worth buying the printed documentation to keep on the shelf. If it's short enough to print conveniently from an electronic version, this is an acceptable option. Don't, however, fall into the trap of wasting more time than the printout is worth—printing the thousands of pages typical of OS documentation will absorb much more time and resources than simply buying it in the first place.

Buying Hardware

You will find that as you get more specialized UNIX hardware, more specialized peripherals might be required to make everything work in harmony. If a Sun CD-ROM drive
works best with a Sun system, make sure your organization gets you the Sun CD-ROM
drive. Just because a machine might take memory that seems like it ought to be the same
kind as what a PC can take, don't let your company buy that cheaper memory. Make sure
they get what will indeed work.

Setting and Sticking to Policies

One example of setting and sticking to policies is requiring ID when users apply for
accounts or change passwords. If a user walks in your door and asks you to reset his
password, you should require him to provide verification of his identity before you
change his password. Don't be concerned that you'll get a reputation as a hard-nose: You
will. It's much better to be a hard-nose though than to be a "nice guy" and have some
disgruntled technician take advantage of the fact that you don't know him, allowing him
to change a co-worker's password with malicious intent.

Requiring Access and Authority

If you have a security problem with a machine, you need the autonomy and authority to
deal with them quickly and effectively. Don't let yourself be put in a situation where you
have to leave a compromised machine up and causing problems just because you either
can't get to the hardware—maybe you need keys to wherever systems you're administrating are kept or, as one reference on system security suggests, a good fire axe—or can't
get the right signature to allow a shutdown.

Finding a Programmer

You're the system administrator. You'll likely have your hands full keeping your machine
up and running smoothly. You probably won't want to spend a bunch of time learning to
program in C, C++, Java, Perl, and the dozen other languages you'll meet along the way.
If you're trying to install a piece of software, many of which involve compiling from
source code, and it just won't work, it's time to find an expert. Don't waste your time
trying to do another expert's job. It's a two-way street, though, so remember to install
the latest version of the compiler for her promptly when she asks the next time.

Remembering Root is Singular

There might be multiple users with administrative authority for your cluster of machines,
but when one of you is logged in as root, there should be only one of you logged in as
root. Too many cooks spoil the soup, and too many roots stepping on each other's toes

can quickly turn a system to chaos. Don't put yourself in a situation where there are dozens of normal users who also happen to have root access "just in case." The less reason they have to actually be root, the less time they'll spend logged on in a state where one mistyped command can erase the entire system.

Effective System Administrators

The job task list you review in this chapter probably seems a bit overwhelming. Just how do you effectively do all that?

Essentially, you will have to find a balance between the machines' best interests and your users' best interests. You have to keep your machines running in a stable condition and as bulletproof to the world as you can make them. At the same time, you have to provide useful software and services to your users so that they can be productive. The users aren't there to praise your everlasting power; rather, you are there to make things run as smoothly as possible for them.

In the process, you will have to make decisions that will make you unpopular. You can try to make each user happy, but inevitably, something that makes one user happy will not make another happy. Believe it or not, some users will actually thank you for some of the unpopular decisions you will have to make, whereas others will accuse you of trying to ruin their research careers and will try to have you fired. How does this all balance out when it's employee review time? I can't tell you that yet because our department just implemented a new performance-rating system that does not seem to take into account that not every job is a popularity contest. Hopefully, you won't be found in a similar situation.

Okay, now that you are probably appropriately fearful and respectful of what can happen out there, how do you deal with it? The best advice for some of it is to choose the route that leads to the fastest solution. Don't make hasty decisions, but your users are depending on you keeping things running smoothly. As a result, you can't always afford to research and ponder each problem looking for a perfect solution. In system administration, a good solution now is frequently better than a better solution later. Here are some examples:

- Having a problem compiling something because you don't know C? Find that programmer who is at your disposal and have him take a look at it for you. The problem you're having might have its roots in the operating system itself.

- You've been told that your machines are causing security problems on another set of machines, but you haven't been given a copy of their logs, and your logs indicate no trouble at all. Nothing out of the ordinary appears to be happening on your machines, yet other evidence suggests there has been some sort of breach of security. You could spend forever trying to track down what might be the problem on your machines, continuing to expose them to the world, and exposing your users' files to possible damage at the same time. Without further information, your best course of action might be to wipe the machines clean and start over. This might take a little longer than your users might like, but it's in their and the machines' best interests.

- Something that was working yesterday isn't working today, and you've investigated everything you can think of. (Did you check the applicable log files?) Don't spin your tires looking at the same things over and over again. If you have a system administration guru at your disposal, ask her. If not, check briefly through your reference books in case they mention something, and then check the newsgroups.

- You're having a problem installing some commercial software. Look at the documentation. If you can't decipher the documentation or if the problem isn't documented, don't even waste your guru's time asking her; go directly to the vendor. You paid good money for the software, and with it should come support: Use it. Reserve your guru for those special occasions when there's no one else to ask.

What about your system's users? They all think that their requests are the most important, and in a way they're right: They are, after all, the reason that you're maintaining the system. How do you accommodate the user requests? You or your facility will have to establish a system and consistently follow that system. Here are some examples:

- Your facility is part of a university whose mission includes both teaching and research. During a time when a class is using your machines to complete an assignment, one of your researchers is taking up a license for the program that the class needs to use, rendering one of your machines useless, as far as the class is concerned. What do you do? If your facility has decided that the needs of a class (many users) have priority over the needs of individuals, you will have to inform the researcher of this policy and ask him to relinquish the license for the time being.

- A user has walked into your office and proceeds to demand that some piece of software be installed this week, or else. At the same time, a piece of software that an entire research group needs has just arrived and also has to be installed this week. What do you do? If you've done your homework, your facility will already have a policy detailing the proper procedure for user software requests—one that says that you accept requests, not demands. If your facility has decided that the needs of a research group have priority over the needs of an individual, you will have to inform your user that your facility has to serve many users and that software package of interest to her will be handled as quickly as possible. You might want to practice doing this as pleasantly as possible because everybody's project is the absolute top priority. If you don't have a policy yet, start thinking about one as soon as possible because this situation is probably on its way to your office as you read this.

- One of your users comes to you asking advice about buying a new UNIX machine for his office. You have two choices: Either let him put a separately (and possibly questionably) administrated machine on the network, or offer support for his machine in return for him making it available as part of the general cluster that you maintain. If at all possible, opt for the latter. Independently maintained systems attached to your network will, over time, be a neverending source of security problems and other assorted trouble for you. If you're already maintaining several machines, adding another to the collection isn't a large addition to your workload, and it reduces potential future problems, solves the problem of administration for your user, and adds more power to the cluster of machines you administrate. It's a win-win situation.

- An amazingly annoying user—say she is verbally abusive, tracks potato-chip crumbs into your office, takes up all your disk-space, heck, the three billy goats would rather meet the troll on the bridge than this person—needs a software package. One of your more polite users happens to need something else at the same time. Which one do you install first? Of course, that all depends on what priorities your facility has. You might personally want to install your pleasant user's package right away and wait a long, long time to install software for your hobgoblin, if you ever do it at all. Remember, however, that you're there to serve your users, and personal likes and dislikes cannot affect your administrative decisions. Your facility might have received a mandate that your annoying user's research is a high priority. If so, you will have to install her software first. Your facility might have a first-come, first-served policy, in which case, whoever made the request first should be serviced first. Your facility might have a policy that requests for software packages that will be of use to more users have priority. Day 2, "Designing Your Cluster: From Planning to Policy," has a section on user request policies and a few sample policies you might choose to implement for your machines.

- You overhear some of your users discussing their department's plans to buy a high-end graphics printer—something your facility could really use. Don't hesitate to contact the department and offer your support. Chances are that you can provide better network connectivity, more convenient access, and better regular maintenance for such hardware than they can. If your facility is on a tight budget (as most are), you'll find it difficult to justify purchasing large specialty pieces of equipment, but you might be able to convince whoever holds the purse-strings to go for a cost-sharing option if someone else will help foot the bill. Don't hesitate to forward the notion of partnering with other departments to increase the capabilities of both your facilities. If you network with the right people, you can add capabilities to your facility, increase value to your users, make useful friends in the right places, and save money all at the same time.

- The user who wanted advice on what UNIX box to buy bought one, and you now administrate it. He urgently needs more drive space for use in a class he is teaching, and you had at one point actually managed to convince your boss that you should keep a spare drive on hand for emergencies. Your user offers to replace your spare drive if you would be willing to install the one you have on hand into his machine. Take advantage of opportunities to barter, especially if you have a tight budget. If you have reason to believe that you won't need your spare drive right away, go ahead with the deal. You will have solved a problem for your user without incurring a cost for yourself, generating good will in the process.

When you are running into problems with software or machines, it is often best to choose (within reason) the fastest path to solving your problem. If that means you have to ask an expert, ask an expert. Make that backup copy before you change anything. To effectively work with the users, it will help you if your facility has some basic policies to guide you. Also, don't be afraid to work out partnering or bartering deals with your users; they have the potential to be beneficial to everyone, and the happier you make your users, the less they'll be upset when you are forced to make unpopular decisions.

Summary

In this lesson, you have learned the following:

- **The power of UNIX lies in abstraction**—Remember that it is your job as system administrator to organize your system so that it takes advantage of UNIX's abstraction and makes a pleasant experience for your users.

- **The power of root is immense**—As system administrator, you now have the power of root. Use this power with caution: A single mistyped command can wipe out your system. With the power comes responsibility.

- **The scope of system administration is wide**—Not only will you sit in front of your computer, but you will open machines, assist users, order supplies, design spaces, and more. You have to expect the unexpected. If you like a job with a wide variety of tasks, you'll like system administration. If you don't like variety, this might be the right time to learn to appreciate it.

- **Only root can perform certain tasks**—Root has certain responsibilities, such as adding devices, which only root can perform, so that your system is not in constant chaos. Remember that the fewer users who can log on as root, the less chaos you will experience.

- **Your facility and users have certain obligations to you**—It is certainly your job to provide services to your facility and users; however, you can't provide the best services for them unless they help you. Some of what you should expect of them includes having copies of the essential software and operating system on the shelf, having the right hardware, having a programmer available, and having fixed policies to guide you.

- **Be there for the users**—Remember that you are there for the users, no matter how annoying you might find them at times. To effectively deal with users' requests, follow the guidelines your facility has in place, or create the guidelines if none exist.

- **Remember win-win**—Partner or barter with your users when it looks beneficial to all involved. Making your users happy is sometimes as easy as thinking ahead and recognizing when you have a ready solution to a problem they are about to experience.

- **Seek help when you need it**—Don't waste a lot of your time trying to solve what seems like an impossible problem. Seek the help of your resident expert, or if you don't have one, check the newsgroups or look on the Web.

Q&A

Q Does that device name `/dev/dsk/dks1d5s0` actually have any meaning?

A Yes, it does. This is one of those instances where you will see differences in the UNIX varieties. In this case, which is from an SGI machine running IRIX, you can tell from the name that the partition is located on a SCSI drive on SCSI controller 1, with ID 5 at partition 0. Other flavors of UNIX have their own naming conventions, but they usually decrypt in a similar fashion. You'll learn more about this in Day 13, "Saving Your World: Making Backups."

Q If you decide to share drives between machines, do all the machines have to run the same operating system?

A You can network machines with different operating systems. However, for your own sanity, you will probably want to keep the number of different operating systems to a minimum.

Q Are users really that bad?

A No, they're worse! Seriously though, 50 percent or more of the job of a system administrator is public relations. I can't teach you to be a good people person or to enjoy doing service-oriented work, but I'll try to warn you throughout the following chapters where to expect friction with your users, and I'll try to help you build a good enough system to reduce the likelihood of that friction.

Workshop

Quiz

1. Why does a UNIX system need a system administrator?

2. Why does root access carry more responsibility on a UNIX machine than on your own personal computer?

3. Assuming that you have settled into your new office space a bit and that you have inherited a UNIX cluster already in place, what are some of the things you might do on your first day on the job?

4. You have just become root to take care of some task, and the phone rings. What do you do?

5. It turns out that the call in the previous question was from a user who has forgotten her password and would like to know if you could tell her what it is so that she can log in again. How do you respond?

DAY 2

Designing Your Cluster: From Planning to Policy

Whether you inherited a cluster of UNIX machines or you intend to put together your own, understanding how to design your cluster and what sort of policies you might need is important. Today's chapter will expose you to many of the factors you need to consider before making decisions. Among these considerations are the following:

- Thinking like a safe-system administrator
- Issues to address when planning a cluster
- Hardware and network terms you need to know
- Your budget
- Physical space considerations
- Policy and political concerns
- Security issues

After you've committed yourself to a particular choice of machines, networking strategy, and other design issues, changing in midstream will cost you downtime and potentially considerable ill will from users affected by the change. Asking that you actually make all the design decisions appropriate for your situation, of course, is silly. You can read here about what sorts of decisions you will face and think about them until you're comfortable that you're on the right track. Take your time making these decisions and be sure that you know why you're making them. When dealing with users who wish you'd done something differently, it's usually more important to have actually had a reason for your decision than to have your users agree with it.

Policies that you decide to implement and enforce are also important to think out ahead of time. Depending on your environment, the policies you need to have will range from the trivial to the exceedingly detailed. If you're in a corporate environment supporting machines for many users, policy decisions will be extremely important to you. Written policies, strictly enforced, are your best way of avoiding conflicts among users and misunderstandings about the way your system is run.

To help you with understanding some of the policy decisions you will probably be faced with, I've included several potential policy documents in this lesson and annotated them with comments. Copies of the policies and forms you might find useful are included in Appendix F, "Useful Sample Forms."

Planning for a UNIX Cluster

If you've just decided to put together a UNIX cluster, you're probably wondering what you need to consider in order to make it all happen. It's obvious that you must decide what hardware best suits your needs and how you will implement your network. Additionally, you need to consider less obvious things such as the layout of the space where you will put the machines. For example, if your facility is supposed to support a large-format poster printer and there's no space in the room with your UNIX machines, you had better be looking at a network-capable printer or have other plans to overcome the length restrictions on serial and parallel cables.

The important thing is that you think things through carefully and plan ahead; it will save you headaches in the future.

 Note

Worst-case scenarios   A good philosophical framework for system administration is that it's productive to always look at any situation in terms of the worst possible situations that could occur. The "cup half full" thinkers among you are already crying "that's a negative way of looking at things!" If you've already thought out how to deal with the worst that can be thrown at you, you'll have a plan for almost everything that comes your way. As a UNIX system administrator, you need to be aware that worst cases sometimes do happen. If one should happen to your machines, all manner of unpleasant things can happen in a short period of time—things you'd much rather avoid if possible. You won't run into the worst case too often, but when you do you can smile and deal with it with confidence.

The downside to this philosophy is that you'll be accused of spreading "doom and gloom," and obviously there is the danger of taking this analysis too far, instead of balancing your decisions with analysis of acceptable risks. As long as you don't go down the path of paralyzing yourself while microanalyzing every situation looking for minute faults, your sanity and your users will thank you when the inevitable "bad thing" eventually does happen and you take it in stride.

Deciding on Hardware

How do you decide what hardware best suits your needs? Among the more important factors in making that decision are the intended purpose of your cluster and your budget.

Purpose

What is the purpose? Do you particularly need to have a reliable machine that can serve Web pages? Do you require special graphics hardware? On what platforms can you run the software packages you and your users would like to use? Is there some piece of specialty equipment you need to support that only interfaces with one manufacturer's equipment? These are some of the issues you will have to research.

Tip

Maintain perspective!   Try not to be swayed by a pretty interface or marketing hyperbole. If you need something such as a rock-solid Web server, do a little research on the Usenet newsgroups and the Web. The search engines, particularly Deja (www.deja.com), are your friends. You might be surprised to find that although one major manufacturer today speaks glowingly of their Web-purposed workstations and the CPU power and memory bandwidth they possess, their hardware is also legendary for its inability to stay running for more than a few weeks at a time. If you examine your need critically and stop to observe that you're hooked to the world on a single T1 connection (only 1/6 as fast as standard 10-megabit Ethernet), you might find that an "antique" (pre-1997) machine from another vendor happens to be just as legendary for stability and that a much less expensive solution would suit your needs just fine.

How do you research these issues? If you know someone or some department that is already doing what you would like to do, you might want to ask how they are doing it and whether they are satisfied with how it works. Be sure to check the various vendors' Web sites for details on their products. If you work for a large entity, such as a university, you might want to check with your central computing office for possible suggestions or for general comments that they have heard for solutions you might be considering. You should also check on newsgroups. Of course, if you have any gurus at hand, be sure to get their thoughts. Make good use of your available resources—you might be concerned that you're annoying your gurus by asking them trivial questions, but chances are, questions won't annoy them nearly as much as you wasting time or money going around in circles trying to find out what they could have already told you.

As part of your research, you will probably be getting quotes from various vendors. Quotes can be confusing to read, but an understanding of some of the terms that might appear in a vendor quote will ease your task.

Learning the Language of Hardware

If you're like many people new to administration, much of the world looks like a confusing whirl of TLAs (three letter acronyms) and technical jargon. Whole books have been written just to define computing terms you might find, so I won't try to address the wide world of terminology you'll encounter. Instead, these are a few of the important terms and ideas you need to be familiar with when comparing machine specifications and deciding on hardware:

- **Ethernet interface**—This is the card or device in your computer that provides the port necessary for it to connect to the network. If you have the option to get a 10/100 ethernet interface, do so. This type of card will sense whether it is connected to 10BASE-T or 100BASE-T and adjust its transmission rate accordingly. To connect older machines to the network, you might have to get an ethernet transceiver, which will adapt the type of connection on your older machine to either thinnet or twisted pair.

- **SCSI (Small Computer System Interface)**—This is the interface standard most UNIX machines use to talk to their hard drives. SCSI interfaces now come in many flavors, including SCSI-1, SCSI-2, SCSI-3, and Ultra2-SCSI. Additionally, there are narrow and wide versions of some, indicating how many bits the data path can carry at once. On top of that, there are single-ended and differential versions that indicate different electronics and signal types used on the interface. Unless you're really interested in the particulars of these interfaces, you shouldn't need to know much beyond which interface your hardware supports, that you want the best drives possible, and that there are ways to convert between most of these interfaces if you absolutely must.

- **SCSI controller**—Generally, this is the device your machine will use to talk to the SCSI devices. The controller and collected connections between the drives are commonly known as the SCSI bus. The SCSI bus will transmit data at the rate of the slowest SCSI device. If you need to integrate older SCSI-2 peripherals with your newer Ultra2-SCSI machine, get two SCSI controllers. This will enable you to hang the slower devices off one controller where they won't slow down any new Ultra2-SCSI devices you have. This way, you can continue to use your older devices without sacrificing the speed of your new machine's SCSI hardware.

- **Tape drive**—A device that uses magnetic tape, generally used for backup storage of large quantities of data. Magnetic tape is not as stable or permanent a storage medium as hard magnetic storage (hard drives) or CD-R/CD-RWs, but it is much cheaper. This enables you to make complete copies of the contents of your drives on a regular basis for archival purposes. Tape drives come in a number of formats. At the moment, the most popular for UNIX platforms seems to be DAT (digital audio tape), but tape technology changes and advances quickly; four years ago, DAT was uncommon, and a digital version of 8mm video tape was popular. On the horizon is DLT (digital linear tape). It has 40GB+ storage capacities and seems a likely contender. Whatever your choice for a tape device, keep in mind that you'll need it to last for a while; backups aren't very useful if you don't have a device to read them. Keep in mind the existence of "tape stacker" devices that will autofeed multiple tapes to the machines so that they can perform unattended backups more easily. Also, be aware that with so many tape formats floating around out there, you're likely to get tapes from software vendors and users coming from other facilities that you do not have a drive to read. Short of keeping a spare drive in each of a dozen tape formats, your best bet is to find out what types of drives are at the disposal of other people you know, other departments in your building, or other system administrators you might have contact with. Then buy a different one. Chances are that they've run into tapes they can't read either, and cooperation between the community of administrators in any given locale is the only way some tapes are ever read. If you've got a different drive, they can borrow yours, you can borrow theirs, and everybody comes out ahead.

- **NFS**—The network file system. UNIX provides abstraction of where data is physically stored by allowing any machine to "serve" disk space to any other machine. Access to disk space that is available over the network is made transparent to the users by the operating system. You can design your UNIX cluster so that all machines are disk servers and are clients of all other machines, thereby distributing the computing and network load evenly among them. This decreases the likelihood of a total failure of service because the loss of any one machine only results in the loss of a portion of your aggregate disk space. It also increases the likelihood of partial failure because the number of failure points increases. On the other hand, you can designate one machine as your server and make all other machines clients. In this case, your entire facility depends on the functioning of a single machine, decreasing the occurrence of failures. Frequently, a higher performance and more reliable machine is picked for this role to decrease the likelihood of total failure.

UNIX Friends and Family: Trusted Peers and Clusters

You will frequently hear the term *cluster* applied to collections of UNIX machines. This term doesn't have a very concise definition. Normally, it is used to describe a set of UNIX machines that are set up to share user environments and data. The term cluster usually implies that the machines are configured in such a fashion as to appear essentially identical to each other from the user's perspective and that they are administrated as a single collective unit. Cluster also seems to imply a sense of proximity because it would be rare to consider one corporation's machines distributed around the globe to be a cluster, no matter how similar the setup is.

The term *trusted peer* is used to describe the relationship between one UNIX machine and another with which it shares data. All machines in clusters are typically trusted peers of one another. A corporate branch–office machine that is configured to function as though it were part of your cluster is also a trusted peer of your cluster, even if you don't consider it a part of your cluster proper.

Administratively, it is a good idea for a cluster to be administrated centrally. UNIX machines that share data share the capability to corrupt each other's data and to compromise each other's security. If you allow independent administration of some machines within your cluster, you are essentially allowing that independent administrator free reign to do what he wants with the machines under your administrative control. Machines in a cluster are linked at a very fundamental level, and it would be exceedingly, if not impossibly, difficult to limit an administrator's access to a subset of machines when that subset freely shares data with the remainder of your machines.

By the same token, any trusted peers of your cluster present the same risk. Think long and hard before allowing an independently administrated machine to become a trusted peer. When you do, you are allowing the administrative staff of that machine, and the consequences of any mistakes they might make, to affect the machines in your cluster.

Of course, there are times when this risk is completely acceptable, such as when you are a member of one of many corporate system administration teams managing a country-wide network of trusted peer clusters. In this case, you can be reasonably certain that the administrators of the other machines you're going to trust are also competent administrators. Your primary responsibility is not just to your local users, but to the corporate computing community spread around the country. The benefit to be gained by the corporation as a whole, a completely transparent nationwide network, outweighs the risk of problems with one site propagating to the others.

On the other hand, there are times when this risk is almost completely unacceptable. If you're running a research cluster for a college at a university, for example, your foremost responsibility is probably to your local user community. If a faculty member buys herself a machine and declares one of her students with minimal UNIX experience to be the administrator, you'd have to be crazy to accept it as a trusted peer of your cluster. This means that sharing disks is out, sharing password files for logins is out, and generally any form of sharing that would allow the new machine to write any data to or access any privileged data from your machines should be forbidden. To do otherwise puts your entire cluster and all your users at risk. If the faculty member really needs her machine to be part of the cluster, you can always assume administrative control and administer it with the rest of your cluster. If you don't have that control, don't put your users' data at risk by granting the authority to cause problems to someone who lacks the knowledge to act responsibly.

The UNIX Filesystem

One of the largest tools you have at your disposal as a UNIX administrator is the UNIX filesystem. UNIX abstracts the physical location of data so that you can make an entire collection of devices look like a single cohesive filesystem with a single root directory.

This is done by allowing any filesystem device, such as physical disk drives, or filesystems that are provided over the network to be mounted to another filesystem so that they appear as directories.

How you choose to lay out the complete filesystem makes a big difference in the way your machines feel to users using them. As a UNIX user, you are probably familiar (if you're used to a well-run system) with the way that any machine you sit down at always seems to have your files in the same place (and many other important files as well). This is all done through the magic of the UNIX filesystem. Your files reside in one place, on one machine, somewhere, but where that is, as a user, is not something you need to be concerned about. Your administrator will have set things up so that your files *appear* to be in the same place on every machine in the cluster. Now, you're the administrator, and it's your job to make that happen for the rest of your users. Improperly done, UNIX machines start to feel like awkward versions of normal desktop computers. Properly done, the only difference you will notice between sitting at a computer in your machine room and sitting at the terminal located in a branch office on the other side of the country is a different machine name and a slight network delay.

Figure 2.1 schematically shows the filesystem layout of a networked cluster of machines. To understand the figure, keep the following points in mind:

- The box around each machine delimits the hardware connected to that machine.
- Smaller shaded areas inside each machine box delimit partitions that are all on the same physical device.
- Square-edged rectangles around directory names indicate real directories physically on the device.
- Round-edged rectangles around directory names indicate that the directory appears to be there and can be accessed and worked in just like any other directory, but it is physically located somewhere other than where they appear.
- Follow the solid lines from round-edged rectangles to the actual physical device if it's on the same machine.
- Follow the dotted lines from round-edged rectangles to the actual physical device if it's on a different machine.
- A doubled line from a round-edged rectangle indicates a directory that's really a link to a directory in another location on the same machine—making it available in two places simultaneously.

FIGURE 2.1

Filesystem layout for a small cluster of machines.

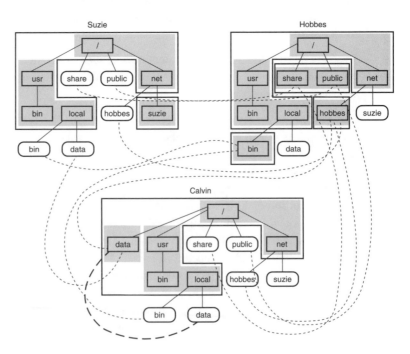

Note that user directories, even though they're served from several different machines, always appear in the same place on every machine. Utility directories, such as /public and /share, all come from the same machine. Also note that the directory at which a filesystem appears (the mount point) does not have to have the same name as the filesystem on the host from which it is being served (exported).

A large part of your job as system administrator will be making, or maintaining this illusion of consistency around your machine's filesystems. When you run out of disk space, you will be moving directories to new locations and then making things appear as though they'd never changed. When you upgrade hardware, you will be rearranging user accounts and consolidating disk services, all transparently to your users. When machines crash, you will be making (or trying to make) it look like nothing more has happened than a CPU being turned off—even though half of your disks just went away.

How well you can manage to perform this collection of magic tricks depends largely on how well thought-out your filesystem schema is in the first place. Take the time to think through the current layout, any plans you have for changes, and what the future holds for your system. Sketch out on paper what you plan to do before making any changes. It's a smart idea to keep the sketch for the day something breaks and you can't look at the system to find out how you had it put together.

Other Issues to Consider

Not only will you have to decide what basic options your machines should have, but you will have to determine what other peripherals your cluster might also need now or in future expansion.

Is it acceptable for your machines to be down when the power goes out? Your facility might decide that the data is too valuable to risk potentially losing during a power outage. You might decide (and rightly so) that it is not good for any of your machines to uncleanly shut down. To avoid potential damage that could come from a power outage, you might want to consider purchasing an Uninterruptable Power Supply (UPS). Most good UPS units have a serial port and communicate with your machines so that your machines can shut themselves down cleanly if the UPS indicates that the power has gone off.

If a hard drive dies, is it acceptable to have that data unavailable for the time that you need to install a replacement drive? If not, perhaps RAID would be another solution for you to consider. RAID stands for Redundant Array of Inexpensive Disks and is a way to both increase disk performance and provide real-time backup of your data. Although not a topic I'll cover in depth in this book, if the utmost in filesystem reliability is a concern, RAID is an important feature to consider.

> **Note**
>
> In brief, RAID systems can provide for data to be written to multiple drives simultaneously such that the failure of any one drive does not compromise the integrity of the data. Without going into the details of the five different levels of RAID, the important thing to know is that RAID systems typically include software that understands how to monitor the drives for problems. If a problem should occur as the system is monitoring, RAID systems know how to rebuild the data of the failed drive automatically from the real-time backup. All that is required on the part of the user when a RAID drive fails is to disconnect the failed device and hook up a new one. Frequently, this can even be done without stopping the system because hardware RAID controllers are capable of handling *hot swaps* of drives. After the fresh drive is connected in place of the failed one, the software automatically rebuilds the drive's contents, and life goes on uninterrupted. If this sounds like a direction in which you would like to go, talk to your hardware vendor about the range of solutions available to you. RAID packages range from plug-in devices that are supported off of your machine's motherboard to networked RAID filesystems that don't even require a parent machine to run to Linux's built-in software RAID capability.

Get a printer. Regardless of whether your users need to print, you as the system administrator require a printer. The facility that I administrate operated for its first three years under the misguided premise that having a printer would encourage users to make unnecessary printouts. When the administrator who preceded me adopted the facility, one of his first actions was requiring that a printer be installed. We do, in fact, now get garbage printouts when users print copies of Web pages that they didn't plan to print (or don't want to admit having printed), and there is a certain cost associated with "waste" printouts that are generated. All this is far outweighed by the fact that now I can print documentation and diagnostic information when I need paper copies.

As a system administrator, you have other issues to consider as well. For example, would you like to be able to write backups to CD-ROM? Perhaps the facility will need a CD-ROM writer. Is software going to be distributed on DVD-ROM? Maybe you will have to consider replacing your CD-ROM drive with a DVD-ROM drive sometime down the road.

No matter what might be decided about these and any other supplemental issues that might arise, remember that you will have to administrate whatever is purchased. Make sure you have some say in what that purchase is. Even if you don't know what solutions would work best, make sure that you are part of the decision-making process. Do whatever you need to do to find information so that you can recommend some options to the people who control your funds. I have observed that when it comes to making actual purchasing decisions, things frequently get decided by committees whose members don't have the expertise or time to research decisions thoroughly. Even though these people usually have the best intentions, they occasionally unknowingly decide to do something in a way that simply cannot be done. You are the best judge of your abilities and what you can and can't do. Don't feel that you're overstepping your bounds by asking to be able to comment on purchasing decisions. People might not be overjoyed to hear "I'm sorry, I just can't make that work" when they propose to buy the latest, greatest three-pronged widget to plug into your burfl server. But, they'll be a lot happier hearing it at the decision-making stage then when the $30,000 box is sitting on your office floor.

Your Budget

Unfortunately, your budget plays an important role in your hardware decision. What hardware gives you the most for your money? If you work for a company that creates special effects for Hollywood, you might have the budget to buy "Big Iron," such as Silicon Graphics Onyx hardware. On the other hand, if you work for an ISP, you might not have a very large budget (regardless of how much you charge your clients), and you wouldn't need the specialty graphics SGI offers. Rather, some flavor of UNIX running on Intel hardware might suit most of your needs.

When you are researching prices, you will encounter a wide range of costs—$20,000+ for various servers to less than $500 for Intel hardware. You will see UNIXes which have a $1,000 base cost, plus $700–$5,000 for the compilers, as compared with the $59 price for the Linux package. As I mentioned in yesterday's chapter, no matter what platform(s) you decide upon, don't be skimpy on the hardware. Shaving a few dollars now is likely to create a number of headaches down the road.

If you're buying new hardware, you usually get what you pay for. For example, if you're buying hard drives, you might be able to get a 4GB drive and enclosure for less than $350 from a discount mail-order source. If you bought from a specialty UNIX hardware provider, that drive would probably cost you almost $600. On the other hand, with the specialty vendor, you get a contract that says that if you need tech support, they'll put a machine together just like yours and sit an engineer down in front of it to walk you through solving your problem. You also get an immediate guaranteed replacement that says if you have a problem, a new drive is on your doorstep the next morning via FedEx. If your time is valuable, you will likely find the no-nonsense guarantee you get when you go through a specialty UNIX dealer to be more than worth the extra monetary cost involved.

Appendix E, "Useful Resources," includes some addresses for retailers that seem to be highly regarded by most administrators.

If you're buying used, you're likely to get a good deal in terms of performance for the money you spend. My husband and I bought our first home UNIX machine in 1994, a rather fully configured Sun SPARCstation, for $1,600. A little research in older Sun literature indicated that the list price in 1991 for the configuration we bought was slightly over $20,000. I recently noticed that the same type of multiprocessor server that a local business I know bought for $700,000 in 1993 was for sale on the Web. The late 1998 asking price was $1,600, and nobody was bidding. If you don't need the absolute cutting edge in performance, used equipment has real potential for saving you money. Make certain that you're buying from a reputable dealer and that you have the right to return the hardware if it doesn't work properly. You can generally be fairly comfortable about buying older UNIX equipment in that UNIX hardware rarely dies; it usually becomes nonviable for the companies that really need cutting-edge performance (or that think that they do) due to performance advances long before it's physically worn out. Usually, you'll find that if a workstation works when it comes in the door, it will still be working when you send it back out again. Again, Appendix E contains pointers to some of the better-thought-of used equipment retailers, as well as suggestions for places to look in the Usenet newsgroup hierarchy.

When you're ready to make your purchase, consider having someone who is good at making deals negotiate for you. Buying computer hardware and software can frequently seem like buying a new car. Because software, especially, costs almost nothing to duplicate, most software sales staffs have significant flexibility in their pricing. A software package that retails for $25,000 might suddenly be available (under a special program, of course) for only $3,500 when the sales person finds out that you don't think you can scrape together more than $3,000 and are considering a competitor's product.

Tell the vendors up front what your budget is so that they can work with you. You'll find that many have rather high-pressure sales tactics, but that simply asking them "I've got $X to spend, what can you do for me?" works wonders to reduce the pressure and get them working for you, rather than on you.

Possibly consider buying at the time of a major computing conference that relates to whatever your computing mission is. You'll find that many vendors have "show special" prices on hardware during such conferences. Better yet, with them all in one place, you can shop around and, if you're good at haggling prices, much more effectively work out a good deal.

Designing Your Network

Hopefully, this is one of the areas where you don't have to do everything. With luck, there's an established network that you will just be adding your machines to and a competent network administrator who takes care of making certain that things work. If not, you're in for a bit more work. Either way, you do need to know a little bit about a network to work with your network administrator or to do the network administration job yourself if you don't have a network administrator.

Learning the Language of a Network

Just as it would be helpful for your users to know a little bit about UNIX when they are communicating with you, your network administrator would appreciate it if you knew some of the basic terminology of her specialty. In the following paragraphs, you'll take a look at some of your network administrator's jargon.

- **Backbone**—Your network administrator might grumble at you from time to time about the backbone of the network and why a machine shouldn't be on the backbone. What is he talking about? The backbone sounds pretty important. In network-speak, it generally indicates a trunk network that provides a connection between smaller network segments. For example, you might find that your building has an archaic thinnet (coaxial) network winding its way through crawlspaces and ductwork throughout the building. Off of this thinnet backbone, you are likely to find twisted-pair networks dangling; each one is isolated physically but is interconnected by the backbone. If your network administrator doesn't want a machine on the backbone, it's probably because he thinks it will generate too much traffic, and he would rather have it isolated in one of the smaller side networks. If he's done his job, traffic generated in the side networks that doesn't need to go out on the backbone will stay isolated in the side network. This way, the machine's traffic won't affect the rest of the networks connected to the backbone.

- **Thinnet**—Your network administrator might also call this nearly obsolete type of cable "coax" (for coaxial cable) or "10BASE-2." Computers are attached in a daisy-chained fashion along the network using lengths of coaxial cable with BNC (British Naval Connector) connectors at the ends. Each machine has a pass-though "Tee" connector installed, and the unused end connectors on the network have resistive terminators installed. Data is transmitted at 10 megabits/second. This type of cabling is the nightmare of system and network administrators. Unfortunately, it's also the inexpensive way to start a network because it doesn't require any hardware other than a wire to connect your first two machines. With thinnet cabling, you will find network problems that are more complicated than the user who disconnects her machine and leaves the network unconnected almost impossible to diagnose. If you're serious about having a system and network with any real sense of stability or thoughts of performance, try to get rid of any thinnet network segments you might find. Once upon a time, when twisted pair hardware was very expensive, it made sense to live with the problems that thinnet causes. Now, if your time is worth more than minimum wage, fighting with the problems that thinnet causes instead of replacing it is irresponsible.

- **Thicknet**—Hopefully, you will never have to know the network horror that was thicknet. This cabling standard was coaxial, like thinnet, but it's thicker. Thicknet cables came in fixed lengths, and instead of attaching computers at Tee junctions in the cable, computers were attached via *vampire* taps directly to the cable. A vampire tap is a type of connector that attaches directly to the still-insulated cable by piercing the jacket and insulation with little teeth and is another thing you should hope to never meet. Each thicknet connection was about the size of a cigar box and had a drop cable that ran from the thicknet connection to the computer. Problems abounded, costs were high, and the standard said both that the minimum length was 10 meters and that all lengths must be integer multiples of 23.4 meters. Thicknet, in today's world, is a bad thing to do and a bad way to do it—or, to quote Nancy Reagan, "just say no."

- **Twisted pair**—"Unshielded Twisted Pair," or UTP, properly. Your network administrator might also call it 10BASE-T. This cable looks a lot like phone wire, which probably makes it seem a bit friendlier to use. Computers are attached in a tree- or star-shaped fashion with wires branching from connection devices called hubs to computers or other hubs. Simply attach a cable to the twisted pair port on the back of your computer and to an empty port on your hub. If you're lucky, your entire network is twisted pair, and your hub plugs into your network simply by connecting to another hub with another twisted-pair cable. If you're unlucky, you're stuck with a thinnet backbone, bringing all the problems of thinnet to your twisted-pair network. Unlike thinnet connections, twisted pair makes diagnosing network problems easy. If you're lucky and your whole network is wired on twisted pair, you can diagnose network problems by simply going to the top-level hub for your building and unplugging wires until the problem disappears. Keep in mind that twisted pair networks are laid out just like UNIX directories—upside-down trees, hubs at the nodes (branch points), cables at the edges (branches), and machines at the leaves (termini). It's a fairly straightforward procedure to simply walk through your network determining which branch to follow at each hub to go directly to a problem machine or piece of wire. Like thinnet, twisted-pair also transmits data at 10 megabits/s.

- **100BASE-T**—Sometimes called "Fast Ethernet," this is a faster twisted-pair network connection that can transmit data at 100 megabits/second. If your network administrator was smart, your twisted-pair wiring will already support the data speeds necessary to carry a 100BASE-T network. Check for markings that indicate "Cat-5" or "Category-5" cabling for 100BASE-T compatibility. "Cat-3" cable will only support 10BASE-T.

- **Ethernet cable**—When your network administrator talks about ethernet cable, he is talking about any of the types previously listed—thinnet, twisted-pair, or 100BASE-T.

In addition to network cabling, you'll also hear your administrator talking about network hardware. The following are some of the terms you might hear used:

- **Hub**—A hub has multiple ports through which you can attach computers or other hubs to the network. Essentially, a hub listens for any data on any port and sends it back out on all the other ports; it provides connectivity amongst any devices plugged in. Some hubs provide activity indicators that show approximate hub utilization percentages and which ports have active connections. Hubs come in a variety of sizes from four ports and up. Regardless of whether you find the indicators useful, your users will like the blinking lights.

- **Repeater**—Network cables have resistance and, therefore, a maximum possible physical length. If you need to extend your network further than the cable can carry the signal, you need some way to amplify it. Repeaters are essentially signal amplifiers that can extend the physical reach of your network. Installed between two ethernet cables, what they hear on one cable, they repeat into the other, and vise versa. Technical details, such as how far you can go before you need a repeater and how many repeaters are too many, are best left for a networking expert.

Note

> **Shameless Plug**   Que's *Special Edition Using TCP/IP*, ISBN 0-7897-1897-9, provides a great in-depth look at the primary network protocol used in UNIX networking, TCP/IP. Written by yet another in the Ray family of system administrators, I find this book a friendly introduction to TCP/IP that doesn't require you to understand too many of the dark secrets to follow the discussion.

- **Bridge**—In correct use, a bridge provides a connection between two networks, with possible source or destination filtering carried out on data transmitted between the networks. The intricacies of TCP/IP networking are too detailed to go into in a book on system administration, but in practice, you'll most usually see bridges used to restrict traffic to a specific segment of the network. You might also occasionally see "bridge" misused to simply indicate a connection between two networks.

- **Firewall**—A machine that acts as a filter to block certain types of traffic from entering or exiting your network. Firewalls are usually implemented as a specific type of bridge.

- **Switch**—A switch is sort of like a very smart hub. Not only does it provide connectivity between the ports, but it remembers which machine it has seen talking on each port and knows to direct traffic for that machine down that wire and only that wire. Switches can be used to reduce network load, improve performance, and to improve your system security—a topic I'll discuss on Day 9, "What About Security?"

- **Router**—A router is a device that connects two networks and determines whether traffic on one network needs to be moved (or "routed") to the other. You will likely have one router on your network, and it will handle all traffic into or out of your network. Traffic that is between machines inside your network will be ignored by the router, thereby keeping this traffic off the outside wires. Also, any outside traffic that isn't destined for machines inside your network will be rejected by the router, thereby decreasing your network load. In popular usage, you will occasionally hear a router called a *gateway*.

- **Gateway**—Nowadays, when you hear someone say "gateway," you can generally think "router" and be safe. A gateway is actually a different type of equipment, but recent advances in personal-computer point-and-click interface obfuscation of details has lead to considerable mixing of the terms. Properly, a gateway provides a connection between two networks that use differing types of hardware and/or signaling, requiring translation of the data carried on one before it can be placed on the other.

The Overall Building Network

Hopefully, you do indeed have a network administrator who will design or has designed an overall network for your building. Figure 2.2 presents an overview of the grand scale in which your network administrator must work. The network administrator for this building has a thinnet backbone running through the building, a cluster of machines behind a bridge, a number of machines on desktops around the building, and several small twisted-pair networks serving individual rooms.

Your Cluster's Network

On Day 9, you will look at how some of the devices your network administrator has included in the network might be helping your security. For now, however, you will concentrate on your cluster's immediate network.

If you haven't guessed this from previous comments, if at all possible, arrange to have your machines connected via twisted-pair. This will cost you a little extra money at start-up time because you'll need to buy at least one hub (as of mid-1999, 4-port 10BASE-T hubs can be had for around $50), but it will save you headaches in the future.

FIGURE 2.2

*A schematic represen-
tation of a typical
building network.*

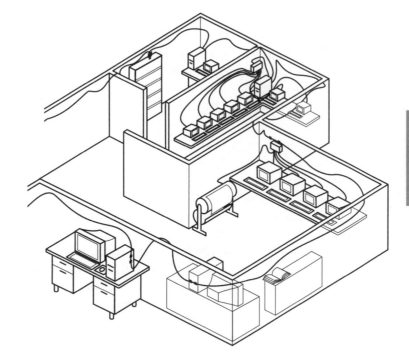

2

Your only plan might be to add more machines to a hub that your network administrator already has in place. Depending on what your network administrator has set up, this could directly expose your cluster to potential security problems on your network. I will implement some software solutions for this scenario next week.

You might want to isolate your cluster as much as possible from the rest of your building network. You can achieve various levels of security by installing bridges, switches, or firewalls.

Switches can do this most transparently for your users, but provide only protection against passive packet-sniffing attacks from inside your network. If your machines will be connected to a large shared network where you don't have physical control over every machine connected to the network, you probably want this type of security.

Bridges, especially a variant known as a Karl Bridge, can be used to restrict some of your cluster's traffic to your local network segment, again reducing the potential for someone to capture your traffic. Using a bridge for this purpose is a little more intrusive than using a switch because it will prevent even authorized outside machines from accessing that traffic, cutting them off from your cluster.

Most secure, and, unfortunately, most annoying to the user, are the infamous firewalls. Firewalls can be regulated in such a fashion that no outside traffic can ever reach your machines, and only authorized outgoing traffic can ever leave them. Users generally find firewalls to be extremely painful to live with, and don't appreciate them in the slightest. Still, if your system contains highly confidential data or requires an extreme level of security, a firewall might be your only choice, short of simply unplugging your network cable.

When making decisions and setting things up, keep in mind the difference that simple niceties can make. For example, you will almost certainly find that using different colored cables to connect your machines, or at least the ones you care about most, to your hub to be a useful way to tell quickly which machine is on which port. Colored patch cables will cost you a few cents more than putting together your own cables from a bulk spool of wire, but the time it will save you when you have to diagnose a problem will be more than worth the cost. If your network administrator won't let you buy colored cables because it's frivolous, buy a set of wire-end identifying tags. (Don't laugh! Some network administrators have been known to be rather jealous of anybody improving their network!) The tags actually are little colored loops sold in pairs so that you can clip one around each end of cables to color-code them. These won't elicit as many comments from users about all your pretty wires, but they'll do the job you need.

Always document in some useful fashion connections to your hubs—even if you think you'll remember where that purple wire on port 12 goes. Two years down the road when you need to find the other end of it, checking a piece of paper will be a lot easier than unlocking a bunch of rooms looking for the cable-end you've lost.

Designing Your Facility's Space

Get out your graph paper, rulers, tape measure, colored pencils/markers, and catalogues! Okay, maybe you don't need all of that yet, but you do need some of it, assuming that you get to pick a room yourself.

The ideal room should have its own air conditioning, or at least be well air conditioned. Remember, you are investing in hardware that will be required to stay on all the time; keep the room cool for your machines. The users can wear jackets in the machine room and go to the sauna when they are done. One of those rooms that is cool in the winter and warm in the summer is not the ideal pick. Try not to let the room be picked by someone who says "The specs say 35–95 degrees F—it's only 92 in here, what's the problem?"

Pull out your furniture catalogues and check out what's available. What kind of shelf space do you want? How much flat table space do you want? The catalogues might give you some ideas if you are having your furniture custom made. Otherwise, you should note the typical furniture measurements.

Pull out your graph paper and map out the size of each prospective room. Find the design that best fits the furniture you need to get into the space available to you. Mapping out the possible furniture arrangements on transparencies worked well for me. I could easily see what each arrangement would look like and rearrange any pieces, all at the same time if I wanted.

When designing spaces, make certain that you've given your users enough room to move around. Sit down in a chair and see if the space you've allotted each is enough that they won't be banging into each other when they slide their chairs back. Make certain that with a user seated at each existing machine, everybody has ample freedom of movement and that the route to the exit is still clear. Don't be tempted to "double-park" your users because your local fire department will probably frown on this arrangement.

If you're crunched for space, try to optimize space usage by overlapping functional spaces. This isn't an easy thing to explain on paper, but consider doors. Doors waste floor space because you can't put anything immobile where a door must be able to open or close. So, put things that can move in the door's space—such as other doors. If you position your furniture so that only one cabinet door can be opened at once, you can potentially save that space for users or equipment. Be certain to adhere to fire and safety regulations if your design calls for cabinet doors or drawers opening into walkway spaces.

Securing Your Facility's Space

After you have picked a room, you will have to consider how you want the users to be able to access it. Should the room have its own key, separate from any building master key? Should it have some sort of pushbutton combination lock that enables you to more finely control access? Should you have key card access instead?

How do you ensure that no one walks off with your relatively small but powerful machines? You might want to use *anchor pads*, a type of security device that locks to your desk. On the other hand, design aesthetics might demand that you don't have bulky and not very attractive metal plates sticking to your new furniture. You might want to consider a video monitoring system. Alternatively, you might just trust that no one would consider taking your hardware.

Even if security is a low priority initially, be sure to address the matter with your boss at some point. If nothing is going to be done about providing for physical security, it's better to have the potential loss of thousands of dollars resting on someone else's head instead of yours.

Designing and Securing Your Own Office Space

You might not actually get the opportunity to design your own office space. In fact, you might not even have enough space to worry about designing your own office space. However, if you do have the room, the same basic guidelines for the machine room apply to your office, with one exception. The machine room only has to have enough room to fit some machines with a few people. However, your space has to fit you, your machines, your reference manuals, and as few of your users as possible.

Although that last item might sound drastic, and even a bit wrong, for a system administrator, it's a necessity. As the "local computer expert," you will become an instant commodity—and also the instant target of any complaints about system performance, user behavior, and just about anything else even vaguely related to the system. If you are not careful, you are likely to be entirely consumed with trying to explain to users that you're trying just as hard as humanly possible to fix that dying machine, rather than spending any time fixing it. You will desperately need a way to insulate yourself from some of this if you every are going to have time to do your job—keeping the machines running for the users.

 Tip

> **Isolationist design**   One of the best ways to achieve this is to have your desk create a barrier between you and the visiting user. You should be behind your desk, and your user should be in front of it. You can provide a guest chair, but it should not be too comfortable. This might sound a bit silly, as you are neither a clerical worker nor an executive, but you'll be glad you did it. I recently got rid of my comfortable guest chair and replaced it with a nice, but nonadjustable, waiting-room chair in an attempt to fend off visits to chat from users who seem to be able to spend hours relaxing and talking about nothing at all in my office. My new boss, who did not take this advice because of the odd shape of his office (and the fact that he's rather new to system administration), has already experienced what can happen if you don't have the barrier. One day when he was talking on the telephone, with his door closed, one of the users burst into his office and walked right up to him behind his desk with a complaint, creating an unpleasant situation. This doesn't happen to me.

Another thing to keep in mind is that if you have your own workstation in your office or if your office should happen to house some of the more important machines in your cluster, be certain that your lock is not keyed to the same key as rooms housing the rest of your machines. Curious and/or determined users tend to see all corporate computing resources as belonging to them. If they've got a key that opens your office, anything in your office is fair game if there's a problem they think needs solved and you aren't around.

Policy: Who, How, What, and Why—In Writing!

It would not be an overstatement to say that successful system administrators live by policy, and many unsuccessful ones die by lack of the same. As I mentioned on Day 1, "What Is a System Administrator?" lack of policy regarding what you'll do for who, and when, leaves you open to constant demands on your time outside the important work you need to do, accusations of favoritism, or worse. Lack of defined policy that is strictly adhered to in other areas of system administration can cause even more damaging problems.

Only with written policies do you, as the administrator, have an on-paper document that details to users the how and why of your actions. Without such a written document, the users are free to interpret your actions and decisions in any way they see fit. If a user doesn't like a decision you have made and there is no written policy that details the reasons, chances are that they're going to try to find someone to overrule your decision. Worse yet, if policies and decision-making processes aren't documented, it will be very difficult for other administrators who work with you to work on a level playing field. You need neither the headache caused by the lack of parity among decisions your administrative staff makes nor the accusations of favoritism that this will inevitably cause.

Lack of written policies also leaves you and your facility open to poor decision making in the name of expediency. If you've just discovered that one of your users is using your machines for trading illegal copies of software in violation of copyright law, what do you do? Remove their account and hand them over to the authorities? Delete the files and do nothing else? Warn them never to do it again? If the user is the son of the chairman of your department, does your decision change? If you have a well thought-out acceptable-use policy, the decision will be clear, and the action will be clearly prescribed.

Written policies additionally serve as recipes to be followed in times of crisis. In the event of a security breach of your site, who is in charge? Does the system administrator sitting at the console who sees a break-in happening have the authority to shut the system down? Is her head going to be on the chopping-block in front of users whose "important work" was more important (to them) than the security of the system at large? Does the apprentice system administrator sitting at the console who observes a break-in in progress even know what to do in a crisis, and is he going to remember how to do it all properly? A written policy that both provides a recipe to follow in case of an emergency and gives the administrator-du-jour the authority to act covers both of these bases.

Written policies should be in place and available for review by both users and administrators alike. Policies should detail what users can expect from administrators, what administrators can expect from users, and, yes, even what administrators can expect from administrators. You should have policies detailing at a minimum, the following:

- User-account request procedures
- Acceptable-use guidelines for the UNIX system
- Acceptable-use guidelines for your network
- Response procedure for security problems
- User responsibilities
- User rights
- Administrator rights and responsibilities
- Mission statement and budgetary policy

To address user account requests, you need a user-account application form that solicits enough information for you to verify the user's identity and to track her down if you need to find her away from the system. Keep in mind that it is actually illegal to use a user's Social Security number for identification purposes, although you will find many corporations that use a copy of the SSN as an ID number as well. You'll want this form to include as much contact information as possible. Address and phone number are a must. Possibly require the name and signature of the user's supervisor. I also find it useful to include some space on the form for administrative comments and data that I need to have on hand when I create the accounts. Figure 2.3 shows a version of the user account form I use for my users. Notice how it makes my "Users who cause trouble get in trouble" policy statement right on the form so that there's no question what they're getting themselves into. You might have some concern that having a password line is a security risk. In practice, I fill this out with an impossible to remember random password and immediately expire it so that it can only be used once. When the user logs in, what's on the paper is no longer valid. If someone other than the user gets to the paper before the user logs in the first time, he immediately gives himself away by being forced to change the password. A blank copy of this form is available in Appendix F. Feel free to make use of it for your facility until you have time to develop something more appropriate. I've left enough space for you to copy it onto your company's letterhead. You should also be able to replace the return-to address with some good old-fashioned cut and paste—you remember, the kind that uses a real pair of scissors?

The second thing to keep in mind when creating your network's policies is generating some acceptable-use guidelines for the UNIX system. You need a detailed document that gives guidelines for acceptable and unacceptable user behavior. You will need to evolve this policy over time as you encounter new problems and situations that need documented. At a minimum, your acceptable-use policy should detail all the reasons you can think of that would make you want to take drastic actions, such as deleting a user's account. You'll obviously want this to include things such as conducting illegal activities, but you might also want to include things such as sharing passwords or reading other user's files without permission. Remember that this document is as much an armor for justifying actions that you need to take as it is a set of requirements for your users. If you can think of any situation in which a user should be denied access for an action, it's best if you codify that in the rules and adhere to the decision with any users that transgress. You should give a copy of your acceptable-use policy to every user who has an account and to any user who requests an account. Make certain that users have a paper copy available, even if you also have an online copy.

FIGURE 2.3

A completed account application form. Always require legible handwriting!

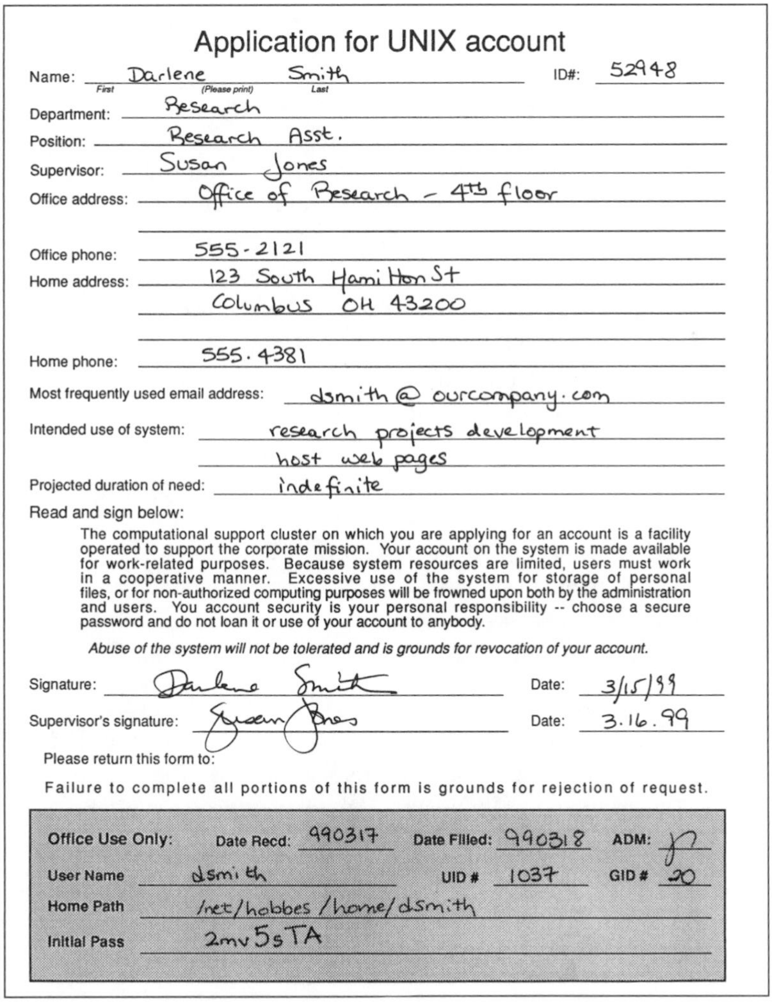

Application for UNIX account

Name: Darlene Smith   ID#: 52948
Department: Research
Position: Research Asst.
Supervisor: Susan Jones
Office address: Office of Research - 4th floor

Office phone: 555-2121
Home address: 123 South Hamilton St
Columbus OH 43200

Home phone: 555-4381
Most frequently used email address: dsmith @ ourcompany.com
Intended use of system: research projects development host web pages
Projected duration of need: indefinite

Read and sign below:

The computational support cluster on which you are applying for an account is a facility operated to support the corporate mission. Your account on the system is made available for work-related purposes. Because system resources are limited, users must work in a cooperative manner. Excessive use of the system for storage of personal files, or for non-authorized computing purposes will be frowned upon both by the administration and users. You account security is your personal responsibility -- choose a secure password and do not loan it or use of your account to anybody.

Abuse of the system will not be tolerated and is grounds for revocation of your account.

Signature: Darlene Smith   Date: 3/15/99
Supervisor's signature: Susan Jones   Date: 3.16.99

Please return this form to:

Failure to complete all portions of this form is grounds for rejection of request.

Office Use Only:	Date Recd: 990317	Date Filled: 990318	ADM:
User Name	dsmith	UID # 1037	GID # 20
Home Path	/net/hobbes /home/dsmith		
Initial Pass	2mv5sTA		

You also need to consider what will be the acceptable-use guidelines for your network. These guidelines might or might not be considered part of your UNIX acceptable-use guidelines. Largely, this depends on whether users can install their own machines on the network and on whether your network administrator has already created a set of network-use guidelines. At a minimum, there are certain requirements that you, as an administrator, should be able to place on the network community at large. These include such things as disallowing cracking attempts against the UNIX cluster or unauthorized sniffing of traffic on the network. Additionally, as the person responsible for security of your machines, you should require physical access to any machines on your network segment; if there's a problem, you will be the person responsible for putting an end to it. If politics prevent you from having direct personal access, either make certain that you have 24-hour, 7–days-a-week access to someone who does or, on the advice of one expert on system security, invest in a good fire axe.

When compiling your network's policies, keep in mind what your response procedure will be for security problems. In addition to the obvious "press this button, shut down that machine, yank that cable" procedural document, you need documented personnel procedures. Who is responsible for acting in response to security problems? Who has the authority to detail this response? If these are not the same people at your site, you are in for a nightmare of administrative problems. Upper-level management often wants to assign some director-level manager to be the person with the authority to make decisions in a security crisis. This is usually a bad idea because frequently the director-type isn't available when a crisis hits or even isn't a system administrator herself. Waiting to find and procure authority for something such as an emergency shutdown can cause extensive damage to user files and long periods of downtime to make repairs. Don't allow the separation of the person with the responsibility (usually you!) from the authority to act. Generally, you want the person with his hands closest to the keyboard to have complete authority to act quickly and decisively. Requiring the person with his hands on the keyboard to track down a manager-type somewhere before executing an emergency halt in response to a break-in is very similar to requiring a pilot to get authorization from the navigator before turning the plane to avoid an imminent crash.

The best possible policy is one that gives the administrator closest to the machines absolute dictatorial control in an emergency and requires him to immediately notify all senior (in experience) administrators available. The procedure for transfer of authority to the most senior administrator (and who this is should be detailed on paper as well) available should also be detailed; the last thing you need in a real security crisis is confusion over who is calling the shots. If you can't get a policy enacted that gives you the authority to act in an emergency, at least get it in writing that you're not responsible for damage to your users' files.

Note

Are break-ins a crisis? You bet. The potential for damage runs the gamut from loss or theft of user data to unknown modifications of your system to break-ins of other systems using your machines as stepping-stones to illegal data trafficking using your machines as couriers. You don't want to be caught in the mess of dealing with any of this. If a malicious attack is directed at your site, your machines can be cracked, user data can be deleted, and attacks can be launched at other systems with the intent of bringing reprisals in your direction. All this can happen in a matter of seconds. If you see a break-in occurring, you usually will not want to wait and find out what is going on. Unless you have a particular reason to need to catch a cracker, your responsibilities to keep your machines running and your user's data secure usually will outweigh any responsibility to chase the cracker. Generally, secure your machines immediately, prevent further attacks by disconnecting or disabling services, notify affected users and any other affected sites, clean up the mess, and get back to business.

Tip

Assigning system administration duties to a person requires an immense amount of trust. If you don't trust a person enough to allow her to make critical decisions regarding your hardware and software, don't give her the root password! Every decision a user makes when logged in as root is a critical decision, and one wrong decision can result in disaster for your entire system. If you trust a user enough to give her the root password, it's silly not to trust her enough to take authoritative actions to protect your system from intruders.

Your network policies should, of course, include guidelines for user responsibilities. When granted an account on your machines, the user should automatically be expected to assume certain responsibilities. Among these are responsibilities such as keeping his password secure and cooperating with other users who need to use the machines. Even though some of these will seem like common sense to you, you need to spell them out for your users. Things such as keeping passwords private might not sound like a serious responsibility, and it might be one that many users might be inclined to ignore. You, however, need that policy on a piece of paper because you will eventually have the user who doesn't believe password loaning is a serious problem. He will lend it to a friend who then uses it to try to crack your root password. You need a written policy that lets you demonstrate to the irresponsible user just how serious a problem it is.

When your policy addresses user responsibilities, it also must address user rights. Along with the responsibilities the user assumes when using your machines, he also gets some rights. Certain rights will be dependent on what the purpose of your site is, such as the right to put up Web pages if your site's purpose is as a Web server. Others are rights that you need to define for the smooth running of your site and tend to run along the lines of enforced common courtesy—such as the right to equal usage of the system (no tying up all the machines with one user's processes). Finally, there are the legal rights that the users have, such as the right to the privacy of their files and electronic communications. You should detail these in a policy document as well.

Whereas users have standard rights and responsibilities, frankly, in most places, administrators don't have many rights, and they have many undocumented responsibilities. For you to retain your sanity and to improve the functioning of any administrative staff you might have to work with, I suggest you work out some detailed documents regarding administrators' rights and responsibilities. Tops on your list—you might want to include things such as "we don't make house calls" and "if you bought it without asking us if it would work, we reserve the right to not fix it." An easy way to get some ideas for this document is to take the time to detail exactly what you spend your time on for a few weeks. You might (or might not) be surprised to find that you spend as much as 75 percent of your time doing work that you don't really consider "part of your job." If you're paid to keep a cluster of machines running and instead of keeping up with the latest security patches and software updates, you're off fixing Macintoshes that refuse to talk to their printers, you're probably wasting your employer's money. Additionally, both you and your users will be happier if you all know what your responsibilities are. If they don't know that your network administrator is the person who has been assigned responsibility for network security and the cluster is offline due to security problems, they're going to blame you, even though there's nothing you can do.

Who watches the watchers? Administrators need administration too. Who makes decisions about granting administrative access? Are there limited administrative accounts, and who can use them? What limitations are there on the administrator's authority? All these are decisions better committed to paper than to memory. The last thing you need as root is to not know who else is root, and if it's other authorized root users who are creating this confusion, you're likely to have a major political problem on your hands.

System policies should also include a mission statement and a budgetary section. You'll be hard pressed to run a facility well if you don't have a written statement of what it's there for. Your life will be much easier if you have a defined budget. A defined budget enables you to make intelligent purchasing decisions and decide when and where you can "splurge" on improvements. At a minimum, your defined budget should include money for any salaries you need to pay, software licenses your facility needs, funds for hardware maintenance, and any consumables (such as backup tapes or printer supplies) that you might have. You should keep in mind that hardware is in fact a consumable and that machines that are the cat's pajamas today will be barely viable antiques in three years. A reasonable budget must include money for replacing machines as they become performance liabilities, rotating them out and putting new machines in on a regular basis. Convince whoever defines your purpose to put these things down in writing; you will sleep much easier with these things as defined quantities, rather than nebulous moving targets.

Additionally, you should consider policies and procedure documents concerning the following:

- **Your first login—getting started**—Include information on how to log in, responsibilities of the users, how to set their password, and how to get help. It's okay if you don't detail all their rights here, but you want a document that both sets their boundaries and provides them the help they need to get started.

- **Account creation and deletion procedures**—How do you create and delete accounts at your site? What logging procedures do you use, where do you put the accounts, who gets notified, and so on? Creating accounts isn't a very interesting or difficult task, but it will run more smoothly if there's a written recipe to be followed. This way, you don't come back from vacation to find that your apprentice administrator has created a number of accounts with conflicting IDs and put them in some strange directory. Written procedures make your life easier. Word-of-mouth tradition, as is used by many facilities, makes your life harder. Save on the grey hairs: Write things down.

- **Shutdown and downtime notification procedures**—What sort of notice do you give your users when you're about to shut the machines down? How do you go about notifying them? It's downright rude (though sometimes necessary) to simply halt a machine out from under a user who's working at it. You should detail scheduled and unscheduled downtime notification procedures and do your best to stick to them. Users might not like having to work around a scheduled shutdown, but they'll like it a lot less if you take machines down while they're in the process of doing real work. If you have to shut a machine down without advance notice, have a policy that states when and how this is to be done, and how users are to be notified of the event. It won't necessarily save you much in the way of hard feelings, but it will at least save you time on the phone if the users know that a console message that says "Emergency Shutdown—happening NOW!" means that the machines won't be back up for at least a few hours.

- **Acceptable passwords**—Users are notoriously bad at choosing good passwords. Help them out by explaining the differences between a good password and a bad password. Additionally, consider helping them out by installing a decent version of the `passwd` utility that makes certain that passwords can't be trivially guessed.

Make it policy that users are held responsible for the security of their passwords and then actually hold them to it. You don't need the security problems inherent in having a user who just cannot pay attention to rules and will not choose and maintain password security.

- **Software installation requests**—As noted on Day 1, having a policy on how software installation requests are accepted and serviced is a very good idea. Generally, you will want a policy that gives you as much control over what you'll accept as possible. Of course, your users will want a policy that says you must jump at their every whim. Remember that you, as a system administrator, really are here to provide a service. That service is making your machines run as smoothly and as productively as possible for your users. Try to strike a reasonable balance on software requests and handle them in a fair way.

- **Hardware installation requests**—Hardware installation requests can be a nightmare, especially if it's some specialty piece of hardware that you have no experience with but that the user has purchased and for which she "absolutely" needs your support. A policy that requires administrative staff purchase pre-approval before hardware will be supported is a good idea; otherwise, you could find yourself spending time on one user's needs and neglecting the needs of many.

- **Backup procedures**—Another dull task, backing up the system can eat a significant amount of your time if you don't have the right hardware. Outline a backup procedure and stick to it. (I'll talk more about this on Day 13, "Saving Your World: Making Backups to Tape.") After you have the backup procedure outlined, estimate the time required. If it's going to mean that you have to baby-sit a tape drive for 24 hours straight every Friday evening, you should probably insist that a better tape drive be purchased. If you can't get hardware to enable you to stick to a good backup schedule, detail your less-than-ideal one so that users know the limitations that have been placed on their data security.

- **Restore from backup requests**—Even duller than backing up is restoring data for users, many of whom seem to have an incredible tendency to overuse the rm (remove files) command. Although your job *is* making the system as usable as possible, if you rush to restore a file from backup every time a user mistakenly types **rm**, you're going to spend your entire work week doing restores. If that's your entire job, go for it. Otherwise, realize that the time spent fixing that one user's problem is time taken away from the needs of the rest of your users. For this reason, many system administrators adopt a policy of only doing restores one day a week or while the user is present and after 5:00 p.m. It's amazing how many users with files that are "absolutely critical that they get restored" manage to find their own backup copies or decide that the file wasn't that important after all if they're required to wait a week or stay late after work.

- **Guest access**—Occasionally, users will come to you with requests that guests be allowed to use the system temporarily. How you handle this is entirely up to you and the purpose of your facility. If you're running a high-security lab for a research project, you probably want to have a "no guests ever" policy. On the other hand, if you're running a university teaching lab, there's no real reason that you shouldn't make guest access available so that students can show friends and family all the fun things they're doing. Whatever your policy, put it down on paper so your users don't get the impression that you're arbitrarily deciding whether their requests should be granted.

Notes on Making Policies

When writing policies, state in plain English what the rules are. Don't obfuscate the issue by making vague references to activities you want to prohibit. State them plainly. A policy that says, "Users will attempt to keep their password secret," is much weaker and much more difficult to enforce than one that says, "Users will not write down or otherwise record their passwords."

When making rules, it's crucial that you state the results of not following the rules. A policy that says, "The system administrator on call will immediately inform the lead administrator in the event of a break-in," is almost useless. If you examine the part of the policy that says, "will immediately inform the lead administrator," you should ask yourself, "or what? What happens if they don't?" A policy with no teeth is almost useless as a policy.

State acceptable practices in terms of hard and fast rules, not personal judgement. A policy that says, "Users will not attach personal UNIX machines to the building network unless the network administrator judges the machine to be secure," leaves the security of the machine up to personal conjecture on the part of the network administrator. A devious user could configure her machine to appear to be secure, thereby passing the "judgement" test, while in fact remaining insecure. Much better would be wording to the effect, "unless the machine adheres to security guidelines as defined by the network administrator."

If your machine or machines are connected to the Internet, remember that the Internet is the great intellectual equalizer and one of the truly great examples of freedom in action. This is kind of a "warm fuzzy" policy comment, but as a system administrator, you and your policies need to stand for open-mindedness and tolerance. A large part of what makes the Internet a great place and makes the UNIX and Internet community such a strong and self-supporting community is the free exchange of ideas. You will undoubtedly have users with whom you have deep philosophical disagreements. If part of your mission is providing Internet connectivity, it's not your place to make judgements regarding their philosophies, skin color, sexual proclivities, or favorite sport. Even if you're providing Web services for something such as a college research lab and you allow users to place some personal material on the Web, you really need to allow them to place *any* (legal) personal material on the Web. Of course, you can make it subject to disk-space or bandwidth constraints. Before you decide that this means that you shouldn't allow any personal material, you need to keep in mind that what makes the Web such a useful tool and such a neat place is people who make useful things available. If the usage isn't affecting your other users' business or research use of the network or machines, what reason is there for you to not let your users give something back to the Web community? So, they might not all have the most brilliant or useful Web pages, remember that if you write policy that bans one, you need to ban them all. If you ban them all, that might mean banning the one person who really would make a valuable contribution back to the community. Don't let the importance of your site's mission get in the way of the benefits of letting users express themselves creatively.

Note

What about questionable material?   The concern of what to do about questionable material might immediately spring to mind. The issue, of course, is what exactly is "questionable." If you run a site that provides software support for an animal hospital, you might write a policy that states that all material on personal pages must relate to animal health concerns; that's perfectly reasonable. Don't, however, make the mistake of assuming that what you consider to be "acceptable" material is acceptable to everybody or that what you consider to be "offensive" is offensive to everybody.

Different people find different things questionable, and for almost anything that you allow a user to put on the Web, there will be someone who finds it offensive. Does this mean that you should have a policy of strict censorship of your users' personal pages? Far from it. As a system administrator, you are responsible for preserving your users' rights to create the wonderful multifaceted world that is the Internet. Impose subject area restrictions if it is in your facility's purpose to do so, but realize that the more restrictions placed on Internet content, even those made with the best intentions, the less useful a place it will be.

Remember lastly that all policies you have must be understood by you, any other administrators, and your users. They must be enforced fairly and consistently. Don't put yourself at risk of users' ire or, worse yet, possible legal actions by using discriminatory enforcement.

Caution

READ THIS PARAGRAPH—READ IT WELL! Never, *never*, NEVER! write policy that indicates that you will enforce any sort of censorship or up-front control over your users' activities. Policies that state that you will react appropriately if informed of inappropriate or illegal actions on the part of your users are fine. Policies that even *hint* that you will attempt to prevent such activities automatically make you liable for their enforcement.

For example, you might be concerned that your users might make use of your system to illegally pirate software. Writing a policy that states "To prevent piracy, any software placed on the FTP site will be checked by the administration" makes the administration liable for any commercial software that is discovered there. You might not like that fact, but that's the way lawyers work the law, and system administrators who claim to monitor their user's activities have been successfully sued as a result of those activities. You're much safer if you write a policy that says, "We do not condone software piracy and will cooperate fully with the authorities in investigations resulting from illegal software found on the FTP site."

Write your policy such that you react to complaints regarding your users' behavior. If you should be the one to notice that behavior, so be it, but do *not* write policy that indicates that you will attempt to preemptively monitor and prevent the activity. This goes for FTP sites, Web sites, and any other data your users own or activities they perform.

2

Never, *never*, NEVER! write policy that indicates that you will enforce any sort of censorship or up-front control over your users' activities. Does that sound like you just read it in the preceding Caution? Good! I can't stress strongly enough the implications of writing policies that claim that you will prevent certain activities. If you claim you'll prevent them, you become responsible if they occur. Just don't do it!

Something to keep in mind is the fact that even though as root you can do it, it's probably illegal for you to look at the contents of your users' files without permission. The government has rather strong privacy laws in place, and rooting through a user's files without permission can subject you to a rude introduction to a user's legal rights. Again, don't go looking for trouble. If there's a problem, even if it's something such as a user collecting potentially illegal pornography and nobody knows it's there, it's not much of a problem. If someone knows it's there, you're sure to find out soon enough. Again, if you try to regulate your users' activities, *you* become responsible for them!

It's never a bad idea to have a lawyer check over any policy documents you have created. If your company has a legal staff, check with them and see if they can identify any places where you have left yourself open to legal liability or where there are loopholes in your rules.

A Sample Security Policy

Here's an annotated copy of a network and security policy that is similar to the one we use at our site. If you'd like to use a copy of this document until you have time to evolve your own document, a formatted copy is provided in Appendix F.

Following each section of the policy are italicized comments on why that respective section of the policy was written in that particular fashion.

Guidelines for System Security Requirements

Users wishing to make use of corporate computing resources or network resources agree to have read and understand the following.

A breach of system or network security is any attempt to connect to, view data on, or otherwise access computing resources without authorization. This includes, but is not limited to; use of computer facilities or network facilities without an account or authorization, accessing files belonging to other users without the written consent of said user, and authorized use of facilities for purposes outside the intent of the authorization. An action which causes a breach of system or network security constitutes a direct violation of corporate computing security policy. Employees found to have willfully violated corporate computing security policies will be remanded to corporate disciplinary affairs.

This is rather Draconian, but it covers the entire gamut of using other's passwords, trying to break into the system, dangling personal computers off of the corporate network, and otherwise causing trouble. We don't get to define disciplinary action such as terminating employment, unfortunately.

Account security on the facility UNIX machines is the responsibility of the account holder. Passwords are not to be shared. Passwords are not to be written down, or otherwise recorded. Loaning of passwords to other users will be considered a direct breach of system security and additionally will be considered grounds for immediate revocation of your account. Discovery of recorded copies of passwords will also be considered a direct breach of system security and dealt with in the same manner.

We take password security seriously. You should too. You would not believe the number of times I find scraps of paper with user IDs and passwords sitting next to machines.

Non-UNIX Machines Attached to the Building Network

Execution of system-crashing or system compromising software such as (but not limited to) "Win-nuke" and "Nestea" constitutes grounds for removal of a system from the building network. This constitutes electronic vandalism and/or theft of service, and subjects the person executing the software to potential legal liability. Users can be assured that facility staff will provide any assistance necessary to track and prosecute anyone found to be conducting such attacks.

There is a whole genre of "crash a PC" programs out there that won't actually crash UNIX machines but that can make life annoyingly slow and can make network connections unstable for UNIX users. Users on your network shouldn't be allowed to run this software against either PCs or your UNIX hardware. Users caught doing this should be punished. We remove their systems from the network wholesale. Users caught doing this to remote sites are likely to have remote site administrators calling and threatening legal action. Users might think it's all fun and games, especially if you're providing support for a college facility, but the person whose computer crashes and who loses a research grant as a result isn't going to think it's so funny.

Collection of network traffic which is not destined for the user and the machine in use (via, but not limited to, such methods as packet sniffers or ARP spoofing) constitutes grounds for removal of a system from the building network. Collection of network traffic without court authorization or a direct and immediate need to diagnose network problems constitutes execution of an illegal wire tap. Users should be comfortable that their data and electronic transactions are secure against eavesdropping.

Check Appendix D, "Legal Stuff," for more information on the legal implications. Suffice it to say, unless you've got a policy in place that says all data on the system can be monitored at any time, anyone caught monitoring network traffic that isn't intended for them could be in deep trouble—including you!

Additionally, users can be assured that facility staff will not intercept network traffic without legal authorization or an immediate need to diagnose an existing network problem.

Always a good idea to tell users what their rights are as well, and the right to privacy is an important one. Users need to feel comfortable that they are not going to be "found out" if they discuss an unpopular opinion with a co-worker and that they do not need to fear reprisals for the content of personal information kept on the system.

Execution of port-scanning software, or other software which attempts to discern or determine vulnerabilities in UNIX or non-UNIX hardware without facility staff approval will not be tolerated. Execution of such software will be considered an attempt to breach system security and will be dealt with as such.

There is a lot of software out there that's freely available and that any user can run, which they should nonetheless be strongly discouraged from running. Among this software is a collection that searches for vulnerabilities in UNIX hosts. Depending on your environment, you might want to treat running this software as a direct attack on your machines.

Users will not run FTP, HTTP, or other data servers which provide illegal data (commercial software, or other illegal data types). The facility staff cannot and will not attempt to police the building network for such behavior, but reports of copyright infringement or other illegal behavior will be forwarded to the appropriate authorities.

Notice that we explicitly claim that we won't monitor the network for this type of usage. If someone reports it, we'll certainly act, but we don't want the legal liability that would come from even trying to monitor for it.

Users will not run software designed to provide unintended gateways into services which are intended to have a limited scope. Depending on the service and the manner in which the service is gatewayed to unintended users, execution of such software may constitute theft of service. The facility staff cannot and will not attempt to police the network for the execution of such software, but will cooperate fully in any investigations brought by users whose services have been compromised.

Again, note that we explicitly refuse to monitor for this sort of activity. The legal status of some of this software is questionable, and we don't want mixed up in legal troubles. If somebody comes to us with a problem, we deal with it.

UNIX Machines

Execution of software similar in purpose to any of the software detailed in the "Non-UNIX" section will be dealt with in the same manner as detailed above, and/or users accounts will be terminated without recourse.

Execution of password cracking software against the computational facility password database will be considered an attempt to breach system security and will be dealt with as such.

Notice that we only prohibit attempts on the facility password database. This might seem a little peculiar, but proactively, we're really only concerned with our facility's security. If one of our users tries to actually break in to some other machine, she'll be violating a law, and we have something on which we can take action. Until she does something like that, she's only behaving questionably, and we get back to the "don't go looking for trouble" idea. If we claimed that we'd prohibit anyone from trying to crack any password file on our machines, we'd instantly be liable for letting the one we didn't notice get away with it.

Users wishing to install UNIX machines on the building network can do this in two ways.

> *Because this policy was designed for a college computing environment, it's important to address that we allow users to connect both lab owned and personal machines to the network. Personally owned UNIX machines have been a big problem, especially the Linux variant, in that lots of people know how to put the CD-ROM in the drive, but very few know how to manage the machines when they're up and running. Unfortunately, Linux comes with just about the world's largest collection of security holes, all wrapped up neatly in one box. The end result is that if you let a poorly administrated Linux machine on your network, you've essentially invited the entire world to come watch all your network traffic and to probe your machines from inside your network.*

Machines that are considered by the computational facility System Manager to be of general use and interest to the facility at large, may, at the discretion of the System Manager, be allowed to be set up as part of the facility. Machines handled in this fashion will be administered by the facility staff as full peers in the facility UNIX cluster, and system security will be handled through the facility staff. Machines administered in this fashion remain the property of their respective owners and are to be considered primarily intended for the use of their owners. As full peers of the facility UNIX cluster they may be used by other facility users (at least remotely) when they are not fully utilized by their owners.

> *We've found it productive to grow our facility resources by offering administrative services in exchange for allowing general facility use of the hardware. This seems to be a productive arrangement for other groups around campus as well. Some go so far as to have an arrangement whereby anybody interested in buying hardware gives their money to their computational facility staff. The staff then seeks out other users interested in the same type of hardware, pools all the money it can find, and provides a far better machine to be shared than any of the "investors" could have afforded individually.*

> *If you decide to go this route, make certain that you have discretionary control over what hardware you'll take on as part of your facility and what you won't.*

Security for these machines will be handled in the same manner as security for all computational facility UNIX cluster machines. Users can be assured that all reasonable security precautions have been taken, and that known potential security problems will be dealt with in a timely fashion.

Should a security violation occur involving one of these machines, it will be dealt with by the computational facility staff and should not require significant time or effort from the owner of the machine.

The users taking this route to machine acquisition and maintenance need to know that they're getting something out of the deal as well. Putting this down in writing also helps when you need to point out to the occasional problem user what the costs and benefits of "working with you" are.

Machines that are to be administered by their owners or their owner's assignees will be maintained at a level of security at a minimum in compliance with the requirements in this document and with security guidelines as defined by the computational facility staff.

Notice how it "requires compliance with security guidelines," rather than something like "requires acceptable security." Don't get caught with wording that's easy to misinterpret, either accidentally or deliberately. Notice also that the guidelines are defined by the facility staff. The "System Manager" referenced a few items in the preceding text isn't actually a UNIX administrator at our facility. He's an overall director type, so he is not the best person to define acceptable administration guidelines for UNIX machines. We wanted to keep this flexible enough so that the staff who actually had the experience to define the guidelines could do the job without having whiney users complaining that "person X doesn't have the authority to tell us we can't...."

Violations of policy laid down in this document are to be dealt with as defined in this document—requirements for account maintenance and termination will be strictly enforced.

Administration security guidelines will be based upon current security problems as reported by corporate network security and the online security community. These guidelines will be provided by the computational facility staff on a set of Web pages dedicated to building network security. It is expected that administrators will bring their machines into compliance with the guidelines within seven (7) days of the guidelines being posted.

The guidelines referenced here are things like the following: Shut off all those $@%@#@#$% services that Linux starts automatically. No outside-accessible accounts for non-employees. Install security patches when CERT® publishes information on them. (CERT® stands for Computer Emergency Response Team, a not-for-profit Internet security task force. We'll talk more about CERT® in Day 9, "What About Security?") This also includes anything else that happens to be pertinent at the time.

Also, seven days is probably too long a period to allow for securing against newfound threats because these things make their way around the Internet amazingly quickly. If you can get away with being more strict with this, you probably should.

Computational Facility staff will keep a database of independently administrated UNIX hardware and administrators and the administrators will be notified immediately when guidelines are updated.

It wouldn't be very fair to the administrators if we didn't make some attempt to notify them when we discover something they need to update.

Periodic scans of the building network for known security problems will be conducted by computational facility staff—results will be made available to administrators of self-administrated machines as soon as the data is available. Facility machines will be protected against any vulnerabilities found by facility staff. Independently administered machines will be brought into compliance by their respective administrators. Failure to bring a machine into compliance will result in the machine being removed from the building network.

No, we're not scanning for security violations here, but for security holes. If a new way to break into the sendmail (a very commonly found mail-handling program) service is discovered, we want to know if any of our users are running vulnerable versions, and we want them to fix it if they are.

Due to the normal speed, potential for rapid damage, and fact that most security problems occur during off hours:

Computational facility staff may require physical access to any computing or network hardware in the building at any time. To facilitate such, master-keys for access will be provided in a sealed package in the facility safe. Access to these keys will be logged, justification given and the party whose area required access notified immediately upon opening this sealed package.

You absolutely need a way to get to any computing hardware that's attached to a network that you have any responsibility for. If there is a security problem and the owner of a machine is not available, somebody needs to be able to get to the machine and stop the problem.

You might think that simply being able to yank a network cable would be enough to stop a problem, but consider the following case. Something very similar did happen here at OSU. Imagine if someone at a desktop machine somewhere in your building sends a threatening email message to the President of the United States' cat, Socks. (Quit laughing. This part really happened!) When the secret service shows up (it's apparently a felony to threaten the first feline, as well as the commander in chief), they're going to march straight to your building's main computer facility. The men in nice dark suits and sunglasses are going to demand that you take them to the machine that this email message originated from, and they're going to demand that you do it now. You are going to comply. You are most emphatically not going to tell them, "Oh, that's Dr. so-and-so's machine in the corner lab on the third floor. I'm not allowed in there, and nobody will be around to let you in until Monday." The men in nice dark suits can be most persuasive.

Computational facility staff may require administrative access to any computing hardware in the building at any time. To facilitate such, administrators of independent machines will provide to the computational facility staff with root or other appropriate administrative passwords, to be kept sealed unless needed in a crisis. Independent administrators will keep these passwords up-to-date at all times. Access to these passwords will be logged, justification given, and appropriate administrators notified immediately should use of these sealed passwords be required.

See previous rationale. Also notice that both here and previously, if access is required to the user's hardware without his presence, we've put on paper that we will log the usage and notify him immediately. Users need to feel secure that their offices and machines won't be invaded needlessly. They're reluctant enough to provide for this type of access, but it's one of the costs of being on the network for them. One of the costs to accessing their machines is a lot of paperwork and apologizing for you. It will help keep you honest.

Responsibility and authority for maintenance of security guidelines and for definition of and action upon network security threats lies with the computational facility System Manager. In the case that the System Manager is not, or is unavailable to be, administrating the facility UNIX cluster, the responsibility and authority pass to the facility UNIX cluster Lead System Administrator. Facility assistant administration staff have the authority to deal with immediate crisis situations as necessary until the Lead System administrator can be contacted.

Our higher-ups here require that the System Manager be at the top of the chain of command. This isn't an ideal situation in an emergency because he isn't a UNIX administrator. Because of this, we've worded this policy in such a fashion that he'll almost never actually be the person who has to call the shots, yet he retains the authority to do so if he needs to.

Our facility has one real full-time administrator and a number of assistant administrative staff (students) who are available on odd schedules. The assistant administrators have the authority, in the absence of the Lead System Administrator, to deal with any security issues that arise. This, as mentioned previously, is a trust issue. So they're students—so what? They have proven themselves trustworthy, and are trusted completely and implicitly whenever they're logged in as root. They're also trusted, within the bounds of facility-defined policy, to make responsible decisions regarding the necessity for actions regarding system security.

Summary

Today, you were introduced to a range of topics that are critical for you to keep in mind while making initial decisions regarding your cluster. You'll probably come up with even more over time. Hopefully, the questions and concerns brought up here will help you in identifying additional areas that you need to consider for your site. Also, you should now have a little better insight into how to analyze the consequences of decisions that you might make as a system administrator.

Q&A

Q I want to build the best and most efficient network for my machines. What should I do?

A If money is no (large) object, invest in desktop smart switches. There are small-capacity switches that can support one to four IP addresses per port that are becoming quite economical. Using these will provide your machines almost the full network bandwidth among all the machines simultaneously. If you've got a collection of machines, some of which support 10BASE-T and some of which support 100BASE-T, make sure your hubs or switches can translate between these two formats in real-time.

Q What is a reasonable budget for my facility?

A My, what a loaded question! It's extremely difficult to identify what a "reasonable" budget is without knowing what your mission is. To get the best answer, find other facilities that are run the way you would like yours to run, and ask what their budgets are or what they think their budgets *should* be. At a minimum, your budget needs to provide for the software you need and hardware maintenance. In any reasonable setting, it will also be sufficient to allow timely updates of your hardware and improvements to your facility.

Q If I write a policy that says, "Thou shalt not," and someone does, what should I do?

A Do whatever your policy says you should do. Write your policies in such a way that they define remedies or punishments for noncompliance, and then stick to them.

Q Should my policies give users who violate policy a second chance?

A That depends somewhat on what your purpose and environment are, but generally, I would recommend not. Giving users a second chance lets them get away with just about any policy violations, secure in the knowledge that they'll only get a warning when they're caught. This is not a healthy situation. Do you really want to give a license to violate policy once? Remember, keep those worst-case scenarios in mind.

Workshop

Quiz

1. Why do you need written policy documents?

2. True or false: A good policy document provides the opportunity for administrator judgement in its enforcement.

3. A good administrator always takes what into consideration when making policies and decisions?

4. What is your first action in the case of a system security breach?

Exercises

1. Define your facility's mission as you see it.

2. Write yourself a five-year plan to sustain that mission.

    (Bonus Exercise!)

3. Get your five-year plan approved and signed by whoever provides your funding.

4. Map your building, or at least cluster network. Decide where you can improve performance by installing switches or bridges.

5. Diagram your cluster's current disk layout.

6. Run though a simulated response to a security breach of your facility. Know what actions to take, who to notify, and how to recover.

7. Decide what your response is if you find a user posting pornographic pictures to the Web from your site. Write it down.

8. Does your boss agree with your answer to Exercise 7?

9. What if the material in question is anti-Semitic literature? Hoplophobic diatribes? Christian rhetoric?

    (Bonus Exercise 2!)

10. Decide why you haven't decided to give up on system administration and run away screaming. Write down your answer. You'll need it someday.

DAY 3

Setting Up a Machine: From the Box to the Desktop

After a few days of philosophy, you're probably ready to start some of the hands-on work. For organizational purposes, today's tasks are listed as one day's work; in practice, depending on your set up, you might need a couple of days to complete everything. Today, you'll learn about the following:

- How to put together machine hardware
- How to talk to the hardware command monitor and what it can tell you
- How to boot from a CD-ROM
- What information you need to give the install procedure
- Selecting partition sizes
- Choosing passwords
- Installing the OS
- Patching the OS
- Things to do as soon as the machine is up

Keep in mind while reading and attempting to follow this chapter that this is more or less a case study of an installation on one particular type of machine, with one particular flavor of UNIX. Unless you are setting up exactly the same machine or one of the ones covered in the appendix, you'll need to use this as a guideline to determine the right decisions and steps to take with your particular hardware.

Connecting the Components

Let the excitement begin! Whether you have just gotten a brand new, expensive system or an older, cheaper, yet stable system, connecting your components should not be too difficult. If you have any experience with personal computers, this should be very similar. Match the appropriate cable type with the appropriate symbol. Plug it in. What could be simpler? SCSI cabling might be one of your biggest problems, with five or more different connector standards. Luckily, adapters are available between all of them. Next might be your ethernet connection, where you might find that your machine comes with only one connection type, and your network is another. If you have a newer machine, it is already likely to be twisted-pair capable, which is the direction you probably want to be taking your network. For your older machine, you might have to get an ethernet transceiver that plugs into its AUI port, whereas if you need to adapt between network standards, an inexpensive hub might be your best bet. In case you've met with a cable that doesn't look familiar and has no identifying markings, Figure 3.1 identifies end views of a number of different connector types and the symbols that are usually associated with them.

FIGURE 3.1

Note that some interfaces share connector types with very different interfaces. Be careful that you don't confuse serial cables with SCSI or parallel cables, or network with phone modem connections!

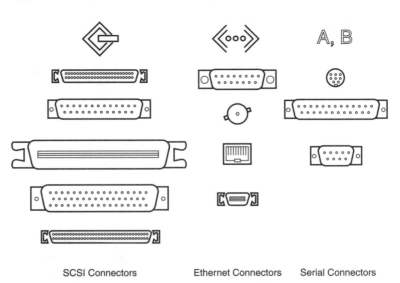

SCSI Connectors   Ethernet Connectors   Serial Connectors

Note

> **Hookup advice to remember** Probably the most important connection detail to remember is that the last SCSI device in your chain should be terminated—that is, have a SCSI terminator attached to its empty port or have the drive internally configured to terminate itself. Be sure to check your system's requirements. In some instances, if you do not yet have any devices to add, you might have to have the connection on the machine itself terminated.
>
> Next most important to remember if you're using thinnet (coaxial) network cabling is that your network cabling also needs to be terminated.
>
> The most common hookup error is to completely forget to plug the machine or peripheral into power. Before getting too confused about a piece of hardware that seems nonresponsive, make certain it's plugged in. If you check the power first, you'll save yourself a considerable amount of embarrassment someday.

3

I was pretty nervous when we got our first new SGI. It was more expensive than any other system I had ever touched. Because I had inherited a cluster of machines from their previous administrator, it was also my first experience installing a machine from scratch. I was amazed that connecting its components was much like connecting my Mac's components—the biggest difference was that the SGI was more ergonomic-looking. So, relax. Pretend you are hooking up your personal computer. Your system should come with hookup instructions, but even though I'm not a hardware wiz, I didn't notice the ones for our new system until it was already put together.

Installing the Operating System

Unfortunately, the similarity between your personal computer and your UNIX system ends with the cabling. On my Mac, I would simply insert the MacOS CD, double-click the install icon, and answer a couple questions, and I would be ready to start installing software shortly.

You will also likely boot your UNIX machine from an OS CD, but depending on your system, you might have to format and partition your hard drive, and of course, you will wait a while for the operating system to install.

Although I could have provided you an example of a more current operating system, one with a graphical user interface and lots of bells and whistles, I am foregoing the pretty pictures for an older operating system, SunOS 4.1.4 on older Sun hardware. With Solaris 7 coming out, you might be asking, "Isn't SunOS 4.1.4 almost dead?" Sure, you can run Solaris 7 on your older hardware, but your older hardware will run faster with less memory on the older operating system. People and facilities are still using this older hardware because the Sun hardware just won't die. More importantly, SunOS is representative of the older, less automated way of doing things. With SunOS, you will do many things by hand that something such as IRIX, SGI's current operating system, does transparently.

> **Note**
>
> **Doing it the hard way?** I've picked SunOS as one of the main representative OS flavors for this book for several reasons. Yes, partly because it's "the hard way." For comparison, you'll run through "the easy way" on an SGI in Appendix B, "Sample Operating System Installations", but there's a lot of merit in knowing how to do things by hand. As a system administrator, you'll find that it's exactly when you most need a tool that the easy interface to it isn't available or won't give you the flexibility you need.
>
> Additionally, almost all UNIX flavors have similar administrative, updating, and maintenance tasks. The interfaces to these tasks might vary wildly, but the concepts are generally the same. SunOS provides you with a selection of examples that are elegant in their simplicity; consider it a sort of lowest-common-denominator OS that makes for a good learning experience.

SunOS will give you a taste of the BSD flavor and provide some extra work (it will be good for you). You will get some basic experience with the SunOS example that you miss from some of the current operating systems that come with a lot of extras. Of course, a full install of SunOS on the stock 500MB drive in my SPARCstation IPX will actually leave me some room to spare, unlike a robust install of IRIX 6.5. On the other hand, you will not get to take any VRML (Virtual Reality Markup Language—the graphical equivalent of HTML) tours of the system, as you would get to do with a new SGI O2. Figure 3.2 shows you a few of the standard UNIX distributions as they come from the manufacturer. Interestingly, the newer the OS, the less paper you get—meaning that with an OS-like IRIX 6.5, all your documentation comes on CD-ROM, and you'd better hope that you have a working machine to read it if you need it.

FIGURE 3.2

From left to right, OS distributions for SunOS 4.1.4, Solaris 2.5.1, and IRIX 6.5—OSes that have come out at roughly two-year intervals since 1994.

Preliminary Advice

No matter what operating system you are installing, read through the instructions first, whether they are in the form of a little booklet or an actual book.

Plan ahead of time your desired drive partitions and sizes if you need to. Although it might seem as if that is work that you would only have to do for an older OS such as SunOS, you will find a drive-partitioning step even in Linux, a current and widely supported OS. Know what your machine's IP address is supposed to be, what your network gateway is, your NIS(YP) information, and any other network information (proxy servers, DHCP servers, and so on) that applies. Write it all out on a sheet of paper, a post-it, or whatever your preference is. Think of a name ahead of time for your machine. It's amazing how much time you can waste at the console trying to think of the right name for the machine! In Figures 3.3 and 3.4, you can see the decisions I've made for the machine I'll be using here. You will find copies of these forms in the back of the book in Appendix F, "Useful Sample Forms." Make a copy of these forms now so that you can fill in these values before you need them.

FIGURE 3.3

FIGURE 3.3

*Here is the information
for this machine. Some
of it, such as the
machine name, is my
own decision. Other
pieces are standard for
my particular network.
You might need to get
some of the pieces,
such as your gate-
way/default-route
address, from your
building network
administrator.*

Host Information Sheet

General Information

Host name: _____Barracuda_____

Manufacturer and Model: ____Sun____IPX_____

Architecture: _____sun4c_____

Operating System: _____SunOS 4.1.4_____

Serial number: _____

System number: _____57219a 1a_____

Location: _____

Network Information

IP Address: _____192.168.1.20_____

Default Route: _____192.168.1.4_____

Netmask: _____255.255.255.0_____

Domain Name: _____killernuts.org_____

NIS Information

Function: __✗__ Server ____ Slave ____ Client ____ None

NIS domain name: _____shipsahoy_____

FIGURE 3.4

Here is how it was decided to partition the drives. Keeping a sheet like this with not only the final values you've decided on, but a record of how you got to them (and any math errors you might have made) can help clear up confusion in the future.

Drive Partioning Sheet

General Information

Host name: Barracuda

Drive and Manufacturer Model: Fujitsu M2624FA-1

Cylinders 1440   Tracks _____   Sectors _____   Heads _____

Location: X Internal ___ External   (system disk)

SCSI ID: 0   SCSI controller: 0   Capacity: 519M

Partitions   → 512-byte blocks

part	type/tag	flag	cylinders	blocks	size	mount pt
a			(145/0/0)	~~102020~~ 102400	~~51M~~ 50M	/
b	swap		(290/0/0)	~~204160~~ 204800	~~108M~~ 100M	
c			(1440/0/0)	1013760	~~519M~~ 500M	
d						
e						
f						
g				665924	~~340M~~ 330M	/usr
h				40128	~~19M~~ 20M	/home

entire → drive (pointing at c)

1MB = 1048576 bytes

$$\frac{1048576 \text{ bytes}}{512 \text{ bytes}} = 2048$$

(a) $\frac{2048}{\times 50}$ = 102400   (b) $\frac{2048}{\times 100}$ = 204800

↓
(145/50) not even # cylinders → (290/10/0)
(145/0/0)   (290/0/0)

start a   0
start b   146
start g   437

initial g   1440
(rest of   145
drive)   290
            1005
skipped   → 2
cylinders   1003
          (1003/0/0)

146 + 290 = 436 + 1 = 437

final start set during OS install

a   0
b   145
g   435
h   1381

final g + h partitions made as part of OS install

Note

> **Assigning hostnames**   The name of your machine, or *hostname*, is not something you can just grab out of thin air and assign.
>
> First and foremost, it must be unique in your domain. It's a unique, plain English identifier for your IP address, and so it and your domain name (hostname + domainname = fully qualified domain name) must not be the same as any other machine anywhere in the world (or more properly, any other machine anywhere in the world that this one can talk to).
>
> Second, it should conform to any naming conventions your company might have defined. If your company names all its machines after Greek and Roman gods (an amazingly common practice—it's not hard to guess their NIS domain names either), they'll probably take a dim view of you naming your machine JimBob.
>
> Finally, you need to know that just because you name your machine something, that doesn't mean that the rest of the world can tell this. Your name must be registered with your name service so that the rest of the world can find out about it. How you do this will differ from organization to organization. Generally, there is one person responsible for updating name-service information. If you're not that person, find your network administrator and ask her who is the correct person. You'll need his help getting your new machine recognized by the world.

Booting from a CD-ROM

I am first going to have to boot from a CD-ROM. For installing the OS, most UNIX machines can be booted not only from a CD-ROM, but also over the network and from a magnetic tape drive. Booting from Magtape is much like booting from a CD-ROM (only a lot slower), and booting over the network is a more advanced topic than I'll cover here. Stick with the simple stuff and keep a copy of your OS installation CD handy while you get settled into your new role. You can experiment with network-booting machines when you're comfortable you know how to make them work the easy way.

To allow adjustments to drive partitioning and so on during installation, the machine will first load a minimal operating system, called the mini-root. From this, you execute the appropriate installation commands.

Here's what happens when I first turn on the machine:

```
WARNING: Unable to determine keyboard type
SPARCstation IPX, No Keyboard
ROM Rev. 2.9, 32 MB memory installed, Serial #2202138.
Ethernet address 8:0:20:d:8d:48, Host ID: 57219a1a.
```

```
Boot device: /sbus/esp@0,800000/sd@3,0   File and args:
The file just loaded does not appear to be executable.
Type b (boot), c (continue), or n (new command mode)
>new mode
Type  help  for more information
ok
```

To make some sense of this, you need to know that I disconnected the keyboard from the machine to make it ignore its screen, and to direct its console input and output to the primary serial port. I've connected a terminal to the serial port, and I'm actually talking to the Sun via a shareware terminal program from my Macintosh.

Note

> The *system console*, or just console, is the device to which the system sends output and from which it receives input by default. This is usually the keyboard and screen combination or, if there is no keyboard, one of the serial ports. When a person is logged into the system, the console is frequently directed to a window in that person's environment. Due to the multiuser abstraction that UNIX provides, frequently every concurrent user has a window that displays the console.

3

The initial response, that what was loaded does not seem to be executable, is a bit disturbing, but not altogether unexpected because I don't know where this machine has been or how it was used before I got it. Before I actually boot off the CD-ROM, I am curious to see what I might be able to learn about the machine. I've already put it in Sun's new command mode, which is a sort of interface for talking to the hardware. Your machine will probably have some sort of interface that provides similar functions—on Sun, it's a command line, on SGI it's a point-and-click interface, and for Linux on Intel hardware, it's your familiar CMOS setup.

See what my machine has to say for itself:

```
ok help

Enter 'help command-name' or 'help category-name' for more help
(Use ONLY the first word of a category description)
Examples:  help select   -or-   help line
    Main categories are:
File download and boot
Resume execution
Diag (diagnostic routines)
Select I/O devices
System and boot configuration parameters
Line editor
Tools:(memory,numbers,new commands,loops)
```

```
Assembly debugging:(breakpoints,registers,disassembly,symbolic)
>-prompt
Power on reset
Floppy eject
Sync (synchronize disk data)
ok
```

From the help command, I find out that there's quite a bit that I can do. What can I find out about the system? Take a look:

```
ok help system
     Category: System and boot configuration parameters
printenv         (−)     show all configuration parameters
     numbers are shown in decimal
setenv  name value       (−)     change a configuration parameter
     changes are permanent but only take effect after a reset
   Examples:
     setenv input-device ttya       - use ttya input next time
     setenv sbus-probe-list 0132    - set sequence of probing sbus slots
     setenv screen-#rows 0x1e       - use 30 rows of display ( hex 1e )
     setenv boot-device net         - specify network as boot device
     setenv auto-boot? false        - disable automatic boot
set-defaults      (−)     revert to factory configuration
ok
```

Look at the configuration parameters:

```
ok printenv
```

Parameter Name	Value	Default Value
selftest-#megs	32	1
output-device	screen	screen
input-device	keyboard	keyboard
sbus-probe-list	0123	0123
keyboard-click?	false	false
keymap		
ttyb-rts-dtr-off	false	false
ttyb-ignore-cd	true	true
ttya-rts-dtr-off	false	false
ttya-ignore-cd	true	true
ttyb-mode	9600,8,n,1,-	9600,8,n,1,-
ttya-mode	9600,8,n,1,-	9600,8,n,1,-
fcode-debug?	false	false
diag-file		
diag-device	net	net
boot-file		
boot-device	disk	disk
auto-boot?	true	true
watchdog-reboot?	false	false
local-mac-address?	false	false

```
screen-#columns        80                                  80
screen-#rows           34                                  34
scsi-initiator-id      7                                   7
use-nvramrc?           false                               false
nvramrc
sunmon-compat?         true                                true
security-mode          none                                none
security-password
security-#badlogins    16                                  <no default>
oem-logo               00 00 00 00 00 00 00 00 ...         <no default>
oem-logo?              false                               false
oem-banner                                                 <no default>
oem-banner?            false                               false
hardware-revision                                          <no default>
last-hardware-update                                       <no default>
testarea               85                                  0
mfg-switch?            false                               false
diag-switch?           false                               false

ok setenv selftest-#megs 2
selftest-#megs =       2
ok
```

Wow! That's quite a bit of information, and I haven't even booted off the CD-ROM yet. From this list, I can see things such as what speed my serial ports are set at, how many columns my screen is set to, and a plethora of specialty settings, such as whether the machine should load an OEM banner instead of the normal Sun banner at startup. Most of these can be adjusted with the `setenv` command you probably noticed in the previous `help` example. One of the changes to the default settings that you might want to consider if this were your machine would be to include the command `setenv selftest-#megs` (using some low number) because the startup time to rigorously test all 32MB gets a bit tedious sometimes. Here, I've set it down to 2MB so that it will only check 2MB of RAM, and starting up won't take all day.

If you don't have Sun hardware, your hardware-level command interface will be rather different. You're likely to have similar options available, however, and it's important that you feel comfortable working with your machines at this base level.

See what diagnostic tools might be available to you:

```
ok help diag
    Category: Diag (diagnostic routines)
test   device-specifier ( — ) run selftest method for specified device
    Examples:
        test /memory         - test memory
        test /sbus/le        - test net
        test net             - test net (device-specifier is an alias)
        test floppy          - test floppy disk drive
```

```
watch-clock        (−)     show ticks of real-time clock
probe-scsi         (−)     show attached SCSI devices
```

In the preceding example, probe-scsi looks useful. You might not always have to take an inventory of your devices, but it can be quite helpful. It's always a good idea to make certain you know exactly what your devices are when you are about to do something major to your system, such as upgrading from an older OS or, as I'll be doing here, installing an OS from scratch. Upon running probe-scsi, I find the following:

```
ok probe-scsi
Target 3
  Unit 0  Disk      FUJITSU M2624F-512      0405
Target 6
  Unit 0  Removable Read Only device TOSHIBA XM-4101TASUNSLCD342412/08/94
```

The CD-ROM drive that I will be booting from is on target 6 (here, SCSI ID 6 as well), and the hard drive destined to get an operating system is on target 3. You will see other ways of looking for this information during the different phases of the installation, just to get you used to looking for that sort of detail with your own system.

On your system, how the machine looks when you first turn it on will vary with the different operating systems. On your machine, you might also have gotten a command-line interface, a menu-driven system, or even a friendly graphical user interface.

Well, perhaps I should be getting on to booting from the CD-ROM. How do you do that? Ideally, you have already looked up the appropriate command in the documentation you received or in online documentation (that you had to use another computer to view because yours isn't working yet). If you're lucky, you might just be clicking a couple icons to accomplish the task. Unfortunately, I am not so lucky, and I have to check what my options might be:

```
ok help boot
   Category:  File download and boot
boot  <specifier>  (−)     boot vmunix ( default ) or other file
   Examples:
      boot                   - boot vmunix from default device ( sd )
      boot net               - boot vmunix from network
      boot cdrom             - boot vmunix (MUNIX) from CD-ROM
      boot tape              - boot default file from tape
      boot disk myunix -as   - boot myunix from disk with flags "-as"
      boot /sbus/esp/st@4,0 oldunix  - boot oldunix from scsi device
                                       'st' target 4 unit 0
```

It looks on this machine, a SPARCstation IPX, as if the boot cdrom command should do the trick. However, if this were a SPARCstation IPC, I would use boot sd(0,6,2) instead. Obviously, the command varies with the hardware, so be sure you have checked ahead of time.

Now, I am going to give it a try:

```
ok boot cdrom
Boot device: /sbus/esp@0,800000/sd@6,0:c    File and args:
root on /sbus@1,f8000000/esp@0,800000/sd@6,0:c fstype 4.2
Boot: vmunix
Size: 770048+2247512+54024 bytes
SunOS Release 4.1.4 (MUNIX) #2: Fri Oct 14 11:07:06 PDT 1994
Copyright (c) 1983-1993, Sun Microsystems, Inc.
mem = 32768K (0x2000000)
avail mem = 5001216
Ethernet address = 8:0:20:d:8d:48
cpu = SUNW,Sun 4/50
zs0 at obio 0xf1000000 pri 12
zs1 at obio 0xf0000000 pri 12
sbus0 at SBus slot 0 0x0
dma0 at SBus slot 0 0x400000
esp0 at SBus slot 0 0x800000 pri 3
sd0 at esp0 target 3 lun 0
sd0: <Fujitsu M2624FA-1 cyl 1440 alt 2 hd 11 sec 64>
sr0 at esp0 target 6 lun 0
le0 at SBus slot 0 0xc00000 pri 5
fd0 at obio 0xf7200000 pri 11
rd0: using preloaded munixfs
WARNING: preposterous time in file system — CHECK AND RESET THE DATE!
root on rd0a fstype 4.2
swap on ns0b fstype spec size 4788K
dump on ns0b fstype spec size 4776K

What would you like to do?
   1 - install SunOS mini-root
   2 - exit to single user shell
Enter a 1 or 2: 1
```

Note how the boot device, /sbus/esp@0,800000/sd@6,0:c, has changed. The 6 indicates target 6, which probe-scsi showed to be the CD-ROM drive. (So far, so good.)

At this point, I can choose 1, load the mini-root, to begin the installation procedure. On your machine, whatever you have to do to boot off the CD might automatically load the mini-root for you without asking if that's what you want to do.

Formatting Your System Disk

Just after I choose to install the mini-root, the computer responds:

```
Beginning system installation - probing for disks.
installing miniroot on disk "sd0", (only disk found).
Do you want to format and/or label disk "sd0"?
   1 - yes, run format
   2 - no, continue with loading miniroot
   3 - no, exit to single user shell
Enter a 1, 2, or 3:
```

Because I am not sure about my disk, I will go ahead and choose number 1, format. (If you are using new hardware, you probably will not want to format your hard drive. It usually comes from the vendor preformatted.) This is a bit of a preview of some of what you'll learn next week when you add a disk drive to your system. In that lesson, I'll spend more time on the details and you will have the luxury of not having to rush through a format.

After I choose to run format, the installation process gives me a menu:

```
Searching for disks...done
selecting sd0: <Fujitsu M2624FA-1>
[disk formatted, defect list found]


FORMAT MENU:
        disk       - select a disk
        type       - select (define) a disk type
        partition  - select (define) a partition table
        current    - describe the current disk
        format     - format and analyze the disk
        repair     - repair a defective sector
        show       - translate a disk address
        label      - write label to the disk
        analyze    - surface analysis
        defect     - defect list management
        backup     - search for backup labels
        quit
format>
```

The software notes that the drive appears to already be formatted and that it contains an accumulated list of defective sectors. If I wanted, I could skip the formatting step with this drive, but because it's to be an example, I'll forge ahead. I will choose type to see if my disk is already listed. On Sun machines, the type menu enables you to define the geometry and access parameters for the disk. When you install a new disk in Week Two, you'll get an example of how to determine and enter the drive parameters. Vendors other than Sun handle drive-geometry definition by configuration files in the configuration directory /etc or by assorted automatic methods that sometimes appear to border on magic. Here, when I ask the machine what drive types it knows about, it responds as follows:

```
format> type
AVAILABLE DRIVE TYPES:
        0. Quantum ProDrive 80S
        1. Quantum ProDrive 105S
        2. CDC Wren IV 94171-344
        3. SUN0104
        4. SUN0207
```

```
    5. SUN0320
    6. SUN0327
    7. SUN0424
    8. SUN0535
    9. SUN0669
   10. SUN1.0G
   11. SUN1.05
   12. SUN1.3G
   13. SUN2.1G
   14. Fujitsu M2624FA-1
   15. other
Specify disk type (enter its number) [14]:
```

If I look at the default offered, I see that it is indeed my disk:

```
selecting sd0: <Fujitsu M2624FA-1>
[disk formatted, defect list found]
```

I've probably dallied around enough now. Shall I take the plunge and do the format?

```
format> format

Ready to format. Formatting cannot be interrupted
and takes 8 minutes (estimated). Continue?
Continue? yes
Beginning format. The current time is Thu Mar 18 07:18:58 1999

Formatting...done

Verifying media...
        pass 0 - pattern = 0xc6dec6de
   1439/9/38

        pass 1 - pattern = 0x6db6db6d
   1439/9/38

Total of 0 defective blocks repaired.
format>
```

Don't believe the estimated time; it took more than 8 minutes, more like 45 minutes actually. Unfortunately, that was enough time for me to forget the menu choices. If you forget your menu choices, always look for some sort of help before continuing. Whether you are formatting your system disk or an additional disk, the wrong choice could result in disaster. Here is what happens when I try help:

```
format> help

'help' is not expected.
```

Only to discover that help doesn't work on this menu.

Typing help doesn't produce the response I would expect from the system, so trying ? seems to work better:

```
format> ?
Expecting one of the following (abbreviations ok):
        disk        - select a disk
        type        - select (define) a disk type
        partition   - select (define) a partition table
        current     - describe the current disk
        format      - format and analyze the disk
        repair      - repair a defective sector
        show        - translate a disk address
        label       - write label to the disk
        analyze     - surface analysis
        defect      - defect list management
        backup      - search for backup labels
        quit
format>
```

Now that the drive has been formatted and I remember what my choices are, I am ready to partition the drive. In this case, the vendor advises only partitioning root and swap at this stage and perhaps cleaning up some overlapping partitions. Any other partitions I might want to create will have to be done during the OS installation process.

Hopefully, you have thought about the partition sizes you would like to have. Be sure to look at the vendor's instructions because you might find that some operating systems prefer certain partitions in certain places. Among the specifics for SunOS are that the root partition will be Partition A and swap will be Partition B. For SunOS, a fairly large /usr partition (on G) is also recommended. SGI once recommended separate / and /usr partitions, but the operating system has grown over the years and now only a / partition is recommended on the system disk. In general, I'd recommend not adhering too closely to the vendor's recommended sizes for partitions. Although they tend to be reasonable sizes if you never have to upgrade your system and never exercise it too hard, they also tend to be rather conservative. It never hurts to have the root partition larger than the vendor recommends. Requirements for the swap partition vary between vendors from roughly the same size as the physical memory on the system to three or more times the size of the physical memory. Again, it never hurts to have it larger than recommended; if your swap is larger than you ever need it to be, you've wasted a little disk space. If it's smaller, you'll eventually hit an out-of-memory condition.

From the partition menu on my machine, I can find out my options and see how the drive is currently partitioned:

```
format> partition

PARTITION MENU:
        a      - change 'a' partition
        b      - change 'b' partition
        c      - change 'c' partition
        d      - change 'd' partition
        e      - change 'e' partition
        f      - change 'f' partition
        g      - change 'g' partition
        h      - change 'h' partition
        select - select a predefined table
        name   - name the current table
        print  - display the current table
        label  - write partition map and label to the disk
        quit
partition> print
Current partition table (original sd0):
        partition a - starting cyl     0, # blocks      704 (1/0/0)
        partition b - starting cyl     1, # blocks   400576 (569/0/0)
        partition c - starting cyl     0, # blocks  1013760 (1440/0/0)
        partition d - starting cyl   570, # blocks   612480 (870/0/0)
        partition e - starting cyl     0, # blocks        0 (0/0/0)
        partition f - starting cyl     0, # blocks        0 (0/0/0)
        partition g - starting cyl     0, # blocks        0 (0/0/0)
        partition h - starting cyl     0, # blocks        0 (0/0/0)

partition>
```

The plan for my 500MB drive is approximately 50MB on / (remember, / is the root directory and typically has its own partition), 100MB on swap, 330MB on /usr, and 20MB on /home (where I would put user directories). In my case, the vendor recommends 16MB on / and 32MB on swap. Ideally, / is only intended to have what the operating system minimally needs. However, if you have to reconfigure your kernel (add or change parts of the software at the most basic level of the system), you want enough room to save the old one and try the new one. As you start to apply patches, the space you start to need in / can grow beyond what you have. This was going to be a problem for me on our older SGIs running IRIX 5.3. With the exception of the machine that's system disk had failed and had been replaced with a larger disk and a larger / partition (by the system administrator who passed this wise advice on to me), the rest had 16MB / partitions and not enough room to apply the Y2K patches. I ended up having to back all the user data up to tape and to completely reformat the drives before upgrading them to the Y2K-compliant IRIX 6.5. The IRIX 6.5 installation recommends that the entire system disk consist of the one / partition. Tearing everything down to overcome the short-sightedness of the default installation was quite annoying, but now at least they are Y2K compliant! (Of course, they are probably also slower than they would be if they were still running 5.3, but that's one of the prices you pay for running antique hardware.)

Note

Some is good, more is better, and too much is just right When deciding on partition sizes, it's always safer to overestimate than to underestimate. If you make your root partition too small, you'll eventually run into a situation where it fills up and something ends up breaking. If you make your swap partition too small, you'll eventually end up out of memory and unable to run something you're trying to execute. Disk space is cheap; your time isn't. Save yourself time and headaches by giving your partitions all the space you imagine that they could ever use and then giving them some more.

/var especially is subject to unlimited space consumption by users and automated processes. The /var directory hierarchy typically contains temporary files, log files, and files waiting around for a system service to deal with them (such as outgoing or incoming mail or printer jobs). It isn't unreasonable to dedicate hundreds of megabytes to /var, and to be ready to replace it with an entire partition or drive if the need arises.

At any rate, see how the plan for the hard drive partitioning unfolds:

```
partition> a

        partition a - starting cyl     0, # blocks      704 (1/0/0)

Enter new starting cyl [0]:
Enter new # blocks [704, 1/0/0]: 50M
'50M' is not an integer.
Enter new # blocks [704, 1/0/0]: 102400
partition>
```

Note that I've chosen to start it on cylinder 0 (zero). To my dismay, I learn that I can't specify 50MB and have to specify 512-byte blocks (50MB×2,048) instead. You might be able to specify the desired size in megabytes with your operating system. Be sure to read your vendor's comments carefully as you partition your drive. In next week's chapters, you will see some different examples for partitioning drives. Now, continue:

```
partition> print
Current partition table (unnamed):
        partition a - starting cyl     0, # blocks    102400 (145/5/0)
        partition b - starting cyl     1, # blocks    400576 (569/0/0)
        partition c - starting cyl     0, # blocks   1013760 (1440/0/0)
        partition d - starting cyl   570, # blocks    612480 (870/0/0)
        partition e - starting cyl     0, # blocks         0 (0/0/0)
        partition f - starting cyl     0, # blocks         0 (0/0/0)
        partition g - starting cyl     0, # blocks         0 (0/0/0)
        partition h - starting cyl     0, # blocks         0 (0/0/0)
```

The numbers in parentheses, (145/5/0) indicate that my 50MB will take 145 full cylinders, 5 additional full tracks, and 0 additional sectors on my drive. Splitting partitions on cylinder boundaries increases performance, so I really don't want those 5 additional tracks. SunOS provides a nice way to fix this: I can specify partition sizes either in megabytes or in Cylinders/Tracks/Sectors format. Because I can get better performance with even cylinder boundaries, I will decrease the size of the partition by repeating the same partition command with slightly different answers to the questions:

```
partition> a

        partition a - starting cyl      0, # blocks    102400 (145/5/0)

Enter new starting cyl [0]:
Enter new # blocks [102400, 145/5/0]: 145/0/0
partition>
```

I am now ready to make a partition for swap space. First, I have to specify a starting cylinder for the swap partition on b. Here, I can't just choose 0. I have to remember that I already have a partition in place. Read your vendor's instructions for how they recommend entering the starting cylinder information. Some systems are zero-based, some are one-based, and yet others use a more convenient scheme where they list partitions by start and stop cylinders instead of start and length. Even after reading your vendor's instructions, you'll probably want to skip one cylinder (or whatever unit your version of format speaks—some ignore cylinders and use tracks), regardless of whether your vendor indicates that you have to. It has been my experience that vendors are sometimes confused about how their own software works. Because of this, I have gotten into the practice of starting new partitions spaced one cylinder past where the last partition ends. Here, although I could probably start the next partition on cylinder 145, I think it will be better for me to choose 146, which is not at all in question. I waste a cylinder but save myself a potential headache:

```
partition> b

        partition b - starting cyl      1, # blocks    400576 (569/0/0)

Enter new starting cyl [1]: 146
Enter new # blocks [400576, 569/0/0]: 204800
partition> print
Current partition table (unnamed):
        partition a - starting cyl      0, # blocks    102080 (145/0/0)
        partition b - starting cyl    146, # blocks    204800 (290/10/0)
        partition c - starting cyl      0, # blocks   1013760 (1440/0/0)
        partition d - starting cyl    570, # blocks    612480 (870/0/0)
        partition e - starting cyl      0, # blocks         0 (0/0/0)
        partition f - starting cyl      0, # blocks         0 (0/0/0)
        partition g - starting cyl      0, # blocks         0 (0/0/0)
        partition h - starting cyl      0, # blocks         0 (0/0/0)

partition>
```

As you can see here, I have then optimized partition b to (290/0/0):

```
partition> print
Current partition table (unnamed):
        partition a - starting cyl       0, # blocks    102080 (145/0/0)
        partition b - starting cyl     146, # blocks    204160 (290/0/0)
        partition c - starting cyl       0, # blocks   1013760 (1440/0/0)
        partition d - starting cyl       0, # blocks         0 (0/0/0)
        partition e - starting cyl       0, # blocks         0 (0/0/0)
        partition f - starting cyl       0, # blocks         0 (0/0/0)
        partition g - starting cyl       0, # blocks         0 (0/0/0)
        partition h - starting cyl       0, # blocks         0 (0/0/0)
```

The c partition spans the entire disk and is supposed to remain so designated. Looking at it, you can see the size of the entire disk in cylinders—1,440 in this case. Which partition is the one to span the entire disk will vary with the vendor, but they all seem to use one. For that matter, the partition-naming conventions will also vary. For example, the partitions are identified in IRIX by number, rather than by letter.

I also try assigning a partition size (to fill the remainder of the disk) to partition g at this point:

```
partition> g

        partition g - starting cyl       0, # blocks         0 (0/0/0)

Enter new starting cyl [0]: 437
Enter new # blocks [0, 0/0/0]: 1005/0/0
'1005/0/0' is out of range.
Enter new # blocks [0, 0/0/0]: 1003/0/0
partition> print
Current partition table (unnamed):
        partition a - starting cyl       0, # blocks    102080 (145/0/0)
        partition b - starting cyl     146, # blocks    204160 (290/0/0)
        partition c - starting cyl       0, # blocks   1013760 (1440/0/0)
        partition d - starting cyl       0, # blocks         0 (0/0/0)
        partition e - starting cyl       0, # blocks         0 (0/0/0)
        partition f - starting cyl       0, # blocks         0 (0/0/0)
        partition g - starting cyl     437, # blocks    706112 (1003/0/0)
        partition h - starting cyl       0, # blocks         0 (0/0/0)
```

By skipping another cylinder, the start cylinder for g is (0 + 145 + 1 + 290 + 1) = 437. I have to remember that I "wasted" these spare cylinders between partitions when I am assigning the total number of cylinders for the g partition. If I just assume that I've used only 145 + 290 cylinders, I might think that I have (1,440 − 435) = 1,005 cylinders remaining, but by spacing my partitions out by a cylinder each, I only have 1,003 cylinders remaining.

If you find this confusing, don't worry. I will go over this more thoroughly next week when I add another disk drive. However, if you do have to partition a drive for your system disk, you might want to look this over a bit. The procedure might not be exactly the same, but you will probably have to deal with similar calculations and concepts.

Here's the final layout:

```
partition> print
Current partition table (unnamed):
        partition a - starting cyl     0, # blocks   102080 (145/0/0)
        partition b - starting cyl   146, # blocks   204160 (290/0/0)
        partition c - starting cyl     0, # blocks  1013760 (1440/0/0)
        partition d - starting cyl     0, # blocks        0 (0/0/0)
        partition e - starting cyl     0, # blocks        0 (0/0/0)
        partition f - starting cyl     0, # blocks        0 (0/0/0)
        partition g - starting cyl   437, # blocks   706112 (1003/0/0)
        partition h - starting cyl     0, # blocks        0 (0/0/0)
```

When you've gotten your drive to this state, you'll want to print this out and save it for future reference. For simplicity, if I need to duplicate this layout, I can name the partition table I've just created:

```
partition> name
Enter table name (remember quotes): "512Mb 50a/100b/350g"
```

Note that I've chosen a name that includes sufficient information for me (or the next system administrator that comes along) to figure out what it was I did. The convenience of having a saved partition table that I can reuse is not so convenient if I have to load every one I've created to find the one I want.

Next, I need to label the disk. The software actually makes the changes indicated to tables it holds in memory. To actually make the changes to the disk itself, you write the data from memory to the drive—in essence, "labeling" the disk. Again, procedures vary from UNIX flavor to UNIX flavor; follow whatever procedures your vendor recommends. Don't use the fact that the data isn't written to disk until you label it as an intentional safety valve. As soon as you learn to trust a safety feature to be there for you, you'll meet a machine that doesn't have it. Constant care is your best safety. Now, continue:

```
partition> label
Ready to label disk, continue? y
```

Now, I check to see if the named table is listed. There's no reason it shouldn't be, but again, a little care now saves headaches later:

```
partition> select
        0. original sd0
        1. 512Mb 50a/100b/350g
Specify table (enter its number) [1]:

partition> q
```

Finally, I think I am ready to continue with the installation proper. It sure is much nicer to work with newer hardware that comes with a preformatted system disk!

```
format> q

checking writeability of /dev/rsd0b
0+1 records in
1+0 records out
Extracting miniroot ...
using cdrom partition number 2
¦

Mini-root installation complete.
```

Performing the Installation

Now that the mini-root has been copied to the swap partition, I have all the tools necessary to install the operating system.

Rebooting from the Mini-Root

After installing the mini-root, the computer asks this:

```
What would you like to do?
  1 - reboot using the just-installed miniroot
  2 - exit into single user shell
Enter a 1 or 2: 1
```

I choose 1. Now, the machine will reboot from the hard drive using the mini-root that was just installed. This time, I do not get any comments about the loaded file not being executable! A quick look at the boot device name shows that the machine has indeed booted off the hard drive, target 3, using partition b, which is the swap partition.

Note

> **Booting from swap partition?** Yes, most OS installation procedures build a small filesystem on the swap partition for the purposes of running the installation software. Although it might not be immediately obvious, this makes perfect sense. The swap partition is only ever used as transient

storage for spare memory. Because the installation process doesn't need much memory, it shouldn't need swap space, and it's the only partition that's guaranteed to not have anything else interesting in it. Of course, this means that if for some reason your installation goes wrong, you might have to start over again because there's no guarantee that the installation filesystem on swap will have survived.

When the system reboots, you should see something similar to the following:

```
rebooting from: /sbus@1,f8000000/esp@0,800000/sd@3,0:b -sw
syncing file systems... done
Rebooting...
SPARCstation IPX, No Keyboard
ROM Rev. 2.9, 32 MB memory installed, Serial #2202138.
Ethernet address 8:0:20:d:8d:48, Host ID: 57219a1a.

Rebooting with command: /sbus@1,f8000000/esp@0,800000/sd@3,0:b -sw
Boot device: /sbus@1,f8000000/esp@0,800000/sd@3,0:b   File and args: -sw
root on /sbus@1,f8000000/esp@0,800000/sd@3,0:b fstype 4.2
Boot: vmunix
Size: 835584+154952+55064 bytes
SunOS Release 4.1.4 (MINIROOT) #2: Fri Oct 14 11:07:35 PDT 1994
Copyright (c) 1983-1993, Sun Microsystems, Inc.
mem = 32768K (0x2000000)
avail mem = 31186944
Ethernet address = 8:0:20:d:8d:48
cpu = SUNW,Sun 4/50
zs0 at obio 0xf1000000 pri 12
zs1 at obio 0xf0000000 pri 12
sbus0 at SBus slot 0 0x0
dma0 at SBus slot 0 0x400000
esp0 at SBus slot 0 0x800000 pri 3
sd0 at esp0 target 3 lun 0
sd0: <Fujitsu M2624FA-1 cyl 1440 alt 2 hd 11 sec 64>
sr0 at esp0 target 6 lun 0
le0 at SBus slot 0 0xc00000 pri 5
fd0 at obio 0xf7200000 pri 11
WARNING: preposterous time in file system — CHECK AND RESET THE DATE!
root on sd0b fstype 4.2
swap on sd0b fstype spec size 102080K
dump on sd0b fstype spec size 102068K
#
```

Note the pound sign after the diagnostic messages. This indicates that I am now in a shell in the mini-root. Before I can begin the installation step, I have to verify that the terminal emulator I'm using to talk to the machine, a vt100, is indeed in /etc/termcap by issuing the following:

```
# grep -i vt100 /etc/termcap
```

If the machine had been hooked up to a Sun keyboard and monitor rather than a terminal, I could have skipped this step. Keep in mind that unless you're installing a machine with no monitor and keyboard (a *headless* machine), this is likely a step that your system will not require.

> **Note**
>
> **Shells on the beach**   Most of the shell syntax you'll see me use in this book is csh (the C shell) or tcsh syntax. Depending on the flavor of UNIX you'll be working with, your default shell might be csh, sh (the Bourne shell), ksh (the Korn shell), bash (the Bourne again shell), or one of a range of lesser-known variants. Each of these has slightly different syntax and slightly differing ways of performing certain tasks. The Bourne shell, sh, is by far the most widely available shell, but its lack of features makes it a poor choice for a user shell. The csh shell is probably the second most prevalent shell. It is a good one to standardize on for day-to-day use because it's friendly enough to be usable, and you'll find it almost anywhere you go. An extended version of csh, the tcsh shell, provides extra features that I like. Don't select a non-ubiquitous shell for root's default shell because you never know when the machine is going to come up with most of its partitions missing. Root's login must be indestructible, so if you want to use an alternative shell such as tcsh for most of your normal work, start it by hand or in your startup scripts after you log on.

Starting the Installation

Now that all the preparatory work has been done, I really am ready to begin installing the operating system. Again, your system might have a different command, or some other way of getting you started:

```
# suninstall
```

This command brings up a screen that looks something like the following:

```
                    Welcome to SunInstall

   Remember:  Always back up your disks before beginning an installation.

SunInstall provides two installation methods:
   1. Quick installation
```

```
This option provides an automatic installation with a choice of
standard installations, and a minimum number of questions asked.
```

```
2. Custom installation
```

```
Choose this method if you want more freedom to configure your
system.  You must use this option if you are installing your
system as a server.
```

```
Your choice (or Q to quit) >> 2
```

Because I'd actually like to make and talk about a couple decisions here, I choose the custom installation. Next, I have to specify my terminal type based on the /etc/termcap entry I determined earlier:

```
Select your terminal type:
        1) Televideo 925
        2) Wyse Model 50
        3) Sun Workstation
        4) Other
>> 4
```

```
Enter the terminal type ( the type must be in /etc/termcap ):
>> vt100
```

Assigning a Time Zone

Next, I have to pick the time zone. I could have entered this at the command line, but it is easier to pick by asking for help, again using ? rather than help. How you specify the time zone will vary from operating system to operating system (one actually puts you in a VRML world where a nice lady in a video screen explains to you how to adjust the settings). If you do not have to indicate a time zone at the initial installation time, you will probably need to edit a file and reboot your machine to adjust the machine's time zone. Here, I begin:

```
TIMEZONE MENU                                     [?=help]

        Select one of the following categories to display
         a screen of tie zone names for that region

                     x   United States

                         Canada

                         Mexico

                         South America

                         Europe
```

```
                      Asia

                      Australia and New Zealand

                      Greenwich Mean Time

Are you finished with this menu [y/n] ? y

[RET/SPC=next choice] [x/X=select choice] [^B/^P=backward] [^F/^N=forward]
```

After selecting United States, I get more choices:

```
UNITED STATES MENU                                    [?=help]

        TIME ZONE NAME                 AREA
    x US/Eastern                       Eastern time zone, USA

      US/Central                       Central time zone, USA

      US/Mountain                      Mountain time zone, USA

      US/Pacific                       Pacific time zone, USA

      US/Pacific-New                   Pacific time zone, USA
                                       with proposed change to Daylight
                                       Savings Time near election time

      US/Alaska                        Alaska time zone, USA

      US/East-Indiana                  Eastern time zone, USA
                                       no Daylight Savings Time

      US/Hawaii                        Hawaii

 Are you finished with this menu [y/n] ? y

[RET/SPC=next choice] [x/X=select choice] [^B/^P=backward] [^F/^N=forward]
```

Next, I have to confirm date and time or change it if necessary:

```
Is this the correct date/time: Thu Mar 18 04:19:16 EST 1999

[y/n] >> n

Enter the current date and local time (e.g. 03/09/88 12:20:30); the date
may be in one of the following formats:

        mm/dd/yy
        mm/dd/yyyy
        dd.mm.yyyy
        dd-mm-yyyy
```

```
dd-mm-yy
month dd, yyyy
dd month yyyy
```

and the time may be in one of the following formats:

```
hh am/pm
hh:mm am/pm
hh.mm
hh:mm am/pm
hh.mm
hh:mm:ss am/pm
hh:mm:ss
hh.mm.ss am/pm
hh.mm.ss
```

```
>> 03/18/99 04:02:00
```

```
Is this the correct date/time: Thu Mar 18 04:02:00 EST 1999
```

```
[y/n] >> y
```

Although this menu might not be identical to what you see when you set your time and
date information, the formats available are likely to be similar.

Assigning Host Information

Finally, I get to the main menu. As I complete a section in the main menu, an additional
section is added. The first section to appear is one on assigning host information. This is
when it's handy to already have a name in mind for your machine. It's time to refer back
to those sheets with host information you were going to fill in. Again, the look and feel
of your OS's installation and configuration procedure will vary with each type system,
but you will still have to provide this type of information at some point, whether it's part
of a menu-driven system or part of a VRML experience:

```
MAIN MENU                                              [?=help]
                    Sun Microsystems System Installation Tool

                      ( + means the data file(s) exist(s) )

                          assign host information


                          start the installation

                          exit suninstall

[RET/SPC=next choice] [x/X=select choice] [^B/^P=backward] [^F/^N=forward]
```

Selecting assign host information prompts me for the following information:

```
HOST FORM              [?=help] [DEL=erase one char] [RET=end of input data]

Workstation information :
    Name :  Barracuda
    Type :  [standalone]   x[server    [dataless]



Network Information :
    Ethernet Interface :   [none]   x[le0]

    Internet address    : 192.168.1.20
    NIS Type            : [none] x[master]   [slave]   [client]
    Domain name         : killernuts.org

Misc Information :
    Reboot after completed :   [y]  x[n]



Are you finished with this menu [y/n] ? y

 [x/X=select choice] [space=next choice] [^B/^P=backward] [^F/^N=forward]
```

Note that if you intend to have multiple machines and users who would like to conveniently use the machines, you will probably want to make use of NIS (the Network Information Service), a sort of user information sharing database that I will discuss in more detail next week. When you are installing your operating system, you will probably have to indicate in some way what type of NIS participant your machine will be. In my case, the machine will be the master, the machine that actually controls and provides the information for other machines. This machine will serve passwords and other important information to client machines. You might also have a machine that will be an NIS slave server, essentially a backup to the master. If you have either type of machine, be sure to indicate on this form that you do not want to reboot. You will have to run a command to set up the NIS databases. Other operating systems will provide the appropriate instructions for anything special you might need to do to implement NIS on your machine. Also be aware that the IP that I've selected is one of a range that has been set aside for personal networks and that can't exist as part of the address range on the Internet. You will have to determine the IP to use for your machine by asking your network administrator or whoever it is that assigns network resources in your location.

Again, remember that if you're not installing SunOS as I am doing in this example, your machine is going to have different ways of specifying this information. All of it is necessary information, and your OS will have some way of asking you for it.

Tip

Answer everything Also, as a quirk of the host information request when you're installing SunOS, I have to select an answer to each item on the form, even if the default is the right choice for me. If I do not indicate something for each question, I will (and did) end up lost in a loop, trying to answer a question that the form doesn't want to take me to.

Assigning Disk Information

After I've filled in the host information, I tell the system that I'm done with the form, which takes me back to the main menu. From the main menu, I will be able to next choose to assign disk information. The disk form asks the following:

```
DISK FORM            [?=help] [DEL=erase one char] [RET=end of input data]
_ _ _ _ _ _ _ _ _ _ _ _ _ _ _ _ _ _ _ _ _ _ _ _ _ _ _ _ _ _ _ _ _ _
Attached Disk Devices :
   x[sd0]

Disk Label :  [default]  [use existing]  [modify existing]
Free Hog Disk Partition :  [d]  [e]  [f]  [g] x[h]
Disk Label :  [default]  [use existing] x[modify existing]
Display Unit       : x[Mbytes]  [Kbytes]  [blocks]  [cylinders]
```

That funny `Free Hog Disk Partition` you see in the preceding listing is what SunInstall uses to adjust other partition sizes as needed for the software I will shortly be installing. It is assigned to the h partition, which usually houses the users' directories. Because its size is determined relative to the sizes of the other partitions, I can't change h directly. I will only be able to change its size by changing the size of another partition.

Now is when I can specify partition sizes that I couldn't specify in the format step. Keep in mind that at this stage, the sizes of / and swap cannot be changed here. Again, how you initially specify this information will vary with your system. You might also have menu-driven options similar to this, or in the case of IRIX, which now wants everything in one partition, this will not even be a worry to you:

PARTITION	START_CYL	BLOCKS	SIZE	MOUNT PT	PRESERVE(Y/N)
a	0	102080	51		
b	145	204160	103		
c	0	1013760	519		
d	0	0	0		
e	0	0	0		
f	0	0	0		
g	435	706112	360		
h	0	0	0		

3

Notice how the system has automatically changed the starting cylinders to numbers that look like they should be all right but that are choices that you can't always rely on as being safe if you entered them yourself. Hope it knows what it's doing and that this change really does work.

Next, I pick some mount points for partitions I've created—/, and /usr. I also assign some space to the h partition by decreasing the size of the g partition. To maintain an overall total, the h partition has to increase to make up for the deficit caused by the change in g. You might have to watch for something similar with your system. Also note that I've marked the preserve field as n for these partitions. I'm starting from scratch here:

```
PARTITION START_CYL BLOCKS   SIZE    MOUNT PT              PRESERVE(Y/N)
================================================================================

    a      0        102080   51      /                        n
    b      145      204160   103
    c      0        1013760  519
    d      0        0        0
    e      0        0        0
    f      0        0        0
    g      435      665984   340     /usr                     n
    h      1381     40128    19      /home                    n
```

Choosing Software

On completing the disk form, I can choose software from the software form. With SunOS, this is a relatively fast, painless procedure. With IRIX 6.5, however, you have to scroll through many CDs of choices, each item with a cryptic description. It can take a while to pick which software packages you want, and you usually end up missing one or two in spite of all your efforts to double-check everything. Ironically, this stage of an IRIX install is command-line based rather than graphical and provides less information than the old SunOS system I'm installing here:

```
SOFTWARE FORM         [?=help] [DEL=erase one char] [RET=end of input data]
Software Architecture Operations:
   x[add new release  [edit existig release]


Media Information:
  Media Device  :  [st0]  [st1]  [st2]  [st_]  [xt0]  [mt0]  [fd0] x[sr0]
  Media Location :  x[local]  [remote]


Choice:   [all]   [default]   [required]   x[own choice]
    Executables path:  /usr
    Kernel executables path:  /usr/kvm

Destination fs:  /usr   (sd0g)
```

As I add choices, I see changes in the figures at the bottom right of the form. My used space increases, whereas my free space decreases. Your system will show you something similar, whether it is with each package you install or after some number of packages depends on the OS.

I select own choice, which automatically chooses required packages and then lets me pick additional optional ones (your vendor will provide instructions on how to select default items, add the defaults, and so on):

```
SOFTWARE FORM          [?=help] [DEL=erase one char] [RET=end of input data]
Software Architecture Operations:
  x[add new release  [edit existig release]


Media Information:
 Media Device   :  [st0]  [st1]  [st2]  [st_]  [xt0]  [mt0]  [fd0] x[sr0]
 Media Location :  x[local]  [remote]


Choice:   [all]  [default]   [required]   x[own choice]
    Executables path:  /usr
    Kernel executables path:  /usr/kvm

Media Filenames:
  root    Install      Sys            Demo
  usr     Networking   SunView_Users  OpenWindows_Users
  Kvm     System_V     Text           OpenWindows_Demo


 OK to use this architecture configuration [y/n] ?

[RET/SPC=next choice] [x/X=select choice] [^B/^P=backward] [^F/^N=forward]
```

Assigning Client Information

When I finish adding software packages, the next choice that appears on the main menu is assigning client information. I only have to complete that form if I will have some diskless clients or want to use this server to provide binaries for machines that don't share the same architecture. Both of these are beyond the scope of this book, but you'll probably be surprised how close to ready you'll be to do even these tasks by the time you're finished with your three-week course. For the time being, if you need to support multiple architectures, you'll be much happier doing it by having a separate server for each. Because I will not have either diskless clients or disparate architecture clients, I am not completing that form. The form asks for such information as client name, architecture, IP address, paths to various directories, and so on.

Rechecking Partition Sizes

Now that I have added some software, I should double-check my partition sizes to see whether I need to make any further adjustments. SunOS is nice in that it doesn't actually partition the drive during the install until after you've selected what software you want to install. If your partition selections aren't sufficient for the software you've installed, it will try to reconfigure things to make everything fit. Other UNIX flavors partition first, then complain that you can't fit all the software, and make you repartition the drive yourself. Depending on your system, you might have a similar step.

The main menu now looks like this:

```
MAIN MENU                                           [?=help]
                Sun Microsystems System Installation Tool

                  ( + means the data file(s) exist(s) )

                 + assign host information

                 + assign disk information

                 + assign software information

                 + assign client information


                 _ start the installation

                   exit suninstall

[RET/SPC=next choice] [x/X=select choice] [^B/^P=backward] [^F/^N=forward]
```

I have to choose assign disk information one more time. To the menu in the listing, an option named data file has been added. If I choose this option, I can look at the new decisions for the partition table. The system might have had to increase and decrease partition sizes, so this is my opportunity to make any changes that might better meet my needs. For my install, none of my partition sizes have changed, so I don't need to do anything. When I finish this form, I will finally be ready to start the ball rolling!

```
Choose    x start the installation
```

Now, I can walk away for quite a while! After the machine has crunched away for a while, it will have spit out a bunch of lines that look something like the following:

```
System Installation Begins:
Label disk(s):
        sd0
```

```
Create/check filesystems:
Creating new filesystem for / on sd0a
newfs /dev/rsd0a >> /etc/install/suninstall.log 2>&1


Creating new filesystem for /home on sd0h
newfs /dev/rsd0h >> /etc/install/suninstall.log 2>&1


Creating new filesystem for /usr on sd0g
newfs /dev/rsd0g >> /etc/install/suninstall.log 2>&1


Setting up server file system for services
Extracting the sunos 4.1.4 sun4c 'root' media file.
Extracting the sunos 4.1.4 sun4c 'usr' media file.
Extracting the sunos 4.1.4 sun4c 'Kvm' media file.
Extracting the sunos 4.1.4 sun4c 'Install' media file.
Extracting the sunos 4.1.4 sun4c 'Networking' media file.
Extracting the sunos 4.1.4 sun4c 'System_V' media file.
Extracting the sunos 4.1.4 sun4c 'Sys' media file.
Extracting the sunos 4.1.4 sun4c 'SunView_Users' media file.
Extracting the sunos 4.1.4 sun4c 'SunView_Demo' media file.
Extracting the sunos 4.1.4 sun4c 'Text' media file.
Extracting the sunos 4.1.4 sun4c 'Demo' media file.
Extracting the sunos 4.1.4 sun4c 'OpenWindows_Users' media file.
Extracting the sunos 4.1.4 sun4c 'OpenWindows_Demo' media file.
Extracting the sunos 4.1.4 sun4c 'OpenWindows_Fonts' media file.
Extracting the sunos 4.1.4 sun4c 'User_Diag' media file.
Extracting the sunos 4.1.4 sun4c 'Manual' media file.
Extracting the sunos 4.1.4 sun4c 'TLI' media file.
Extracting the sunos 4.1.4 sun4c 'RFS' media file.
Extracting the sunos 4.1.4 sun4c 'Debugging' media file.
Extracting the sunos 4.1.4 sun4c 'SunView_Programmers' media file.
Extracting the sunos 4.1.4 sun4c 'Shlib_Custom' media file.
Extracting the sunos 4.1.4 sun4c 'Graphics' media file.
Extracting the sunos 4.1.4 sun4c 'uucp' media file.
Extracting the sunos 4.1.4 sun4c 'Games' media file.
Extracting the sunos 4.1.4 sun4c 'Versatec' media file.
Extracting the sunos 4.1.4 sun4c 'Security' media file.
Extracting the sunos 4.1.4 sun4c 'OpenWindows_Programmers' media file.
Copying /a/export/exec/proto.root.sunos.4.1.4 to /a/
Copying binaries

Setting up tftpboot files

Updating bootparams
Updating server's exports file
Configuring inetd for tftpd operation
```

3

```
Bootblock will contain a.out header
Boot block installed
No sunos 4.1.4 sun4c clients to add.
Copying /etc/install to /a/etc/install
Cleaning disk(s):
        / (/dev/sd0a)
/dev/rsd0a: is clean.
        /home (/dev/sd0h)
/dev/rsd0h: is clean.
        /usr (/dev/sd0g)
/dev/rsd0g: is clean.

System installation completed:

Reboot the system single user.
Remember to run 'ypinit -m' before booting multi-user!
#
```

Note that I've created a little bit of an advantage for myself by using a headless machine with a terminal to talk to it. I have a scroll-back buffer in which I can look at messages that would have scrolled off the top of the screen on a directly connected monitor. This way, I can leave the machine alone while it installs, and I don't need to baby-sit it to make certain I get any diagnostic messages.

Configuring the NIS Master or Slave

As mentioned previously, the NIS service is essentially used as a database of user information. It stores user passwords, where their home directories are, and other information that needs to be shared among multiple machines in a cluster. NIS databases can also be used for other purposes, but you're not likely to be interested in them unless your site already uses them or you truly enjoy pain. This database system needs a name that it can use for identifying itself to other machines on your network—its domain name. Each NIS domain potentially contains multiple maps, tables of information that are provided by this domain. Essentially, other machines subscribe to these databases.

The security implications are rather staggering. The server for a given NIS domain provides things such as password maps for all the users. Any machine that asks that server for its password maps can retrieve the password database! To somewhat limit the potential for trouble, you should attempt to make your NIS domain names hard to guess. The NIS server doesn't advertise what domains it has available, so if an intruder can't guess what NIS domain to subscribe to, he can't ask the server for any information.

To configure my NIS master, I have to follow the final instructions left on the screen. Note that the presence of the pound sign at the end means that I am still in a shell in the mini-root. If the machine had rebooted instead, I would have gotten a login prompt. How you initially set up the NIS master or slave will vary; be sure to check your vendor's documentation. You might just have to click on the appropriate box.

In my case, I will begin by rebooting to single-user mode:

```
# sync;sync;reboot — -s
syncing file systems... done
rebooting...
SPARCstation IPX, No Keyboard
ROM Rev. 2.9, 32 MB memory installed, Serial #2202138.
Ethernet address 8:0:20:d:8d:48, Host ID: 57219a1a.


Rebooting with command: -s
Boot device: /sbus/esp@0,800000/sd@3,0    File and args: -s
root on /sbus@1,f8000000/esp@0,800000/sd@3,0:a fstype 4.2
Boot: vmunix
Size: 1343488+218832+131992 bytes
SunOS Release 4.1.4 (GENERIC) #2: Fri Oct 14 11:08:06 PDT 1994
Copyright (c) 1983-1993, Sun Microsystems, Inc.
mem = 32768K (0x2000000)
avail mem = 30478336
Ethernet address = 8:0:20:d:8d:48
cpu = SUNW,Sun 4/50
zs0 at obio 0xf1000000 pri 12
zs1 at obio 0xf0000000 pri 12
audio0 at obio 0xf7201000 pri 13
sbus0 at SBus slot 0 0x0
dma0 at SBus slot 0 0x400000
esp0 at SBus slot 0 0x800000 pri 3
sd0 at esp0 target 3 lun 0
sd0: <Fujitsu M2624FA-1 cyl 1440 alt 2 hd 11 sec 64>
sr0 at esp0 target 6 lun 0
le0 at SBus slot 0 0xc00000 pri 5
cgsix0 at SBus slot 3 0x0 pri 7
cgsix0: screen 1152x900, single buffered, 1M mappable, rev 8
fd0 at obio 0xf7200000 pri 11
root on sd0a fstype 4.2
swap on sd0b fstype spec size 102080K
dump on sd0b fstype spec size 102068K
checking / and /usr filesystems
/dev/rsd0a: is clean.
/dev/rsd0g: is clean.
```

Note that this time, I am finally rebooting off the root partition, target 3, partition a.

Booting into single-user mode puts me back at the # shell prompt. Be careful when you're in single-user mode because this mode gives you root privileges, often without requiring a password. Unfortunately, I find that literally following the instructions that Sun provides does not quite work:

```
# ypinit -m
ypinit: not found
```

Instead, I must specify the complete path:

```
# /usr/etc/yp/ypinit -m
The local host's domain name hasn't been set.  Please set it.
```

This is not quite what I wanted. Here, I can have an interesting problem. domain name could refer to the domain name part of my internet address, or it could refer to the name of my NIS domain. In this case, it happens to refer to my NIS domain, which I thought I set back there on one of those forms. To set it again, I issue the command domainname <whatever_name_I_pick>. Because I'm starting out fresh here, I have to make sure that I pick something hard to guess in an attempt to deflect possible intruders. If you're adding a machine to an existing cluster, you'll need to know the NIS domain to answer this question.

I did experience some trouble with the domain name on the host form and the domain name issued here. After issuing the ypinit command, it would have been best to check /var/yp for a directory with the name I had intended to use for my NIS domain. (NIS domain information is typically stored in subdirectories in /var/yp.) If I had found a directory with the wrong domain name, I could have removed it and reissued the domainname and ypinit -m command. However, I didn't have this foresight, wound up in a loop, and had to shut down and redo that part.

> **Stuck at startup?**   If you've gotten yourself stuck in a loop during startup, try using Ctrl+C or Ctrl+\—sometimes many, many times in a row. This is not always guaranteed to work, but it might be your only choice. You might also have some other way to force your machine to boot into single-user mode, where many of the services don't start, enabling you to get to your configuration files to edit them and repair problems. Check your vendor's documentation for specifics.

Customizing Your Machine

After the operating system has been installed, there are still some things you might want to take care of right away.

You will have to set a password for root. Pick something that you can remember, but not something easily guessed. If your machine comes with open accounts (that is, accounts with no passwords), you need to block those accounts. This is especially a problem with SGIs and might be as well with other operating systems. You will want to close as many services as you can, a step to reducing your machine's vulnerability to attacks. You will look at some of these issues in more detail in several chapters later this week and next week.

If you did not have to specify a default route or netmask during the initial setup, you might have to do that at this stage. Depending on your initial setup, you might have to supply your machine's name now. You might have decided what your machine's name really ought to be, and you will have to look for the file that contains the information or the menu that enables you to change that information. If you are going to change your machine's name, it's easier to do it now, when its IP address might not yet be registered. You might also have to supply information on the nameserver somewhere in a file, if you didn't have to do that earlier.

You will take a brief look at some of the common ideas you will see across the various operating systems.

Choosing a Root Password

When the machine finishes its system installation, the root account has no password. At this point, you, or whoever walks in the room, can have absolute power. You will most likely be able to assign a password to root by logging on as root and issuing the `passwd` command. Do not pick dictionary words or anything that can be easily guessed. Instead, pick something you can remember. Be sure to have some combination of upper case, lower case, and alphanumeric characters.

Tip

> **Picking passwords**   Most people think passwords that are hard to guess are also hard to remember. If you just pick a random collection of characters and numbers, this is probably true. On the other hand, you can generate a very convincing simulation of random characters and numbers, one that can't be guessed using dictionary or "look up your personal information" attacks, and one that can be remembered, using a very simple trick. Make up passwords by thinking up a phrase you can easily remember, and then pick the first letters (or first and second, or—you get the picture) from each word in the phrase. For example, you might chose the phrase "My oh my I can't remember my password!". This would generate a password something like "Momlcrmp!", which would be extremely difficult to guess, but which you can probably remember easily.

Locking Accounts

In the case of locking accounts, you will actually look at an IRIX example rather than SunOS as you have been so far in this chapter. Because SGIs try to be as friendly as possible, they come with some open accounts that are not protected by passwords. One of those accounts is the one that provides you with the VRML tour of your SGI world when you first install the OS. Right away, you should lock those open accounts. There's no need to make your machine any more vulnerable than is necessary.

Here is an original /etc/passwd file that comes with an SGI:

```
root::0:0:Super-User:/:/bin/csh
sysadm:*:0:0:System V Administration:/usr/admin:/bin/sh
cmwlogin:*:0:994:CMW Login UserID:/usr/CMW:/sbin/csh
diag:*:0:996:Hardware Diagnostics:/usr/diags:/bin/csh
daemon:*:1:1:daemons:/:/dev/null
bin:*:2:2:System Tools Owner:/bin:/dev/null
uucp:*:3:5:UUCP Owner:/usr/lib/uucp:/bin/csh
sys:*:4:0:System Activity Owner:/var/adm:/bin/sh
adm:*:5:3:Accounting Files Owner:/var/adm:/bin/sh
lp::9:9:Print Spooler Owner:/var/spool/lp:/bin/sh
nuucp::10:10:Remote UUCP User:/var/spool/uucppublic:/usr/lib/uucp/uucico
auditor:*:11:0:Audit Activity Owner:/auditor:/bin/sh
dbadmin:*:12:0:Security Database Owner:/dbadmin:/bin/sh
sgiweb:*:13:60001:SGI Web Applications:/var/www/htdocs:/bin/csh
rfindd:*:66:1:Rfind Daemon and Fsdump:/var/rfindd:/bin/sh
EZsetup::992:998:System Setup:/var/sysadmdesktop/EZsetup:/bin/csh
demos::993:997:Demonstration User:/usr/demos:/bin/csh
OutOfBox::995:997:Out of Box Experience:/usr/people/OutOfBox:/bin/csh
guest::998:998:Guest Account:/usr/people/guest:/bin/csh
4Dgifts:*:999:998:4Dgifts Account:/usr/people/4Dgifts:/bin/csh
nobody:*:60001:60001:SVR4 nobody uid:/dev/null:/dev/null
noaccess:*:60002:60002:uid no access:/dev/null:/dev/null
nobody:*:-2:-2:original nobody uid:/dev/null:/dev/null
```

Each line is a colon-delimited set of fields. The second item in the line is where the encrypted password goes. Notice how some accounts have * in this field. The accounts are locked, and you can't log in as those users. Notice how root, lp, nuucp, EZsetup, demos, OutOfBox, and guest don't have * in the second field? This means that they are not password-protected and that anyone who discovers your machine can log in to those accounts without a password.

Here's a modified /etc/passwd file:

```
root:ciMUgYtVCh2CM:0:0:Super-User:/:/bin/csh
sysadm:*:0:0:System V Administration:/usr/admin:/bin/sh
cmwlogin:*:0:994:CMW Login UserID:/usr/CMW:/sbin/csh
diag:*:0:996:Hardware Diagnostics:/usr/diags:/bin/csh
daemon:*:1:1:daemons:/:/dev/null
```

```
bin:*:2:2:System Tools Owner:/bin:/dev/null
uucp:*:3:5:UUCP Owner:/usr/lib/uucp:/bin/csh
sys:*:4:0:System Activity Owner:/var/adm:/bin/sh
adm:*:5:3:Accounting Files Owner:/var/adm:/bin/sh
lp:*:9:9:Print Spooler Owner:/var/spool/lp:/bin/sh
nuucp:*:10:10:Remote UUCP User:/var/spool/uucppublic:/usr/lib/uucp/uucico
auditor:*:11:0:Audit Activity Owner:/auditor:/bin/sh
dbadmin:*:12:0:Security Database Owner:/dbadmin:/bin/sh
sgiweb:*:13:60001:SGI Web Applications:/var/www/htdocs:/bin/csh
rfindd:*:66:1:Rfind Daemon and Fsdump:/var/rfindd:/bin/sh
EZsetup:*:992:998:System Setup:/var/sysadmdesktop/EZsetup:/bin/csh
demos:*:993:997:Demonstration User:/usr/demos:/bin/csh
OutOfBox:*:995:997:Out of Box Experience:/usr/people/OutOfBox:/bin/csh
guest:*:998:998:Guest Account:/usr/people/guest:/bin/csh
4Dgifts:*:999:998:4Dgifts Account:/usr/people/4Dgifts:/bin/csh
nobody:*:60001:60001:SVR4 nobody uid:/dev/null:/dev/null
noaccess:*:60002:60002:uid no access:/dev/null:/dev/null
nobody:*:60001:60001:original nobody uid:/dev/null:/dev/null
```

Now notice how root has a funny collection of characters, whereas the rest of the accounts are now locked with a *. The funny collection of characters is the encrypted copy of root's password. The encryption algorithm used is set up to be one-way. The password cannot be decrypted. How, then, does the machine make sure that a user enters the proper password? It encrypts the password that the user enters and compares the encryption of what the user enters with the encrypted password in the file. This provides security against someone reading your password file and decoding the passwords while still allowing the system to determine whether a user is valid. So, with this password file, root can now log in with a password, and no one else can log in.

Interestingly, on some machines, you might notice an account named sync, with a shell of /bin/sync that doesn't have a password. Contrary to what you might think from the demo accounts, it's not a huge security hole waiting to bite you. Instead this is actually a utility account that can do nothing but sync the disk. If your machine has a sync account and a user tries to log in as sync, all it does is flush the disk cache tables from memory to disk—a generally healthy and innocuous thing to do. If you're really super paranoid about security, you might want to consider closing it, but it seems fairly unlikely that it presents a significant threat.

Don't worry if this file looks odd to you right now. You will examine the contents of the password file and the purpose of some of those users who come automatically with your system when we make user accounts in Chapter 12, "The Basics of Making User Accounts." For right now, all you need to know is that if your machine has some open accounts, lock them down and make sure you don't lock out root in your enthusiasm.

Closing Down Unnecessary Services

It is also important for you at this point to close down services on your machine that you don't need. One of the common areas to do this is in the `/etc/inetd.conf` file. The `/etc/inetd.conf` file controls what services the `inetd` daemon will make available as needed. It is a good idea to close down as many services as possible. For some systems, it might be hard to guess what services you can safely close. For example, SGIs come with a lot of SGI-specific services listed, so you might have to leave a number of those open for your SGI to function properly. Before I had made good notes about all the services my machines are running, I once closed off a service that resulted in my machine no longer having a display. That's how I determined that it must be one that I need. To close down services, put a # sign in front of each service that you do not need. If you are running a Linux box, you will especially want to take care of this right away. Within four days of putting up a cluster of Linux boxes with their services wide open during the summer of 1998, the machines were cracked.

> **Note**
>
> **Hackers or Crackers?**   Real hackers aren't at all happy with how the media has perverted the sense of "their" word to mean people who break into machines. In the world of "real programmers", hackers are people who write devilishly clever code to perform seemingly amazing tricks. They're the people who seem to eat and breathe code and who think in binary.
>
> Although the origins of the name are obscure, many believe the term "hacker" is derived from the usually small and frequently brutal bits of code that they write. If you haven't a proper saw and need to make a piece of wood into two pieces, you eventually resort to hacking at it, with whatever you have at hand. Likewise, hackers, in the programmer use of the word, are people who traditionally make pieces of software perform new and different tasks, frequently in ways unintended by their original authors. Hackers tend to do this in whatever manner is most expedient, and they are not often concerned with the elegance of the modifications they make.
>
> Crackers, on the other hand, are the variety of computer criminal who break into people's machines. True, there have been hackers who are crackers, but the majority of crackers nowadays are buffoons who found cracking software on a Web site and who want to impress their friends.
>
> If you have one, make friends with your local hacker. Not only does the true hacker dislike the cracker as much as you do (for sullying his good name), but she can also do magical things with software if you should ever need help.

Here are a few lines from a Linux `/etc/inetd.conf` file.

```
# daytime      dgram   udp    wait      root    internal
# chargen      stream  tcp    nowait    root    internal
```

```
# chargen          dgram   udp    wait    root    internal
#
# These are standard services.
#
ftp      stream  tcp    nowait  root    /usr/sbin/tcpd  in.ftpd -l -a
telnet   stream  tcp    nowait  root    /usr/sbin/tcpd  in.telnetd
# gopher          stream  tcp    nowait  root    /usr/sbin/tcpd  gn
# pop-2   stream  tcp    nowait  root    /usr/sbin/tcpd      ipop2d
# pop-3   stream  tcp    nowait  root    /usr/sbin/tcpd      ipop3d
# imap    stream  tcp    nowait  root    /usr/sbin/tcpd      imapd
#
# Finger, systat and netstat give out user information which may be
# valuable to potential "system crackers."  Many sites choose to disable
# some or all of these services to improve security.
#
# finger          stream  tcp    nowait  root    /usr/sbin/tcpd  in.fingerd
```

3

Lines with # signs in front of them are ignored by inetd when it reads the file, so not only can you disable but keep potentially useful lines, like the pop services, but you can also include configuration comments as with Finger.

It's not important that you understand the format of this file, especially at this point. Simply understand that if you don't need a service, you can edit the file and add a # in front of the undesirables. Reboot your machine to get the changes to take effect.

Note

There's actually another way to make the changes take effect as well.

ps -elf ¦ grep inetd (use ps -auxww on BSD systems)

This command should show you the process ID for inetd. Make sure you read your man page for ps so that you know which column is the pid:

kill -HUP <inetd processid>

This will make inetd restart and reread your configuration file. It's a lot faster than restarting your machine, but make sure you know that you've got the right inetd process ID before you try it.

This trick isn't so much a trick as a semitypical way of causing many different parts of UNIX to restart or to reread their configuration information. When you're comfortable with the notion of HUPing processes, it's certainly a faster solution than rebooting.

Be somewhat cautious when you decide to go this route because you never really know if everything that might be affected at startup is really affected by the HUP. This can result in odd and unaccountable behavior when you finally reboot three months later and things no longer work as before. HUP is expedient and usually all you need, but a reboot gives you confidence that everything is really alright.

It is appropriate to comment out the popular protocols, such as pop and imap, especially right now. In my /etc/inetd.conf, I have turned off everything except telnet and ftp. I am leaving those on for some convenience for the moment. But in the coming weeks, I will show you how to make even those services more secure. If you have actual console access to your machine, you might want to turn off even telnet right now. Because I am accessing my machine from a terminal, I am taking a risk and leaving some less secure network services open in case I should need them. Closing them down and making the machine as secure as possible will be a large part of next week's topics.

Other Configurations

As I mentioned earlier, there might still be other customizations you might have to put in place if your operating system did not already ask for them. For example, because I answered the domain question wrong on my host form, I had to add the domain part of my Internet address in the /etc/resolv.conf file. I also added nameserver information because my operating system did not ask for that information. Here is what my /etc/resolv.conf file looks like:

```
Barracuda# more /etc/resolv.conf
domain killernuts.org
nameserver 204.210.252.252
nameserver 204.210.252.250
nameserver 128.146.1.7
```

My operating system did not ask for a netmask either. If you don't know what your netmask should be, check with your network administrator. I added my netmask to the /etc/netmasks file on my machine:

```
Barracuda# more /etc/netmasks
#
# Network masks database
#
# only non-default subnet masks need to be defined here
#
# Network        netmask
192.168          255.255.255.0
129.144          255.255.255.0
129.145          255.255.255.0
129.146          255.255.255.0
129.147          255.255.255.0
129.148          255.255.255.0
129.149          255.255.255.0
129.150          255.255.255.0
129.151          255.255.255.0
```

On other systems, however, you might find that the netmask is given as a number in hexadecimal. Here is a sample from `/etc/config/ifconfig-1.options` in IRIX:

```
netmask 0xffffff00
```

The netmask here is also `255.255.255.0`, but in hexidecimal.

Note

> **Netmask troubles**   If you end up with networking almost working properly on your machine and the symptom that suggests a problem is that your machine can't connect to some nearby machines, even though it can connect to other distant machines, suspect a netmask problem. Many manufacturers ship their OSes with a default netmask of `255.255.0.0`. This is cause for more than a little confusion as the netmask is essentially a definition of what constitutes machines on the same subnet or local network. Few installations are set up with a single subnet that spans an entire B-class network address space, and this is what a `255.255.0.0` netmask implies.

Because my operating system did not ask for my default route, I included that information in `/etc/defaultrouter`:

```
Barracuda# more /etc/defaultrouter
192.168.1.4
```

Note

> **Route problems**   If your machine can connect to other machines on the local subnet but can't connect to any machines outside the local subnet, you probably have not set a default route. The default route is the address to which all traffic is sent when it doesn't match the netmask's definition of a local destination. If you have no default route set, your machine has no idea where to send traffic to get it off the local network.
>
> You can check to see if you have a default route set by using the `netstat` command. Depending on your operating system, `netstat -i` or `netstat -r` should show you a list of network destinations. If you have a default route set, one of them will be indicated as `default`. Appending the `-n` option to the `netmask` command might be necessary in some instances as well.

Remember that the precise locations of some of this information will vary with the operating system. The lack of most of this information will pose a problem for you, so you'll want to track down where these things get defined on your machine.

Finally, be sure you have added your host's name to the /etc/hosts file if your machine has not already done so. That is one of the locations that the machine is most likely to use to look up information about itself. Here is what my machine's file looks like:

```
Barracuda# more /etc/hosts
#
# Sun Host Database
#
# If the NIS is running, this file is only consulted when booting
#
127.0.0.1        localhost
#
192.168.1.20     Barracuda loghost
```

Note

> **Host information brain-damage** Some completely insane versions of UNIX duplicate host information in both the /etc/hosts file and in cryptic configuration files usually buried several layers deep in a subdirectory under /etc/. This is just plain wrong—and can be a source of considerable potential for confusion—but that doesn't stop it from being done.
>
> If you need to update your machine's IP address, make certain that you have found all the places where its IP is defined in files. The behavior of the system in the case where this information is not consistent is not well defined. A prime example of this is evident with Linux. Some versions can be accidentally configured to believe they have and respond to one IP address from the console and command line, but to advertise and respond to a different IP from the network, because different parts of the OS get their information from different configuration files.

Installing Operating-System Patches

While the machine is still new and no one is used to using it yet, this is a good time to install any operating-system patches, such as security updates or Y2K patches. If you are running a new operating system, you might find this suggestion ludicrous. Really, it is not. IRIX 6.5 was released only months ago as I write this, but security and bug-fix patches come out for it on an almost weekly basis. If you are running a current operating system, you have probably saved yourself the Y2K patches step, but you might still have to install some operating system patches.

Follow your vendor's instructions for installing patches. You might end up running an install script that you download at the same time or some other special program that is already part of the operating system. Follow the instructions carefully. You might have to be in single-user mode to install certain patches. SGI is currently trying to phase out patches altogether and issue updates to the operating system as streams. IRIX 6.5 has only been out for a few months, and I am already on the third maintenance upgrade. Keeping up with the latest stream has been important because IRIX 6.5 was initially buggy enough to cause a brand-new machine to go down in a panic several times. Even though you might have the latest operating system, it might be important, perhaps even more important, for you to get the latest patches because the operating system might still be in its infancy.

Installing a Nice, Simple Patch

With SunOS, each patch comes with a README file. Definitely read each README. You might find that a particular patch requires certain other patches. The README, of course, will present the instructions for installing the patch.

This patch installation you are about to see is for patch 100478-02, an xlock patch. Here are the instructions from the README:

```
Install Instructions:

    1) cd to $OPENWINHOME/bin
    2) su to root
    3) get patch id from current xlock using strings xlock ¦ grep -i patch
    4) if patch_id exists
            mv xlock xlock.patch_id_123456_89
            where patch_id_123456_89 is recorded from step #3
       else
            mv xlock xlock.30fcs
    5) cp patched xlock to xlock
    6) chmod 755 xlock
```

I will actually install the patch from the patch directory rather than performing Step 1, mostly because that is how I am used to seeing the instructions, and it requires greater thought from me to do it the other way. By all means, if you have a routine, stick to it. Developing and following a routine when doing this sort of "menial labor" is a good way to keep from making mistakes.

Root is my only user right now, so I can skip Step 2. Also, because I have just finished installing the operating system, I already know that xlock has not been patched. This means that I can skip Step 3, where I'm supposed to check what version of xlock I have installed.

Before I start with the else portion of Step 4, I double-check what $OPENWINHOME is on my machine:

```
Barracuda# echo $OPENWINHOME
OPENWINHOME undefined variable
```

Well, that's not what I expected. Because this is a Sun machine, though, I've got a good guess what it should be if it were set. If I didn't, I'd have to use the `find` command to search the entire filesystem for the `xlock` file, and depending on the size of the filesystem, that could take days!

```
Barracuda# ls /usr/openwin/bin/xlock*
/usr/openwin/bin/xlock
```

That looks promising, so I start Step 4 now:

```
Barracuda# mv /usr/openwin/bin/xlock /usr/openwin/bin/xlock.30fcs
```

Because I am in the patch directory, I have to take a moment to see what's actually there (I suppose I don't really have to do this, but it makes me feel better; when I've done a bunch of these, I probably won't feel so obligated to check):

```
Barracuda# ls
README  sun4

Barracuda# ls sun4
xlock
```

Good. The promised `xlock` really is there. I would have had to undo Step 4's instructions if it were not there.

Next, I complete the instructions:

```
Barracuda# cp sun4/xlock /usr/openwin/bin/xlock
Barracuda# chmod 755 /usr/openwin/bin/xlock
```

Because I always like to see the results of what I've done, I check to see that there are now two `xlock` versions:

```
Barracuda# ls -l /usr/openwin/bin/xlock*
-rwxr-xr-x  1 root       245760 Mar 18 15:46 /usr/openwin/bin/xlock
-rwxr-xr-x  1 root       245760 Sep 26  1991 /usr/openwin/bin/xlock.30fcs
```

Indeed, there are two! Although I don't have a monitor on the machine right now, I'm ready for one. Because this new `xlock` doesn't look all that different from the old one, based on the `ls` results the system generated, I decide to run the `strings` command from Step 3 that I didn't run earlier:

```
Barracuda# strings /usr/openwin/bin/xlock.30fcs ¦ grep -i patch
Barracuda#
Hmm...  That's not very interesting.
Barracuda# strings /usr/openwin/bin/xlock ¦ grep -i patch
Patch Id: 100478_02.
Barracuda#
```

Yep, I really do have the latest `xlock`. Funny how they're the exact same size. My programmer friends tell me that this isn't all that uncommon. I'd say I'd better not rely on things such as file sizes to determine whether I've got the right file.

Installing a Patch that Requires Single-User Mode

This patch, `102545-12`, a `libc` patch, is actually going to serve two purposes for me. Not only is it a patch that requires single-user mode at some point in the process, but it is also a Y2K patch. This is a patch that I actually avoided doing on a different machine at one point because its README contains this most horrible instruction: "Bear in mind that `/usr/lib/libc.so.X.Y` dynamically binds the *entire* SunOS and any corruption to this particular library will render a system virtually useless." I decided that there were still a few more months before Y2K was really an important issue.

I won't go into the full details for this one's instructions because the instructions themselves take a few pages (providing, of course, another reason to avoid doing it!). First, I had to rename the old versions of various files and back up a couple of directories. Then, I had to copy the files in the patch directory to the appropriate locations. Next, I had to boot the machine into single-user mode. The README suggested I type the following:

```
Barracuda# sync
Barracuda# halt
```

The computer's response was this:

```
Mar 22 19:18:00 Barracuda halt: halted by root
Mar 22 19:18:01 Barracuda syslogd: going down on signal 15
syncing file systems... done
Halted

Program terminated
Type b (boot), c (continue), or n (new command mode)
>
```

At this point in the patch process, I was able to issue this:

```
>b -s
```

I had to rename some of the new files that I had already copied in a previous step to their correct names and then issue the `date` command, which responded with the date:

```
# date
```

```
Mon Mar 22 19:24:17 EST 1999
```

That hardly seems scary or the least bit exciting, does it? However, when the README describes typing `date` as "Do this last step CAREFULLY. If the `date` command does *anything* else but show a proper date, then IMMEDIATELY do...," then suddenly the tension builds as you type `date` and contemplate whether you really want to press return!

In the final steps, I had to rename new files that I had already copied to a different directory. The README provided another advisory on carefully issuing some `ranlib` commands, but it did not follow up with a warning on what to do immediately afterwards, thereby making the `ranlib` commands seem less dramatic.

Upon issuing ^D to terminate single-user mode, as the README instructed, the computer responded in a friendly fashion:

```
# Multiuser startup in progress...
Mon Mar 22 19:30:27 EST 1999
```

The first thing I tested after reboot was date, which also seemed to work in multiuser mode. In spite of the many pages of instructions that come with this patch, you really don't need to wait until the end of 1999 to do this one if you have a SunOS machine.

Installing a Patch that Requires Reconfiguration of the Kernel

This type of patch sounds as if it should be especially traumatic, given that the READMEs for those patches tend to end with instructions along the lines of "configure, make and install your new kernel following the instructions in the System and Network Administration handbook."

Note

> **IRIX makes kernel updates nice—sort of**   This type of patch on IRIX is far less disturbing. You just sit there while the console tells you that it is reconfiguring the kernel (and you wonder if you have remembered to save a copy of the old one). Now that IRIX is moving away from patches, any changes you make to IRIX will result in the system reconfiguring the kernel. Always remember to save a copy of the kernel that was already working.

Reconfiguring the Kernel: Streamlining Your Kernel

Before installing a patch that required reconfiguration of the kernel, I decided to fine-tune the kernel a bit, which also requires rebuilding the kernel.

Most standard off-the-shelf kernel configurations include support for devices you don't have and services you won't need. In SunOS, for example, even the smallest default kernel includes support for two SCSI controllers. The kernel is the most fundamental basis for your operating system, and every additional kernel resource adds a little bit of code to the kernel and absorbs a little bit of execution time. Optimizing your kernel so that it doesn't include unnecessary resources can improve your machine's performance.

If you want to streamline your kernel, now is also a good time to do that while the machine is still in its early stages of development. Carefully read the appropriate man pages on reconfiguring your kernel before you proceed. Remember, save a copy of the working one.

To actually modify your kernel in SunOS, you edit a file, build a new kernel, and reboot with the new one. In IRIX, you run `autoconfig`. With Linux, you can have a pretty point-and-click interface to kernel configuration options.

> **Caution**
>
> Did you read where I said to keep a copy of your old kernel? Don't forget it! If something breaks and your newly reconfigured kernel won't work properly, you will need to be able to boot your machine using the old kernel. If you've deleted it, you're a good ways up the proverbial creek.
>
> Keep a copy in the root directory, and make sure you know what it's named so that you can get back to it in an emergency.

For SunOS, you will find detailed instructions on reconfiguring the kernel in the README in `/sys/'arch -k'/conf`.

> **Tip**
>
> **Saving keystrokes**   You might initially find the preceding path list a little odd—especially the `'arch -k'` portion of it. That's because the portion of the path enclosed in the `'` quotes tells the system to execute that part as a command and to replace the quotes and their contents with the results of the command. In my case, issuing the command `arch -k` results in the response `sun4c`. Therefore, issuing the command `more /sys/'arch -k'/conf/README`, executes the `more` command on `/sys/sun4c/conf/README`.
>
> It doesn't really save me keystrokes here, but if I can't remember what my machine's architecture is, it saves me having to issue the `arch -k` command and the `more` command separately.

In my case, I started with a generic, small version of the kernel configuration file that was provided and made a few changes. Here are some of the changes I made:

```
# Name this kernel GENERIC_SMALL.
#
ident           "GENERIC_SMALL"
# Put the kernel configured this way in a file named 'vmunix'.
#
config vmunix           swap generic
```

I gave the kernel the customized internal name and changed the output filename to `vmunix_small`:

```
ident           "BARRACUDA_SMALL"
# Put the kernel configured this way in a file named 'vmunix'.
#
config vmunix_small     swap generic
```

I increased my maximum users number from 4 to 15. The maximum users number is more of a maximum simultaneous connections number, so it also includes windows under windowing systems. I am allowing here (as well as that xlock patch) for future expansion of my system to include a monitor and my wanting to display lots of windows on it.

I also removed the option of a second tape drive and replaced that with the option to include yet another hard drive on SCSI controller 0:

```
# The following section describes SCSI device unit assignments.
#
scsibus0 at esp                         # declare first scsi bus
disk sd0 at scsibus0 target 3 lun 0     # first hard SCSI disk
disk sd1 at scsibus0 target 1 lun 0     # second hard SCSI disk
disk sd2 at scsibus0 target 2 lun 0     # third hard SCSI disk
disk sd3 at scsibus0 target 0 lun 0     # fourth hard SCSI disk
disk sd5 at scsibus0 target 5 lun 0     # fifth hard SCSI disk
tape st0 at scsibus0 target 4 lun 0     # first SCSI tape
# tape st1 at scsibus0 target 5 lun 0   # second SCSI tape
disk sr0 at scsibus0 target 6 lun 0     # CD-ROM device
```

Also, I commented out a similar entire section for SCSI controller 1. Because my machine only has one SCSI controller, the additional allowances certainly are not necessary. You can take a look at the fully modified configuration file in Appendix C, "Sample Configuration Files."

From /sys/sun4c/conf, I ran the following:

```
Barracuda# /etc/config BARRACUDA_SMALL
Doing a "make depend"

Barracuda# cd ../BARRACUDA_SMALL
Barracuda# make
```

When it was done, I then renamed the current working kernel, /vmunix, to /vmunix.old and copied the just made kernel, vmunix_small, to /vmunix:

```
Barracuda# mv /vmunix /vmunix.old
Barracuda# cp vmunix_small /vmunix
```

In my usual paranoia, I then had to double-check that I really had all the vmunix files I hoped I would have:

```
Barracuda# ls -l /vmunix*
-rwxr-xr-x  1 root        1466130 Mar 22 20:20 /vmunix
-rwxr-xr-x  1 root        1740330 Mar 18 05:30 /vmunix.old
```

I did! I rebooted, and this comment, indicating that the system was loading my customized kernel, was included among all the introductory startup messages:

```
SunOS Release 4.1.4 (BARRACUDA_SMALL) #1: Mon Mar 22 20:15:29 EST 1999
```

It seemed to have worked! Because the machine seemed functional when I logged back in, I then went on to installing a patch that required yet another reconfiguration of the kernel.

Now for that Patch

After successfully streamlining the kernel, installing a patch that requires reconfiguring the kernel seems like a breeze!

In this case, I installed patch 102517-05, a tcp patch. The procedure began very simply as it instructed that I renamed certain current kernel files:

```
Barracuda# cd /sys/'arch -k'/OBJ
Barracuda# mv tcp_input.o  tcp_input.o.FCS
Barracuda# mv tcp_output.o tcp_output.o.FCS
Barracuda# mv tcp_timer.o  tcp_timer.o.FCS
Barracuda# mv tcp_usrreq.o tcp_usrreq.o.FCS
```

Next, I went back to my patch directory, copied the new files, and changed their permissions:

```
Barracuda# cp 'arch -k'/tcp_input.o  /sys/'arch -k'/OBJ
Barracuda# cp 'arch -k'/tcp_output.o /sys/'arch -k'/OBJ
Barracuda# cp 'arch -k'/tcp_timer.o  /sys/'arch -k'/OBJ
Barracuda# cp 'arch -k'/tcp_usrreq.o /sys/'arch -k'/OBJ
Barracuda# chmod 444 /sys/'arch -k'/OBJ/tcp_*.o
```

I was now ready for Step 3. Yes, Step 3 was that infamous "reconfigure-your-kernel-as-described-in-a-manual-you-probably-don't-have" step. Following my own previous kernel-compilation instructions, the results of Step 3 appeared in yet another message from the system:

```
SunOS Release 4.1.4 (BARRACUDA_SMALL) #2: Mon Mar 22 20:33:01 EST 1999
```

Regardless of whether your operating system requires as much manual intervention in installing patches and reconfiguring the kernel as SunOS required, you have worked hard today! You end today's activities here and will slow down for the next couple of days before you return again to the hard work.

Summary

Today, you learned how to take a tour of your hardware and bring your machine to life from a collection of components. because every machine and every OS is different, unless you're installing SunOS on a Sun4c machine, most of what you read today will be done a little differently on your machine. A few alternative installs are shown in Appendix B, "Sample Operating System Installations." In general, simply remember that your OS will ask similar questions and have at it. Covering every UNIX install procedure in even this much depth would fill several books this size, and you still have a lot of work to do!

You also have done a few of the important tasks that need to be done as soon as any machine you configure is alive, such as locking open accounts and setting passwords. Keep the lessons learned today in mind when you create and administer user accounts in later lessons.

Q&A

Q My OS came on a tape rather than a CD-ROM. What do I do?

A Find yourself a tape drive, plug it in, and navigate your hardware command monitor to "boot from tape". UNIX is an amazingly flexible OS, and when you've told it where to get the software necessary to build the mini-root, it will handle almost everything else automatically.

Q I rather like the guest accounts. They've got neat demo software. Do I have to lock them?

A No, but you should assign them passwords if you're not going to lock them completely. You do this with the same command that you use for assigning any other password, `passwd<accountname>` (or `yppasswd<accountname>` if it's a network account), and then follow the directions. If you do assign passwords to guest accounts, make sure you always log guests in yourself, or change the password as soon as they've left. You don't want to have any account on the machine that multiple people know the password to, and a guest account that doesn't even have an assigned user is the worst possible case.

Q I just rebuilt my kernel and copied it over my old one. I forgot to make a copy of my old kernel first. Is it safe for me to reboot?

A Well, you're going to have to do it someday, you might as well find out just how big a mess you might have made now. Reboot the machine and cross any fingers, toes, or other appendages that you feel inclined to. If your machine doesn't boot, you're probably going to have to go back to your OS installation media and install a mini-root. With luck, you have another machine of the same architecture and can figure out some way to get a functional kernel from it onto your new doorstop. The kernel from the mini-root might do in a pinch. Remember to try to undo the changes you made that broke your kernel, or you're just going to be back in the same boat the next time you rebuild.

Workshop

Quiz

No quiz today—just reading this lesson has been enough work! You do get some exercises, though, because they'll help you with your own machine install.

Exercises

1. Go to Appendix F, "Useful Sample Forms," and make some copies of the host information sheet. Fill one out for each of your existing machines.

2. Also, fill out a host information sheet for any machines you're about to install or for a hypothetical machine if you're not doing an install just now. Make a record of who you have to talk with to get things such as your IP address or to register your hostname with your nameserver.

3. Decide what services your machines really need. Web services? FTP? What else?

4. Justify your answers to Quiz Question 3. Remember that if you're keeping a service "just in case," you're keeping a security risk "just in case." Have you kept services you could turn off now and turn back on when you actually need them?

5. Examine your kernel configuration procedure and current configuration. Make a set of notes on how you configure, build, and install a new kernel.

6. Go install a machine! It's good for you!

3

DAY 4

A Stroll Through Your System

After an intensive day of putting together your new machine, I thought it might be fun to relax for a little while and take a tour of your machine. I personally haven't taken the time to do this yet myself, so I've been looking forward to today's activities.

Getting to Know Your System

As was mentioned on Day 1, "What Is System Administration?" the UNIX filesystem is organized as a hierarchy from the root directory, /, on down. That is where you will begin your tour.

Directories You Should Get to Know

I could probably go on for pages about all the directories you should get to know, but you will only look at some of the most important ones. After all, you are supposed to be relaxing a bit today.

In the tour, you will look at a representative from each of the UNIX flavors: IRIX as a System V flavor and SunOS as a BSD flavor. Grab a comfortable chair and go sit in front of your new machine.

The Top of the Tree: /

The best place to start on a tour of your new machine is at the top, the root directory. This will give you a sort of table-of-contents view of the machine.

Here is a look at the root directory on yesterday's SunOS machine:

```
Barracuda# ls -l /
total 2124
lrwxrwxrwx  1 root              7 Mar 18 05:30 bin -> usr/bin
-r--r--r--  1 root         110352 Mar 18 05:31 boot
drwxr-sr-x  2 root          11264 Mar 18 12:32 dev
drwxr-sr-x  9 root           2048 Mar 19 13:12 etc
drwxr-sr-x  5 root            512 Mar 18 04:56 export
drwxr-xr-x  4 root            512 Oct 14  1994 home
-rwxr-xr-x  1 root         252913 Mar 18 05:31 kadb
lrwxrwxrwx  1 root              7 Mar 18 05:30 lib -> usr/lib
drwxr-xr-x  2 root           8192 Mar 18 04:53 lost+found
drwxr-sr-x  2 root            512 Oct 14  1994 mnt
drwxr-sr-x  2 root            512 Mar 18 04:56 pcfs
drwxr-sr-x  2 root            512 Mar 18 05:31 sbin
lrwxrwxrwx  1 root             13 Mar 18 05:30 sys -> ./usr/kvm/sys
drwxr-sr-x  2 root            512 Mar 18 05:31 tftpboot
drwxrwsrwt  2 root            512 Mar 19 04:15 tmp
drwxr-xr-x 27 root           1024 Mar 18 05:22 usr
drwxr-sr-x 10 root            512 Oct 14  1994 var
-rwxr-xr-x  1 root        1740330 Mar 18 05:30 vmunix
```

Notice how a couple of the directories have -> after their names, indicating that they are links that point elsewhere. On this machine, vmunix is the kernel.

Note

If you're not familiar with the concept of a link, think of it as a way to make a file that is physically in one location appear to be in another location at the same time. In the preceding listing, lib is actually a link to /usr/lib. That is, there's something named lib in the root directory that you can access as though it were in the root directory, but it is really located in the /usr directory with the name lib. In this case, /usr/lib is a directory, so you could actually type cd /lib and end up in /usr/lib. Note that the thing at the end of the link doesn't have to have the same name as the thing linked, so if I wanted to make /usr/lib appear in the root directory as a directory named libbey, I could do that just as easily.

Here is another root directory, this time on an IRIX machine:

```
SUZIE  71 > ls -l /
total 38303
drwxr-xr-x   2 root      sys              9 Jan 28 13:40 CDROM
drwxr-xr-x   2 root      sys             66 Jan 15 19:10 Desktop
lrwxr-xr-x   1 root      sys              7 Jan 15 15:24 bin -> usr/bin
lrwxr-xr-x   1 root      sys              4 Jan 15 19:05 debug -> proc
drwxr-xr-x  13 root      sys           4096 Mar  5 18:10 dev
drwxr-xr-x   2 root      sys             27 Jan 15 19:10 dumpster
drwxr-xr-x  16 root      sys          12288 Mar 18 14:16 etc
drwxr-xr-x   2 root      sys              0 Mar 19 15:24 hw
drwxr-xr-x   2 root      sys            109 Feb 12 15:23 lib
drwxr-xr-x   2 root      sys             58 Feb 12 13:43 lib32
drwxr-xr-x   5 root      sys             53 Feb  3 15:35 net
drwxr-xr-x   1 root      sys             21 Mar  5 18:09 ns
drwx------   2 root      sys              9 Jan 19 12:15 nsmail
drwxr-xr-x   8 root      sys            101 Jan 15 17:25 opt
drwxr-xr-x   2 root      sys              9 Jan 15 19:43 patches
dr-xr-xr-x   2 root      sys           4784 Mar 19 15:24 proc
drwxrwsrwx   8 bioftp    ftponly       1536 Mar 17 11:02 public
drwxr-xr-x   3 root      sys           4096 Feb 12 15:25 sbin
drwxr-xr-x   4 root      sys             44 Dec 31 09:10 share
drwxr-xr-x   2 root      sys             20 Feb 12 13:41 stand
drwxr-xr-x   2 root      sys              9 Jan 19 13:12 testing
drwxrwxrwt   5 sys       sys           4096 Mar 19 15:20 tmp
-rwxr-xr-x   1 root      sys        6765172 Feb 12 15:48 unix
-rwxr-xr-x   1 root      sys        6686124 Feb 11 17:17 unix-old
drwxr-xr-x  42 root      sys           4096 Mar  5 18:09 usr
drwxr-xr-x  33 root      sys           4096 Jan 25 09:06 var
```

A couple of the directories here point elsewhere too. On this machine, the kernel is unix. Notice the unix-old file stored there as well? You can already tell from this quick glance that the kernel has been recently reconfigured.

Central Configuration Location: /etc

As you might have noticed in yesterday's discussion, /etc is an important place to search for your machine's configuration files.

Here's some of the /etc directory on my SunOS machine:

```
Barracuda# ls /etc
.install.d      fastboot        link            publickey       sm
adm             fasthalt        magic           rc              sm.bak
aliases         fbtab           mkfs            rc.boot         spool
aliases.dir     filetype        mknod           rc.ip           state
aliases.pag     format.dat      motd            rc.local        svdtab
arp             fsck            mount           rc.local-orig   syslog.conf
bootparams      fstab           mount_rfs       rc.single       syslog.pid
chown           fuser           mtab            rdump           termcap
```

4

```
chroot        gettytab      ncheck         reboot     tmp
clri          group         netmasks       remote     ttys
config        halt          netmasks-orig  renice     ttytab
```

On IRIX, here's a look at some of /etc:

```
SUZIE joray 101 > ls /etc
config             init           prfstat        stdlogin
cpr_proto          init.d         profile        stdprofile
cron               inittab        project        sulogin
cron.d             install        projid         swap
cshrc              ioconfig.conf  protocols      sys_id
cshrc-orig         ioctl.syscon   prtvtoc        sysinfo
datemsk            irix.cap       pwck           syslog.conf
default            killall        rc0            telinit
device.tab         labelit        rc0.d          tt
devnm              link           rc2            ttytype
dmedia_tools.cap   lnsyscon       rc2.d          uadmin
dump               magic          rc3            umount
dvhtool            mipsabiversion rc3.d          umountfs
```

On the SunOS machine, a number of the items actually point to /usr/etc, whereas on the IRIX machine, a number of the items point to /sbin or /usr/sbin.

In addition to being a storage place for your machine's configuration files and links to various useful commands, /etc is the place to look for your startup scripts. Some software you install might instruct you to place a line in your startup script to start it up at boot time. You would look for your startup script in /etc.

On the SunOS machine, you would probably add that line to /etc/rc.local. If you have a BSD-flavor machine, you might want to take a quick look at /etc/rc.local, just to get a feel for what it looks like.

On the IRIX machine, the startup scripts are organized a little differently. Take a quick look at some of /etc/rc0.d:

```
SUZIE joray 67 > ls -l /etc/rc0.d | more
total 0
lrwxr-xr-x   1 root      sys              14 Jan 15 15:36 K02midi ->
../init.d/midi
lrwxr-xr-x   1 root      sys              13 Jan 15 16:23 K02pcp ->
../init.d/pcp
lrwxr-xr-x   1 root      sys              16 Jan 15 15:36 K02videod ->
../init.d/videod
lrwxr-xr-x   1 root      sys              13 Jan 15 15:24 K02xdm ->
../init.d/xdm
. . .
```

Now look at some of /etc/rc2.d:

```
SUZIE joray 68 > ls -l /etc/rc2.d ¦ more
total 8
lrwxr-xr-x    1 root     sys        18 Jan 15 15:24 S00announce ->
➥../init.d/announce
lrwxr-xr-x    1 root     sys        20 Jan 15 15:24 S00disk_patch ->
➥../init.d/disk_patch
lrwxr-xr-x    1 root     sys        13 Jan 15 15:24 S04usr ->
➥../init.d/usr
lrwxr-xr-x    1 root     sys        21 Jan 15 15:24 S12filesystems ->
➥../init.d/file_systems
. . .
```

In both directories, you see that the files are simply links to files in /etc/init.d. The
scripts starting with S start the appropriate processes at boot time, whereas the scripts
starting with K kill them at shutdown. In fact, they're mostly the same script, and the
main startup and shutdown routines look through the rc.* directories, calling the appropriate scripts in order and passing start or stop to the script depending on whether its
name starts with an S or a K. If your machine is organized like this instead, you might
want to take this opportunity to look at a couple of the scripts.

Note

> **Tradition** It seems that some manufacturers are now hiding initialization
> scripts in the /sbin directory instead of in their more traditional /etc/*
> homes. I haven't met such a configuration as yet, but I'm told that this is just
> one more point of confusion that you're likely to meet along the way.

4

Here's a brief look at how two different systems start syslogd, the daemon that handles
logging system messages. On SunOS, the lines in /etc/rc.local have three lines,
including a comment, like the following:

```
# syslogd doesn't belong here, but needs to be started before the others.
if [ -f /usr/etc/syslogd ]; then
        syslogd
```

On an IRIX machine, this is handled in /etc/rc2.d/S20sysetup with these lines:

```
#   Start the syslog-demon
    /sbin/suattr -M dbadmin -c "killall syslogd"
    /sbin/suattr -M dbadmin -C CAP_DAC_WRITE,CAP_MAC_WRITE,CAP_NETWORK_
➥ MGT,CAP_PRIV
_PORT+ip -c "/usr/etc/syslogd ""`cat /etc/config/syslogd.options 2>
➥/dev/null`"
```

It's not all that much longer, but it looks more complicated.

What /etc/rc.local does on SunOS, all the various scripts do on IRIX. Next week,
you too will get to edit your /etc/rc.local or make a new S** startup script.

A Bit of Everything: /usr

As you might have gathered in yesterday's chapter, /usr is a fairly important directory. It
contains a bit of everything: man pages, files, libraries, locally installed software, games,
demos, and so on.

On SunOS, /usr looks like the following:

```
Barracuda# ls /usr
5bin            dict        lib           openwin       tmp
5include        etc         local         pub           ucb
5lib            export      lost+found    sccs          ucbinclude
adm             games       man           share         ucblib
bin             hosts       mdec          spool         xpg2bin
boot            include     net           src           xpg2include
demo            kvm         nserve        stand         xpg2lib
diag            lddrv       old           sys
```

On IRIX, it looks like this:

```
SUZIE joray 103 > ls /usr
Cadmin        bin         gfx         mbase       share
CosmoPlayer   bsd         gnu         nds         sitemgr
Imgtcl        cms         include     ns-home     spool
Motif-1.2     cpu         java        pcp         stand
Motif-2.1     custlink    lib         people      sysadm
NetVis        demos       lib32       preserve    tmp
ToolTalk      diags       lib64       relnotes    tmp_rex
adm           etc         local       sbin        var
adobe         freeware    mail        sgitcl      webdocs
```

Because /usr has so much variety, I wanted the /usr partition on my machine to be
rather large. You will most likely store any software you add to your site in /usr/local,
and more preferably, /usr/local/bin. It will sometimes make sense to not put some of
the software you add to /usr/local/ or /usr/local/bin, but those instances will probably be rare. You will, however, look at a couple of software examples next week that you
might prefer to store in a nonstandard location.

Log and Temporary/Dynamic Storage: /var

As system administrator, you will get to know the /var directory. Your logs are probably
stored in a subdirectory of /var—likely /var/log or /var/adm. Your NIS maps and
other system dynamic or temporary files are often kept in /var as well—things such as
printer spool files, outgoing mail, and editor temporary files are frequently found in subdirectories of /var.

Here's a look at /var on SunOS:

```
Barracuda# ls /var
adm             log             preserve        tmp
crash           net             spool           yp
```

Here it is on IRIX:

```
SUZIE joray 105 > ls /var
X11             dmedia          ns              sysadm
adm             flexlm          opt             sysadmdesktop
arch            inst            pcp             sysgen
boot            lib             preserve        tmp
cms             mail            saf             tmp_rex
config          mps             share           www
cron            netls           spool           xfsdump
dhcp            netscape        statmon         yp
```

Here's an example of the kind of information you will find in your logs. This comes from my SunOS machine's /var/adm/messages file:

```
Mar 18 12:32:05 Barracuda vmunix: rebooting...
Mar 18 12:32:05 Barracuda vmunix: SunOS Release 4.1.4 (GENERIC) #2: Fri
➥Oct 14 11:08:06 PDT 1994
Mar 18 12:32:05 Barracuda vmunix: Copyright (c) 1983-1993,
➥Sun Microsystems, Inc.
Mar 18 12:32:05 Barracuda vmunix: mem = 32768K (0x2000000)
Mar 18 12:32:05 Barracuda vmunix: avail mem = 30478336
Mar 18 12:32:05 Barracuda vmunix: Ethernet address = 8:0:20:d:8d:48
Mar 18 12:32:05 Barracuda vmunix: cpu = SUNW,Sun 4/50
Mar 18 12:32:05 Barracuda vmunix: zs0 at obio 0xf1000000 pri 12
Mar 18 12:32:05 Barracuda vmunix: zs1 at obio 0xf0000000 pri 12
Mar 18 12:32:05 Barracuda vmunix: audio0 at obio 0xf7201000 pri 13
Mar 18 12:32:05 Barracuda vmunix: sbus0 at SBus slot 0 0x0
Mar 18 12:32:05 Barracuda vmunix: dma0 at SBus slot 0 0x400000
Mar 18 12:32:05 Barracuda vmunix: esp0 at SBus slot 0 0x800000 pri 3
Mar 18 12:32:05 Barracuda vmunix: sd0 at esp0 target 3 lun 0
Mar 18 12:32:05 Barracuda vmunix: sd0: <Fujitsu M2624FA-1 cyl 1440 alt 2
➥hd 11 sec 64> Mar 18 12:32:05 Barracuda vmunix: sr0 at esp0
➥target 6 lun 0
Mar 18 12:32:05 Barracuda vmunix: le0 at SBus slot 0 0xc00000 pri 5
Mar 18 12:32:05 Barracuda vmunix: cgsix0 at SBus slot 3 0x0 pri 7
Mar 18 12:32:05 Barracuda vmunix: cgsix0: screen 1152x900, single
➥buffered, 1M mappable, rev 8
Mar 18 12:32:05 Barracuda vmunix: fd0 at obio 0xf7200000 pri 11
Mar 18 12:32:05 Barracuda vmunix: root on sd0a fstype 4.2
Mar 18 12:32:05 Barracuda vmunix: swap on sd0b fstype spec size 102080K
Mar 18 12:32:05 Barracuda vmunix: dump on sd0b fstype spec size 102068K
Mar 18 13:34:05 Barracuda login: ROOT LOGIN console
Mar 18 13:49:39 Barracuda login: ROOT LOGIN console
Mar 19 01:27:13 Barracuda login: ROOT LOGIN console
Mar 19 12:49:43 Barracuda login: REPEATED LOGIN FAILURES ON console, root
Mar 19 12:49:57 Barracuda login: ROOT LOGIN console
```

4

In this case, the comments from vmunix are from when the machine booted. As you can see, most of your startup diagnostic comments are stored here in case you need them after startup has finished. In addition to startup information, you will see various additional comments in the logs. Your system can be configured to keep track of all manner of diagnostic and error information in the log files, which is something I will show you how to do on Day 9, "What About Security?" when you get to learn about enhancing your machine's security. Keep in mind, however, that most machines are set up to occasionally rotate the logs to keep disk usage down. Because of this, logs eventually rotate out of existence.

Bunches of Binaries

Among some of the directories accompanying UNIX, /bin, /usr/bin, /sbin, /usr/sbin, and /usr/ucb are where you will find a lot of the basic UNIX commands that you're already familiar with. In general, expect these directories to contain system-installed binaries—things that are a part of the standard distribution of the operating system. The sbin directories usually tend to contain administrative, configuration, or diagnostics commands, whereas the bin directories usually tend more towards commands regular users would find more useful. On some System V machines, /usr/ucb will contain BSD flavors of some commands; these are there for the people who are more comfortable with the BSD syntax or options. Occasionally, commands are also there because the manufacturers realize that the BSD way of doing things is less troublesome than the System V way for some things.

Special Devices: /dev

The /dev directory contains special filenames for some devices. For example, /dev/rmt/ on a Solaris machine is where you can find special device names for tape drives. Of the special devices names, /dev/null is probably one that you will see a lot. Anything written to /dev/null, is discarded, as the name might suggest.

User Directories

User directories can be found lurking in /home, /usr/people, and just about anywhere else on your system. As a system administrator, you will have some control over that yourself. On SunOS, the default location for home directories is /home. On IRIX, however, the default location is /usr/people. You, of course, might have another arrangement already in place or might decide to make yet some other arrangement to your liking. Of the two mentioned here, it seems that /home would be an easier convention to work with. If you use /home for users, as you add more diskspace and more user partitions, you could perhaps call them /home, /home2, and so on.

Lost and Found: `lost+found`

As the name might suggest, `lost+found` directories contain files that that the system lost and now doesn't know what to do with. You will only find `lost+found` directories at the top of individual partitions. For example, if you have a / partition and a /usr partition, you will have a /lost+found and a /usr/lost+found.

Useful Commands

A tour of your system wouldn't be complete without a look at some of the more useful UNIX commands for a system administrator.

Space Management: `df`, `du`, and `ln`

As system administrator, you now care about the overall use of space on your system.

`df` is a command that you will use fairly regularly to see how much space is available on your machines. It reports how much free space is available on your filesystems. To get your figures in kilobytes, which are more meaningful to the average user than 512-byte blocks, simply issuing `df` is sufficient on some systems, but you might have to issue `df -k` on others. Here's how my machine looks already, rather full, and I haven't even started to add any extra software:

```
Barracuda# df
Filesystem            kbytes    used   avail capacity  Mounted on
/dev/sd0a             47575    3818   39000     9%    /
/dev/sd0g            311975  195702   85076    70%    /usr
/dev/sd0h             18671      10   16794     0%    /home
```

Here is a more interesting `df -k` example. In this one you can see that this machine is using resources from other machines. This example is especially interesting for me. The `df` command might report the space available on the drives, but it can also be a convenient tool to give a quick diagnosis of the health of your system. For example, we had a lengthy, scheduled power outage today, and I took the day off to stay home and write. I'm hoping that the machines at work come back up properly without intervention so that I don't have to go in and talk to them myself. As soon as the machines start reappearing on the network, a quick glance at `df` is one way for me to tell right away that either not everything has been turned back on or that some drives failed. Unfortunately, this sample output should include directories from two other machines if everything was working properly (I guess I'll have to go in this evening and check on the status of the world):

```
SUZIE testing 7 >df -k
Filesystem             Type  kbytes     use     avail %use Mounted on
/dev/root              xfs  4111320 2857156  1254164  70  /
catbert:/var/spool/mail      nfs   93759   43037    50722  46  /usr/mail
waashu:/1a/share       nfs  3887200 3593076   294124  93  /share
waashu:/1a             nfs  3887200 3593076   294124  93  /net/waashu/1a
waashu:/1b             nfs  3887200 3189224   697976  83  /net/waashu/1b
```

You will probably find yourself using du when you suddenly discover that a filesystem that you thought had plenty of space doesn't seem so spacious any more. du displays the amount of disk space a directory or file takes up. Again, you will find that on some systems, the default is already in kilobytes and that du -s will provide the summary you want, whereas on others, you might have to issue du -sk instead.

Running du -s * in my /usr directory quickly reveals that /usr/openwin is taking up a lot of space on my machine. Here's a look at /usr/openwin itself:

```
Barracuda# du -s openwin
74888   openwin
```

The ln command is more useful to me as a system administrator than it ever was as a regular user. You will use it to give your users that seamless appearance that UNIX has. As you start to run out of space and have to move directories to other drives, you will be using ln -s to link. Your users might be more inclined to use it for linking whatever they have called their main Web page to whatever your Web server expects to find.

Sharing Resources: exportfs and mount

To allow your machine to export its resources to other machines in your cluster, use the exportfs command. Some directories you will export for a while, others you will export only to complete a specific task. Some systems might use another command that calls exportfs or substitutes for its functionality.

exportfs, when invoked without any arguments, lists what is being exported. Here's an example:

```
WAASHU testing 3 >exportfs
/1a             -anon=-1,root=catbert:rosalyn:suzie:hobbes:calvin:moe:halo,
➥access=catbert:rosalyn:suzie:hobbes:calvin:moe:halo
/1b             -anon=-1,root=catbert:rosalyn:suzie:hobbes:calvin:moe:halo,
➥access=catbert:rosalyn:suzie:hobbes:calvin:moe:halo
/1c/GCG_user -anon=-1,root=catbert,access=catbert
/usr/local      -anon=-1,root=halo,access=halo
```

mount is the command that allows your machine to mount what another is exporting. As with exportfs, when mount is invoked without any arguments, you get back a listing of what is currently mounted:

```
SUZIE testing 8 >mount
/dev/root on / type xfs (rw,raw=/dev/rroot)
/hw on /hw type hwgfs (rw)
/proc on /proc type proc (rw)/dev/fd on /dev/fd type fd (rw)
catbert:/var/spool/mail on /usr/mail type nfs
➥(rw,vers=2,hard,intr,bg,rsize=512,wsize=512,dev=c0000)
waashu:/1a/share on /share type nfs
➥(rw,vers=2,hard,intr,bg,rsize=512,wsize=512,dev=c0001)
waashu:/1a on /net/waashu/1a type nfs
```

```
➥(quota,vers=2,rw,hard,intr,bg,rsize=512,wsize=512,dev=c0002)
waashu:/1b on /net/waashu/1b type nfs
➥(quota,vers=2,rw,hard,intr,bg,rsize=512,wsize=512,dev=c0003)
```

I can use mount as another quick way for me to tell that the other directories that this machine should be mounting still haven't been mounted yet. It confirms my suspicion that I'll have to go in this evening.

Process Management: ps, top, and kill

ps is one of the commands that you will use to look at what processes your machine is running. This is another one of those commands where you will find differences in the operating systems. If you type **ps -elf ¦ more** and the machine complains, try typing **ps -auxww ¦ more** instead.

Note

> **elf and auxww?** This is one of those annoying differences between System V and BSD UNIX flavors. System V uses elf, whereas BSD uses auxww. In both cases, the arguments say "show everything, not just processes I personally own" (e for "everything," versus a for "all" and x for "I really meant all"). The arguments also say "show me as much useful information as possible" (l for "long" and f for "full, because long's not enough" versus u for "user friendly"). The BSD version also includes ww, which gives the system a hint about how many times you'd like to have long lines wrapped when the information is insanely long.
>
> Additionally confusing, some versions of ps don't like it when you give them the - in front of the arguments. These versions will complain about the dash but will work properly even with it.
>
> Don't worry if you can't remember what these options mean right now; Appendix A, "Useful UNIX Commands for the System Administrator," gives you a list of useful commands and details on their options. Also, you'll probably find that you won't really care what the options to ps mean. As root, you're going to be asking for the most detailed process listing possible every time you type the command; soon your fingers will be typing -elf or -auxww automatically for you every time you enter the ps command.

4

Here's an example of the kind of information you will get. Note that I've piped the output through the pager command more, just in case the output is long and I want to look at it one page at a time:

```
WAASHU joray 87 > ps -elf ¦ more
    UID        PID    PPID  C   STIME TTY  TIME CMD
   root          1       0  0  Mar 05 ?   0:11 /etc/init
  nobody    191000     572  0  Mar 15 ?   0:00 /usr/SeqWeb/httpd/httpd
➥-d /usr/SeqWeb/httpd
```

```
    root          566      1   0   Mar 05 ?   0:01 /usr/etc/sshd
    root          568      1   0   Mar 05 ?   0:07 /usr/etc/sshd1
➥-f /etc/sshd_fix_config
    nobody     223579    572   0   Mar 17 ?   0:00 /usr/SeqWeb/httpd/httpd
➥-d /usr/SeqWeb/httpd

    root          572      1   0   Mar 05 ?   2:05 /usr/SeqWeb/httpd/httpd
➥-d /usr/SeqWeb/httpd

    root          578      1   0   Mar 05 ttyd0:00 /sbin/getty ttyd1 console
```

In the `UID` column, you see who is running the process. In the `PID` column is the process ID. You'll need that number when you have to kill a process. `PPID` is the parent process's ID. For example, you see that the Web server process `191000` is a child of `512`.

`top` is useful for seeing what processes are taking up how much of your machine's resources. You might find this command to be especially useful when your machine seems rather slow. It will give you machine load averages, the number of processes running, and so on. It is also rather interesting to run because it updates dynamically. Unfortunately, this command isn't present by default on all versions of UNIX, but I've included instructions on how you can build and install your own in Day 19, "Optional Software." Here's one moment in time, as captured by the `top` command:

```
last pid: 12321;  load averages:  0.83,  0.86,  0.72          15:36:21
65 processes:  62 sleeping, 3 running
Cpu states:      % user,     % nice,     % system,     % idle
Memory: 24360K available, 24232K in use, 128K free, 2212K locked

  PID USERNAME PRI NICE   SIZE   RES STATE    TIME  WCPU    CPU COMMAND
12199 ray       32    0 14872K 5148K run      0:55 14.50%  8.20% netscape
12312 joray     15    0   472K  688K sleep    0:00  3.85%  1.56% tcsh
24421 ray        1    0 22708K 2280K sleep1229:46  1.17%  1.17% X
12320 joray     29    0   468K  580K run      0:00  3.95%  0.39% top
12065 lists      1    0  1084K  776K sleep    0:06  0.39%  0.39% sendmail
12321 ray        3    0   364K  504K sleep    0:00  7.69%  0.39% vi
12219 lists     -5    0  1072K  776K run      0:04  0.00%  0.00% sendmail
```

Also, you will run into various occasions when `kill` will be a necessary command for you to run to terminate a process. One year I ran into the problem of students not cleanly quitting a program that they had to use for their class. The process would still be running, taking up a license, yet no one else could run that program at that machine until the process had been killed. So I would have to look up the PID with the `ps` command and issue `kill -9` to terminate the process. You will sometimes have to use `kill` to send a signal to the process to hang up but not to actually terminate.

Useful Utilities: `grep` and `find`

`grep` is useful for searching for certain character strings. At first, I didn't think this would actually be all that useful, but as time goes on, I find that I am regularly using `grep`. When you are installing software, `grep` can help you find where certain information is set. I used `grep` yesterday to give me a quick idea of which patches would require that the kernel be reconfigured. The results looked like the following:

```
Barracuda# grep "kernel" *
102394.readme:Config, make and install a new kernel.
102394.readme:for details on building and installing a new kernel.
102436.readme:Keywords: hangs kernel looping bootup hat_pteunload
➥segu_get performance xbox
102436.readme:1171171 -> Machine soft hangs under load with kernel
➥looping
102436.readme:3. Rebuild the kernel and reboot the system.
102436.readme:  building and booting new kernels using config(8) and
➥make(1).
102516.readme:3. Rebuild the kernel and reboot the system with the
➥new kernel.
102516.readme:for details on building and installing a custom kernel.
102517.readme:3) Config, make and install a new kernel.
102517.readme:   for details on building and installing a custom kernel.
```

You might find `grep` especially useful in combination with other commands. For example, if you were looking for certain types of processes, you might issue a `ps` command like this:

```
Rosalyn joray 95 > ps -elf ¦ grep "ftp"
   joray  6830  6358  1 13:54:17 pts/8    0:00 grep ftp
```

In this case, you see that the only command running that contains the pattern `ftp` is your `grep` command. From this you can see that no one is using `ftp` for anything.

The `find` command can be quite useful. I tend to use it mostly to look for a file whose name I know but whose location I don't know. However, you can do much more with the command. You can have it search for files that are a certain age, size, or whatever and then have `find` execute some command on the files it finds. Take a look at root's crontab (`crontab -l` is a reasonable try) for some examples of what you can do with `find`. Don't worry if you don't have time to check your root's crontab right now; you will look briefly at one tomorrow.

Monitoring Your Machine's Usage: `who` and `last`

The `who` command tells you who is currently logged on your system. I find this command to be most useful if I have to do something that might require that the machine be rebooted. It helps me decide whether it is okay to reboot the machine now, or if I can't wait, it tells me who I have to inform about the reboot.

You will find last to be a surprisingly useful command. For example, if you see in your logs a login that shouldn't have occurred, you can get more specific information about the login for further use. Here's a good example from an IRIX machine:

```
Moe joray 146 > last -W
jane       ttyq1         Mon Nov  2 10:05 - 10:11  (00:06)
           soyokaze.biosci.ohio-state.edu
joray      ttyq1         Mon Nov  2 09:42 - 09:58  (00:15)
           rosalyn.biosci.ohio-state.edu
larry      ttyq0         Mon Nov  2 09:34 - 12:44  (03:09)
           rosalyn.biosci.ohio-state.edu
larry      ttyq0         Mon Nov  2 08:26 - 08:27  (00:00)
           rosalyn.biosci.ohio-state.edu
lp         ttyq0         Sun Nov  1 23:36 - 00:08  (00:32)
           ip122.pontiac.mi.pub-ip.psi.net
lp         ttyq0         Sat Oct 31 17:00 - 17:09  (00:09)
           ip122.pontiac.mi.pub-ip.psi.net
lp         ttyq0         Sat Oct 31 16:14 - 16:54  (00:40)
           ip122.pontiac.mi.pub-ip.psi.net
lp         ttyq0         Sat Oct 31 13:24 - 13:34  (00:09)
           ip122.pontiac.mi.pub-ip.psi.net
lp         ttyq0         Sat Oct 31 13:11 - 13:23  (00:11)
           ip122.pontiac.mi.pub-ip.psi.net
lp         ttyq0         Sat Oct 31 12:53 - 13:03  (00:09)
           ip122.pontiac.mi.pub-ip.psi.net
lp         ttyq0         Sat Oct 31 12:30 - 12:52  (00:21)
           ip122.pontiac.mi.pub-ip.psi.net
ted        ttyq1         Fri Oct 30 14:47 - 14:49  (00:02)
           :0.0
ted        ttyq0         Fri Oct 30 14:45 - 18:48  (04:03)
           :0.0
harry      ttyq1         Fri Oct 30 14:33 - 14:42  (00:08)
           :0.0
harry      ttyq0         Fri Oct 30 14:33 - 14:42  (00:08)
           :0.0
wanda      ttyq1         Fri Oct 30 13:41 - 13:42  (00:00)
           suzie.biosci.ohio-state.edu
ted        ttyq0         Fri Oct 30 09:59 - 14:33  (04:33)
           :0.0
```

Here, last reveals that one of those accounts that should be locked out has logged in, and it gives you an IP address that you can give to the security group to further pursue. You can also see that some of your users logged in on the console (:0.0) as well as from other machines in the biosci.ohio-state.edu domain.

vi: The Editor You Should Get to Know

A tour of your system can hardly ignore a tour of the system administrator's favorite editor: vi. The vi editor is a quick editor that's found almost everywhere you go. It doesn't have a fancy interface, and the command syntax is cryptic, but it gets the job done and is always there when you need it. Although vi can do some impressive things in the right hands, for the purposes of making a quick change to a configuration file, you don't really need any of the more powerful features. Excerpted from *Sams Teach Yourself UNIX in Ten Minutes* is the following short vi tutorial. It doesn't contain any of the fancy keystrokes, but how fancy do you need to get to edit a small file anyway?

Quick and Dirty Editing: vi

The vi editor (some pronounce it "vee-eye", others pronounce it "vie". There seems to be no consensus, but the people who call it "Vie" are still wrong!) is UNIX's most universal editor. It isn't an easy editor. It isn't a friendly editor. It is, however, a quick-starting editor with a very small memory footprint, which you will find on every UNIX machine that you sit down in front of. Because of its ubiquity, knowing the basics of vi will enable you to work with your files even if more convenient editors are not available.

If you need to use vi, you should do the following:

1. Determine what file you want to edit.
2. Issue the vi command as: **vi <filename>.** The vi editor can also be started with no filename if the mood strikes you.

When you start vi, there are a number of things you need to know to make it useful. The Return key has been included here as some of these commands take effect immediately upon pressing the respective keys, and some require <return> to be pressed after them.

vi operates in one of two modes: Command Mode and Insert Mode. In Command Mode, you have control of things such as cursor position, deleting characters, and saving files. In Insert Mode you can insert characters. This distinction is bound to be confusing at first, but you'll find vi's speed and universal presence outweigh its odd interface when faced with some tasks.

When in Insert Mode, hit the <esc> (escape) key to get into Command Mode.

When in Command Mode, you will use the following key(s) and key combinations:

- Position the cursor with the following four keys: **L** to move right, **H** to move left, **J** to move to the next line, and **K** to move to the previous line. Some versions of vi also work with the arrow-keypad cursor keys, but you can always control your cursor with the **H,J,K,L** key set.
- To delete a character, position the cursor on the character you want to delete and hit the **X** key.
- To delete an entire line (including when you need to delete an empty line), hit the **D** key twice.

4

- Switching to Insert Mode—To append to the end of a line, position your cursor on the line you would like to append to, and hit **A**. The **I** and **A** keys will also enter Insert Mode, either before the character under the cursor or after the character under the cursor, respectively. (When in Insert Mode, you can type characters into the file. The Backspace and Delete keys should work properly, but only for data that you have just inserted.)

- To save the file, enter Command Mode (it never hurts to type **<esc>**, even if you're already in Command Mode—it might beep if you're already in Command Mode, but don't let it bother you), and type **:w<return>**.

- To save the file to a new name, enter Command Mode and type **:w <filename><return>**.

- To exit vi, enter Command Mode and type **:q<return>**.

- If you're in too deep and need to quit without saving, enter Command Mode and type **:q!<return>**.

Because it would be impossible to walk through a step-by-step example, try typing the following, compare what you're typing to the short list of commands above, and see what happens. Although the finer details will not be revealed by this example, you should pick up enough to at least let you get useful work done and get you out of any sticky vi situations you get yourself into.

Try typing the following exactly as it appears, and see what happens. Where a new line appears in the text, hit <return>. (remembering that <esc> is the escape key):

```
> vi mynewfile

iThis is my new file
This is line one of my new file
This is a test
This is line four of my new file<esc>kddkA
This is line three of my new file<esc>khhhhhhhhhhhhhhhhhhhxxxitwo<esc>:wq!
```

Your machine should respond with the following:

```
"mynewfile" [New file] 4 lines, 119 characters
```

Now look at what you've got:

```
> cat mynewfile

This is my new file
This is line two of my new file
This is line three of my new file
This is line four of my new file
```

Planning Your System's Future

You conclude the tour of your system with a look to the future. Yes, planning was discussed in great detail on Day 2, "Designing Your Cluster: From Planning to Policy," but I take this opportunity to remind you to be thinking a bit about your facility's future.

The Immediate Future

If you have not yet had a chance to do this, you will want to start to think about the overall organization of your cluster. Decide where your local software will go. Decide where your user directories will go. Do you need more drive space for these directories? Will you need more drive space for these directories at some point? At some time, you might want to add a drive that will simply be storage for your stuff—`tar` files of software you have already installed, patches, and so on. Draw a map of your cluster as it develops.

The Future

In addition to the immediate plans, your facility should be thinking about what kind of expansion and upgrade plans it will be making. Remember that computer technology rapidly changes, and you don't want to be left completely behind. Put some sort of plan in place to add new machines (perhaps one every year), up to some maximum number of machines that your facility thinks might be sufficient. Of course, your plans can change as necessary, but you will be happier if there is some sort of expected plan. You do not want to just buy a few computers and let them sit in a room for so long that the new versions of the software no longer run on your hardware. Remember that you should have a plan for the machines too, not just the software.

Don't be afraid to consult as many resources as necessary to plan your facility, whether it is the immediate organization of your cluster or the overall planning for your facility.

Summary

In this lesson, you took a brief tour of your system and learned the following:

- / is the highest directory on your machine. Under it, the system is typically organized as follows:

  /etc has configuration files and startup scripts.

  /usr has a bit of everything, from man pages and include files to locally stored software.

  /var serves as dynamic/temporary storage for logs, printer spool files, and other such things.

bin directories tend to store regular user commands, whereas sbin directories tend to store administrative commands.

/dev is the special devices directory, housing most notably /dev/null, which discards anything output to it.

/lost+found is the machine's lost and found room.

User directories can go just about anywhere.

- Some of the commands useful to the system administrator include the following:

  df, du, and ln help monitor space usage or link files or directories to make space seem the same to the users.

  mount and exportfs share resources.

  ps, top, and kill monitor or terminate processes.

  who and last find out who is/has been using a machine.

- vi is an editor that is almost everywhere. Learn its basic usage.

- Plan, plan, plan. From planning your facility to planning your machine's disk space, you should always stay focused if you want your facility to grow.

Q&A

Q How full can a drive get before you have to worry about freeing up space on it?

A That depends entirely on what you're doing with it. Generally, you should leave the drive with at least a small percentage of free space so that the OS has room to do any behind-the-scenes work it needs to do. This isn't as necessary with drives that store large files that don't get modified as it is with drives that store smaller files that are modified frequently. With some filesystem implementations it's not really a concern at all because 100 percent full actually leaves the system some spare room. As root, you can frequently go over 105 percent full on a drive.

Q I want to add a new application, and /usr/local/ says I have 35MB free. Is this enough?

A Presuming you're putting the software in /usr/local/, which is where most third-party software goes, the answer depends entirely on the size of your /user/local partition and on the size of your application. If 35MB will fit the application and still leave enough room that your OS doesn't have trouble accessing the drive, sure. (Remember that small percentage of free space from the question above? Violating it can incur a severe performance decrease.) If not, you need to clean house or add some more disk space.

Q **What happens to the files in `lost+found` directories? Do they just stay there, or does the system eventually do something with them?**

A Sometimes, these files are deleted by root `crontab` entries if they sit around too long. Usually, they just sit around and take up disk space until an administrator gets tired of them being there and deletes them. Unless a user lost something really important, it's probably not worth trying to piece together whatever it was that ended up in `lost+found`.

Q **Are there any editors other than `vi` that are likely to come with multiple operating systems?**

A Not ones that you want to use. `sed`, the stream editor, is available almost everywhere. Plain old `ed` shows up frequently, too. Neither of these are things you want to have to use as an editor. A number of additional editors are available for almost all flavors of UNIX. Chief among these is `emacs`, the editor with everything including the kitchen sink, but you'll usually have to install these if you want them.

Workshop

Quiz

4

1. What's the root of the filesystem?
2. How do you find out what processes are running?
3. How do you find out what users are using your machine?
4. How do you get rid of a process that you want stopped?
5. Where are your executables coming from?

Exercises

1. Look around your system and see if there are any places that have executable files that aren't in your path. Catalog the interesting ones for future reference.
2. Look at your current disk layout. Decide where you would grow it if you had another disk drive to add.
3. What resources on this machine could be shared with other machines in your cluster to conserve disk usage and to make maintenance easier?
4. Practice using the `find` command. Read the `find` command. Read the `find` man page, and then practice finding things by date, ownership, name, and size.

DAY 5

On Root's Best Behavior

I hope you enjoyed taking a tour of your machine yesterday. Today will be another short day to give you still a bit of a chance to recover from the task of setting up your machine. Although today's discussion will be brief, it is very important. Remember, you are root now. What you do affects everything.

Caring for the Root Password

One of the first things you had to do as root was make a password. Remember that root's password should always be something that is hard to guess. Use some combination of uppercase and lowercase alphanumeric characters. Do not use dictionary words, the name of your significant other, and so on. At the same time, you want the password to be something that you can remember. You do not want to casually write down root's password and leave it somewhere; however, it would probably be a good idea to leave the root password in a safe location, should it become absolutely necessary for someone to access the root account when you are not available. As you'll remember from Day 3, "Setting Up a Machine: From the Box to the Desktop," you might find turning a phrase into a password to be a method that is hard to guess but is easy for you to remember.

How often should you change the root password? Precisely how often is at your discretion, but you should probably change it at least every few months. Certainly change it after someone who previously had root access has left. Any time that you discover that a machine on your network has been compromised, change the root password. Don't change it so often that you have trouble coming up with a password or that you have to write it down to remember it.

Don't follow the same sort of pattern all the time, even if it does make for a terrific password. If someone uncovers your pattern, it's not so terrific any more. Also, pick something you can easily type. I have rejected many passwords that seemed like they would be great passwords but that I had difficulty typing.

Only give the root password to those who really need it. Remember, the fewer of you who can be root, the less likely it is for someone to accidentally cause serious damage or even wipe out the system.

Becoming Root

At this stage, your options on how to become root are fairly limited: You can log in directly as root. However, when you start adding users to your system, your options will grow.

After You Have Added Users

After you have added a couple users to your system, never log in as root. Logging in as root leaves no trace of the user attached to the login and no accountability path if there is a problem. If possible, disable root logins on your machine for both network connections and for console logins. If you need to become root, you should su to the root account. This leaves a log entry and enhances the security of your system.

Even Better than su

When possible, don't use root at all. The less time you spend at a root prompt, the less opportunity you have for making a catastrophic mistake. When compiling software, compile as a normal user—only become root for installation steps that require writing to protected directories. If possible, use the sudo package instead of the su command. You'll learn how to install and configure sudo next week. Briefly, sudo enables users to assume partial root privileges. The users who are enabled to use these privileges and exactly what privileges are granted to a particular user are controlled by a set of configuration files. Additionally, sudo logs all commands used, so you have better accountability of your administrative staff.

Root Do's and Don'ts

As root, you've got to be a bit more careful than the normal UNIX user. Although not a complete list by any stretch of the imagination, here are a number of things that fall under the imperative "do" or "don't do" category if you want your machines to remain stable and secure.

Use \rm -rf with Care

As you are cleaning up things manually as root in addition to what root is doing in the background in cronjobs, you will use \rm -rf regularly. You might even practice appropriate caution and resist using \rm -rf at first, but eventually you will tire of having to answer "yes" to everything you want to delete. When you reach that point, you can use \rm -rf, forcing everything to be deleted recursively.

> **Note**
>
> **Why \rm -rf instead of rm -rf?** Adding the backslash (\) before a command causes the command to be executed without paying attention to any aliases that you might have set for it. If you already have rm aliased to rm -i and you issue the command as rm -rf, the actual command executed is rm -i -rf. Because the -i, interactive flag, takes precedence over the -f, force flag, the remove procedure asks you to confirm each delete. Issuing the command as \rm -rf causes the shell to ignore your alias and execute the command exactly as typed.

Use this command with caution. Be sure you have checked and double-checked where you are when you issue this command. If you hear the machine crunching away for what seems to be much longer than you thought it would take, you might want to interrupt that command. I have been told that it's only a matter of time before I will issue that command and start deleting the contents of the entire machine. So I pass that warning on to you. So far, I have only accidentally deleted /usr/local. I was fortunate in that I had just run a full backup of /usr/local the day before, so I was able to restore the contents relatively painlessly. Due to the condition of the network in our building, however, I did take the all network activity in the building to a grinding halt for several hours, but at least /usr/local was recovered.

If You Don't Know What It Is, Don't Run It

Never, ever, run an unknown shell script or program as root. When you're root, every application you run does so with your permissions. If you run a program or script as root, it has the capability to do absolutely anything you can do as root. Always test applications as a normal user, and always read scripts to attempt to determine what they do. If you can't figure out what a script does and it doesn't come from somewhere considered to be an extremely reliable source (hint: the Web in general doesn't qualify—your application vendors might), you should seriously examine whether you really need to do whatever the script claims to do.

Never Give Normal Users Root Access

Never give normal users root access—not even for a little while. Regardless of whether they can be trusted, normal users should not be allowed to enter commands as root. Not only is there the basic question of trust involved, but normal users are not conditioned to the same level of paranoia regarding precise use of commands. The fact that simple typographical errors in commands can be devastating to the system as a whole is not something a normal user is faced with on a day-to-day basis. If a normal user accidentally tries to delete the entire filesystem from the top down, he gets the message "permission denied." Root is root—it never gets "permission denied."

Don't Needlessly Share with Others

Never share administrative access with users who don't actually need it. If you have an administrative staff, that's one thing, though even there you should carefully consider whether everybody really needs the root password. If you have an environment where some users own hardware that is a part of your cluster, you might be pressured to give the owners root access to their machines. Don't do it unless you absolutely are required to. If these users are not part of your administrative staff, they don't need the root password. You might think it safe to give their machines a different root password from the root password for the rest of your cluster, which would limit any possibility for damage to each user's machine. Unfortunately, this is not true. If their machines share disk space with the rest of your machines, a root password on each of their machines allows them root-privileged manipulation of any filesystems on the machine—including the space of other users on filesystems shared from other machines. This is a security risk you should not be prepared to take.

Whether normal users are trustworthy is not the question. They are not administrators, and like any other non-administrator, they do not understand the scope of administrator-related concerns. If you give a normal user the root password to her machine, chances are that she will write it on a sticky note and put it in her desk drawer. Someday, she will have a project and not have enough disk space. She'll look around a bit and find a likely looking directory to do a bit of housecleaning, and bingo, half your users just lost their files. This one is an issue that's worth "going to the mat" for, when discussing it with your superiors. Giving a normal user—any normal user—root access to any trusted hardware is giving him the access required to generate a complete disaster.

Root Should Not Have . in Its Path

Your friends might already have told you early on to make certain root does not have . in its path. Why is this important? What does it mean anyway? It took me a while to catch on to this....

Your path is the list of directories that the system consults when you ask it to execute a command. If you want to know what is currently in your path, issue the command `echo $path`. The system will print out the contents of your path. For security reasons, because it is very important that root always knows exactly what software it is executing, root's path tends to be a bit more minimal than a regular user's path, and it is often advised that . not be in root's path.

What's that dot? It refers to the current directory. If . is in your path, commands in the current directory will be executed. For a programmer, this is a good thing, but for root, this is cause for concern. For example, imagine you are moving through the system as root, examining the contents of directories. On your tour, you happen to `cd` into a directory in which someone has placed a command named `ls`, creating a command with the same name as the system directory listing command `ls`. When you are in that directory and issue `ls` to list the contents, you might be executing the `ls` command from your current directory, rather than the system `ls`, and you have no way of knowing what this look-alike command might do.

The order of the contents of your path also makes a difference. The directories listed in the path are searched for commands to execute in the order that they appear in the path. If root were to include . in its path, at the end would be a better place for it so that the system looked in more standard places before looking in the current directory for commands. However, root always has to be paranoid. Including . in root's path, even at the end, would allow a devious user to create a malicious program and name it with a common misspelling of a normal command. If root should happen to be in the directory with the fake command and mistype the normal command, placing the . last in the path won't protect root from executing the user's substitute program.

In short, root has to be paranoid. To be completely safe, root really should issue commands in the form of their full paths and avoid all possibility of confusion. Because that's impractical, leaving . out of your path is your safest alternative.

Good Habits and Good Ways to Do Things

As root, it's important that you develop some good habits in your daily routine. In this section, I'll discuss a few of the things that should become second nature to you and some of the better ways to do things as root. Because it would be impossible to even scratch the surface of an exhaustive list of such topics, you should look at this section as a primer in the way that you should be thinking when developing your own habits and procedures.

Backups, Backups

As root, you can change anything with a keystroke or two. Sometimes, however, those changes won't result in everything you had hoped for. It's for those occasions that you always make a backup copy of whatever you plan to change, whether it's as major as the kernel or something seemingly minor instead. If the change is very minor, as in something that you think you can remember, you might think it is pointless to make that copy. Go ahead and do it anyway. That change might not seem to have had any noticeable effect now, but it might farther down the road. With a backup copy in place, you'll be able to retrace your steps. As you work over time, you will develop a feel for when you can get away with not making a backup copy. Until you reach that point, however, always make a backup copy. If you get in the habit of regularly making a backup before you change something, you will remember to make a backup for those occasions when it really counts, such as when you are reconfiguring the kernel.

A Look at Root's `crontab`

As was mentioned in yesterday's tour of the system, a look at root's `crontab` will probably give you a good idea on what can be done with the `find` command. Not only that, but you might want to take a look at root's `crontab` just to see some of what root does at odd hours of the day. If you happen to be at the machine at 5:00 a.m. (yes, that will eventually happen) and the machine starts grinding away all of a sudden, it might just be one of root's `cronjobs` cleaning up the machine for you.

Here's a look at only a small part of root's `crontab` on an IRIX machine. It comes, out of the box, nicely commented and spells out the format of the lines as well as commenting what each entry is doing. Note how a number of the entries ask `find` to search for certain types of files, often last modified or last accessed within a specific period of time, and then remove them. Root runs jobs that remove old or core files, rotate logs, and perform various other tasks, depending on your system. As a comparison, this is only a small portion of root's `crontab` on this IRIX machine, but the one that root has on my SunOS machine is only three lines long and has no comments:

```
WAASHU joray 92 # crontab -l
# $Revision: 1.48 $
#
# The root crontab can be used to perform accounting data collection
#       and cleanup.
#
```

```
# Format of lines:
#min      hour    daymo    month    daywk    cmd
#
#
# General SGI practice
#
# Remove old trash
0         5        *        *        *        find / -local -type f '(' -name
➥core -o -name dead.letter ')' -atime +7 -mtime +7
➥-exec rm -f '{}' ';'
#
# Remove old sendmail mail files
2         5        *        *        *        find /var/spool/mqueue -local
➥-type f -mtime +30 -exec rm -f '{}' ';'
#
# Remove old rwhod files
2         5        *        *        *        find /var/spool/rwho -local
➥-type f -mtime +7 -exec rm -f '{}' ';'
#
# Remove old vi/ex 'preserved' files
3         5        *        *        *        find /var/preserve -local
➥-type f -atime +30 -mtime +30 -exec rm -f '{}' ';'
#
# Rotate the logs
1         1        *        *        0
➥umask 033;cd /var/cron;if test -s log &&
➥test "`/sbin/stat -qs log`" -ge 10240; then
➥mv -f log OLDlog;touch log; killall 1 cron; fi
1         1        *        *        0
➥umask 077;cd /var/adm;if test -s sulog &&
➥test "`/sbin/stat -qs sulog`" -ge 10240; then
➥mv -f sulog OLDsulog;touch sulog; fi
```

By adding useful commands that you run regularly to your crontab, you can have them executed automatically whenever you want. If you need to remove your Web server logs periodically, if you want to search for accounts that have been logged on but have been idle for long periods, or if you have any other sort of useful routine maintenance, you can automate the process by putting it in your crontab. This both removes some of your day-to-day typing load and makes sure that you don't forget some routine-but-trivial task that might slip your mind.

Gracefully Shutting Down

Do not just power off your UNIX box when you have to shut it down! Your machine has a lot to do before it is turned off. Instead, you will issue some combination of the following commands, depending on your needs.

5

Shutdown Alternatives

When initiating a graceful shutdown on your machine, you'll find yourself faced with the first option of using `sync;sync;sync;halt`, rather than `shutdown -h now` (or `shutdown -g0 -i0 -y` if your OS is System V–ish). Some traditions say that two `sync`s are sufficient, whereas others say that three is the way to go. Whichever tradition you prefer, if you are going to use `halt`, include multiple `sync`s in front for good luck. Using `sync;sync;sync;halt` does not give your users any warning before the machine is shut down, whereas `shutdown -h now` does provide some warning, however brief. If you want to be more polite to your users, `shutdown` is certainly the appropriate command to use. At this stage, you are the only user, and it doesn't much matter. But do keep your users in mind when you have to shut down the machine. Try to do anything that will require a shutdown during less popular times, so that as few of your users as possible are interrupted.

Why would you ever have to turn off the power anyway? Unless you have a machine with hot-swap capabilities, you will turn off the power each time you add a peripheral to your machine. If you do not, you will eventually end up destroying your machine's SCSI controller. We have a few machines in our cluster that suffer from this ill fate. In addition, the powers that be might decide that planned power outages are necessary for whatever reason. If you do not have a UPS on your system, you will have to turn off power to your machines. Be sure to inform your users ahead of time so that they can plan their work accordingly.

When you turn your machine back on, remember to turn on any peripherals before turning the machine itself on. This will give the machine the opportunity to identify all its devices at startup.

If what you need to do is reboot your machine rather than turn it off, you will issue one of these reboot commands: `sync;sync;sync;reboot` or `shutdown -r now` (`shutdown -g0 -i6 -y`). The different commands for rebooting your machine are similar to the different ways for halting your machine: `shutdown` will give your users some brief notice ahead of time (brief to them, forever to you), whereas `reboot` will not. The same traditions also apply. Pick your preferred number of `sync`s before `reboot`, if you choose `reboot`.

Things to Keep in Mind

To be effective as a system administrator, it's imperative that you keep several nontechnical things in mind when doing your job. At the top of this list is what your responsibilities are and who they are to. Many potential system administrators "burn out" or become adversarial impediments to their users because they fail to keep these simple things in mind when making policy or interacting with their users.

Why Are You Here?

Always remember why you're there. System administrators are there to keep machines running for their users. Your job is to facilitate the work of the user community you support. Because of the technical nature of the work, many people unsuited for the public-relations half of system administration gravitate to this job. These people unfortunately frequently develop the attitude that the machines are their toys and that the users are there to appreciate them for keeping the machines running. System administration really is a rather thankless service position. If you're the type of person who doesn't much enjoy the "helping" part of it, at least keep in mind that it is why you get to do the technical tweaking. If you do enjoy the helping part, take comfort in the fact that what you do is a great help to all your users, even if they don't know it or bother to thank you for it.

What Do Your Users Want?

Users can sometimes be strange creatures. Frequently, they try to define solutions to problems when they haven't adequately defined the problem. This usually manifests itself as a user with a problem to solve and a purchase order for a piece of software that won't solve it. After that software is purchased, the user will likely blame you for the fact that it doesn't do what she wanted. A large part of your job as a system administrator will probably be helping to identify the actual needs of your users, as opposed to their perceived needs. After you have accomplished this, you then have the job of coaxing them in the direction of making the right choice. If you're friendly and supportive and you make yourself available to your users, perhaps even more than they would like initially, you can derail some of these impending train wrecks before they occur.

To help keep yourself on the "asked before making decisions" list, keep in mind that the computers are supposed to be a productivity tool for your users. It's not uncommon to see users trying to accomplish some goal where the problem of working with the computer has become a larger task than the original problem was. Learn to recognize this when it happens, and provide helpful solutions to those who will listen. You'll be surprised how often you don't even need to have any knowledge of the field they're in or the goal they're working towards to solve the more immediate problems they're having.

Know When a Computer Is the Wrong Tool

A subset of the "help identify the real problem" situations you will encounter are those where the real problem doesn't have a good computer solution. Many users brought up in today's world of high-tech electronic widgets have completely forgotten that there was a way to do things that doesn't involve a mouse and keyboard. Sometimes the "old way" is better: Keep an eye out for it, as you can probably save your users a lot of time this way. To illustrate, I'll give you two recent examples from the world of user weirdness.

It was 3:00 a.m. on a Friday night (or Saturday morning, depending on how you define these things), and I was still at the office arguing with a rebellious printer. Two of my users walked in (they keep as oddball hours as I do) and were discussing a flyer that they needed to put together to advertise a campus event. One of them had a paper copy of a beautifully designed version of the flyer with great eye-catching graphics, but had an error in the date and time. The other had a flyer he'd made, which was, quite frankly, ugly, but at least the information was correct. They'd come in to use the machines to download the better flyer from the user's ISP (Internet service provider) account, correct, and print it. Unfortunately, our printer was down. They spent about 20 minutes arguing in the background and calling all the campus computing labs trying to find one that was open, while I puttered about printer configurations. Eventually, it filtered through to me that they had completely failed to find a lab with a network connection and a functioning printer. They had, however, found one with a scanner and a functioning printer, and so were headed off to go scan the pretty flyer, make the change and print out more copies. The shocked looks of slowly dawning comprehension on their faces when I handed them a pair of scissors and introduced them to the photocopier were a sight to behold.

Another example of doing things the "old-fashioned" way includes a user of whom I am not particularly fond. The user was working on putting together a set of overheads for a presentation. One of the overheads required a simple flow-chart diagram with three connected ovals, a word in each, and arrows between them. Regardless of the fact that she's not my favorite user, it's still my job to help. So, when I noticed that she was sitting in front of the PC fighting a graphics package with a steep learning curve for the second day in a row, I tried to help. I mentioned that the PC really wasn't the right tool for the job and that I could help her solve her problem easily. She retorted that she despised Macintoshes and that this was the best graphics program available. Some users can't be helped. I didn't stay to tell her about the drafting-oval templates I have in my desk.

In brief, even though you're the system administrator and it's your job to help your users use the system and to make that system as useful for them as possible, sometimes it's in your user's best interest to not use your system. It's almost as important for you to be able to catch these situations and explain potentially better solutions as it is to be able to point them at the best computational solution. Even if you have the world's greatest hammer, not everything is a nail, and you as an outside observer can be a great help to your users by recognizing when they have developed tunnel vision regarding a computational solution for which there is a better noncomputational alternative.

Summary

In this lesson, you learned the following:

- **Caring for the root password**—Pick a password that can't be easily guessed but is one that you can remember. Change it every few months—particularly after someone who had root access has left and whenever you have discovered that a machine has been compromised. Be sure to leave the root password in a safe, rarely accessed place for emergencies that might occur when you aren't available.

- **Becoming root**—Never log in as root. When you have to become root, use su, which leaves you an audit trail, or better yet, use sudo, which leaves even better logs.

- **Use \rm -rf with care**—Think twice before you force the system to recursively remove files. You wouldn't want to wipe out your system!

- **If you don't know what it is, don't run it**—Don't risk giving away your "rootly" powers to an unknown shell script or program. Try it out as a normal user first. If you still can't tell what it does, don't risk running it as root until you know more.

- **Never give normal users root access**—You are well-trained, but you know you can devastate the entire system with one typographical error. Just imagine what a normal user without your training could accidentally do.

- **Don't needlessly share with others**—Administrative staff or not, don't give out root access to those who do not really need it. Don't risk the potential damage.

- **Never dot root's path with .**—Again, it is in root's best interest to be paranoid. Do not include the current directory in root's path, so that root can't potentially be tricked into using the wrong command.

- **Backups**—Better safe than sorry. Back it up before you make that change.

- **Root never rests**—Even at odd hours of the morning while you are asleep, root is cleaning up your system for you in one of its cronjobs.

- **Gracefully shutting down**—Treat your machines with care. Do not just turn off the power; invoke the proper shutdown procedure for your machine and your users.

- **Why are you here?**—Your purpose is to facilitate your users' productivity. Don't forget that, no matter how annoying they can get.

- **What do they want?**—Your users frequently will have difficulty choosing solutions to their problems primarily because they haven't well enough defined the problems. You can make your job easier and more pleasant by helping your users to clearly define problems.

5

- **Doing it the right way**—Keep in mind that the computer is just a tool and is sometimes the wrong tool for whatever job your user might be trying to do. Recognize when the computer is part of the problem, rather than part of the solution, and when to point your users in the right direction.

Q&A

Q **Are you really serious that root can destroy the entire filesystem with a single typo?**

A Dead serious.

Q **Okay, how's that possible?**

A Consider the possible typos of the command \rm -rf ./*.

Q **Could you be more specific?**

A If you don't see the danger inherent in that statement, you're not nearly paranoid enough yet. First, consider what the command was intended to do, which is to recursively delete anything and everything that's in the current directory. This particular command is more or less innocuous, if somewhat violent, as commands go. It's not something you'd do every day, but it's not something that's outside the ordinary for root either. Now, what happens if you have a minor typing error, and an extra space creeps in there? Specifically, what is the result if \rm -rf . /* ends up being the command you issue?

Q **Okay, I understand why it's a bad idea to give inexperienced people the root password, but doesn't this create hard feelings if you tell users they can't have the root password to their own machines?**

A Yes, generally, it does. Do you prefer the occasional hard feeling or the occasional loss of user data?

Q **Just how do I get my boss to buy into this philosophy of appropriate paranoia? He's concerned about upsetting the engineers with their own machines.**

A Chances are, you don't. You can try to explain it to him in terms of the number of users that will be upset when one of the engineers with his own machine pulls a "whoopsie" and deletes all the rest of the engineers' data. Chances are this will not work. Luckily, you have another option in addition to educating him—namely replacing him with a boss that, if he doesn't understand the problem, at least understands when to listen to the experts he's hired. The downside, of course, is that you will need new business cards.

Workshop

Exercises

1. Pick any shell script that you've installed on your system, and try to figure out what it does without running it. Consider the security implications of the result of this analysis. Turn paranoia control two clicks clockwise.

2. Check through your filesystem for files that have been recently modified by root. Check through your last log and any other system logs you have and try to figure out a) what the changes were and b) who was actually responsible for the changes.

3. Based on the results of Exercise 2, seriously consider shutting off all root logins and doing everything via sudo.

5

DAY **6**

Deciding What Kind of Software to Install: Free Versus Commercial

After a long week of wading through the sometimes harrowing experience of bringing a machine to life for the first time, you're probably ready for a bit of a break before starting in on the task of enhancing your machine. Today, you'll take a bit of a breather and look at some of the decisions you'll need to make when deciding what software to install to suit your needs:

- What is UNIX free software?
- Why is it so much better than most personal-computer shareware?
- When is free software better than even commercial software?
- When is commercial software a must?

UNIX Freeware

You are probably already familiar with shareware on personal computer systems, and maybe you're even familiar with the occasional completely free program that's available. UNIX, on the other hand, has many completely free programs and very little in the way of "pay if you like it" shareware. I've chosen to call this freely available software for UNIX systems "freeware," for the sake of being able to differentiate it while writing about it. However, you won't find this to be a universal naming convention. To most UNIX users, regular software is generally free, and the exceptional few pieces that cost money are thought of as "commercial software."

Based on your experience with most freely available software for personal computers, you might initially expect that the lack of shareware or commercial software means that UNIX platforms are starved for quality programs. Nothing could be further from the truth.

To understand this, you need to recall the roots of UNIX and the strong network ties and connectivity that have been with UNIX from the very beginning. The "UNIX community" is a large, amorphous and undefined, yet strangely cohesive, collection of all the UNIX users around the world. The UNIX community has been rightly described as the world's largest functioning anarchy, and as an anarchy, it is an amazingly good demonstration of the basic decency of human beings. This community has been working together on projects where the lead programmers all worked for different, highly competitive rival companies. This community has been having a chat over tea about politics with participants located on every continent. It has read first-hand, up-to-the-minute reports from frightened-to-tears college students watching the Tiannemen Square tragedy from a dormitory, and it has shared in real-time the hope and trepidation of a writer watching the activity in the Red Square at the close of the Soviet Union. Email and other forms of electronic communication span countries and the globe almost instantly, making friends of people who have never met and family of those who's lives are only vicariously shared. This connectivity and level of communication among so many and for so long has bred a spirit of cooperation among UNIX users that is unparalleled in the personal computer world.

When one UNIX user writes a useful piece of software, traditionally she makes it available to other users in the community. If it is truly useful, other users modify it, update it, and over time the software grows and becomes more robust and more useful. All this happens for free and because of the genuine interest of the community in perpetuation of this tradition.

Large pieces of software are frequently adopted by entire groups of volunteer developers who spend their own free time and resources keeping the software up-to-date.

Unlike personal computer shareware, where one or a few individuals maintain a piece of software and make only an executable available, UNIX freeware is usually available in source form, and normally has a large group of developers to whom a user can turn for help. In addition, whereas the personal computer shareware author is motivated (or not, in the case of little generated income) to update the software and fix bugs based on income from the product, the developers of UNIX freeware do it mostly for enjoyment and because of enlightened self-interest.

This is not to claim that there's anything wrong with writing software for profit—far from it! Programmers are an extremely important commodity, and the work they do should be well rewarded. It is simply an observation that online communities of programmers have recognized that the utility software that they use every day to make their jobs easier is written and supported by other online communities of programmers. These programmers realize that the fruits of other people's labors are making their lives easier, and that the best way to perpetuate this situation is to return the favor.

With this sort of programming expertise backing the UNIX freeware programs, it is not uncommon for bugs that users discover to be fixed within days of the bug report. Features that users request are also frequently added in similar timeframes. No single programmer can hope to compete with the power of the online developer community.

Commercial (for money) software frequently fares similarly when compared to UNIX freeware solutions. If you look, for example, at the realm of software compilers, you will be hard pressed to find a better compiler than the Gnu C compiler, a completely free compiler that is provided and supported by the Free Software Foundation.

Note

Gnu's not UNIX   Gnu software goes beyond just being free. If you're interested in the philosophy, you can learn more at the Free Software Foundation's Web site www.fsf.org. Even if you're not interested in the philosophy, you need to know a little bit about the license agreements involved. Gnu software is software which has been written and placed under the Gnu Public License (GPL).

GPLed software goes far beyond being simply freely available. The Free Software Foundation believes very strongly that all monetary worth comes from the material and intellectual investment in making a product. As there is little to no investment involved in making a copy of a piece of software, in their estimation it has no monetary value and should not cost anything. This is not to say that they believe everything should be free, but that if a price is to be charged it should be for things like customer support or manuals, not copies of the software. To this end, they have written the GPL in such a way

continues

6

> that it requires that any products created using GPLed products automatically carry the GPL. Notice that this means that if a programmer wants to create a piece of commercial software, they can't use the GNU compilers to build it, as their use would force the programmer's product to be GPLed and therefore free.

Because of the GPL, if your site is going to be developing commercial applications, you'll probably want to look into other compilers, even if gcc is the one that your programmers love the best. Alternatively, you can take the path that the FSF recommends and make your support commercial, but your software free.

Commercial Software

Of course, not all commercial software is overshadowed by UNIX freeware. Although freeware tends to win in the utility department, there is a large body of specialty application software for which there is no freeware alternative.

Here, you're at the mercy of the vendor's accounting department because UNIX commercial software, which has a much smaller audience than personal computer software, generally carries a much larger price tag. Although you might have found yourself thinking, "What, are the FSF people loonies? People should be allowed to charge whatever the market will bear!" a few minutes ago, the first time a vendor quotes you $30,000 for a single piece of software, you're almost certainly going to think, "Yowza! $30K? Are they nuts? It doesn't cost that much to make me a copy!" Then, you'll think, "I've got $2K to spend. I think they should be willing to take that, at least that way they make *some* money from me."

UNIX commercial software, like personal computer software, varies widely in quality. Unfortunately, the selection of products available to solve a particular problem is much more limited than personal computer products. Don't take the appearance of a package or the extent to which it has been "polished," into too great a consideration when making purchasing decisions. Frequently, it seems that products with horrid user interfaces were written by a bunch of engineers or scientists who knew the right way to solve a problem but did not know how to write user-friendly software. Equally as frequent are packages that appear to have been written by a group of human-computer interface wizards with no clue whatsoever how to properly approach the problem they've chosen to solve. You'll find that you often have to weigh the value of your users' ease of use against the importance of them getting proper results. Depending on your users, this decision could go either way.

Free Versus Commercial: A Comparison

To round out the comments on freeware versus commercial software, here are some observations and comments on certain commercial and free products.

License Key Woes

Many commercial software packages have "licenses"—controlling pieces of data that allow the software to only execute some limited number of simultaneous copies of itself. Additionally, most software licenses are tied to a physical hardware ID or serial number from your machine and so disallow execution on other nonlicensed hardware.

Licenses are a perfectly reasonable thing and a fine way to prevent software piracy and other illegal activities. Unfortunately, it is not uncommon for every software publisher to have a different idea of how they want their license software to work, and to have written custom solutions for enforcing licenses with their software. This leads, at the best, to you having to maintain multiple poorly documented license programs and keep them from interfering with each other.

At the facility that I manage, one software product that we license, and this is a product with a $30,000 up-front charge and a $10,000 yearly maintenance fee, retail (or $10,000 up-front and $3,000 yearly if you've got a good negotiator), has a 44 page manual for installing and maintaining the software and a 58 page manual on installing the licenses.

The Land of Milk and Compilers

Gnu's C compiler, gcc, is without a doubt the most widely available, most supported, and most popular C compiler in the UNIX world. In some instances, it's even the only compiler available because some OS vendors have taken to not including compilers with the operating system anymore. If you are trying to install a software package that involves compiling the software and you're having problems, check to make sure you're using gcc. A large percentage of software you'll encounter includes notes indicating problems compiling with various OS vendor's versions of C.

If you need to support the development of commercial software, you'll need to look into what commercial compilers are available for your system. Most BSD UNIX flavors seem to have compilers bundled with the OS, whereas most System V flavors seem to require that you pay extra.

Investigate whether your OS vendor's compilers are well thought of by other program-mers before buying. If developing a commercial product is a major mission, you might want to look into different manufacturer's hardware just to get access to a good compiler suite.

6

An opinion that is growing less popular as time passes (but only, according to long-time programmers I know, because of the brainwashing of the masses and the lack of education of new blood) is that SunOS 4.1.X is the ideal platform for program development. In the opinion of those who adhere to this belief, SunOS offers everything programmers could want and none of the overhead they don't need. A decent compiler comes with the system, Gnu compilers build easily and cleanly, and man pages are conveniently completed. Many programmers who have worked in this environment refuse to leave—keeping older Sun hardware available for development and only moving code to the target machine when it's ready to go into production.

The Server's Server

The Web server Apache is another great example of free UNIX software. Apache compiles and configures easily and runs on almost every flavor of UNIX in existence. It is also easy to customize and to extend if you need additional power. What it does not provide automatically that are available from some commercial packages are things like administer-through-the-Web forms and proprietary data-encoding protocols. Unless you need to serve some form of Microsoft proprietary Web-data format, and you need it to only be accessible to users running the latest version of Internet Explorer, you probably don't need to look further than Apache. It's free. The support community fixes problems within days. What more could you ask for?

When You Can't Afford to Get it for Free

Sometimes, commercial software is a better choice than free software for reasons entirely outside the amount of support it receives or the rapidity of bug fixes. If your company has a mission-critical task and you're assigned the responsibility of deciding on a software package that will carry out that task, you need to evaluate your options carefully.

If there are competing commercial and free alternatives, which do you pick? At some point, the quality of the respective offerings must come into the picture, but there are other considerations as well.

If you opt for the free alternative, how good is the support? If the online community is actively supporting the package and updates are prompt, are you sure they'll stay that way in the future? With free software, you usually don't get any sort of guarantee of anything.

If you opt for the commercial alternative, what sort of guarantee do you get about the functionality of the software? Many software packages have amazingly anticustomer licenses and guarantees that would be the laughingstock of any nonsoftware business. Many of them state, in much more elegant legal terms, that the user should be happy if the software does anything at all and that the authors have a sneaking suspicion that there's nothing but random data on the disks. If you're about to spend your company's money, is this the best place to spend it?

This is a good place to think about applying that "look for the worst case" philosophy. First, you have to define what the worst case scenario is—worst case for you, worst case for your company, or what? Note that worst case for you and worst case for your company are likely to frequently be different things—especially here. In making software purchasing decisions, one can frequently apply the adage that "Nobody has ever been fired for buying IBM." If you go with a commercial package and there is a failure due to the software you purchased, you're not likely to be fired if you bought the best commercial package available. If you went with a freeware solution, you're likely to be toast. Both of these statements are true regardless of whether the commercial package was better than the freeware package. The "better" solution for your company, in terms of features and capability, might well be the freeware solution, but the better solution for you, in terms of job security, might be the commercial package.

Note that a similar analysis applies at the corporate level as well. If your company is responsible for providing a service to some other company and ends up failing this task because of a software fault, your CEO is going to be a lot happier if there's a company you paid for that software to whom the blame can be passed.

It will have to be your decision how you want to deal with these situations, which will inevitably arise. The world of system administration is unfortunately also one of politics, and sometimes there just isn't a good "right" answer.

Should I Pay or Shouldn't I?

In a turn of events you might find truly bizarre, there are even UNIX packages that are free if you want them for free or tens of thousands of dollars if you want to pay for them. A good example of this is the BIND package, the Berkeley Internet Name Daemon. BIND is the software that provides the majority of the Internet name service for the world. Recognizing exactly the issues discussed in the "When you can't afford to get it for free" section, the organization that produces BIND makes it available for free or for $80,000. If you need the best and you want support, you can pay for it and satisfy management that you've made the best possible decision (and have supported a very worthy cause at the same time). If you want a good nameserver but don't think it's worth $80,000 to your company, you can have it for free and support it yourself. If you're MCI and you're handling a large fraction of the nation's Internet-switching load, you might be inclined to think $80,000 is pretty cheap to ensure that your name service is running all day, every day. If you're installing a little UNIX cluster in your building and just want a backup name server in case your primary is down, free might be just the price you're looking for.

6

Summary

While reading this chapter, you learned a bit of the philosophy behind UNIX software distribution and the options you might have. Hopefully, a knowledge of the strengths and weaknesses of each model of software distribution will help you in making decisions for your cluster. Always keep in mind that it's the needs of your users that should drive the software you choose. Buying the latest, greatest, whiz-bang 3-Dimensional rendering tool won't help your users at all if they're using the machines for database servers. As completely unamusing as some of their software needs are going to seem, it's what they need that you need to be researching and buying. For software you're personally interested in, free is almost *always* better.

Q&A

Q I've written a nifty program and compiled it with gcc. Can I sell it?

A Probably not. Read the GPL to be absolutely sure, but if your software includes any GNU-supplied code (such as header files or library functions), you might have obliged yourself to give it away for free if someone asks. Of course, you can still charge for documentation and user support if you want to.

Q ˙How much money should I budget for software?

A Lots, if you have to actually buy software to serve your mission. Figure that UNIX software costs about ten times what comparable personal computer software costs. Remember that there is probably some potential for negotiation in any price you are quoted.

Q I think I'm going to like the UNIX community model of software development. What can I do to contribute?

A Get out there on the Usenet Newsgroups and look around. There is a multitude of newsgroups dedicated to supporting this or that software package, and there are probably even more mailing lists. Find a package you'd like to support and get on the developer list. Fix a few bugs, develop a warm fuzzy feeling, and sit yourself down beside this here virtual campfire and have a cup o' cocoa. Glad to have you along!

Workshop

Quiz

1. How is UNIX "freeware" different from freeware in the personal computer world?

2. Say that you wrote a useful utility script to scan backup tape inventories to determine what filesystem they belong to. What should you do with it after you get it working?

Exercises

1. Read the GPL. What are the requirements it places on you if you use gcc to compile a product?

2. Itemize the computational needs of your users. Actually go and talk to them to find out what it is they want to do; don't just assume that what's on the system is what they want or that what you've been told by other administrators is correct.

3. Ask your users what software they want. Make a list.

4. Investigate what this software does and compare this list with the list of things they want to do. Does the software actually match the list of capabilities? Frequently, users don't know what software they really need to solve a problem. They know about one package, and that's it. You can make yourself a popular person very quickly by actually talking to the users and helping them with these decisions.

5. Investigate the commercial and freeware solutions available that meet your users' needs. Write up a comparison of the various solutions so that your users can make better recommendations for software. (This comparison could also help you negotiate prices when it comes time to purchase commercial packages.)

6. Write up a list of installed software and capabilities. If you've access to a graphic-artist type, have her make it into a nice little brochure for you. Stuff it in your users' mail and hand it out to prospective new users. (You'll be surprised how many of your users come to you within a few days and say, "Hey, I never knew you had *** on the system. I've always wanted to...").

6

DAY 7

The Most Important Accessory: The C Compiler gcc

I think you've had some time to recover from your operating system and patch installations. Now get back to work! Today you install some of the most important tools you will need for a lot of your work in the next two weeks, and well afterwards.

If you run an operating system that provides extra goodies, you might not need to actually install any of these packages. However, it is still a good idea to look over the information to see what you might have to do, should you ever need to. Even if your operating system distribution does make some of these packages available, you might want to get in some compilation practice by trying to compile some of the packages—you won't need to install them anywhere.

This chapter is going to be a little odd, in that for every different version of UNIX, there are different paths through some of the installation processes. There are also places that you might have to go to find source, or binary, distributions for the software. As the particulars of the installs and who makes them available on the Internet change on an almost daily basis, you should consider what is today to be representative of the process, but not necessarily of the particulars. I attempt to provide pointers to the best online resources for you to access when you are ready to attempt these installs yourself.

I should also point out that much of this is "Cross your fingers and have faith" territory. You shouldn't have too much trouble with the software that I cover today, but today you are firmly in the camp of the programmers. Some install steps ask you to do things or produce results that would be difficult for even most programmers to understand. As a system administrator, this is where you follow directions and hope that the programmer who wrote the documentation did a good job. If something doesn't work as the directions indicate that it should, you're almost certainly going to need a programmer to fix it for you.

At the end of the install, to show you what happens and how easy recovery can be, I take the opportunity to strategically run out of disk space. Tomorrow's lesson is about adding devices, including an additional disk drive, so you have the chance to see how to simply deal with an installation that broke due to too little disk space—something that you might think nearly impossible if you come from the world of personal computers.

Here's an overview of what you'll do today, so that you don't get lost in the details in the middle:

- Finding or installing at least a rudimentary compiler. To proceed with today's tasks you need the ability to compile software, and for that you need a compiler. You will start off with some simple software that can be compiled without a particularly sophisticated compiler, so if your system provides one out of the box, that will do. Otherwise you need to find a binary installation online (help with this will be provided) or find a nearby machine that can do your initial compiling for you.

- Installing some simple utility software that is required to make use of most freely available software packages.

- Installing a much more sophisticated compiler—one that is the darling of most UNIX programmers. You will use your system's provided compiler, or one that you have downloaded, to build one that is specific to your machine and OS.

- Seeing what to do when you encounter that bane of all system administrators, too little disk space.

- Finally, walking through a very simple software debugging job—for the truly adventurous system administrator!

If you are running IRIX 6.2 or later, go to `http://freeware.sgi.com`, SGI's official freeware site, to get the latest precompiled, inst-packaged (IRIX's automated "put everything where it belongs" utility) versions of gcc and gdb. If you are running Solaris 2.5 or later, go to http://smc.vnet.net, home of the Solaris Freeware Project, to get precompiled, pkgadd (Solaris's automated "put everything where it belongs" utility) format versions. If the latest version of gcc does not happen to be available, get the most recent version that there is. Installation differs from platform to platform, but it should be detailed relatively well in the README file you will find accompanying the compiler distribution.

No matter what version of UNIX you're running, you can ftp source distribution packages of everything today from ftp.cis.ohio-state.edu, which is one of many mirrors of the GNU software collection.

Tools More Basic Than gcc

Although you will focus on gcc later today, you will also need to install some basic utilities: gzip, patch, and gnu make. To install these you need a compiler and the associated development libraries and include files. If your system does not provide these, you need to find a system that has them or install a precompiled executable compiler that you have downloaded from the Internet.

Note

> **Lifting oneself by one's bootstraps**   If your system doesn't come with at least rudimentary compilers and development tools, you need to find a compiler somewhere before you can complete any of these tasks. The gcc compiler is frequently available in binary form for UNIX versions that don't include development tools, so you can probably fill this need by browsing the Web for a bit. Start with the Free Software Foundation's Web site at http://www.fsf.org, which should point you in the right direction for most popular UNIX versions, or the Web sites listed earlier for Solaris and IRIX platforms. If you're running an oddball UNIX variant on hardware that only a few people own, you might have to hit the newsgroups or do a bit more general Web searching to find a version for your configuration.
>
> Of course, you always have the option of breaking down and buying the commercial compilers for your system as well.
>
> You need to purchase, or find, and install this compiler before proceeding with the rest of this chapter.

7

Installing gzip

When you have determined that your system provides compilers or have found a working version via the Free Software Foundation site, you can proceed to build some software.

As you download software packages, you will probably notice that a lot of them are compressed with gzip, the compression tool that appends .gz to filenames. It's rather difficult to do anything with these files without being able to use gunzip. The GNU software mirror site at ftp.cis.ohio-state.edu, from which I downloaded gzip, had two versions of it—a .gz version and a .shar version—but not a plain .tar. Needless to say, there was little point to considering the .gz version, so I got the .shar version, which is a shell archive. Unpacking a shell archive is much like extracting tar files. Here is a look at some of it:

```
Barracuda# sh gzip-1.2.4a.shar
WARNING: not restoring timestamps.  Consider getting and
installing GNU 'touch', distributed in GNU File Utilities...

x - creating lock directory
x - creating directory gzip-1.2.4a
x - extracting gzip-1.2.4a/README (text)
x - extracting gzip-1.2.4a/NEWS (text)
x - extracting gzip-1.2.4a/INSTALL (text)
x - extracting gzip-1.2.4a/Makefile.in (text)
x - extracting gzip-1.2.4a/configure.in (text)
x - extracting gzip-1.2.4a/configure (text)
x - extracting gzip-1.2.4a/COPYING (text)
x - extracting gzip-1.2.4a/TODO (text)
x - extracting gzip-1.2.4a/THANKS (text)
x - extracting gzip-1.2.4a/ChangeLog (text)
x - extracting gzip-1.2.4a/gzip.c (text)
x - extracting gzip-1.2.4a/zip.c (text)
x - extracting gzip-1.2.4a/deflate.c (text)
```

Before you actually do your compile of gzip, be sure to check the README for any notes on your system. The default installation locations for this package are /usr/local/bin, /usr/local/lib, and so on. You can change these default locations if your site places locally installed software in other directories.

The installation, done in the source directory, is straightforward:

```
Barracuda# ./configure
Barracuda# make
Barracuda# make check
./gzip -6 < ./texinfo.tex > _gztest.gz
rm -f _gztest
./gzip -d _gztest.gz
gzip test OK
rm -f _gztest*

Barracuda# make ZCAT=gzcat install
```

Each of the `configure`, `make`, and `make check` commands can produce copious output. Other than the output of the `make check`, which is the expected output for a clean bill of health, I haven't reproduced any of it here. The `ZCAT=gzcat` is included so that the software will not potentially overwrite an existing `zcat`, but will instead call itself `gzcat`.

After you have installed the `gzip` package, you will want to read the README file and add the lines that it recommends to your `/etc/magic` file. You will do this so that the `file` command can recognize files made by `gzip`.

Installing `patch`

Armed with your system's `tar` tools and your newly installed `gzip` package, you are ready to face the world of software acquisition! The first conquest will be `patch`. Again, `patch` is a GNU product, so it should be easy to find, and, with any luck, easy to install.

When you have gotten `patch`, look at the README to see whether there are any special settings you need to enable for your system. As with the `gzip` package, patch installs its tools in various `/usr/local` directories. If this is not where your site stores locally installed files, be sure to specify the right location. Because the default locations are where I want the files, and because my machine does not require any special options, the simplest steps should work to compile `patch` on my machine.

Here's the procedure from the source directory on my machine, without any of the transcripts:

```
Barracuda# ./configure
Barracuda# make
Barracuda# make install
```

This compilation was a success!

Installing GNU `make`

You will sometimes see that applications require, or highly recommend, that you create them with GNU `make` rather than the standard system `make`. So GNU `make` is the next utility you will install.

I think you are probably getting used to the standard procedure for making GNU products. First, check the README for any system-specific information you might need to know. My machine again does not require any special options to be set. Default installation directories are once again in `/usr/local`.

Here's how it looks in the source directory on my machine. As with `gzip`, I have chosen to do the optional `make check` test for this one. Note that you use make from the current

7

directory (that is, the GNU version of make that you just built) rather than the system make. I thought it would be interesting to see those results:

```
Barracuda# ./configure
Barracuda# make
Barracuda# ./make check
/usr/local/source/make-3.77/./make check-recursive check-local
make[1]: Entering directory '/usr/local/source/make-3.77'
Making check in glob
make[2]: Entering directory '/usr/local/source/make-3.77/glob'
/usr/local/source/make-3.77/./make
make[3]: Entering directory '/usr/local/source/make-3.77/glob'
make[3]: Nothing to be done for 'all'.
make[3]: Leaving directory '/usr/local/source/make-3.77/glob'
make[2]: Leaving directory '/usr/local/source/make-3.77/glob'
ln ./getloadavg.c loadavg.c ¦¦ \
  cp ./getloadavg.c loadavg.c
cc -g  -o loadavg -I. -I. -DHAVE_CONFIG_H -DTEST  loadavg.c
➥-L/usr/local/lib -lkvm
The system uptime program believes the load average to be:
uptime
  1:05am  up 1 day,  3:38,  1 user,  load average: 0.26, 0.34, 0.11
The GNU load average checking code believes:
./loadavg
1-minute: 0.257812  5-minute: 0.339844  15-minute: 0.113281
/usr/local/source/make-3.77/./make all-recursive
make[2]: Entering directory '/usr/local/source/make-3.77'
Making all in glob
make[3]: Entering directory '/usr/local/source/make-3.77/glob'
make[3]: Nothing to be done for 'all'.
make[3]: Leaving directory '/usr/local/source/make-3.77/glob'
make[2]: Leaving directory '/usr/local/source/make-3.77'
Couldn't find make-test-* regression test suite.
make[1]: Leaving directory '/usr/local/source/make-3.77'

Barracuda# make install
```

Unfortunately, these check results are not as clear-cut as the gzip check results—the gzip make check clearly said "Okay," whereas "Nothing to be done for," and "Couldn't find" sound less positive. However, it hasn't told me specifically that something broke, and because everything has been going well up to this point, I have decided to do the make install.

Now the major disk and time-consuming work is about to begin. This is a good time to run make clean in all the source directories to get rid of as much junk as you can, particularly if you have as little drive space available as I do.

Why gcc?

Finally you get to the heart of today's activities! What makes gcc so important? You must be doing this as a favor for your resident programmer, right? Although it is certainly good practice to do what you can to make your resident programmer happy, you're actually doing this for yourself. That is not to say that your resident programmer isn't going to appreciate having gcc. Quite the contrary, she will. However, in the goal to make your machine useful, you will find that gcc is an important tool.

It is not unusual for the software out there to compile better with gcc than with the native compiler. Why is that? I don't really know. Perhaps as a freely available package, it's the most accessible one for the community at large to use for developing applications. No matter what the reason, I have run into packages that simply cannot be compiled with anything else. I have also found some that won't allow you to compile them with anything other than gcc if you have it installed, even if you specify your native C compiler at compile time. The gcc compiler seems to be the darling of the UNIX free software author, and given its ubiquitous distribution, it is rightly so. At this stage you might also find gcc to be useful in that you might not have the licenses in place to use your vendor's native compilers. Of course, if you don't have any compilers and you need to compile gcc, you're in a bit of a catch-22. Thankfully, the good folks at the Free Software Foundation and other programmers in similar straits as yourself generally have taken care of this problem for you. If your machine doesn't include a working C compiler (if the response to typing cc is "command not found" or some complaint about not having license keys, it means you don't have a compiler), it's very likely that some kind person has made a precompiled binary available. As noted earlier, start browsing from the Free Software Foundation's site (http://www.fsf.org) or your OS vendor's Web site looking for "freeware" links and you're likely to find a precompiled copy of gcc relatively quickly.

Note

> Even if you have no compilers on the machine that you are currently working on, you can build a cross-compiler version of gcc on another machine to use to build gcc for your machine, the target machine. Yes, that is to say that if you do have a compiler on another machine, you can make a version of gcc on that machine and use that just-built gcc to build a copy of gcc for your compiler-less machine. You will not actually walk though that scenario, but it could be useful information for future reference or perhaps your actual situation. The instructions are included in the documentation that comes with the gcc source code if you need them.

7

Installing gcc

There appear to be several ways to install gcc: Compile it separately or compile it as part of a big batch of GNU tools. The first way to install gcc involves compiling it with your native cc (or gcc that you've downloaded precompiled), recompiling it with the gcc you just built, and double-checking the version you compiled with gcc by recompiling it with itself again. This method actually worked on my machine, but there are many options you will have to think about. I have also seen this method fail miserably on IRIX…and this was even when there was a programmer at the keyboard.

When you compile gcc, you might decide that you want C++ to be included in the languages that are finally built. Part of what is needed with the C++ package is libstdc++, which does not get compiled as part of the gcc package. You have to download libstdc++ separately. In the README that comes with gcc 2.8.1 proper (the version I will be installing here—it has undoubtedly changed by the time you are reading this), you will see instructions that say you should compile gcc first and use the gcc you just compiled to compile libstdc++.

The README that comes with libstdc++, however, says that starting with libstdc++ 2.8.1, it is recommended that you not compile gcc separately first, but rather, build it as part of the libstdc++ compile.

Which method is correct? Which one is better? Both are good questions. Installing gcc separately takes more of your attention, whereas using the libstdc++ method is more automatic—when you compile using the second method you compile gcc as well as libstdc++. Furthermore, the general README that comes with the libstdc++ suggests you could probably compile a number of additional GNU development tools at once when you compile libstdc++. On the other hand, the all-at-once method doesn't give you any opportunity to reorganize while it's building, so if space is a consideration you might want to consider the first, more labor-intensive, approach.

Here I will walk through the install-each-separately method, so that you can see more of what is actually going on behind the scenes.

Method 1: Installing gcc as a Separate Package

I begin the discussion on installing gcc with the option to install it as a separate package. Whether you choose to install gcc using this method or as part of a larger package, it is probably a good idea to read the README several times to be sure you catch any special options you might need to include. It is indeed a bit intimidating at over 30 pages long, but read it anyway. Some of the README file contains operating-system specific notes, so be sure to read what's important to your system. If you plan to install gcc separately, make sure you understand approximately what you'll be doing.

Because the README is over 30 pages long, I will summarize the important steps here. I hope that this summary might make the actual README seem a bit less intimidating. Remember, the README contains a lot of system-specific information. I recommend that you print it out, and go over it with a highlighter marking all the steps that you need to take. Attempting to actually follow instructions interspersed in 30 pages of text is difficult and can easily lead to overlooking a step in the middle.

Brief Summary of the Installation Procedure

This summary assumes that you are building gcc for the first time on your machine in the directory with the source files.

1. If you are building gcc on a System V variant, make sure that /usr/bin precedes /usr/ucb because the cc in /usr/ucb uses libraries with bugs. You can check your order by issuing echo $path, and you can rearrange the order by using set path=(*list of directories in the preferred order*).

2. Install the bison parser generator (available from any GNU software mirror) if you need to. What the README doesn't tell you is that you will not need to install it if the files c-parse.c and cexp.c in your gcc source distribution directory are more recent than the c-parse.y and cexp.y files in the same directory, and you do not plan to change the .y files. Thankfully, I have a programmer who knows something about bison and who can tell me these things. Because the .y files are used to make the .c files, if the .c files are newer than the .y files, the .c files must have been generated from those .y files. Otherwise the parser definition .y files have been updated since the last time the parser code (.c files) was generated, and you will need to run bison to regenerate the parser code.

3. Determine what configuration options you need:

   - Determine what your -build option should be. A canonical configuration build name is of the form CPU-COMPANY-SYSTEM. You might be able to substitute nicknames in various parts of that canonical formula. Check the README for the summary of supported configuration types. In my case, I will use —build=sparc-sun-sunos4.1.4.

   - Determine whether you have to specify -with-gnu-as. This option does not build the GNU assembler gas, but does modify gcc's output to work with gas. You will have to build and install gas yourself. Some systems that require this include some HP-PA, i386, m68k, and mips systems. Check the README to see whether this option is required for your system. Many of the systems that require the GNU assembler will also require the GNU linker.

7

- Determine whether you have to specify `-with-gnu-ld`, the option which will modify gcc to work with GNU linker. Again, check the README to determine whether this options applies to your system. Additionally, this option does not install the GNU linker; you will have to do that yourself.

- Determine whether you have to specify the `-with-stabs` option, which specifies the debugging format. This option appears to be especially important for mips machines. Apparently the default can't fully handle languages other than C, whereas the BSD-style stabs can handle other languages, but only works with the GNU debugger, gdb. Sound confusing? Definitely check the README here.

- Determine whether you have to specify whether your machine has a floating point unit by specifying `-nfp`. This must be done for at least m68k-sun-sunosN and m68k-isi-bsd systems, but be sure to check the README to see whether any other systems might also have this requirement.

- Determine whether you should specify the `-enable-threads=TYPE` option. Apparently some systems, particularly Linux-based GNU systems, default to single-threaded runtime for Objective C, but threads can be enabled with this option. TYPE can be single, posix, win32, solaris, irix, or mach.

- If you want to install gcc in a location other than its default location, `/usr/local`, specify `-prefix=DIR`, where DIR is what to use in place of "`/usr/local`".

- No matter where you install the compiler, `/usr/local/include` is searched for header files. If you want the compiler to search some other directory, `DIR/include`, for locally installed header files, specify `-local-prefix=DIR`, where DIR again is what to use instead of `/usr/local`. Do not specify `/usr` as DIR because the local prefix must not contain any of the system's header files.

4. If your configuration for gcc requires any of the other GNU tools, such as gas, instead of the standard system tools, install those tools in the build directory under subdirectories as defined by their README files. This allows the compiler to find all the tools it needs. Alternatively you could do a compilation of the compiler such that the necessary GNU tools come before the system tools in the PATH environment variable.

5. Issue the appropriate configure command for your system.

6. Build the compiler by typing **make LANGUAGES=c** in the compiler directory. You could specify other languages in your list, but C is the only language certain to work with non-GNU C compilers. Check the README for the list of warnings that it is safe to ignore.

7. Now you have made the first stage, a version of the compiler built with the native compiler. Move the first stage files to the stage1 subdirectory by typing **make stage1**.

8. If your configuration requires other GNU tools, install the required tools in the stage1 subdirectory. Or use the alternative method that requires setting your PATH variable.

At this point, you have built what is hopefully a functional version of the gcc C compiler. This version, however, has been built with your system's compiler and so includes bits of system libraries that didn't come from GNU. To be certain that your compiler is "clean", you will build another version of gcc using your freshly built gcc—it will be built by, and include only, GNU parts. Finally, you will build a third version using your second version, and the second and third will be compared to make certain that the "clean" second version produces exactly the same output as the version produced by your system's compiler. The installation procedure then continues as follows:

9. Build the stage2 compiler. Recompile the compiler with itself by executing make CC="stage1/xgcc -Bstage1/" CFLAGS="-g -O2".

10. This version of the command builds compilers for all the supported languages, but you can specify certain ones by including LANGUAGES="LIST", where LIST can be one or more of the following separated by spaces: C, C++, objective-c, proto. (Proto refers to the programs protoize and unprotoize, which you shouldn't need to be concerned about unless a programmer has asked for them.) If you plan to build the stage2 compiler, you might want to build only C again. If you are short on space after compiling stage2, do rm -r stage1 to remove the now-unnecessary stage1 hybrid compiler.

11. If you want to test the compiler with itself one more time, first install any other tools you might need, such as the assembler, in the stage2 subdirectory. Then type **make stage2**.

12. Assuming that the third stage build is likely your last build, you might build for all the languages, or at least you might have objective C as one of your language choices. Configure picks the appropriate objective C thread implementation for you. However, you might want a different back-end, or you might want to disable thread support. For whatever reason, you might want to specify a value for OBJC_THREAD_FILE. Check the README for possible values, but some of the options include Sun Solaris and SGI IRIX. Your make statement might look like:
```
make CC="stage2/xgcc -Bstage2/" CFLAGS="-g -O2"
➥OBJC_THREAD_FILE=thr-single
```

7

If you do not want to specify a thread value for objective C, your `make` statement might look like this, where the lack of a `LANGUAGES` value provides support for all the possible languages:

```
make CC="stage2/xgcc -Bstage2/" CFLAGS="-g -O2"
```

13. If you do not require any additional GNU tools, you can bypass steps 7–11 by issuing this command instead:

    make bootstrap LANGUAGES=LANGUAGES-LIST BOOT_CFLAGS=OPTION-LIST

14. Compare the stage3 object files with the stage2 object files with `make compare`. Here you find out whether your stage2 compiler is capable of making a duplicate of itself. Many lines of comparisons are likely to scroll by, but you only need to be worried if it says "files differ". If it doesn't, you're all set. If it does, you're finished for the day because it's time to find an expert.

15. Install everything. Use the same values for `CC`, `CFLAGS`, and `LANGUAGES` that you used when compiling because some versions of `make` can recompile for you at this step, and using the same variable values results in a correct recompile. If you used your stage2 compile as the install version, your command might look like:

    make install CC="stage2/xgcc -Bstage2/" CFLAGS="-g -O2"

Doing an Actual Installation

So that you know what the responses at the various stages as you do your own install should look like, I will now walk through an actual installation of gcc.

First I check to see whether I should install bison. A quick check in my source directory reveals the following:

```
Barracuda# ls -l c*parse* cexp*
-rw-r--r--  1 9225      147772 Mar  2  1998 c-parse.c
-r--r--r--  1 31184       2231 Apr  9  1993 c-parse.gperf
-rw-r--r--  1 9225        1318 Mar  2  1998 c-parse.h
-r--r--r--  1 5200       85046 Feb 14  1998 c-parse.in
-rw-r--r--  1 9225       66577 Mar  1  1998 c-parse.y
-rw-r--r--  1 9225       58770 Mar  2  1998 cexp.c
-r--r--r--  1 9225       30014 Feb 18  1998 cexp.y
```

It turns out that `c-parse.c` and `cexp.c` are more recent than my `c-parse.y` and `cexp.y`. Note that `c-parse.c` is only one day newer than `c-parse.y`, but it is newer nonetheless. Because the README indicates that I only need bison if I need to reparse the `.y` files, I see that I don't need bison. Generally, you shouldn't either, unless you've decided to make changes to the parser or are working on a very atypical installation.

Now I run `configure` and the build with the existing c compiler:

```
Barracuda# ./configure —build=sparc-sun-sunos4.1.4
Barracuda# make LANGUAGES=c
```

Then I move everything from the first build to the stage1 directory and then build gcc with itself:

```
Barracuda# make stage1
'stage1' is up to date.

Barracuda# make CC="stage1/xgcc -Bstage1/" CFLAGS="-g -O2"
```

Because stage1 won't be needed anymore, I can remove the first build and recover some disk space at this point. I move the stage2 files to the stage2 directory and test gcc by compiling it with the stage2 version of itself. If you paid close attention to the README, you'll note that because I was planning to do a third build anyway, I could probably have saved some time by specifying LANGUAGES=c earlier.

```
Barracuda# rm -r stage1
Barracuda# make stage2
'stage2' is up to date.

Barracuda# make CC="stage2/xgcc -Bstage2/" CFLAGS="-g -O2"
```

Now I have to compare the stage2 compiler with the stage3 compiler. There should not be any differences present:

```
Barracuda# make compare
for file in *.o; do \
  tail +16c ./$file > tmp-foo1; \
  tail +16c stage2/$file > tmp-foo2 2>/dev/null \
    && (cmp tmp-foo1 tmp-foo2 ¦¦ echo $file differs) ¦¦ true; \
done
for dir in tmp-foo cp objc; do \
  if [ "'echo $dir/*.o'" != "$dir/*.o" ] ; then \
    for file in $dir/*.o; do \
      tail +16c ./$file > tmp-foo1; \
      tail +16c stage2/$file > tmp-foo2 2>/dev/null \
        && (cmp tmp-foo1 tmp-foo2 ¦¦ echo $file differs) ¦¦ true; \
    done; \
  fi; \
done
rm -f tmp-foo*
```

These compare results show nothing wrong, but if there had been something wrong, I would have gotten results that look more like this:

```
Barracuda# make compare
for file in *.o; do \
  tail +16c ./$file > tmp-foo1; \
```

7

```
   tail +16c stage2/$file > tmp-foo2 2>/dev/null \
     && (cmp tmp-foo1 tmp-foo2 || echo $file differs) || true; \
done
tmp-foo1 tmp-foo2 differ: char 1, line 1
genpeep.o differs
for dir in tmp-foo cp objc; do \
  if [ "`echo $dir/*.o`" != "$dir/*.o" ] ; then \
    for file in $dir/*.o; do \
      tail +16c ./$file > tmp-foo1; \
      tail +16c stage2/$file > tmp-foo2 2>/dev/null \
        && (cmp tmp-foo1 tmp-foo2 || echo $file differs) || true; \
    done; \
  fi; \
done
rm -f tmp-foo*
```

If the compare doesn't work, you will get some feedback on what file(s) are different. Note that in the code example, the system reports "genpeep.o differs". Any difference, however small, indicates that something is wrong. Investigate the problem. Start to recompile gcc again from a fresh untar of the distribution. If the compare fails again, you might have encountered a bug. If you do have a bug, you've discovered one disadvantage of playing outside the system administrator's home ballpark. Unless you're also a gifted programmer, at this point you're stuck. Find your resident programmer and see whether she can fix it, or hop on the Internet and find out whether anyone else has reported the same problem. Unfortunately, there's very little that you as a system administrator can do about fixing software bugs. You obviously already have at least rudimentary compilers on your system; you will have to make do with them or turn to a commercial solution unless you can find someone to fix your problem for you.

Because my results indicate no problems, I decide to do the install step:

```
Barracuda# make install CC="stage2/xgcc -Bstage2/" CFLAGS="-g -O2"
```

A significant amount of diagnostic output is generated at this point because the installation copies bits of itself to their permanent homes on your system. Unless the installation step reports a "Fatal Error," you should be able to ignore almost all of what it has to tell you. When it finishes, you can clean up disk space by deleting the various stage directories, and by issuing the command **make clean**.

Installing libstdc++

Now you enter that fuzzy zone I mentioned earlier. If you chose to include C++ as one of the languages, you will have to install libstdc++. If you believe the README that comes with gcc, "one method" for installing libstdc++ is to compile gcc and use the gcc you just installed to make libstdc++. If you choose to try this method, do the following:

1. Build and install gcc.

2. Download the corresponding libstdc++ distribution.

3. In the top directory of the libstdc++ distribution directory, execute the following, where the CONFIGURE-OPTIONS are the same as you used to build gcc:

```
CXX=gcc .configure CONFIGURE-OPTIONS
make
make install
```

Instead of walking through this process, take a look at the multipackage installation process that libstdc++ recommends. Although the process that you're about to see looks much easier than that which you just went through, there might be times when you're required to follow the long process listed earlier. An attempt at installing gcc as part of a package on IRIX failed miserably. My programmer determined that he had no option but the step-by-step process that you have already looked at.

Method 2: Installing gcc as Part of a Package

The README that comes with the libstdc++ distribution suggests that rather than building and installing gcc, and then using that gcc to build libstdc++, it is better to move your gcc source directory into the libstdc++ source directory and build everything you need at once. Before starting on this path, you might want to examine the README files for each package that you need and determine what the space requirements for your configuration are for them. Most software takes up a lot of temporary space while it's compiling, and many /usr/local partitions don't have the room to install packages that can suck up over 200MB of temporary disk space. Furthermore, the general README that comes with the libstdc++ distribution and the gdb distribution suggests that you should be able to build multiple GNU development tools all at once. If you have a bit of space, you might want to try building gdb and gcc simultaneously with libstdc++. I do not have the luxury of such space, so I will try building gcc as part of the libstdc++ package, and then build gdb in another step.

Brief Summary of the Method 2 Installation Procedure

As always, read the README before performing any software installation. This is intended to give you an idea of what is in the README but does not serve as a substitution for the README itself.

1. Move your gcc source distribution directory to a directory in the libstdc++ source directory. When there you will call it gcc (libstdc++/gcc).

2. Run patch on the INSTALL file in the top level of the libstdc++ distribution directory. The patch allows you to test the built compiler.

3. Get a test suite for gcc and move it to the gcc subdirectory in the libstdc++ directory.

4. Make a directory called objdir in the libstdc++ directory and run **configure [options]**, specifying a target machine if you are building a cross-package and specifying any pertinent options for which the default is not satisfactory.

7

Each enable option also has a disable option available; each with option, a corresponding without option.

-prefix=dirname   Use this option to specify a top level directory other than /usr/local, which is the default.

-with-local-prefix=dirname   Use this option to specify an installation directory for local files. The default is /usr/local/.

-with-gxx-include-dir=dirname   Use this option to specify the directory for g++ header files. The default is /usr/local/include/g++.

-enable-shared   Use this option to build shared versions of the C++ runtime libraries, if supported. The default is -disable-shared.

-with-gnu-as   Use this option if the compiler is to assume availability of GNU assembler.

-with-gnu-ld   Use this option if the compiler is to assume availability of GNU linker.

-enable-multilib   Use this option to build multiple target libraries to support different target variants. This is the default.

5. In the same directory, objdir, use GNU make to build libstdc++.

6. Test the built compiler by running make check in objdir.

7. Run make install in objdir to install the software.

Installation with Method 2

Now I can begin an installation of gcc using the method described in the README that comes with the libstdc++ distribution.

First, I move my gcc distribution to a subdirectory of the libstdc++ distribution called gcc:

```
Barracuda# mv gcc-2.8.1/ libstdc++-2.8.1/gcc/
```

Here I run the patch command as instructed by the libstdc++ README. I'll warn you ahead of time that for the versions of the software I am using, this isn't going to work quite as planned because it turns out that slightly out-of-sync versions of files are being distributed while I am writing this. I've included the process here so that you can recognize whether this happens to you, and a bit of diagnostic detective work so that you can tell whether it's for the same reasons.

```
Barracuda# /usr/local/bin/patch < INSTALL
can't find file to patch at input line 145
Perhaps you should have used the -p or —strip option?
```

To my dismay, the patch doesn't seem to quite work. To check my options, I check patch's online help, using its nonstandard "minus minus help" option. I only show here a small number of the available options:

```
Barracuda# /usr/local/bin/patch —help
Usage: /usr/local/bin/patch [OPTION]... [ORIGFILE [PATCHFILE]]

Miscellaneous options:

  -t  --batch  Ask no questions; skip bad-Prereq patches;
➥assume reversed.
  -f  --force  Like -t, but ignore bad-Prereq patches,
➥and assume unreversed.
   -s  --quiet  --silent  Work silently unless an error occurs.
   --verbose  Output extra information about the work being done.
```

From the patch error I'm not sure what the problem is. However the patch option, -t, which suggests that it will cause patch to skip bad patches and not ask me any questions, seems promising. I'm playing dumb system administrator here—if a patch is bad, I've no way to fix it, and I doubt I know how to answer any questions it might ask. You're on full autopilot right now—either the software is going to work the way it is supposed to, or you're going to give up. Following the same logic, I also like the idea of it not telling me about anything but errors, so I also specify the -s option as well. I try to run patch again. Here I again only show a small portion of the output:

```
Barracuda# /usr/local/bin/patch -t -s < INSTALL
The text leading up to this was:
--------------------------
|        Configuring libstdc++-2.8.1
|
|--- gcc/Makefile.in.orig      Fri Feb 20 13:53:00 1998
|+++ gcc/Makefile.in    Fri Feb 20 13:58:33 1998
--------------------------
No file to patch.  Skipping patch.
4 out of 4 hunks ignored
```

I was rather hoping that the patch file might have acquired some garbage that needed to be skipped (this sometimes happens when patches are posted to newsgroups by their authors), and that simply skipping error sections would solve the problem. However, even with the "skip bad" option specified, there seem to be errors. Apparently worse, they're errors complaining about specific files, rather than simply complaints about possible garbage in the file. My initial hope and supposition appears to be wrong. However, this error message actually has some information content. It appears to be looking for a Makefile.in.orig and a Makefile.in. On checking my gcc directory, I learn that there is no Makefile.in.orig, so it is understandable why patch can't patch that file.

7

```
Barracuda# ls gcc
INSTALL          caller-save.c   fixcpp          genemit.c        pself2.c
Makefile.in      calls.c         fixinc-nt.sed   genextract.c     pself3.c
NEWS             cccp.1          fixinc.dgux     genflags.c       real.c
ORDERS           cccp.c          fixinc.irix     genmultilib      real.h
```

Furthermore, I discover that my `Makefile.in` is more recent than the file `patch` would have patched (look at the dates in the patch error output). Apparently my `Makefile.in` already has the patch incorporated.

```
Barracuda# ls -l gcc/Makefile.in
-r--r--r--  1 9225        105910 Mar  2  1998 gcc/Makefile.in
```

Because my machine really does not have a whole lot of free space available, I decide not to download the test suite. My resident programmer tells me that gcc builds rarely fail, so I move on to the configure step. I have chosen to enable shared C++ libraries.

Shared libraries allow all programs that make use of a given "common system routine" (things like looking up remote host IP addresses from hostnames) to access this routine out of a single shared copy of the executable code. If this routine weren't shared, each program that wanted to use this code would have to keep a copy locally inside its own executable.

Both shared and nonshared libraries have their advantages and disadvantages. With shared libraries, you only have to update one piece of software, the library, if a common routine needs to be updated. Also, common routines can make up a large percentage of any given program's size, and keeping them as shared libraries can decrease the amount of storage space you require for software. The downside is that every program that wants to use the code has to take extra time to open the library and load the code, decreasing performance.

Nonshared (static) libraries are actually excerpted and the relevant portions inserted into a program at compile time. This speeds execution of the program and can make a significant performance boost, but it also costs extra disk space and requires that all software that uses a library be recompiled if there is an important update to a library routine.

Because I'm working on a limited-space installation, I will choose to enable shared libraries in this example.

```
Barracuda# mkdir objdir
Barracuda# cd objdir
Barracuda# ../configure —enable-shared
Configuring for a sparc-sun-sunos4.1.4 host.
Created "Makefile" in /usr/local/source/libstdc++-2.8.1/objdir
➥ using "mh-frag" a
nd "mt-frag"
Links are now set up to build a native compiler for sparc-sun-sunos4.1.4
```

Then I run make: `Barracuda# make`

I wait awhile for the machine to crunch away, as the README warns that this can take huge amounts of disk space, and I am somewhat concerned about whether I have enough. On a Sparcstation IPX, you might want to consider taking a four-to-six hour nap at this point. On a Sun Enterprize 250 dual-UltraSparc system, plan on a short lunch hour or a really long coffee break. However, a check of my available disk space indicates that I have to stop here…no more disk space! It's a good thing you will be adding a disk drive tomorrow! When I have my disk set up, I'll be able to continue with this installation method.

```
Barracuda# df
Filesystem          kbytes    used   avail capacity  Mounted on
/dev/sd0a            47575    6705   36113    16%     /
/dev/sd0g           311975  305664       0   109%     /usr
/dev/sd0h            18671      10   16794     0%     /home
```

Those of you with space can continue with the commands make check, and if that works, make install, and you're all finished. As noted earlier, if make check doesn't complain about files that differ, you're good to go with the install. The make install process will, as is usual, put everything where it belongs, and then you're all finished.

If you ever find yourself in a position where you've run out of space like this, or actually, run out of space anywhere in the install, not all is lost. Unlike in the personal computer world, software installations are not monolithic, all-or-nothing propositions. In tomorrow's lesson I'll show you how easy it is to finish that installation after adding sufficient disk space to hold it.

A Complement to gcc: gdb

As a system administrator your first responsibility is not as a programmer, but there will be times when knowing a little bit about programming and debugging will be helpful. Code is rarely perfect, so if you're installing third party software that you have to compile, you'll eventually find something that's broken. If you have the time, send a bug report to the author and wait for it to be fixed. If you have a programmer on duty, use her services to identify the problem and fix it. And then send the fix to the author—UNIX freeware authors rely on people who find bugs to let them know there's a problem! If you need to accelerate the process and don't have a programmer at hand, it's time for you to roll up your shirtsleeves and get a bit dirty.

First off, you'll need a debugger. Just as the Free Software Foundation's Gnu C compiler, gcc, is the king of C compilers, its debugger, gdb, is a mighty fine debugger.

7

Installing gdb

Installing gdb is relatively simple. You will want to read the README first to check for the available options and any machine-specific information you might need, but chances are this one will configure itself and build properly right "out of the box."

The README suggests that installation should not require many steps. From the top of the gdb distribution directory, you can run

```
./configure
make
cp gdb/gdb /usr/local/bin/gdb
```

As you can see, there is no default installation location, unlike the rest of the packages you have worked with today.

Using gdb

Before you start, remember that you're treading in the land of the programmer here. Both the language and the debugger are capable of many more things that I can't show you, but I can give you the beginning of a hint of how you can actually use this tool, even with little knowledge of the C programming language. It's always frustrating as a system administrator when you find a piece of software that claims to do exactly what you need something to do, but that won't run properly. Frequently the errors in these pieces of software are due to a programmer writing and testing the program on one machine and never checking it on any others. Little differences in the OS or configuration of the machine might make a the program work in his case, even with a small error, but break when run on your machine. With the help of a debugger, you might, just *might*, be able to find and fix that error yourself.

To use gdb, you first need something on which to use it. Type this little program as it appears here. Name the file addme.c.

```
/* addme.c    A really silly C demo program */
/* 990325 WCR                               */
/* Usage is <progname> <filename>           */
/* adds all the values in <filename> and    */
/* returns the result                       */

#include <stdio.h>

int addem(a,b)
int a, b;
{
  return a+b;
}
```

```
void main(argc,argv)
int argc;
char *argv[];
{
  int i;
  char infilename[8];
  int j;
  FILE *infile;
  char number[100];
  char *infilename2=infilename;
  strcpy(infilename2,argv[1]);
  i=0; j=0;
  infile = fopen(infilename2,"r");

  if(infile==NULL)
  {
     printf("couldn't open file %s please try again\n",infilename2);
     exit(1);
  }

  i=0;
  while (fgets(number,90,infile) != '\0')
  {
     sscanf(number,"%d",&j);
     i=addem(i,j);
  }
  printf("Your total is %d\n",i);
  exit(0);
}
```

This is a really simple little C program that takes a list of integers from a file, one per line, and adds them together. So that you have a file to work from, create a file named numbers with the following contents:

```
1
2
13
15
```

Make sure there are no blank lines above or below the data. Also create a file with a very long name, such as supercalifradgilisticzowie, and put the same data in it.

Note

My programmer tells me that there's a little bit of trickery involved in the way this code is written that's there to generate an error. Specifically, I'm told that even though there are a few errors in this code, some systems are sloppy enough with memory management that it runs correctly intermittently. Also, if you rearrange the definition of the variables i and j it decreases the likelihood of a crash. Weird, huh?

7

> If it works properly once, try running it again. Maybe start up a bunch of other programs and try some more. There really is an error, and it really should break, but this can't be guaranteed with all systems and all mixes of running software.
>
> If it consistently works properly for you, you luckily (or unluckily, depending on how you look at it) are running on a system that is somewhat more tolerant to sloppy programming. You'll have the benefit of having more software run on your machine without complaining, but your programmers might end up distributing code that no one else can run.

Now see what you have. Time to compile the program. You don't have a makefile, so you'll have to do it by hand. Issue the following command:

```
soyokaze testaddme 271> gcc -g -o addemup addme.c
```

After a few seconds your machine should return you to a command line. You've typed the program incorrectly if your machine does anything else, especially like the following:

```
addme.c: In function 'main':
addme.c:15: parse error before 'char'
addme.c:23: subscripted value is neither array nor pointer
```

Specifically, if you got this error, in all likelihood you forgot the semicolon after the line that says int argc;.

When you get the program to compile cleanly with no errors, you're ready for the next step—trying it out. Issue the command **./addemup** and see what happens. Note that the command is addemup, not something related to addme. I could actually have named it anything I wanted, simply by changing the -o addemup part of the gcc command. If you don't specify any output filename, gcc names the output file a.out by default. Also, so you know, the -g flag tells the compiler to turn on debugging output for use by the debugger. This slows the program down a little but gives the debugger important information. You should see this when you run the program:

```
soyokaze testaddme 273>./addemup
Segmentation fault
```

Well, that doesn't sound good. What could be wrong? You probably can figure it out by looking at the code at this point, but on a more complicated program that would not be possible. Instead, start up the gdb debugger and take a look.

```
soyokaze testaddme 274> gdb ./addemup
GDB is free software and you are welcome to distribute copies of it
 under certain conditions; type "show copying" to see the conditions.
There is absolutely no warranty for GDB; type "show warranty" for details.
GDB 4.13 (sparc-sun-sunos4.1.3_U1),
```

```
Copyright 1994 Free Software Foundation, Inc...
(gdb)
```

Now you're at a prompt. What do you do? The gdb debugger actually has a rather complete selection of online help available. To access the help system, simply enter the command help:

```
(gdb) help
List of classes of commands:

running — Running the program
stack — Examining the stack
data — Examining data
breakpoints — Making program stop at certain points
files — Specifying and examining files
status — Status inquiries
support — Support facilities
user-defined — User-defined commands
aliases — Aliases of other commands
obscure — Obscure features
internals — Maintenance commands

Type "help" followed by a class name for a list of commands in that
➥class.
Type "help" followed by command name for full documentation.
Command name abbreviations are allowed if unambiguous.
(gdb)
```

Rather than walk you through some of the interesting items there, I'll leave that for you to explore. Right now get back to debugging the program. To start the program, simply issue the command r:

```
(gdb) r
Starting program: /home/ray/testaddme/./addemup

Program received signal SIGSEGV, Segmentation fault.
0xf7733194 in w4str ()
(gdb)
```

So gdb knows something. Not a very intelligible something at this point, but something nonetheless. Now see whether gdb can be a bit more informative if you use the where command to ask it to expand on that "in w4str()" comment:

```
(gdb) where
#0  0xf7733194 in w4str ()
#1  0x409c in fopen ()
#2  0x2340 in main (argc=1, argv=0xf7fff744) at addme.c:23
(gdb)
```

7

gdb says the program broke in a procedure named w4str, which was called from a procedure named fopen, which was called from line 23 of the file addme.c. Look at this region of the code. Using the command l followed by a line number lists the region around that line.

```
(gdb) l 23
18          char infilename[8];
19          int j;
20          FILE *infile;
21          char number[100];
22          char *infilename2=&infilename;
23          strcpy(infilename2,argv[1]);
24          i=0; j=0;
25          infile = fopen(infilename2,"r");
26
27          if(infile==NULL)
(gdb)
```

You have an fopen in the program, but it seems to be on line 25. Line 23 is doing something else entirely. Must be an fopen that's called somewhere invisible to you at this point. Hard to tell, without being a programmer. Still, line 23 is a hint. Set a breakpoint using the b command (a place you want the program to stop running and wait for you) at line 23 and see what happens.

```
(gdb) b 23
Breakpoint 1 at 0x2320: file addme.c, line 23.
(gdb)
```

So far so good. Now to run the program again and see where this takes you.

```
(gdb) r
The program being debugged has been started already.
Start it from the beginning? (y or n) y
Starting program: /home/ray/testaddme/./addemup

Breakpoint 1, main (argc=1, argv=0xf7fff744) at addme.c:23
23          strcpy(infilename2,argv[1]);
(gdb)
```

Note that gdb asks me whether I want to restart from the beginning and I told it to go ahead. Now it's run up to the breakpoint and is waiting for me to do something. I don't know quite what strcpy does but something's obviously wrong with this line. I know I've got a variable named infilename2 and a funny variable named argv[1]. See what gdb has to say about them, by using the p command to print their contents.

```
(gdb) p infilename2
$1 = "L\000\000@"
(gdb)
```

Well, that's not too informative. What about this argv[1]?

```
(gdb) p argv[1]
$2 = 0x0
(gdb)
```

0x0 is a hexadecimal 0, or NULL in the C world. Examining the code again certainly suggests that something useful should be happening here; after all, it looks like infilename2 gets used to open a file in a few lines, and neither L\000\000@ nor NULL look promising as a filename. Nulls get used in C, but frequently they're signs of a problem, so think about this.

The program is trying to do something with a variable named argv[1]. The only other place this variable (argv) appears is in the main statement, the statement that starts off the actual program execution. Certainly looks like there should be something other than a NULL here. Wait a minute, what was it that it said in the comments at the top? It said I needed to give it a filename! I didn't give it a filename, and it's trying to copy something that doesn't exist to get one. Silly programmer; he should have checked for that!

Now I'll see whether I'm right. I'll rerun the program with a filename this time. I can simply use the r command, and follow it by any command-line parameters or options that I might want.

```
(gdb) r numbers
The program being debugged has been started already.
Start it from the beginning? (y or n) y
Starting program: /home/ray/testaddme/./addemup numbers

Breakpoint 1, main (argc=2, argv=0xf7fff73c) at addme.c:23
23          strcpy(infilename2,argv[1]);
(gdb)
```

I started it over, but I forgot to turn off my breakpoint. Still, this is a good opportunity for me to check to see whether I was right.

```
(gdb) p infilename2
$3 = "\000\000\200\000\000\000 "
(gdb)
```

That's as useless as before. Given the name of the variable involved, I was hoping I might see my filename here. Still, you have that argv[1] variable that also appeared to have a problem last time. Now look at it again.

```
(gdb) p argv[1]
$4 = 0xf7fff80f "numbers"
(gdb)
```

7

Okay! Now you're getting somewhere. If you remember to give it a filename, it actually gets one! To continue past the breakpoint, I can enter c.

```
(gdb) c
Continuing.
Your total is 31

Program exited normally.
(gdb)
```

And the program now does exactly what it should—it adds up all the numbers in the file numbers and gets the correct answer, 31. If I'd like to test it again without stopping at the breakpoint, I can delete the breakpoint with the d *breakpointnumber* command and run it again.

```
(gdb) d 1
(gdb) r
Starting program: /home/ray/testaddme/./addemup numbers
Your total is 31

Program exited normally.
(gdb)
```

The command d 1 deletes breakpoint 1 (you can have multiples if you need them). Note that I don't have to give it the command-line argument numbers this time when I hit r because it conveniently remembers command parameters and options for me. As you can see, it runs properly to completion.

Quitting gdb with the quit command and trying it on the command line produces the same results.

```
soyokaze testaddme 286> ./addemup numbers
Your total is 31
```

Now see whether you can demonstrate another type of error. Do you still remember what your very long filename is? Try using that filename instead of numbers and see what happens.

```
soyokaze testaddme 287> ./addemup supercalifragilisticzowie
couldn't open file supercalifra please try again
```

Huh? I didn't call it supercalifra. Something happened to my filename. Time to break out gdb again and have another look.

```
soyokaze testaddme 288> gdb ./addemup
GDB is free software and you are welcome to distribute copies of it
 under certain conditions; type "show copying" to see the conditions.
There is absolutely no warranty for GDB; type "show warranty" for
➥details.
```

```
GDB 4.13 (sparc-sun-sunos4.1.3_U1),
Copyright 1994 Free Software Foundation, Inc...
(gdb)  r supercalifragilisticzowie
Starting program: /home/ray/testaddme/./addemup supercalifragilisticzowie
couldn't open file supercalifra please try again

Program exited with code 01.
(gdb)
```

So it says basically the same thing. There must be something more you can find out though. Try looking at the code and see whether you can figure out where that weird truncation came from.

```
(gdb) l
14       int argc;
15       char *argv[];
16       {
17         int i;
18         char infilename[8];
19         int j;
20         FILE *infile;
21         char number[100];
22         char *infilename2=infilename;
23         strcpy(infilename2,argv[1]);
(gdb)
24         i=0; j=0;
25         infile = fopen(infilename2,"r");
26
27         if(infile==NULL)
28         {
29             printf("couldn't open file %s please try again\n",
➥infilename2);
30             exit(1);
31         }
32
33         i=0;
(gdb)
```

So line 29 seems to be where the error message is coming from. Set a breakpoint there and see what happens.

```
(gdb) b 29
Breakpoint 1 at 0x2374: file addme.c, line 29.
(gdb) r
Starting program: /home/ray/testaddme/./addemup supercalifragilisticzowie

Breakpoint 1, main (argc=2, argv=0xf7fff72c) at addme.c:29
29             printf("couldn't open file %s please try again\n",
➥infilename2);
(gdb)
```

7

So you're at the breakpoint. infilename2 is supposed to be supercalifragilistic-zowie, and it is:

```
(gdb) p infilename2
$1 = "supercalifra"
(gdb)
```

Something's very wrong here! Time to back up to the trusty breakpoint at line 23 and watch what happens from the top down.

```
(gdb) b 23
Breakpoint 2 at 0x2374: file addme.c, line 23.
(gdb) r
Starting program: /home/ray/testaddme/./addemup supercalifragilisticzowie

Breakpoint 2, main (argc=2, argv=0xf7fff72c) at addme.c:23
23          strcpy(infilename2,argv[1]);
(gdb) p argv[1]
$1 = 0xf7fff7ff "supercalifragilisticzowie"
(gdb)
```

So the previous culprit isn't a problem here, it's not something preventing the filename from getting into the program.

```
(gdb) p infilename2
$2 = "\000\000\200\000\000\000 "
(gdb)
```

Nothing interesting there. See what happens on the next line—use the gdb command n to step to the next line. When you step to the next line, this line executes, so you should expect to see the results of that strcpy after stepping forward.

```
(gdb) n
24          i=0; j=0;
(gdb) p infilename2
$1 = 0xf7fff6b0 "supercalifragilisticzowie"
(gdb)
```

As expected, infilename2 contains the atrociously long filename. Nothing wrong here. Still, by the time it hit line 29, it was broken, so step forward again and see what happens.

```
(gdb) n
25          infile = fopen(infilename2,"r");
(gdb) p
$3 = 0xf7fff6b0 "supercalifra"
(gdb)
```

Wait a minute! Now it's wrong! What happened? All that the program did was assign the variables i and j to both be zero, and somehow it affected infilename2? You wouldn't think this could happen—variables just changing their values willy-nilly.

In fact, if the program had been written properly, this wouldn't have happened. As a system administrator, this is where you usually give up. That isn't to say that the exercise has been useless however. With this information you can much more easily explain to the author or online support community what problems you've observed, so that they can fix it more easily and quickly. Program authors hate it when they get bug reports that say "it didn't work." This doesn't mean anything to them because if they could duplicate the problem on their end, they'd probably have found and fixed it already. The information you can provide by taking these few steps to figure out where the program is going wrong on your end, can mean the difference between a fix that takes a few minutes to appear, and a fix that never appears.

> **Note**
>
> **Note from the programmer**   If you're curious, and keep a C handbook around, fixing this particular error isn't that difficult. The error here is that the variable `infilename` has only been defined to be long enough to hold eight characters. `infilename2` is essentially an alias to `infilename1` that's needed to fool the debugger into not telling you about the problem immediately. The assignment of the very long filename to `infilename2` actually works most of the time because there's enough slop in the assignment of memory space that it's not going to write over anything important, even though the `supercalifragilisticzowi` value hangs out the end of it and into unknown memory space. The thing that actually makes the error show up almost all the time though is the placement of the definitions of `i` and `j` around the definition of `infilename`. Most compilers order variables in memory in the same order they were defined in the program. Because the compiler doesn't know you're going to stuff a huge string into `infilename`, it chooses memory fairly close to `infilename` for the storage of `i` and `j`. With most compilers they will flank `infilename` in memory, and a sufficiently large value in `infilename` will overlap the memory used by `i` and `j`. By assigning both `i` and `j` to 0 after assigning `infilename`, I've almost guaranteed that part of `infilename` will be damaged and that the program will fail. To fix the program so that this can't occur with any reasonable filename, simply change the definition of `infilename` to something such as `char infilename[256];` instead of `infilename[8];`.

Summary

In today's lesson you installed various useful software packages that will be useful to you in the coming weeks and beyond. You installed

- gzip, which provides an alternative tool for compressing files and, more importantly, allows you to uncompress with gunzip the many .gz files you will download.

7

- `patch`, which allows you to update one file with another. Some of the packages you install will have a base package and a number of files, or patches, which you will apply to the base package.
- GNU `make`, an alternative tool with which some applications might prefer to be built.
- `gcc`, which is a free C compiler used to build many of the packages you will find out there.
- libstdc++, which is a set of libraries needed for the C++ component of the `gcc` package, if you chose to install that particular language.
- `gdb`, which is a debugger for `gcc`. Your programmer will find this package especially useful, and you might find it useful for solving minor problems you might encounter when you are compiling a package, or for being able to provide a starting point for a software author to fix a bug.

Q&A

Q Installing this stuff was a lot of fun. What other basic utilities would you suggest I get for my machine?

A Oh wow. Fun question! Look into almost anything GNU—it's comprised of almost universally great code and useful utilities. Depending on what you find amusing, spend some time browsing the Usenet newsgroups to see what other people with similar interests are running and where they're getting it from. The World Wide Web has turned into a great clearinghouse for UNIX freeware because there are literally hundreds of sites where individuals have collected and categorized the software they find most interesting. Chances are one or more of them will agree with your tastes.

Q What do I do if I don't have any compilers available on my machine?

A Hard answer: Find another machine that has compilers, build a `gcc` cross-compiler, and use it to create a compiler for your machine. Much easier answer: Check the Web, starting from `www.fsf.org`, looking for a precompiled binary of `gcc`. If that's not fruitful, search Usenet news through Deja (`www.deja.com`), or ask on the newsgroups yourself. You're very unlikely to be the only person who's had this problem, and in the UNIX world, that means that the solution is out there.

Q I have a program and it won't compile properly, what should I do?

A Go find a real programmer and ask that person to help. You're a system administrator and you're not expected to be a wonder-programmer. If there's a problem with a program, get an expert.

Workshop

Quiz

1. What command do you use to compile a program?
2. What is the first thing you do when you have a new package to install?
3. What do you do if a compile results in a "Fatal Error"?
4. True or False: A "Segmentation Fault" is a bad thing.

Exercises

1. Install everything you've been shown today, even if you've already got a copy of gcc.
2. Find, download, and install unzip. It works with personal-computer type pkzip files, whereas gunzip works with gnuzip files. They are not interchangeable commands.
3. Fix the silly sample program so that it exits gracefully instead of breaking if you forget to give it a filename. Hint—There's an example of everything you need to know in the file itself.

7

WEEK 2

At a Glance

The topics in Week 2 take you through several software installations and the process of securing your machines. You will also learn about real-life security horror stories, the decisions you'll need to make, and policies you'll need to enforce.

- Day 8, "Adding Basic Devices," coaches you on adding basic devices to the system.
- Day 9, "What About Security?," examines today's security problems as well as basic approaches for dealing with them.
- Day 10, "Defending Your Machines and Encrypting Traffic," trains you to implement common sense software solutions for your machine.
- Day 11, "Making Your Machines Communicate with Each Other: NIS and NFS," helps you enable your machine to communicate with another machine by implementing the Network File System and the Network Information Service.
- Day 12, "The Basics of Making User Accounts," gets you up to speed on how to create user accounts.
- Day 13, "Saving Your World: Making Backups to Tape," looks at how to make a tape backup of your machine and how to restore from that backup should the need arise.
- Day 14, "Other Useful Software: Useful Utilities," walks you through the installation and usage overview of Perl and MySQL.

DAY 8

Adding Basic Devices

When I was originally planning this book, this chapter came much later, everything fit where it belonged, and installations worked out neatly. Somewhere between there and here I decided that you'd probably get more out of the book if it were more representative of things you'll encounter in real life. So, as you might recall from yesterday, I took the opportunity to run out of disk space in the middle of the second method of gcc installation, thereby precipitating the need to add a drive to my system. (I meant to do that—really!) Today, you will add some basic devices to the system: a disk drive, a tape drive, a CD-ROM drive, and a printer. Some devices will entail a bit of work, whereas others will simply involve a reboot of the system. Are you ready to forge ahead?

Adding a Disk Drive

Whether your machine originally came with a 4GB drive or a 500MB drive, you will find that there is no such thing as too much disk space. Regardless of whether you feel you need extra disk space right now, you'll be amazed at how easily you'll be able to fill up what you have! Today, you will add a SCSI drive to the system. If you are running Linux on Intel hardware, you might be adding an IDE drive instead, or if you're playing with older hardware, it might be one of those one-pound-per-megabyte xylogics or other proprietary format pieces of hardware. In any case, the decisions you'll have to make will be similar, though the exact syntax might vary slightly.

Anatomy of a Drive

Before you actually start adding the extra drive, take a look at the structure of a disk drive. As is often the case with technology, older disk drives were physically larger and did not hold as much information, whereas newer disk drives are smaller and hold more data. In case you've ever wondered what a disk drive actually looks like, take a look at Figure 8.1, which shows a few points along the evolution of hard drives from prehistoric times (1980!) to 1999. The drives look pretty neat, don't they? When your drive is no longer working, you're at least left with an interesting piece for your shelf.

FIGURE 8.1

Drive internal evolution over the years.

Some operating systems automatically determine the physical drive parameters, whereas others require that the operator provide this information. On the SunOS machine I am currently configuring, I will have to supply some of this type of information for my drive. To give you an idea of what the `format` program will be asking about, take a look at Figure 8.2, which diagrams the basic drive parts. As you probably noticed in Figure 8.1, a disk drive is composed of a set of stacked platters that spin. Not surprisingly, each platter is composed of two surfaces. Each surface is composed of concentric tracks, which are delimited by the areas where the heads can position themselves. The heads are what actually do the reading and writing, and they move as a unit, accessing the data from the same track on each surface simultaneously. If you observe the arrangement of the same track on each surface, you will see that it forms a cylindrical shape in the stack of surfaces—hence the term "cylinder." Finally, a surface can be further subdivided by making pie pieces, known as sectors.

FIGURE 8.2

The anatomy of a hard disk drive.

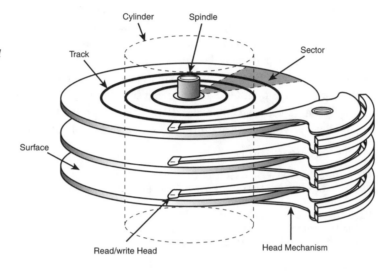

Depending on who you talk to, parts of drives might be referred to by slightly different names. Just to be clear, these are the definitions as I use them.

Platters are the physical flat metal plates that make up the drive.

The *spindle* is the axis around which the platters rotate.

Surfaces are the part of the platters that the data is written on—two per platter.

Tracks are the physical concentric areas on each surface that contain data, so if the heads can be positioned at 100 discrete positions, you have 100 tracks per surface.

Sectors are the pie-slice shaped sections into which each surface can be broken.

Cylinders are stacks of tracks, all the same distance from the spindle. If you have 20 surfaces with 100 tracks per surface, you have 2,000 tracks on the drive, arranged in 100 cylinders.

Blocks are the smallest unit and are the result of tracks being subdivided by the sectors. If your drive uses 45 sectors and 100 tracks, each surface has 45×100=4500 blocks.

More typical than the sample numbers I've used here are cylinder numbers in the thousands and sector numbers in the hundreds. Also, you'll very rarely see a drive with an even number of surfaces because most drives use one surface as a control for head-positioning purposes.

Picking Your ID

SCSI, the drive connection hardware used for almost all modern UNIX hardware, communicates among the devices by assigning each device an ID between 0 and 7 (or between 0 and 15 for the new UltraSCSI format). You will have to pick an ID number for your drive. Be sure to pick a number that is not already in use or that is not already intended for some particular device type. For example, you would want to reserve 6 on a Sun for your CD-ROM drive. If you aren't sure what numbers are already in use, check with your machine first. On Suns, you can sort through the startup comments to look for IDs by issuing the dmesg command. IRIX comes with the hinv command, which very neatly displays your hardware inventory. Here's a sample of hinv output:

```
HOBBES joray 201 > hinv

CPU: MIPS R10000 Processor Chip Revision: 2.7
FPU: MIPS R10010 Floating Point Chip Revision: 0.0
1 195 MHZ IP32 Processor
Main memory size: 128 Mbytes
Secondary unified instruction/data cache size: 1 Mbyte on Processor 0
Instruction cache size: 32 Kbytes
Data cache size: 32 Kbytes
FLASH PROM version 4.11
Integral SCSI controller 0: Version ADAPTEC 7880
  Disk drive: unit 2 on SCSI controller 0
  CDROM: unit 4 on SCSI controller 0
Integral SCSI controller 1: Version ADAPTEC 7880
  Disk drive: unit 3 on SCSI controller 1
  Disk drive: unit 5 on SCSI controller 1
On-board serial ports: tty1
On-board serial ports: tty2
On-board EPP/ECP parallel port
CRM graphics installed
Integral Ethernet: ec0, version 1
Iris Audio Processor: version A3 revision 0
Video: MVP unit 0 version 1.4
AV: AV1 Card version 1, O2Cam type 1 version 0 connected.
Vice: TRE
```

From the owner's manual for this particular SGI, you would already know that this model can't take an additional internal drive (only one internal drive bay), so you would not be able to add anything to what is identified as SCSI controller 0. However, you can still add many external devices to this machine. The hinv command shows you that you can't pick ID 3 or 5 on SCSI controller 1, which controls this machine's external devices, because these devices are already in use.

8

> **Note**
>
> **Sun hardware is weird** A bizarre naming exception for SCSI hardware is found with Sun equipment. On Suns, SCSI ID 3, the default boot device, shows up as sd0, and SCSI ID 0 shows up as sd3. Other sd numbers correlate directly to their SCSI ID numbers:
>
> If your Sun hardware indicates something like:
>
> ```
> sd0 at esp0 target 3 lun 0
> sd0: <Fujitsu M2624FA-1 cyl 1440 alt 2 hd 11 sec 64>
> ```
>
> When you look at the startup/dmesg information, you cannot add a drive with SCSI ID 3, but you can add one with SCSI ID 0 (or 1 or 2). IDs 4 and 6 are reserved for tape and CD-ROM drives. ID 5 is reserved for a second tape in the default kernel, but because most don't have two tape drives, it can be reconfigured to take an additional hard drive.

If you are adding an external drive to your system, you will probably be able to set a switch on the back of the drive enclosure to set the appropriate SCSI ID number. To actually pick the number you want, you might either have to press a + or - sign (with something like a pencil point) to adjust the number until the one you want appears, or you might have to move a dial. If you are adding an internal drive to your system, you will be indicating the ID number with little jumpers that cover up pins. Be sure to look at the manufacturer's documentation to see what combinations of covered and uncovered pins make the ID number you are looking for.

If you're stuck trying to determine how to set the SCSI ID for a device without literature from the manufacturer, here's where to start. Consult Figure 8.3 to see what the SCSI ID jumpers on an assortment of drives look like. Yours will probably be something like one of these. If you're lucky, the drive's logic-board will have the ID numbers silk-screened on it near the SCSI ID jumper pins. If you're not lucky, you'll have to guess. Pick an open SCSI ID, guess which end of the pin array is the ID 1 side, and use the data from Table 8.1 to attempt to set your ID. Notice that this is simply the binary representation of the numbers 0 to 7.

TABLE 8.1 SCSI ID Jumper Settings

ID	ID Jumper 2	ID Jumper 1	ID Jumper 0
0	0	0	0
1	0	0	1
2	0	1	0
3	0	1	1

continues

TABLE 8.1   continued

ID	ID Jumper 2	ID Jumper 1	ID Jumper 0
4	1	0	0
5	1	0	1
6	1	1	0
7	1	1	1

 Caution

You won't often be able to use ID 7 for devices because this is usually reserved for the SCSI host controller. Unless your system specifically enables you to use this ID, you're best off just avoiding it.

FIGURE 8.3

Typical SCSI selection pin sets.

Plug in the drive, attach it to your machine (making sure your machine is off), turn it on, and bring your machine up. If you don't see the drive at the ID it's supposed to be at, especially if you see it at the reverse of the binary value (001 = 1 is the reverse of 100 = 4), guess that the other end is the ID 1 side and try again.

 Tip

When trying to install SCSI ID selection hardware that's more sophisticated than jumpers, such as ID wheels or push-button selectors, you also have to pay attention to what side of the pin-set is the ground side and what side is the selection side. Sometimes, you will find that one side of each pair of ID pins is attached to what is called electrical ground and that one side of your selector connector is also connected. The correct hookup is with the common (connected) side of the selector connector hooked up to the ground side of the ID pin set. If you hook it up with the common side of the selector connector on the nonground side of the ID pin set, you'll most likely end up with a drive that appears only at ID 0 or ID 6.

You don't need to know what the technical electronics terms here mean. Just be aware that if you plug in a SCSI ID selector to a drive and you end up with a bizarre SCSI ID that isn't what you thought it should be, trying to hook the connector up in other orientations is likely to help. It might seem an odd recommendation, but if you have a drive with no documentation and you can't contact the manufacturer or find the information anywhere else, the best solution is to "fiddle with it." You won't break anything by experimenting with the SCSI ID selector; the worst thing that will happen is that you will duplicate an existing ID and neither drive is recognized. As with most things, this is much easier to actually do than it is to explain or to follow in written form. If you have a drive and no way of acquiring documentation, don't be afraid to simply experiment with the jumper settings. Things will start to make sense much faster than you might expect.

What's in a Name?

When you ran df on your machine during the tour of your system on Day 4, "A Stroll Through Your System," you might have noticed that each filesystem had a long, unusual name as well as a directory name. What can you tell from those weird names?

Here is df -k output on the same IRIX machine from which you have the hinv output. Only the information on the filesystems that are physically stored on this machine is shown:

```
HOBBES joray 208 > df -k

Filesystem          Type  kbytes    use      avail   %use  Mounted on
/dev/root           xfs   4307492   3124812  1182680  73   /
/dev/dsk/dks1d3s6   efs   3911360   3486154  425206   90   /archive
/dev/dsk/dks1d5s7   xfs   1096800   281224   815576   26   /space
/dev/dsk/dks1d5s6   xfs   3887200   3008904  878296   78   /mnt
/dev/dsk/dks1d5s0   xfs   3887200   3593116  294084   93   /people
```

/dev/root is the name for the root partition. From hinv, you know that this drive is also SCSI device 2 on SCSI controller 0. However, you can see a bit more information about the external drives. From hinv, you already know that SCSI controller 1 has drives 3 and 5 attached. From df, you see that /dev/dsk/dks1d3s6 has a filesystem called /archive. From the name that df shows, you can break the name into its parts. In IRIX, a disk drive's name is in the form /dev/dsk/dksXdYsZ, where X is the SCSI controller number, Y is the drive's ID number, and Z is the partition number. So for /archive, you learn from its name, /dev/dsk/dks1d3s6, that it is partition 6 on drive 3 at SCSI controller 1.

Note

> **Raw or block devices versus character devices** You will probably notice that there are (at least) two device descriptors for each drive you have attached to the machine—one for a "raw" or "block" device and one for a "character" device. There are slight differences in the way that the OS treats reading from and writing to the same device depending on whether you ask it to treat the device as a raw/block device or a character device. These differences revolve around whether the OS expects buffering for the device I/O to be handled at the OS level or at the software level. Generally, you shouldn't need to know much about these differences. Software that has a preference for one device type over the other will tell you in its documentation.
>
> As a general rule of thumb, you will find that software that wants to read data as though it were in files or distinct records on a device will probably prefer that you use the character device. Software that wants to simply read data from the device as a continuous stream will probably prefer that you use the block device. Neither choice is critical unless your software specifically insists on one instead of the other. The only usual detriment to choosing the wrong device (block or character) will be a performance penalty.

Because the final steps to adding your disk drive will include telling the machine which partition goes with which filesystem, you should take a few moments to learn the naming conventions for your operating system. Run df, look at /etc/fstab, and check the man pages. You might find that your drive names are longer than the IRIX example I've given, as is possible with Solaris, or you might find shorter names are the convention, as is the case with SunOS.

Planning Your Partition Sizes

Before you add your drive, you will want to plan your partition sizes. Does your operating system have any limits? I will be adding a 3GB drive to my system. The largest partition size that SunOS recognizes is 2GB, so I will have to have at least two partitions. You should also consider any limits that your backup device might produce. Your life will be easier if your partitions are not larger than what you can fit on a tape. For example, if I were adding my 3GB drive to an SGI, I could have one large partition if I wanted. But if I also had a tape drive that could only read DDS1 DAT tapes with their 2GB limit, I would probably prefer to keep my partition sizes at 2GB or less. This would enable me to easily back up one partition onto one tape.

Table 8.2 shows some common tape formats that might limit your partition sizes.

TABLE 8.2 A Selection of Common UNIX Tape Formats and Capacities

Tape	Format	Length	Estimated Capacity
DAT(4mm)	DDS1	90m	2.0GB
DAT(4mm)	DDS2	120m	4.0GB
Video8(8mm)	8200	106m	2.0GB
Video8(8mm)	8500	106m	4.0GB
QIC(1/4in)	6100	600ft	40MB
QIC(1/4in)	6150	620ft	150MB
QIC(1/4in)	2000	205ft	40MB
9-Track(1/2in)	6250	164m	40MB

What's the plan for your drive? I am planning to have a 1.2GB partition for software, a 1.0GB partition for user space, 100MB for swap, and 630MB for storage for making a backup to CD-ROM.

If you have a CD-ROM writer available or plan to get one, you might want to consider making a partition that you can use for storing data to be written to CD-ROM, too. CD-ROM backups of important software or configuration files are much more convenient and stable than magnetic tape backups.

A CD-ROM can hold up to 640MB, and by choosing a partition that will be approximately 630MB, I won't have to worry about accidentally going over the capacity of a CD-ROM.

Adding the Hard Disk Drive

I have chosen an ID, examined the drive-naming convention for my OS, and planned approximate partition sizes. I think I am finally ready to start adding a disk drive to the system.

Attaching the Drive

Before you can attach the drive to your system, you will have to cleanly shut down your machine and turn it off. For an external drive, set the ID number, hook the drive up to the computer with the appropriate cable, and don't forget that power cord. It's amazing how poorly the drive functions without power! Turn the machine back on. If you are adding an external drive, turn it on before turning the machine on. This will give the operating system the opportunity to detect the new device.

SCSI Termination   Make sure your SCSI chain is properly terminated. Perhaps more properly, start off trying to make it properly terminated, and if that doesn't work, play with things until it is. SCSI termination, although theoretically a well-defined procedure, frequently more closely resembles some form of black magic. Proper termination is for a SCSI chain to be terminated at each end of the chain and only at the ends. Beyond external terminator packs that can be plugged into your external drive's empty SCSI connector, many drives also carry termination hardware on the drive logic board. Some of these are simply resistor packs plugged into the drive logic board that you pull out with pliers to disable. Others are enabled and disabled by setting jumpers on the logic board.

I find it convenient to disable termination on all external devices and to terminate external chains with termination packs that plug into the last empty SCSI connector. This enables me to add a new drive without opening the case on any old equipment. I can simply move the terminator to the new drive, and I'm all set.

Again, SCSI termination can sometimes be rather like black magic. For some systems, hooking things up properly will result in odd behavior and failures. For these systems, the only way you will approach a stable system is with exhaustive rearrangement of parts and termination. The order of devices along the SCSI chain can make a difference, the IDs that each device has can make a difference, adding and removing termination at seemingly random locations along the chain can make a difference. If you run into one of these nightmarish SCSI chain problems, your only recourse is experimentation and a fair amount of colorful language.

Formatting and Partitioning the Drive

If your drive comes preformatted, you might only have to repartition the drive. If your drive comes from a cheaper vendor, you might have to format the drive as well as repartition it. For my machine, I will have to go through both steps.

Formatting the Drive

If you haven't turned your machine back on, do so now. Upon turning mine on, I see that the operating system has indeed detected the new device:

```
sd2 at esp0 target 2 lun 0
sd2:    corrupt label - wrong magic number
sd2: Vendor 'MICROP', product '1936-21MW1092407', 5906128 512 byte blocks
```

If your machine has not detected the new device, you might have to run a special reboot command. In Solaris,

```
reboot -- -r
```

will pass the -r option to the boot command and get the machine to look for all its devices. This special reboot command saves you the trouble of halting the machine and manually issuing boot -r.

> **Note**
>
> Some operating systems save time at startup or kernel resources in general by always "believing" the previous configuration and never checking for new devices. This eliminates quite a bit of time wasted probing various busses on the average startup and eliminates kernel resources wasted on devices that don't exist, but it means that your system won't see new hardware unless you tell it that the new hardware is there. If you're having trouble getting a device to be recognized by your system and you think you've followed all the man pages regarding your device, check to see if there are any notes about recognizing new devices. You might need to boot or reboot your machine with a special command to make it aware of the new device.

If you haven't already looked at the man pages for your operating system's format command, this is a good time to do so.

I am ready to begin, so I type format:

```
Barracuda# format
Searching for disks...done


AVAILABLE DISK SELECTIONS:
       0. sd0 at esp0 slave 24
          sd0: <Fujitsu M2624FA-1 cyl 1440 alt 2 hd 11 sec 64>
       1. sd2 at esp0 slave 16
          sd2: <drive type unknown>
Specify disk (enter its number):
```

Great! My latest drive appears as a choice. With your operating system, you might have to enter the device number as an argument to format. You might have to interactively provide SCSI controller number, ID number, and so on. Make sure that you have your drive information correct because one wrong move here sends you back to Day 3, "Setting Up a Machine: From the Box to the Desktop." No matter how you have to indicate your disk drive, make sure that you are indicating the new one, and not your system disk. Remember to read the man pages for your operating system carefully before you proceed. You probably don't literally have only one shot at getting this right, but you certainly can set yourself back a bit if you do it wrong. Treat each step in the format command as though you only have one chance to get it right, and you'll hopefully take the time to research it well enough that you can avoid any problems.

I enter the number for my new drive, and `format` shows me a list of available drive types. However, mine is not listed, so I have to pick `other` to create a new drive type:

```
Specify disk (enter its number): 1


AVAILABLE DRIVE TYPES:
        0. Quantum ProDrive 80S
        1. Quantum ProDrive 105S
        2. CDC Wren IV 94171-344
        3. SUN0104
        4. SUN0207
        5. SUN0320
        6. SUN0327
        7. SUN0424
        8. SUN0535
        9. SUN0669
        10. SUN1.0G
        11. SUN1.05
        12. SUN1.3G
        13. SUN2.1G
        14. Fujitsu M2624FA-1
        15. other
Specify disk type (enter its number): 15
```

Next, `format` becomes a bit tricky for me. The operating system that I'm using, SunOS, doesn't hold the system administrator's hand through the formatting process, and it doesn't provide highly useful diagnostic information about mistakes you might make. Other operating systems make some parts of this process much easier, but as I've stated before, it's always good to look at the worst case. SunOS requires a lot from the system administrator doing a format, and so if you understand how to deal with it, you will be ready for any less-demanding operating systems that you might encounter.

Before I continue, I will explain a bit about the magic that is about to happen. `format` will ask me for the number of data cylinders, alternative cylinders, heads, and data sectors/track. For a SCSI disk on a SunOS system, the specifics are not truly important, but `format` asks for the information anyway. If I have the actual information, I can go ahead and enter it. If I don't, I will have to give `format` guesses, and I'll have to keep guessing until the guesses work. I'll show you what kind of responses you'll get from `format` when things work and when they don't work.

> **Note**
>
> **Pin the tail on the physical parameters**   On many recent systems, this information is either calculated automatically by the OS, or it comes from a lengthy drive definition table that is supplied by the vendor. This means that your life is generally much easier than what is depicted here. When these

systems work, they work neatly and enable you to get on with more important things. On the other hand, you'll find that many of these new OS versions will refuse to work with a drive that's not defined in their drive-type table. If you have a drive that's not supported, it is simply not supported, and you have little in the way of options for making it work.

OS flavors that let you tweak the parameters by hand can be made to work with almost any device to at least some level of compatibility. You might not get optimum performance out of a device using made-up parameters, but you can make almost anything work.

The key to making all this work is the number of blocks for this device that appeared just as the machine booted. I already knew that I would need the number, so I have it safely written down. If I didn't, I could still quit `format` and run `dmesg` to get the number. Another look at the message that appeared at startup shows me that the new drive is 5,906,128 512-byte blocks in size:

```
sd2 at esp0 target 2 lun 0
sd2:    corrupt label - wrong magic number
sd2: Vendor 'MICROP', product '1936-21MW1092407', 5906128 512 byte blocks
```

A set of cylinders, heads, and data sectors/track numbers can be derived from this number. You can make many guesses for all three numbers. When I finish formatting my drive, I will show you another set of numbers that worked on the exact same drive type for someone who didn't notice that he had any vendor documentation. Because I have noticed that I have vendor documentation, I am not going to guess all three numbers, but I will give you an idea of how you might guess all three if you needed to.

To get started, the vendor indicated that there are 2,772 cylinders and 21 heads. However, the vendor has not provided a data-sectors per track figure, so I will be trying to determine this number. Also, when I enter the cylinders number, I have to remember that `format` wants to automatically set aside 2 cylinders as alternative cylinders, so the number of data cylinders I will enter is (*total number*) – (*alternate number*), which is 2,772–2, or 2,770. I will make a guess for data-sectors/track as follows:

```
Enter number of data cylinders: 2770
Enter number of alternate cylinders [2]:
Enter number of physical cylinders [2772]:
Enter number of heads: 21
Enter number of data sectors/track: 1000
'1000' is out of range.
```

`format` clearly does not like my guess of 1,000. I will enter a few more guesses:

```
Enter number of data sectors/track: 500
'500' is out of range.
```

```
Enter number of data sectors/track: 300
'300' is out of range.
```

These are no good either, so I decide to try 250:

```
Enter number of data sectors/track: 250
Enter rpm of drive [3600]:
```

Wow! format buys that value and has brought up the next question. Because I want to get as close as possible to the total number of blocks available to me, I need to have the sector count as close as possible to the real number of sectors. I will quit format and start it again to try to find the highest value for the data sectors/track that it considers acceptable:

```
Enter number of data cylinders: 2770
Enter number of alternate cylinders [2]:
Enter number of physical cylinders [2772]:
Enter number of heads: 21
Enter number of data sectors/track: 275
'275' is out of range.
Enter number of data sectors/track: 260
'260' is out of range.
Enter number of data sectors/track: 259
'259' is out of range.
Enter number of data sectors/track: 258
'258' is out of range.
Enter number of data sectors/track: 257
'257' is out of range.
Enter number of data sectors/track: 256
Enter rpm of drive [3600]:
```

256 data sectors/track looks good. At the rpm of drive prompt, I enter what comes with the documentation, although for SunOS, this value really doesn't matter because it doesn't really use the information for anything. Even though it doesn't use it, the highest value that SunOS's format accepts is 5,400.

Note

Drive RPM and interleave factor If your version of format asks for a drive rotation speed or an interleave factor, it's trying to gauge how to place the data on the drive to most efficiently access it during extended reads or writes. If your system actually makes use of this information for anything (SunOS doesn't), you can affect the performance of your system considerably by varying the interleave factor and/or supposed RPM information. If you have specific numbers that came with your drive or that your manufacturer suggests, use these. Otherwise, unless you are adventurous and feel like spending a lot of time experimenting, stick with your system's defaults.

8

```
Enter rpm of drive [3600]: 5400
Enter disk type name (remember quotes):
➥"Micropolis 2772CYL 21HD 2ALT 256SEC"
selecting sd2: <Micropolis 2772CYL 21HD 2ALT 256SEC>
No sense error during read
ASC: 0x0    ASCQ: 0x0
Apr  1 19:43:59 Barracuda vmunix: sd2c:   Error for command 'read(10)'
No sense error during read
ASC: 0x0    ASCQ: 0x0
[disk formatted, no defect list found]
No defined partition tables.
```

So much for what looks good! At last, the system finally spits out some information that is slightly more diagnostic:

```
format> Apr  1 19:43:59 Barracuda vmunix: sd2c:   Error Level: Fatal
Apr  1 19:43:59 Barracuda vmunix: sd2c:   Block 14896896,
➥Absolute Block: 5906128
Apr  1 19:43:59 Barracuda vmunix: sd2c:   Sense Key: Illegal Request
Apr  1 19:43:59 Barracuda vmunix: sd2c:   Vendor 'MICROP' error code: 0x21
Apr  1 19:43:59 Barracuda vmunix: sd2c:   Error for command 'read(10)'
Apr  1 19:43:59 Barracuda vmunix: sd2c:   Error Level: Fatal
Apr  1 19:43:59 Barracuda vmunix: sd2c:   Block 14897152,
➥Absolute Block: 5906128
Apr  1 19:43:59 Barracuda vmunix: sd2c:   Sense Key: Illegal Request
Apr  1 19:43:59 Barracuda vmunix: sd2c:   Vendor 'MICROP' error code: 0x21
```

From the additional comments, it becomes apparent that format has run into a problem trying to format the drive beyond its capacity.

I start over with a few more guesses. Without showing you all the details, I keep guessing lower sectors/track values until one actually works. Usually, it's best to do this by stepping over large ranges of numbers until one works and then working back up until the highest acceptable value is found. In my case, 200 doesn't work; 150 doesn't work. To my eventual surprise, 125 works! I decide not to play any more games with trying to find the highest instance when format doesn't complain. Instead, I decide to continue with the formatting, suspecting that it isn't quite optimal but that the annoyance of repeating this process over and over while trying to find the highest acceptable value between 125 and 150 sectors/track is not worth the potential 20 percent in disk space that I might gain.

```
format> format
Ready to format. Formatting cannot be interrupted
and takes 24 minutes (estimated). Continue?
Continue? yes
Beginning format. The current time is Thu Apr  1 20:17:45 1999

Formatting...
```

Recalling how the previous drive format estimated 8 minutes for my system disk and that it took more like 40 minutes, I decide to take a break for a bit. Several hours later, I see this:

```
Formatting...done
No sense error during write
ASC: 0x0   ASCQ: 0x0
Warning: error saving defect list.
No sense error during write
ASC: 0x0   ASCQ: 0x0
Warning: error saving defect list.
Apr  1 21:34:37 Barracuda vmunix: sd2c:   Error for command 'write(10)'
No sense error during write
ASC: 0x0   ASCQ: 0x0
Warning: error writing backup label.
No sense error during write
ASC: 0x0   ASCQ: 0x0
Warning: error writing backup label.
No sense error during write
ASC: 0x0   ASCQ: 0x0
Warning: error writing backup label.
No sense error during write
ASC: 0x0   ASCQ: 0x0
Warning: error writing backup label.
Apr  1 21:34:37 Barracuda vmunix: sd2c:   Error Level: Fatal
No sense error during write
ASC: 0x0   ASCQ: 0x0
Warning: error writing backup label.

Verifying media...
        pass 0 - pattern = 0xc6dec6de
Apr  1 21:34:37 Barracuda vmunix: sd2c:   Block 7273875,
➥Absolute Block: 5906128
Apr  1 21:34:37 Barracuda vmunix: sd2c:   Sense Key: Illegal Request
Apr  1 21:34:37 Barracuda vmunix: sd2c:   Vendor 'MICROP' error code: 0x21
Apr  1 21:34:37 Barracuda vmunix: sd2c:   Error for command 'write(10)'
Apr  1 21:34:37 Barracuda vmunix: sd2c:   Error Level: Fatal
```

format doesn't seem to be as pleased as it was at the beginning of this. I decide to quit the program. Having wasted a couple of hours with that guess, I finally decide to see if there is any pattern to the madness. At my 256 sectors/track guess, format first complains about block 14,896,896; at 200, 11,638,400; at 150, 8,728,650; at 125, 7,273,875. A quick check on the calculator reveals that the block number about which it initially complains divided by my sectors/track guess is always equal to 58,191 (except for one that comes out 58,192). Regardless of whether format intended to give me a pattern, I finally feel like I am getting somewhere! Where exactly this recurring 58,191 value came from, I'm not certain. With it, it looks like I can divide my known total number of blocks by 58,191 and get a corresponding value for sectors/track.

Dividing my known number of blocks, 5,906,128, by 58,191 gives me 101.49555, just over 101. It seems sort of odd that it doesn't come out to a whole number, but 102×58,191 gives me 5,935,482, slightly more than my number of blocks, and 101×58,191 gives 5,877,291, just less than the number of blocks. 101 looks like the best choice for my data sectors/track value.

To double-check that choice, I decide to do what I could have done to start off with, but didn't so that you could see how to do things when you don't have manufacturer numbers. Given that the total number of cylinders, heads, and data sectors/track factor to make the total number of available blocks, it seems reasonable that *(total # blocks)/(total # cylinders)/(total # heads)* should give me the data sectors/track. 5,906,128/2,772/21=101.4589, also suggesting that 101 should be a good guess.

So I try again, this time with 101 for my guess. It still takes me a few tries to even get that right because I am trying to include as much information about the configuration as I can when naming the disk type:

```
Enter number of data cylinders: 2770
Enter number of alternate cylinders [2]:
Enter number of physical cylinders [2772]:
Enter number of heads: 21
Enter number of data sectors/track: 101
Enter rpm of drive [3600]: 5400
Enter disk type name (remember quotes):
➥"Micr1936 3GB cy2770 al2 hd21 sec101"
selecting sd2: <Micr1936 3GB cy2770 al2 hd21 sec101>
[disk formatted, no defect list found]
No defined partition tables.
```

Notice that there's no defect list found. Although you might think this is a good thing—no defects—it's actually a bit problematic with some OS versions. Almost all drives have some number of defects, usually a small number (in the low hundreds on a 1GB drive), and some versions of `format` appear to have been written by a programmer who never thought that zero was a valid number of defects. If your `format` fails unexpectedly on a drive for no apparent reason, check whether there are any defects in the defect list, and if there aren't, add one by hand. I've only heard of one other person with this problem, but I've seen it myself with one of my drives, so it's become something I check out of habit.

I run `defect` to extract the manufacturer's defect list, and so there is a defect list on record for the `format` step:

```
format> defect


DEFECT MENU:
        restore  - set working list = current list
        original - extract manufacturer's list from disk
```

```
        extract  - extract working list from disk
        add      - add defects to working list
        delete   - delete a defect from working list
        print    - display working list
        dump     - dump working list to file
        load     - load working list from file
        commit   - set current list = working list
        create   - recreates maufacturers defect list on disk
        quit
defect> original
Extracting manufacturer's defect list...Extraction complete.
Working list updated, total of 94 defects.

defect> quit
Warning: working defect list modified; but not committed.
Do you wish to commit changes to current defect list? yes
Current Defect List updated, total of 94 defects.
Disk must be reformatted for changes to take effect.
```

If there had not been a manufacturer's defect list on the drive, I would have used the defect menu add command to force the addition of one supposedly bad block. I lose a small amount of drive space this way, but this trick has been known to fix problems with drives that won't format for unknown reasons.

Then, I run the actual format:

```
format> format
Ready to format. Formatting cannot be interrupted
and takes 24 minutes (estimated). Continue? yes
Beginning format. The current time is Thu Apr  1 22:17:34 1999

Formatting...done

Verifying media...
        pass 0 - pattern = 0xc6dec6de
    2769/20/59

        pass 1 - pattern = 0x6db6db6d
    2769/20/59

Total of 0 defective blocks repaired.
```

Between two and three hours later, I discover that format is successful this time! Then, I label the drive and quit format. To recap what figures work with my drive, I have a total of 5,906,128 blocks available. The vendor information indicates that there are 2,772 total cylinders and 21 heads total. 101 appears to be a good guess for data sectors/track. $(2,772) \times (21) \times (101) = 5879412$ blocks, which falls within the right range.

If you should have to work through an install where you have none of the physical parameters except for the number of blocks, you will have to make guesses at each of the stages of format, not just at the sectors/track step. Remember that *(tracks)×(heads)×*

8

(*sectors/track*)=(*number of blocks*). It might take some playing with the math to find values that work well, but it can be done. I find it is usually easiest to start by trying different numbers of heads until I find a value (or values) for which (*blocks*)/(*heads*) is (or is very close to) a whole number. From that value, I can work on guessing track and sector values that are factors of (*blocks*)/(*heads*). Because of some slight strangeness (described in the following text) in the way that many drives are made, it might not be possible to determine whole number values for each parameter that multiply out to the entire number of blocks. If you manage to get fairly close, you've done well enough.

Here's the data that was derived from a drive identical to mine by a person who didn't realize that he had the manufacturer's documentation and worked all the numbers out the hard way:

```
sd5: <Micropolis 1936 3GB 16HD 1475CYL 250 cyl 1470 alt 5 hd 16 sec 250>
```

From the naming he chose, you see that he picked 1,475 total cylinders, 16 total heads and 250 data sectors/track. What does that give you? (1,475)×(16)×(250)=5,900,000 blocks. Not bad! He got even more usable disk space without using any vendor-supplied data. He probably had a more miserable time doing it, though.

Tip

On the oddness of variable-sector formatting   You've probably noticed and started wondering by now how it's possible for a drive with geometry as I've drawn in the preceding text to have physical parameters that don't multiply out neatly to exactly the total number of blocks on the drive. Actually, it's because I told a little white lie when I described the physical structure of disk drives. The structure that I showed is sort of the classical way that disks are laid out, and there have been modern advances beyond this. The imbalance in numbers is due to the fact that as drives have gotten more sophisticated, manufacturers have actually moved to a mechanism where different areas of a surface have different numbers of sectors. Near the spindle, tracks are broken into fewer sectors than near the rim of a platter. This makes more efficient use of the space on the disk, but it also makes a mess of platter/head/track/sector calculations.

Older operating systems such as SunOS use the old definition for access, and you can simply fudge the numbers to get them to believe something reasonable is going on. Who cares what's physically happening on the drive so long as it's working and you've got access to almost all the space available. Newer operating systems keep tables of exact drive definitions for different drives and manufacturers and load the physical parameter data directly so that you don't have to know anything about the drive. There are advantages to each way of doing things because you can make almost any drive work with SunOS by doggedly fiddling until you have a working set of parameters. More modern operating systems work automatically with most drives, but they often can't be made to work at all with ones that aren't in their drive tables.

Hopefully, your drive does not come from a cheaper vendor, and you did not have to go through the formatting step of format. However, now you have seen an example of the formatting process, should you have to do it yourself one day.

Partitioning the Drive

Now, my drive has been formatted and is ready to be partitioned. If you did not have to format your drive because it came pre-formatted, you might just be starting your OS's version of format so that you can partition your drive. Proceed with caution, nonetheless. You do not want to partition the wrong drive. Read your man pages carefully, and make sure you know the drive-naming conventions for your operating system. Make sure you know pertinent SCSI controller information, drive ID, and so on. That being said, I'll start the partitioning process for my drive.

First, I decide that partition A will be my 1.2GB partition for software, B will be the swap, and C will be the entire drive.

 Note

> **The whole drive, in its partition**   When partitioning drives, it's customary to always have one partition that's the size of the entire drive. This gives you the capability, should you need it, to use something like a block copy command to duplicate an entire drive simply by block-copying the entire (whole drive) partition onto another physically identical drive.
>
> Different flavors of UNIX will have different partitions that are held to customarily be the "whole drive" partition.

Additionally, I find it convenient to have one partition approximately the same size as a CD-ROM so that I can use it to build convenient CD-ROM images for backup purposes. Partition D will be the CD backup partition at about 630MB, leaving partition E for the user space. You'll have a lot easier time justifying adding space for user directories than for system support space when you have to ask for money to upgrade later. My choices for the assignment of the B and C partitions are based on Sun convention.

Before I can do too much work, I have to recall that the block sizes in SunOS are in 512-byte blocks. To convert the MB figures into 512-byte block figures, I will have to multiply by 2,048 (*# of MB*×1,024=*# of 1KB blocks* and *# of 1KB blocks*×2=*# of 512-byte blocks*). Fortunately, newer operating systems have expanded their format's vocabulary to include KB and even MB. Figure 8.4 shows my drive partitioning worksheet, which gives a preview of what you will be doing in this section.

FIGURE 8.4

Partition choices for a new drive.

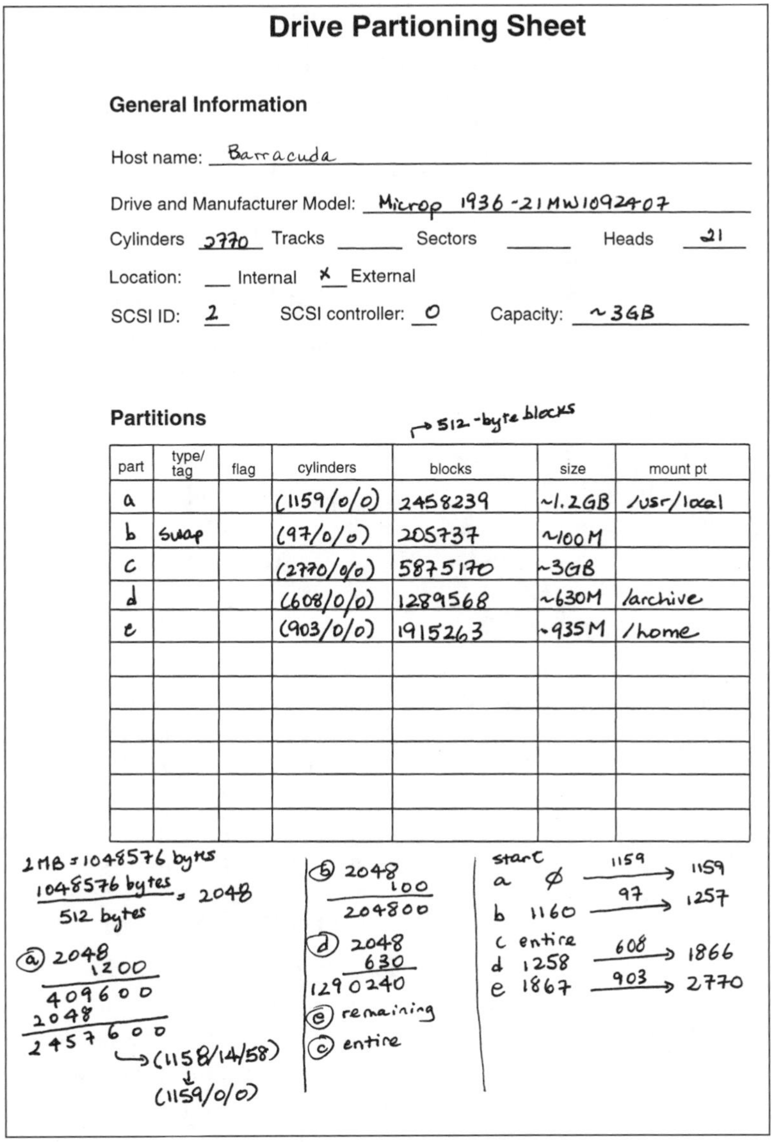

8

Drive Partioning Sheet

General Information

Host name: _Barracuda_

Drive and Manufacturer Model: _Microp 1936-21MW1092407_

Cylinders _2770_ Tracks _____ Sectors _____ Heads _21_

Location: ___ Internal _X_ External

SCSI ID: _2_ SCSI controller: _0_ Capacity: _~36B_

Partitions

→ 512-byte blocks

part	type/tag	flag	cylinders	blocks	size	mount pt
a			(1159/0/0)	2458239	~1.2GB	/usr/local
b	swap		(97/0/0)	205737	~100M	
c			(2770/0/0)	5875170	~3GB	
d			(608/0/0)	1289568	~630M	/archive
e			(903/0/0)	1915263	~935M	/home

```
1MB = 1048576 bytes
1048576 bytes
─────────── = 2048
512 bytes

a) 2048
  × 1200
  ─────
  409600
  2048
  ────────
  2457600
  → (1158/14/58)
        ↓
    (1159/0/0)

b) 2048
   × 100
   ──────
   204800

d) 2048
   × 630
   ──────
   1290240

e) remaining

c) entire

         start    1159
a   ∅  ─────→  1159
              97
b  1160 ─────→ 1257
c  entire
              608
d  1258 ─────→ 1866
              903
e  1867 ─────→ 2770
```

Now, begin the actual partition process:

```
format> partition

PARTITION MENU:
        a      - change 'a' partition
        b      - change 'b' partition
        c      - change 'c' partition
```

```
d       - change 'd' partition
e       - change 'e' partition
f       - change 'f' partition
g       - change 'g' partition
h       - change 'h' partition
select - select a predefined table
name   - name the current table
print  - display the current table
label  - write partition map and label to the disk
quit
```

As you can see, running partition brings up my partition menu. To set the size of partition A, all I have to do is enter a. Then, I have to provide a starting cylinder and a block size. I decide that my starting cylinder will be 0, and because it will be my software partition, my target block figure will be (1,200MB)(2,048)=2,457,600.

```
partition> a

        partition a - starting cyl     0, # blocks        0 (0/0/0)

Enter new starting cyl [0]:
Enter new # blocks [0, 0/0/0]: 2457600
```

To see the resulting partition, I enter print:

```
partition> print
Current partition table (unnamed):
        partition a - starting cyl     0, # blocks  2457600 (1158/14/68)
        partition b - starting cyl     0, # blocks        0 (0/0/0)
        partition c - starting cyl     0, # blocks        0 (0/0/0)
        partition d - starting cyl     0, # blocks        0 (0/0/0)
        partition e - starting cyl     0, # blocks        0 (0/0/0)
        partition f - starting cyl     0, # blocks        0 (0/0/0)
        partition g - starting cyl     0, # blocks        0 (0/0/0)
        partition h - starting cyl     0, # blocks        0 (0/0/0)
```

The description that you see for partition A is that it is 2,457,600 blocks in size, or (1,158/14/68) cylinders. That (1,158/14/68) cylinders value actually represents 1,158 complete cylinders, 14 additional sector segments of a cylinder, and 68 additional blocks. Remember, however, that to get the best performance out of my disk, I want my partition sizes to be whole numbers of cylinders because I want them to end on cylinder boundaries. This means that I would prefer my cylinder size to appear as either (1,158/0/0) or (1,159/0/0), which would be either exactly 1,158 cylinders or exactly 1,159 cylinders. Because it doesn't hurt to have a lot of space for software, I pick a size of 1,159. To do this, I enter a at the partition prompt and repeat the process. Then, I check the results with the print command:

```
partition> a

        partition a - starting cyl     0, # blocks  2457600 (1158/14/68)

Enter new starting cyl [0]:
Enter new # blocks [2457600, 1158/14/68]: 1159/0/0
partition> print
Current partition table (unnamed):
        partition a - starting cyl     0, # blocks  2458239 (1159/0/0)
        partition b - starting cyl     0, # blocks        0 (0/0/0)
        partition c - starting cyl     0, # blocks        0 (0/0/0)
        partition d - starting cyl     0, # blocks        0 (0/0/0)
        partition e - starting cyl     0, # blocks        0 (0/0/0)
        partition f - starting cyl     0, # blocks        0 (0/0/0)
        partition g - starting cyl     0, # blocks        0 (0/0/0)
        partition h - starting cyl     0, # blocks        0 (0/0/0)
```

Next, I will have to specify a starting cylinder for partition B, the swap partition. I could pick 1,159, but because I have run into problems in other operating systems when I go with a choice that starts the next partition on the cylinder that ended the previous partition, I decide to pick 1,160. This is likely to waste a cylinder, but it will definitely work and could potentially save me the trouble of having to repartition the drive. It's always difficult to determine whether an operating system has decided to consider the partition boundary information to mean "include up to and including cylinder 1,159" or "include up to, but stop before, 1,159." Even operating systems that claim to tell you which they use sometimes seem to be confused on the issue. Choosing 1,159 might cause overlapping partitions to be made, which would then cause a problem later when I try to mount filesystems on my partitions. Remember that drives are cheap, and your time probably isn't. To be safe, just skip a cylinder.

For partition B, I enter a starting cylinder, 1,160, and a target number of blocks, this time (100MB)(2,048), or 2,048,000 512-byte blocks. Then, I check how many cylinders 204,800 blocks comes out to be:

```
Enter new starting cyl [0]: 1160
Enter new # blocks [0, 0/0/0]: 204800
partition> print
Current partition table (unnamed):
        partition a - starting cyl     0, # blocks  2458239 (1159/0/0)
        partition b - starting cyl  1160, # blocks   204800 (96/11/73)
        partition c - starting cyl     0, # blocks        0 (0/0/0)
        partition d - starting cyl     0, # blocks        0 (0/0/0)
        partition e - starting cyl     0, # blocks        0 (0/0/0)
        partition f - starting cyl     0, # blocks        0 (0/0/0)
        partition g - starting cyl     0, # blocks        0 (0/0/0)
        partition h - starting cyl     0, # blocks        0 (0/0/0)
```

Again, my first try does not come out to a whole number of cylinders—(96/11/73).
For this partition, I could choose a size of 96 or 97 cylinders. Again, I opt for the larger
cylinder number, 97, as shown below. The target block sizes rarely result in whole
numbers of cylinders, but they provide a good starting point:

```
Enter new starting cyl [1160]:
Enter new # blocks [204800, 96/11/73]: 97/0/0
partition> print
Current partition table (unnamed):
        partition a - starting cyl       0, # blocks   2458239 (1159/0/0)
        partition b - starting cyl    1160, # blocks    205737 (97/0/0)
        partition c - starting cyl       0, # blocks         0 (0/0/0)
        partition d - starting cyl       0, # blocks         0 (0/0/0)
        partition e - starting cyl       0, # blocks         0 (0/0/0)
        partition f - starting cyl       0, # blocks         0 (0/0/0)
        partition g - starting cyl       0, # blocks         0 (0/0/0)
        partition h - starting cyl       0, # blocks         0 (0/0/0)
```

I have decided partition C will be the entire drive. Even though I have 2,772 cylinders
total, I've listed 2,770 as being the data cylinders with 2 alternative cylinders. Therefore,
I make partition C 2,770 cylinders.

When I start partition D, I again decide to skip another cylinder between B and D
so that I will have a convenient starting point. So my partition D will start at cylinder
1,159+1+97+1, or cylinder 1,258. I again play with my totals until all my partitions are
whole numbers of cylinders. Here's the final partition table:

```
partition> print
Current partition table (unnamed):
        partition a - starting cyl       0, # blocks   2458239 (1159/0/0)
        partition b - starting cyl    1160, # blocks    205737 (97/0/0)
        partition c - starting cyl       0, # blocks   5875170 (2770/0/0)
        partition d - starting cyl    1258, # blocks   1289568 (608/0/0)
        partition e - starting cyl    1867, # blocks   1915263 (903/0/0)
        partition f - starting cyl       0, # blocks         0 (0/0/0)
        partition g - starting cyl       0, # blocks         0 (0/0/0)
        partition h - starting cyl       0, # blocks         0 (0/0/0)
```

I then name the partition table, label it, and quit:

```
partition> name
Enter table name (remember quotes): "a1.2G b100M d629M e935M"

partition> label
Ready to label disk, continue? yes

partition> quit
```

For the partition name, I again try to include as much information as I can about the
partition sizes for easy future reference.

Making a New Filesystem

Now that the drive has been partitioned and formatted, it is ready for me to install
filesystems on the partitions. In SunOS and Solaris, I would use newfs, which calls mkfs.
In IRIX, I would use mkfs directly. Check the man pages to see what command your
operating system uses.

If you haven't already checked the naming conventions used by your operating system,
do so now. The names that you enter for newfs must be correct. Double-check what
you've typed before you press Return because you do not want to accidentally wipe
out your system.

Here's what I do to make a filesystem on partition A of my new drive:

```
Barracuda# newfs -v sd2a
mkfs  /dev/rsd2a 2458239 101 21 8192 1024 16 10 90 2048 t 0 0 8 7
Warning: 1 sector(s) in last cylinder unallocated
/dev/rsd2a:    2458238 sectors in 1159 cylinders of 21 tracks, 101 sectors
         1258.6MB in 73 cyl groups (16 c/g, 17.38MB/g, 7936 i/g)
super-block backups (for fsck -b #) at:
 32, 34080, 68128, 102176, 136224, 170272, 204320, 238368, 272416,
 306464, 340512, 374560, 408608, 442656, 476704, 510752, 544800, 578848,
 612896, 646944, 680992, 715040, 749088, 783136, 817184, 851232, 885280,
 919328, 953376, 987424, 1021472, 1055520, 1085984, 1120032, 1154080,
 1188128, 1222176, 1256224, 1290272, 1324320, 1358368, 1392416, 1426464,
 1494560, 1460512, 1528608, 1562656, 1596704, 1630752, 1664800, 1698848,
 1732896, 1766944, 1800992, 1835040, 1869088, 1903136, 1937184, 1971232,
 2005280, 2039328, 2073376, 2107424, 2141472, 2171936, 2205984, 2240032,
 2274080, 2308128, 2342176, 2376224, 2410272, 2444320,
```

With the -v option to newfs, newfs shows the results verbosely as the filesystem is made.
Particularly useful is what this option prints out about superblock information, which you
might find to be useful sometime in the future when the drive starts to die. If you can find
an option in your operating system's version of newfs that prints out the superblock information, make your filesystem with that option turned on. If your drive is malfunctioning
and you need to run the disk-repair utility fsck, you might need to provide information
such as where to find alternative superblocks. Keep printed copies of this information,
even though there's an option to read the superblock locations off the drive with software.
If it's not working, how likely is it that you'll be able to read it to get the information?

Mounting a New Filesystem

My new drive has been formatted and partitioned, and I have made filesystems for each
partition, except swap.

> **Tip**
>
> **No filesystems for swap**   Swap is read and written as a raw storage space for data. It doesn't need or want a filesystem. The OS won't be bothered if you do put a filesystem on swap. So, if you're ever in a bind and need some emergency disk space—like temporary space to finish a large compile—you can get away with trading your virtual memory for diskspace temporarily. Just remove the swap definition from your `fstab` and reboot the machine to get the OS to release the partition (most flavors of UNIX can't release swap space after they've claimed it without a reboot). `newfs` it, `mount` it, and work away. When you're ready to turn it back into swap, just add it back to your `fstab` as swap and reboot.

Now, I have to tell the system where to mount each new filesystem.

First, I will have to make the new mount points:

```
Barracuda# mkdir /new1
Barracuda# mkdir /archive
Barracuda# mkdir /home2
```

> **Note**
>
> **What's this about mount points**   Mount points are just directories. A partition looks like a big directory, right? To have that big directory show up in a specific location on the system, you simply specify a real directory that you want everything on the partition attached to. After you've done this, the OS will take care of making certain that everything behaves as though the space for that partition actually was at that directory.

Then, I have to mount each filesystem. To mount partition A, I type the following:

```
Barracuda# mount /dev/sd2a /new1
```

If I run `df`, I see that the new filesystem has indeed been mounted:

```
Barracuda# df
Filesystem           kbytes     used    avail capacity  Mounted on
/dev/sd0a             47575     6840    35978    16%     /
/dev/sd0g            311975   305664        0   109%     /usr
/dev/sd0h             18671       11    16793     0%     /home
/dev/sd2a           1155517        9  1039957     0%     /new1
```

Although it's all right to do this manually, you will not always want to manually mount your filesystems. To get your filesystems to mount at boot time, you must add entries to your `/etc/fstab`, which contains a listing of what filesystems to mount where.

8

Each line of data in the /etc/fstab contains this information:

```
filesystem    directory    type    options    frequency    pass
```

The following list describes what each item of information means:

- filesystem is the filesystem that is to be mounted.
- directory is the mount point.
- type is the type of filesystem. The main distinctions you are likely to find here are whether the filesystem is a type native to your operating system (such as 4.2 for SunOS, xfs or efs for IRIX, ufs for Solaris) or swap or nfs.
- options is a listing of any useful options to be included, such as rw to mount the filesystem as read/write.
- frequency is the interval between dumps.
- pass indicates whether fsck should check the partition, and on what pass. Filesystems with pass 0 would not be checked, and the root partition should be alone in pass 1.

Tip

Flavored fstabs Be sure to read the man pages for your operating system's explanation of the /etc/fstab file. Some things might be handled slightly differently. For example, fsck doesn't run on IRIX's xfs filesystems, and you have to specify fsck as an option for efs filesystems. Solaris does not even use an /etc/fstab. Instead, apparently just to be annoying, Solaris uses /etc/vfstab, and the table contains slightly different information.

To help you build your new /etc/fstab entries, it might be a good idea to take a look at the original /etc/fstab with your system:

```
Barracuda# more /etc/fstab
/dev/sd0a   /       4.2 rw 1 1
/dev/sd0b   swap    swap rw 0 0
/dev/sd0h   /home   4.2 rw 1 3
/dev/sd0g   /usr    4.2 rw 1 2
/dev/fd0    /pcfs   pcfs rw,noauto 0 0
```

In the one that comes with my machine, you see that filesystems are mounted read/write and have been assigned a pass during which they will undergo the fsck process. You also see that a floppy drive is listed, which never undergoes this process.

> **Note**
>
> **Fsck passes?**   You might be wondering what it means to be specifying `fsck` passes. Remember that `fsck` is the command that is used for disk checking and repair. You always want your disks to be checked at startup for potential problems, and this can take quite a while. What can you do? You can take advantage of the fact that the SCSI standard is capable of asking every drive to perform some specific task simultaneously. In the case of startup `fsck` passes, you can specify that `fsck` be run on certain partitions simultaneously, thereby cutting down on the overall startup time. Of course, it only helps to specify partitions that are on different drives to be checked simultaneously. As you see in the preceding code, the three different partitions on `/dev/sd0` here are being checked in three passes total.
>
> You will see that when another drive is added, I can specify that its three data partitions also be checked by `fsck` in the same three passes. Both drives will be checked simultaneously this way.
>
> Swap, not having a filesystem, never undergoes an `fsck` pass.

I am next going to add entries for my new swap and my new filesystems, and I will assign `fsck` pass numbers to the filesystems.

Moving Data

If you are adding a disk drive because you had run out of space somewhere, you will next want to move your existing data to your new partition. If you were adding a disk drive just to have more space, you might not have any data to move yet.

Use the situation where I have run out of room on my original drive because of everything I tried to store in `/usr/local`. I plan to move all my data from `/usr/local` to my new partition, `/new1`. I will remove unnecessary material from my original `/usr/local` and mount the new partition over the original `/usr/local` partition. I could remove my original `/usr/local` entirely, but I will keep it as a minimal backup, just in case. If my new drive should happen to malfunction before my system disk, I will still have a minimal amount of software I can work with in my original `/usr/local`.

First, I have to move my data to my new partition. I am choosing to use `tar`, but I could also use a combination of `dump` and `restore`. From my original `/usr/local`, I do this:

```
Barracuda# tar -cf - . ¦ ( cd /new1; tar -xf - )
```

The `tar` command here simply tars everything in the current directory, and instead of putting it in a file, puts it on `stdout`. The `stdout` socket is piped into a subshell in which I `cd` to my destination directory and then re-use `tar` to extract everything that's coming into the shell on the pipe.

This is a very convenient way for root to move large quantities of data around the system without any changes in ownership or modification date.

A quick ls of my new partition, /new1, compared with an ls of the original /usr/local reveals that the overall contents of both directories look the same. The new partition has a lost+found directory that the original /usr/local does not have, but this is because you are looking at the top level of the new partition:

```
Barracuda# ls /new1
bin                     lib                     source
include                 lost+found              sparc-sun-sunos4.1.4
info                    man
Barracuda# ls /usr/local
bin                     lib                     sparc-sun-sunos4.1.4
include                 man
info                    source
```

As another check, I also verify how much space each directory takes up, just to make sure nothing is wrong:

```
Barracuda# cd /usr/local
Barracuda# du -s *
1368     bin
1        include
1910     info
1        lib
221      man
133244   source
4        sparc-sun-sunos4.1.4

Barracuda# cd /new1
Barracuda# du -s *
1368     bin
1        include
1910     info
1        lib
8        lost+found
221      man
133240   source
4        sparc-sun-sunos4.1.4
```

This check reveals that the contents of the new directory take up slightly less space than the original directory does. Specifically, /new1/source takes up 133,240KB, whereas the original, /usr/local/source, occupies 133,244KB. Although this might seem odd, it is not unusual to see slight differences in reported sizes across different disks. I can be reasonably certain that my tar has been successful.

Before I delete some of my original /usr/local, I decide to make certain that the new partition will mount as I expect it to. To do this, I first make a garbage directory in /new1

called `fooble`. This is going to be a simple way to track around which directory I'm really looking at because they look almost identical at this point. Although /new1 already has
a `lost+found` directory that /usr/local doesn't have, `fooble` is a bit more noticeable at
a quick glance. Then, I double-check the contents of both directories:

```
Barracuda# ls /new1
bin                     info                    man
fooble                  lib                     source
include                 lost+found              sparc-sun-sunos4.1.4

Barracuda# ls /usr/local
bin                     lib                     sparc-sun-sunos4.1.4
include                 man
info                    source
```

Yes, /new1 has a directory `fooble`, and /usr/local does not.

Then, I run `df` to double-check which partition is mounted as /new1:

```
Barracuda# df
Filesystem            kbytes    used    avail capacity  Mounted on
/dev/sd0a              47575    6720    36098    16%    /
/dev/sd0g             311975  305664        0   109%    /usr
/dev/sd0h              18671      11    16793     0%    /home
/dev/sd2d             606463       9   545808     0%    /archive
/dev/sd2e             900158    1153   808990     0%    /home2
/dev/sd2a            1155517  136755   903211    13%    /new1
```

Now, I've got the information I need to mount /new1 as /usr/local. Before I unmount
/new1 and mount it as /usr/local, I should first make certain that I am not in /new1, or
the `umount` command will fail and complain that the filesystem is busy:

```
Barracuda# pwd
/
Barracuda# umount /new1
Barracuda# mount /dev/sd2a /usr/local
```

A quick `ls` shows success:

```
Barracuda# ls /usr/local
bin                     info                    man
fooble                  lib                     source
include                 lost+found              sparc-sun-sunos4.1.4
```

/usr/local has a `fooble` directory! I'm ready to do it for real now. I will unmount
this /usr/local partition so that I can delete some of the contents of the original
/usr/local. Note that when I delete my source directory, I decide to use `\rm -rf`.
Recall that by using `\rm`, I am forcing `rm` to not adhere to any aliases that might be in
place, which in this case means `rm -i`, the interactive mode that asks before deleting.

8

Remember to not use \rm -rf unless you are absolutely positive of your location. I will mount the new partition as /usr/local again:

> **Note**
>
> **Wait a minute! What just happened there?**   You remember that partitions mount at mount points and that mount points are directories. Nothing in that description says that the directory used as a mount point has to be empty! It's a bit of a poor use of space usually if a directory used as a mount point contains data because data in the directory will never be available while something is mounted on the directory containing it. In this case, however, I'm going to use my original /usr/local as an emergency backup, so if my new /usr/local ever fails, I still have some useful software in /usr/local.

```
Barracuda# umount /usr/local
Barracuda# df
Filesystem            kbytes    used    avail capacity  Mounted on
/dev/sd0a              47575    6720    36098    16%     /
/dev/sd0g             311975  305664       0   109%     /usr
/dev/sd0h              18671      11    16793     0%     /home
/dev/sd2d             606463       9   545808     0%     /archive
/dev/sd2e             900158    1153   808990     0%     /home2
Barracuda# cd /usr/local
Barracuda# ls
bin                   lib                      sparc-sun-sunos4.1.4
include               man
info                  source
Barracuda# \rm -rf source
Barracuda# ls
bin                   info                     man
include               lib                      sparc-sun-sunos4.1.4


Barracuda# mount /dev/sd2a /usr/local

Barracuda# ls /usr/local
bin                   info                     man
fooble                lib                      source
include               lost+found               sparc-sun-sunos4.1.4
```

Another look at the results of df reveals that everything has gone well. Because /usr/local used to be a directory under /usr, when I deleted the source directory out of it, I freed up space in the partition that /usr is mounted on. /usr is down to 61 percent in use, rather than the previous 109 percent! I've also got lots of new, available space in /usr/local:

```
Barracuda# df
Filesystem            kbytes    used    avail capacity  Mounted on
/dev/sd0a              47575    6720    36098    16%     /
```

```
/dev/sd0g          311975  172420  108358  61%  /usr
/dev/sd0h           18671      11   16793   0%  /home
/dev/sd2d          606463       9  545808   0%  /archive
/dev/sd2e          900158    1153  808990   0%  /home2
/dev/sd2a         1155517  136755  903211  13%  /usr/local
```

Because I would like to have this partition mount at boot time, I have to fix my /etc/fstab to reflect /usr/local as the mount point for /dev/sd2a rather than /new1:

```
Barracuda# more /etc/fstab
/dev/sd0a   /              4.2 rw 1 1
/dev/sd0b   swap          swap rw 0 0
/dev/sd0h   /home          4.2 rw 1 3
/dev/sd0g   /usr           4.2 rw 1 2
/dev/sd2a   /usr/local        4.2 rw 1 4
/dev/sd2b   swap          swap rw 0 0
/dev/sd2d   /archive       4.2 rw 1 2
/dev/sd2e   /home2         4.2 rw 1 3
/dev/fd0    /pcfs   pcfs rw,noauto 0 0
```

To enable swap now, I issue the swapon command:

```
Barracuda# swapon -a
Adding /dev/sd2b as swap device
```

If you made a swap partition on your new drive and your system does not have swapon, you might try swap.

Note

> **Temporary storage**   You can add all defined swap space with the swapon -a command or specific swap space with the swapon <device> command. Adding swap by the swapon <device> command adds it only for the duration of this boot. As you will note that I have done, if you want your additional swap to come back the next time you reboot, add the definition for your swap partition to your fstab. swapon -a gets its definition of all swap space from the fstab information, so if this command adds your new swap, things will also work the next time you reboot.

With the addition of my new drive, you might be wondering if there is really any point to my small /home partition, which is less than 20MB in size. What would any user store there? Contrary to what you might believe, this small partition is actually ideal for storing emergency copies of certain commands and the kernel.

I will store the emergency backups on the partition currently mounted as /home. Then, I will umount it and remove the entry from the fstab. If the machine is ever compromised, I will have these hidden backups conveniently available. Of course, this plan does rely on my original mount still being available and on my remembering where I put things.

To figure out where in my path the commands are stored, I run which on each command. Here's what it looks like with the ls command:

```
Barracuda# which ls
/bin/ls
```

So here, I would use the command cp /bin/ls /home to copy the executable command ls to my small /home partition. After copying emergency commands to /home, I double-check that the permissions of the copies agree with the original permissions. Here is my current backup collection:

```
Barracuda# ls -l /home
total 2487
drwxr-sr-x  2 root           512 Mar 18 04:56 Barracuda
-rwxr-xr-x  1 root          7152 Apr  6 00:16 cp
-rwxr-xr-x  1 root         11264 Apr  6 00:26 dd
-rwsr-sr-x  1 root         57344 Apr  6 00:19 dump
-rwxr-xr-x  3 root         49152 Apr  6 00:26 ed
-rwxr-xr-x  1 root        172900 Apr  6 00:23 format
-rwxr-xr-x  1 root        205199 Apr  6 00:19 fsck
-rwxr-xr-x  1 root        180224 Apr  6 00:24 ifconfig
drwxr-xr-x  2 root          8192 Mar 18 04:53 lost+found
-rwxr-xr-x  1 root         13352 Apr  6 00:16 ls
-rwxr-xr-x  1 root        172032 Apr  6 00:19 mount
-rwxr-xr-x  1 root         24784 Apr  6 00:16 mv
-rwxr-sr-x  1 root         40016 Apr  6 00:23 ps
-rwxr-x---  1 root        147456 Apr  6 00:19 restore
-rwsr-xr-x  1 root          6944 Apr  6 00:25 rsh
-rwxr-xr-x  1 root        147456 Apr  6 00:16 tar
-rwxr-xr-x  1 root         16384 Apr  6 00:19 umount
-rwxr-xr-x  7 root        204800 Apr  6 00:25 vi
-rwxr-xr-x  1 root       1466167 Apr  6 00:25 vmunix
```

I would include top if I had it, but I don't have it yet because it does not come as a part of the SunOS operating system. If you should decide to take this route to making yourself a backup of some of your software, feel free to add whatever you think might be important. In any case, I can always add to the collection as I discover more commands I might need. Now, I'm ready to umount the current /home:

```
Barracuda# umount /home
```

I'll leave this partition unmounted and just hanging around on the disk. This way, if I ever experience a break-in or have some reason to think that some of my more important commands or the kernel have been tampered with, I have a hidden backup of them that I can simply mount and use to make repairs.

The final change I will make is with my new /home2 partition. Because I no longer want people to know about my original /home partition anymore, I think I will mount the current /home2 as /home. I will also have to make a note on my original drive partitioning sheet from Day 3 that my /dev/sd0h will no longer be mounted as /home. I will have to adjust the final mount points for today's drive-partitioning sheet.

Speaking of final, here's how my setup should look for a while:

```
Barracuda# more /etc/fstab
/dev/sd0a  /              4.2 rw 1 1
/dev/sd0b  swap         swap rw 0 0
/dev/sd0g  /usr           4.2 rw 1 2
/dev/sd2a  /usr/local       4.2 rw 1 4
/dev/sd2b  swap         swap rw 0 0
/dev/sd2d  /archive     4.2 rw 1 2
/dev/sd2e  /home        4.2 rw 1 3
/dev/fd0   /pcfs  pcfs rw,noauto 0 0

Barracuda# df
Filesystem            kbytes    used    avail capacity  Mounted on
/dev/sd0a             47575    6722    36096    16%     /
/dev/sd0g            311975  172420   108358    61%     /usr
/dev/sd2d            606463       9   545808     0%     /archive
/dev/sd2a           1155517  136755   903211    13%     /usr/local
/dev/sd2e            900158    1153   808990     0%     /home
```

Getting Back to Work—Recovering a Partial Install

For those following along a little too closely, here's all you would now need to do to finish that gcc install that I aborted due to lack of disk space on Day 7, "The Most Important Accessory: The C Compiler gcc."

At this point, you've added a new drive, put everything back where, from the point of view of the user, it always was, and have the system running again. Thanks to UNIX's power and convenience, from the point of view of the compiler, and the partially compiled and installed software, everything really is back to exactly where it previously was.

The tar command I used to move files from one drive to the other maintained not only the ownership of the files, but also all the correct creation and modification date information. Because of this, the make program will be none the wiser about the fact that everything is all on a completely different drive, and everything will work just as though you hadn't taken a break to install a drive in the middle.

That means that to recover from the somewhat hair-raising problem of running out of space in the middle of the install, all you have to do is keep going where you left off!

You will in general find it to be the case that UNIX's powers of abstraction cause things like this to work surprisingly well and surprisingly frequently. If you are ever stuck halfway done with an install and have to rearrange things to find room to finish, you should be able to pick up where you left off easily.

Adding CD-ROM and Tape Drives

In addition to an extra disk drive, you will find that a CD-ROM drive will be helpful because most commercial software is distributed on CD-ROM. If you hope to back up your system, you will also want to add a tape drive to your setup.

Adding a CD-ROM Drive

If your system didn't come with a CD-ROM drive, you might have already had to add a CD-ROM drive to your system. If someone added a loaner CD-ROM drive for you and took his back, you might have to add one now.

The procedure for adding a CD-ROM drive begins like the one for adding a disk drive. Cleanly shut down the system and turn off the power. If you added an external drive, remember to power it down, too. Assign an ID number to your CD-ROM drive (for SunOS, SCSI ID 6 should be used—other operating systems aren't as picky), attach it to the computer with the appropriate cable, provide appropriate termination, attach the power cord, and plug it in. Turn on any external devices and then your machine. The CD-ROM drive is likely available in some way now. If you are running Solaris, you will likely have to run reboot -- -r.

On my machine, this comment appears at startup:

```
sr0 at esp0 target 6 lun 0
```

On an SGI, you can run hinv to see if the CD-ROM drive has been recognized.

To test if your CD-ROM drive works, put in a CD (ISO 9660 format, please) and try to list the contents.

In SunOS, you mount -t hsfs /dev/sr0 /mnt and then ls /mnt, and you should see the contents of the drive.

In IRIX, because it will mount (or attempt to mount, presuming your object server and directory server processes haven't succumbed to one of the long-standing IRIX bugs and gone away) the CD automatically, you type ls /CDROM.

In Solaris, you use ls /cdrom/cdrom0, provided that vold is running, which it is by default. If it isn't, you'll have to add the cdrom line definition to your /etc/vfstab as specified in the mount man page for your version of Solaris and mount the drive by hand.

To eject the CD-ROM in SunOS you use eject cdrom, but to be safe, it would be a good idea to umount the directory on which you mounted it first; in IRIX, eject /CDROM; in Solaris, eject cdrom, provided again that vold is running—otherwise, you'll need to manually umount here as well.

Adding a Tape Drive

When you add your tape drive, again follow the same basic procedures as you would for any other device. As with adding any device, make sure you have the cables you need.

It took me a while to get the appropriate cables, but when I did, I shut everything down, connected the tape drive, and turned everything back on. At startup, this comment now appears:

```
st0: <Archive Python 4mm Helical Scan>
```

Depending on your operating system, you might not get such instant feedback. Running dmesg on my Solaris machine provides no indication of the presence of a tape drive, but one with SCSI ID 4 is indeed attached.

If you do not find any useful comments anywhere on your system to indicate whether you were successful in adding your tape drive, try to talk to the tape drive itself instead. You will find mt to be the most useful way to communicate with the tape drive, and these will probably be the best general options to start off with:

- mt status will give the status of your tape.
- mt rewind rewinds your tape.
- mt offline takes the tape offline so you can eject it.

Although dmesg does not obviously indicate the presence of a tape drive on my Solaris machine, I can communicate with it using mt. If I put a tape in the drive but haven't actually loaded it, or even if I haven't put a tape in the drive at all, here is the response I get:

```
Rosalyn joray 275 > mt status
/dev/rmt/0: no tape loaded or drive offline
```

If I've just loaded a tape, I get this response instead:

```
Rosalyn joray 277 > mt status
SCSI tape drive:
    sense key(0x6)= Unit Attention    residual= 0    retries= 0
    file no= 0    block no= 0
```

After finishing a set of backups, I get this:

```
Rosalyn joray 284 > mt status
SCSI tape drive:
    sense key(0x0)= No Additional Sense    residual= 0    retries= 0
    file no= 11    block no= 0
```

In this preceding listing, you can see that the tape drive is positioned at the eleventh file on this tape.

When you use the mt command to access tapes on your system, you should see similar, but probably not quite identical information. For example, some tape drives give more, and some less, diagnostic information when you ask them for their status. The basic information however should be the same—whether there is a tape, what file the drive is on, and what tape block the tape is at.

One thing that you should be aware of is that the mt syntax shown will work only with a tape at the system's default SCSI ID. If you need to access a tape at a different SCSI ID, you will need to use mt -f <devicename>, where <devicename> is the /dev/somedevice name of your tape drive. See the man pages for mt for your operating system's specific requirements for naming and any alternative naming conventions that you might be able to use.

Note

Tape Drive Silliness   You'll learn how to actually make and restore backups on Day 13, "Saving Your World: Making Backups to Tape." For the time being, the one thing you'll need to know or look up somewhere about your tape drive and system is how to address the tape as a "no rewind" device.

Tape drive interfaces almost universally have the capability to be addressed in a mode that rewinds the tape automatically after every command and in a mode that doesn't. The mode that does this tends to be almost completely useless. Who wants a tape drive that, when you try to back up 10 files to it, rewinds the tape between each one so that you end up writing over every backup with the next one? Naming conventions for the rewind versus the no-rewind interfaces vary considerably. You might expect rewind interfaces to have an r in the name and no-rewind interfaces to have an n, or perhaps nr.

For example, with SunOS I actually have a choice of addressing my tape drive as st0, which is an indeterminate name, rst0, which is a rewind version of the driver, and nrst0, which is the no-rewind version.

You can make certain that you are using the no-rewind version of the device by checking the status of the drive with the mt status command. If you perform some action that advances the tape, run mt status and find that the file no value (file number value) is greater than zero, and then run mt status and find that the file no value has reset to zero, you're using the rewind version, and the drive dutifully rewound after telling you the status.

Some operating systems have other flags built in to the names of the tape devices as well. IRIX, for example, provides interfaces that perform byte-swapping operations on the data from the tape as it is read, in an attempt to make IRIX compatible with tape formats from other UNIX vendors.

Adding a Printer

Adding a printer to your setup is most unlike anything else you've done so far. As a matter of fact, it's so unlike anything that you'd ever actually want to do voluntarily that I'd almost suggest that attempting to hammer nails into your skull would be a more useful and enjoyable experience. UNIX printing is a nightmare, and it's liable to completely consume the unwary. Entire books could be written on how to configure one particular printer for one particular operating system, and even then, the likelihood that it would work robustly and consistently is minimal.

Instead of confusing the issue further by attempting to adequately cover the range of the topic here, I'm going to outline some of the strengths and weaknesses of the various printing schemes, explain some of the commands, and recommend a possible course of action.

Two Printing Flavors: BSD and AT&T/System V

Just as there are two major variations in the flavors of UNIX available, there are two major variations in the printing software. You might expect that System V systems come with System V printing and BSD systems come with BSD printing, but this is, due to the nature of UNIX printing, not quite the case.

BSD printing, using the `lpd`, `lpr`, `lpq` system of commands, is clunky, difficult to configure, and cryptic. Error messages are terse and not particularly meaningful. It frequently requires the installation of special-purpose filters to print new data types. The configuration files require that you actually know particulars about your printer, such as the following: what hexadecimal character to send to it to put it in graphics rather than character mode; how long it takes the print head to return after printing a line of text; and whether to translate <carriage-return> to <carriage-return><linefeed>, <linefeed>, or what.

System V printing, using the `lpsched`, `lp`, `lpstat` system of commands, is polished, user-friendly, and in a heterogeneous environment, almost completely broken. Error messages are verbose, friendly, and frequently wrong. There is no way to install special-purpose filters to print new data types, even though the system requires them. The configuration files are unreadable and built entirely by pieces of software that don't have the options that your printer needs.

> **Note**
>
> **System V versus BSD printing**   To be entirely fair, I should point out that System V printing works fairly well for local printers for which the OS has a built-in description. The problems with it come in the fact that it, like much System V software, attempts to be too user-friendly and puts software

> between the administrator and the configuration files. Because the configuration files usually aren't written in human-readable form, if the configuration software doesn't know about the particular model of printer you have, there's no way for you to enter the correct data and no way for you to make the system work.
>
> BSD printing, on the other hand, requires that you do absolutely everything by hand, but it's possible to configure almost any printer to work with almost any BSD system with sufficient patience and enough time. The problems that this system has are in the difficulty in configuration and in the poor reporting of error information, making diagnosing problems quite difficult.

Because of the clunky nature of BSD printing configuration, many vendors have tried to put a more System V–type face on their BSD printing software. Because of the broken nature of System V printing, many System V vendors have provided BSD printing capabilities as an alternative to their System V native solutions.

Unfortunately, although these both seem like reasonable responses to the problem, they don't solve the underlying difficulties. The System V faces on BSD printing systems don't make fixing configuration errors any easier. In addition, few of the System V user-friendly features translate well to the BSD model, so functions such as printer load balancing and printer classes (providing "print to any available color printer" under System V) don't work. In the other camp, many of the System V vendors, secure in the knowledge that System V is really the one true way, have tried to make BSD capabilities available through hacks into the pre-existing System V printing software. This doesn't work for quite obvious reasons.

BSD Printing

BSD printing works through the printer daemon lpd. The lpd daemon handles receiving requests for printing services and routing them off to the appropriate device. The lpd daemon is completely configured by the file /etc/printcap, which contains a cryptic but complete description of every printer known to the system. For every printer, it contains every piece of data necessary to access that printer. A typical /etc/printcap file might be as follows:

```
soyokaze joray 202> more /etc/printcap

# Soyokaze printcap 950214
0¦lp¦IMG¦imagewriter¦ImageWriter II:\
        :lp=/dev/ttya:sd=/var/spool/lpd:br#9600:fs#06020:fc#0300:\
        :sh:lf=/var/adm/PRINTLOG:
```

```
1¦lp1¦jiji¦PostScript LaserWriter:\
        :lp=/dev/null:lf=/var/adm/lpd-errs:pw#80:hl:rs:\
        :of=/usr/local/atalk/etc/ofpap:\
        :mx#0:\
        :if=/usr/local/atalk/etc/ifpap:\
2¦lp2¦lw360¦Apple Laserwriter Select 360¦PostScript LaserWriter:\
        :lp=/dev/null:lf=/var/adm/lpd-errs:pw#80:hl:rs:\
        :rm=hobbes.biosci.ohio-state.edu:\
        :mx#0:\
        :sd=/var/spool/bounce:
Pretty2¦lpc¦HP Deskjet via lpr:\
        :lp=/dev/null:lf=/var/adm/lpd-errs:pw#80:hl:rs:\
        :rm=halo.biosci.ohio-state.edu:\
        :mx#0:\
        :rp=Pretty2:\
        :sd=/var/spool/bounce:
```

This system has four printers configured on it, three remote printers and a local printer. The remote printers require much more simple configuration information because almost all the lpd daemon needs to know about them is where to send the data to get it printed. The local printer, on the other hand, which is connected to one of the serial ports on this machine, is configured with a cryptic collection of data. Included is a collection of hints about how it's connected. Because it's used only for text, it has no output filters, but the definition could include information on software to make it print each of many specific types of data.

Analyzing this printcap listing slightly, you can see the following:

- Each of the printers can be referred to by several names. Pretty2 and lpc are the same printer, for example. The system administrator for this system has even included rather verbose names for each printer, probably more as a description for his own use than for users to use at the command line.

- Every line after a printer definition, until the last line before the next printer definition, is trailed by a \ character. This is the continuation character for UNIX and indicates that the next line is a continuation of this one.

- Fields are all separated by colons.

Additionally, you will notice that two of the remote printers have rm: fields. These specify the remote machine. Only one of them has an rp: field, however. This is because lw360 is the only printer available on the remote machine hobbes, so it doesn't need to specify a printer destination there. On halo there are actually multiple printers, so in addition to specifying halo.biosci.ohio-state.edu for the rm: field for Pretty2, the file must also specify which printer to use (coincidentally also named Pretty2 on halo).

8

The definition for the printer jiji doesn't include an rm: definition, even though it's not a local printer to this machine. How can this be? jiji is actually a printer hooked up to a Macintosh in another part of the building. The printcap definition for jiji includes an of: field, which says, "Take any data that the user says to send to this printer, and send it to this output-filter". The output-filter here happens to be a program that translates print requests into the AppleTalk printer language and sends them off to their appropriate destination.

The scariest definition by far is the one for the Imagewriter. This printer is an old-fashioned serial dot-matrix printer hooked up to serial port /dev/ttya. The rest of the definition for this printer specifies things like the baud rate at which it communicates and other interface-configuration parameters. Although you might not expect it, with only a few (grueling, but few) changes to this printer definition, I could make this old dot-matrix printer print PostScript. By using a publicly available PostScript interpreter such as ghostscript and combining this with an appropriate "of:" definition for this printer, I could use it as a (very slow) PostScript printer. BSD printing is certainly clunky, but if you're willing to slog through the details, it's an amazingly tweakable system.

The most common entries you see used in this /etc/printcap file are detailed here in Table 8.3, but don't imagine that this is a complete listing. If you're trying to configure a BSD printer, you'll need your man pages, your printer's technical documentation, and a lot of patience and luck. Table 8.3 shows you a selection of some of the most frequently encountered printcap options. Use your own man pages to find out what your machine supports because UNIX flavors that implement BSD printing as an interface into a System V printing system generally lack the more useful options here.

TABLE 8.3 Typical BSD *PRINTCAP* Variables

Variable Name	Use of Data
af	Accounting file.
br	Set the baud rate for tty printers.
ff	String to send to generate a form-feed.
fo	Send a form-feed at the beginning of every job.
fs	Set interface-specific flag bits (see your man pages).
hl	Print the job-identification banner page last.
if	Name of the input filter program through which to preprocess all data.
of	Name of the output filter through which to send otherwise uncategorized data.

continues

TABLE 8.3 continued

Variable Name	Use of Data
lf	Name of the log file. This file must exist on some systems, so touch it before trying to use it.
mx	Maximum file size; 0 = unlimited.
pl	Length of page in lines.
pw	Width of page in characters.
px	Width of page in pixels.
py	Length of page in pixels.
rm	Name of machine with remote printer.
rp	Name of remote printer on remote machine.
rs	Restrict remote printing to users with local accounts.
sc	Refuse to print more than one copy.
sd	Spool directory.
sf	Suppress form-feeds.
sh	Suppress printing of job-identification banner page.

When you've got printing working on a BSD system, lpr -P<printername> <filename> will get your file printed on printer <printername>. lpq -P<printername> will check the status of the print queue for <printername>, and lprm -P<printername> <job number> will delete job <job number> from the print queue on printer <printername>.

Note

> **More rootly powers** You alone as root have the ability to delete a printer job that doesn't belong to you. If a user accidentally sends a huge print job and doesn't realize that the Web page she just selected Print on will take seven hours to print, your other users are going to expect you to step in and cancel the job. Keep an eye on the print queue and if you see jobs start to stack up, check to see if either something is wrong or if an oversized or slow job is holding everything up. If it's not an important print job (you'll find these are quite easy to tell, usually), kill it off so that others can use the printer.

BSD Printing the Easy Way

If you're using a BSD printing environment, consider investing in a printer that comes with the LPD facility built in. Many network printers support lpd printing directly. All

8

that is necessary to make them work from a BSD printing environment is to put the printer on the network and specify its IP address in the `remote printer` description field in `/etc/printcap`. This solution can save you considerable time and headaches.

System V Printing

System V printing works through the magic of the `lpsched` daemon, which, depending on implementation, might use other daemons to control specific printers. I can't show you a configuration file for a System V printer because these are typically not humanly readable. The configuration files are created (usually) by a program named `lpadmin`. If you were to look at the manual page for `lpadmin`, you would see that it wants you to issue the command as `lpadmin`, with arguments (among others) of `-p<printername> -m<model>`. The `lpadmin` program then creates the appropriate configuration files for a new printer named `<printername>` of whatever `<model>` you specified. What if you don't know what model you should call your printer? Well, you can look in `/usr/spool/lp/model` for hints, but don't count on finding your printer there. If you can't guess a model to make `lpadmin` and your printer happy, with System V printing, you're out of luck.

If you should happen to be lucky enough to get System V printing working, you enable printing by starting the `lpsched` daemon, and then using the `enable <printername>`. Jobs are sent to the printer with `lp -d<printername> <filename>`, status is checked with `lpstat -t`, and jobs are cancelled with `cancel <jobname>`.

A Better System V Way

If you should happen to be on a System V machine, check out the software available from ESP Software (`http://www.easysw.com/`). This company makes a program called ESP Print that solves many System V printing problems by containing an enormous printer database and an actually useful front-end for configuring the printer. Configuring a System V printer with the ESP Print package is as simple as pointing and clicking your way through a set of configuration menus. Although I usually am not a big fan of configuring UNIX things with GUI tools, this is one case where the tool works well and solves many more problems than it creates. Figure 8.5 shows a selection of the configuration panels available for each printer. As you can see, this software enables you to treat non-PostScript printers as PostScript printers and to configure a great variety of printing and imaging options for each printer. Currently (early 1999) available for the Solaris, IRIX, and HPUX flavors of System V, it might even be worth your time to install one of these machines just to run this software if you're obliged to support System V printing for a network.

FIGURE 8.5

*ESP Print
configuration panels.*

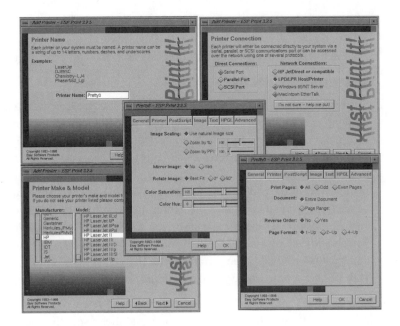

Summary

In today's lesson, you learned a lot about adding devices to your machine. Don't expect to actually absorb all this in one sitting or to be able to add all these devices in one day when you try it the first time. Waiting for disk formats to finish, fighting with printer definitions, and just plain silly mistakes will conspire to make this impossible. Don't rush, but most of all, don't be intimidated. Installing a new piece of hardware for the first time can be a somewhat traumatic experience, especially if all your users expected you to have it done last week. Don't push and make mistakes. These things take time, and you're better off doing it right the first time than making a mistake and formatting your root disk by accident.

Specifically, in today's reading, you learned the following:

- A bit about the technology of disk drives
- What sort of decisions you need to make when installing a new drive
- A brute-force approach to deriving physical parameters for drives when you don't have manufacturer information
- How you can rearrange your files after you have a new drive online
- How to install and use a CD-ROM drive
- How to install and access a tape drive

8

- A brief glimpse of the horrors of UNIX printing
- A trick or two that might help you avoid the horrors of UNIX printing

Q&A

Q Could you go through that drive parameter calculation again? Say that I have a drive that claims to have 4,848,291 blocks.

A Okay. You start by trying to guess the head count. It's almost always odd, and it's probably somewhere between 15 and 29. #blocks/#heads should be a whole number because there are always the same number of blocks per surface:

```
4,848,291/15 = 323,219.4 · 4,848,291/25 = 193,931.6
4,848,291/17 = 285,193.6 · 4,848,291/27 = 179,566.3
4,848,291/19 = 255,173.2 · 4,848,291/29 = 167,182.4
4,848,291/21 = 230,871.0
4,848,291/23 = 210,795.3
```

The value 21 looks like a likely pick because it divides out neatly to a whole number, whereas none of the others do. So you pick 21 as the number of heads, and start making guesses about the number of sectors. The number derived in the preceding text must be the number of blocks-per-surface. Using the approximation that the drive is classically configured, blocks-per-surface should divide evenly by the number of sectors, giving you a value for the tracks-per-surface number, or number of cylinders. The number of sectors can vary widely, but usually seems to be between 100 and 300 (guessing this can take a long time!):

```
230,871/100 = 2308.7 · 230,871/200 = 1154.4
230,871/101 = 2285.9 · 230,871/201 = 1148.6
230,871/102 = 2263.4 · 230,871/202 = 1142.9
...
230,871/120 = 1923.9 · 230,871/250 = 923.5
230,871/121 = 1908.03 · 230,871/251 = 919.8
230,871/122 = 1892.4 · 230,871/252 = 916.2
230,871/123 = 1877.0
230,871/124 = 1861.9
```

Without going through the entire collection to demonstrate, you find that a guess of 123 sectors happens to divide out to a whole number of tracks. It looks like this drive really does use the classical definition of drive parameters. In the end, you have a drive with 4,848,291 blocks, 1,877 cylinders, 123 sectors, and 21 heads.

If you were not able to find values that caused the math at each step to work out to exactly whole numbers, your drive probably uses variable sectoring. Choose a set of values that produce numbers that are almost whole numbers and try the format. If it works, you're in luck, you've probably wasted a few blocks of space, but you have a working drive. If it doesn't work, back off on your numbers slightly and try again—starting by decreasing your cylinder count by one. Relatively quickly you'll hit a collection of values that will cause your drive to work and that won't waste too much space.

Q I installed my drive, but it isn't being recognized. What did I do wrong?

A Don't you hate it when users ask imprecise questions like that? The range of "not being recognized" is rather large, but here goes, anyway.

Things to check include the following:

1. Did you plug it in, attach it, and turn it on?
2. Is it spinning?
3. Is the SCSI chain terminated at each end, and only at each end?
4. Is the SCSI ID correctly set? (Try turning off all your other devices and see if this one suddenly appears at an unexpected ID.)
5. Does it show up in your SCSI-hardware list? (If you plug it into a Macintosh or PC, can you see it on their SCSI chain?)
6. Did you `mkfs` it?
7. Is it in your `fstab`?
8. Did you buy a generic drive for a System V machine that only recognizes certain vendor's hardware?
9. Did you reboot your machine using its "recognize new hardware" flag?

Q What's a good partitioning scheme for my drive?

A That depends heavily on your needs, but you can't go wrong keeping a few simple rules in mind:

1. Be aware of any maximum partition-size limitations of your OS.
2. Having more swap space split among more devices almost never hurt anybody.
3. You'll frequently end up running out of room for general system maintenance and upkeep functions.
4. Your users will frequently run out of room for home directories. (It's amazing how quickly they can fill space with downloaded pictures from Web pages. No, don't look at them; you're happier not knowing—trust me on this one.) They also have no problem calling your supervisor at 3:30 a.m. on a Sunday morning to complain about being out of space.
5. Data storage areas for things such as building images of CD-ROMs are always useful. You'll find that as a system administrator, you become quite a data packrat.

Q I'm having trouble configuring a printer. What should I do?

A Apply for vacation. Hope that a miracle has occurred and that everything is working when you get back. Even if it's not, you'll be in a much better mood for dealing with what you're about to get into. On a more serious note, however, contacting your OS vendor is your best bet. They wrote the thing, they should be able to figure out how to make it work. If it means you have to pay them a bit for a support call, it's still going to be a lot cheaper than the time you're likely to waste on this yourself. If that's not an option, seriously consider a network-capable printer or a package like ESP Print.

Workshop

Quiz

1. What does the author think of System V's general way of doing things?

2. If your drive has 12 platters, how many heads is it likely to have?

3. If you have a network printer already installed and want to configure BSD printing, the following is true:

   a. Life is good.

   b. It's time for a change of career.

   c. Be prepared for long nights and learn to like coffee.

4. If you have a band-printer (you do remember band-printers, don't you? The "antique" impact line-printers that printed at rates in the pages-per-second on fanfold paper?) and want to configure System V printing to use it, the following is true:

   a. Life is good.

   b. It's time for a change of career.

   c. Be prepared for long nights and learn to like coffee.

5. If you have a HPGL printer (an alternative graphics language to PostScript for printer page imaging) and want to make it available in a BSD environment, the following is true:

   a. Life is good.

   b. It's time for a change of career.

   c. Be prepared for long nights and learn to like coffee.

Exercises

1. Imagine that you are going to double your facility's current disk space by adding two new drives. Map out what you would change, what would stay the same, and where you would put new partitions.

2. Find out whether your OS has any limitations as to support for specific drives and, if so, what drives are supported.

3. Find out whether your OS has support for any specific printers. If it does, which ones?

DAY 9

What About Security?

Whether you are setting up a home machine, a cluster for a small research group, or machines for a major corporation, security is an issue these days. In this chapter, you will take a look at today's security problems and some basic approaches to dealing with those problems.

The Cold Cruel World: Crackers

Although it is possible that your researchers' data is so valuable that your cluster could be facing industrial espionage, in all likelihood, your greatest danger comes from the cracker wannabe. The person who seems to have nothing better to do with his time than compromise your system. Fortunately, he generally has so little of an idea of what he's really about that he leaves much more telltale evidence than a professional would. Unfortunately, he's more concerned with impressing his buddies than anything else. Being spectacularly destructive or using your system to break into others to do the same is going to be much higher on his list than peeking at your files and slipping away unnoticed.

UNIX, an operating system that was intended to facilitate productivity and cooperation, sometimes does not lend itself to being secure. Software that takes advantage of known security problems is readily available today for download.

As UNIX becomes a more popular alternative operating system for the home and small-business user, more people are downloading software that could compromise your system and are just looking for a system to install it on. Sometimes, the goal might just be to do it because they can. Sometimes, the crackers are simply looking for sites to connect through. They might be using yours to cover their tracks as they hop from site to site until they finally attack the site of real interest—perhaps that of a former employer or a former ISP. They don't have to know anything about programming; today's cracker wannabes only need to know where to find the packages and how to read the README that comes with them.

This means that your cluster of machines or even your one home machine is at risk. Do not believe you are secure simply because you are not a public target. Entire networks can be easily scanned for vulnerable machines using software easily accessible from many Web sites. If you are on the Internet, you are vulnerable. If you are vulnerable and are on a network with other machines (almost every UNIX machine is, to some extent), you contribute to their vulnerability.

I did not realize how easy it was for people to download the software necessary to compromise a system until the summer of 1998. I had put up a cluster of Linux boxes for use in a course and was installing the software necessary for the course's students. I was peripherally aware that Linux came with a great number of security holes and that I still had a bit of work to do to tighten up the security. I also had a number of other things to do at the same time and had put security concerns on the back burner. After all, they were only a few machines, and they were newly plugged in. Who would attack them? Within four days of plugging in the network cables, they had already been cracked. Someone probed our entire network, found the Linux boxes, and installed software that sniffed network traffic. Included in the traffic that they collected was a file of users' passwords in clear (unencrypted) text.

Security Problems Overview

There are six common classes into which I will divide attacks that crackers will try to use against your system. Broadly categorized, these are physical attacks, exploitation of OS and software flaws, computational/predictive attacks, denial of service attacks, brute-force attacks, and social engineering.

Against a dedicated cracker who seriously wants to compromise your system, there is little that you can actually do. Using any of these methods, a seriously interested individual will be able to compromise your system or affect its performance. A rather defeatist attitude, yes? Also a rather practical one. It has been suggested that a not inappropriate answer to the question "what can you do to make this system secure?" is "lock it in a safe, seal that in a block of concrete, and drop it in the middle of Hudson Bay—and then you still can't be sure." If your system is network-accessible, and even very likely if it is not, the best you will ever be able to do is enhance security and discourage the casual invader.

Thankfully, the vast majority of people who will try to invade or damage your system are much less than dedicated. Today's breed of cracker wannabe is not out for knowledge, money, or industrial secrets. Few are even out for the thrill of entering a previously unassailable system. You are very unlikely to meet the ingenious thrill-seeking cracker whose greatest adrenaline rush comes from changing the message-of-the-day file on supposedly "secure" government sites, the international spy, or the cracker version of Billy the Kid. These people are never going to have their exploits chronicled in best-selling books or movies. Instead, most people who will try to crack or crash your system today are a "Beavis and Butthead" parody of the crackers you might have heard about from earlier days. These individuals are, in a cruel joke upon themselves, out for personal glory and admiration from their peers and are also largely incapable of effectively compromising your system on their own. Stupid and dangerous at the same time, these people rely on "pre-packaged" break-in scripts available easily on the Web and Usenet newsgroups, and they think it's "funny" to break your machine just to prove that they (or rather the script that they downloaded) can. Although they are considerably more dangerous in terms of the type of damage they're likely to cause, you can also effectively protect yourself against most of their attacks by simply keeping your machine up-to-date with the latest patches and fixes to block the popular break-in scripts of the day. The old joke about carrying running shoes while hiking so that you can out-run your hiking-partner if attacked by a bear applies well here. To dissuade the vast majority of attacks you're likely to meet, you need only to make your system a little harder to catch than average, and the common bear will attack somewhere else instead. I've even considered keeping an isolated machine vulnerable and carefully monitored as a decoy to lure attacks away from important machines.

Now, take a look at each of the classes of attacks you're likely to meet and what you can and cannot do about them in general terms. Later in this chapter, I'll cover some of the specific physical measures you can take to protect your systems and which of these attacks they'll help against. In tomorrow's chapter, "Defending Your Machines and Encrypting Traffic," I'll cover the installation of software that will address some of the others.

Social Engineering

Starting with the variety of attack that is probably the easiest to implement, the one you think about the least, and the most insidious, social engineering is the one variety of attack that no amount of software or physical security can hope to defeat. Social engineering is the easy way for a cracker to access your system. No matter how thorough

9

your software security measures are, they are not proof against simple failures of human nature. Passwords are often hard for users to remember, so users write them down. It's impolite to not trust spouses, significant others, and even casual friends, and so passwords and accounts are loaned to others. If all else fails, it doesn't take much effort at all to casually look over a user's shoulder as she's logging in and memorize her keystrokes. Simply put, social engineering is the art of the cracker who uses your users, rather than software, to break into your system. In the world of corporate espionage, this is the new worker who is immediately friendly with the secretarial pool and always makes sure he's hanging around their offices when they're logging in in the morning. In the world of college computing-lab pranks, it's the student who comes to the lab early and does nothing but on-paper homework.

Of course, you'll have a considerably greater number of legitimate and perfectly harmless users who exhibit exactly these sorts of behaviors than you will have crackers. This makes it almost impossible to block social engineering attempts by proscribing behaviors. The only things effective against social engineering attacks are education, policy, and punishment. Educate your users to the problem, establish a policy, and strictly enforce it. It's hard to prevent users from writing down passwords or from having their shoulders looked over. If your users know that their accounts will be terminated if you ever discover that their account is compromised, they'll be more likely to jealously guard their passwords than if they know you as the kind and forgiving type.

> **Note**
>
> Also under social engineering (or, more properly, under "human idiocy") comes the brain damage known as a .rhosts file. This is a file that a user can create in her home directory that will allow no-password access to her account from a specified remote machine. The security implications should be obvious, but many users still try to use these files.
>
> You'd be best off making installing one a violation of your security policy, whether it's been used in violation or not.
>
> To prevent their use, some system administrators create .rhosts files in all user directories, make them empty and owned by root, and then turn off all the permissions. It is nearly impossible for the users to make any modifications to such a file, neatly preventing them from installing insecure versions of their own.

To prevent, or at least mitigate, the possibility of social engineering attacks on your machines, in general you should do the following:

- Write an acceptable use policy and stick with it. I've provided a generic version of the policy that I use in Appendix F, "Useful Sample Forms." Feel free to make copies from the appendix and use them until you have time to make a policy that's tailored to your site.

- Make certain that your users have read all your policies and have signed a statement certifying that they will comply.

- Make certain that your users know that their account security is their own responsibility and that lending the use of their accounts to anyone is considered a violation of system security and policy. Many of your users will have the impression that "don't lend anyone your account and password" means "only give it out to people you've known for at least a few weeks."

- Make it clear to your users why sharing accounts is not acceptable. Many users will find it rude and ruthless of you to suggest that they can't share their account with their roommates, classmates, or friends. They seem to understand more easily if you explain the difficulty associated with maintaining security and the necessity of keeping a clear accounting trail of who logged in, when, and where. The fact that they're each the only name associated with the account and that they will have to be held legally responsible for anything that happens with, to, or from it is something that most of them have not considered. Invoking the user's basic mistrust of everyone else is an effective way to get most users to guard their information a bit more jealously.

- Watch for suspicious activity or persons conspicuously "out of place" around your machines. If you have a user who's constantly looking over other people's shoulders as they log in, spend some time hanging over her shoulder and see if you can't put the fear of root in her.

Denial of Service

Denial of service attacks are generally destructive attempts rather than attempts to access your system. These attacks are targeted at preventing you and your users from using your machines instead of at providing an intruder access. Because this can be effectively accomplished without the aid of your system, there's little that you can do about many of these attacks. Because the denial of service attack rarely results in an actual security violation or illegitimate access of your system, your best defense is detection and elimination.

Although the specific methods employed in different varieties of denial of service attacks vary, they share a common feature—the exhausting of some service or resource that your machines require or provide. Why do people do this? Good question. You might expect this sort of behavior from a disgruntled ex-employee attacking a former employer or from a student who thinks it's a funny practical joke. Less expected are denial of service attacks that seem to happen as random vandalism just because the attacker can do it.

Certain denial of service attacks can be mitigated or prevented with software or hardware updates. In general, these updates tend to be the installation of OS patches to disallow certain types of connections or the installation of filtering hardware to block certain types of network traffic. Unfortunately, with denial of service attacks, which can range from flooding a user's email to absorbing all your http server connections to running your printer out of paper to flooding your network with ICMP ping packets, there's little you can count on to be reliably effective other than constant vigilance and swift retribution.

 Caution

> Not all denial of service attacks are devoid of security risks. Some denial of service attacks are targeted at services that are known to break inelegantly and that sometimes enable privileged access when broken. Just because a denial of service attack looks relatively "harmless," don't allow yourself to be complacent. It could be less harmless than it looks, or it could be a prelude to more unpleasant attacks.

The possibility of denial of service attacks can never be completely eliminated because they originate outside your system and by definition make use of publicly available services. However, you can minimize the risk and impact by keeping the following in mind:

- Against denial of service attacks, vigilance is your best defense. Watching your machine's load and network performance is the best way to discover an attack in progress.

- Consider building yourself a monitoring Web page that collects this information from all your machines and provides you with a continuously updated representation of the state of the world.

- A gateway between your cluster and the outside world can be used to deny traffic from an outside host that decided to be a problem. Unfortunately, this can't prevent an outside host from effectively denying you network services just by banging away at your gateway until your network bandwidth is consumed.

- Enlist the help of system administrators upstream from your site in tracking and blocking denial of service attacks as they occur. Because you can't effectively prevent a user on the other side of the world from running flood-ping (an attack in which an outside site simply attempts to overload your system's built-in ICMP responder) against your machines, you'll need to find someone between you and them who can help.

Physical Attacks

Next on the list of varieties of attack in terms of frequency, and also on the list of almost impossible to completely prevent attacks, are physical attacks to your machines.

Categorized under physical attacks are all methods of compromising your machines through physical access to or modification of your machines or network. These attacks could be further subdivided into direct abusive attacks to your hardware and attempts at illegal entry that only require physical access. Rather than use that fine a distinction on the subject, I will discuss them as a united class because the preventative measures are common between the subsets.

By far, the easiest physical attack on your hardware is the power switch combined with the capability to boot the machine into single-user mode or off of a device specified at startup, either without a password. No matter how good your software security and network security measures are, if all a user has to do is come in to a lab, cycle the power on a machine, and tell it `boot -s` or click `Stop for System Maintenance`, you've all but given your local users unlimited root access. Even if you are using a UNIX flavor that won't let a machine boot single-user without entering the root password, if you're using a machine on which the boot device can be specified at startup without a password, a person intent on entering your system illegally can simply boot from a CD-ROM. Most flavors of System V now include a check in the single-user start-up scripts to require the root password before giving the user a shell prompt. Whether these scripts are proof against Control+C and other forms of subversion will vary from implementation to implementation. Unfortunately, even with this level of protection, these operating systems provide no way of preventing a user who would go to this length from simply specifying a different boot device. The user can still bring your machine up from the OS install disk, build himself a miniroot partition in your swap space, and become the new root user in complete control of the machine. Near-complete protection from this sort of attack can only be had with the combination of an OS that provides this level of security and hardware that also requires password access to do anything other than execute a default startup. Sun hardware, for one, gives you the capability to set a hardware password, without which the machine will refuse to enter its hardware command monitor. Intel hardware running Linux is at the other end of the scale as almost unsecurable because it can be easily booted from and compromised by a person with a floppy disk. A UNIX flavor that always requires a password for single-user mode and that is run on hardware that requires a password for configuration changes effectively prevents both single-user startups and alternative-device startups. It has the "downside" of just as effectively preventing you from making any changes to the boot information on the machine if you forget the hardware password. If you set the hardware password and forget it, you'll need to send your machine off to have the password removed by a technician.

9

Note

> **"Near-complete" as opposed to "complete" protection** The entire issue of whether a system administrator should ever believe that anything provides complete protection aside, there are tricks to get around even hardware passwords. With physical access to the machine, a user can always swap drives on you and install a boot drive that will fool your machine. With some systems, there are also ways for users to erase hardware passwords. These usually involve rather risky (from the equipment's point of view) electronic procedures and shouldn't be considered a viable alternative to sending a machine in for service if you've forgotten your own hardware password.

Following immediately from points that the preceding note should bring to mind, you also need to be concerned about users who "just want your stuff." Just as an unscrupulous individual who wanted access to your system could swap a "Trojan disk drive" for your boot drive and hijack your entire machine, one who really wants your data can just physically steal your drives. Many system administrators don't seriously consider this variety of threat when designing computing labs. Your hardware is usually small, expensive, and might contain interesting data. It makes prime "swiping" material for the thief who wants your data and for the scum who thinks your SGI workstation would look better on his desk than on yours. It is not at all uncommon for a system administrator to note that a machine is running more slowly than it should and after considerable investigation of the software installed, network statistics, and every configuration change made in the previous six months, to discover that the machine mysteriously has only half the physical memory that it previously had. Memory is easy to pocket, CPUs (especially Intel CPUs) are easy to swap for lower-performance cheaper models, hard-drives disappear, and even motherboards get swapped. Some protection is offered by lockable cases and fiber-optic alarm systems. You also have the option of physically attaching your hardware to some relatively unmovable object. Remember that whatever you do is essentially an attempt at deterrence; if someone wants your stuff, they're going to get it, no matter how big a lock you buy.

The other variety of physical attacks to your hardware are ones that require physical access but are non-invasive. Chief among these, and a good example of the overall type, are the ever-present "sniffing" attacks. In the sniffing attack, a machine located near your machine on the network is used to "sniff" the data intended for your machine that is moving over the network. Near in this context means somewhere on the same unfiltered network segment.

Network traffic does not actually travel point-to-point. Given the physical size of a typical subnet and the speed of propagation of the electrical signals through the wire, a signal that is being written by machine A and is destined for machine B is everywhere on the subnet simultaneously.

9

Messages from one machine to another are written onto the network as a sequence of packets, each containing a variety of information, including the source and the intended destination. Quite frequently and for the majority of major protocols, this information is transmitted in "clear text": Characters that are typed or displayed are transmitted just as they were typed or displayed. Machine B receives messages intended for it by looking at the headers of all packets it sees on the network, ignoring those that specify other destinations and reading those that are marked as destined for it. Machine C (hopefully) does not receive messages destined for machine B because C's ethernet interface should reject packets that say they're destined for B.

If you're paying attention, your "well *that* sounds like a brilliant security idea!" warning klaxon should be going full blast about now. Yes, this networking model actually relies on the cooperation of every other machine on your network to keep your data secure; if it's data that's coming from across the country, it relies on every other machine on every other subnet that your data touches along the way. You might be surprised to know that once upon a time, before the commercialization of the Internet and the proliferation of mismanaged computers attached to it, this wasn't actually *that much* of a security threat. It was a threat even then, but UNIX hardware was expensive, and root access was jealously guarded and was generally understood to mean that the person was trustworthy (you need root access to tell your ethernet interface to ignore what it knows is right and collect all traffic instead of just what's destined for its host). DOS and Macintosh computers could sniff traffic but couldn't be accessed remotely, making them much less of a threat. Today, however, any yahoo can grab an old Intel box, slap Linux on it, declare herself root, and start causing trouble.

I've classified sniffing attacks as physical attacks here because they require physical access to your network or access to a machine that has physical access. A person interested in capturing all that clear-text data going to and coming from your machine, such as people's logins and passwords when they Telnet in or out or their email when they read it, needs a machine attached to your network where it can see this traffic. To accomplish this, she has two choices. She can bring a machine to your network and plug it in close enough to your machine that there are no gateways or other packet-filtering devices to prevent it from seeing the data. Alternatively, she can find a machine that fits this criteria, crack her way into it, and use it illicitly to sniff your traffic. In the second case, the attack used to gain entry to the machine used for sniffing can be just about any other way of gaining access.

In trying to prevent all these varieties of physical attacks, you need to consider the physical protection of your cluster and its network. Think about it in terms of, "If a user can touch this, what does it give him access to, and what can he do?" If the answer is that "he could theoretically do bad things with information that he shouldn't be able to see," you need to find some way of preventing him from touching it.

Physical protection measures range from "keep people from taking it" to "keep people away from it" to "keep people from knowing it's even there." When considering physical means that you can employ to protect your hardware, system, and network, keep these things in mind:

- If theft of your machines is a concern, bolt your hardware to the table—especially things such as drives. If aesthetics are a factor in your decision, you might consider one of the fiber-optic loop-though security cable systems because they are fairly unobtrusive. You might also want to consider investing in a computer-controlled video-capture program. This would enable you to selectively video-monitor your hardware only when faults (machines not responding, drives offline, and so on) occur, or with the image-analysis variety, only when motion is sensed during off-hours.

- Use those case locks so that your internal drives can't be altered without leaving tell-tale marks (every case of security system I've seen can be defeated easily with bolt-cutters or pliers), and keep an eye on them so you know if anyone has been tampering.

- Use your machine's hardware password and any capability to protect single-user mode.

- Do what you can to defeat or disconnect front-panel power switches and reset buttons. An ugly blob of epoxy putty stuck over the power-on-reset button is a worthwhile tradeoff against the users who think that they should hit Reset to reboot the machine whenever Netscape hangs. Not only is this behavior bad for the machine (and almost impossible to break users of doing), but it will eventually corrupt a drive badly enough that the machine will come up into single-user mode automatically just to let you run `fsck`.

- Put critical machines behind tightly controlled gateways or behind packet filters. One highly recommended option is to get a set of smart switches and dedicate them only to your cluster. This will isolate any traffic between your machines to their own piece of twisted-pair wire. The unscrupulous can still get to your signals by disconnecting your machine, adding a hub, and plugging your machine and his sniffer into the hub, but you're far more secure than in a situation where your network traffic can be seen all over the building.

- Don't discount Macs and PCs as sniffing troublemakers, but don't obsess about them. Both can sniff your traffic easily. The thing that makes them somewhat less of a problem than other UNIX boxes on your wire is that Macs and PCs can't easily be broken into from unknown outside sites. A Mac on your network can sniff all your traffic for its user—hopefully, someone you can track down and clobber if necessary. A Linux box on your network in its out-of-the-box configuration is an open door for anyone on the planet to sniff your traffic.

Brute Force Attacks

Finally, moving on to attacks over which you actually have some control, you come to the brute force attack. The simplest application of this attack is sitting at the console and trying to log in by iteratively guessing passwords. The most sophisticated variation is running a piece of software that does the very same thing. The largest variation is in how "smart" the guessing software tries to be and in moving the password off to some other machine so you don't see your CPU crunching away running `crack -file /etc/passwd`. Because there's absolutely nothing you can do to prevent people from trying, many of your best defenses are already built in to the way that UNIX works in general.

For example, you might have noticed that when you log in to a UNIX machine, it takes a second or two to actually accept a proper login and to reject an improper one. This is actually an intentional delay, using intentionally designed inefficiencies in the password-checking routine. The password-checking routine is intentionally designed this way to make it almost impossible to run a brute-force attack by sequentially entering password guesses; it simply would take too long to attempt to make more than a few password guesses.

Another feature built in to most UNIX flavors is the capability to log password attempt errors.

Four things you might want to look into to further improve security in this area are the following:

- See if your operating system has any facility to make your password file inaccessible to normal users. In general practice, users can access the encrypted password file, and if they have sufficient time and resources, they can run a brute-force cracking attempt on it. If they try this on your machine, catching them and giving them the boot isn't too difficult: A process named `crack` that occupies 90 percent of your CPU and runs for two or three days is a pretty good giveaway that somebody is up to no good. More dangerous are the users who grab your password file and move it off to another machine where you can't monitor their activities. Some vendors have an advanced security option that enables you to make even the encrypted password file inaccessible. If you value your security, look into this.

- Look also for a version of `login` that not only logs incorrect login tries, but that also locks accounts if too many attempts are made. Require that users come to your office and present identification to reinstate accounts. This also usually comes as a vendor upgrade.

- Replace your standard `passwd` package with one that places more strict requirements on the user for choosing good passwords. The smart cracker will try choosing dictionary words and personal information about the user as password information first. There are versions of the passwd program available that check potential pass-words against all known user data and against a dictionary before allowing the user to set that password. These are available both as vendor upgrades and occasionally as publicly released software. The sophistication of the publicly available versions is generally better than that of the vendor's versions, but it is frequently superceded as new algorithms appear in the cracker's world.

- If your users are allowed to pick poor passwords, you'll be amazed at how many will do so. Smart system administrators run the most sophisticated cracking soft-ware they can find against their own password files. They do this to make sure that their users' passwords can't be cracked with the latest technology and to allow them to force the users with bad passwords to change them. You'll probably want to spend time regularly perusing the cracking software sites and trying the software against your site. Unless you're relatively certain your site is impervious, you might want to avoid the stuff that's supposed to crash your machines, but running the cracker's latest password-breaking software against your password database is the only way to be sure that the crackers can't get in with it.

Computational/Predictive Attacks

Sitting near the brute force attack in method, but showing considerably more sophistica-tion, are computational or predictive methods of breaking system security. These methods rely on using knowledge of the system or the user to aid in breaking system security. The use of fields from the user's name and address data in the password database would almost count as a predictive attack, but fails the definition I've chosen here in that it requires brute force application of all this data until a match is found. A creative cracker can supplement this information and allow a program to make predictions about which data it might be. At the simple end of the spectrum, these methods include things such as remotely turning on a machine's microphone and listening to login keystrokes. At the more sophisticated end, they include things such as analyzing the sequence of random numbers generated by a machine's random number generator (which very rarely are actually random) and using this information to predict connection port numbers to hijack a user's terminal session.

As an example of the level of creativity and analysis that some crackers will display (yes, there are some creative ones out there as well; it's just that the majority that you'll meet are only capable of using the fruits of these creative few's labors), one of the major Web browser vendor's secure–form submission method was cracked by application of a trivial observation. Some person brighter than the programmer who wrote the algorithm observed that, although the encryption algorithm used a 128-bit key, which should be quite safe, the key was actually generated by an 8-bit random number generator. Because almost no random number generators are at all random (technically, they're pseudo-random, providing a predetermined set of random numbers), all that a person had to guess was what hardware and software was running the server, and the 128-bit "random" keys could be predicted directly.

Protection against most sorts of predictive attacks comes in the form of vendor-software updates and paying a bit of attention to newsgroup postings of newfound vulnerabilities. No one can predict where the next one of these will come from, so mostly you'll be operating in a reactive mode. Thankfully, the opportunities for a cracker to make useful predictions that can make your system vulnerable, without the presence of other significant security flaws, are few and far between.

Exploitation of OS and Software Flaws

Finishing out the list are the variety of attacks that you will most frequently face and that you will most frequently be making modifications to your system to prevent. It has been claimed that, due to human errors and the immense complexity of programming tasks, "Every piece of software has at least one bug, and at least one extraneous line of code." Although this seems perhaps a little extreme, in reality, it does seem that the vast majority of software packages that you meet will have at least a few problems. UNIX is no exception. Bugs in the operating system and basic flaws in the way that certain parts of it were designed are discovered on a regular basis. As time goes by, the more serious ones are uncovered and fixed, but it seems that UNIX and the software that runs on it has, just like any other OS, a never-ending supply.

The handful of creative crackers out there seem to have a knack for analyzing these bugs and finding ways to exploit them to gain access to a machine. The variation in methods used is quite large because UNIX is made up of such a great number of cooperating processes, but they tend to share a few characteristic features. If you're curious and would like more complete information, I highly recommend perusing the CERT and 8lgm Web sites and reading the archives. (The sites `http://www.cert.org` and `http://www.8lgm.org` are worthwhile to check out. See Appendix E, "Useful Resources," for pointers to more security sites.) Here, I'll give you a brief overview because it's not nearly as important that you understand the methods these creative, but misguided, individuals might use, as that you understand what to do to fix the holes as they appear.

Briefly, the majority of attacks against OS and software bugs exploit areas where a programmer did an insufficient job of error-checking arguments in some routine.

Consider a subroutine in the OS that is designed to take as an argument a filename, and the subroutine is supposed to open the file with this name and execute some particular UNIX command on the file. What does the subroutine do if instead of getting a filename as an argument, it gets an entire paragraph of data? The answer is "hard to tell." If the programmer did her job carefully, the first thing that the subroutine does is check to make certain that it really does only have a single word as an argument, and it exits with an error otherwise. Unfortunately, the range of possible errors is sometimes difficult to see. A programmer who had just been stuck in a four-hour meeting about why productivity was down (not uncommon, from what I hear from those in programmer land) might miss the possibility of too much data being provided. This slightly off-peak programmer might only check the argument to make certain that it contained data and might forget the case where it contained too much data. Along comes a cracker who observes that this routine doesn't error-check its arguments completely. With a little experimentation, it is discovered that if just the exactly right data is passed into the subroutine, not only can a filename be given as an argument, but the UNIX command to be run on this filename can be modified. A quick bit of shell-script crafting later, and the cracker provides an exploit tool on the Web. The new tool enables any user who runs it to set the root password to anything he likes. The cracker used the bug to take advantage of the fact that the OS runs as root to execute a command to update root's password. This sort of attack is called a *buffer overflow* attack and is a very common theme.

The other large class of OS and software flaws that can be exploited fall under the category of design flaws rather than simple bugs. The original NIS/YP database system fits this description. The NIS/YP database is used to provide password information from a server to all client machines, allowing them to share accounts and to look seamlessly identical. As a client/server system, it was decided that the less the client knew, the better. Therefore, when a client machine is started, all it knows about the server is that it's looking for a server that serves a password database (called a *map* in NIS/YP terminology) with a particular name.

Because the system needed to be proofed against a server failure, the system was designed with the idea of a single *master* server and multiple *slave* servers. The master kept the "final word" copy of all the information, but it regularly provided update maps to the slave servers so that, in the event of a failure of any one machine, the cluster could continue to function. In this model, when a client starts up, it broadcasts a message on the network saying essentially, "Hey, I'm looking for a server who will provide me with a password map named 'splart'" (splart's just a funny word). The first server machine that responds (master, slave, or otherwise) and claims "Sure, I'll give you a password map named 'splart'" will be believed by the client and the client will download its password information from this server. Did you notice the "otherwise" in with the master and slave in the previous aside? Nothing in this model prevents a Trojan-server from being inserted in your network. The client machine doesn't know which machines are allowed to be servers; it will believe any server that claims to have the information it needs. If a cracker wants to take over your machine using this system, all that's needed is to guess the name of your password map, plug your machine into a fake server that will serve a doctored copy of it, reboot, and away he goes.

What can you do about these attacks? Here, you're basically relying on your vendor to provide timely patches in response to problems as they are found. Following are a few things to keep in mind:

- Keep an eye on the CERT email announcement list and make certain to take any protective measures that are recommended.

- Apply vendor OS update patches as they become available. It's not always clear whether a patch to the C compiler will enhance security, but why take the chance? If you're running a program you've compiled as root, who knows what the bug might do?

- Occasionally, you will have to live with a problem and hope that there is no widely accessible exploit for it. The NIS/YP flaw is one such area where the protocol is inherently unsafe, but there is no standardized replacement (NIS+ is an attempt but has so many problems of its own that most prefer to live with the original NIS) that provides the same cohesive presentation of a group of machines as a cluster. Thankfully, exploiting the NIS/YP flaw requires knowledge of what map your client is looking for and access to your network to insert a fake server. The lack of an "outside" exploit for the flaw makes it much less appealing for the cracker-wannabes, so it is overlooked as uninteresting by the ones you're likely to need to worry about.

- Turn off any services or protocols that you don't actually need. The less you have running, the less likely it is that there's an easily accessible hole in something. It is especially important to turn off data-sharing protocols when possible. If you only occasionally mount disks from other machines, don't start the NFS daemons at machine startup. Start them by hand when you need them, and kill them off when you're done. If a machine doesn't handle any of its own mail, make certain that `sendmail` is turned off. Additional software provides additional risks; make informed decisions before turning on anything unnecessary.

General Comments on Break-Ins by Any Means

As a system administrator, you are likely to encounter many more break-in situations than what I can outline in this book. However, the following are a few words of wisdom from experiences that I've encountered:

- If you discover an unauthorized access to your system by way of any attack, publicize it. Don't just expire everyone's passwords and force them all to change them; tell them why you're doing it and who forced you to do it. Peer pressure and the thought of hundreds of users wanting the person's head on a platter can be an effective deterrent.

- If you discover an unauthorized access to your system, presume that everything is compromised. It takes only milliseconds for a cracking script, when it has breached your system, to install numerous back-door entrances and to download your entire password database. Finding and closing all the back-door entrances is an almost impossible task, and the perpetrator now has your password file to bang away at until he's guessed all your passwords anyway. Change *everything*. All users' passwords need to be changed, and if your system is at all important, you really should be wiping the machine and reinstalling the operating system.

- Remember that users don't have clear knowledge of just how much you, as root, know about what they're doing. This can work to your advantage. The closer they believe you are to all-seeing and all-knowing, the less likely they'll be to think they can get away with doing something stupid. Of course, this lack of knowledge on the users' part can work against you as well because some less than bright users don't realize just how much information you do have at your disposal. A casual look at who's logged in will occasionally find the same user to be "dialed in" (connected remotely by phone and modem) to several machines and simultaneously to be sitting at a machine in your lab.

- Don't take your concerns about security to the point that you've violated your user's rights to privacy. I'll go into considerably more depth on this in Day 20, "How to Be a Good System Administrator," but be aware that your behavior in monitoring users is likely governed by law. If you aren't aware of and don't follow the laws, there's a reasonable chance that you could land your own backside in jail if you discover a user doing something illegal or against policy that you had to break the law to find out about.

Detecting the Break-In

So, how did I detect the break-in on our Linux boxes? Actually, I didn't. The university's security group, which monitors the university's network traffic, among their various duties, told our administrative staff that we had a break-in. Not only did they tell us that we had a break-in, but they were able to tell us where on our machines to find the culprit software and evidence. Obviously, the security group keeps up-to-date on the latest vulnerabilities and popular cracking software. The break-in was well hidden from us. Common commands such as ls had been replaced, and the software had been placed in a directory called ... that not only usually requires using ls -a rather than ls to see, but that their replacement version of ls wouldn't show at all. They also replaced the ps command with one that wouldn't show their sniffing processes, even though the processes were still running, and tried to delete all other traces of their presence off the machines. A couple people from the security group came with a floppy that had uncompromised versions of useful commands, and we were indeed able to see this ... directory and the unusual processes that were running.

9

At the time when we experienced a break-in, the university was being scanned about twice a month. As time goes by, the number increases every time I ask the security group. The last I heard, which was a while ago, we were up to about twice a week. So, even though our security group can detect a number of problems, it can't get to each and every incident right away, requiring that we, and all the other UNIX facilities around campus, take a proactive role in enhancing security. Is there anything that you can do to complement your security group's efforts?

There are some things you and your facility can do to detect a break-in. Who knows— you might detect one in progress. Your network administrator, who is probably monitoring network traffic, might be able to tell you if the network is being probed or if it was recently probed. This might give you the opportunity to check your logs for any unusual activity. If your machines seem sluggish, someone else could be tying up your resources. Check your logs, check to see who is logged on, check what processes are running. It's possible that you will discover that a normally rather inactive account has had a recent flourish of activity. Depending on how far along the cracker might be in the process, your useful commands for detecting unusual activity might have been replaced. Try using `ls-F` in `tcsh` instead of your normal `ls` to see if you can detect the presence of any unusual software or directories. Even if your network administrator hasn't alerted you to any unusual network activity or even if your machine isn't sluggish at the moment, check your logs regularly. You never know what you might find.

Note

> **tcsh has a built-in ls**   The `tcsh` shell has a built-in `ls` command named `ls-F`. As most of these cracker wannabes don't really know what they're doing, most of them aren't bright enough to add a fake `ls-F` or to replace `tcsh` with a broken version, as well as replace the normal `ls` command in `/usr/bin`. Of course, you shouldn't rely on this as a 100 percent certain way of detecting problem directories or compromised commands. Just as soon as you start trusting something, some cracker wannabe of above average smarts will add that to one of the automated scripts. It's just another tool in your arsenal, and you need all the tools you can get.

Be especially paranoid around holidays. Crackers know that users and many system administrators won't be around on holidays. This makes holidays, weekends, and early morning hours prime cracker-time because they know they'll have at least a few hours to play before any human is likely to notice them.

Responding to the Break-In

A break-in has been detected. How do you respond? Your response will depend on the circumstances surrounding the break-in.

If your security group is the one that discovers the break-in, do whatever it tells you to do. You will see that what it tells you will somewhat depend on the circumstances of the break-in. In the case of a sniffer, it will advise you on securing your machines and tell you to have everyone change their passwords. By changing passwords, they will mean passwords for any accounts the users on your network might have accessed during the time in question. Yes, that's all passwords on any accounts they might have accessed from your network—including ones on other machines on other networks that they've accessed from your machines. I'll say it again: All information that anyone has typed while connected to a machine on your network, regardless of whether it was a password for a local machine or a credit-card-number on a Web site halfway around the world, are likely to now be compromised and will need to be changed. If you have a sniffer, all the traffic that's been across your network has been compromised, including outgoing traffic to other sites, so this might impact machines far beyond just your cluster of machines.

If your security group learns that one of your machines was that final hop that I mentioned earlier, the one that is used for attacking another site, the response that security will suggest might surprise you. You might find that this time it is not asking you to secure your machine right away. The site that was attacked might request the cooperation of your site in capturing the culprit.

Our facility experienced one of these when someone gained access to an open `lp` account on an SGI. (I thought I had just checked that the month before. See what I mean about having to regularly check the status of everything?) That person used that account to launch an attack on an ISP over a holiday weekend. When I got in that Monday morning, I had email from the ISP as well as our security group, so I didn't have to do much to detect the break-in. Although security had information on how much traffic had been generated on our machine, it didn't actually know how the culprit got in, unlike with the Linux experience. So the first response I had to make to this break-in was to determine what the security hole might have been. In this case, it didn't actually take too long because the response from the `last` command, which you got to see in Day 4, "A Stroll Through Your System," indicated that `lp` had been logged on a few times. The `lp` account should never have anyone logging in to it because it's just a utility account for handling ownership of printer resources. After determining the cause, I then checked `lp`'s directory to see if any unusual software had been installed. As expected, something had been installed. I saved that evidence along with the `last` output, for security. In this instance, the ISP had asked that we leave our machine open in the hope that we could catch the culprit. So, I left the machine open for a week. Because a class was going to be using the cluster starting the following week, I was reluctant to keep the machine open any longer. Security understood, and I again closed out that lp account.

If you detect a break-in before your security group does, you will have to decide for yourself what that response will be. This is actually something that you should have a policy about, to go with the rest of your policies. Here, you will probably want to leave yourself and your administrative staff some leeway to deal with problems in whatever manner is most effective. Every break-in is different, and each will require individualized responses. You will need to consider things such as the following: Do you close down the machine? Do you keep it open to try to catch a culprit? Do you ask your security group what to do? There is certainly nothing wrong with asking your security group, but depending on the time of day and level of security problems this week, you might not be able to find your security group. Think about how you personally might respond to a break-in before one actually occurs. If the break-in is similar to the sniffer break-in we had where no obvious damage seems to have been done to anyone else's site, swiftly closing down services on your machine and fixing what was done to yours might be the right solution. If damage has been done to someone else's site, you might want to keep your machine open for a while in a cooperative effort to catch the culprit. On the other hand, if your site appears to be being used to break in to someone else's site and she doesn't know about it yet, you have the responsibility to stop the attack before the crackers can do any more damage. Cooperation is the name of the game here, including behaving in as reasonable and professionally courteous manner as possible. If a remote site requests your help, do everything you can to help—you'd want the same courtesy. If a remote site is being attacked through yours, bend over backward to limit its damage. You wouldn't want someone to tell you, "Oh, we could have stopped that, but we were in the middle of a game of Quake and didn't want to shut down."

No matter what you do decide to do, if you have a security group in your company, be sure to tell it about the incident and what you did. It needs to know everything in order to best assess your company's security needs.

If you have reason to believe that your cluster might have been compromised, but you can't find any obvious evidence in your logs, and any logs that might help you haven't been made available to you, then you might have no recourse but to wipe out your machines and start over. Your users might not like this (nor might they understand that you don't either), but it is better for you to have machines that you know you can trust, even if that means starting over from scratch. Your users would probably prefer the downtime to the potential loss of their data, although they probably haven't thought about that yet. Again, tell your security group what you have done. In all likelihood, it will support your decision to wipe out your machines and start over from scratch.

It would rather have you do that if you have any doubt about your machines, than have you let suspect machines stay on the network. Roughly a third of our campus network and a related government site were taken down for several days recently when someone persisted in allowing one single compromised machine to stay on the university's network. Fortunately, my machines weren't involved in that one.

Fighting the Cold Cruel World

Although it is important to think a bit ahead of time about how to deal with a break-in, it is also important to do your best to armor your machines. Yes, UNIX does not lend itself to being secure, but there is some preventive medicine you can apply without installing that loathed-above-all measure, the firewall. Some of what you can do does not take long. The extra peace of mind you gain makes it worth taking the extra steps.

What You've Done Thus Far

"What have I done thus far?" you might be wondering. All you have right now is one machine that appears to have little more than the operating system, right? But your machine does have a bit more than the operating system. You had to FTP some software, and depending on your operating system, you had to FTP patches, too. So, you are connected to the world. You can harm and be harmed by the world. But because you don't want to harm or be harmed, you have already begun to take some of those precautionary measures to secure your machine!

Shortly after installing your operating system, you assigned a hard-to-guess password for the root account, and you locked down any open accounts by editing the /etc/passwd file. Right now, no one can take advantage of any open accounts that come with your operating system. In addition, you closed down unnecessary services by editing your /etc/inetd.conf file. This is the file from which inetd starts certain services as needed. For example, you can control whether Telnet, POP, imap, FTP, and finger are started just from this file. You commented out any services that you didn't need and either rebooted the machine to get the changes to take effect or told the inetd to re-read the configuration file. Your machine is hopefully not running any services that it does not need to run at this time; if it is, don't worry too much. I'll cover what you can shut off in inetd.conf in depth in tomorrow's lesson, among other specific measures you can take.

Depending on your operating system, you might have had to install some patches or maintenance streams already. This is another good habit to continue. On Sun's site, the non-Y2K patches are described as "security and recommended patches." Not only did you install patches that fundamentally improve your operating system, but you also installed security patches—ones that the vendor has issued to take care of security holes discovered with the operating system.

Doesn't seem like much, does it? Wasn't all that complicated, was it? Nonetheless, your machine is already more secure than the Linux boxes I put up for that course in the summer.

What you've done thus far is simply a part of some common sense security practices. You have locked nonpassword-protected user accounts. You have closed down unnecessary services. You already know that you need to check your logs regularly for any unusual activity and that you need to check your password file regularly to make sure that those locked accounts are still locked. You have even updated your operating system.

Physical Approaches to Security

Beyond the obvious recommendation of physically attaching your hardware so that it can't get up and walk away, by far the next most important aspect of physical security is physical security of your network. Your machines are probably relatively secure in terms of OS updates and resistance to common attack schemes. You're a good system administrator, and you spend 30 percent of your week keeping up with OS security patches and recommended configuration settings. What about the rest of the hardware on your network? Is it as trustworthy? Even if you are the administrator for every single machine attached to your building network, there is almost no way for you to prevent a user from dragging in his or her personal laptop and plugging it into your network—instant security hole.

The largest practical threat you are likely to experience is the ongoing insecurity of the machines that are your immediate network neighbors. These machines are the ones that sit near you on the network and can sniff your traffic. If you don't administrate them, you're best off thinking of them as direct threats to the security of your system and attempting to isolate your machines from them to the greatest extent possible. Here is where the smart-switch network hardware mentioned earlier comes in handy. Smart switches can be used to isolate network traffic so that only the wire with the machine for which the traffic is destined sees the messages for that machine. Smart switches are not yet inexpensive, but as of mid-1999, they will cost you roughly $60 per machine that you want to protect. This is a small investment compared to the amount you've spent on hardware and software already and an even smaller amount in terms of the potential cost to productivity if your user's data is compromised.

By installing smart switches to handle all the machines in your cluster, you will decrease your overall building network load and at the same time significantly increase your cluster's security. With your machines communicating through smart switches, your network neighbors can't be used to sniff any traffic between your machines, reducing their level of threat considerably. Even if a neighbor were to be compromised, it couldn't see anything about your machines. Following up on installation of smart switches by installing the encryption software as discussed in tomorrow's chapter will make your machines just about as bullet-proof as a UNIX machine can be. After this software is installed and all clear-text protocols on your machines are disabled, not only will your network neighbors not be able to sniff your traffic, but even if they could, all they'd see would be strongly encrypted traffic. No more filling in a form on a Web page and sniffing traffic from *your* machines for the cracker-wannabes. Let them go bother someone else!

> **Tip**
>
> You should probably enlist the help of your network administrator for choosing and installing smart switches, but if you're the multipurpose network administrator as well as system administrator, you'll have to make these decisions yourself. I would recommend, somewhat counter to what you might expect, that you buy the lowest capacity switches possible for installing the end-run to your machines. Ideally you'd have switches that supported only one IP address per twisted-pair wire because this would make it more difficult for someone to install a hub between your machine and the switch to use as a port for sniffing. If you can't find such a switch to suit your needs, use network-monitoring software to flag the appearance of any machines that shouldn't be inside your protected network. Most switch manufacturers provide monitoring software to let you check traffic patterns and what IPs are seen on what ports. There is also a fair amount of shareware and publicly available software for this purpose as well (again, Appendix E provides links).
>
> Installation of a high-capacity smart-switch for your entire building can also help reduce overall network congestion. Additionally, if you can convince the powers that be to allow the construction of a second network chain through the building, you can use one port of a high-capacity switch to make an unrestricted, nonsecure network. This network could be reserved for users to plug in their laptops or own personal machines without significant concern that their insecurity will affect any other network resources.

Where to Go from Here

You will continue implementing some of those common-sense security practices with software you will install tomorrow.

Here's what our security group recommends to provide your machine with basic security: Patch your operating system regularly, disable all services you do not need, do not use Telnet, use secure shell, tunnel all traffic via encrypted socket connections, and start thinking about using some sort of filtering hardware (like a firewall—yikes!) between you and the world.

You've already covered patching your operating system, and you have started disabling services you don't need. Tomorrow, you will install TCP wrappers, which will enable you to log connections to TCP services, such as Telnet, and restrict those services. Then, you will install secure shell with TCP wrapper support. You will still be able to restrict your services while encrypting your traffic. After you've done this, you'll be ready to disable Telnet, which transmits traffic in clear text. Next week, you will look at securing FTP and POP services.

Don't think that your security administration ends there. Remember that the word "regularly" keeps appearing to describe how often you will be doing things. In addition to the common-sense things I've already indicated are important, you should also be keeping current in the field, as some of your users are probably required to do in their specialty fields. Don't worry if you don't become an expert in security. Hopefully, your security group will serve as the expert. However, whenever a bug has been found in your operating system, you want to know about it. This might mean getting yourself on a security mailing list with your vendor. If your company participates in a special support program, you might want to get on that mailing list as well.

Caution

> **Paranoia, paranoia, paranoia** Did you notice the implicit paranoia in saying "get on that list as well," rather than saying "get on that list instead"? The more information you have, the safer you are. Some days, you might find that the only productive thing you get done is wading through piles of system-related email. If it finds you that tip that enables you to block a soon-to-be-popular flavor of attack, it's time well spent. Remember that as a system administrator, you frequently must gauge the relevance of your tasks in terms of "what might be the consequences if I don't."

When the vendor discovers a security hole, the vendor might provide a patch, or the vendor might provide an advisory to disable a feature. In either case, you want to know about it. The downside to relying on vendors and one of the reasons that you want to keep an eye on CERT mailings and newsgroup discussions is that many vendors still believe in security through obscurity. You're unlikely to hear about a security hole from a vendor if it doesn't have a fix ready for it. Its logic is that until it has a fix, the fewer people who know about the hole, the fewer who will try to exploit it. The completely interconnected nature of the Internet today means that generally, as soon as one cracker knows a new way to break a service, they all do. The end result is that you will usually hear about breaking security-threat news on the Usenet newsgroups related to security (`comp.sys.unix.security` is good) or your operating system from other system administrators who have been attacked before you hear it elsewhere. If you watch these sources, and any system administrator–populated security mailing lists that you find relevant, you will hear about new security threats at least slightly before you hear about them from CERT (which takes some time to compile and analyze the reports) or the vendors (who take some time to try to figure out how to fix it). Without a vendor-supplied fix, you might find that you don't have many options other than either to wait out the fix with your machines up and hope nobody notices the flock of sitting ducks or to yank your network connection. At the least, you will have the knowledge to decide whether the level of threat deserves the isolationist strategy or just increased vigilance until a patch is available.

If your security group, your expert, sponsors users' group meetings, attend. This is your opportunity to learn more about security issues, including current events. Even if you are not interested in the day's topic, this is also your opportunity to ask questions one-on-one and to make your face known to your expert. The more it believes you're concerned about doing security right, the more helpful it's likely to be. If you've sent email and called but haven't gotten a response from security, it's not that it hates you or thinks that your question is not worthy of a response. Its job is to help you make your machines as secure as possible. It's just that it is so busy doing that job for so many people that your query has probably gotten lost in the pile. The meetings, however, are the occasions when you are sure to see one or more of the group. Take that opportunity to ask that not-so-earth-shattering question that's been burning in your mind. They'll be happy to answer it, and chances are that they'll recognize your next email and might answer it even if it's not the most pressing thing on their list. Human networking is almost as important here as the copper variety.

You should also regularly check the CERT Coordination Center Web site for any security alerts at `http://www.cert.org`. Better yet, get on the mailing list, which you can do from its Web site. The CERT Coordination Center grew out of the Computer Emergency Response Team, which was formed in 1988 by the Defense Advanced Research Projects Agency (DARPA) in response to the Internet worm that made the headlines of the day. Today, it's the Melissa virus that's making the headlines, and, needless to say, the CERT Coordination Center has information on it. A few months ago, CERT issued an advisory for a Trojan Horse version of TCP wrapper! If you weren't keeping current on the latest security events, you might have unwittingly installed the Trojan Horse TCP wrapper in an effort to make your machines more secure.

You might also want to check out the National Infrastructure Protection Center's site at `http://www.nipc.gov`. The center is currently trying to issue security reports every two weeks in PDF format. The reports, which seem to be rather thorough, break down into three sections: Bugs, Holes & Patches; Recent Exploit Scripts; and Viruses.

In addition to keeping up with the news, you might also want to consider installing other security-enhancing software packages. Tripwire monitors important system files and reports any changes. This could alert you to potential damage to your system. Tcpdump is a packet sniffer that you might want to install on your system to assist in further identifying why a machine might be acting sluggish or to help track what a cracker is doing with your machine. You or your security group might want to consider getting Internet Security System's scanning software that scans your machines for technical vulnerabilities. This is very helpful in further securing your machines, as are the Satan and COPS suites of tools. Keep in mind that anything that's out there that can break your system is likely to be tried by somebody. If you find a package that finds a security vulnerability with your system before the bad-guys get to it, you're one step ahead in protecting your machines.

Summary

In this lesson, I've hopefully instilled the notion that everyone *is* out to get you. As a system administrator, a healthy dose of paranoia is a good thing. Your supervisors might not initially understand the time commitment required to keep your system secure, so it is imperative that you explain this to them in terms that make sense to them. Explain the security problems that are regularly seen and the consequences to the users if security is compromised. Following are some tips:

* If you want to maintain your sanity, insist that you have the authority to make the decisions that your responsibilities require. No system administrator can survive long in a situation where she is responsible for maintaining security without having the authority to implement needed security changes.

* Expect most attempts to compromise security to come from individuals who are incapable of doing more than running prebuilt cracking scripts. If you defend effectively against these, you will eliminate *most* threats.

* By far, the easiest way for a user to steal another user's password is to simply watch him type it.

* Any code or security precaution can be broken if enough time can be spent trying. Brute force attacks are crude, but they are quite effective at cracking passwords.

* If your security is compromised, you really should be reinstalling everything and starting fresh.

* Your network can provide just as many vulnerabilities as physical access to your machines. Restrict network access by restricting the motion of traffic. Restrict the information available from network traffic by encrypting everything you can.

* Keep up-to-date with all sources of security information. The more you know, the safer you are.

- Don't run unnecessary services.
- Especially don't run unnecessary services as root. If a service is useful, see if it can be run as a nonpriveleged user so that if it can be compromised, the compromise is limited to normal user permissions.

Q&A

Q **A research group has come to me and wants one account to share between them. Should I let them have one?**

A Not if you want to maintain any sort of accountability for who does what with the system. If the entire research group is comfortable with the notion that if there is any compromise to the account, they all will be banned from the system, then sure, give them the account and kick them all back off two days later when you discover the scratch paper with their password left beside a machine. You and they will both be much better off if you insist that they have individual logins and simply give them a private group in /etc/groups so that they can all work on the same files if they want.

Q **I've noticed occasional logins from users when I'm almost certain that they're not really logged in. What should I do?**

A Ask them about it! I wouldn't suggest starting a full-scale investigation into what the user does and when because this might be an invasion of privacy and land your backside in hot water, but talk to them. It might be something as simple as them having configured a terminal package on their home machine with their login information, and whenever the machine is on, it logs in. This is generally a bad idea to let users do, but most of them won't even be aware that this is what their software does when they click Remember Password. It could also be a long-standing bug in many versions of System V, which for some reason seems occasionally incapable of recognizing when a user has logged off.

Q **A CERT advisory just came out saying that the version of XYZ that we run is insecure. What do I do?**

A Did the CERT advisory have information on available vendor patches? If so, install them. If not, follow its recommended procedure. If its recommended procedure is to decide whether this is a critical problem for you, you have some thinking to do. Will an exploit of the problem affect your users more than shutting down the affected service and hoping for a prompt fix? What do your users want to do? If the affected service is mission-critical, you might be in a position where you really can't shut it down without making your facility completely useless. In this case, you'd better plan on some late nights babysitting your machines until a fix appears.

Workshop

Exercises

1. Visit CERT and read though the advisory archives. Check over your machine records. How many patches don't you have installed?

2. Install them all!

3. Using the resources available or linked from CERT and 8lgm, find a system exploit-checking script and run it against your system. Did your system pass? Did you know it would pass before you ran the script?

4. Again using CERT and 8lgm, find a copy of `crack` or another password-cracking program. Run it against your user's password file. How many users chose passwords that are directly related to their job, hobbies, or friends? Expire all these user's passwords and make them all change them.

5. Just for good measure, unless you know it's been done in recent history, expire everyone's passwords and make everybody change them.

6. Rerun `crack` and see how many changed their previously bad passwords to `<previously bad password>.1`. Make them change them again.

7. Find out who in your organization is responsible for network and system security at the "oversight and contact for system administrators" level. Go introduce yourself. Consider doing lunch. You might not think you'll have anything to talk about, but they'll be overjoyed that you care enough about security to find out who they are and will probably be overflowing with useful information.

8. If your network administrator hasn't provided a securely switched network segment for your machines, call a smart-switch vendor and have him come discuss network security with you. If your network security administrator hasn't done this, add him to your mental list of irresponsible users who shouldn't be trusted.

9

DAY **10**

Defending Your Machines and Encrypting Traffic

Yesterday, you took a brief look at what you have to defend your machines against. Today, you will implement some of the basic common sense software solutions for your machine—namely, the TCP wrapper package, ssh1, and ssh2. As you might recall, in addition to regularly patching your operating system, turning off services you do not need, not using Telnet, and using secure shell are all good common sense practices for improving the security of your system. Today, you will make sure that services you don't need have been turned off. Then, you will install TCP wrapper, which monitors and filters requests for TCP services, and two versions of secure shell, which encrypt traffic.

Turning Off Those Services

Shortly after you installed your operating system, you turned off services you didn't need by commenting out the appropriate lines in your /etc/inetd.conf file. As you might have noticed, your machine comes with a lot of strange and not-so-strange services already on. Believe it or not, you and your machine will function fine without a number of these services, and your machine will be that much safer from the world.

Editing `/etc/inetd.conf`

`inetd` is the Internet services daemon that runs on your system. It starts at boot time, and when it starts, it reads its configuration file, `/etc/inetd.conf`. `inetd` listens for requests for any of the services that are turned on in `/etc/inetd.conf` and in turn invokes the appropriate daemon for the request. The presence of `inetd` is intended to reduce the load on your system. Rather than having a bunch of daemons running continuously that might not get many requests and just eat up some of your resources, there is only one running instead.

Each service line in `/etc/inetd.conf` has the following basic form:

```
<service_name> <socket_type> <proto> <flags> <user> <server_path> <args>
```

The order of entries in `/etc/inetd.conf` varies with the operating system, and some operating systems have entries that others don't, but I will cover a lot of common `/etc/inetd.conf` items. You will walk through the basic file in the order that items appear in my SunOS version.

`/etc/inetd.conf` on my machine starts with entries for FTP and Telnet. At this point, you might still need those services for your own purposes, so you should leave those services on. By the end of the day, though, you'll be turning off Telnet.

If you have a gopher entry in your `inetd.conf`, turn that service off by placing # in front of the line. Nobody uses gopher anymore.

My `/etc/inetd.conf` next has an entry for a name server protocol, which it already describes as obsolete. If you are running a more current operating system, you probably don't have that entry. If you do, I think you would be safe in commenting it out.

Next, I have entries for what `inetd.conf` describes as BSD protocols:

```
# shell stream  tcp     nowait  root     /usr/etc/in.rshd      in.rshd
# login stream  tcp     nowait  root     /usr/etc/in.rlogind   in.rlogind
# exec  stream  tcp     nowait  root     /usr/etc/in.rexecd    in.rexecd
# comsat dgram  udp      wait    root    /usr/etc/in.comsat    in.comsat
# talk  dgram   udp      wait    root    /usr/etc/in.talkd     in.talkd
```

Here is how the code breaks down:

- `shell` and `exec` enable a user to remotely access your machine without actually having to be logged in.
- `login` supports the somewhat more secure than Telnet, but still completely insecure, `rlogin` protocol.
- `comsat` notifies users who want to know when incoming mail has just arrived.
- `talk` enables users to converse with one another in real time, rather than sending email and replying back and forth.

Although most of these are convenient capabilities to have, they're all security risks and are not necessary. You should comment out all these entries unless you absolutely need them.

What follows the BSD protocols in my `inetd.conf` is an entry for `uucp`, UNIX-to-UNIX copy, and an entry for `tftp`:

- The `uucp` protocol was used to network UNIX machines in the dark ages and has been largely abandoned.
- `tftp` is "trivial file transfer protocol", a service used to boot diskless or near-diskless clients.

You can safely comment out the `uucp` line, unless you're trying to provide virtual network services for a transiently connected node—not something for the faint of heart!

Comment out the `tftp` service, unless your machine serves as a boot server for other machines.

10

Next, I have entries for `finger`, `netstat`, and `systat`:

```
# finger  stream  tcp    nowait  nobody  /usr/etc/in.fingerd  in.fingerd
# systat  stream  tcp    nowait  root    /usr/bin/ps              ps -auwwx
# netstat  stream  tcp   nowait  root    /usr/ucb/netstat    netstat -f inet
```

These services can provide information about your system that could be of more use to crackers. Some of these might already be disabled in your file:

- `systat` provides information on processes running on your machine to remote users.
- `netstat` provides network information for your machine to remote users.
- `finger` provides information about users on your machine to remote users.

Both `systat` and `netstat` should be disabled. If `finger` isn't disabled, disable it. `finger` could be helpful for someone who communicates with one of your users and who would like to double-check on information about her. On the other hand, it also unnecessarily provides information about who your users are for those who might just be trying to guess potential usernames that they could try to use to get in to your system.

My `inetd.conf` continues its entries with a couple of time entries for clock synchronization as well as entries for `echo`, `discard`, `daytime`, and `chargen`, which are described as being used for testing purposes. It's okay to comment out all those services.

If your `inetd.conf` has any entries for `pop` or `imap`, both providing mail reading services, disable them. These are certainly unnecessary services at this point. In addition, IMAP is becoming more popular among the crackers.

Next my `inetd.conf` lists RPC (Remote Procedure Call) services. These services are listed in the basic form:

`<rpc_prog>/<vers> <socket_type> rpc/<proto> <flags> <user> <path> <args>`

Overall, their appearance in `/etc/inetd.conf` does not look much different from the TCP services. Some services you will see listed here are `mountd`, `rexd`, `ypupdated`, `ruserd`, `sprayd`, `walld`, and `rquotad`.

- `mountd` is used by NFS server machines.

If your machine is not going to serve any file systems to other machines, disable this service. Although you might see this service listed here, on some operating systems, such as SunOS, it might be listed with a note that it really starts from elsewhere. On others, such as IRIX, it really does start from `inetd.conf`. On others, such as Linux, it might not appear at all in the `inetd.conf`. Look for it and disable it if you don't need it.

- `ypupdated` is used for NIS updating.

I was running this service on my SunOS machine in the office until recently, when after a security scan, I got a recommendation to disable it. Because the SunOS machine is currently the NIS master, I was a bit reluctant to do this, but after some investigating, I discovered that it didn't seem to actually be doing anything anyway. It has a bug and Sun recommends disabling it.

- `rexd` provides your machine with a minimalistic form of authentication.
- `ruserd` provides user information to remote users.

Both `ruserd` and `rexd` are security risks and should be disabled.

- `rquotad` is used to enforce local user quotas to nfs-mounted machines.

Whether you need this service will in part be determined by whether you have to enforce disk usage limits on your users.

- `rsprayd` is used for network testing. It accepts packets sent from the `spray` program on remote machines and can be used for network diagnosis. More on the `spray` program and its possible uses appears in Chapter 21, "Troubleshooting."

If you don't need this service, disable it. It isn't much of a security risk, but it can be exploited in denial-of-service attacks.

- `rwalld` enables remote users to write messages to the consoles of other users on the machine.

You can safely disable this service. The SunOS `/etc/inetd.conf` file amusingly describes this service: "The `rwall` server lets anyone on the network bother everyone on your machine."

Included in the RPC services section of your /etc/inetd.conf might appear some vendor-specific services. Disable what you are certain you don't need. If you discover that you do need it, turn it back on again. In this section of the IRIX /etc/inetd.conf, I once inadvertently disabled my display (I believe that was the sgi_fam service). You might want to make certain you can remotely access your machine before you start to play with some of the vendor-specific services.

> **Note**
>
> If you're using an SGI or Sun and have any entry for the ToolTalk Database Server, disable it unless you are certain that you are using it. SGI and Sun both recently advised that this service be disabled.

My /etc/inetd.conf ends here. However, the IRIX version does go on to list TCPMUX services. Under IRIX 6.5, these services at the moment only include print and scanner services. Again, disable whatever you don't need.

Finish with your updates and save your changes. Editing the file isn't quite enough to instate the changes. Now you have to tell the inetd to re-read its configuration file. You have a couple ways to do that. If your /etc/inetd.conf file lists a recommended procedure, use that one. If it doesn't, use ps to find the PID of inetd and send a hangup signal to inetd. The next time there is a request for one of the services it monitors, it will re-read the configuration file. This second method will work no matter what the operating system is. However, if your operating system recommends a method that doesn't require looking for any numbers, it's just that much easier to execute.

Here's what I have to do on my machine:

```
Barracuda# ps -aux ¦ grep "inetd"
root       197  0.0  0.6   32  196 co S    11:50   0:00 grep inetd
root       149  0.0  0.0   52    0 ?  IW   03:29   0:00 inetd

Barracuda# kill -HUP 149
```

Beyond /etc/inetd.conf

Is /etc/inetd.conf the only place you should look for services to disable? There might be services that start out of your /etc/rc.local or /etc/rc*.d that you could also disable. If you have an /etc/rc.local, you could do what you have done with the /etc/inetd.conf and comment out appropriate lines to disable the service. If your services start out of /etc/rc*.d, you might want to rename the startup files for the service. Then either kill the process you have disabled or reboot the machine.

Seriously scrutinize the services started in places like /etc/rc*.d or rc.local. Especially on some of the newer versions of UNIX, the vendors are falling over themselves to make the user environment more friendly and more like what users are used to on personal-computer systems. To do this, the vendors are inventing and adding all sorts of automatic services that do all manner of wonderful things. Unfortunately, many of these have not been well tested and present serious security risks. A particularly egregious example, Linux, right out of the box is a collection of disasters just waiting to happen. The best way to deal with all these wonder-services is to turn off absolutely everything that isn't critical for the functioning of the machine and then turn back on only those items that are mission-critical for your facility.

Is it nice to have, for example, an automount service running that enables any user to insert a CD-ROM or floppy and have the mount command run for it automatically? Certainly! Users can use their own CD-ROMs, they don't have to bother root to use privileged commands to mount the device, and everybody's happy. Heck, they can even write CD-ROMs on their Linux boxes at home with a set-uid script owned by root, drop the CD-ROMs in your machine, and have instant root privileges on your machine themselves—what could be better?

It might seem overly draconian to turn everything off and not turn things back on unless it "really hurts," but it's the safest way of preventing you from needing to kick yourself in the butt for having something turned on that was insecure at a later date.

Tip

A Personal Suggestion From Your Opinionated Author

rant mode on

Many newer versions of UNIX include an automagical NFS drive-mounting service. This service might be called automounter, or autofs, or automountd, or something similar on your machine. The preceding text's comments on auto-mount devices aside, as they really only apply to the variety that automatically mounts removable devices, *please* turn this service off! This automagical auto-mounting service will cause any NFS device that you access to magically appear in the directory /net. It will remember this information forever and will mount the device in /net without you ever touching anything.

I'm sure this service was added with the best of intentions. It sort of autoclusters machines without you having to do any work. It neatly and transparently handles devices that are transiently available or unavailable on the network. It requires absolutely no thought whatsoever. It's the most annoying piece of UNIX software I've ever met, and aside from some of the more drastic cracking software, it is the most deserving of a worldwide witch hunt to find and punish the perpetrator.

If you leave this particular service enabled, you will have almost no control over when and where devices are mounted. It automatically puts them where it wants to, and there's not a thing you can do about it. The slight benefit of having something that transparently handles transiently missing devices is completely outweighed by the fact that if it gets to a mount first, any mount point you've specified in your `fstab` will fail.

Help stamp out this software abomination. Find and destroy any NFS `automount` services that your OS includes. You, as the system administrator, need complete control over your machine, what happens, when it happens, and how it happens. This software removes that control. It's a bad thing to do and a bad way to do it.

```
# rant mode off
```

10

Rebooting the machine probably gives you the best diagnostic information, especially if you are not sure what the service you just disabled does.

As an example of what can happen if you disable services without understanding what you're doing, in the same security report that it was suggested that I disable `rpc.ypupdated`, it was also suggested that if I didn't need it, to disable `keyserv`. I read the man page for `keyserv`, and although it somehow involves encryption, it didn't look like I would really need to have `keyserv` running. So, I commented it out of `/etc/rc.local`. On one machine, the service was commented out and its process was killed. On a second machine, I commented it out and happened to reboot the machine. It turned out that I could still use the encrypted secure shell connection `ssh` to connect to the first machine, but I could not `ssh` to the second machine. Apparently, more functionality was disabled by commenting the `keyserv` service out than I wanted. If I hadn't rebooted one of the machines, I might not have noticed that anything had broken for quite a long time, as the machine on which I simply killed the `keyserv` process kept working just fine.

Unfortunately for me, `telnetd` happens to be disabled on the machine that I rebooted, so I couldn't `telnet` to it either. To make matters worse, this particular machine does not have a monitor and keyboard attached, so I could not log in on the console right way. I shut the machine down and borrowed a keyboard and monitor from another machine. After I undid the changes I had made, I rebooted and tested `ssh` while I still could log in on the console. I could remotely log in again! Then, I had to make the hardware switch again. Obviously, `keyserv` is useful for the encrypted secure shell software even if my security scans are telling me to turn it off!

All this goes to show that it's important to know that your machine will reboot and work properly after making a configuration change. Sometimes, this means rebooting it even if you don't think it needs it so that you can break it earlier, rather than later. If I hadn't rebooted either machine, their first reboot could have come at some time when I was unavailable to repair the problem, and my staff would have had a difficult time determining exactly what it was that had gone wrong.

Whether you are disabling services through /etc/inetd.conf or through the startup scripts, make sure that you have a way to access your machine. In the case of my SGI display problem, I had to be able to access the machine remotely. In the case of my Sun, I had to add a keyboard and monitor so that I was able to access the machine at the console.

TCP Wrapper

Now that you have taken the time to investigate at least the services that appear in /etc/inetd.conf and have disabled the ones you know you don't need, you are ready to start wrapping the TCP-based services with TCP wrapper. TCP wrapper is a package that monitors and filters requests for TCP (Transmission Control Protocol) services. You will not look at the protocol in any detail—that is a book subject in itself. Suffice it to say that the protocol has enough control information in it that you can use a package such as TCP wrapper to filter some of that traffic.

What Is TCP Wrapper?

TCP wrapper is a package that provides a way for you to monitor incoming requests for TCP services and filter what machines are allowed to access what services. The package produces a daemon, tcpd, which you will use to wrap services. When you are done installing and configuring TCP wrapper, for any TCP daemon needed, inetd will call tcpd, rather than calling the actually requested daemon. tcpd, in turn, will decide from its access files whether to grant the request.

By default, TCP wrapper will log its decisions in the same place where the sendmail daemon logs its information. To see where that will be, likely somewhere in /var, check your /etc/syslog.conf file.

Installing TCP wrapper consists of two parts:

- Building and putting the package somewhere useful on your system.
- Configuring the package.

Building and Installing TCP Wrapper

If you are running Linux, you already have TCP wrapper installed somewhere. Look for it, and to prepare you for the ssh portion of today's work, search for tcpd.h and libwrap.

a and remember those locations. Because Linux already comes with TCP wrapper, you might be able to find the location of the daemon itself in your inetd.conf.

If you're not running Linux, you might have to get the source code and start from scratch. There are also places where precompiled versions are available for some flavors of UNIX. If you have a source for a precompiled version, make sure that you know where the package was intended to be installed. This might be one instance where you are likely to want to perform the compilation yourself. You can get the source for TCP wrapper from many places, but ftp.cert.org is a good one to try.

Why all the confusing advice above? You have two options for how you can install TCP wrapper: easy and advanced. In the easy method, after you build TCP wrapper, you will move the real daemons that you want to wrap to a hard-to-find directory and put tcpd in the original daemon directory in place of the real ones. The documentation suggests a ... directory in the directory where the real daemons are regularly stored. In other words, if your real daemons are stored in /usr/etc, you would make /usr/etc/..., move the daemons you want to wrap in /usr/etc/..., and put tcpd in /usr/etc/tcpd. The precompiled version available for IRIX at SGI's freeware site is intended for this installation method. The drawback to this method is that whenever you upgrade your operating system, you have to remember to look for and move any upgraded daemons to the alternative directory.

In the advanced way of installing the program, you edit your /etc/inetd.conf directly to call tcpd. This method can also have its drawbacks; don't put it past an operating system upgrade to replace your inetd.conf with a new one. Even if your operating system should do this, I'm sure you're keeping backup copies of the file on hand anyway, as a good practice. When I upgraded from IRIX 6.5.2 to IRIX 6.5.3, my inetd.conf was replaced.

I find it easier to remember to check for any configuration files that might have changed than to go chasing around moving executables, so I use the advanced option. In the case of IRIX, the configuration files you had in place tend to be kept, either as the file that is still the default or as a backup to the new improved installed version.

You will look at the advanced installation method today.

Building TCP Wrapper Building TCP wrapper is not at all painful. The instructions for what to do appear at the beginning of the makefile, and the makefile contains many templates for different systems, including some for IRIX.

Table 10.1 shows the options available at compilation.

TABLE 10.1   TCP Wrapper Compilation Options

Option	Function	Default
-DHOST_ACCESS	Enables access control per host, service, or combination.	Enabled
-DPARANOID	Double-checks hostname/ address. Refuses services when there are discrepancies.	Enabled
-DKILL_IP_OPTIONS	Refuses to service connections with IP source routing options. Usually not needed with current operating systems.	Disabled
RFC 931	Performs username lookups, but only when access control files require it (this is in the makefile rather than a command-line option).	Enabled by default with 10 second timeout
-DPROCESS_OPTIONS	Language extensions. Provides additional keyword support for access control files, including banner messages.	Disabled

Decide which options you need. Read the README and the makefile to see if you need to edit the makefile to compile.

In my particular case, I am interested in being able to have a banner up to notify people that they are being refused access so that they don't wonder what is happening with their connections. I am able to issue this command to build my version:

```
Barracuda# make REAL_DAEMON_DIR=/usr/etc STYLE=-DPROCESS_OPTIONS sunos4
```

Installing TCP Wrapper   After you have built TCP Wrapper, you have to decide where to put the daemon. You might want to store it in the directories where your real daemons reside, or you might want to store it in some form of /usr/local, or wherever you store your local software. You might decide you want to store tcpd in /usr/local in a directory of the same approximate hierarchy as your real daemon storage. For example, if your real daemons are in /usr/etc, perhaps you will want to store this one in /usr/local/etc. After you have decided where you want tcpd, copy it to the appropriate location. The compilation also produces a libwrap.a and tcpd.h. Copy those to where you store locally installed libraries and include files.

Edit your /etc/inetd.conf so that inetd will call tcpd. For example, to wrap telnetd, your line might look like this:

```
telnet  stream  tcp     nowait  root    /usr/local/bin/tcpd     in.telnetd
```

Remember to restart your inetd.

Now you're done with the installation!

Configuring TCP Wrapper

Now you are ready for the more confusing part—configuring TCP Wrapper. TCP Wrapper has two control files, /etc/hosts.allow and /etc/hosts.deny. Be sure to read the man page on host access and host options.

Here is the format of the access control files:

```
daemon_list : client_list : option : option ...
```

Through /etc/hosts.allow you can allow specific services for specific hosts.

Through /etc/hosts.deny you can deny services to hosts and provide global exceptions.

The easiest way to think of and use these configuration files is to think of TCP Wrapper as putting a big fence up around all the services on your machine.

The specifications in /etc/hosts.deny tell the fence what services are on the outside of the fence and are therefore *not* denied. The fence can appear to be around different sets of services for different clients. For example, an /etc/hosts.deny file might look like this:

```
ALL EXCEPT ftpd : 192.168.1. : banners /usr/etc/banners
ALL : 140.254.12.100 140.254.12.135 : banners /usr/etc/banners
ALL EXCEPT ftpd sshd : ALL : banners /usr/etc/banners
```

This file says the following:

- For the subdomain 192.168.1., deny all connections except connections to the FTP daemon, ftpd.

- For the specific machines 140.254.12.100 and 140.254.12.135 (maybe they're troublemakers) deny absolutely all connections.

- For all other IP addresses, deny everything except connections to ftpd and to the secure-shell daemon sshd.

The banners /usr/etc/banners entry is an option that tells tcpd that if it denies a connection to a service based on this entry, try to find an explanation file in this location.

For example, in `/usr/etc/banners`, I have a collection of files named `ftpd`, `rlogind`, and `telnetd`. (I've been a little lazy and not created one for every service; they're only necessary if you want to tell people who shouldn't be connecting to your machines, why you've denied them a connection.) The TCP wrapper package actually comes with some prototype files you can edit if you'd like to make use of this facility, but creating your own isn't too difficult.

Simply create a file in the banners directory with the name `<servicename>` for whatever service you want to give explanations for, and put the message you'd like displayed in it. If you look at the contents of my `/usr/etc/banners/telnetd` file, you see the following:

```
Mother 234> cat /usr/etc/banners/telnetd

             Welcome to Mother

     For security reasons the network access
          to Mother has been restricted.

       If you have an established account on
    Mother and would like to have network access
             please send E-mail to
          access@mother.politically.correct.com
```

This is exactly what you should see if you try to Telnet to my home machine, `mother.politically.correct.com`.

The specifications in `/etc/hosts.allow` make little gates through the fences erected by `/etc/hosts.deny` for specific host and service combinations. For example, an `/etc/hosts.allow` file might look like this:

```
ALL: 140.254.12.137 192.168.2. 192.168.3.
popd: 140.254.12.124 140.254.12.151 192.168.1.36
```

This file says the following:

- Allow connections to any TCP service from the host `140.254.12.137` and all hosts in the `192.168.2.` and `192.168.3.` subdomains. (Perhaps the `192.168.2.` and `192.168.3.` subdomains are known highly secure networks, and you really trust `140.254.12.137` because it's so well run.)
- Allow connections to the `popd` service for three specific machines `140.254.12.124`, `140.254.12.151`, and `192.168.1.36`.

If used in combination with the previous `/etc/hosts.deny` file, these allowances still stand. They override the denials in `/etc/hosts.deny`, so even though the `192.168.1.` subdomain is denied all access except to `ftpd` by `/etc/hosts.deny`, the specific machine `192.168.1.36` has its own private gate that enables it access to the `popd` service as well.

Tip

> **Giving an allowance**   The `/etc/hosts.allow` and `/etc/hosts.deny` files are supposed to work with IP addresses. Usually, they do. However, I have observed that on occasion, these files require a hostname. I don't pretend to understand the how or why of this, but should you encounter a situation where you're certain that you have everything configured correctly and an `/etc/hosts.allow` entry just refuses to work, give it a try with the fully qualified hostname.

Note

> **Services with a smile, or without?**   There can be a bit of confusion as to the name of the service to put in an `/etc/hosts.allow` or `/etc/hosts.deny` file. If it's a service out of `inetd.conf`, generally the name to use is the service name from the left-most column of the file. If this doesn't work, try adding a `d` to the end of the service name (for example, changing `ftp` to `ftpd`). In other implementations, it seems that you need to add `in.` before the service name.
>
> Other services use names that don't seem to be recorded officially anywhere. From experimentation, I've found that X11 appears to be simply X11, and versions of portmapper that obey the `/etc/hosts.allow` and `/etc/hosts.deny` files go by portmapper. The secure shell `ssh` daemons seem to respond both to their actual name, `ssh1` and `ssh2`, and to `sshd`. Other services that you encounter and decide to wrap with the TCP wrappers might require a bit of experimenting on your part. Thus far my experience has been that their names are relatively easy to guess.

10

Secure Shell

Now that you have your services wrapped, you are ready to encrypt some of that network traffic. Secure shell provides for a secure connection to your machine by encrypting the connection. By using secure shell rather than Telnet, your password and any other information in your terminal session will no longer be transmitted in clear text. It uses encryption and cryptographic authentication to achieve a more secure connection. There are currently two SSH protocols, SSH1 and SSH2. Because you can't be sure what type of client software your users will have, it is best to install both `ssh1` and `ssh2`, in that order. Install `ssh` version 1.2.26 or later and the most recent version of `ssh` version 2.0.*. You can find a wealth of information on the protocols, plus where to find the packages and whether you should get the commercial versions or the free versions at `http://www.ssh.fi/sshprotocols2`.

Installing ssh1

Your experience with installing ssh1 can range from quite pleasant to nightmarish. If you run into problems, be sure to check the comp.security.ssh newsgroup to see if someone already has a solution posted. That being said, get on with the installation.

Installation Overview

As always, read the documentation before you begin. Read INSTALL and any available READMEs. Be sure to look for tips for your operating system and on general common problems.

The installation procedure is much like what you've seen so far with other packages. You will run the following:

```
./configure
make
make install
```

If you run configure and then decide you want to supply some options or different options than you did originally, run make distclean before running configure again.

If you have to share binaries among machines, you can compile on one machine as described above and then run make hostinstall on other machines that share the same binary executables. In my facility, I have two SGIs of one architecture and four SGIs of another. One machine of each architecture type is serving binaries for the machines of similar architecture type. The make hostinstall feature enabled me to speed up the overall installation on the SGIs after everything was finally working.

After you have installed the software, take a look at the two configuration files that are generated, /etc/sshd_config and /etc/ssh_config, to see if there is anything you want to edit. The files are very self-explanatory, and generally, you will be happy with the defaults in them.

Finally, start and test the daemon. When you are satisfied that the daemon works, edit your /etc/rc.local file or make a script in your /etc/rc*.d directory to start the daemon at boot time.

If for some reason you should have to remove ssh, run make uninstall.

Configuring ssh1

Table 10.2 shows some of the options you can specify when configuring ssh1.

TABLE 10.2 Configuration Options for ssh1

Option	Function	Default
Standard Options		
--prefix=PREFIX	Where to install files	Default: /usr/local
--exec_prefix=PREFIX	Where to install executables	Default: /usr/local
--srcdir=DIR	Source directory location	Default: where configure is
Specific Options		
--enable-warnings	Enables –Wall if using gcc	
--with-x	Uses the X Window system	
--with-idea	Uses IDEA	Default
--without-idea	Doesn't use IDEA (avoids patent problems in commercial use)	
--with-blowfish	Includes blowfish encryption	Default
--without-blowfish	Doesn't include blowfish encryption	
--with-des	Includes single-DES support	
--without-des	Doesn't include single-DES support	Default
--with-arcfour	Includes arcfour. Don't do without reading README.CIPHERS	
--without-arcfour	Doesn't include arcfour	Default
--with-none	Includes support for unencrypted connections	

10

continues

TABLE 10.2 continued

Option	Function	Default
Specific Options		
`--without-none`	Doesn't support unencrypted connections	Default
`--with-login[=PATH]`	Uses `login -f` to finish login connections	
`--with-rsh-PATH`	Specifies where to find `rsh`	
`--without-rsh`	Does not use `rsh` at all	
`--with-path=PATH`	Default path passed to user shell by `sshd`	
`--with-etcdir=PATH`	Directory for `ssh` system files	Default: `/etc`
`--with-securid[=PATH]`	Enables support for Security Dynamics SecurID card	
`--with-tis[=DIR]`	Enables support for TIS authentication server	
`--with-kerberos5=[KRB-PREFIX]`	Compiles in Kerberos5 support	
`--enable-kerberos-tgt-passing`	Passes Kerberos ticket-granting-ticket	
`--with-libwrap[=PATH]`	Compiles in TCP wrapper support	
`--with-socks`	Compiles in SOCKS firewall transversal support	
`--with-socks5[=PATH]`	Compiles in SOCKS5 firewall transversal support	
`--with-socks4[=PATH]`	Compiles in SOCKS4 firewall transversal support	

Option	Function	Default
Specific Options		
`--with-rsaref[=PATH]`	Uses RSAREF (to try to avoid patent problems in the U.S.)	
`--without-rsaref`	Uses normal RSA routines	Default
`--enable-group-writeability`	Enables group writeability in `auth-rsa`	
`--enable-deprecated-linux-pw-encrypt`	Enables use of deprecated Linux `pw_encrypt` function	
`--disable-server-port-forwardings`	Disables all port forwardings in server except X11	
`--disable-client-port-forwardings`	Disables all port forwardings in client except X11	
`--disable-server-x11-forwarding`	Disables X11 forwarding in server	
`--disable-client-x11-forwarding`	Disables X11 forwarding in client	
`--enable-suid-ssh`	Installs `ssh` as suid root	Default
`--disable-suid-ssh`	Installs `ssh` without suid bit	
`--disable-asm`	Disables assembly language optimizations	

Table 10.3 lists environment variables you might want to configure.

TABLE 10.3 Environment Variable Configuration

Variable	Function	Default
`CC=compiler`	Name of C compiler	Default: `gcc` or `cc`
`CFLAGS=flags`	Flags to C compiler	Default: `-O -g` or just `-O`
`LDFLAGS=flgs`	Flags to linker	Default: none

10

You might especially want to set some of these variables if you have some files stored in nonstandard places. For example, gcc seems to automatically look in /usr/local/ include for include files. That is where I put my tcpd.h. However, if I had put my tcpd.h in some unusual location, I might have wanted to specify that location for configure.

If you are running csh, here's a way to do that:

```
 (setenv CC=xcc; setenv CFLAGS="-O2 I/yyy/include";
➡ setenv LDFLAGS="-L/lib/zzz"; ./configure)
```

I recommend enabling TCP wrapper support. With this added support, sshd will process the controls specified in /etc/hosts.allow and /etc/hosts.deny. Don't disable any of the port forwardings, X11 or otherwise. Not only can ssh be used to encrypt your network traffic, but it can also be used to forward TCP services over an encrypted channel. You will use this feature next week when you secure FTP and pop services.

If some of the options don't mean anything to you, you probably don't need them.

Installing ssh1

I am pleased to report that installing ssh1 is a fairly pleasant experience in SunOS 4.1.4. A bit into the original configuration process, I do have a slight problem:

```
Barracuda# ./configure --with-libwrap=/usr/local/lib/libwrap.a
checking for xauth... no
configure: error: configuring with X but xauth not found - aborting
```

SunOS does include a version of X11 though, so I want the X11 authentication code to work. A bit of digging around shows that the directory for the X11 executables (in Sun's nonstandard /usr/openwin/ hierarchy) is not in my path. I set my path to include the binary directory for xauth, and all goes well for a bit:

```
Barracuda# set path=($path /usr/openwin/bin)
Barracuda# ./configure --with-libwrap=/usr/local/lib/libwrap.a
Barracuda# make
```

At the make step, I discover that I have forgotten to put tcpd.h somewhere that the compiler can find on my system, so I get this error:

```
ssh.c:199: tcpd.h: No such file or directory
ssh.c: In function 'main':
ssh.c:875: warning: assignment makes pointer from integer without a cast
make: *** [ssh.o] Error 1
```

After putting tcpd.h in /usr/local/include, where I had intended for it to go, the make succeeds, and I can continue:

```
Barracuda# make install
```

Don't be surprised if during the `make install` step, you get comments such as the following:

```
mv: /usr/local/sbin/sshd1: Cannot access: No such file or directory
mv: /usr/local/sbin/sshd: Cannot access: No such file or directory
```

The directories or files might not yet exist, and the install process is trying to be polite and back them up before installing new ones. By the time `make install` is done, though, everything will be where it belongs.

If during `make install`, the machine spends an extraordinary time making the host keys, there is probably something wrong. Suspect this especially if the process seems to be stuck in a loop making `p key...` `making k key...` over and over. Check the documentation to see if you missed any hints, and check the newsgroup for any useful postings.

> **Note**
>
> **Busted IRIX compilers and libraries** IRIX seems to have more than its fair share of bugs with the system libraries and compilers.
>
> If you are building `ssh1` on IRIX, you will want to fix the `int err;` line in `sshd.c`. Find the line containing `int err;` in `sshd.c`. The section will look much like the following one. Change it to `int err=0;` as follows:
>
> ```
>     */
>     int sgi_project_setup(char *username)
>     {
>       int err=0;
>       int naccts;
>       projid_t pbuf;
>
>       /* Find default project for a particular user */
> ```
>
> With this fix, `ssh1` ought to function in IRIX, although your logging information, at least in 6.5, will indicate that connections are coming from `255.255.255.255`. Check the `ssh` newsgroup for various proposed solutions.

Testing the `sshd`

Now, you've got `sshd` installed. Does it actually work? It's almost time to give it a try.

Before you actually start up the daemon, edit your `/etc/services` file to include this new service. A look at the `/etc/sshd_config` file indicates that `sshd` is running on port 22. Your new entry should look like this:

```
sshd1           22/tcp
```

You'll find that it helps when you add items to `/etc/services` to insert them into the body of the file in port-number order, rather than adding them at the end of a file. This way, you can more easily determine whether a particular port is free when you want to add a new service.

Knowing, because I've done this before, that I will be adjusting the configuration file for sshd1 when I am done with sshd2, I copy my /etc/sshd_config file to /etc/sshd_fix_config and start the daemon like this:

```
Barracuda# /usr/local/sbin/sshd1 -f /etc/sshd_fix_config
```

You do not have to choose to do it this way. Instead, you might just want to back up your /etc/sshd_config file to make sure you have a backup copy. Later in this lesson, you will be changing a configuration setting in /etc/sshd_config. Because I wanted to be sure I wouldn't forget the change, I renamed my configuration file and invoked the -f option to use a nonstandard configuration file. If you choose to use /etc/sshd_config, the default file, as the configuration file for sshd1 to read, all you need to do to start the daemon is this:

```
Barracuda# /usr/local/sbin/sshd1
```

In anticipation of having both sshd1 and sshd2 installed fairly soon, I update /etc/hosts.deny to include both. Here is what my /etc/hosts.deny looks like:

```
Barracuda# more /etc/hosts.deny
ALL EXCEPT sshd1 sshd2 sshd : ALL : banners /usr/etc/banners
```

Now, I do the actual test to verify that ssh works:

```
Barracuda# /usr/local/bin/slogin 192.168.1.20
Host key not found from the list of known hosts.
Are you sure you want to continue connecting (yes/no)? yes
Host '192.168.1.20' added to the list of known hosts.
root@192.168.1.20's password:
Last login: Wed Apr  7 22:56:10 1999 from 192.168.1.4
SunOS Release 4.1.4 (BARRACUDA_SMALL) #2: Mon Mar 22 20:33:01 EST 1999
No mail.

Barracuda# exit
Barracuda# logout
Connection to 192.168.1.20 closed.
```

It works! Now all I have to do is edit my /etc/rc.local file so that the daemon will start at boot time.

Installing ssh2

Again, I am pleased to report that installing ssh2 is a fairly pleasant experience in SunOS. Unfortunately, I must warn the IRIX users that if ssh1 was unpleasant, ssh2 will be even more unpleasant. Check the newsgroups for solutions for IRIX. I had to have my programmer work on this for my IRIX install. He actually had to write his own working version of some things that were being done incorrectly by the OS to get this working with IRIX 6.5, but there might be other solutions. True to the UNIX and Internet way of solving problems, the secure shell authors are supposed to be incorporating the fix that my programmer wrote for me into future versions of the product, so you might not experience this unpleasantness in your installs.

Configuring and Installing ssh2

Although the SSH2 protocol might be different from the SSH1 protocol, the installation procedure is not. As usual, read the README, plus the SSH2.QUICKSTART files. Remember to check for any tips for your operating system.

The installation overview notes for ssh1 already describe the installation procedure for ssh2, except that you can no longer run make hostinstall on machines that are sharing binaries. However, if you are in the source directory cd apps/ssh and run make generate-host-key, you can perform the same trick.

The configuration options are the same for ssh2, except that—disable-asm is no longer an option.

Editing System Configuration Files for ssh2

Here is where you have to do a little more work than you did with ssh1.

In our area we have both Mac and PC users, as you might expect. We were planning to use the DataFellows F-Secure Tunnel and Terminal client for the Mac and PC. Because I have many IRIX machines in my cluster, when I first installed the ssh programs, I was not able to install both in the same day. After ssh1 was successfully installed, I went home, tried the Mac client program, and connected to the cluster without any problems. I then downloaded the trial version for the PC and tried to connect from the PC, but I couldn't. I determined that the PC version must speak SSH2 protocol and that the Mac version speaks SSH1 protocol. Given the already joyous experience I had had with ssh1 and IRIX, I was less than excited to see that ssh2 needed to be installed immediately.

As soon as IRIX, with the diligent help of a programmer, permitted ssh2 to be successfully installed, I again tried to log in to the cluster from home on the PC. It worked! However, the problem this time was that I could no longer speak to the cluster from the Mac. I had assumed that by enabling ssh1 compatibility in ssh2 that things would work out by themselves, but that didn't seem to be the case. The easiest solution to that problem turned out to be running ssh1 on a different port from ssh2. I recommend running ssh2 on the default port, 22, and picking a common unused port among all your machines for running ssh1.

10

After you have installed ssh2, edit your /etc/services file. This time, indicate that for port 22, the service is sshd2. Assign your commonly available unused port to sshd1. Here, I picked port 24 and added an sshd1 line at port 24 to /etc/services as well.

Now, you need to indicate to ssh2 that you want ssh1 compatibility. This will (theoretically—remember that it didn't work for the DataFellows Macintosh client) enable a user from a remote site that is only running ssh1 to log in to your system. sshd2 will call sshd1 when it receives the request—or at least it's supposed to. That method is slower than if the user sshes in directly to the sshd1 port, but with this setup, the remote user doesn't have to know the specifics about your setup to be able to log in. When ssh2 is installed, it will become the default secure shell. If you use ssh2 to ssh to a remote site only running ssh1, it will revert to ssh1 mode. This fallback method does seem to work for UNIX ssh clients, even though it seems to have some problems for clients on personal computers.

To enable ssh1 compatibility, edit /etc/ssh2/sshd2_config to include these lines, of course pointing to wherever sshd1 resides on your system:

```
Ssh1Compatibility           yes
Sshd1Path                   /usr/local/sbin/sshd1
```

With ssh-2.0.12, you might find both of those lines already in the file in whole or in part.

Next, edit /etc/ssh2/ssh2_config to add these lines, this time pointing to wherever ssh1 resides on your system:

```
Ssh1Compatibility           yes
Ssh1Path                    /usr/local/bin/ssh1
```

Now, edit the configuration file for sshd1 to reflect the new port. In my case, the configuration file I have picked for sshd1 is /etc/sshd_fix_config, where I need to change the default port from 22 to 24. If you are using the standard configuration file, edit /etc/sshd_config.

Testing SSH2

Now, you are ready to test ssh2.

First, kill the current sshd processes. The current ones are named sshd1. I do this as follows:

```
Barracuda# ps -aux ¦ grep "ssh"
root 11852  0.0  0.6   32  196 co S    02:40   0:00 grep ssh
root  6861  0.0  0.0  456    0 ?  IW   01:20   0:02 /usr/local/sbin/sshd1 -f
root  6797  0.0  0.0   96    0 ?  IW   00:48   0:45 /usr/local/sbin/sshd1 -f

Barracuda# kill -9 6861 6797
```

Then, I start sshd1 and sshd2:

```
Barracuda# /usr/local/sbin/sshd1 -f /etc/sshd_fix_config
Barracuda# /usr/local/sbin/sshd
```

Remember, sshd is now running sshd2 by default:

```
Barracuda# /usr/local/bin/ssh2 192.168.1.20
Accepting host 192.168.1.20 key without checking.
root's password:
Apr 8 02:45:59 Barracuda sshd[11861]: User root's local password accepted
Apr 8 02:45:59 Barracuda sshd[11861]: Password authentication for
➥user root accepted
Apr 8 02:45:59 Barracuda sshd[11861]: User root, coming from
➥Barracuda, authenticated
Last login: Thu Apr  8 01:20:09 1999 from 192.168.1.254
SunOS Release 4.1.4 (BARRACUDA_SMALL) #2: Mon Mar 22 20:33:01 EST 1999
No mail.

Barracuda# exit
Barracuda# logout
```

To double-check that sshd1 is still working, I explicitly try ssh1:

```
Barracuda# ssh1 192.168.1.20
root@192.168.1.20's password:
Last login: Thu Apr  8 02:46:00 1999 from Barracuda
SunOS Release 4.1.4 (BARRACUDA_SMALL) #2: Mon Mar 22 20:33:01 EST 1999
No mail.

Barracuda# exit
Barracuda# logout
Connection to 192.168.1.20 closed.
```

It all seems to work!

As everything is currently set up, ssh2 commands are the defaults. slogin now points
to ssh2. If users want to use ssh1 commands, they have to explicitly add the 1 to the
commands. For example, to explicitly use ssh1 rather than the default ssh2 (slogin)
to log in to a machine, you would do the following:

```
WAASHU joray 201 > ssh1 rosalyn

Enter passphrase for RSA key 'joray@Halo':
Last login: Tue Jul  6 09:42:36 1999 from ryoohki.biosci.o
...Remote login...


Rosalyn joray 201 >
```
On our machines, at least with ssh version 2.0.11, ssh2 had problems working cleanly
on the Suns, so we used ssh1 commands for navigating the Suns. By ssh version 2.0.13,

this bug has been fixed. Both versions of ssh, although they were very painful to install on IRIX, work nicely when installed, so we use the default SSH2 commands on the IRIX machines.

Final System Configuration Edits

After you've tested that the daemons are working, you must edit the appropriate startup script to have them start at boot time. Provided here are sample entries for both an /etc/rc.local and an /etc/rc*.d file.

Here's the addition to my /etc/rc.local file:

```
if [ -f /usr/local/sbin/sshd1 ]; then
    /usr/local/sbin/sshd1 -f /etc/sshd_fix_config; echo "started sshd1"
fi

if [ -f /usr/local/sbin/sshd ]; then
    /usr/local/sbin/sshd; echo "started sshd2"
fi
```

Here's a sample startup script for a System V machine. It doesn't use any fancy testing of the existence of the daemons, but it gets the job done:

```
#!/sbin/sh
echo "Starting sshd2"
/usr/etc/sshd
echo "sshd2 started"
echo "Starting sshd1"
/usr/etc/sshd1 -f /etc/sshd_fix_config
echo "sshd1 started"
```

With secure shell running now, it is recommended that you disable Telnet.

Note

> **The grinch who stole Telnet**   Your users are going to think that you're an evil (unspeakable text deleted) for taking away Telnet. They've used Telnet for years, it's worked for years, they don't want to change, and you're a bad person. This is an occasion for "tough love." Telnet is a supremely insecure protocol, and it leaves your machines and your users open to loss of data, downtime, and all manner of unpleasant problems. Your users will probably hate you now for disabling Telnet and forcing them to all go purchase a secure connection program. I wish I could say that they'll love you later when the secure connection program saves them hundreds of hours of downtime and thousands of dollars of lost productivity, but they won't—they won't even notice that things worked smoothly where previously things might not have. Instead, you need to be satisfied that you're doing the right thing here and know in your heart of hearts that you've done the right thing, even if your users think you're the grinch.

User Configuration: Setting up an ssh Client

This section is included here so that a lot of the basic ssh configuration material is located in the same section for easy reference. However, because root is currently your only user, you are not actually expected to try this until Day 12, "The Basics of Making User Accounts," when you finally make some user accounts. Here, I will demonstrate setting up an ssh client on the Mac.

Installing F-Secure SSH Tunnel and Terminal

For information on how to purchase F-Secure SSH Tunnel and Terminal, check `http://www.datafellows.com`. Install the program, which on a Mac is simply double-clicking the install icon and following the onscreen instructions.

10

Note

SSH client availability In addition to the DataFellows clients for the SSH protocols, you might be able to find shareware or freeware clients for the SSH protocols. Unfortunately, due to a particularly dim-witted concept known as a software patent and the equally uninspired notion held by the U.S. government that encryption software is military munitions subject to export controls, it is probably not legal to import and possibly not legal to use this software.

As an aside, have you ever noticed that if you want to download the most secure version of something like Netscape Navigator, you have to download it from a site outside the United States? This is because of the bizarre notion that the strong-encryption software that this program uses is a military technology and therefore cannot be exported. An *on-paper listing* of the software, however, is considered to be a written work, is subject to freedom-of-speech guarantees provided by the First Amendment, and therefore can be exported. If you need to provide an encryption technology worldwide, it seems that the only legal way to do it is to export it in code form as a listing, in which form it is a protected written work. When out of the country, you can have it typed in, compiled, and served to the world from a foreign site not afflicted by this particular brand of idiocy. For a more complete dissertation on this silliness, do a Web search on the PGP program and its author. The story of the adventures that this man and his extremely useful "Pretty Good Privacy" encryption software have experienced at the hands of the U.S. government reads like a made-for-TV late-night conspiracy theory movie.

In any case, should you be located outside the United States or care to exercise a bit of civil disobedience, you might want to check out the following Web sites:

`http://www.lysator.liu.se/~jonasw/freeware.html`

`http://www.zip.com.au/~roca/ttssh.html`

The former serves an ssh-enabled version of `niftytelnet` for the Macintosh, and the latter serves an ssh-enabled version of `teraterm` for the PC.

Connecting to a Remote Host

Secure shell provides two ways to connect to a remote host: password authentication and RSA authentication. With password authentication, your password is encrypted as it is transmitted. RSA authentication provides yet another level of security by creating a set of passphrase-protected keys that you can use for accessing your account.

When you start F-Secure, the program brings up an empty window, as seen in Figure 10.1.

FIGURE 10.1

Initial empty terminal window.

This is a rather unintuitive beginning to your session. It does get better, however. When you start the program for the first time and every now and then as you use the package, you have to generate some random numbers. Move your mouse around. This is lots of fun. It's even more fun if you have a pen and tablet connected. Figure 10.2 shows the random generator.

FIGURE 10.2

Generating random numbers by hand.

After you have generated some random numbers, press Enter to bring up a connection dialog box, as shown in Figure 10.3.

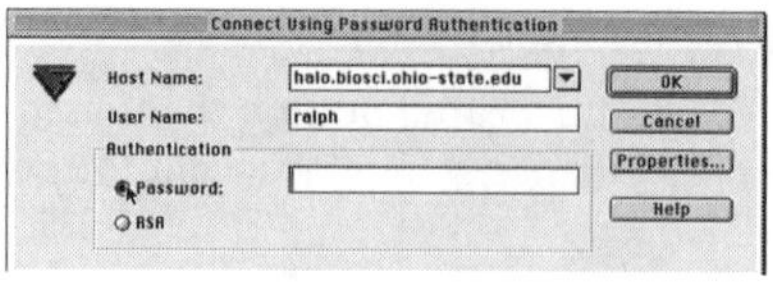

FIGURE 10.3

Connect Using Password Authentica-tion dialog box.

Click Properties. Figure 10.4 shows that connection properties will come up in the Properties dialog box. Change the port to the sshd1 port, which if you've set yours up like I did, is 24 in this case, and click OK.

FIGURE 10.4

Properties dialog box—change sshd1 *port here.*

Now, you're back to the Password Authentication dialog box. Enter your username. Enter your password precisely. Remember that case does count. Okay, so you already know that case does count. Just getting you in practice for dealing with your users. When you log in to a remote host for the first time, F-Secure notifies you of the unknown host key that it has encountered and asks you what to do. Choose Accept and Save if you expect to regularly log in to this host. Figure 10.5 shows you the New Host Key dialog box.

FIGURE 10.5

New Host Key dialog box—click Accept and Save.

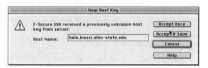

Now, you're logged in! It looks just like a Telnet window, only it's secure. Figure 10.6 shows a successful login.

FIGURE 10.6

Terminal session in progress.

As Figure 10.7 shows, choose Save Properties under the File menu, and save to your desktop for your convenience.

FIGURE 10.7

Saving your settings to the desktop.

Setting up RSA Authentication

Now, you will look at setting up another level of security by setting up RSA authentication. RSA authentication in the ssh suite enables you to use a passphrase, rather than simply a password, for connecting to your UNIX machine. Although I won't cover the more advanced configuration options here, it can even be configured to accept different passphrases from different clients so that you can conditionally enable and disable your access from certain places as you see fit.

Generating an Authentication Key on the UNIX Side   While you are still logged in, go ahead and generate an authentication key on the UNIX side.

At the prompt, run ssh-keygen1 and press return. After the machine generates an authentication key for you, it will ask you where to store it. As a default, it will offer $HOME/.ssh/identity, where $HOME denotes the location of your account. Press Return to choose the default. Next, you will be prompted to enter a passphrase to enable you to use the key. A good passphrase is 10–30 characters long. Avoid simple sentences or anything that can be easily guessed, but make sure it's something you'll remember. A favorite quote or witticism would be appropriate, but make sure it's not something that someone else could conceivably associate with you. Now, copy the key you just generated to an authorized_keys file:

```
HALO ralph 2 >cp ~/.ssh/identity.pub ~/.ssh/authorized_keys
```

Now, test out your new authentication key:

```
HALO ralph 3 >ssh1 waashu
Host key not found from the list of known hosts.
Are you sure you want to continue connecting (yes/no)? yes
Host 'waashu' added to the list of known hosts.
Enter passphrase for RSA key 'ralph@HALO':
/usr/bin/X11/xauth:  creating new authority file
/net/waashu/1b/usr/ralph/.Xauthority
No mail.

WAASHU ralph 1 >
```

It works! Just as the Mac client notifies you about unknown host keys, so does the UNIX client.

Exit your session and quit the program, just to give yourself a fresh start.

Generating an Authentication Key on the Macintosh   This time, start F-Secure by using your desktop alias. Notice how the alias brings up the Password Authentication dialog box without your having to press Enter in the empty terminal window.

Enter a hostname, enter your password, and click OK. Then, under the Edit menu, select Connection Properties, as shown in Figure 10.8. Notice that another user has already generated an authentication key from this Mac. You are not likely to see this unless you are working on a Mac that already has F-Secure and that is used by more than one person or by one person who has multiple accounts.

FIGURE 10.8

Editing connection properties.

Choose RSA Identity (which is likely to be what already appears), and click New. Figure 10.9 shows the RSA Identity Generation dialog box. Enter a comment of suggested form user@macintosh to identify the authentication key that will be generated (for example, fred@bedrock, where fred is your username and bedrock is your Mac's name). Then enter a passphrase to enable you to use the key and enter the passphrase again to verify a match. Use the same good practices you used when you generated an authentication key on the UNIX side. Finally, click Generate Key.

FIGURE 10.9

RSA Identity Generation dialog box.

More fun! Move your mouse around again to generate the key. Then save the file. It is recommended that you call it IDENTITY. If you have more than one user on your Macintosh who needs to access your UNIX machine or if you have more than one account, you might want to make a separate folder in your F-Secure folder for each user/account and save the IDENTITY file in the appropriate folder. Figure 10.10 shows the Save dialog box.

Figure 10.10

Saving your identity.

Click OK, and click OK again. In Figure 10.11, you see that the RSA identity generation is a success.

Figure 10.11

Successful identity.

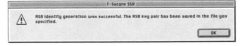

Choose Save Properties under the File menu to update the alias you have saved on your desktop. Then quit the program to give yourself another fresh start.

Setting up Your Account to Use the Key Generated on Your Macintosh

Now, you are going to provide your UNIX account with the authentication key you just generated on your Macintosh.

Start F-Secure as usual, entering your password. Under the Edit menu, select Connection Properties. Select RSA Identity. If you do not see a file that lists the comment that you just included when generating your authentication key, click Select and select the appropriate identity file, as shown in Figure 10.12.

Figure 10.12

Selecting your identity.

Now, the Properties box should show the right identity. Select Copy. As you see in Figure 10.13, this brings up a dialog box warning you that your public key is being copied to the clipboard.

Click OK, and click OK again. Now, your terminal window is all that is up. In your window, type the following:

```
HALO ralph 1 >cd .ssh
```

Start the editor of your choice to edit the authorized_keys file. Paste in the key that you generated on your Macintosh in the usual Mac fashion. Now your file looks approximately like this:

```
HALO .ssh 3 >more authorized_keys
1024 37 11956829057726354520385433858868315057460665214784976537
333481350197593827496204823544379616383727143318958679156430900069
35553185948960077061432874178962147790350138119582666082913725432
1507380015014414113068044972188820515032689003615469171461726346
9171197976371831173919079748832382506796582663003138118 9 ralph@HALO

1024 33 64666568643883184244277364702035003909485444162189368010 7
923797002901328334194383496977474528050344895697241204823419762 45
634803045378857935643003139010689610557871628993812186943744484 44
7415883946416697135230856333526711780087367780500877558511179325 9
4909189289776127302916729803619738644127403060529367188 3 ralph@ryoohki
```

Please note that the file that you have edited consists of three actual lines. The first line is the key you generated on the UNIX side. The second line is a blank line. The third line is the key you generated on your Macintosh. If it turns out that for some strange reason, the copy request you had made in the RSA Identity window chose only to copy the comment field, don't bother to save the changes. Just quit the editor and the program and start the copy over.

Please note that you can generate your key on the Mac first and then generate one on the UNIX side. The problem that you might encounter involves the fact each key has to be one long line.

Because you have to paste the second one into a pre-existing file, if you make the key on the UNIX side second and try to do typical Mac-style copy-and-paste, you'll find that the key generated on the UNIX machine is pasted in as several lines, rather than one long line. For you, this is not particularly a problem because you can easily edit your file. However, fixing things in this scenario could prove to be a challenge for your users. It's easier to have them do this on the UNIX side first and avoid the problem in the first place.

Now, you are ready to try out your key from the Macintosh!

Connecting to a UNIX Host from your Macintosh Using a Passphrase

Start F-Secure as usual. This time, however, select RSA rather than Password and click OK. If you can't select RSA, try generating a passphrase again. In Figure 10.14, notice that the box becomes the Connect Using RSA Authentication dialog box.

FIGURE 10.14

Selecting a connection using RSA Authentication.

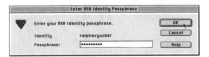

Now, for the big excitement: Enter your passphrase, as shown in Figure 10.15.

FIGURE 10.15

Entering your passphrase.

Now, you're logged on!

User Configuration: Setting up RSA Authentication in ssh2 on the UNIX Side

Setting up the Mac client also provides instruction on setting up ssh1 on the UNIX side. Because I will not be doing an actual walk-through on setting up a PC client, you will not get to see setting up RSA authentication in ssh2 on the UNIX side in quite the same fashion. However, I will provide a brief summary of the procedure that is included in the documentation.

To log in from a local machine to a remote machine, follow these steps:

1. On your local machine, run ssh-keygen2 to generate your public and private keys. As in ssh1, you will be asked for a passphrase. Private and public keys will be stored in ~/.ssh2 with names similar to the following:

```
id_dsa_1024_a       1024-bit DSA private key
id_dsa_1024_a.pub   Corresponding public key
```

These are equivalent to identity and identity.pub in SSH1.

2. Make the file ~/.ssh2/identification in the following format, where the entry that follows IdKey is the filename of your private key:

   IdKey id_dsa_1024_a

3. On the remote machine, run ssh-keygen2, protect it with a passphrase, and make ~/.ssh2/identification with the appropriate line entry for the private key for the remote machine.

4. Copy the contents of the public key you generated on the local machine to ~/.ssh2 on the remote machine under a name you can identify, such as local_machine_name.pub.

5. On the remote machine, make the file ~/.ssh2/authorization in the following format, where the entry following Key is the filename for the public key for your local machine:

   Key local_machine_name.pub

6. Now, you can log in to the remote machine from the local machine using the local machine's passphrase.

To log in from the remote machine to the local machine, follow these steps:

1. Copy the contents of the public key you generated on the remote machine to ~/.ssh2 on the local machine, as some filename you can identify, such as remote_machine_name.pub.

2. On the local machine, make the file ~/.ssh2/authorization in the following format:

   Key remote_machine_name.pub

3. Now you can log in to the local machine from the remote machine using the remote machine's passphrase.

Summary of the Programs that Come with ssh1 and ssh2

The programs that come with ssh1 end in 1, and the programs that come with ssh2 end in 2. When ssh1 is installed, all the programs are linked to their non-numbered equivalent, with the exception of ssh1, which is also linked to slogin. When ssh2 is installed, the non-numbered equivalents are linked to the ssh2 programs instead. Likewise, slogin is linked to ssh2 instead.

Provided in Tables 10.4 and 10.5 are brief summaries of the programs that come with ssh1 and ssh2. Be sure to read the man pages to get the full details.

TABLE 10.4 ssh1 Program Summary

Program	Function
sshd1	ssh1 server
ssh1	ssh1 client
scp1	Secure copy program (remote file copy program)
ssh-keygen1	RSA keys creation tool
ssh-agent1	Holds authentication private keys
ssh-add1	Registers new keys with the agent ssh-agent1
make-ssh-known-hosts	Creates /etc/ssh_known_hosts file

TABLE 10.5 ssh2 Program Summary

Program	Function
sshd2	ssh2 server
ssh2	ssh2 client
sFTP-server2	Secure FTP server
sFTP2	Secure FTP client
scp2	Secure copy program (remote file copy program)
ssh-keygen2	RSA keys creation tool
ssh-agent2	Holds authentication private keys
ssh-add2	Registers new keys with the agent, ssh-agent2
ssh-askpass2	X11 utility for querying passwords

Limited Root Access: sudo

Finally in today's work, you will install a convenient little utility called sudo that provides a method to create accounts with limited root access, but not complete root powers. This is a very useful facility if you want to be able to assign responsibilities for something such as the maintenance of a file repository or for backups to some willing and capable user who is not otherwise trusted with root access. In these cases, you can configure sudo to enable the user to execute only those commands necessary to perform the task that she has been given with the permissions of root. For all other commands, she behaves as her normal user and has no other root privileges.

Installing sudo

Installing sudo can range from simple to highly complex in difficulty. Here, I will walk you through a simple installation, and if you want to investigate the more powerful options at a later date, you can do this at your leisure.

The latest version of sudo, currently 1.5.9, is available at http://www.coutesan.com/sudo.

After you have downloaded and unpacked your distribution, you should do the following to install sudo:

1. Read the READMEs. If you are upgrading your sudo from a previous version you inherited, check the notes on upgrading in the INSTALL document. Also, be sure to check INSTALL for any comments on your operating system.

2. If you are installing from a shared directory on a cluster of machines and you have already run configure on a different host, run **make distclean** to remove the config.cache file, or type **rm config.cache**.

3. If you have not yet looked at the configure options listed in INSTALL, do so now. There are pages and pages of options, which range from the standard prefix, directory, and CC options to the --with-insults option, which when turned on will cause sudo to insult you when you mistype a password.

4. In the source directory, run ./configure. Include any special options you might need or want on the same line with this command. For a basic installation, you should require nothing special here.

5. Edit the configure-generated makefile to change any default paths that you might want changed but did not specify on the ./configure line. Specifically, you will want to make sure that the installation directories correspond to where your facility keeps third-party software.

6. Run make. If you have any problems running make, be sure to check the TROU-BLESHOOTING and PORTING files. The sudo package is well supported on a large number of platforms, so it compiles out of the box without any problems in almost all cases.

7. As root, run make install. This will install sudo, visudo, the man pages, and a skeleton sudoers file, and it will not write over an existing sudoers file.

8. Examine the sample.sudoers file and the sudoers man page for tips on editing your sudoers file. Then edit sudoers with the visudo tool.

The sudoers file is the file that is used to control access to root privileges. The file can be simple or quite complex.

10

Here is a sample `sudoers` file, which must be located in `/etc/sudoers`. It must be edited with the `visudo` editor, which is a tweaked version of `vi` that can edit this protected file:

```
# sudoers file.
#
# This file MUST be edited with the 'visudo' command as root.
#
# See the man page for the details on how to write a sudoers file.
#

# Host alias specification

Host_Alias  MYHOST=mother.politically.correct.com
Host_Alias  THATHOST=barracuda.politically.correct.com

# User alias specification

# Cmnd alias specification

Cmnd_Alias SHUTDOWN=/etc/shutdown,/etc/reboot
Cmnd_Alias MISC=/usr/bin/ls,/usr/bin/cp

# User privilege specification
george      MYHOST=MISC
ralph               THATHOST=SHUTDOWN
```

The preceding example is quite simple, but it should start to get you thinking about some of what you will be able to do with `sudo`. What you should be able to see from this example is that user `george` is now allowed to issue `ls` and `cp` as root on `mother`, and user `ralph` is now allowed to issue `shutdown` and `reboot` on `barracuda`. If the cluster had a few more users, I could include a user alias to group selected users and in turn grant privileges to that aliased group as a whole.

To make use of the increased privileges that these users now have, they simply issue the commands with `sudo` prepended to the command they want to execute. For example, if george wanted to copy a file named `bismark` that was owned by root and had permissions set to only be readable by root, he could issue the command `sudo cp bismark <destination>`. The file `bismark` would be copied to `<destination>` as though ralph were actually the root user.

In this file, you can allow a user access to any command on any host, a small selection of commands on certain hosts, access to a group of commands except one or two out of the group, and so on.

With `sudo`, you can grant privileges to users who might need certain privileges or grant emergency privileges to users whom you can trust. You can grant privileges as simply or as complexly as required for your site. Furthermore, `sudo` creates an extensive log of the use of these commands, giving you an audit trail.

Caution   **Don't shoot yourself in the foot!**   The sudo package is supposed to enable you to grant some small set of privileges to users who aren't trusted as full administrators for whatever reason. Be cautious of the commands that you do give access to because a creative user with access to something like root-privileged cp, or worse, vi, can manage to assume full root privileges with only a little creativity. Editing or replacing a commonly run root script, such as a startup script, and causing it to make changes or run commands on her behalf is all it takes.

Summary

In today's lesson, you learned how to configure your machine to be much more secure than its out-of-the-box configuration that you originally set up. In fact, if you've followed along and done each of the steps as advised here, your machine is probably more secure than 99 percent of the UNIX machines out there. Although I'd argue that it's impossible to ever be completely secure, the point you've reached should be good enough. With the plethora of machines that are so much less secure than yours, you've drastically decreased the likelihood that anyone will bother with trying to crack your machine.

Specifically, in today's reading, you learned the following:

- All about your inetd.conf file, what services it starts, and which ones you don't need.
- Where to look for other services that your machine might be starting.
- That you have to be on watch for poorly written or thought-out services, even if they come from your OS vendor.
- All about how to install and configure TCP wrapper, your first line of defense in stopping most intruders at the door.
- All about how to install and configure the Secure Shell packages, enabling you to encrypt the majority of your network traffic and protecting you from sniffing attacks.
- How to install and configure a basic installation of sudo, one of the useful packages that enables you to grant partial administrative privileges to selected users.

Now, you only need to keep up with your security patches and any updates to the software you've installed today. If you do, your machines should purr along almost perpetually with few, if any, security problems. What more beautiful thing could a system administrator ever ask for?

10

Q&A

Q **I don't know what half of these services that start in `/etc/rc*.d` are. What should I do?**

A Well, there are always the man pages. If reading those is too much trouble, you're still pretty early in your install, so you could try killing them all off and finding out what breaks. Seriously, though—even if you have to resort to breaking things as badly as to require going back to day one and starting over repeatedly until you have the minimal set that is absolutely required to run, you're likely to be further ahead in the long run. It might take you a whole week to repeatedly install the OS and delete things until you have the minimal set that runs. If, on the other hand, you left IMAP installed because you didn't know what it was, you could end up spending that week in a nice U.S. government–funded country-club while the lawyers sort out whether the threatening email that the president received really came from you or was forged using your buggy server.

Q **Yikes! Are you really trying to scare the bejeezus out of your readers?**

A I think I've heard this one before, haven't I? In any case, the answer (still) is "You bet!" You're a system administrator now, and with that comes a lot of responsibility. I'd rather have you think that I'm pedantic, overbearing, and heavy-handed and you be safe, than pretend that this is all fun and games and have you get burned because of it. I refuse to water down potential problems, and might even embellish some, just to make sure that you have the proper respect for the power that now rests in your hands and the responsibility you have for using it properly.

Q **I know FTP is carried in clear text on a TCP connection just as Telnet is. Is there a way of protecting it?**

A Yes. This can also be done through the facilities of Secure Shell by using it to act as an encrypted port forwarder. I'll cover exactly this issue next week, during Day 16, " Securing Services: FTP and POP."

Q **I think I'm having a problem with Secure Shell. I can log in, but when I log out, the connection just hangs forever. What can I do?**

A This problem has been fixed in `ssh` version 2.0.13. If you must use an older version for some reason, try reverting to using `ssh1` (for me it seems to only happen with `ssh2`). If you end up with a hung connection, you can disconnect it by finding the `slogin` process on the client machine and killing it off manually.

Q **The sshd2 server refuses to accept connections from any client on my machine. It reports errors containing an incorrect IP address for the client. Any suggestions?**

A You're using an SGI and gcc, aren't you? Rumor has it that using SGI's compilers might fix this. Rumor also has it that a fix to the client code is in the works, so check with DataFellows regularly for ssh2 source updates.

Workshop

Quiz

1. Where do you look to turn off services on your machine?
2. Is it a good idea to leave on a service that provides support of a networked multiplayer game?
3. What do you always do with configuration files before you make changes to them?
4. Why is it important to turn off Telnet?
5. Why don't you put sshd in /etc/inetd.conf?

Exercises

1. What would be the effect of completely turning off inetd after you have sshd installed on your system?
2. Install an ssh client on a personal computer and connect to your UNIX machine (if you can connect as root or have a user to connect to).
3. Document the experience in a format that you can use as a guide for your users when they ask for connection assistance.
4. Make a list of all the services that you've left running on your machine, and then use deja (www.deja.com) to browse the newsgroups to see what security problems they might present.

10

DAY 11

Making Your Machines Communicate with Each Other: NIS and NFS

Today you will get your machine to communicate with another machine by implementing NFS, the Network File System, and NIS, the Network Information Service. With NFS you will be able to share your machine's resources with another machine and vice versa. Combined with NIS, NFS enables you to set up a cluster of machines that trust each other. In turn, by unifying your machines into a cohesive cluster, your users' accounts should look the same to them across all the machines. Unfortunately, both practices are not secure.

Before you begin your implementation of NFS and NIS, make sure that all the machines involved have undergone the same security measures and are at the same general level of "installedness," even if they're of differing operating systems.

You will take a basic how-to approach in today's activities. I will not discuss the details behind NFS and NIS, but will try to help you do what is necessary to set up a small machine cluster which is sharing its resources. Much of this might look like black magic at this point, but like many other things, UNIX understanding can come later, if necessary.

Setting Up Your NIS Master

As you learned on Day 3, "Setting Up a Machine: From the Box to the Desktop," NIS is used as a means for storing user information: passwords, home directory information, and so on. NIS is also used for storing host information: trusted hosts, untrusted hosts, and, as a matter of fact, just about any list-oriented databases you could want. You will set up a small cluster of two machines sharing their resources. Even with what is currently planned to be a cluster of two machines, you need to have one machine serve as an NIS master—that is, one machine that stores the bulk of user and host information. This machine will also serve some resources. You will have one client machine that will also serve some resources but will get the bulk of its user and host information from the master. This might seem a bit extreme right now, with only two machines, but it's always a good idea to design for the future and leave room for a machine cluster to grow.

Initializing the NIS Master

To start to set up my cluster, I am first going to set up NIS. The NIS function of my machine was one of the questions I was asked during installation of the operating system. Depending on your operating system, you might not have done that yet. How the setup works varies from one operating system to another. With SunOS, I had to set a domain name for my NIS domain and then build NIS databases by issuing `domainname` `whatever_name_I_pick` followed by `/usr/etc/yp/ypinit` `-m`. In IRIX a graphical user interface is available instead.

Before you start setting up your NIS master, run **rpcinfo -p *hostname***. This gives you a good idea of what, if any, NIS services the machine is already running.

Here is some sample output:

```
Barracuda# rpcinfo -p barracuda
   program vers proto   port
   100000    2   tcp    111  portmapper
   100000    2   udp    111  portmapper
   100004    2   udp    662  ypserv
   100004    2   tcp    663  ypserv
   100004    1   udp    662  ypserv
   100004    1   tcp    663  ypserv
   100007    2   tcp   1024  ypbind
   100007    2   udp   1027  ypbind
   100007    1   tcp   1024  ypbind
   100007    1   udp   1027  ypbind
```

```
100029   1   udp    666   keyserv
100005   1   udp    711   mountd
100005   2   udp    711   mountd
100005   1   tcp    714   mountd
100005   2   tcp    714   mountd
100003   2   udp   2049   nfs
100026   1   udp    723   bootparam
100024   1   udp    727   status
100024   1   tcp    729   status
100021   1   tcp    730   nlockmgr
100021   1   udp   1033   nlockmgr
100021   3   tcp    734   nlockmgr
100021   3   udp   1034   nlockmgr
100020   2   udp   1035   llockmgr
100020   2   tcp    739   llockmgr
100021   2   tcp    742   nlockmgr
100021   2   udp   1036   nlockmgr
100012   1   udp   1038   sprayd
100009   1   udp   1021   yppasswdd
```

Note that if you can't run `rpcinfo`, you might have to start the `portmap` or `rpcbind` program, depending on your operating system. Search through your `/etc/rc.local` or `/etc/rc*.d` for how to start it.

Note

> **Non-working information services** Chances are, if things such as `portmap` didn't start at boot time, it's because no services required them and they're smart enough to not bother taking resources if they're not needed. After you have things running once, and have created resources, such as an NIS database, that require the portmapper, these services will probably start automatically at the next boot.

Setting Up Important NIS Files

Some of the important maps (files used by NIS) your NIS server hosts are the `/etc/netgroup` and `/etc/hosts` maps. The NIS master provides content for these maps, and the data provided from the master (depending on your client's implementation) replaces or supplements these files on your client. The NIS master also serves files such as `/etc/passwd`, `/etc/aliases`, and `/etc/group`. These files, however, the master simply adds to the client's listings.

Setting Up `/etc/netgroup`

The `/etc/netgroup` file is where netgroups are stored. Netgroups can be used for specifying hosts to be trusted or untrusted, and any other groupings of machines that you might find that you need. You can use groups defined in /etc/netgroup to give specific permission to access certain filesystems, hosts, or to specifically deny access to certain resources for specific groups of hosts. You also can use /etc/netgroup to group users, or really any form of data that you might want to represent in the hierarchical BNF format, which you'll discuss further directly.

The format of an entry in the /etc/netgroup file is

```
groupname member1 member2 ...
```

A member might be another group, or it might be a triple in the form of

```
(hostname, username, nis_domain)
```

Note

This format is technically known as Bachaus-Naur Form (BNF). You might find other places in UNIX where you are asked to provide a BNF-format description of something. This simply means providing a description where the left-hand column contains terms, and everything to the right of the term is a definition. Definitions can be other terms, ordered lists of terms, or terminal nodes. Terminal nodes are final non-subdivideable entries.

As an example, a simple BNF description for the structure of a few simple English sentences:

sentence : (subject verb object) (subject verb)

subject : phrase

object : [a] phrase

phrase : (noun) (adjective noun)

verb : [hit] [threw] [chased]

noun : [tommy] [ball]

adjective : [red] [big]

If you consider things in parenthesis to be ordered lists of terms, and things in brackets to be terminal nodes, you have a BNF definition that can be used to build potential sentences. Using this BNF to construct "valid" sentences you can come up with things such as:

"tommy hit a ball"

"tommy hit a big ball"

"big tommy hit a red ball"

or

"tommy hit"

Because I didn't put much effort into making a good English definition for my BNF description, this BNF description can also be used to construct sentences such as:

"ball threw" and "red ball chased a big tommy."

Your UNIX machine uses the BNF descriptions you give it for things such as netgroups to construct exactly this sort of "valid" collection of data. As you see, it is important that you make certain that your definition really parses to what you want it to.

Setting up the /etc/netgroup file is rather tricky. It is easiest to begin the listing with definitions for various groups, and then break down the group definitions further with the host, user, and NIS_domain definitions. Especially tricky about the /etc/netgroup file is that each definition must be one line long. You can break the line up with \ at the end of each entry line. However, there must not be a space after that \. It will be hard to tell when that is even a problem.

Here's a sample of what I've set up so far in my /etc/netgroup:

```
our-machines \
        our-sun-server \
        our-pc-clients \
        our-mac-clients

our-sun-server \
        (barracuda.politically.correct.com,,shipsahoy) \
        (barracuda,,shipsahoy)

our-pc-clients \
        (mother.politically.correct.com,,shipsahoy) \
        (mother,,shipsahoy)

our-mac-clients \
        (lagendra.politically.correct.com,,shipsahoy) \
        (lagendra,,shipsahoy)
```

So far I have one main group that I have called our-machines. It in turn is made up of our-sun-server, our-pc-clients, and our-mac-clients. Each group definition that makes up our-machines at this time has only one machine listed. Note that in the definitions of the form (host, user, nis_domain) nothing is listed in the user portion. This means that all users on those machines fall in to those groups.

Setting Up /etc/hosts

Whether your machine is the master or the client, you will have to make an /etc/hosts file. This file serves as a hostname database for your machine. It looks here for hostname information first before it searches elsewhere.

11

An entry in the `/etc/hosts` file is of the form

```
IP address  official_name   alias
```

Here is how my `/etc/hosts` file looks so far:

```
127.0.0.1       localhost
#
192.168.1.20    Barracuda loghost
192.168.1.254   lagendra.politically.correct.com        lagendra
192.168.1.4     mother.politically.correct.com          mother
192.168.1.2     challenger.politically.correct.com      challenger
```

Setting Up `/etc/passwd`

The NIS master stores the main `/etc/passwd` file and simply appends its entries to those of the client machines, if they are so configured. Therefore, the NIS master's `/etc/passwd` file must not end with this line

```
+::0:0:::
```

This indicates that the main NIS `/etc/passwd` file should be appended, which would lead to the master running in circles chasing its tail.

Also, the NIS master, as keeper of passwords, is the machine to actually change passwords. When a user on a client invokes `yppasswd` to change her password, the client then makes a request to the master to change the password. The master must run `yppasswdd` to handle these requests. This entails either editing your `/etc/rc.local` file or starting a script in `/etc/rc*.d`. Alternatively you could force all your users to log in to your NIS master to update their passwords with `passwd`. I don't recommend this for general purpose use because it's a nuisance for users to have to know that one machine in particular is "in control" (and teaching them otherwise if you change it is even worse!), but in some heterogeneous environments you might be forced to do this.

When all your configuration files are in place, you can start up your yp master server. This is usually `ypserv`, but you can check your `rc.local` or `rc*.d/*` files to find the exact syntax for your version of the OS. I'd actually recommend doing this by rebooting the machine, to make certain that everything actually is found as intended and that the server starts automatically as it should. With some installations, even after all the right configuration files are in the right place you have to tell the OS to enable the master server. This can be done by removing a comment from a `rc` file, by running a program such as `chkconfig`, or by modifying the contents of configuration files in a directory such as `/etc/config`.

Note

On your system, the configuration option to turn on NIS might be named *ypsomething*. This stems from its old naming convention. When Sun invented the system, they called it the "yellow pages," for obvious reasons. However, it turns out that the name "Yellow Pages" is trademarked by a British tele- phone company, and so Sun had to rename the service. They renamed it to NIS, but most of the software remained named yp*. If you can't find an entry for nis-master, look for yp-master.

Tip

SunOS Name Service weirdness   On most modern UNIX flavors, name lookup information comes from information in the file /etc/resolv.conf. SunOS however doesn't seem to know how to use a DNS server properly. To fix this problem, on SunOS the ypserv process can be configured to talk to the DNS and to provide DNS lookups for client machines via the NIS service.

1. This means that even if you have only one SunOS machine and noth- ing else, you're probably going to want to have it be an NIS master to itself so that DNS works.

2. Sun's man page for how to make ypserv function in this capacity are wrong. The man pages say to use ypserv -d to make ypserv function as a DNS. I have never seen this work properly. Starting ypserv as ypserv -i however does cause it to work.

11

Initializing the NIS Client

After your NIS master is running, start the setup for your NIS client.

Setting Up /etc/hosts and /etc/passwd

Although the NIS client ultimately gets its /etc/hosts information from the master, it still needs an /etc/hosts of its own for boot up or if it has to stand on its own for awhile, should the master be down, intentionally or unintentionally.

In addition, because the NIS client does want to have information from the NIS master appended to its copy of /etc/passwd, add this line to the end of the client's /etc/passwd file:

```
+::0:0:::
```

You could also choose to append only a subset the password file by creating a netgroup of selected users in the /etc/netgroup file, and then add a line similar to this to your client's /etc/passwd:

```
+@good-staff::0:0:::
```

You could also remove a subset of passwords in the same fashion, replacing the + with -. You actually have the ability to build quite sophisticated databases and automatically configure and reconfigure your users access through the NIS system. The technical issues involved range far beyond the scope of this book, but the interested reader is encouraged to examine the O'Reilly title *NFS/NIS* for a thorough treatment of the subject.

For some operating systems, the /etc/nsswitch.conf file, the name service switch file, is used instead of the /etc/passwd file to configure the client to incorporate the NIS master's information. The file contains a list of databases and their sources and the order in which they should be consulted. Here is a sample /etc/nsswitch.conf entry that does the same thing as the +::0:0::: notation earlier:

```
# the following two lines obviate the "+" entry in /etc/passwd and
# /etc/group.
passwd:     files nis
```

If your system uses /etc/nsswitch.conf, check your man pages. There might be a compatibility flag available that obeys the +/- notation.

Starting NIS

To start NIS on your client machine, you will have to somehow tell the machine what its domain name (NIS domainname) is and start ypbind. On the SGI, you can do this in a graphical user interface. In Solaris you run ypinit -c. The system will respond with information on how you should provide the domain name.

On my Linux client I set the domain name information in /etc/yp.conf and start ypbind. Check the man pages for your operating system to see what the recommended procedure is. Unfortunately this is one place where every flavor of UNIX handles things in its own distinct way. Thankfully, the information that you'll need to provide should be identical. You'll certainly need to set the NIS domain name, possibly using the domainname command. After that, it might be as simple as using the ypbind command with no arguments and letting it figure things out for itself, or it might involve adding information to a configuration file.

On my Linux machine, which uses a configuration file, my /etc/yp.conf looks like this:

```
 [root@mother sbin]# more /etc/yp.conf
# /etc/yp.conf - ypbind configuration file
# Valid entries are
#
#domain NISDOMAIN server HOSTNAME
#       Use server HOSTNAME for the domain NISDOMAIN.
#
#domain NISDOMAIN broadcast
#       Use  broadcast  on  the local net for domain NISDOMAIN
#
#ypserver HOSTNAME
```

```
#       Use server HOSTNAME for the  local  domain.  The
#       IP-address of server must be listed in /etc/hosts.
#
domain shipsahoy server 192.168.1.20
```

Note

> Observe that I have a "broadcast" option for binding to the NIS domain name. This is the least secure, but the most portable and most flexible implementation. Because the network on which I'm demonstrating has only one NIS server, specifying a particular server is no detriment here. If, however, I had a master server and several slave servers as backup, I'd defeat the purpose of the slaves by forcing the binding to a particular machine.

To check whether the Linux box recognizes the NIS master, I try ypwhich:

```
[root@mother sbin]# ypwhich
Barracuda
```

Great! Now I have an NIS server and an NIS client set up! I can log in to the Linux machine (mother) using accounts that I have set up on the SunOS machine (Barracuda).

Tip

> The ypwhich command is a very useful tool. If you're having NIS problems, using the ypwhich command can give you much more informative diagnostic information than what's likely to be appearing in your log files.

11

At this point it's probably a good idea to reboot the client, to make sure it picks the binding back up properly after a reboot. If it doesn't, you'll need to figure out where in your configuration files the ypbind statements need to be enabled. Check your man pages and sort through your start up scripts for that information. If you still have problems, don't forget that a wealth of information is available on the newsgroups. Search or ask on newsgroups dedicated to your OS.

From now on, when you want to change a password, you should do it with the yppasswd command instead of the passwd command. If you use the passwd command (or if your yppasswd command is broken), when you change the password on the NIS master, it is changed in the /etc/passwd file but isn't updated in the yppasswd map. The result is that you can use the new password on the master machine but not on client machines. To fix this, you need to go to your yp database directory on the master server and issue a make (or on some machines, ypmake). This updates and pushes the new maps to the clients. If you want to avoid having to do this on a somewhat regular basis, make yourself a crontab entry that runs a `make` and pushes the maps every 15 minutes or so. It won't hurt anything to have it being updated when nothing has changed, and this seems to be the most reasonable route to a solution. (There is a service that's supposed to handle this automatically—`ypupdated`—but it's been declared a security risk by the vendors.)

Setting Up NFS

For each machine that will export a filesystem, NFS must be turned on. This might mean starting a script or two or setting a configuration flag somewhere. Check the man pages for your operating system. Your `/etc/exports` or equivalent file, which you will look at later, can also be a useful source for information on how to start NFS on your system. A good way to also check to see whether NFS services are on is to run `rpcinfo -p` *hostname*.

Exporting Resources

Each filesystem or directory that will be exported to NFS clients must have an entry in `/etc/exports`. An entry in `/etc/exports` is typically of the form:

```
directory   -option[,option ]...
```

Common options for `/etc/exports` are listed in Table 11.1.

TABLE 11.1 Common Options for `/etc/exports`

Option	Function
ro	Export directory read-only. If not specified, directory is exported read-write.
rw=hostname:hostname...	Export directory read-mostly, that is, read-only to most machines, read-write to specified machines. If not specified, directory is exported read-write. In Solaris, rw is read-write.
anon=uid	Maps root's uid (0) to another value so that a root user on a client machine is not also treated as root when accessing the NFS server. Default mapping is to nobody (-2 or 65534). Mapping to -1 or 65535 disables access from unknown users or from root on hosts not included in root option.
root=hostname:hostname...	Allows root access only for root users on the specified hosts.
access=client:client:...	Gives mount access to only the clients specified. Client can be a hostname or a netgroup.

The form of an entry in /etc/exports in Linux is

```
directory  hostname(option,option)
```

Linux comes with a number of other options than what is listed for the common options in Table 11.1.

Solaris uses /etc/dfs/dfstab rather than /etc/exports to identify resources to be exported, or shared, in Solaris's terminology. An entry in /etc/dfs/dfstab takes the form:

```
share [-F fstype] [ -o options] [-d "text description"]
➥ pathname [resource]
```

When you have NFS running on your machine and have an /etc/exports file in place, you must tell the machine to export the directories specified in /etc/exports. You can do this with the exportfs command on SunOS and IRIX. In Solaris, use shareall with no options, and shareall shares all resources listed in /etc/dfs/dfstab. On Linux you kill -HUP your mountd and nfsd processes to accomplish the same thing. Table 11.2 provides a listing of common options for exportfs.

TABLE 11.2 Common Options for exportfs

Option	Function
no options	Lists what is currently exported.
-a	Exports everything specified in /etc/exports.
-u	Unexports the specified directory.
-u -a	Unexports all the currently exported directories.
-v	Prints each directory as it is exported or unexported.
-o	Applies a comma-separated list of options. The potential options are the same as the options that can be included in /etc/exports itself.

Here is a sample /etc/exports from my machine:

```
Barracuda# more /etc/exports
/home       -anon=-1,root=mother,access=mother
```

Here, I've chosen to export the /home directory, with anonymous mapping set to -1 so that root access from hosts not listed in the root option is disabled, and with root access set to a host I trust and client access given to a specific client. Most important about the settings I have chosen is that root on mother has the same root privileges on Barracuda's /home as root on Barracuda does. I trust myself to handle the root privileges appropriately. However, if you are exporting a filesystem to a host for which you do not have root privileges, you should not trust that root with your filesystem.

A quick check with `exportfs` shows what the machine is currently exporting:

```
Barracuda# exportfs
/usr
/home
/var/spool/mail
```

Oops! It turns out that the machine is exporting what it was originally listed in `/etc/exports` as a result of the system installation—changes don't take effect until a reboot or until the change is manually enforced. But I can change that by unexporting what is currently being exported, having `exportfs` reread `/etc/exports` and checking the results:

```
Barracuda# exportfs -u -a
Barracuda# exportfs -a
Barracuda# exportfs
/home -anon=-1,root=mother,access=mother
```

From this listing you see that Barracuda is now exporting its `/home` filesystem to mother with the options I specified in its `/etc/exports` file. In other words, Barracuda is sharing its `/home` with mother.

Mounting Resources

When an NFS server has exported its resources, the client must mount them. Here you have to think a bit about how you might want to mount the new resource. Do you need any special naming convention? If the machine is mounting storage space, a special naming convention might be required if you want your users to be able to access the directory using the same name across all machines. This is especially true of users' home directories.

In my case, I have chosen to export a directory that stores users' home directories. I also can't mount it as `/home` on the client machine because the client machine already has a `/home` directory and I would like the client machine to be able to access both. Instead, I pick a naming convention that can be used on both machines. I mount Barracuda's home on mother as `/net/barracuda/home`. I then use a link to point `/net/barracuda/home` on Barracuda to the real directory, `/home`.

Now that I have decided how the hierarchical structure for users' directories will appear on both machines. I am ready to edit the `/etc/fstab` on mother. Table 11.3 provides a list of the common NFS options for `/etc/fstab`. If you're running Solaris, you edit `/etc/vfstab` instead, which has the same types of common NFS options.

TABLE 11.3 Common NFS Options for /etc/fstab

Option	Function
rw	Mounts resource read-write.
ro	Mounts resource read-only.
bg	Retries mount in the background if first attempt fails.
fg	Retries mount in the foreground if first attempt fails.
retry=n	Number of times to retry a mount.
rsize=n	Sets read buffer to n bytes.
wsize=n	Sets write buffer to n bytes.
timeo=n	Sets NFS retransmission timeout to n tenths of a second.
retrans=n	Sets the number of retransmissions to n.
vers=(NFS version number)	Specifies NFS version number to use.
soft	Returns an error if server does not respond.
hard	Retries request until server responds.
intr	Allows keyboard interrupts on hard mounts.
nointr	Disallows keyboard interrupts on hard mounts.

Here's mother's /etc/fstab with the additional line to mount Barracuda's /home
directory:

```
[ray@mother]# more /etc/fstab
/dev/sda1              /                    ext2    defaults        1 1
/dev/sda6              /innerspace          ext2    defaults        1 2
/dev/sda5              /usr                 ext2    defaults        1 2
/dev/hda1              /var                 ext2    defaults        1 2
/dev/sda7              swap                 swap    defaults        0 0
/dev/fd0               /mnt/floppy          ext2    noauto          0 0
/dev/cdrom             /mnt/cdrom           iso9660 noauto,ro       0 0
none                   /proc                proc    defaults        0 0
barracuda:/home        /net/barracuda/home  nfs     rw,hard,intr,bg 0 0
```

I've chosen some basic options—read-write mount, hard mount, interrupts permitted, and
backgrounding mount requests. I don't have to specify a version because both machines
only speak version 2 of NFS, or NFS2. Machines that can use NFS2 or NFS3 typically
start with NFS3, and if that doesn't work, they drop back to NFS2. However, when IRIX
6.5 first became available, it was recommended that NFS2 be specified explicitly because
NFS3 was the default, but it did not quite function properly. At this point, I am not going

to worry about some of the other option types, unless I should discover that I am having network problems.

 Note

> **Why these mount options?**   Read/write should be obvious; I want to be able to both read and write to the drive.
>
> I've hard mounted it as soft-mounts simply error-out and go away if there's a problem. If there's a transient network problem, I want the machine to keep trying until it gets the mount back, so it has to be a hard mount.
>
> Interrupts turned on because if the device really does go away, I want to be able to <Control>-C out of the loop the machine will get stuck in perpetually trying to get the mount back.
>
> Backgrounded because if the device isn't there when the machine is being rebooted, I don't want it to sit around forever waiting for the drive to appear. This way it goes on with life and retries the mount occasionally in the background. If you leave hard mounts in the foreground you are almost guaranteed to deadlock machines at reboot because each will sit waiting for another to provide disk services, and each will refuse to budge before the other does. If you really want to make your life difficult, put your hard mount in the foreground and turn off interrupts.
>
> You can get a little performance mileage out of your network mounted devices by playing with the timeout and retry count parameters, especially if you have to live with a flaky network. I am not concerned about that here because my in-home network is small and very robust. If you do have a problematic network, however, no matter how you play with the parameters you will never have a truly pleasant NFS experience because the algorithm used to guarantee robustness over a problem network leads to extreme slowdowns.

On adding the entry in /etc/fstab I can issue

```
[ray@mother]# mount -t nfs -a
```

This will mount all NFS-type filesystems specified in /etc/fstab. To check whether the mount has taken, I can issue mount without any options:

```
[ray@mother]# mount
/dev/sda1 on / type ext2 (rw)
none on /proc type proc (rw)
/dev/sda6 on /innerspace type ext2 (rw)
/dev/sda5 on /usr type ext2 (rw)
/dev/hda1 on /var type ext2 (rw)
barracuda:/home on /net/barracuda/home type nfs
➥(rw,hard,intr,bg,addr=192.168.1.20)
```

Great! It has taken. Let's see what I've got:

```
[ray@mother]# ls /net/barracuda/home
lost+found
```

Not too much yet. If I check directly on Barracuda:

```
Barracuda# ls /home
lost+found
```

Indeed not much.

I've also exported mother's /innerspace, and mounted that storage space as /innerspace on Barracuda.

```
Barracuda# mount
/dev/sd0a on / type 4.2 (rw)
/dev/sd0g on /usr type 4.2 (rw)
/dev/sd2a on /usr/local type 4.2 (rw)
/dev/sd2d on /archive type 4.2 (rw)
/dev/sd2e on /home type 4.2 (rw)
mother:/innerspace on /innerspace type nfs (rw,hard,intr,bg)
mother:/home on /net/mother/home type nfs (rw,hard,intr,bg)
```

If I look at /innerspace on Barracuda, I get

```
Barracuda# ls /innerspace
bison-misc          gunzip-misc          patches-barracuda
gcc-misc            libstdc++-misc       security-misc
gdb-misc            lost+found
gmake-misc          patch-misc
```

And if I check /innerspace on mother, I get

```
[ray@mother]# ls /innerspace
bison-misc      gmake-misc       lost+found          security-misc
gcc-misc        gunzip-misc      patch-misc
gdb-misc        libstdc++-misc   patches-barracuda
```

That's a bit more interesting. Isn't it exciting to have your machines sharing their resources? If you are having any problems getting any of this to work, be sure to read your man pages, double-check your files for any typos and check your system logs for feedback.

11

> **Tip**
>
> **Your system logs are your friends!**   System administration training, when you're not teaching yourself from a book, is usually a master/apprentice thing. I can't guess how many times that I was chastised during my training as a system administrator when my master observed me fighting with a configuration problem for hours without checking the system logs. It's so very tempting to "try another variation" and reissue commands with minor modifications ad nauseam. I was usually amazed at how quickly he could look at

what I was doing on the screen, flip to the bottom of a log file, point an accusing finger at a diagnostic message, snort in irritation, and go back to doing whatever he was doing. I was also usually amazed at my lack of common sense for wasting hours fighting with a problem that had an answer waiting a dozen keystrokes away the whole time.

To this day I still find myself having to fight the urge to fiddle with something when it doesn't work properly the first time. Because I can't be there to give you an appropriate apprenticeship, should you ever find yourself tweaking things without checking the logs to find out what you should be tweaking, imagine me standing behind you glaring at the screen and tapping my foot impatiently—I've never managed to get the snort down right.

Note

Many will meet one very predictable problem at this point. If you manage to get everything mounted by hand and it all works great, reboot your machine. If everything mounts up properly again and it continues working properly, great! You're all set to go. If on the other hand, your mounts suddenly stop working and no amount of work will get you past a cryptic message that says something like "resource already in use," your machine is running an NFS automounter. You can't mount the drives where you're trying to because an automatic service that you didn't find and disable when you were trying to earlier this week is already using your drives. It noticed that you mounted them during the last reboot and has remembered this. Now it has them mounted somewhere of its choosing and is making your life difficult. Find out where this service started by checking and rechecking your startup scripts, fix things so it can't and reboot again. If you've found all the places where your OS vendor has hidden pieces of this problematic software, all should be well.

Setting Up `/etc/hosts.equiv`

This file sets up trusted remote hosts and users. Trusted users are allowed access to the machine without having to specify a password. You might find, however, that with ssh, the trusted users might have to supply their passwords anyway.

Note

More to the story   There's a way around this with ssh as well, but that falls under more advanced topics. Using passwords to log in until you're comfortable reading the ssh documentation for this procedure shouldn't be much of a burden.

An entry in /etc/hosts.equiv can be of the form:

```
hostname   username
hostname
```

The first form specifies a hostname and username, whereas the second line specifies any user from that hostname. An entry can be made negative by adding -. You can also use netgroups by using a netgroup in either the hostname or username field.

My /etc/hosts.equiv looks like this so far:

```
+@our-machines
```

Which is to say, I can log in from any machine in the our-machines netgroup without issuing a password. Because I serve this netgroup only to members of this netgroup, I've essentially defined a trusted cluster. All machines in our-machines trust all other machines in our-machines, and trust no others. Were I to later develop a group of troublemaking machines and define it in /etc/netgroup as something like our-machines-lockout, I could then add an entry to /etc/hosts.equiv in the form

```
-@our-machines-lockout
```

This entry would deny access to users in that particular group. This could still be done while allowing them to be part of our-machines for other purposes, such as sharing the password database or NFS-mounting drives.

Note

> **.rhosts files are evil!**   You might find that your users try to install .rhosts files to allow themselves no-password access from remote machines not under your control. .rhosts files have the same syntax as the hosts.equiv file, but you have no control over the contents. It's entirely possible for a user to install a .rhosts file that says to allow no-password logins for every user on aol.com. You're best off deleting any .rhosts files that you find without even asking questions—most system administrators do this with an automatic job run regularly from the crontab. Remove .rhosts files with all prejudice, because they should be against security policy.
>
> The only valid use for .rhosts files is as root in situations where the root user needs to run remote-shell software such as dump and restore to a remote tape drive. In these cases the .rhosts file should contain specific host and user information making it as difficult as possible for a user to spoof the remote machine identity.

11

Summary

You learned today of two great tools that are used to make collections of UNIX machines function as cohesive units—as clusters. The NIS service, as you now know, is what provides the seamless availability of user logins and permissions across an entire group of machines. NFS-mounted diskspace completes the illusion and makes any user login truly location-independent on that cluster.

Specifically, today you learned about

- Providing the NIS information—the creation of the NIS master and the maps that you want it to provide.
- Receiving the NIS information—the creation of an NIS client, and how to attach it to an NIS domain to get information.
- Serving NFS resources—getting your NFS server ready to go.
- Exporting filesystems.
- Controlling client access to exported filesystems.
- Using NFS resources—planning mount points and preparing your NFS client.
- Mounting filesystems.
- The hosts.equiv file—its uses and a few of its security implications.

Q&A

Q I have some users who should have access to all the machines all the time and others whom I need to limit to only off-hours access. Is there a way I can do this?

A Yes. It's a bit more complicated than can be answered in a book of this nature, but if you research the NIS literature you will find that password sharing can actually be handled with a syntax similar to the netgroup sharing I discussed here.

At a conceptual description level, it is possible to create net-user-groups that with the appropriate password syntax can be added to and deleted from the password information on client machines. One solution would be to make an "all users" password map that was stably served to all machines, and an "occasional users" database that was transiently subtracted back from the "all users" database. Of course, there are other, equally valid paths to the solution as well. All that remains is to update the master files at the appropriate time and remake the maps.

Q **Can I mount the same directory on multiple different machines?**

A Absolutely! UNIX wouldn't be nearly as useful if you couldn't!

Q **Can I mount the same directory in multiple different places on the same machine?**

A Not really, or at least not generally. To make it look like you've done this, mount the directory in one place, and make links to it from the other places you'd like it to appear.

Q **I've mounted a directory named /hoopy from machine#1 onto /net/ machine1/hoopy on machine#2. I also want to mount /hoopy/local on /usr/ local on machine#2, but it keeps saying that it can't because the parent is already mounted. What's up?**

A With the exception of a few newer and odder UNIX flavors, NFS won't allow you to mount subdirectories of a parent directory that's already mounted. The solution to your problem is the same as in the question earlier; use links to make the subdirectories appear where you'd like copies of them to appear.

Q **I've successfully exported and mounted my drives, but my client machines can't seem to write anything on them, even though they're supposedly exported and mounted r/w. Any suggestions?**

A Make certain that your export definition has a root= entry. I've also met machines that refused to accept certain other machines in an access=netgroup entry and required that the problem machines be specified by name or IP. This happened even though other identical machines worked fine with the access=netgroup setup and even though the machine that was being denied access was the master server for the netgroup. If neither of those work, you might need to put an entry for your clients in your server's /etc/hosts.equiv.

Workshop

Quiz

1. Where do you specify disk export information?
2. As a paranoid system administrator, do you think NFS is secure?
3. If your drive doesn't mount, what's the first thing you should do?
4. Given its obvious security implications, why do you put up with NIS?
5. A user has changed their password, but can't use the new password to log on. What's wrong?

Exercises

These exercises require that you've got a preexisting cluster to administer and that there's some work that needs to be done to bring it into tiptop shape. If you have only one machine and no users at this point, turn on the services and create configuration files, but you're not going to see any really spectacular changes.

1. Go through all machines in your domain and try to create a conflated `/etc/passwd` file with no duplicate entries, and no conflicting numerical userids.

2. Go through all the machines from Question 1 and update their password files and numerical userids to match your master database. You'll use the `chown` command frequently here, so make sure you back everything up before you go mucking about.

3. Be daring. Cross-mount your drives and start trying to conflate duplicate user directories. Again, keep complete backup copies of everything so that if you do make a mistake, you can fix it before a user calls for your head.

DAY 12

The Basics of Making User Accounts

Have you been feeling the pressure of constantly having to be root, knowing that anything you might mistype could result in disaster? I'll bring an end to that with today's topic—making user accounts.

Preliminary Files to Get to Know

Before you look at making user accounts, there are a couple of files you should get to know: /etc/passwd and /etc/group. In addition, your system might use /etc/shells, a file to list approved shells. Check the man pages to see if your system uses it.

> **Note**
>
> **She sells C shells**   Some UNIX flavors won't provide for login shells that aren't specified in the file /etc/shells. Some provide for all shells if there is no /etc/shells file and only shells in /etc/shells if the file exists. If that's too much of a tongue twister to remember, just remember that if you can start a shell at the command line with no problems but you get kicked off the system with an "illegal shell" message if you try to use it in /etc/passwd, it's because the shell is not listed in /etc/shells. Oh well, if it's not a tongue-twister, it's a run-on sentence—some days you just can't win.

/etc/passwd

/etc/passwd is the file you will work with the most because each user has to have an entry in the password file. This being the case, it is important to know what the fields in /etc/passwd represent.

An entry in /etc/passwd is of the following form:

```
user:password:UID:GID:user information:home directory:shell
```

Table 12.1 provides a more detailed description of the password file fields.

TABLE 12.1   /etc/passwd Fields

Field	Description
user	The username for logging in to the account. It is best to keep the length to a maximum of eight characters. On most systems, if the username is over eight characters, the user will not be able to establish a shell login, although many other services will work fine.
password	An encrypted copy of the user's password.
UID	User ID provides a unique number to identify the user.
GID	Primary group ID to which the user belongs.
user information	A comma-separated list of information about the user, such as name, address, and phone. If you had the finger service running, this is where it would get information about the user.
home directory	Path to where the user's files are stored. This directory is the user's own top-level directory.
shell	Path to the user's shell. The shell is what the user will use to communicate with UNIX. Common shells include the following:
	sh—Bourne shell. The ubiquitous UNIX shell. Not particularly good for user interaction, but good for shell scripts because it's everywhere.

Field	Description
	csh—C shell. A shell with some programming capabilities reminiscent of C. The C shell is probably the second most prevalent UNIX shell.
	tcsh—Extended C shell. This shell has some useful extensions to C shell. If you like C shell, upgrade to tcsh. Command completion and other features make this shell a winner.
	bash—Bourne again shell. This shell is the default with the Linux distribution and is an attempt to make the sh environment more user friendly.

If the password field in your /etc/passwd has an x rather than an encrypted password, your system is using the shadow password file, /etc/shadow. The normal /etc/passwd file is readable by all users, and this makes for a bit of a security problem as it enables brute-force attacks against the encrypted passwords. Some systems use a shadow password file system where the encrypted password information is stored in a file that is readable only by root.

/etc/group

The /etc/group file defines the groups recognized by your system and allowable in entries in /etc/passwd. An entry in /etc/group is of the following form:

```
group name:password:GID:user list
```

The fields are as defined in Table 12.2.

TABLE 12.2 /etc/group Fields

Field	Description
group name	Name of the group.
password	Encrypted password for the group. If the field is empty, a password is not needed.
GID	ID number unique to the group.
user list	Comma-separated list of users belonging to the group.

A minus in front of a group name disallows that group entry. A plus in front of a group name indicates that NIS entries should be incorporated for that group. If an entry with a plus has a password or user list in it, the entries in those fields override NIS entries. A plus by itself on a line indicates that the NIS /etc/group entries should be appended there.

Whatever GID entries you make in /etc/passwd have to be defined in /etc/group.

The contents of the group file control membership in arbitrary groups that you as the system administrator can define. The capability to group users goes largely underused in most UNIX installations. The group ID is what controls access according to the second set of read/write/execute permissions in the rwxrwxrwx permission triple. These fields define the permissions granted to users with a group ID identical to that of the file.

By clever manipulation of the /etc/group file and group permissions, you can satisfy collections of users who want to all have access to the same files but who you want to keep as separate IDs for administrative purposes. If you have a research laboratory with many students who all need access to the same files but you don't want the headache of giving them all the same userid, you can create a new group in /etc/group for their lab and assign that GID to all the users in the lab. After you have done this, any file that any of them creates with group read/write/execute permissions turned on will be accessible to other members of the lab because they all share the same group.

Users can also be members of more than one group. The passwd file GID entry defines the default group to which they belong when they log in. However, the /etc/group file defines both groups and users that are in the groups. One user can occur in multiple groups in /etc/group and can switch between which group he is currently acting as a member of by using the newgrp command, which invokes a new shell under the requested group. If he needs to change the group ownership of a file that he owns to be owned by a different group of which he is also a member, he needs to use the chgrp command.

Some special groups you might end up making might be for departmental accounts, temporary accounts, and administrative users, as well as one for regular users. You might also have groups for special projects or certain software packages.

Note

A turn of the wheel Historically, a group named wheel was used for administrative users. This does not seem to be adhered to very closely anymore, but you will still find the occasional piece of UNIX software designed for system administrators that will refuse to run unless the user running it is a member of group wheel. This is a simple security precaution from the "old days" when UNIX and the Internet were kinder and gentler. If you come across a piece of software that refuses to run with nothing more than a cryptic message such as "not wheel," it's because it is checking to see if your user ID is considered to be an administrator by checking the /etc/group definition for the wheel group.

Predefined System Users and Groups

A look at your /etc/passwd and /etc/group files shows that there are a few predefined system users and groups. Which ones you have depend on your operating system, but Table 12.3 shows some of the common predefined users.

TABLE 12.3   Common Predefined System Users

User	Function
root	The superuser. Has access unrestricted access to everything.
daemon	Frequently used to run or own daemons.
bin	Owns most executables.
sys	Frequently used to run or own system processes.
uucp	Used to connect for uucp network transfers. Should definitely be disabled!
adm	Administrative user, use is sporadic and seems random.
nobody	Used to own things that you want to be available to users, but that you want to be locked from ever possibly having a shell, executing commands, or otherwise doing anything other than sitting on your drive.

Making Accounts: The Basic Way

You're finally there! On some systems, you might have to make user accounts by hand, whereas other systems might provide graphical or script-driven tools for adding a user to the system.

You will look at the steps needed to make a user account by hand. Even if your system provides a tool for adding user accounts, a look at how to do it by hand will give you an idea of what the system is doing for you.

12

Note

Hard work is good for you!   I highly recommend avoiding graphical tools for maintaining user accounts, and I generally recommend avoiding automated tools unless you know and understand their inner workings. Having an add-user script is fine, and being able to control user access by clicking virtual buttons on a Web page is pretty darned neat. If, however, you come to rely on these tools and you have an emergency where you need to deal with a problem account or something goes wrong and the utility makes incorrect accounts, you're going to be in trouble.

> Understanding how accounts are created and modified by hand is important. It's much faster to tweak settings in vi than in a graphical interface, and users are going to ask that you fix things on a regular basis. Learn the manual way now, and then use the fancy tools later if you're comfortable with them. That way, you'll be ready for any problems that should arise.

The basic procedure for making a new user account is the following:

1. Make certain that the account you're about to create does not duplicate an existing account or reinstate an account that you have closed for cause. Initially, this won't be a problem, but when you have hundreds of users, making certain that you aren't about to duplicate a user account for someone who has forgotten that she has an account will take a bit of time. Even more important is preventing users who have had their accounts terminated for misconduct from sneaking back on with a new user ID.

2. Create an entry in the password file for the user. As a security precaution, you might want to list * as the initial password.

3. Verify that the username and UID are indeed unique.

4. Make sure the GID assigned to the user is defined in /etc/group.

5. Update your NIS master when you are satisfied with the entry.

6. Create the directory that will house the user's account.

7. Copy initialization files to the user's directory. For your convenience, store basic initialization files in a central location.

8. Change ownership of the directory to the new user.

9. Assign a password. Expire it if you need to, and update the NIS master. (You will have to experiment with how ssh behaves with password expiration. ssh ignores password expiration information on my system. As a substitute, I've written a replacement shell that forces users to update their password when they log in and to do password expiration by changing their shell.)

10. Apply any quotas if you need to. edquota is the likely command to help with this if you use quotas.

I will add a user with the user ID ralph to my system. I first create an entry for him in the password file:

```
ralph:*:1001:200:Ralph, 555-1234:/net/barracuda/home/ralph:/bin/csh
```

In my entry, `ralph` has a user ID of `1001` and a group ID of `200`. I picked numbers that seem to be out of the general range of the current password file. Now, I must define group `200` in the `/etc/group` file:

```
user:*:200:
```

This will be my general user group.

Next, I update the NIS master, which on my system is the following:

```
Barracuda# cd /var/yp
Barracuda# make
updated passwd


pushed passwd
updated netid

pushed netid
couldn't find /etc/timezone
couldn't find /etc/auto.master
couldn't find /etc/auto.home
```

Note

> **The things that aren't there**   Notice the complaints that the `make` process made about various `/etc/*` files that don't exist on my system. These are some of the other default maps that are served by my version of the NIS server. I don't have a use for them here, but leaving them in the makefile definition so that I get a regular reminder that I should take care of them is probably a good idea.
>
> I can also add other maps to the database if I want to. NIS provides the capability to serve arbitrary table-based databases to your client machines.

12

Next, I create the directory for the account:

```
Barracuda# cd /net/barracuda/home
Barracuda# mkdir ralph
```

I provide initialization files for the account. Because the user's default shell is `csh`, `ralph` needs a `.cshrc` and `.login`. If `ralph` used `sh`, he'd need a `.profile` instead of a `.cshrc`. Other shells you might choose to use might have different configuration files as well. I'm particularly partial to `csh` and `tcsh`, which both use `.cshrc`, so that's what I use here.

To make my life easier in installing user accounts, I keep a copy of a dummy user account with all the necessary bits and pieces in a directory named `/usr/local/extras`. This enables me to easily do installs just by copying files and to simply replace files if a

user mysteriously loses one. I've provided copies of the .login and .cshrc files that I
use for my user defaults in Appendix C, "Sample Configuration Files."

> **System administrator syntax ahead!**   Watch out for this next cp command!
> It's going to copy all files with names that start with a dot (period), followed
> by a lowercase letter in the range a to z, followed by anything. It will place
> copies of these files in the target directory /net/barracuda/home/ralph,
> which is where the user ralph lives.
>
> As a system administrator, you will find this sort of ranged regular expres-
> sion shell syntax to be very useful.

```
Barracuda# cp /usr/local/extras/.[a-z]* /net/barracuda/home/ralph/
```

Next, I change the ownership of the directory and its contents to the new user, ralph:

```
Barracuda# cd /net/barracuda/homeBarracuda# chown -R ralph.user ralph
```

A couple checks of the command shows that the files and directory are indeed now
owned by ralph:

```
Barracuda# ls -alg ralph
total 4
drwxr-xr-x  2 ralph    user          512 Apr 14 18:34 .
drwxr-xr-x  4 root     wheel         512 Apr 14 17:17 ..
-rw-r--r--  1 ralph    user          904 Apr 14 18:34 .cshrc
-rw-r--r--  1 ralph    user          719 Apr 14 18:34 .login

Barracuda# ls -ldg ralph
drwxr-xr-x  2 ralph    user          512 Apr 14 18:34 ralph
```

Next, I assign a password for ralph:

```
Barracuda# passwd ralph
Changing password for ralph on Barracuda.
New password:
Retype new password:
```

> **The Invisible Password**   Yes, I actually did enter a password for ralph in the
> previous example. As a security precaution to make life a little more difficult
> for people looking over your shoulder, most UNIX programs that accept
> passwords shut off the screen echo while you're typing the password. Others
> display asterisks (*) instead of the password you're typing.

> **Tip**
>
> **Responsible password assignment** If you're assigning passwords responsibly, you really should assign the password to the account and immediately expire it. Check your man pages for `passwd` to find exactly how to do this for your version of the OS.
>
> By doing this, you guarantee that the user has to change her password on her very first login and that nobody has any capability to know that password other than the user. Keeping passwords secure is serious stuff, and they need to be secure even from you and your administrative staff.
>
> This is as much for your protection as for your user's protection. If you don't force them to change their passwords immediately and there is a problem, you can be accused of knowing the password and being the source of the problem. If you can't know the password, then this accusation cannot be made.

I again update the NIS master by `cd`ing to `/var/yp` and typing `make`. Because I only want to update one NIS map, it is also sufficient to type `make passwd`.

At this point, I am not concerned about quotas for the users, so I will not apply a quota here. You don't have to apply any quotas to start off with, if you don't want to. As a matter of fact, if you don't expect to have problems with your users, I'd strongly advise not using quotas. Enabling quota checking makes logins take considerably longer and can consume a fair amount of CPU resources, just to enforce what should be basic polite behavior.

At the facility I administrate, we have a policy that users will not use more than 100MB of disk space. Most of our users tend to be polite about adhering to the quota on their own—most actually manage to stay in the 20–40MB range without any administrator prompting at all. Unfortunately, some do need to have quotas applied to provide that extra bit of inspiration to play nice.

Situations where you might want to consider turning on quotas, even though they are a resource drain, include the following:

- For systems that provide unlimited data storage for a more or less anonymous facility. For example, if you provide a Web-based image drop-off for an in-house printing facility, you might need to enable quotas to prevent a spike in job submissions from overwhelming your diskspace.

- For systems where some users simply cannot contain themselves and make life difficult for the other users by completely consuming resources. If your choice is between only a small subset of users being able to use the machines at all and everyone being mildly inconvenienced by quota checks, opt for the quota checks.

12

- For systems where maintaining adequate diskspace for all users to be "comfortable" is impossible. The only way you will be able to make them live in an uncomfortably cramped amount of space is by enforcing quotas.

If you do find a need to enforce quotas, you need to be aware of the following:

- Users who are over quota when you turn on quotas will not be able to write anything to disk until they are under quota. Error messages regarding the fact that operations have failed due to lack of diskspace are sometimes not particularly clear. Be prepared for confusion.
- Users who are over quota when you turn on quotas will be able to log in and use the machines. They just will not be able to add to their disk quota. This enables them to log in and clean up after themselves.
- Most quota systems have a soft quota and a hard quota. Users who are over the soft quota get warning messages and in some implementations, some period of time to get back under quota before being prevented from writing. Users who are over the hard quota cannot write.
- The procedure for enabling quotas appears different for different flavors of UNIX, but the NFS shared drive quota information appears to be cross-platform compatible.

To enable quotas, you will have to do the following:

- Enable quotas on your drives. This appears to commonly be done by inclusion of a configuration file named quotas at the root level of each affected partition and by subsequently executing the quotaon command. Check the man page for quotaon to learn whether you need the quotas file and what the correct syntax is.
- Start a quota-checking server on the machine holding the users' home directory. Check the man pages for quota and quotacheck.
- Set a quota for your users. Some systems support creation of universal quotas for all users; others require assignment of quotas for each user individually. Check the man pages for edquota.
- Enable quota sharing of NFS volumes. This involves adding options to your NFS mount statements in your fstab entries.

Now that I am done installing ralph as a user and have decided that I'm not interested in quotas at the moment, I'll see if both machines in my cluster know about ralph. Not surprisingly, barracuda, the NIS master, knows about the account:

```
Barracuda# cd ~ralph
Barracuda# pwd
/home/ralph
```

Note **Commands on the half-shell** If you should try to access a user directory by the ~username syntax and get an error that it's not found, it's probably because you're using sh. The bourne shell is a wonderful shell for making universally executable scripts, but it is a very poor shell to use at the command line. For this reason, I'm sticking with csh and tcsh syntax in this book.

The password file specifies /net/barracuda/home/ralph as the directory, but on barracuda, /net/barracuda/home points to /home, so /home/ralph is the right place.

Note **System administrator bag-o-tricks** After you've mastered this way of making your user's directory look like it's in the same place on all your machines, do a bit of reading about the finer points of NFS. Although the tricks are more than you want to know about just yet (by my second week I sure wasn't doing NFS mounts from scratch!), you can use some NFS magic to make these machines look even more identical.

If I check on mother, I see that the NIS client also recognizes the account:

```
[ray@mother]# cd ~ralph
[ray@mother]# pwd
/net/barracuda/home/ralph
```

More importantly for ralph, can he log in? On barracuda, he can:

```
SunOS Release 4.1.4 (BARRACUDA_SMALL) #2: Mon Mar 22 20:33:01 EST 1999
No mail..
Barracuda ralph 1
```

He can log in on mother, too:

```
No mail.
mother ralph 1 >
```

You'll probably want to double-check the functionality of new accounts as you make them, especially as you are the first person doing this. Find out before your users will that everything is or is not working properly.

Your system probably does not require that you manually make accounts this way. It might have a useradd command that takes arguments such as the user's directory, group, location of basic initialization files, and so on. What has been shown here is essentially what useradd is doing for you.

12

Making User Accounts—The Exotic Way

Some operating systems might provide you with more exotic user account–making tools than the average `useradd` tool. Take a look at what you can do in IRIX. IRIX provides both a graphical interface for creating user accounts and a command-line alternative, `addUserAccount`. Because you've already seen the manual way to do things, I'll show you the graphical interface here. Be aware that the graphical interface isn't available in all IRIX installs and that you might get stuck if you came to rely on it.

Now begin the adventure! First, I bring up the System Manager from the Toolchest. Figure 12.1 shows you the System Manager.

FIGURE 12.1

Security and Access Control Panel as part of the System Manager.

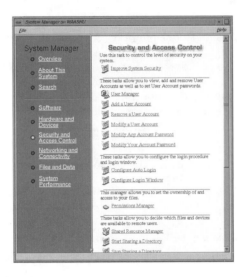

Next, I start the User Manager, shown in Figure 12.2.

FIGURE 12.2

User Manager in IRIX.

Now, the machine brings up an introductory instruction panel, as shown in Figure 12.3.

FIGURE 12.3

*Introductory informa-
tional panel for adding
a user account.*

Finally, I get to do something! Figure 12.4 shows the panel where the username is
entered.

FIGURE 12.4

Entering username
betty.

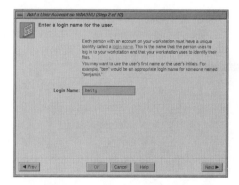

Next the machine requests the full name of betty as you see in Figure 12.5.

FIGURE 12.5

*Here's where the
user's real name gets
entered.*

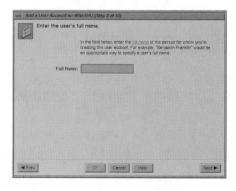

12

In Figure 12.6, the machine asks what type of account the user should have. Because this machine is not the NIS master, I can't make an account that would be recognized throughout the cluster. My only choice is an account local to the machine. I pick the default.

FIGURE 12.6

Selecting the user's account type.

Next, I have the option of assigning a password to the account. Although Figure 12.7 already shows the box for adding a password selected, that was not the default.

FIGURE 12.7

Choosing to password protect the new account.

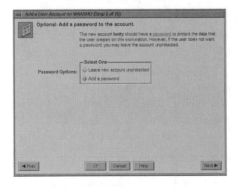

Notice in Figure 12.8 that the number of total panels I will have to visit has increased by one. Now, I assign a password to the account.

The next panel, shown in Figure 12.9, is where the user ID is assigned. I accept the number that is already there. Presumably the machine verifies whatever entry you make.

As you might expect, the next panel, shown in Figure 12.10, is the one used for assigning the group ID. The panel doesn't actually offer a group number, but rather a group category. Here, I also accept the default. Again, I assume that the machine verifies the validity of the group number.

FIGURE 12.8

Assigning a password to the new user account.

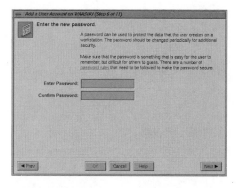

FIGURE 12.9

Assigning the user ID.

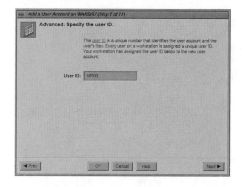

FIGURE 12.10

Assigning the group ID for the new user account.

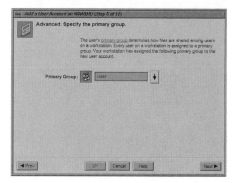

12

The user's home directory is assigned in the panel shown in Figure 12.11. Again, I accept the default and ask that it verify and create the directory.

In Figure 12.12, I indicate that the default shell should be csh.

The machine then brings up a panel for confirming the settings as shown in Figure 12.13. Everything looks good.

FIGURE 12.11

Assigning a home directory for the new account.

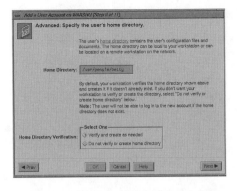

FIGURE 12.12

Assigning a shell to the account.

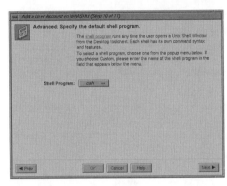

FIGURE 12.13

Confirming the settings for the new account.

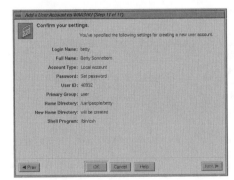

Now, everything looks even better as the machine indicates that the account has been successfully made in Figure 12.14.

So what did the machine do, anyway? Take a look behind the scenes.

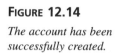

FIGURE 12.14

The account has been successfully created.

You'll notice that `/etc/passwd` has a new entry:

`betty:.gjVN64oiZoy2:48932:20:Betty:/usr/people/betty:/bin/csh`

Right now, even `betty`'s account is as minimal as `ralph`'s account on the other machine, with only `.cshrc` and `.login` present:

```
WAASHU 10% ls -al ¦ more
total 48
drwxr-xr-x    8 betty    user         4096 Apr 14 13:14 .
drwxr-xr-x    5 root     sys            50 Apr 14 13:11 ..
-rw-r--r--    1 betty    user          552 Apr 14 13:11 .cshrc
-rw-r--r--    1 betty    user          631 Apr 14 13:11 .login
```

Can `betty` log in to an SGI with so few initial files? Figure 12.15 shows you her desktop after she has logged in.

Here, you can see the Toolchest in the upper-left corner, where you can find buried such options as opening a UNIX shell. In the lower-right corner, you can also see her icon catalog, which provides a way for her to point to and click on many applications to start them. Not everything, even on an SGI, starts that way, though. For some packages, she will still have to be able to open a UNIX shell.

After `betty`'s first log in, she now has a few more files in her directory:

```
WAASHU 1% ls -al ¦ more
total 48
drwxr-xr-x    8 betty    user         4096 Apr 14 13:14 .
drwxr-xr-x    5 root     sys            50 Apr 14 13:11 ..
-rw-r--r--    1 betty    user          126 Apr 14 13:14 .Sgiresources
-rw-r--r--    1 betty    user          552 Apr 14 13:11 .cshrc
drwxr-xr-x    7 betty    user          128 Apr 14 13:16 .desktop-WAASHU
drwxr-xr-x    3 betty    user           24 Apr 14 13:14 .desktophost
-rw-r--r--    1 betty    user          631 Apr 14 13:11 .login
```

12

```
drwx------    2 betty     user          29 Apr 14 13:14 .netscape
-rw-r--r--    1 betty     user         640 Apr 14 13:11 .profile
drwxr-xr-x    2 betty     user          87 Apr 14 13:14 Desktop
-rw-r--r--    1 betty     user          69 Apr 14 13:14 betty.outbox
drwxr-xr-x    2 betty     user          27 Apr 14 13:14 dumpster
drwxr-xr-x    4 betty     user         105 Apr 14 13:14 public_html
```

FIGURE 12.15

This is what the desktop of betty, *my new user, looks like.*

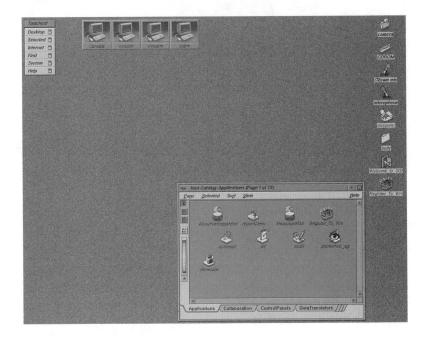

Unlike betty, ralph, after a few logins to the other machine, only has a few new ssh-related files in addition to his initial files:

```
Barracuda ralph 18 >ls -al
total 6
drwxr-xr-x  3 ralph           512 Apr 14 23:01 .
drwxr-xr-x  4 root            512 Apr 14 17:17 ..
-rw-------  1 ralph           105 Apr 14 23:01 .Xauthority
-rw-r--r--  1 ralph           904 Apr 14 18:34 .cshrc
-rw-r--r--  1 ralph           719 Apr 14 18:34 .login
drwxr-xr-x  3 ralph           512 Apr 14 19:19 .ssh2
```

The SGI OS does many magical things behind your back, including creation of all manner of configuration files to handle information about where the user has put icons on the desktop, what programs were left open, and other history information. SunOS does much less of this, though if I started using the X-Window System (X11) with it, I'd start seeing automatically created configuration files cropping up there as well. Generally, you should-n't be worried about this automatic behavior. Users will accumulate configuration files and directories over time, but the files tend to run between benign and mostly harmless. The only time you need to worry about this behavior is when an automagic tool goes awry and decides that it absolutely must write a 230MB configuration file in a hidden directory in a user's account. You generally find out about these fairly quickly, though, either from the user or the OS.

Just as when you make accounts by hand, it's good practice, even with a graphical tool available, to verify that the account works. Although `betty` was able to successfully log in, the system did not prompt her for a new password. If that was not the behavior you wanted, you would have to figure out a way to expire the password.

Deleting User Accounts

Just as with making accounts, on some systems, you will have to do deletions by hand. With others, you will be able to use a tool like `userdel`. With others, there will be a graphical user interface. You will look at IRIX's graphical user interface for this discussion because it looks more interesting than command lines and also because one of the panels that the process generates brings up important issues for everyone.

Just as with adding an account, the first panel is an introductory panel, as shown in Figure 12.16.

FIGURE 12.16

IRIX's introductory panel for deleting a user account.

12

In the panel in Figure 12.17, I indicate a user account to delete.

Then, as you see in Figure 12.18, the machine asks how to handle the account's files. I could leave them there, but they would remain accessible only to the system administrator, presumably achieved by changing permissions on files. I also can delete all the account's files. Wisely, the machine advises backing up the files before deleting them, just in case I should later discover a need for them. The final choice is that I could keep the files and reassign ownership. In this particular case, `betty` had no data that was needed elsewhere by anyone, so I decide to have everything deleted.

Figure 12.17

Indicating the account to be deleted.

When deleting an account, disposition of the files is something you will have to consider. Various schools of thought recommend such things as the following:

- Leave the user's entry in the password database, and change the password to an asterisk (*) to lock the account. Accountability traces and the ability to find information about the user without going back to backup tapes could be a useful thing.

- Zap everything and remove every trace of the user. You never have any idea what might happen to files that are "abandoned" on your system, and the less opportunity for trouble, the better.

- `tar` and compress the user's directory and keep it online for some reasonable period. Users lose files when moving to new homes and frequently come back asking for their old files. Your life will be easier if you anticipate this and have the files online already instead of having to go to tape to retrieve them.

- After a user is gone, he has no right or recourse to his data. Keep anything that looks interesting, and do whatever you please with the rest.

Personally, I lean towards the first and third suggestion, but you'll have to make up your mind just how you want to handle these things. I'd suggest you make a decision and put it in your written system policy document.

Figure 12.18

Indicating how to handle user files when the account is deleted.

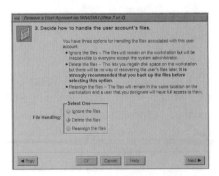

Figure 12.19 shows the panel that asks for a confirmation of the account and disposition.

FIGURE **12.19**

*Confirming the
account to be deleted.*

After I select OK, the machine informs me that this might take a while. I instantly hear the drives start to chew. The machine wasn't kidding about the possibility that it could take a while! The machine is checking everywhere for betty's files, not just in her home directory, but in /tmp directories and anywhere else just in case. Eventually, however, the machine reports success, as shown in Figure 12.20.

FIGURE 12.20

*The account has been
successfully deleted.*

Poor betty! Her account was so short lived.

Summary

In today's lesson, you learned how to create and manage user accounts. There's not too much to summarize about it, but in condensed form, you should now know about the following:

- /etc/passwd and /etc/group file entries.
- How to update your NIS master maps.
- How to create the user account information.
- How to create the user directory and properly assign properties.
- How the lucky people with fancy GUI interfaces get to do this stuff.

12

Q&A

Q **Sometimes when I do a long listing of a directory, I get funny numbers instead of usernames for the owners of files. What does this mean?**

A It means that you're missing entries from your password database. Those files were created by a user with the numeric user ID that you see being displayed instead of the username. Now, your /etc/passwd file or NIS yppasswd map does not contain a user for this numeric ID. Most likely, the user previously existed and was deleted from the passwd file. Alternatively, these files might have come from another system by way of a tar file that maintained the user information and untarred to an unknown user ID.

Q **I know that my user's files are available on all the machines on my cluster and that her password is served to all the machines by NIS. Does this mean that she can log in to multiple machines in the cluster simultaneously?**

A Yes it does. UNIX really handles each user process like it's from an independent login. Because a user ends up running dozens, if not hundreds, of simultaneous programs when she's logged into any machine, it makes no difference to UNIX if those are all from one physical login or from multiple separate logins. Similarly, the rest of the machines don't care whether the user is logged in to them multiple times as well.

Q **What happens if I assign multiple different usernames in /etc/passwd to have the same numeric user ID?**

A Tricky person, aren't you! The numeric user ID is really the differentiating factor for users. All usernames with the same numeric user ID are "the same user." If you absolutely must have a group account with multiple people having access to the same login, you can do it this way. Give each of them a different username and a different password, but give them all the same numeric user ID and the same home directory. The only time I've ever seen this actually be acceptably useful was with an email-only account that had to be accessed by multiple different people, but maybe you'll come up with a creative use for this possibility.

Workshop

Quiz

1. How do you lock a user account so that he can't log in?
2. What's the first thing you should do after assigning a password to a new account?
3. Why do you need to create the passwd file entry before taking care of the user directory?
4. A user who is over quota can or cannot log in to the machine?

Exercises

1. Create a new user account using the most sophisticated tool that your OS provides. Almost all now provide at least a command-line script for you to use.

2. Create a new user account using just the manual tools as you've been shown here. How close can you get to an equivalent installation to the one that was created automatically?

3. If you have a pre-existing system at hand, pick an existing user on your system and search through the system for all the files owned by this user. The older the account, the better, in terms of this exercise being illustrative. You might want to check the manual pages for the find command to help you with this.

4. If you have a pre-existing system at hand, find a dead or dormant account. Search through the contents of this account, and try to decide what disposition you should make of the files if you were to decide to delete the account.

12

DAY 13

Saving Your World: Making Backups to Tape

Now that you have a bit of data on your machine, it's about time to make some use of your tape drive. Today, you will take a look at how to make a backup of your machine and how to restore from that backup.

Backing Up Your Machine to Tape: Using dump

Some form of dump is the basic command used to back up your machine to tape. Read the man pages for your operating system's version of dump multiple times to find any useful specific information you might need.

Understanding Incremental Dumps

No matter what version of dump your operating system supports, the type of backups you will perform are incremental backups. As the name might suggest, you will not back up everything on the system every time. Instead, you will decide on a backup schedule that consists of doing whatever is necessary to maintain reliability for your site. At the very least, you will run full backups every few months. At the very best, you will run full backups every few months, a monthly, a weekly, and a daily. In practice, your schedule might fall somewhere in between.

The key to understanding incremental dumps is understanding that you will not be backing up everything on your system every time you run the dump command. You will be able to issue different levels, or degrees, of the dump command. You can issue the dump command from levels 0 through 9. Except for level 0, which is the level used for a complete backup that backs up everything, you will have the freedom to assign what number means what. Each dump level with a level number higher than 0 will only back up files that have changed since the most recent dump *that has a lower level number.* Note that I didn't say since the most recent dump, but rather, since the most recent dump with a lower level number. This facility enables you to conserve tapes and save on equipment wear by doing most of your backups only of files that change, and infrequently backing up files that stay the same for long periods of time.

In the example you will look at, the level numbers I have chosen have the following meaning:

- 0—full
- 2—monthly
- 4—weekly
- 6—daily

I don't have to choose even numbers. Odd numbers are just fine too. I've chosen to space mine out so that I can add an unexpected backup for whatever reason. It doesn't matter what arbitrary values you assign so long as the numeric values increase with the frequency of the scheduled dump, but to make your life easier, be consistent from use to use.

It's fairly easy to be confused by the idea of incremental backups, but an example should help to clear things up.

Say that last month I ran a full dump (level 0) on a filesytem. Every day initially following the full dump, I ran dailies (level 6). A week after the full dump was made, I decided to run a weekly dump (level 4). In the days following the weekly dump, I ran dailies (level 6). The second week after the full dump, I ran another weekly (level 4). I continued the pattern until today, a month after the full dump. Today, I decide to run a monthly (level 2). Table 13.1 shows a sort of calendar of the sample backup schedule I will follow. For purposes of the example, today is the last identified day in the schedule, Monday of Week 5.

TABLE 13.1   Sample Backup Schedule

Week	Mon	Tues	Wed	Thurs	Fri	Sat	Sun
1	0	6	6	6	6	6	6
2	4	6	6	6	6	6	6
3	4	6	6	6	6	6	6
4	4	6	6	6	6	6	6
5	2						

To reiterate, remember that dumps are incremental. Keeping that in mind, what do the numbers mean in Table 13.1? Here is what lands on each of the tapes:

On Monday of Week 1, a full dump, `level 0`, was done. Everything on the filesystem was backed up to the dump `level 0` tape.

On Tuesday of Week 1, a daily, `level 6 dump` was done. That is, everything that had changed since the most recent dump with a lower level was backed up. In this case, Monday's dump `level 0` has a lower level, and is the most recent dump with a lower level. So, anything that changed between Monday's `level 0 dump` and Tuesday's `level 6` was backed up to the dump `level 6` tape.

What about Wednesday of the first week? Again, with the Wednesday dump, `level 6`, only files that have changed since the most recent dump with a lower level were backed up. What's the most recent dump with a lower level number? Yes, it's the `level 0 dump` from Monday. Again, only files that changed between Monday, `level 0`, and Wednesday, `level 6`, were backed up. Wednesday's dump is not a reflection of the changes in files between Tuesday and Wednesday because both of those dumps are a `level 6`.

Thursday, Friday, Saturday, and Sunday's dumps for the first week mimic the behavior of Tuesday's and Wednesday's. For each of these dumps, the most recent dump with a lower number will be Monday's `level 0 dump`, and each of these contained a backup of all files that changed between Monday and the day of the dump.

On Monday of the second week, a dump `level 4` was done. What does this mean? Again, the files that changed between the most recent dump with a lower dump level number and the current date were backed up. Again, the dump `level 0 dump` from the previous Monday was the most recent dump with a lower number. The dump from Monday of the second week reflects changes that were made between the previous Monday and that Monday. The significance of using `level 4` for this dump will appear with the dump for the next day.

13

What about Tuesday of the second week? On this Tuesday, I run a dump `level 6`, but this time the most recent dump with a lower dump level than 6 is not the first Monday's `level 0 dump`, but the second Monday's `level 4` dump instead. Tuesday's dump, then, consists of the files that changed between Monday of Week 2 and Tuesday of Week 2.

Likewise, the dump from Wednesday of Week 2 reflects the changes between Monday of Week 2 and Wednesday of Week 2.

What files did the dump `level 2` on Monday of Week 5 capture? If you look at the chart, you see that the most recent dump with a dump level lower than the dump level of 2 is the dump `level 0` of Monday on Week 1. So the dump `level 2` on Monday of Week 5 is a dump of the files that changed between Monday of Week 1 and Monday of Week 5.

Note

> **Tomorrow, tomorrow, and all tomorrow's tomorrows…** Notice that if I do a dump `level 6` tomorrow, that today's dump `level 2` will be the most recent lower number. The "most recent lower number" isn't looking for any sort of order in the numbers; it just goes back looking for the most recent lower numbered dump performed in the past and backs up everything since then.

When you are restoring files, the same incremental approach applies. Dumps are incremental, so the restores must be incremental as well. If a user deletes a directory, to rebuild that directory to its most recent state will take one restore at each of the dump levels that your facility uses.

For example, if I accidentally delete a directory midday on Tuesday of Week 5, sometime after the daily dump (`level 6`) was done, I would have to restore my directory from the dump `level 0` of Monday of Week 1, the dump `level 2` of Monday of Week 5, and Tuesday morning's daily dump, `level 6`.

Why do I have to restore my directory from multiple different archives? Because other than the `level 0 dump` that provides a complete snapshot of my directory, the others only provide differences over time. I need to restore the dump `level 0` to get back files that have been around in my directory for ages, the dump `level 2` for changes in the last week, and the dump `level 6` for changes since yesterday. What comes from each tape is as follows:

The dump `level 0` tape would provide the base level restore of my directory as it existed on Monday of Week 1 because it's a full dump and captures everything as of when it is made.

To this, the dump `level 2` tape adds any changes that occurred between the dump `level 0 dump` of Week 1 and the date of the `level 2` dump, the day before I made the mistake. Any new files that I had added during that time or older files that I had changed would be backed up on this tape, but files that I had not changed would not be included.

Tuesday's dump `level 6` fills in any changes that occurred between the dump `level 2` of the day before and Tuesday.

As you can see, the directory has to be restored incrementally. If Tuesday's daily dump ran at 4:00 a.m. and I made some spectacular changes at noon, just before I accidentally deleted everything after lunch, I can't get the spectacular changes back. I can only restore to the state of the directory as it was at 4:00 a.m.

Using dump

What options you will use for `dump` will vary with your operating system and possibly with what type of machine the tape drive itself is attached to. Options that you want to make sure you include are the dump level, a blocking factor, any special tape size information you might have to provide, and the name of the tape device. The blocking factor is information used by `dump` to determine how to group the data and control information on the tape. Your man pages will provide advice on a useful blocking factor to use. Some operating systems use a streaming `dump` that does not require any tape specifications. However, for those dumps, you might have to provide an arbitrary session name that you can use as a key for searching when you have to restore something. If you haven't already done so, read the man pages for your operating system's version of `dump`. Other versions of `dump` require that you provide information in as fine a detail as the storage density of your tapes in bytes per inch and the lengths of your tapes. Again, your man pages will give you advice on what is appropriate.

Always record on the tape packaging the date, the dump level, the blocking factor, and the filesystems that were dumped in the order they were dumped. For systems that use a streaming `dump`, also record the session label that goes with what you dumped. Record the blocking factor, even if you are just using a default. It might save someone else time restoring from your tape if she knows the blocking factor right away instead of having to guess.

The clever system administrator will work out a schedule whereby tapes that are used for weekly or daily dumps will be rotated into duty as full-dump tapes are (semi)permanently archived after some period of time. Magnetic media has a finite lifetime when running over record and playback heads, so moving a frequently-used tape to a "use once and forget" status near the end (or middle, more practically) of its useful life is a way to economize on tape costs.

13

Here's the basic form of a dump command:

```
dump options filesystem_to_dump
```

To give you an idea of what kind of output to expect from a dump command, here is a sample from SunOS, which uses dump for dump:

```
catbert# dump 4bdsfu 128 48000 6000 rosalyn:/dev/rmt/0n  /
  DUMP: Date of this level 4 dump: Tue Mar 23 11:31:56 1999
  DUMP: Date of last level 2 dump: Mon Mar  1 09:52:06 1999
  DUMP: Dumping /dev/rsd0a (/) to /dev/rmt/0n on host rosalyn
  DUMP: mapping (Pass I) [regular files]
  DUMP: mapping (Pass II) [directories]
  DUMP: mapping (Pass II) [directories]
  DUMP: estimated 23690 blocks (11.57MB) on 0.01 tape(s).
  DUMP: dumping (Pass III) [directories]
  DUMP: dumping (Pass IV) [regular files]
  DUMP: level 4 dump on Tue Mar 23 11:31:56 1999
  DUMP: Tape rewinding
  DUMP: 23620 blocks (11.53MB) on 1 volume
  DUMP: DUMP IS DONE
```

In this particular instance of dump, 4 is the level. After the 4, you see the string bdsfu. This string specifies that it is followed by a collection of data values:

b is the blocking factor.

d is the density in bytes per inch.

s is the size of the tape in feet.

f is the tape device.

u is an indication to update /etc/dumpdates on successful completion of dump.

Following the bdsfu string are the numeric values corresponding to each item specified, in the order specified. The filesystem to be dumped is specified as the last thing on the line; here, it's /. As you can see by the naming convention, rosalyn:/dev/rmt/0n, the tape drive is not local to the machine. The magical numbers used for density and size have been determined from various man pages as something that ought to work for 90m DAT most of the time.

Note

Most classical versions of dump have arguments more appropriate for 9-track streaming tape drives like the type you see in 1960s and 1970s sci-fi films. The parameters were not really designed to accommodate today's high-capacity cartridge drives, and so you must fudge the length and density values until a working selection that makes reasonable use of the tape's capacity is achieved. It is usually sufficient to provide size and density such that it is bigger than the actual tape capacity because most modern tape drives will detect when EOM (end of media) is reached. However, if the value is significantly larger, dump's estimate of the number of tapes required will be useless, so you probably will want to attempt to make a reasonably accurate guess. The man pages usually make helpful suggestions on making these guesses, but given the rapid advances in tape capacity in recent years, even the man pages seem to be out-of-date as far as accurate predictions go.

In this example, you see that the tape drive is local to the machine. This example shows the Solaris variant to dump, ufsdump:

```
Rosalyn joray 205 # ufsdump 4bdsfu 128 48000 6000 /dev/rmt/0n /mnt2
  DUMP: Writing 64 Kilobyte records
  DUMP: Date of this level 4 dump: Tue Mar 23 11:39:25 1999
  DUMP: Date of last level 2 dump: Mon Mar 01 10:19:59 1999
  DUMP: Dumping /dev/rdsk/c0t2d0s7 (Rosalyn:/mnt2) to /dev/rmt/0n.
  DUMP: Mapping (Pass I) [regular files]
  DUMP: Mapping (Pass II) [directories]
  DUMP: Mapping (Pass II) [directories]
  DUMP: Estimated 987046 blocks (481.96MB) on 0.27 tapes.
  DUMP: Dumping (Pass III) [directories]
  DUMP: Dumping (Pass IV) [regular files]
  DUMP: 987006 blocks (481.94MB) on 1 volume at 941 KB/sec
  DUMP: DUMP IS DONE
  DUMP: Level 4 dump on Tue Mar 23 11:39:25 1999
```

Notice that the same options that worked in SunOS work here in Solaris. They also work for IRIX's variant of dump for its native efs filesystems, dump.

This sample shows you what output from a streaming dump can look like:

```
WAASHU joray 205 # xfsdump -l 2 -b 245760 -m -f rosalyn:/dev/rmt/0n
➡-M apr991 -L 990406_waashu_2a /1a
xfsdump: version 3.0 - type ^C for status and control
xfsdump: level 2 incremental dump of WAASHU:/1a based on level 0 dump
begun Fri Jan 22 14:38:46 1999
xfsdump: dump date: Tue Apr  6 09:32:10 1999
xfsdump: session id: cb03fced-7bfd-1022-802d-08006905bc41
xfsdump: session label: "990406_waashu_2a"
xfsdump: ino map phase 1: skipping (no subtrees specified)
xfsdump: ino map phase 2: constructing initial dump list
xfsdump: ino map phase 3: pruning unneeded subtrees
xfsdump: ino map phase 3: pass 2
xfsdump: ino map phase 3: pass 3
xfsdump: ino map phase 3: pass 4
xfsdump: ino map phase 3: pass 5
xfsdump: ino map phase 3: pass 6
xfsdump: ino map phase 3: pass 7
```

13

```
xfsdump: ino map phase 4: estimating dump size
xfsdump: ino map phase 5: skipping (only one dump stream)
xfsdump: ino map construction complete
xfsdump: estimated dump size: 1019299072 bytes
xfsdump: preparing drive
remote shell program that invoked /etc/rmt does not exist
xfsdump: WARNING: media contains non-xfsdump data or a corrupt xfsdump
media file header at beginning of media

   ======================= media overwrite dialog =========================

overwrite data on media in drive 0?
1: don't overwrite (timeout in 3600 sec)
2: overwrite (default)
 -> 2
media will be overwritten

   -------------------------- end dialog ---------------------------

xfsdump: creating dump session media file 0 (media 0, file 0)
xfsdump: dumping ino map
xfsdump: dumping directories
xfsdump: dumping non-directory files
xfsdump: ending media file
xfsdump: media file size 276971520 bytes
xfsdump: creating dump session media file 1 (media 0, file 1)
xfsdump: dumping ino map
xfsdump: dumping directories
xfsdump: dumping non-directory files
xfsdump: ending media file
xfsdump: media file size 274022400 bytes
xfsdump: creating dump session media file 2 (media 0, file 2)
xfsdump: dumping ino map
xfsdump: dumping directories
xfsdump: dumping non-directory files
xfsdump: ending media file
xfsdump: media file size 274022400 bytes
xfsdump: creating dump session media file 3 (media 0, file 3)
xfsdump: dumping ino map
xfsdump: dumping directories
xfsdump: dumping non-directory files
xfsdump: ending media file
xfsdump: media file size 204226560 bytes
xfsdump: dumping session inventory
xfsdump: beginning inventory media file
xfsdump: media file 4 (media 0, file 4)
xfsdump: ending inventory media file
xfsdump: inventory media file size 491520 bytes
xfsdump: I/O metrics: 3 by 240KB ring; 4186/4207 (100%) records streamed;
 526090 B/s
xfsdump: dump size (non-dir files) : 1006325552 bytes
xfsdump: dump complete: 2228 seconds elapsed
```

This is an xfsdump statement for an IRIX xfs filesystem, one of the filesystems that provides for a streaming dump. In this statement, -l is the dump level, -b is the blocking factor, -m is a flag needed to indicate that the remote machine with a tape drive is not an SGI, -f identities the tape device, -M gives the tape a name, and -L gives the session a name. The filesystem to be dumped is /1a. With xfsdump, you can also provide a pathname to a specific directory or file that you might want to dump. Traditional dump can only dump filesystems. You don't need to provide xfsdump with any special tape specifications. Here, the blocking factor is whatever was recommended in the man page for my needs, and in this instance, it is only needed because the tape device is not on an SGI.

Notice that the traditional dump output from the Sun gives dump sizes in kilobytes, whereas the xfsdump gives dump sizes in bytes. Even with the latest version of IRIX, you can't get away from measurements in bytes!

Here's an example of unexpected output:

```
xfsdump: WARNING:could not open regular file ino 5655013 mode 0x000081a4:
 Inval id argument: not dumped
xfsdump: WARNING:could not open regular file ino 5655019 mode 0x000081a4:
 Inval id argument: not dumped
xfsdump: WARNING:could not open regular file ino 5655025 mode 0x000081a4:
 Inval id argument: not dumped
xfsdump: WARNING:could not open regular file ino 5655036 mode 0x000081a4:
 Inval id argument: not dumped
xfsdump: WARNING:could not open regular file ino 5655046 mode 0x000081a4:
 Inval id argument: not dumped
xfsdump: WARNING:could not open regular file ino 5655056 mode 0x000081a4:
 Inval id argument: not dumped
```

I have gotten output similar to this for drives that die soon thereafter. If you get output similar to this when you run dump, it might be time to make a full backup and start drive shopping.

Troubleshooting dump

If dump works fine on the machine with the tape drive but not on any other machines, you might have to make a .rhosts file for root on the machine with the tape drive. The .rhosts file should have an entry for each machine that will be allowed access to the tape drive in a form such as the following:

```
mother.politically.correct.com   root
```

Also, when you closed your services in /etc/inetd.conf, you likely disabled rsh. You should probably reenable the service on the machine with the tape drive only and add an entry to your /etc/hosts.allow file that resembles this:

```
in.rshd: 192.168.1.4
```

13

Specify only those machines that are allowed to access the tape drive. So if the machine with the tape drive is supposed to allow your cluster of three other machines to access its tape drive, your /etc/hosts.allow file would include all three of those IP addresses only for rsh:

```
in.rshd: 192.168.1.4 192.168.1.20 192.168.1.8
```

Restoring to Your Machine from Tape: Using restore

It's one thing to get dump to work and another to successfully restore from tape. Make sure you test restoring data from tape before you actually have to do it. Take notes as you do it. Do your testing in noncritical locations on your system. Get an approximate idea of what you have to do. You might not end up restoring to the exact location you hope for, but you can always move the data around.

Preparing to Restore

The information that you will most likely need for traditional restore is the blocking factor and the name of the tape drive. For a restore of a streamed dump, you will probably also need the name of the session that contains the data you want to restore. If you choose an interactive restore session, you might not have to worry about too many other options. As with dump, be sure to read the man pages for your operating system's version of restore.

What tapes you will need for your restore will vary with what you have to restore. If you only have to restore a file that you last updated yesterday before today's dump, today's tape is sufficient. Recall, however, that you might need to restore from the appropriate combination of the most recent full, monthly, weekly, and daily tapes.

When you restore from tape using a traditional form of restore, you have to navigate the tape to the location that has the filesystem with the data you need to restore. This shouldn't be too problematic, assuming that you have written on the tape package somewhere the dump date, dump level, blocking factor, and what was dumped in the order it was dumped. If you do not write this information down, your tapes are all but useless. You might be able to determine the contents of a tape for which you haven't recorded this information with sufficient experimentation, but realistically, you should consider the contents of a tape with no written information to be lost.

Doing a Traditional Restore

I am going to restore a directory that I deleted from my home directory. To complete this task, I will need the tapes from the most recent appropriate levels. In my case, I need the most recent `level 0`, `level 2`, and `level 4` tapes.

I will first restore the base contents from the `level 0` tape. My label indicates that I used a blocking factor of `128` and that the directory I'm looking for is on the first filesystem on the tape. What luck!

When I put the tape in the drive, located at device `/dev/rmt/0n` in this example, I decide to rewind it for good measure:

```
Rosalyn joray 223 > mt -f /dev/rmt/0n rewind
```

Because what I need is at the beginning of the tape, I don't have to navigate the tape any further. I can go ahead with the restore command, which on Solaris is `ufsrestore`:

```
Rosalyn joray 202 # ufsrestore ibf 128 /dev/rmt/0n
```

The options I have indicated are `i` for interactive, `b` for blocking factor, and `f` for tape device.

Because I have chosen an interactive restore mode, I am given a prompt from which I can run `ls`, which, as you might expect, lists the contents of the tape:

```
ufsrestore > ls
.:
 apache.tar      college.tar     joray.tar      restoresymtable
 andy/           geri/           jack/          testing/
 college/        joray/          lost+found/
```

The `/` at the end of names indicates directories.

 Note

> **Is it live, or is it Memorex? A Memorex DAT, that is** Yes, you're reading correctly. In interactive mode, you get an interface to the dump that is very similar to actually "being there" on the device that was dumped.

13

What I want to restore is located on this tape in the directory `joray`. I `cd` to `joray` on the tape and run `ls`. Shown here is only the directory that needs to be restored. Remember, this is the `level 0` tape, so everything is here (no need to bore you with the contents of my entire home directory at the time that the tape was made):

```
ufsrestore > cd joray
ufsrestore > ls
./joray:
 work/
```

The work directory is the one I want to restore. To select it, I issue the add command:

```
ufsrestore > add work
```

Because that's all I want, I can tell ufsrestore to extract it now:

```
ufsrestore > extract
```

The ufsrestore command responds with a request for which volume to read. I've always backed up one tape at a time, so I enter 1. If you end up doing multitape dumps for one filesystem, you will want to answer this question with the highest tape number for a given filesystem. The restore process will instruct you as to how to proceed from there. It's much more convenient to work with single volume dumps and restores, however, and with today's high-capacity tape drives and a bit of planning, you should be able to avoid the necessity for multitape dumps entirely. Here is the request:

```
You have not read any volumes yet.
Unless you know which volume your file(s) are on you should start
with the last volume and work towards the first.
Specify next volume #: 1
```

Then, I wait a while. Finally, ufsrestore asks if I want to set modes:

```
set owner/mode for '.'? [yn] n
ufsrestore > quit
```

You might want to experiment with the set owner/modes question if your version of restore has such a question. The results of choosing yes and no are similar but not exactly identical. When I choose y, the hierarchy of the filesystem on the tape is restored to the restore directory, with permissions and ownership of the restore directory itself ('.') set to those of the filesystem on the tape. If root owns the filesystem that you're restoring from on the tape and you used your home directory as the temporary restore location, your home directory is now owned by root.

Suppose that my home directory is /users/joray and I want to restore a directory I previously had in my home directory called work, just as you saw earlier. If I choose to restore directly into my home directory and choose to answer yes to the set owner/modes question, my home directory is now owned by root, which owns the filesystem /users that is on the tape. The hierarchy that is on the tape is restored into my home directory as joray/work, with expected permissions and ownerships. A /users/joray/joray/work directory now exists, with my home directory, /users/joray, now being owned by root.

If I choose no, the permissions and ownerships of the filesystem that is on the tape are not given to the directory that I'm restoring in, but the hierarchy as it appears on the tape is still restored into the restore directory. Because my home directory, /users/joray, is still owned by joray, n makes sense for me. The directory is still restored as joray/work in the hierarchy that appears on the tape, so I again have a /users/joray/joray/work directory. In this particular instance, to retain joray's ownership of the joray home directory, I choose n. However, for restoring an entire filesystem, you would probably be better off with y.

Next, I decide to verify what I already suspect about the location of my restored directory by searching for a file that I know should have been restored:

```
Rosalyn joray 210 > find ./ -name macuserssh-1.tex -print
./joray/work/facletters/macuserssh-1.tex
```

As I suspected, it's not quite where I wanted it. I only wanted a directory called work in my home directory, not one called joray/work, but at the moment, I take what I can get. This is an incremental restore, so I don't want to move anything just yet.

I go on to the next tape, the level 2 tape, and this time I have to navigate the tape. The filesystem I'm looking for is the ninth one listed on the tape. So, I have to tell the tape drive to fast forward to the end of the filesystem that's just before the one I want. In other words, I tell the tape drive this:

```
Rosalyn joray 235 > mt -f /dev/rmt/0n rewind
Rosalyn joray 236 > mt -f /dev/rmt/0n fsf 8
```

fsf 8 tells the tape drive to fast forward to the end of the eighth file. That puts me at the beginning of the ninth, which is where I want to be. If you don't like using mt to navigate your tape, check to see if your restore has an option to skip to the *nth* file on the tape. Solaris' ufsrestore does have this option available. So, rather than issuing the mt command where I tell the tape drive to fast forward to the end of the eighth file, I could instead issue a ufsrestore command, like this:

```
ufsrestore ibfs 128 /dev/rmt/0n 9
```

Note

> **Always something there to rewind me**   If you can't seem to get off file number 1 on the tape drive, it's because you're using the rewind version of your tape device. Read your man pages to find out how to use the non-rewinding interface to your tape. Currently, your tape is being helpful by automatically rewinding itself after every command. If you're using the rewind device and ask the drive to skip forward eight files, it will dutifully do so. It will then be most helpful and automatically rewind itself again before you can issue another command.

13

In my case, after having the tape drive fast forward to the end of the eighth file, I then issue an interactive ufsrestore again, cd to my directory on the tape, run ls, and extract what I'm looking for as follows:

```
Rosalyn joray 206 # !ufsres
ufsrestore ibf 128 /dev/rmt/0n
ufsrestore > ls
.:
 college/   joray/

ufsrestore > cd joray
ufsrestore > ls
./joray:
 .Xauthority                   .xinitrc
 .history                      newacct.sun.script
 .netscape/                    newacct.sun.script-bk2-most-used
 .ssh/                         work/
 .ssh2/

ufsrestore > add work
Warning: ./joray: File exists
Warning: ./joray/work: File exists
Warning: ./joray/work/facletters: File exists

ufsrestore >ufsrestore > extract
You have not read any volumes yet.
Unless you know which volume your file(s) are on you should start
with the last volume and work towards the first.
Specify next volume #: 1
set owner/mode for '.'? [yn] n
Directories already exist, set modes anyway? [yn] n

ufsrestore > quit
```

Then, I go on to the next tape, the level 4 dump, which also lists the filesystem I'm looking for as the ninth one. I navigate the tape as I did before:

```
Rosalyn joray 242 > mt -f /dev/rmt/0n fsf 8
```

With the tape positioned where I want it, I again run ufsrestore:

```
Rosalyn joray 207 # !ufsre
ufsrestore ibf 128 /dev/rmt/0n
ufsrestore > ls
.:
 college/   joray/

ufsrestore > cd joray
ufsrestore > ls
./joray:
 .Xauthority
```

```
.history
.netscape/
.ssh/
.ssh2/
.xinitrc
orphanage/
work/
```

```
ufsrestore > add work
Warning: ./joray: File exists
Warning: ./joray/work: File exists
Warning: ./joray/work/facletters: File exists
ufsrestore > extract
You have not read any volumes yet.
Unless you know which volume your file(s) are on you should start
with the last volume and work towards the first.
Specify next volume #: 1
set owner/mode for '.'? [yn] n
Directories already exist, set modes anyway? [yn] n
ufsrestore > quit
```

Afterward, I checked the newly restored directory to make sure it had everything I had hoped it would have. Everything I was expecting to find was there, so I moved the newly restored directory to where I really wanted it.

Success!

Doing a Restore of a Streamed Dump

Doing a restore of a streamed dump is a little different from a traditional restore. I don't have to navigate the tape at all! Instead, the pertinent information I need to know is the session name.

Of course, I rewind the tape for good measure before I begin. I then enter into interactive restore by using xfsrestore with the -i option.

```
WAASHU restore_test 1 #>xfsrestore -i -b 245760 -m -f rosalyn:/dev/rmt/0n
➥ -J -L 981012_waashu_0a -a /tmp ./
xfsrestore: version 3.0 - type ^C for status and control
xfsrestore: using online session inventory
xfsrestore: searching media for directory dump
xfsrestore: preparing drive
remote shell program that invoked /etc/rmt does not exist
xfsrestore: examining media file 0
xfsrestore: reading directories
xfsrestore: directory post-processing

======================== subtree selection dialog ========================
```

13

```
the following commands are available:
        pwd
        ls [ <path> ]
        cd [ <path> ]
        add [ <path> ]
        delete [ <path> ]
        extract
        quit
        help
```

I do have to provide a few more flags to the IRIX xfsrestore than I do to a traditional
restore. Here the -J indicates not to update any records because this is just an example
for testing. The -a indicates a location for xfsrestore to store a temporary directory
that it will make to carry out the restore, and ./ specifies a destination directory for the
restore.

I then run ls:

```
-> ls
        29891968 .desktophost/
           52998 .profile
        16810848 .cosmocreate/
             285 floppy/
           52994 .login
           83360 lib64/
        20971648 lib32/
          164164 .Sgiresources
        17560127 .desktop-RYOKO/
         5579597 hosts/
           52999 .varupdate
           52996 .wshttymode
          164163 public/
        21057518 .desktop-WAASHU/
           52995 debug
        16810849 patches/
         8388737 stand/
           74179 .cshrc
        29678385 nsmail/
        25546968 Desktop/
        29678389 share/
        16793345 CDROM/
           63767 PlayG.map
           52993 public_html
          164162 .backgrounds
             132 .webcache/
        20971650 .netscape/
           29777 unix
        16806963 dumpster/
        29360258 sbin/
         4194435 proc/
```

```
29891969 .web/
 8388739 var/
 4194468 usr/
   63743 tmp/
29360441 opt/
16806975 net/
12583274 lib/
16793530 etc/
16793532 dev/
    3624 bin
12972039 ns/
     136 hw/
```

As with traditional `restore`, files ending in / signify a directory. Notice how everything is not arranged in any sensible order. Also, the numbers here do not indicate file sizes.

Next I `cd` to where I want to go and extract what I want:

```
-> cd patches
 -> ls
      16810856 patchSG0003262
      16810855 README.patch.3262
      16810857 patchSG0003262.eoe_sw
      16810858 patchSG0003262.idb
      16810854 patchSG0003262.tar

 -> add patchSG0003262.tar

 -> extract

---------------------------- end dialog ----------------------------

xfsrestore: examining media file 1
xfsrestore: examining media file 2
xfsrestore: examining media file 3
xfsrestore: examining media file 4
xfsrestore: seeking past media file directory dump
xfsrestore: restoring non-directory files
xfsrestore: read_record encountered EOD : end of data
xfsrestore: I/O metrics: 3 by 240KB ring; 1128/1148 (98%) records
 streamed;
464122B/s
xfsrestore: restore complete: 604 seconds elapsed
```

13

`xfsrestore` restores the file into the current directory in the originating hierarchy, in this case as `patches/patchSG0003262.tar`:

```
WAASHU restore_test 4 #>ls -l patches
total 3440
-rw-r--r--   1 root      sys      1761280 Oct  8 05:23 patchSG0003262.tar
```

Here is what the original /patches directory looks like:

```
WAASHU restore_test 6 #>ls -l /patches
total 6872
-rw-r--r--    1 root      sys       3703 Jul 20 16:12 README.patch.3262
-rw-r--r--    1 root      sys        644 Jul 20 16:00 patchSG0003262
-rw-r--r--    1 root      sys    1741506 Jul 20 16:00 patchSG0003262.eoe_sw
-rw-r--r--    1 root      sys       1673 Jul 20 16:00 patchSG0003262.idb
-rw-r--r--    1 root      sys    1761280 Oct  8 05:23 patchSG0003262.tar
```

The same date and size are associated with the file from tape as with the original. Because this was the only file I wanted, this one tape is sufficient for my needs. However, like traditional restore, xfsrestore is incremental. If I had to restore more, I might have had to go through multiple tapes, as I did with the ufsrestore example.

Whether you're using traditional or nontraditional restore, the interactive modes for both types have many options in common, as shown in Table 13.2.

TABLE 13.2   Common Options in Interactive Restore Mode

Option	Function
add	Adds the specified file or directory to the list of files to be extracted. If the argument is a directory, it and all its descendants are added to the list.
delete	Deletes the current file or directory and its descendants from the list of files to be extracted.
extract	Extracts all files on the extraction list from the dump.
cd	Changes to the specified directory.
ls	Lists the current or specified directory.
pwd	Prints the full pathname of the current working directory.
help	Lists the available commands.
quit	Ends session, even if there are files selected for extraction.

Summary

In today's chapter, you learned how to save and recover the state of your world. Making backups is a very important thing to system administrators because losing things is an incredible nuisance, especially if you've worked on them for ages. If your users lose things (if...*Hah!*), they'll probably want you to restore things for them as well. As much as I preach that you're there to provide a service for your users, when you start down the path to jumping at every user restore request, you'll never get a minute away from the tape drive. Most UNIX system administrators that I know consider the tape backup facility an absolute requirement for system stability and system administrator use, but they frown on normal user restore requests. You'll have to make your own decisions about how you want to handle this.

Specifically, in today's reading, you learned the following:

- How to plan a dump schedule
- How to determine what information will be on what tape in a dump schedule
- How to perform a dump
- How to perform an interactive restore
- What the different flavors of dump and restore you might encounter are likely to look like

Q&A

Q The "blocking factor" field must mean something. You used it, but glossed over the details. Could you elaborate?

A I glossed over that point because so long as you a) specify it, b) record what you specified, and c) stay consistent, it isn't really likely to make that much difference in your life. Because you asked, though—The blocking factor is information used by dump to determine how to group the data and control information on the tape. Historically, tapes weren't 100 percent reliable (not that they are today, either). So, instead of simply writing the data from the device you're backing up, the dump program writes the data and then some control and diagnostic information that can be used to make sure that the data was written properly. If you have a very reliable device, you specify a large blocking factor, and your device writes away happily, rarely needing to stop and insert diagnostic and control information. If you have a flaky tape or drive, you specify a small blocking factor, and your device writes the control information much more frequently. With today's drives, a blocking factor anywhere between 40 and 200 is probably a safe bet, although your man pages or tape device might have specific hints that you'd want to follow. The one thing that you do need to be aware of is that the diagnostic information takes up room, and if you specify a small blocking factor, you slow down your writes and decrease the tape capacity available for your backup data. So, you're looking at a tradeoff between a slow and reliable factor and a fast and less reliable factor.

The only time you'll probably end up having to actually worry about blocking factors is if you get a tape from another person who doesn't tell you, or worse, doesn't know, what blocking factor he used. If he uses the same OS as you use, hope that he followed the hints in his man pages, and use yours to make a guess. If he uses a

13

different OS, your best bet will be asking on the appropriate Usenet newsgroups to see if anyone with the same type of machine can give you suggestions. Other than that, it's a guessing game—pick one, see if it reads, and repeat as necessary.

Q Is there a way to make a dump "outside" the normal dump schedule without affecting your normal "what goes where" plan?

A Yes. Simply leave off the u flag to dump, and it won't write the control information to the dumpdates file. This will prevent future dumps from ever knowing that this one occurred. This is exactly what you want to do if you need to give someone else a copy of your dump and don't want making that copy to affect your normal dump schedule or layout.

Q How many times can I reuse tapes before I should remove them from service?

A That question is very difficult to answer. It depends on what variety of tape device you are using, what the manufacturer and grade of the tape is, and how clean (or not clean) your tape drive is. All in all, it's a judgement call on your part. Most system administrators who I know reuse tapes for "noncritical" (read *daily*) backups, but they insist on fresh tapes for full archival backups. The manufacturers of the tape you use will almost certainly have recommendations for tape use that you can acquire with their products to help you make an informed decision.

Workshop

Quiz

1. Say it's now Friday of Week 3. Also, say that Friday's daily dump was done early in the morning. As soon as you get in, one of your users tells you that he was logged in Thursday evening to do some work, he accidentally deleted the contents of one of his directories, and he wants to know if you might be able to restore his data for him. To what state can you restore his account?

2. You've completely confused your dump schedule and can't figure out what's going to go on any dump you make. You can easily create a known state for your world by doing what?

3. A user needs a directory restored to the condition it was in on a particular date in the past. Without knowing the details of your dump schedule, what tapes do you need to pull?

4. Are you going to need as many tapes for each of the higher-level dumps as you do for the full dumps?

Exercises

1. Do a dump of your root / filesystem (or some other small filesystem if / is a large partition in your world). Move to another filesystem, create for yourself a safe sub-directory, cd to it, and restore the root filesystem there. Experiment with the restore process to learn where to expect things to land.

2. Do some more dumps of your root filesystem. Experiment with the numerical parameters to the dump command. Observe the changes in estimated tape capacity and tape drive behavior. If you have a streaming tape drive, such as an old QIC mechanism, you will be able to cause some wildly differing behavior by playing with the blocking factor.

3. Grab a calendar and plan a dump schedule for yourself. Invent a tape labeling scheme to go with it.

4. Try out your plan from Exercise 3. Pick a day on your calendar. See if you can tell what tapes you have to pull and which position each dump file is at on each tape from your plan and your labeling scheme.

5. Full-dump (level 0) all your partitions. Your backup rotation has just begun!

13

DAY **14**

Other Useful Software: Useful Utilities

Last week you installed some very basic useful software for your machine with gcc and gdb and the tools you needed simply to unpack your downloads. Today you will install some more useful software: Perl and MySQL. Then you will take a brief look at using each of them.

Perl will be useful to both you and your users. It is a language that you can use to carry out system administration tasks, and it is the most common language used for writing CGI scripts, which your users might want to use for their Web sites.

MySQL is a database package that implements the SQL database language. Your users probably have many uses for databases, and it is likely that you will discover some uses in your own work along the way.

After you install these two packages you will actually have the opportunity to play with them a little bit today. The potential uses to which you can put these packages are almost limitless, and their value to you in your job is similarly significant. As you experiment with Perl and MySQL, keep in mind that these are only two of the many interesting and useful free UNIX software packages available on the Internet. These two are important and appropriate to install right now, but when you've completed this book, don't neglect the opportunity to explore the wide range of utility software out there that can make your life and your users' lives so much more productive.

Installing Perl

Before you install Perl, you should check whether your system already comes with Perl and if it does, what version of Perl you might already have. As of this writing, IRIX 6.5, for example, already comes with Perl 5.004_04. If you want to consider upgrading to Perl 5.005_0X, carefully read the section in the perl5.005XX/INSTALL file on upgrading from Perl 5.004_XX to Perl 5.005_0X. The biggest problem if you have an earlier 5.004_0X version of Perl can come with any extensions that you might have installed to work with it. You will likely have to recompile the extensions to work with 5.005_0X. You might also want to keep your older version of Perl around to ensure that scripts written with it will still run. You have to know where the script looks for Perl to include the actual Perl version number, 5004XX.

Today you will also install MySQL, which requires that at least Perl 5.004 be installed, if you would like to use Perl support for MySQL. Its documentation for the most part indicates only Perl 5.004, but the Linux note that comes with it says at least 5.00403, so I'll assume they mean 5.004 or newer.

At any rate, I will demonstrate how to install Perl 5.005_03 on a machine that doesn't have any version of Perl yet. As you recall, my machine has an initial no-frills set up.

Installation Overview

You can get the latest version of Perl from `ftp.cpan.org`. The Perl Web site is `http://www.cpan.org`.

As always, read the READMEs before installing anything. The basic installation process is to do the following in the source directory:

```
sh Configure
make
make test
make install
```

Although you can customize your configuration, INSTALL emphasizes that accepting the defaults is a good beginning, and it emphasizes over and over that running `Configure` interactively is the best way to assure that everything is put where you want. Installation prefix questions are near the beginning of the interactive `Configure` because those are the questions where the defaults might not necessarily suit your needs.

The default installation directories are `/usr/local/bin`, `/usr/local/lib`, and `/usr/local/man`. The only quirk to the default directories is that man1 pages default to `/usr/local/man/man1`, whereas man3 pages default to `/usr/local/lib/perl5/man/man3`. The current explanation for the logic is that some of the Perl man pages end up overriding other man pages. The example given is that when Perl man pages are in `/usr/local/man/man3`, and a user issues `man less`, she gets the Perl man page for Perl's `less.pm` module, rather than the man page for `less`. INSTALL indicates that the default in a future release will probably be `/usr/local/man/man3`; however, INSTALL does not indicate whether the current problem would still persist.

If the location where you want Perl components to be stored includes the string `perl`, the storage is slightly simplified. If you wanted everything in `/opt/perl`, your directory structure would look like `/opt/perl/lib/` instead of something longer such as `/opt/perl/lib/perl5`.

The approach I recommend for installing Perl for the first time is to decide where you want Perl to be installed. Check the hints directory, INSTALL, and the README for your OS, if it has one, for any suggestions and issue a `Configure` command that incorporates those suggestions.

If you want to entirely trust the defaults, you can specify `Configure` as

```
sh Configure - des
```

But you would likely miss out on that interactive experience of `Configure` asking you questions.

Doing a Perl Installation

As you probably guessed, I have taken my own advice. I checked for any comments pertinent to SunOS, issued a `Configure` command that incorporated those suggestions, and manually accepted many defaults.

Let me take you on a partial tour of interactive `Configure`, so that you can see some of what `Configure` will ask.

First, I issue my `Configure` command in the source directory:

```
Barracuda# sh Configure -Dcc='gcc -B/bin/'
```

`Configure` responds:

```
Beginning of configuration questions for perl5.
```

14

```
Checking echo to see how to suppress newlines...
...using -n.
The star should be here—>*

First let's make sure your kit is complete.  Checking...
Looks good...

This installation shell script will examine your system and ask you
questions to determine how the perl5 package should be installed. If you
get stuck on a question, you may use a ! shell escape to start a subshell
or execute a command.  Many of the questions will have default answers in
square brackets; typing carriage return will give you the default.

On some of the questions which ask for file or directory names you are
allowed to use the ~name construct to specify the login directory
belonging to "name," even if you don't have a shell which knows about
that.  Questions where this is allowed will be marked "(~name ok)".

[Type carriage return to continue]
```

So I press Return a few more times to get the rest of the introductory comments.
Eventually `Configure` tells me

```
Locating common programs...
```

It then lists the numerous programs and the paths to them. Then it lists another section of
programs prefaced by this comment:

```
Don't worry if any of the following aren't found...
```

So I take `Configure`'s word for it and I don't worry about the missing programs. `Configure`
goes on to check a couple other things before providing some system-specific information:

```
First time through, eh?  I have some defaults handy for some systems
that need some extra help getting the Configure answers right:
```

3b1	dynix	irix_6_1	next_3_0	stellar
aix	dynixptx	isc	next_4	sunos_4_0
altos486	epix	isc_2	openbsd	sunos_4_1
amigaos	esix4	linux	opus	svr4
apollo	fps	lynxos	os2	ti1500
aux_3	freebsd	machten	os390	titanos
beos	genix	machten_2	powerux	ultrix_4
bsdos	gnu	mint	qnx	umips
convexos	greenhills	mips	sco	unicos
cxux	hpux	mpc	sco_2_3_0	unicosmk
cygwin32	i386	mpeix	sco_2_3_1	unisysdynix
dcosx	irix_4	ncr_tower	sco_2_3_2	utekv
dec_osf	irix_5	netbsd	sco_2_3_3	uts
dgux	irix_6	newsos4	sco_2_3_4	uwin
dos_djgpp	irix_6_0	next_3	solaris_2	

You may give one or more space-separated answers, or "none" if
appropriate. A well-behaved OS will have no hints, so answering "none" or
just "Policy" is a good thing. DO NOT give a wrong version.

After the warning to not give a wrong answer I cautiously proceed:

Which of these apply, if any? [sunos_4_1]

Look! Configure gives me hints on what I'll have to do sometime later:

You will probably see *** WHOA THERE!!! *** messages from Configure for
d_tzname and i_unistd. Keep the recommended values. See
hints/sunos_4_1.sh for more information.

Then Configure goes on to provide more operating system advice:

Configure uses the operating system name and version to set some defaults.
The default value is probably right if the name rings a bell. Otherwise,
since spelling matters for me, either accept the default or answer "none"
to leave it blank.

Operating system name? [sunos]

Operating system version? [4.1.4]

Configure then warns about an experimental feature. Sometimes experimental features
are a good thing; the tcsh shell I use daily was an "experimental feature" for quite a
while. In this case, however, I want a rock-solid stable Perl, so I am not interested in
experimental features and gladly accept the default:

Perl can be built to take advantage of threads, on some systems.
To do so, Configure must be run with -Dusethreads.

Note that threading is a highly experimental feature, and
some known race conditions still remain. If you choose to try
it, be very sure to not actually deploy it for production
purposes. README.threads has more details, and is required
reading if you enable threads.
Build a threading Perl? [n]

Then Configure goes on to ask my architecture and asks where I want the various
directories to go. I choose the defaults for everything, so my installation will go in
subdirectories under /usr/local.

Eventually I get to the compiler question with the flags I specified as recommended in
INSTALL, if I were to choose gcc on SunOS. It lists as the default what I specified on
the command line:

Use which C compiler? [gcc -B/bin/]

14

After pressing Return many times to respond to questions about the compiler and libraries, I get this question from Configure:

```
Do you wish to attempt to use the malloc that comes with perl5? [y]
```

Again, I choose the default. INSTALL indicates that Perl relies heavily on malloc (routines involving memory allocation) and that its performance can be affected by the system's malloc. Perl comes with its own version of malloc, optimized for Perl's needs, but this might take some space. The default, to use Perl's malloc, is what I choose. Apparently there could be some conflicts between with large applications or modules using third-party libraries that make malloc calls and Perl's malloc. In some cases, then, it appears that the system malloc might be the better choice, but here I trust the wonderful community of Perl developers to have these problems fixed before I even know that they exist. Keep this in mind if you choose the default and discover some problems later.

Here's the one question where I deviate from the default:

```
Build a shared libperl.so (y/n) [n] y
```

As I decided last week for gcc, I decide to try the shared library. I guess I'll have to remember that it's not the default option, should I discover some problems as a result of this choice.

 Note

> **Space and Time Wizards** The idea of a shared library is to reduce the amount of disk space taken up by software. If a routine is going to be needed by many applications, put it in one file, and let the applications load the file when they need it. On the opposite side of the coin, having to do another file open, load an external bit of executable, and fiddle around the program internals to make use of an external routine costs time.
>
> If space is at a premium, use shared libraries because they will drastically cut down on the size of applications that use them. If execution speed is at a premium, use static libraries because these get directly included into every application that needs them.
>
> If you've got an old, slow machine, with not all that much disk space, your choice will be a tough one.

Configure asks many more questions, to which I respond by pressing Return to accept the default. Eventually Configure asks if I would also like to install Perl as /usr/bin/perl:

```
Many scripts expect to perl to be installed as /usr/bin/perl
I can install the perl you are about to compile also as /usr/bin/perl
(in addition to /usr/local/bin/perl).
Do you want to install perl as /usr/bin/perl? [y]
```

Here I choose the default. This ends up being a link to /usr/local/bin/perl after installation. However, on a system that comes with Perl, you might find that this is the location of your current Perl.

After a few more returns, Configure asks

```
Are you getting the hosts file via yellow pages? [n]
```

My machine, Barracuda, is the NIS master, or in older parlance, the ypmaster which serves the maps. Barracuda is also a client of itself, but can read its own /etc/hosts file fine. In the final analysis, the /etc/hosts file is at least as complete as anything the machine might receive from itself via NIS(yp), so I claim that Barracuda does not get its hosts file via yellow pages and can answer no. If another machine were the NIS master, Barracuda would only be an NIS client, and as such would be getting its /etc/hosts file via yellow pages. In that instance I would definitely have to respond with yes.

Configure continues with a few administrative questions and then asks about how a Perl script should be started on my site:

```
I can use the #! construct to start perl on your system. This will
make startup of perl scripts faster, but may cause problems if you
want to share those scripts and perl is not in a standard place
(/usr/local/bin/perl) on all your platforms. The alternative is to force
a shell by starting the script with a single ':' character.
```

Because I have never seen a Perl script that doesn't start with #!, I choose #! and tell Configure to start with /usr/local/bin/perl for my site. I think not choosing #! as the start sequence would confuse your users, who come with their books on learning Perl that tell them to start their scripts with #! followed by the location of Perl at their site.

```
What shall I put after the #! to start up perl ("none" to not use #!)?
[/usr/local/bin/perl]

I'll use #!/usr/local/bin/perl to start perl scripts.
```

Configure seems agreeable to this. Now it goes on to ask many more questions, to which I again respond by pressing Enter. Although Configure starts to look for more information about my system, this message pops up all of a sudden:

```
*** WHOA THERE!!! ***
    The recommended value for $i_unistd on this machine was "undef"!
    Keep the recommended value? [y]
```

Just as Configure promised early on, I get one of those odd warnings to which I have been already instructed by Configure to respond with the default. So I do.

Configure continues investigating the system, when again I get an odd message:

```
*** WHOA THERE!!! ***
    The recommended value for $d_tzname on this machine was "undef"!
    Keep the recommended value? [y]
```

14

There's that other warning that `Configure` already told me to expect! I accept the default and hope that there are no other warnings to come.

`Configure` goes on to check this, that, and the other thing when I finally get this comment:

`End of configuration questions.`

Now I can sit back and relax for a few moments while `Configure` goes to work.

Or so I thought. One more question pops up, and I again accept the default:

`Run make depend now? [y]`

Eventually `Configure` finishes and instructs me to run `make`, which I do:

`Barracuda# make`

Note

> If you should run into an unfortunate accident while you are in the middle of your `make`, such as your connection unexpectedly dropping, don't despair. According to INSTALL, you run `make realclean`. For Perl, this cleans up any changes to the Perl source directories. It also keeps all the information that was entered as answers to `Configure` questions and use them as the default next time. You would still have to rerun `Configure`, but at least this time you don't have to pay as much attention.

And lots of information spews forth, until I eventually get this message:

`Everything is up to date. 'make test' to run test suite.`

So I run `make test`:

`Barracuda# make test`

It passes everything except one test, and I follow the instructions for running the tests again:

`Barracuda#./perl harness`
`ld.so: libperl.so.5: not found`

I search, see that it has made such a library, and tell it where to look by setting my `LD_LIBRARY_PATH` to `/usr/local/source/perl5.005_03`. Note that the syntax shown here only works for the csh shell variants.

`setenv LD_LIBRARY_PATH /usr/local/source/perl5.005_03`

I rerun the test, and it fails the same one (the `lib/ipc_sysv.t` test) but does not make the `ld.so` complaint. Perl claims that it is 98.95% correct, which looks good enough for me. Because the test's name appears to be System V–related, I decide that it probably doesn't matter for my machine and I finish with

```
Barracuda#make install
```

Installing MySQL

The MySQL home page is located at `http://www.mysql.org`. The site provides a number of download locations around the world. Pick the site nearest you. The installation of MySQL is not nearly as friendly as Perl. MySQL comes with an incredibly long manual with dozens of pages devoted to installing it.

Binaries are available for some platforms, whereas others must use the source. If there is a binary already available for your platform, definitely install that.

If you want to use Perl to access MySQL, you'll need to get the following Perl modules (all available at `ftp.cpan.org`):

- Data-Dumper (if you have Perl 5.004_71 or later, it is part of the standard distribution)
- DBI
- Data-ShowTable
- Msql-Mysql

Installing Perl Modules

Installing any Perl module will be an identical experience to installing any other Perl module, or at least this has been my experience. After unpacking your distributions to wherever you prefer, do the following in each module's source directory:

```
perl Makefile.PL
make
make test
make install
```

The main note here is that you can't run `make test` on the Msql-Mysql modules until mysql is installed and running.

Also, rebuild and reinstall the Msql-Mysql modules whenever you upgrade MySQL, especially if you notice your DBI scripts dumping core after such an upgrade.

The MySQL manual does not indicate any preference as to whether the Perl modules should be installed before or after MySQL, only that server should be running to complete the testing steps for the Msql-Mysql modules.

14

The first time I try the first step in building a Perl module I encounter this problem:

```
Barracuda# perl Makefile.PL
ld.so: libperl.so.5: not found
```

There's that shared library biting me again! I know the library was made when I ran `make` during the Perl build, so in `/usr/local/lib` I run:

```
Barracuda# find ./ -name \*.so\* -print
./pic/v8/libstdc++.so.2.8.1
./pic/libstdc++.so.2.8.1
./libstdc++.so.2.8.1
./ucpic/v8/libstdc++.so.2.8.1
./ucpic/libstdc++.so.2.8.1
./v8/libstdc++.so.2.8.1
./perl5/5.00503/sun4-sunos/auto/B/B.so
./perl5/5.00503/sun4-sunos/auto/Data/Dumper/Dumper.so
./perl5/5.00503/sun4-sunos/auto/Fcntl/Fcntl.so
./perl5/5.00503/sun4-sunos/auto/IO/IO.so
./perl5/5.00503/sun4-sunos/auto/IPC/SysV/SysV.so
./perl5/5.00503/sun4-sunos/auto/NDBM_File/NDBM_File.so
./perl5/5.00503/sun4-sunos/auto/ODBM_File/ODBM_File.so
./perl5/5.00503/sun4-sunos/auto/Opcode/Opcode.so
./perl5/5.00503/sun4-sunos/auto/POSIX/POSIX.so
./perl5/5.00503/sun4-sunos/auto/SDBM_File/SDBM_File.so
./perl5/5.00503/sun4-sunos/auto/Socket/Socket.so
./perl5/5.00503/sun4-sunos/auto/attrs/attrs.so
./perl5/5.00503/sun4-sunos/auto/re/re.so
./perl5/5.00503/sun4-sunos/CORE/libperl.so.5.3
```

I knew the library was there! When I link the expected library location with the real one, my module installations become much more pleasant.

Note

> **Share and share alike**   Shared libraries are nice for cutting down on disk usage, but they have the problem of causing software to not run if they can't be found. Any time you see a message of the form "blah blah blah.so* not found", it's because a shared library isn't being found in the places the system is looking. You have two ways of fixing this:
>
> 1. You can find the library and put it in one of the standard places that the system looks on your version of the OS. Usually this will be `/lib`, `/usr/lib`, and maybe `/usr/local/lib`. On some versions of Solaris it includes `/opt/lib`.
>
> 2. You can find the library and add its location to the path that your system searches for shared libraries. To do this, add the path to the directory it lives in to the environment variable LD_LIBRARY_PATH.
>
> Both solutions work. Generally I like the first one better because I like having all my user-installed binaries in one place and all my user-installed

> libraries in another place (/usr/local/bin and /usr/local/lib). Doing it
> this way should speed things up a bit because the more places that you ask
> the system to look for things by extending paths, the more time it's going to
> need to spend looking.

```
Barracuda# ln -s perl5/5.00503/sun4-sunos/CORE/libperl.so.5.3
➥libperl.so.5.3
```

When you install the Msql-Mysql module, don't choose the default answer for the first question unless you really do already have mSQL. If you choose to install support for both, 10 minutes later in the install it's going to break because it can't find your msql installation.

```
Which DBMS do you want to use?

  1) MySQL
  2) mSQL (1 or 2)
  3) Both MySQL and mSQL

  4) mSQL1 and mSQL2
  5) Everything (MySQL, mSQL1 and mSQL2)

Enter your choice:  [3]
```

Just as Perl provides friendly comments while you run Configure, so do the Perl modules. Don't be surprised or concerned if you get helpful messages after issuing the perl Makefile.PL command. When you type that command for the DBI module, you first get

```
*** Note:
    The optional PlRPC-modules (RPC::PlServer etc) are not installed.
    If you want to use the DBD::Proxy driver and DBI::ProxyServer
    modules, then you'll need to install the RPC::PlServer, RPC::PlClient,
    Storable and Net::Daemon modules. The DBI CPAN Bundle may help you.
    You can install them any time after installing the DBI.
    You do *not* need these modules for typical DBI usage.
```

Relax. Don't let the comment disturb you. Perl module authors are gregarious sorts who really like trying to be helpful. You'll find that almost every module you install will have useful hints about other modules that it can work with and suggestions for other things you might want to consider installing. In the immediate case, none of these optional proxy modules are needed for the MySQL install.

Binary Installation Overview

If you do not plan to modify the C and C++ code for MySQL, installing a binary distribution should be sufficient. Many platforms are supported, and it's a lot easier to

14

put together than trying to work from a source distribution. Check to see whether a binary distribution version is available for your platform.

Before you begin an installation of the binaries, you'll need GNU `gunzip` and GNU `tar` (both available at `ftp.cis.ohio-state.edu`). Get and install those if you haven't already. As you might recall from Day 7, "The Most Important Accessory: The C Compiler," the steps will likely be

```
./configure
make
make install
```

After you have unpacked the MySQL distribution, run the following:

```
cd /usr/local
ln -s mysql-VERSION-OS mysql
cd mysql
scripts/mysql_install_db
bin/safe_mysqld &
```

The `scripts/mysql_install_db` step creates MySQL grant tables, which are the lists of users, hosts, and databases, and must be run the first time you install MySQL.

After running `scripts/mysql_install_db`, you will get a notice to set the root password:

```
PLEASE REMEMBER TO SET A PASSWORD FOR THE MySQL root USER !
This is done with:
./bin/mysqladmin -u root password 'new-password'
See the manual for more instructions.
```

The `bin/safe_mysqld &` step actually starts the server. If you want the server to start at boot time, add the following line to your startup scripts:

```
/usr/local/mysql/support-files/mysql.server start
```

If you put your binary distribution in a nonstandard location, you might have to edit the `mysql.server` script.

If your system uses `/etc/rc.local`, add this line instead, assuming you put your binary distribution in the standard location:

```
/bin/sh -c 'cd /usr/local/mysql ; /bin/safe_mysqld &'
```

Source Installation Overview

If there is not a binary available for your platform, or if you think you might want to modify the code, you are installing directly from source.

Before you begin the installation, you will need

- GNU `gunzip`, GNU `tar`, GNU `make`
- A working ANSI C++ compiler. Recommendations include

  `gcc 2.8.1` or later (don't use if you are running Solaris)

  `egcs 1.0.2` or later (available from `ftp.egcs.cygnus.com`; if you are running Solaris, you need version 1.1.2 or later)

  SGI C++

  SunPro C++

After you have unpacked your distribution wherever you want it, you will run the following in the source directory:

```
./configure --prefix=/usr/local/mysql
make
make install (run as root)
scripts/mysql_install_db (needed only with the first installation)
<BINDIR>/safe_myqld & (<BINDIR> is location of safe_mysql on your system)
```

If you want the server to start at boot time, add the following line to your startup scripts:

```
<installation_dir>/share/mysql.server start
```

If your system uses `/etc/rc.local`, add this line instead:

```
/bin/sh -c 'cd <installation_dir> ; /bin/safe_mysqld &'
```

Hopefully, everything goes smoothly. If not everything goes smoothly, search the online manual and mailing list archives, which are available at the MySQL Web site. If that doesn't help, ask a question on the appropriate mailing list. Information on how to subscribe to MySQL mailing lists is also available at the MySQL Web site.

Using MySQL

Although it might be the users who request MySQL, if you investigate it a bit you will also find MySQL useful for assisting you in storing information that you need for your job. Because it's such a neat tool, take a peek at what you can do with MySQL. (Keep in mind that the following little tour contains many more `quit`s and printing of data than you'd need to do in real life.) This tour was constructed by my programmer to be a complete enough demo of what you can do with SQL and Perl; you can be up and running relatively sophisticated databases instantly, by tweaking what you see here.

14

A Brief Tour of MySQL

Say you've already got MySQL installed and you decide that you want to play with it. As you already know from your intensive system administration work, you probably don't want to play as root. So you make a MySQL test account for yourself.

 Note   **An account by any other name**   MySQL accounts are separate from UNIX accounts. A MySQL account allows the user certain privileges for using the database, but no other access to your UNIX cluster. MySQL stores its own userid and password files as well—all handled internally.

You start the mysql client as root:

```
soyokaze testdb 199>mysql -u root -p
Enter password:

Welcome to the MySQL monitor.  Commands end with ; or \g.
Your MySQL connection id is 158 to server version: 3.22.17

Type 'help' for help.

mysql> GRANT SELECT,INSERT,UPDATE,DELETE,CREATE,DROP
    -> ON usertrack.*
    -> TO demo@localhost
    -> IDENTIFIED BY 'demopassword';
Query OK, 0 rows affected (0.00 sec)

mysql> quit
Bye
```

Then you log back in as user demo with the password demopassword, and you ask to see what databases are available. Please note that the output you see here is from a MySQL server that has been running for a bit and has some user-created databases. When you are starting from a clean install of MySQL, test and mysql are the only available databases.

```
mysql> show databases;
+-----------+
| Database  |
+-----------+
| agf       |
| mjan      |
| mth       |
| mysql     |
| pyro      |
| test      |
+-----------+
6 rows in set (0.00 sec)
```

For some reason you decide that even though pyro sounds like an interesting name for a database, you'd rather work with the database mjan:

```
mysql> connect mjan
ERROR 1044: Access denied for user: 'demo@localhost' to database 'mjan'
```

Only you discover that you can't access that database. You don't have permission! Offended, you terminate your mysql client:

```
mysql> quit
Bye
```

After you log out, you remember that you just created the user demo and gave it permission to access only the database usertrack. Of course you couldn't see mjan!

Note

> **On how to cheat in demos**   My programmer says that disconnecting in the previous example is really a clever trick to avoid an error message in the example. If you didn't disconnect at that point, a bug in the connection code would have sneaked up to bite you by continually complaining that you didn't have permission to access the mjan database, regardless of what other commands you entered.

So you decide to log back in and make your own database. After all, you did want to play.

```
soyokaze testdb 201> mysql -u demo -pdemopassword
Welcome to the MySQL monitor.  Commands end with ; or \g.
Your MySQL connection id is 162 to server version: 3.22.17

Type 'help' for help.

mysql> create database usertrack;
Query OK, 1 row affected (0.00 sec)
```

You decide to check whether your database is in the database list:

```
mysql> show databases;
+-----------+
| Database  |
+-----------+
| agf       |
| mjan      |
| mth       |
| mysql     |
| pyro      |
| test      |
| usertrack |
+-----------+
7 rows in set (0.00 sec)
```

14

Cool! It's there. You decide to connect to your database:

```
mysql> connect usertrack;
Connection id:    163
Current database: usertrack
```

Yes, you can. However, you remember that you have to define some tables first, so you quit again. You decide that you need to have a table for personal information, a table for project information, a table for project members and a user information table.

Note

> **The wily programmer tries to be helpful**   The database example here is rather targeted at the sorts of things that a system administrator might want to do. Without going into deep details on database design philosophy, you want to keep the data in your tables in discreetly related collections. User information includes things such as the user's userid and home directory. Users also happen to (usually) be people, and people have characteristics such as names and addresses. Although all this information might be attached to one individual, good database design dictates that you create separate database tables for the two types of information and "relate" them together. As well, "user information" is about accounts on your machine, and "person information" is about actual human beings. A person owns each userinfo record though, so there's a shared userid field that relates the data in these two tables together.
>
> The form of the database as designed here includes information about people and information about UNIX user accounts. To make the example interesting, it includes the notion that there might be collections of users that have accounts because they work together on some project. Therefore the database also includes information about projects and information about who is involved with each project.

You have created some files in your directory containing proper SQL definitions for each of the SQL tables that you are going to use. You have chosen to name them `mysql.`*`tablename`*`.def` so that you can find them easily. This also lets you use the definitions in the file to create the database tables from the command line, rather than having to type them into the interface by hand.

```
soyokaze testdb 202> ls *.def
mysql.personinfo.def       mysql.projectmembers.def
mysql.projectinfo.def       mysql.userinfo.def
```

In the personal information table you decide you should collect the basics: first name, last name, address, phone number, userid. You specify a maximum number of characters per field, such as 10 for the zip code.

```
create table personinfo (
userid CHAR(20),
firstname CHAR(20),
lastname CHAR(20),
address1 CHAR(40),
address2 CHAR(40),
city CHAR(40),
state CHAR(40),
zip CHAR(10),
phone CHAR(14))
;
```

In the project information table you specify information relating a project itself, such as the project name and termination date. You have more a greater variety of field types in this table: characters, date, and text.

```
create table projectinfo (
supervisorfirstname CHAR(20),
supervisorlastname CHAR(20),
projectname CHAR(40) NOT NULL PRIMARY KEY,
termination DATE,
description TEXT)
;
```

Note

Pedantic programmers This example doesn't use the fields defined to anywhere near the best of their ability, but the programmer wanted to show several other data types. The DATE data type takes YEAR-MO-DY numeric information, and the TEXT data type takes up to 32KB (in MySQL's implementation) of textual data. The programmer says he included these fields so that the hypothetical user could use them to hold interesting data about their project—and so that the system administrator could tell what projects had expired to determine what users might need to be removed.

The NOT NULL definition is fairly self-explanatory—require that this field contain data for every record.

The PRIMARY KEY definition says that this is what this particular table will be indexed on and that it had better be a unique entry for each record.

The project members table only has two fields:

```
create table projectmembers (
projectname CHAR(40),
userid CHAR(20))
;
```

14

The user information table that you define has a lot of the type of information present in /etc/passwd.

```
create table userinfo (
userid CHAR(20) NOT NULL PRIMARY KEY,
usernum MEDIUMINT,
defaultgroup MEDIUMINT,
homedir CHAR(120),
shell CHAR(40))
;
```

Now you feed those table definitions to your database, usertrack:

```
soyokaze testdb 204> cat *.def ¦ mysql -u demo -pdemopassword usertrack
```

Note

> **Sloppy programmers!**   Notice that the sloppy programmer specifies his password right there on the command line! Programmers aren't nearly as concerned about security as are system administrators.

Then you connect directly to your database:

```
soyokaze testdb 205> mysql -u demo -pdemopassword usertrack
Reading table information for completion of table and column names
You can turn off this feature to get a quicker startup with -A

Welcome to the MySQL monitor.  Commands end with ; or \g.
Your MySQL connection id is 165 to server version: 3.22.17

Type 'help' for help.
```

You thought that the statement you had given for feeding your table definitions to your database should work, but you decide that you had better check that:

```
mysql> show tables;
+--------------------+
¦ Tables in usertrack ¦
+--------------------+
¦ personinfo         ¦
¦ projectinfo        ¦
¦ projectmembers     ¦
¦ userinfo           ¦
+--------------------+
4 rows in set (0.00 sec)
```

Wow! Your database knows about your tables!

What good are tables without any data? Well, you were wondering that too, so you decide that you had better get some data in there. You tell MySQL that you want to insert a data row into your table, projectinfo, by defining each field line by line:

```
mysql> INSERT INTO projectinfo
    -> SET supervisorfirstname='Henry',
    -> supervisorlastname='James',
    -> projectname='Wine Tasting 101',
    -> description='A very important experiment in grape yield',
    -> termination='2000-01-01'
    -> ;
Query OK, 1 row affected (0.00 sec)
```

You decide that the line-by-line method seemed a bit cumbersome. This time you choose to go with a more up-front method. You hand the table a list of the fields you plan to define. Then you hand the table a list of corresponding values for the fields.

```
mysql> INSERT INTO projectinfo
    -> (supervisorfirstname,supervisorlastname,
    -> projectname,description,termination)
    -> VALUES ('Martin','Dooley','Hydroponics',
    -> 'Heat dissipation in hydroponics systems',2020-04-01);
Query OK, 1 row affected (0.00 sec)
```

And you add another row to the projectinfo table:

```
mysql> INSERT INTO projectinfo
    -> (supervisorfirstname,supervisorlastname,
    -> projectname,description,termination)
    -> VALUES ('Burt','Dunler','Negative Space Phenomena',
    -> 'Sealant lifetimes vs packaging atmosphere in buried containers',
    -> '0001-06-06');
Query OK, 1 row affected (0.00 sec)
```

Now it's time to check whether all that typing did any good. Even though your project info table has the supervisor's first name and last name, and a name, description, and termination date for each project, it won't all fit neatly on one page. For the convenience of fitting your results into a narrow book page, instead of your wide UNIX monitor, you decide to only look at the project name and supervisor information at this point:

```
mysql> SELECT projectname,
    -> supervisorfirstname,supervisorlastname
    -> FROM projectinfo;

+--------------------------+---------------------+--------------------+
| projectname              | supervisorfirstname | supervisorlastname |
+--------------------------+---------------------+--------------------+
| Wine Tasting 101         | Henry               | James              |
| Hydroponics              | Martin              | Dooley             |
| Negative Space Phenomena | Burt                | Dunler             |
+--------------------------+---------------------+--------------------+
3 rows in set (0.00 sec)
```

The information is really there! Pleased with the outcome, you decide to quit mysql for the moment.

14

As you are sitting back in your chair, thinking about your exciting mysql experience, you see one of your users walk in with his Perl book. That's when you suddenly remember your Perl and Perl module installations. "I bet I could write a Perl script to talk to mysql, so I don't have to remember to put those quotes around my values!"

So you decide to play with Perl for a bit. Now you've written a Perl script to talk to mysql. You know it's not quite polished yet, but you can't wait to give it a try:

```
soyokaze testdb 201> ./adduser.pl
usage is adduser.pl <databasename>
```

Note

The actual code for the Perl program that talks to MySQL and generates this interface is included later today in the "Using Perl" section, where the intrepid programmer comments on his code. It is also included as an uninterrupted listing in Appendix C, "Sample Configuration Files," if you should care to enter it and use parts of it on your machine. For now, if you want to see how things work between MySQL and the script, you're going to have to flip back and forth a bit for the next few pages.

In your excitement to try out the script, you forget to provide the script with the database name that it needs! But you think it's clever that you remembered to have the script tell you what you did wrong. Anyway, you try again, with the proper syntax this time:

```
soyokaze testdb 202> ./adduser.pl usertrack
Enter user's first name: Henry
Enter user's last name : James
Enter user's street address - use the form
address line 1
address line 2
City, State Zip code
134 Bayaard St.
Room 1214
Clifton, OK 13754
Enter the user's phone number : (614)-555-1322
Built userid hjames
Is this OK?  (Y/N) : Y
Is this user attached to a project? (Y/N) : Y
Project 0 Wine Tasting 101
   Supervised by Henry James
Project 1 Hydroponics
   Supervised by Martin Dooley
Project 2 Negative Space Phenomena
   Supervised by Burt Dunler
Please pick a project (0-2) : 0
User Added.  Exiting
```

You try another one, although this one doesn't have a two-line address; you'll see why this comment is significant when you look at the code and its comments:

```
soyokaze testdb 204> ./adduser.pl usertrack
Enter user's first name: Burt
Enter user's last name : Dunler
Enter user's street address - use the form
address line 1
address line 2
City, State Zip code
41254 County Rd 7

Hallyute, MT 64210
Enter the user's phone number : (976)-555-0666
Built userid bdunler
Is this OK?  (Y/N) : Y
Is this user attached to a project? (Y/N) : Y
Project 0 Wine Tasting 101
   Supervised by Henry James
Project 1 Hydroponics
   Supervised by Martin Dooley
Project 2 Negative Space Phenomena
   Supervised by Burt Dunler
Please pick a project (0-2) :2
User Added.  Exiting
```

After this, try another one. This time you don't like the userid that the script assigns, but luckily, you've left a way for the user to override the script's judgement. Again, this is mostly a demonstration of a part of the Perl script's functionality, but you need to see where some of these values come from for the MySQL discussion:

```
soyokaze testdb 201> ./adduser.pl usertrack
Enter user's first name: Billy
Enter user's last name : TheKid
Enter user's street address - use the form
address line 1
address line 2
City, State Zip code
14 Mulbery Lane
Apartment 41b
Smilesville, CT 01324
Enter the user's phone number : (900)-432-1432
Built userid bthekid
Is this OK?  (Y/N) : n
Enter an acceptable userid : btkid
You entered btkid
Is this OK?  (Y/N) : Y
Is this user attached to a project? (Y/N) : Y
Project 0 Wine Tasting 101
   Supervised by Henry James
```

14

```
Project 1 Hydroponics
   Supervised by Martin Dooley
Project 2 Negative Space Phenomena
   Supervised by Burt Dunler
Please pick a project (0-2) : 2
User Added.  Exiting
```

You run your script a couple more times before you decide to see what, if anything, you got in your database. Then you log in and decide to see what names and phone numbers go with what userids in the personinfo table:

```
soyokaze testdb 201>  mysql -u demo -pdemopassword usertrack
Reading table information for completion of table and column names
You can turn off this feature to get a quicker startup with -A

Welcome to the MySQL monitor.  Commands end with ; or \g.
Your MySQL connection id is 207 to server version: 3.22.17

Type 'help' for help.

mysql> SELECT userid, firstname,
    -> lastname, phone
    -> FROM personinfo;
+----------+-----------+----------+----------------+
| userid   | firstname | lastname | phone          |
+----------+-----------+----------+----------------+
| hjames   | Henry     | James    | (614)-555-1322 |
| mdooley  | Martin    | Dooley   | (888)-432-1345 |
| bdunler  | Burt      | Dunler   | (976)-555-0666 |
| btkid    | Billy     | TheKid   | (900)-432-1432 |
| mbelper  | Marge     | Belper   | (888)-555-1234 |
| rhiggins | Rambold   | Higgins  | (800)-123-9944 |
| awolsach | Alice     | Wolsach  | (800)-432-1111 |
| mboyle   | Marty     | Boyle    | (976)-125-3223 |
| rhelmer  | Roger     | Helmer   | (555)-800-0001 |
+----------+-----------+----------+----------------+
9 rows in set (0.00 sec)
```

Look at that! I guess quite a few users got entered without being memorialized in the text! Then you decide to look at everything in the userinfo table:

```
mysql> SELECT * FROM userinfo;
Empty set (0.00 sec)
```

Not much there. That's a bit disappointing, but the Perl script doesn't handle that information yet.

> **Note**
>
> **The programmer thinks watching sys admins program is funny**   As an
> incentive to get you to play with Perl and learn to use it, the ever-helpful
> programmer left out the functionality that's most important to you and
> I—the part that creates and installs user account information! He thinks this
> is quite amusing for some reason. Overall, I have to agree with his logic.
> With the Perl code that he's provided for us here, you're well on the way
> to filling in the rest of the script so that it can generate the data for the
> userinfo table as well.
>
> The programmer also suggests that when experimenting with this that you
> will quickly learn why it's good to always keep syntactically correct table
> definitions conveniently stored in separate files.

Moving on, you ask for all the data from the projectmembers table instead:

```
mysql> SELECT * FROM projectmembers;
+--------------------------+----------+
| projectname              | userid   |
+--------------------------+----------+
| Wine Tasting 101         | hjames   |
| Hydroponics              | mdooley  |
| Negative Space Phenomena | bdunler  |
| Negative Space Phenomena | btkid    |
| Hydroponics              | rhiggins |
| Wine Tasting 101         | awolsach |
| Wine Tasting 101         | mboyle   |
| Wine Tasting 101         | rhelmer  |
+--------------------------+----------+
8 rows in set (0.00 sec)
```

To be certain of what else is in the database, you'll look at some of the information in the
projectinfo table again:

```
mysql> SELECT projectname,
    -> supervisorfirstname,supervisorlastname
    -> FROM projectinfo;
+--------------------------+---------------------+--------------------+
| projectname              | supervisorfirstname | supervisorlastname |
+--------------------------+---------------------+--------------------+
| Wine Tasting 101         | Henry               | James              |
| Hydroponics              | Martin              | Dooley             |
| Negative Space Phenomena | Burt                | Dunler             |
+--------------------------+---------------------+--------------------+
```

To generate a completely contrived example where this is good for something, imagine
that you are about to quit mysql, when you get a call from the dean's secretary. She tells
you that the dean needs to contact everyone in Henry's project group right away. What

14

timing the dean must have! You entered all that data into your database as a test only moments ago. You decide that a listing of the names and phone numbers for the members of Henry's project ought to provide enough information for the dean.

So what do you need?

- You need to correlate which project is Henry's from the projectinfo table. You don't know any more than the fact that the project belongs to someone named "Henry" though, so this will have to do for a search criteria for the project.

- You have to match that project name with all the members who belong to that project from the projectmembers table.

- You need names and numbers from the personinfo table.

- However the personinfo table doesn't contain any project-specific information, so you will have to use the userids that correlate to the project name from the project-info table to get the personal information from the personinfo table.

You try:

```
mysql> SELECT personinfo.userid, personinfo.firstname,
    -> personinfo.lastname, personinfo.phone, projectinfo.projectname
    -> FROM personinfo, projectinfo, projectmembers
    -> WHERE projectinfo.supervisorfirstname LIKE '%enry%' AND
    -> projectmembers.projectname = projectinfo.projectname AND
    -> personinfo.userid = projectmembers.userid;
+----------+-----------+----------+----------------+-----------------+
| userid   | firstname | lastname | phone          | projectname     |
+----------+-----------+----------+----------------+-----------------+
| hjames   | Henry     | James    | (614)-555-1322 | Wine Tasting 101 |
| awolsach | Alice     | Wolsach  | (800)-432-1111 | Wine Tasting 101 |
| mboyle   | Marty     | Boyle    | (976)-125-3223 | Wine Tasting 101 |
| rhelmer  | Roger     | Helmer   | (555)-800-0001 | Wine Tasting 101 |
+----------+-----------+----------+----------------+-----------------+
4 rows in set (0.00 sec)
```

First you identify the fields that you want in your resulting table: userid, firstname, lastname, and phone from personinfo and projectname from projectinfo.

Then you tell mysql to search three tables: personinfo, projectinfo, and projectmembers.

From those three tables you want to produce a table where the following hold true:

- The supervisorfirstname contains the string enry (to be sure you capture Henry, whether he's capitalized or not).

- The projectname fields collected from the projectmembers table are identical to the projectname from the projectinfo table (that is, Henry's project).

- The userids fields from the personinfo table to be identical to the userids from the projectmembers table (that is, all the userids that belong to Henry's project).

Having trouble following that? Make a picture of the tables and draw out what is happening in the query statement. I would include a picture of it for you here, but it's so much more informative to watch the lines being drawn than to see a static picture, and I can't include a QuickTime clip in this book.

Knowing that the dean is an avid wine connoisseur himself, you figure that your query must have worked. With confidence in your results, you give his secretary a list much sooner than she had hoped.

With this brief tour of MySQL you are on your way to discovering the many potential uses you will have for the program.

A View From the Outside

You've gotten to see what MySQL can be like from a user's perspective. Let's get back to your perspective, that of the system administrator.

As you saw earlier in this example, the table definitions are being stored in the user's home directory; but, as you also saw in the example, some databases were made. Where are they?

A look at the mysql directory gives us a clue:

```
soyokaze# ls -l /usr/local/mysql/data
drwx------  2 root          512 Apr 15 15:47 usertrack
```

Here's what usertrack looks like from outside MySQL:

```
soyokaze# ls usertrack
personinfo.ISD     projectinfo.ISD     projectmembers.ISD  userinfo.ISD
personinfo.ISM     projectinfo.ISM     projectmembers.ISM  userinfo.ISM
personinfo.frm     projectinfo.frm     projectmembers.frm  userinfo.frm
```

What does this ultimately mean to you? If you expect that MySQL will be in high use, you might want to consider having a separate drive partition to store your users' databases. Remember, it's your job to provide what your users need to carry out their jobs. Sometimes your users' needs and yours even overlap!

Now that you've seen how to install and a hint of how to use the MySQL package, take a look at using another one of the useful pieces of software you now have on your system—the Perl programming language. Both of these packages are representative of the immense power and utility of the free software that is available for UNIX. Although I won't have space to tell you about even a small fraction of this software, you should consider these to be not only great tools but representatives of the UNIX free software experience in general.

14

Using Perl

As you saw in the MySQL tour, you can write Perl scripts to serve as interfaces to your MySQL databases. Now look at the Perl code that was used to enter data into the database.

My programmer has, in his usual helpful fashion, commented his code so that I can follow what he did. However, I'll add a few more comments interspersed here and there about what you saw happen at the command line and things that you need to watch out for with Perl. Here you will look at a complete listing of the code, and I won't repeat the comments that are in it, but I might respond to some of them. You'll want to follow what the programmer wrote about the code as well as my comments to get the most out of this section.

```perl
#!/usr/local/bin/perl
require DBD::mysql;
$|=1;                    # set perl for non-buffered output

$databaseuser="demo";        # bad form to put passwords in here
$databasepass="demopassword";    # but this is just a demo
```

The programmer has set his userid and password information right in the script...can you believe it?! Notice that the programmer at least knows this is bad form. If you were to do this and leave the root password for your mysql database in a publicly readable script, you'd be creating a large security problem. Investigate the MySQL documentation on security issues for suggestions on how to avoid this problem.

```perl
$databasename=$ARGV[0];        # arguments from the command line
                # come in in the ARGV[] array
                # Remember that UNIX and perl
                # are zero based.

# be good, check our arguments
if(@ARGV != 1) {print "usage is adduser.pl <databasename>\n"; exit 1};

# establish a connection to the database
$dbh=DBI->connect("DBI:mysql:$databasename",
                "$databaseuser",
                "$databasepass")
                || die "Couldn't open the database you specified\n";

# get some responses from the user
# <STDIN> is the standard input stream
print "Enter user's first name: ";
$firstname = <STDIN>;
print "Enter user's last name : ";
$lastname = <STDIN>;
```

The $variable=<STDIN>; syntax causes Perl to read data from the standard input—usually the keyboard, up until the first <return>.

```
print "Enter user's street address - use the form\n";
print "address line 1\n";
print "address line 2\n";
print "City, State Zip code\n";
$addressline1 = <STDIN>;
$addressline2 = <STDIN>;
$citystatezip = <STDIN>;
```

Here you see that the programmer wasn't working very hard on error-checking the data. Instead of letting the user enter data in any format and figuring out whether there was a second line of the address or coming up with some other way of cleanly handling both one and two line addresses, the script always requires two.

```
print "Enter the user's phone number : ";
$phoneno = <STDIN>;
```

And even worse, the programmer is not going to error-check the phone number to make sure it resembles a phone number. Of course, he did say that this script was intended to help a person *learn* Perl, so he probably expects that an interested reader would go about learning by doing—things such as adding error checking.

```
# chomp deletes the return off the end of the values that
# the user supplied.  perl is very literal
chomp($firstname); chomp($lastname);
chomp($addressline1); chomp($addressline2);
chomp($citystatezip); chomp($phoneno);
```

Perl collects up to and including the first <return>, so if you want the line as entered, you need to strip the return off the end of the data.

```
# split splits things up into arrays based on the first
# argument.  The comma between the city, state zip
# lets us pull the city off by splitting into an array
# containing [city][ state zip]
@splitaddress = split(/\,/,$citystatezip);
$city = $splitaddress[0];
```

The Perl split command is a really nifty function. It lets you take any collection of data in a string and break it up based on the occurrence of a character or pattern of characters. This is an amazingly powerful feature. If you look at your log files, you'll almost certainly see items of interest interspersed among material that's routine diagnostic information. With a little creative thought, you can probably find a pattern that you can use to split the data and extract exactly the bits you're interested in.

I notice that the programmer hasn't included anywhere here the global substitution command or the find-matching-lines command, but these are other really useful features that you will want to look into.

14

```
# Now we need to separate the state and zip - use the
# space.  Note that it comes in with a leading space, so
# the result is [][state][zip]
@moresplitaddress = split(/ /,$splitaddress[1]);
$state = $moresplitaddress[1]; $zip = $moresplitaddress[2];

# Split the first name up on nothing, to make it an array
# of letters.  Build the potential username from the first
# character of the first name, and the entirety of the last
# name.  In perl, the period is a concatenation operator.
@nameletters = split(//,$firstname);
$userid = $nameletters[0].$lastname;

# Translate the userid into all lowercase
$userid=~tr/[A-Z]/[a-z]/;
```

The translation command is a lot like the substitution command. The syntaxes are similar, but the translation command substitutes many with many, whereas the substitution command finds patterns and replaces them with other patterns.

```
# Make sure that the derived userid is OK with the user
# entering data
print "Built userid ",$userid,"\n";
print "Is this OK?  (Y/N) : ";
$getok = <STDIN>;
chomp($getok);
if ($getok ne "Y")
{
```

Beware of using the wrong comparison command. Perl doesn't actually care whether you use the string comparison ne or the numeric comparison != on any given piece of data. Either will *run*, but only one will *work*. Perl is a little irritating in that it happily floats along comparing strings as integers and giving odd results, rather than reporting an error and dying.

```
# ne is one of the perl ways of saying "not equal"
# for numeric values you use the more "C" like != syntax
  print "Enter an acceptable userid : ";
  $userid = <STDIN>;
  chomp($userid);
  print "You entered ",$userid,"\n";
  print "Is this OK?  (Y/N) : ";
  $getok = <STDIN>;
  chomp($getok);
  if ($getok ne "Y") {print "Sorry, please try again\n"; exit 2};
}
```

Notice that the syntax of the Perl SQL INSERT command is almost identical to when it was typed on the command line? You don't have to wrap it neatly like this, by the way. This nice formatting for display probably actually slows things down.

```
# Do the SQL database insert
$dbh->do("INSERT INTO personinfo
         SET firstname='$firstname', lastname='$lastname',
         address1='$addressline1', address2='$addressline2',
         city='$city', state='$state', zip='$zip',
         phone='$phoneno',userid='$userid'");
```

A Perl point to note: Perl autocreates variables that don't exist when you first use them. This might seem like a convenience, but it turns out to make debugging very difficult. If, for example, you forgot that you used the variable $phoneno and thought that you had called it $phone, the preceding Perl statement and SQL INSERT would execute just fine. There would be no error reported, and there would be no complaints or warnings. The only evidence you would have that something was wrong would be when you went back and looked in the database by hand, you would see that the phone field would be empty. Perl would have noticed your previously unused $phone variable, created it for you, and helpfully used the virgin variable to enter its lack of data into the database.

```
print "Is this user attached to a project? (Y/N) : ";
$getok = <STDIN>;
chomp($getok);
if($getok eq "Y")
{
  # eq is the perl way of saying "equal" character strings
  # == is the syntax for numeric values.
  # NOTE  if you mistakenly use "=" instead of "==" in an
  # if statement, you're actually making an assignment between
  # the "compared" values and evaluating the if based on the
  # success or failure of the assignment!
```

If you write a Perl numeric comparison, and for some reason it constantly evaluates to true regardless of the values of the arguments, it's probably because you used = instead of == in your comparison. This makes your comparison into an assignment. It will almost always succeed, making the comparison come out to be true, and fouling up the values of your variables at the same time.

```
# Build the SQL query
  $sql=$dbh->prepare("SELECT projectname, supervisorfirstname,
                      supervisorlastname FROM projectinfo");
  $sql->execute;

  # Get the results back in a multi-dimensional array
  $allproj=$sql->fetchall_arrayref;

  # Clean up after ourselves
  $sql->finish;
```

SQL SELECT statements are handled with multiple Perl statements. Notice that the syntax again is almost exactly the same as what you used at the interactive interpreter earlier today.

14

The results of the SELECT are returned into a Perl array of arrays, and you get to deal with them at your leisure.

```perl
# One of several perl "for" syntaxes - for each entry returned
  for $i (0..$#{$allproj})
  {
      print "Project ",$i," ",$allproj->[$i][0],
            "\n   Supervised by ",$allproj->[$i][1],
            " ",$allproj->[$i][2],"\n";
  }
  print "Please pick a project (0-",$#{$allproj},") : ";
```

That odd little bit of syntax $#{$variable} counts the entries in the array.

```perl
$getproj=<STDIN>;
  chomp($getproj);

  # Based on the number we pick, insert the userid and the
  # corresponding project name into the project member
  # table
  $dbh->do("INSERT INTO projectmembers
          SET projectname='$allproj->[$getproj][0]',
          userid='$userid'");
}
```

Note that you've collected enough information by now to go and fill in the userinfo table if you wanted to. You could df the drives, find out where the most space for new user directories is, check for conflicting IDs in the password database, make all the appropriate entries, and create an account right here, with very little additional code.

Using a route such as this is beneficial above and beyond what your system-supplied user-addition facility provides in that it can give you a much more complete record of your users, automatically created and maintained when you create the account.

```perl
# And we're out of here!
print "User Added.  Exiting\n\n";
```

Well, that was fun, wasn't it? Some days I really envy programmers!

Hopefully you will find what you learned about using Perl and MySQL even more useful than what you learned about installing them. Using these and other freely available UNIX software can make your life as a system administrator significantly easier and much more enjoyable as well. It also has the added benefit of making you a much more valuable commodity as a system administrator who can innovate, moving facilities forward and increasing their capacity, rather than allowing them to stagnate—a fine feather in your cap!

Summary

In today's lesson, you did quite a bit of installation, as well as learned a few things about using the MySQL database system, and about programming in Perl.

Specifically, you

- Installed Perl, a language which is especially good at pattern matching and text manipulation. It is especially popular for writing CGI scripts for Web pages.
- Installed Perl modules for writing interfaces to MySQL databases.
- Installed MySQL, a powerful database program.
- Installed any GNU software you need to complete the MySQL installation.
- Got a chance to play around a bit with MySQL and might even have started on the road to learning Perl.

Q&A

Q Today you saw that a regular UNIX user can log in to the MySQL database server. Do you have to have a UNIX account to access the MySQL server? Can you access the server directly from a PC or Mac?

A No, you don't need a UNIX account. The user you installed today needs one because of the way you installed it, but MySQL can be set up so that it can be accessed from remote users using ODBC compatible clients such as Microsoft Access and Claris FileMaker.

Q Learning Perl seems like it would be a lot of work. You said I should leave programming to programmers. Should I spend time learning this?

A That does sort of depend on what your complete job description really is, but in general, I'd say yes. You can write useful Perl programs in as little as two lines of code. This isn't too much effort to invest in something that can save you hours of system administration work each week.

Q Do you have any suggestions on where I should look to learn more about Perl and SQL?

A My suggestion is to go straight to the camel's mouth, so to speak. Larry Wall, the creator of Perl, has a wonderful and quite definitive book on the subject. A minimal search on the Web will point you in the direction of his book as well as other available texts on Perl.

MySQL includes a quite-voluminous reference manual of its own that is available online. The MySQL site also provides many useful pointers to other online SQL resources and references.

14

Q I created a Perl script, but when I try to run it, it says "command not found". What's the matter?

A Check the path you've given in the #! line at the top of the file. This almost always means that the path to the Perl executable is incorrect.

Q I created a Perl script, but when I try to run it, it says "permission denied". What's up?

A Did you remember to chmod it so that it has execute permission? If you did, make sure that any scripts that you call *inside* it also have execute permission turned on.

Workshop

Quiz

1. Suppose it has been decided that your new machine will become the Web server. You have installed the latest Perl in /usr/local/bin/perl, and the latest version of Apache, a Web server, on the machine (As a matter of fact, you will look at installing a Web server on Day 17, "WWW Connectivity: Netscape, Apache, Statistics.") After you are finished with your installations, but before you make the new machine the official Web server machine for your facility, you decide that it might be a good idea to verify that some of the main pages that rely on some Perl code working properly still work. So you start Netscape on your PC and try to load one of the pages, but you get an error page instead. Fortunately the error page suggests that you might want to look at the error_log for more details. On looking at the log, you see the following:

```
[Wed Jun 30 10:01:40 1999] [error] (2)No such file or
➥directory: exec of
/net/suzie/usr/people/kyoko/public_html/diagnostic.cgi
➥failed
[Wed Jun 30 10:01:40 1999] [error] [client 140.254.12.124]
➥Premature end
of script headers: /net/suzie/usr/people/kyoko/public_html/
➥diagnostic.cgi
```

You don't really understand the error messages, but you understand enough to suspect that there must be something wrong with the Perl script that Web server is trying to access. Here are the first few lines of that script:

```
#!/opt/bin/perl

if (-f "/usr/local/apache/cgi-bin/johnclient.pl") { require
➥'/usr/local/apache/cgi-bin/johnclient.pl';
 }
```

What should you check?

2. For what reasons is the MySQL package recommended to be installed as a precompiled binary?

3. What is required to use Perl to access a MySQL database?

Exercises

1. Today you installed three Perl modules. Browse `http://www.cpan.org` and see whether there are any other modules that you think might be interesting or useful sometime in the future.

2. Create a SQL database with at least two tables. Put some data in them and practice getting data out of one table based on references in the other.

3. Using the simple Perl code that has been provided here and a little bit of online research, write a Perl program that will parse your password file looking for entries with asterisks (*) in the password file. For each of these give the user the opportunity to reset the password.

4. Consider keying in the Perl code for the sample program and building the usertrack database. It will definitely take more than a day's work to do everything necessary. If you complete the `adduser.pl` script to the point that it can be used as a database for creating your accounts, you will not only have made your user-account maintenance much easier, but learned an invaluable programming skill as well.

14

WEEK 3

At a Glance

During Week 3, you will be adding useful functional enhancements to your machine. You also will be taking a look at troubleshooting some of the most common system administration common problems.

- Day 15, "Communicating Locally and Globally: Mail," looks at the traditional way to read and send mail, how to install a basic working version of sendmail, and what other mail reading options are available.

- Day 16, "Securing Services: FTP and POP," enables you to set up FTP and POP mail servers and takes a look at how you can make them secure.

- Day 17, "WWW Connectivity: Netscape, Apache, and Statistics," helps you install a browser and a Web server. In addition, you'll get a brief look at some Web site statistics packages.

- Day 18, "Multi-OS Connectivity: AppleTalk and Samba," presents how to enable your machines to talk to one another.

- Day 19, "Optional Software," explores the installation of software packages that can further enhance your network.

- Day 20, "How to Be a Good System Administrator," is a rather lengthy day where you might want to consider taking a break midway in order to process your thoughts. Today, you'll take a look at some of the things it takes to be a good system administrator.

- Day 21, "Troubleshooting," presents you with some of the annoying "spontaneously occurring" sorts of problems you're likely to encounter as a system administrator.

15

16

17

18

19

20

21

DAY 15

Communicating Locally and Globally: Mail

Today you start expanding your communications horizons beyond being able to read local filesystems within your cluster. It's time to take a look at mail! You will look at the traditional way to read and send mail, how to install a basic working version of sendmail, and what other mail reading options are available.

Reading and Sending Mail: `mail/Mail/mailx`

A basic method for reading and sending mail on a UNIX machine is to use some incarnation of mail/Mail/mailx. One or more of those is likely to be an interactive system for reading and sending mail. Although mail/Mail/mailx might seem unfriendly, like vi, it is ubiquitous. It is a good idea to familiarize yourself with its basic usage, in case you should ever need to use it.

Note

> **Three little mailers** It's hard to determine, from outside, whether you'll want to use mail, Mail, or mailx (or yet some other incarnation of mail) on your system. On many systems you meet, /usr/bin/mail is a system utility mailer without a friendly interface, and /usr/ucb/mail is the mailer I discuss here. Depending on which is in your path first, the command mail might result in differing behavior. Frequently, on systems that have both versions of mail, the command Mail points to the one with the more user-friendly interface discussed here. On systems where that is not the case, mailx seems to be a popular name. You'll need to do a bit of experimenting to determine what the proper command is locally for you.

Table 15.1 provides you a list of the basics you need to know to adequately use mail/Mail/mailx. As you will note, overall there are not too many things you need to know to adequately use mail, so don't let it scare you.

Here how a mail listing looks:

```
catbert ralph 1 >mail

Mail version SMI 4.0 Fri Oct 14 12:50:06 PDT 1994  Type ? for help.
"/usr/spool/mail/ralph": 4 messages 4 new
>N  1 joray              Fri Apr 23 21:48    14/376    testing
 N  2 joray              Fri Apr 23 21:49    13/379    Re:  testing
 N  3 joray              Mon Apr 26 18:14    15/409    today is a fine day
 N  4 joray              Mon Apr 26 18:14    14/416    how is it going?
&
```

TABLE 15.1 Basics for Reading and Sending Mail with mail/Mail/mailx

Option	Function
mail *no argument* Mail *no argument* mailx *no argument*	Opens your mail spool so you can read mail
1	Reads message 1
h21	Lists the next batch of messages, starting with message number 21
d	Deletes the message you just read
d 2	Deletes message number 2
d 2 4	Deletes messages 2 and 4
d 1-5	Deletes messages 1–5
u	Undeletes a message. The same types of arguments used with d can be used with u.
inc	Lists messages that have arrived since you started reading your mail

Option	Function
quit q	Quits the program, making the modifications you indicated, such as deleting the messages you specified
exit xit x	Exits the program, not making any modifications you indicated. Any messages that you indicated should be deleted will not be. Replies to the sender of the original message
r	Replies to the sender and the other recipients of the original message
^C	Interrupts the message you are working on
^D	Sends the message
~r *filename*	Includes *filename* in your message
s *filename*	Saves the message you just read as *filename*
mail *username* Mail *username* mailx *username*	Starts a mail message to *username* on your local system
mail *username@somewhere* Mail *username@somewhere* mailx *username@somewhere*	Starts a mail message to a user at the address specified

Installing sendmail

Whether or not you realize it, your operating system probably comes with some version of sendmail, which as the name might suggest, is a program for sending mail. Specifically, it routes mail to other (remote) computers or hands mail to programs on a local computer for local delivery. It is likely stored in /usr/lib/sendmail, which on some systems might be a link to /usr/sbin/sendmail. Even my minimal machine has sendmail. What came with your system might be adequate for now, but it is only a matter of time before you will have to update your sendmail. The latest version is available at ftp.sendmail.org. A wealth of online documentation is available at http://www.sendmail.org.

Today the goal with sendmail is to install an adequately usable sendmail daemon. A discussion of the fine details of sendmail is beyond the scope of this book. If you are interested in the inner workings of sendmail, pick up a copy of the sendmail bible, the O'Reilly book *sendmail*. This is definitely one of those areas of black magic. I might not have remembered to mention this earlier, but along with your C programmer guru and your system administrator guru, you should probably make sure you have a sendmail guru (who is likely also one of your system administrator gurus). Keep a list of his favorite foods handy because you will periodically have to stoke his fire to convince him to deal with any special customizations that might become necessary over time for your sendmail configuration.

Because you might not be able to bother your sendmail guru right away, I will get you started today with the basics you need to get the latest version of sendmail up and running on your system.

Installation Overview

Here is roughly what you will be doing to install sendmail. If your installation does not work quite the way it should at first, don't panic. Check your logs for the error messages, and then check the FAQ at the sendmail Web site to see whether you are having a common problem. The FAQ covers many issues. However, if it does not cover your problem, check the newsgroups listed on the Web site.

1. As usual, read the READMEs. Be sure to also take a look at the document in the sendmail-8.x.y/doc/op directory. The document, like some of the READMEs, is long, but the first few pages are especially helpful.

2. After you unpack the sendmail distribution, your source directory will look like this:

```
[ray@mother]# ls

BuildTools      Makefile        contrib       makemap      src
FAQ             README          doc           praliases    test
KNOWNBUGS       RELEASE_NOTES   mail.local    rmail
LICENSE         cf              mailstats     smrsh
```

In the sendmail-8.x.y/src directory, you will run ./**Build**. This will build everything necessary for your operating system.

Here is what src looks like before running Build:

```
[ray@mother]# ls

Build           conf.c          mailq.0       queue.c      stats.c
Makefile.m4     conf.h          mailq.1       readcf.c     sysexits.c
README          control.c       mailstats.h   recipient.c  sysexits.h
TRACEFLAGS      convtime.c      main.c        safefile.c   trace.c
alias.c         daemon.c        makesendmail  savemail.c   udb.c
aliases         deliver.c       map.c         sendmail.0   useful.h
aliases.0       domain.c        mci.c         sendmail.8   usersmtp.c
aliases.5       envelope.c      mime.c        sendmail.h   util.c
arpadate.c      err.c           newaliases.0  sendmail.hf  version.c
cdefs.h         headers.c       newaliases.1  snprintf.c
clock.c         ldap_map.h      parseaddr.c   srvrsmtp.c
collect.c       macro.c         pathnames.h   stab.c
```

Here it is after running Build:

```
[ray@mother]# ls
Build              err.c                 safefile.c
Makefile.m4        headers.c             savemail.c
README             ldap_map.h            sendmail.0
TRACEFLAGS         macro.c               sendmail.8
alias.c            mailq.0               sendmail.h
aliases            mailq.1               sendmail.hf
aliases.0          mailstats.h           snprintf.c
aliases.5          main.c                srvrsmtp.c
arpadate.c         makesendmail          stab.c
cdefs.h            map.c                 stats.c
clock.c            mci.c                 sysexits.c
collect.c          mime.c                sysexits.h
conf.c             newaliases.0          trace.c
conf.h             newaliases.1          udb.c
control.c          obj.Linux.2.0.34.i486 useful.h
convtime.c         parseaddr.c           usersmtp.c
daemon.c           pathnames.h           util.c
deliver.c          queue.c               version.c
domain.c           readcf.c
envelope.c         recipient.c
```

Note the appearance of a directory with objects for Linux now. Of course, if I were building on a different flavor of UNIX, the appropriate directory would have appeared.

3. Install sendmail by running ./Build install.

4. Build a sendmail.cf configuration file. You will start off with what you would need to do to build a sendmail.cf file for your mail server.

You will do this in the sendmail-8.x.y/cf/cf directory. Notice how there are already a number of generic cf files that you can start with:

```
[ray@mother]# ls
Build              generic-hpux10.cf      huginn.cs.mc
Makefile           generic-hpux10.mc      knecht.mc
chez.cs.mc         generic-hpux9.cf       mail.cs.mc
clientproto.mc     generic-hpux9.mc       mail.eecs.mc
cs-hpux10.mc       generic-nextstep3.3.mc mailspool.cs.mc
cs-hpux9.mc        generic-osf1.cf        python.cs.mc
cs-osf1.mc         generic-osf1.mc        s2k-osf1.mc
cs-solaris2.mc     generic-solaris2.cf    s2k-ultrix4.mc
cs-sunos4.1.mc     generic-solaris2.mc    tcpproto.mc
cs-ultrix4.mc      generic-sunos4.1.cf    ucbarpa.mc
cyrusproto.mc      generic-sunos4.1.mc    ucbvax.mc
generic-bsd4.4.cf  generic-ultrix4.cf     uucpproto.mc
generic-bsd4.4.mc  generic-ultrix4.mc     vangogh.cs.mc
```

a. First, `cp generic-<your_os>.mc <your_machine_name>.mc`. You are using
    the `<your_machine_name>.mc` notation because you can build sendmail config-
    uration files for your various machines and operating systems in the same
    source directory, if you choose. Naming the files initially by machine name
    reduces potential confusion in the future for you.

b. If you do not see your OS listed in the generic files, check for the existence
    of your OS in `../ostype`. There are lots of known operating systems in that
    directory:

```
[ray@mother]# ls ../ostype

aix2.m4            domainos.m4        mklinux.m4         solaris2.ml.m4
aix3.m4            dynix3.2.m4        nextstep.m4        sunos3.5.m4
aix4.m4            gnuhurd.m4         osf1.m4            sunos4.1.m4
altos.m4           hpux10.m4          powerux.m4         svr4.m4
amdahl-uts.m4      hpux9.m4           ptx2.m4            ultrix4.m4
aux.m4             irix4.m4           qnx.m4             unixware7.m4
bsd4.3.m4          irix5.m4           riscos4.5.m4       unknown.m4
bsd4.4.m4          irix6.m4           sco-uw-2.1.m4      uxpds.m4
bsdi1.0.m4         isc4.1.m4          sco3.2.m4
bsdi2.0.m4         linux.m4           sinix.m4
dgux.m4            maxion.m4          solaris2.m4
```

From the listings in that directory you will see how your operating system is
known.

Then pick some generic file to copy to `<your_machine_name>.mc`. Edit the
generic file so that the item listed as OSTYPE reflects the name of your OS as
you saw it in `../ostype`.

Here's a sample `generic.mc` file:

```
[ray@mother]# more generic-sunos4.1.mc
divert(-1)
#
# Copyright (c) 1998 Sendmail, Inc.   All rights reserved.
# Copyright (c) 1983 Eric P. Allman.   All rights reserved.
# Copyright (c) 1988, 1993
#      The Regents of the University of California.   All rights
➥reserved.
#
# By using this file, you agree to the terms and conditions set
# forth in the LICENSE file which can be found at the top level of
# the sendmail distribution.
#
#


#
#  This is a generic configuration file for SunOS 4.1.x.
```

```
#  It has support for local and SMTP mail only.  If you want to
#  customize it, copy it to a name appropriate for your environment
#  and do the modifications there.
#

divert(0)dnl
VERSIONID('@(#)generic-sunos4.1.mc       8.8 (Berkeley) 5/19/1998')
OSTYPE(sunos4.1)dnl
DOMAIN(generic)dnl
MAILER(local)dnl
MAILER(smtp)dnl
```

In this one, for example, where you see OSTYPE(sunos4.1)dnl, you would make this replacement to build a Linux configuration file:

```
OSTYPE(linux)dnl
```

c. There is only one change that you might want to consider making to the <your_machine_name>.mc file. If you have procmail, or would like to use procmail, add the procmail feature.

As you can see from the feature directory, there are a lot of available features that you might someday want to learn about and work in to your configuration as you get more experienced with sendmail.

```
[ray@mother]# ls ../feature
accept_unqualified_senders.m4    nodns.m4
accept_unresolvable_domains.m4   notsticky.m4
access_db.m4                     nouucp.m4
allmasquerade.m4                 nullclient.m4
always_add_domain.m4             promiscuous_relay.m4
bestmx_is_local.m4               rbl.m4
bitdomain.m4                     redirect.m4
blacklist_recipients.m4          relay_based_on_MX.m4
domaintable.m4                   relay_entire_domain.m4
genericstable.m4                 relay_hosts_only.m4
limited_masquerade.m4            relay_local_from.m4
local_lmtp.m4                    smrsh.m4
local_procmail.m4                stickyhost.m4
loose_relay_check.m4             use_ct_file.m4
mailertable.m4                   use_cw_file.m4
masquerade_entire_domain.m4      uucpdomain.m4
masquerade_envelope.m4           virtusertable.m4
nocanonify.m4
```

To add the procmail feature you would add a FEATURE line before the MAILER lines. The MAILER lines must appear last.

```
FEATURE(local_procmail,/usr/bin/procmail)dnl
```

The first part of the FEATURE line indicates that the local_procmail feature should be included. The second part of the line indicates where to find procmail.

If you do not have procmail, but would like to get it, it is available from http://www.procmail.org or ftp.procmail.org. procmail is a local delivery program with powerful filtering abilities. procmail allows you and your users to automatically parse and sort incoming mail, providing functionality much like a vastly more powerful version of the desktop-computer popmail client "mailbox filters." It can even conditionally execute other programs based on the contents of mail messages, allowing for such things as the creation of mailing lists, automatic remailers that send important email to alphanumeric pagers, or that automatically capture special messages to perform special administrative tasks. If you don't have it but think you would like it, you could take a detour now to get and install procmail.

d. To build the sendmail.cf file, run make *your_machine_name*.cf.

e. Take a brief look at what the generated files looks like:

Early on you see the sendmail version number:

```
# level 8 config file format
V8/Berkeley
```

You might want to consider uncommenting this next entry, the DontBlameSendmail entry, an enhancement included in Sendmail 8.9.x. that checks for directory permissions. You might particularly find surprises with users' .forward files, a file that a user might have in her home directory to forward her mail, and :include: files, which I will touch on later in this chapter in the discussion of the /etc/aliases file. Replace the safe flag with the appropriate flags for your needs. For a listing of what flags are available and a more detailed discussion, check the sendmail Web site.

```
# override file safeties - setting this option compromises system
# security
# need to set this now for the sake of class files
#O DontBlameSendmail=safe
```

In this next section, note that your mail server will know for which local machines it receives mail by the listing you will make in the file /etc/sendmail.cw:

```
#################
#   local info   #
#################
```

```
Cwlocalhost
# file containing names of hosts for which we receive email
Fw/etc/sendmail.cw
```

You should be able to leave this entry alone, unless you discover that send-mail can't automatically determine your domain.

```
# my official domain name
# ... define this only if sendmail cannot automatically determine
➥your domain
#Dj$w.Foo.COM
```

At the end of the local info section, the specific sendmail version is listed:

```
# Configuration version number
DZ8.9.3
```

The next section in the configuration file is options. Note that sendmail will expect to find the aliases listing in /etc/aliases:

```
# location of alias file
O AliasFile=/etc/aliases
```

Right now a maximum message size is not listed by default, which means that there is no maximum by default. At some point, you might discover that you might have to change the maximum message size. Here is where you would do it:

```
# maximum message size
#O MaxMessageSize=1000000
```

This is a setting that you would probably want to turn on by uncommenting:

```
# send to me too, even in an alias expansion?
#O MeToo
```

With this option turned on, when you send a message to an alias in which you are included, you will get a copy of the message you sent.

The only timeouts that are already set by default are two settings: the setting for how long sendmail should attempt to send a message before returning it in the event of a problem (currently set at five days) and the setting for how long after attempting to deliver a message sendmail should send a warning to the sender about the problem (currently set at four hours). Here's a snippet from the timeouts section showing these defaults:

```
#O Timeout.fileopen=60s
O Timeout.queuereturn=5d
#O Timeout.queuereturn.normal=5d
#O Timeout.queuereturn.urgent=2d
#O Timeout.queuereturn.non-urgent=7d
O Timeout.queuewarn=4h
#O Timeout.queuewarn.normal=4h
#O Timeout.queuewarn.urgent=1h
```

Overall the timeout settings should be fine. If you need to tweak anything, tweak only those two.

If you have a large mail server, you might find sometime that you have to set the maximum number of daemons that can run. The option for that is here:

```
# maximum number of children we allow at one time
#O MaxDaemonChildren=12
```

Never edit the following setting. It is off by default. Keep it that way.

```
# shall I avoid expanding CNAMEs (violates protocols)?
#O DontExpandCnames
```

Shortly after the options settings section is a bit of information on header formatting, rewriting rules, and so on. Don't touch any of this. If you do, make sure you have your *sendmail* book and sendmail guru at your side. If you do feel brave at some point in time and decide to edit this portion of the file, remember that the spacing is in tabs, not spaces. Here's a glimpse of what you don't want to touch:

```
###########################################
###  Ruleset 3 — Name Canonicalization  ###
###########################################
S3

# handle null input (translate to <@> special case)
R$@                      $@ <@>

# strip group: syntax (not inside angle brackets!) and trailing
➥semicolon
R$*                      $: $1 <@>              mark addresses
R$* < $* > $* <@>        $: $1 < $2 > $3        unmark <addr>
R@ $* <@>                $: @ $1                unmark @host:...
R$* :: $* <@>            $: $1 :: $2            unmark node::addr
R:include: $* <@>        $: :include: $1        unmark :include:...
R$* [ $* : $* ] <@>      $: $1 [ $2 : $3 ]      unmark IPv6 addrs
R$* : $* [ $* ]          $: $1 : $2 [ $3 ] <@>  remark if leading
col
on
R$* : $* <@>             $: $2                  strip colon if
marked
R$* <@>                  $: $1                  unmark
R$* ;                         $1                strip trailing
semi
R$* < $* ; >                  $1 < $2 >         bogus bracketed
semi
```

Pretty scary looking, isn't it? The only thing in the "don't touch" section you should look at is the local and program mailer information. Make sure the path to your local mailer is correct.

15

```
#################################################
###    Local and Program Mailer specification    ###
#################################################

#####  @(#)local.m4      8.30 (Berkeley) 6/30/1998  #####

Mlocal,     P=/usr/bin/procmail, F=lsDFMAw5:/¦@qSPfhn9, S=10/30,
➥R=20/40,
            T=DNS/RFC822/X-Unix,
            A=procmail -Y -a $h -d $u
Mprog,      P=/bin/sh, F=lsDFMoqeu9, S=10/30, R=20/40, D=$z:/,
            T=X-Unix,
            A=sh -c $u
```

   f. When you are satisfied with the <your_machine_name>.cf file, save your
      changes and copy it to /etc/sendmail.cf.

5. For the server machine, make an /etc/sendmail.cw file listing the local hosts it
   serves.

6. To start the sendmail daemon include somewhere in your startup scripts a line such
   as the following:

```
/usr/lib/sendmail -bd -q1h
```

   The -bd tells sendmail to start as a daemon. The -q1h tells sendmail to wait one
   hour between redelivery attempts on messages that have previously failed to be
   delivered and are therefore stuck in the queue. Depending on your needs you might
   decide to change that to -q30m. The document in the sendmail-8.x.y/doc/op
   directory provides a couple more complete startup script examples.

7. For your client machines, you will also have to make a configuration file.

   a. Starting to build the configuration file on a client machine is similar to building
      one on the server. This time, however, you will start your build with the
      clientproto.mc:

```
cp clientproto.mc <your_client_machine_name>.mc
```

      Here is what this file will then look like:

```
divert(-1)
#
# Copyright (c) 1998 Sendmail, Inc.  All rights reserved.
# Copyright (c) 1983 Eric P. Allman.  All rights reserved.
# Copyright (c) 1988, 1993
#       The Regents of the University of California.  All rights
        ➥reserved.
#
# By using this file, you agree to the terms and conditions set
# forth in the LICENSE file which can be found at the top level of
# the sendmail distribution.
```

```
#
#

#
#   This the prototype for a "null client" — that is, a client that
#   does nothing except forward all mail to a mail hub.  IT IS NOT
#   USABLE AS IS!!!
#
#   To use this, you MUST use the nullclient feature with the name of
#   the mail hub as its argument.  You MUST also define an `OSTYPE'
    ➥to
#   define the location of the queue directories and the like.
#   In addition, you MAY select the nocanonify feature.  This causes
#   addresses to be sent unqualified via the SMTP connection;
    ➥normally
#   they are qualifed with the masquerade name, which defaults to the
#   name of the hub machine.
#   Other than these, it should never contain any other lines.
#

divert(0)dnl
VERSIONID('@(#)clientproto.mc    8.12 (Berkeley) 5/19/1998')

OSTYPE(unknown)
FEATURE(nullclient, mailhost.$m)
```

b. Edit your OSTYPE, and edit the FEATURE line to include the name of your mail server. Your FEATURE line might look something like this:

```
FEATURE(nullclient, mail.mycompany.com)
```

As before, run make to make your client's sendmail.cf:

```
make <your_client_machine_name>.cf
```

In your client's configuration file, you will see the mail host listed:

```
# hub host (to which all mail is sent)
DHmail.killernuts.org
```

There is little to edit in the client's configuration file.

c. When you are satisfied with the client's configuration file, save the file and copy it to /etc/sendmail.cf.

8. Although your client machine does not need to have sendmail running as a daemon, it does need to have a sendmail executable. The easiest way to build your client's sendmail executable is to unpack a copy of the sendmail source distribution on your client, run ./**Build** in the sendmail-8.x.y/src directory and copy the resulting executable, sendmail, to /usr/lib/sendmail. As a precaution, be sure to keep your machine's original sendmail before you actually do this.

Note

Although I have listed /etc as the likely location for your sendmail configuration files, these files might be located in /etc/mail on some systems instead. The documentation included with the latest sendmail, currently version 8.9.3, indicates that by version 8.10, /etc/mail will likely become the standard location for these files.

15

9. Test your sendmail installation. You can start your testing by directly speaking to the server, from the server machine or other machines. What follows is an example of how you can do this. The commands that you see in uppercase are commands that you can issue to the server. Obviously, HELO is not necessary, but it's friendly.

```
ryoko joray 247 > telnet ryoko 25
Trying 140.254.12.240...
Connected to ryoko.
Escape character is '^]'.
220 ryoko.biosci.ohio-state.edu ESMTP Sendmail 8.9.3/8.9.3;
➥Tue, 6 Jul 1999 16:49:43 -0400 (EDT)
HELO ryoko
250 ryoko.biosci.ohio-state.edu Hello ryoko [140.254.12.240],
➥pleased to meet you
MAIL FROM: joray@biosci.ohio-state.edu
250 joray@biosci.ohio-state.edu... Sender ok
RCPT TO: joray
250 joray... Recipient ok
DATA
354 Enter mail, end with "." on a line by itself
This is a test
.
250 QAA03306 Message accepted for delivery
quit
221 ryoko.biosci.ohio-state.edu closing connection
Connection closed by foreign host.
ryoko joray 248 >
```

When you have determined that the server is up, send mail from as many machines to as many machines as you can think of to verify that everything works as you expect it to. Remember, if things do not work as they should, check the FAQ at the sendmail Web site and the newsgroups the Web site recommends.

Usage Overview

Now I will briefly go over some details that might make your use of sendmail more helpful.

Forwarding Mail: MX Records

If you have the kind of setup you have been working with today, you have a mail server and local clients whose mail is directed to the mail server. You can direct mail from the outside to those client machines to go directly to the mail server by having whoever maintains the name server set the MX (mail exchanger) record to your mail server.

You can see this setup by querying Ohio State University's name server:

```
catbert log 234 > nslookup

Default Server:  nisca.acs.ohio-state.edu
Address:  128.146.1.7


> set query83=MX
> waashu.biosci.ohio-state.edu
Server:  nisca.acs.ohio-state.edu
Address:  128.146.1.7


waashu.biosci.ohio-state.edu     preference = 10, mail exchanger
➡= catbert.biosci.ohio-state.edu
catbert.biosci.ohio-state.edu    inet address = 140.254.12.236
```

If you look at the MX record for `waashu.biosci.ohio-state.edu`, you see that any mail directed to that machine from the outside automatically goes to `catbert.biosci.ohio-state.edu`.

Forwarding Mail: `/etc/aliases`

In the installation overview I mentioned that sendmail would expect to find aliases in `/etc/aliases`. On each of your client machines you will want a minimal version of `/etc/aliases`. Probably the file that is already there is fine because it most likely contains basic aliases, such as root and postmaster, which you would want in a minimal `/etc/aliases` file.

On your mail server, however, you will want the complete `/etc/aliases`. Just what is `/etc/aliases` good for anyway? It's a convenient way to forward mail. Suppose you had some entries like this:

```
root:action
action:staff
staff:george,harry,susan
```

Here you can see that anything sent to root will go to action. Anything sent to action goes to staff. So in the first two lines you see that an alias can be defined by an alias.

Suppose the security group runs regular security scans for you. To make it easy for them to remember who should receive reports, you can add a security alias for your site by adding a line to the `/etc/aliases` file:

```
security:staff
```

To make it easy for the world to contact your Webmaster, you might decide to add an alias for Webmaster:

```
webmaster:elaine
```

One of your staff members might decide that because he is online at home as much as he is at the office, he would like to have his mail go to his local account as well as the account he has with his ISP. To do that you would add a line such as the following:

```
george:george, george@home.account.com
```

Now mail sent to george goes to his local account as well as his home account.

You can also include files in /etc/aliases, which makes a quick way to set up a mailing list.

If you have a group of users who want to exchange advice on using some software, you could set up a list for them by including a file that has one user's email address per line. You would then include an entry in /etc/aliases that might look like this:

```
graphics-soft: :include:/usr/local/misc/graphics.list
```

You can also discard mail by having it go to /dev/null:

```
nobody:/dev/null
```

Anytime you touch or change /etc/aliases, remember to run newaliases so that a new database is built.

You'll get output that looks like the following:

```
catbert# newaliases
/etc/aliases: 14 aliases, longest 43 bytes, 276 bytes total
```

Please Take a Number

In the same way that you take a number in line at the deli section of the grocery store, so does your outgoing mail. Here is some sample output from running mailq on a machine:

```
                Mail Queue (1 requests)
--Q-ID-- --Size-- -----Q-Time----- ----------Sender/Recipient----------
UAA02195*    316 Mon Apr 26 20:04 lists
```

Under Q-ID you see the messages number in the queue.

The * in the ID tells you that this message is still being processed.

If you look at the mqueue directory on the machine you see this listing (probably located somewhere like /var/spool or /var/mail):

```
soyokaze# ls mqueue
dfUAA02195  qfUAA02195  xfUAA02195
```

The df file is the contents of the message itself. The qf file contains the message's headers. The xf file contains the list of recipients who have not received the message and the reason why. Such reasons include "User unknown" and "Deferred".

An outgoing message typically contains two entries in your logs. Here's a sample:

```
Apr 26 20:13:32 soyokaze sendmail[2251]: UAA02251: from=joray, size=57,
class=0, pri=30057, nrcpts=1, msgid=<199904270013.UAA02251@soyokaze.
biosci.ohio-state.edu>, relay=joray@localhost
Apr 26 20:13:33 soyokaze sendmail[2253]: UAA02251: to=ray.3@osu.edu,
ctladdr=joray (2001/21), delay=00:00:01, xdelay=00:00:01, mailer=esmtp,
relay=orb1.osu.edu. [128.146.225.191], stat=Sent (ok 925171534 qp 29254)
```

Included in the information you'll see in your logs is the queue ID and a message ID. You'll see a relay, if known, and the status of the message. In this example, you see that the message has been sent.

Optional Mail Reading Software

Although mail/Mail/mailx is perfectly adequate for reading mail, you might want to consider installing additional mail reading software.

A couple packages you might want to consider installing are menu-driven mail readers. One is called elm and is available at ftp.viriginia.edu. Additional information is available at elm's Web site, http://www.math.fu-berlin.de/~guckes/elm. The other package is called pine and is available at ftp.cac.washington.edu. The Web site is http://www.washington.edu/pine.

Check your system because you might already have one or both. If you do, check your version in case you would like to update to the latest version. You can most easily determine which version you might have by starting each program with the appropriate command: pine or elm.

Here is what a listing of your mail messages would look like in elm:

```
      Mailbox is '/var/spool/mail/ray' with 3 messages [ELM 2.4 PL25]


  N  1   Apr 26              (14)    ready now?
  N  2   Apr 26              (14)    how goes it?
     3   Apr 26              (15)    testing



 You can use any of the following commands by pressing the first character;
  d)elete or u)ndelete mail,  m)ail a message,  r)eply or f)orward mail,  q)uit
   To read a message, press <return>.  j = move down, k = move up, ? = help

Command:
```

Starting `elm` takes you directly to the mailbox listing, as shown earlier. On the other hand, `pine` requires a bit more navigation. Your users, however, would probably find either one friendlier than `mail/Mail/mailx`.

This is how `pine` looks when you start it up:

```
PINE 3.96   MAIN MENU                    Folder: INBOX  4 Messages


            ?    HELP             -  Get help using Pine

            C    COMPOSE MESSAGE  -  Compose and send a message

            I    FOLDER INDEX     -  View messages in current folder

            L    FOLDER LIST      -  Select a folder to view

            A    ADDRESS BOOK     -  Update address book

            S    SETUP            -  Configure or update Pine

            Q    QUIT             -  Exit the Pine program




     Copyright 1989-1997. PINE is a trademark of the University of Washington.
                    [Folder "INBOX" opened with 4 messages]
     ? Help                 P PrevCmd                    R RelNotes
     O OTHER CMDS   L [ListFldrs]  N NextCmd             K KBLock
```

Summary

In today's lesson you learned

- Enough to adequately use `mail/Mail/mailx`.
- What is necessary to get a basic version of sendmail up and running.
- How MX records can be useful.
- How to forward mail by using the `/etc/aliases` file.
- How to navigate through some sendmail logs and directories. The information could be useful for diagnosing problems in the future.
- What the interfaces to the `elm` and `pine` mail reading programs look like.

Q&A

Q **Does the mail server also have to be the NIS master?**

A No, that is not necessary. The mail server can be its own machine, if that is the sort of mail requirement you have. It is rather common for clusters where one machine can handle the complete load, however, to put the basic services—NIS master, mail, Web server, and so on—all on one server machine.

Q **Suppose I have machines `cherry.mycompany.com`, `pineapple.mycompany.com`, and `mango.mycompany.com`. If I make `pineapple` my mail server, I understand that I can have mail sent to `cherry` and `mango` forwarded directly to `pineapple`. How do I get mail addressed to `user@mycompany.com` to go directly to `pineapple`?**

A Have an MX record for your root domain, `mycompany.com`, point to your mail server, `pineapple.mycompany.com`. Just as it is a good idea to have MX records for your other machines point to the mail server, you should also do the same for your root domain. Users outside your area don't have to remember to add a specific machine to your mail address. This makes it easier overall for the world to communicate with you.

Q **I know that users can have their mail forwarded with a `.forward` file in their home directories. Apparently, I could also have their mail forwarded for them in the `/etc/aliases` file. Is one method preferred over the other?**

A Some of that depends on how much control you need or want to have over mail. If no actual account is associated with the user, you will have to use the `/etc/alias` file. If you don't allow `.forward`, you will have to use `/etc/aliases`. If you do allow `.forward` at your site, you might want to reserve `/etc/aliases` for use with usernames that have no associated account, such as postmaster, or a nickname that a user might want to use. The `.forward` allows the user more control over his own mail, especially if he wants to have his mail redirected for when he is on vacation or otherwise gone.

Workshop

Exercises

1. Visit the procmail Web site to see whether procmail is a package you would like for your facility. If so, get it and install it.

2. Get the latest version of sendmail and install it. Keep around your old sendmail and configuration files as backups.

3. Visit the `pine` and `elm` Web sites. Is your site interested in either of those applications?

DAY 16

Securing Services: FTP and POP

Although your users can log in to your system and manipulate files in their own accounts, sometimes they will need the files at their local personal computer. Today, you will set up an FTP server so that your users can do just that. Additionally, you will install a POP mail server to enable your users to access their mail from a POP mail reader on their Mac or PC instead. To make you happy too, you'll look at how you can make those and some other services secure.

FTP

In addition to the vendor FTP server that comes with your operating system, there are also a number of other publicly available FTP servers that tend to provide more access control than the OS-provided servers. One of the more popular alternative FTP servers is wu-ftpd. There are a couple FTP servers derived from wu-ftpd, wu-ftpd VR series and BeroFTPD. wu-ftpd VR is essentially the wu-ftpd, but it is updated regularly. BeroFTPD, also updated more regularly, is supposed to provide more extensive support for virtual FTP servers. Because wu-ftpd is quite popular, you will look at it.

Installation Overview

The basic procedure for installing wu-ftpd after you have unpacked that file is to do the following:

- Enter **./build** *xxx* where *xxx* is the three-character designation for your platform. If you want to specify an alternative CC, then enter **./build CC=***yyy* *xxx*

- If your platform is not available, you will type the following:

```
cp src/config/config.gen src/config/config.xxx
cp src/makefiles/makefile.gen src/makefiles/Makefile.xxx
cp support/makefiles/Makefile.gen support/makefiles/Makefile.xxx
```

- Then try the build statement. The README file indicates that trying to build for a platform not already built is not trivial and that you would probably want to join the mailing list to get some help.

- If you are upgrading your version of the server, keep your old configuration files, or they will be replaced with sample copies.

- Type **./build install**.

- Edit /etc/inetd.conf to reflect the new wu-ftpd. If you hope to use some of the features of the server controlled by the ftpaccess file, start it with -a option after you have edited the ftpaccess file.

- Have inetd re-read /etc/inted.conf by running kill -HUP <inetd PID>, or whatever is appropriate for your system.

Setting Up the FTP Server

Basic steps in setting up the FTP server include the following:

- Add an entry to /etc/passwd for a user ftp. Make sure the account is locked out with an * in the password field and that the ftp user does not have a real shell.

- Make a group for ftp in /etc/group.

- Make a home directory for user ftp. The ftp user's directory and its subdirectories should not be owned by ftp or any user belonging to the same group as ftp. It is generally recommended that ~ftp and its subdirectories be owned by root and not be writable by anyone other than root.

- Make a bin directory for ~ftp and copy commands to that directory that might be useful in ftp sessions. Copy ls, GNU tar, compress, gzip, and gunzip to that directory, all with execute-only permission (chmod 111), along with any other commands you think you might need.

- Make an `etc` directory in ~ftp to store dummy versions of ~ftp/etc/passwd and ~ftp/etc/group for the `ftp` server to use to display ownership information. These files should be read-only (`chmod 444`).

- Make a pub directory.

- Make an incoming directory if you would like to allow people to upload files.

- If your operating system uses shared libraries, and the commands you copied to the `bin` directory are not statically linked, copy the relevant libraries to the appropriate locations in ~ftp. If you have a Sun, you'll need to copy the runtime linker, the shared C library, some device files, and zoneinfo files to ~ftp directories. See the specific information in a file on setting up FTP on a Sun. Look for this file at download time because it is not part of the general `wu-ftpd` source distribution.

Edit the `ftpaccess` file to suit your site's needs.

Editing the `ftpaccess` File

The `ftpaccess` file enables you to set many controls. You will probably find it wherever the FTP server was installed or possibly in `/etc`. Definitely read the man pages on `ftpaccess` carefully for full details.

Table 16.1 shows some selected useful controls available in `ftpaccess`.

TABLE 16.1 Controls in `ftpaccess`

Control	Function
`loginfails <number>`	After `<number>` of repeated login failures, logs a "repeated login failures" message and terminates the FTP connection.
`class <class> <typelist> <address>`	Sets up classes of users and valid access addresses. `<typelist>` is a comma-separated list of any of these keywords: `real`, `anonymous`, or `guest`. If `real` is included, the class can include users ftping to real accounts. If `anonymous` is included, the class can include anonymous `ftp` users. If `guest` is included, the class can include members of guest access accounts.
`guestgroup <groupname>`	Defines what groups are considered guests.
`limit <class> <number> <times> <message file>`	Limits the number of users belonging to `<class>` to access the server during the `<times>` indicated and posts `<message file>` as reason for access denial.

continues

TABLE 16.1 continued

Control	Function
log comands <typelist>	Logs individual commands issued by users in <typelist>, where <typelist> is a comma-separated list of any of the keywords real, anonymous, or guest.
log transfers <typelist> <direction>	Logs the transfers of users belonging to <typelist> in the specified <direction>. <direction> is a comma-separated list of the keywords inbound or outbound, where inbound refers to transfers to the server and outbound refers to transfers from the server.
passwd-check <level> <enforcement>	Defines how the password will be checked. <level> can be none, trivial (must contain an @), or rfc822 (must be an RFC822-compliant address). <enforcement> can be warn (warns user but enables them to log in) or enforce (warns user and logs them out).
upload <root-dir> <dirglob> <yes/no> <owner> <group> <mode>	<root-dir> specifies the ftp root directory. <dirglob> specifies a directory under the <root-dir>. <yes/no> indicates whether files can be uploaded to the specified directory. If yes, files will be uploaded with <owner>belonging to <group> in <mode>.
<setting> <yes/no> <typelist>	Permission settings can be set for delete, overwrite, rename, chmod, and umask as yes or no for users in <typelist>. The defaults are yes for everyone.

Understanding `ftpaccess` Controls

Take a look at some possible ways to configure some of those controls in `ftpaccess`.

class

Look at this statement:

```
class    staff    real    *.biosci.ohio-state.edu
```

In this example, a class called `staff` is defined as being a real user coming from anywhere in the `biosci.ohio-state.edu` domain.

In the following statement, a class called `local` is defined as being a guest user coming from anywhere in the `ohio-state.edu` domain:

```
class    local    guest    *.ohio-state.edu
```

As a guest user, anyone belonging to this class does not have a real account.

In this statement, a class called `remote` is defined as being an anonymous user whose connection comes from anywhere:

```
class    remote  anonymous        *
```

In the preceding example, if a user attempting to log on to the FTP server does not fall into any of the available classes, her access will be denied. In other words, with the classes described in the example, a "real" user would not be able to access the server unless her attempt originates from a machine in the `biosci.ohio-state.edu` domain. This will play a role in securing your FTP server. Later today, you will see how a "real" user will access the server.

limit

In the following statement, there is a limit of five users belonging to class `remote` who can access the machine on Saturdays and Sundays and on any day between 6:00 p.m. and 6:00 a.m.:

```
limit    remote  5    SaSu¦Any1800-0600    /usr/local/etc/msgs/msg.toomany
```

When the limit has been reached, any such additional user will see a posting of the message file, `msg.toomany`, in `/usr/local/etc`.

In the following statement, no users belonging to class `staff` can access the server at any time:

```
limit    staff   0        Any             /usr/local/etc/msgs/msg.notallowed
```

Whenever they attempt to log in, they will see a message telling them they are not allowed to access the server.

upload

In the following statements, the guest user, `bioftp`, can upload files to the `~ftp` public directory, and files will be uploaded with permissions `600`, that is, read and write permissions for guest user `bioftp`:

```
upload  /home/ftp  /public      yes    bioftp   ftponly    0600
upload  /home/ftp  /public/*    yes    bioftp   ftponly    0600
```

However, in the following statements, no user can upload to `~ftp/bin` directory:

```
upload  /home/ftp  /bin         no
upload  /home/ftp  /bin         no
```

Setting Up the Guest User

The `ftpaccess` file enables you to specify guest account controls, most notably, upload controls. For the guest account to work, you will have to make a directory for the account and a proper entry in the `/etc/password` file, along with the dummy entry in `~ftp/passwd`. Make the guest account's home directory fall somewhere under `~ftp` hierarchy. The entry in /etc/passwd for the guest account looks a bit unusual. It has the following form:

```
<guest_username>:<passwd>:<UID>:<GID>:<Idendifying_Information>:
➥<roodt_dir>.<home_dir>:<nonexistant_shell>
```

A valid entry might look like this:

```
guestftp:<encrypted_passwd>:3000:200:Guest FTP Account:
➥/home/ftp/./incoming/guestftp:/etc/ftponly
```

You're not imagining the /./ notation. The first part is the root of the ~ftp directory. The second part is the location of the guest user account's home directory relative to the root directory.

Also, for guest login or login for real accounts to work properly, make sure if you use /etc/shells that it has an entry for your <nonexistant shell> and entries for your users' valid shells.

Anonymous FTP and Secure Shell

Although you might want to make anonymous FTP available, you also might be wondering if anonymous FTP can co-exist in the secure shell environment you have set up for your cluster. The answer is that it can. One way to do this is to set up an FTP server to handle anonymous FTP and any guest FTP accounts that you might need to have. At the same time, set up another server, running on different ports, to allow access to only the real users.

Set up your anonymous FTP to run off the standard ports, 20 and 21. If you look in /etc/services, you will see those ports already defined as FTP ports. Allow anonymous and guest users to access this server. Do not allow any of your real users to access this one. Have them receive messages indicating that they must use the alternative server instead.

You should also set up an alternative server on an alternative set of ports. Pick ports not already in use, with the data port number being one less than the command port number. Specify those ports in /etc/services. Set up the ftpaccess to allow only the real users and no anonymous or guest users. When I built my alternative FTP server, I edited the Makefile in the source's makefiles directory and pathnames.h in the source's src directory to specify the location where I wanted it and its ftpaccess file to be installed.

Statements such as

```
class   staff   real       *.biosci.ohio-state.edu
class   remote  anonymous       *
limit   staff   0    Any               /usr/local/etc/msgs/msg.notallowed
limit   remote  5    SaSu¦Any1800-0600     /usr/local/etc/msgs/msg.toomany
```

in the anonymous FTP server's `ftpaccess` file become

```
class   staff   real    *.biosci.ohio-state.edu
class   remote  anonymous       *
limit   staff   10  Any                 /usr/local/etc/msgs2/msg.toomany
limit   remote  0   SaSu¦Any1800-0600
➥/usr/local/etc/msgs2/msg.notallowed
```

in the alternative FTP server's `ftpaccess` file.

You should edit `/etc/inetd.conf` to list both FTP servers. Also, edit `/etc/hosts.deny` to provide FTP services to all machines. Your `/etc/hosts.deny` might contain a statement similar to the following:

```
ALL EXCEPT ftpd sshd1 sshd2 sshd: ALL : banners /usr/sbin/banners
```

Edit `/etc/hosts.allow` to allow the alternative FTP service only from the server machine itself. If your server's IP address were `192.168.1.20`, your `/etc/hosts.allow` might have a statement like the following:

```
w2ftpd: 192.168.1.20
```

This setup will cause your real users to tunnel their FTP connections. This setup will impose an extra step in the FTP process, especially if they are using Web-editing suites with built-in FTP programs. However, it is being set up with their best interests in mind. This setup also conveniently provides for anonymous FTP, should you or your users have a need to provide such services. If you don't need to provide anonymous or guest FTP services, it might be sufficient for you to provide only a secure service for your regular users on the regular FTP ports.

Later in the chapter, I will show you how to forward connections in the secure shell client.

POP

In addition to an FTP server, you might want to install a POP mail server. Qpopper, a POP mail server, is available from `http://eudora.qualcomm.com/freeware/qpop.html`.

The basic procedure for installing Qpopper after unpacking the distribution is the following:

1. `./configure`.
2. Check `config.h`, `popper.h`, and the `Makefile` for any settings you might want to change.
3. `make`.

4. Copy the executable that was made, `popper`, to wherever you'd like to have it.

5. Edit `/etc/services` to include the following:

   ```
   pop3          110/tcp                          # Post Office
   ```

6. Edit `/etc/inetd.conf` to include an entry of this form:

   ```
   pop3    stream  tcp    nowait  root    /usr/local/bin/tcpd
   ➥/usr/local/bin/popper -s
   ```

7. Edit `/etc/hosts.allow` to include an entry for your POP server machine:

   ```
   popper: <host machine's IP address>
   ```

8. Update the NIS maps to re-read the services.

9. Have `inetd` re-read its configuration file by issuing `kill -HUP <inetd PID>` or whatever command your system prefers.

10. Test Qpopper to make sure it's really working.

Table 16.2 lists the primary options for configuring Qpopper. However, the README file also instructs you to check `config.h`, `popper.h`, and the `Makefile` before you run `make` to change other possible options. When you check the files, particularly `config.h` and `popper.h`, make sure you make a backup copy before you edit anything, if you are inclined to edit anything.

What kind of files are these? Two of the files that the Qpopper README

Note

suggests you might want to edit, `config.h` and `popper.h`, are written in C. Comments work differently in C from what you've seen so far. The lines written in the following form are comments:

```
/* Define if you have the bcopy function.   */
```

The `/* */` delimit comments. Lines that look like this are actually part of the code:

```
#define HAVE_BCOPY 1
```

TABLE 16.2 Primary Configuration Options for Qpopper

Option	Function
—enable-apop=FILE	Enables with APOP alternative authentication method, with the authentication file specified. This method authenticates without sending the password in clear text. DBM or GDBM libraries must already exist on the system.
—with-popuid=USER	Used in conjunction with -enable-apop. It identifies the user account that administers APOP users.

Option	Function
—enable-bulletins	Enables bulletins, plain text files that can be sent to all POP users.
—enable-servermode	Enables server mode. This mode is intended to work with a large POP account user base.
—enable-specialauth	Enables the use of different libraries for authentication on certain systems with other security enhancements, such as shadow passwords.

Be sure you have read the README file before enabling any of the options listed in Table 16.2.

When you are ready to test Qpopper, make sure you have a couple messages in your mail spool so that there will be something there to list.

To test your installation, do this:

```
telnet <machine> 110
user <user>
pass <password> (the password will appear in clear text on the screen)
list
uidl
quit
```

Here is an example of what to expect when you run the test:

```
Barracuda ralph 217 >telnet barracuda 110

Trying 192.168.1.20 ...
Connected to Barracuda.
Escape character is '^]'.
+OK QPOP (version 2.53) at Barracuda starting.
user ralph
+OK Password required for ralph.
pass n6tB3Dx
+OK ralph has 4 messages (1280 octets).
list
+OK 4 messages (1280 octets)
1 321
2 350
3 341
4 268
.
uidl
+OK uidl command accepted.
1 3fe0e4ed4fd9d921791bb853ee0bbf3c
2 17c5c984a21917e7d2ba2bf903e2dcf0
3 c44abb90135ce317c8684ba8c70b4088
4 aa7d14b8d4ef7f226bd001f78ca3fd67
.
```

```
quit
+OK Pop server at Barracuda signing off.
Connection closed by foreign host.
```

In the preceding test, `list` lists messages by size, whereas `uidl` lists the message by ID. Of course, you'll probably want to check the server again using a popmail reader. Continue reading to see how to securely set up that connection.

Note

> **POP versus IMAP** Isn't there some kind of mail access called IMAP? Yes, there is. POP, Post Office Protocol, and IMAP, Internet Message Access Protocol, are two protocols for remotely accessing mail.
>
> The default settings on popmail clients tend to be set to delete mail from the server after it has been read. This means that the user's mail can get sprinkled over various machines if the user reads his mail at different computers. This does not happen with IMAP. A person can read his mail at different machines without having it spread everywhere.
>
> Unfortunately, POP and IMAP are both security risks. I have my POP server wrapped by TCP Wrapper, as I have done here. I do not have an IMAP server because at this time, IMAP is more popular to exploit than POP. POP works for me because my users also have POP accounts with the university. You might find IMAP to be more suitable and might decide to install and wrap it instead.
>
> For more information on IMAP, check `http://www.imap.org`.

Securing Services: Forwarding Connections

The final step in securing your services is setting up port forwarding in your secure shell client on your PC or Mac. Again, I will show you how this is done on the Mac version of the DataFellows product, F-secure Tunnel and Terminal. The procedure for tunneling FTP and POP is the same. Because you might also have some applications on your UNIX machines that have X-windows licenses allowing them to be displayed elsewhere, I will also show you how to forward your X11 connection.

Forwarding FTP Connections

If you have not yet gone back and set up your SSH client for your general account, do so right now. Go back to Day 10, "Defending Your Machines and Encrypting Traffic," and do the section on setting up an SSH client for a user.

Although you can save many of your settings in one bookmark on your desktop, I find it much easier to save separate bookmarks for each service and/or machine. If one machine is the FTP server and another is the popmail server, I suggest saving a bookmark with connections to the FTP server saved and another with the popmail settings saved. Everything is easier to use that way, although you can end up with a slightly messier desktop.

Start F-Secure and enter in the hostname box the name of the FTP server. Then click Properties to bring up the Properties box. Figure 16.1 shows the Properties dialog box.

16

FIGURE 16.1

Properties dialog box with local forwarding panel.

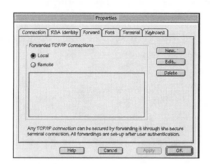

Click Forward. Select Local (which is probably already selected). Click New. You will be asked for a name for this connection. Provide whatever name you think will be useful to you. Then pick a source port. I tend to use 21 and 20 as my source ports on the Mac. For destination host, you should enter your FTP server. Enter an appropriate port number on the destination port, based on your /etc/services entries. Check the Allow Local Connections Only box. Click OK. Figure 16.2 shows the Edit Local Forwarding dialog box.

FIGURE 16.2

Creating a local port forwarding entry for FTP.

Note   **Only one channel or two?**   I have heard that SSH actually only encrypts the command channel and not the data channel of FTP. I tend to include both port numbers in my setup, just in case it can do any good. However, it is likely sufficient to just forward the command port, 21 on a basic FTP server or whatever yours might be if you are using alternative ports.

Assuming that only the command channel is encrypted, your password will be sent via an encrypted channel, but your data would still be open to attack. Because I have experienced the most problems tryin to collect passwords, even this partial security is just what I am looking for.

In the Properties box, you should now see listed the setup you just made. Click New again and set up another forwarded connection to the other FTP port listed in /etc/services. When you finish with your second one, you should see both connections listed in the Properties box, as shown in Figure 16.3.

FIGURE 16.3

Completed local port forwarding entries.

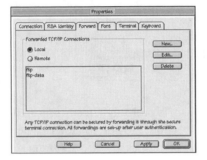

Finish logging in to the FTP server and save your settings to your desktop. When you finish, don't log out.

Now open your favorite FTP client. It might or might not work, so you will have to try and see what happens. I have had very good luck with my favorite FTP client, Anarchie. Before you make any connections, find a place to set the mode as PASV. I have now successfully tried three different versions of Anarchie, ranging from 1.4.0 to 3.5. In that program, the PASV setting tends to be located under something like Firewalls or Internet Configuration. If you have a version that uses the Internet Configuration scenario, you are likely to find PASV either under User Advanced, which you might have to access under the Edit menu, or you'll find it in a box labeled Firewalls. Finding the PASV setting in Anarchie is the most difficult aspect of using it.

When you have located the PASV setting in your FTP client, you're ready to enter the server name. For the server name, enter either localhost or 127.0.0.1, rather than the actual name of the FTP server. F-Secure will forward everything properly for you. You should now see your directory!

I have not had luck with Fetch since I upgraded to the most recent wu-ftpd. However, I have had luck with Fetch on a vendor-provided FTP server, and I have had luck with Anarchie for everything.

As for PCs, WS_FTP has been recommended to me as well as FTP Explorer.

Remember, to tunnel your FTP connections, first connect to the server machine with the SSH client. Set up port forwarding in the SSH client. Start the FTP client, and have it FTP to localhost. The connection will be handled as specified in the SSH client.

Forwarding POP Connections

The procedure for forwarding POP connections is like the one for FTP connections. If your POP server is a different machine from the FTP server, you might want to make a separate F-Secure bookmark for it. Set up port forwarding to forward to the POP server machine as the destination host, with the port listed in /etc/services, likely to be port 110.

You might have to experiment with popmail readers to see if yours works. I have Claris Emailer, and it does work. However, as I understand it, the program is no longer supported by Claris, so unfortunately, it's not one I can recommend. In your program, locate the dialog box that enables you to set up another account. For an email account, enter *username@localhost*, where *username* is whatever your username is. Answer the other questions as usual.

As with FTP, whenever you want to read your mail with the popmail reader, log in to the popmail server with the SSH client. Make sure port forwarding has been set up properly. Then have the popmail reader check the mail for *username@localhost*.

Forwarding Telnet Connections

Forwarding telnet connections? Hopefully, after you've disabled telnet, it is out of your life for good. However, if you should happen to have a user who is using a very specialized telnet terminal, you might have to make telnet available again.

If the need for telnet should arise, do exactly what you have done for FTP and POP. You will uncomment the telnet line in /etc/inetd.conf and wrap the entry with TCP wrapper. Add a line to /etc/hosts.allow for telnetd to be allowed for the host machine only. If the host machine were 192.168.1.20, your /etc/hosts.allow might look like this:

```
telnetd: 192.168.1.20
```

Then set up the SSH client to forward the telnet connection to the telnet port specified in the host machine's /etc/services. When the SSH client is set up, start your favorite telnet program, and telnet to localhost.

Hopefully, you won't need to do this because for most people, the SSH client should make an adequate, if not better, telnet substitute. However, if the need should arise, both you and your users will be happy with this solution.

Forwarding X11 Connections

Forwarding X11 connections sounds like it ought to be difficult and mysterious. Surprisingly, it isn't difficult. However, some of it is indeed mysterious.

UNIX Box to UNIX Box

You'll start off with basic X11 forwarding—from UNIX box to UNIX box. When you were first playing with UNIX, you probably learned that, if you were logged in to one machine remotely but wanted to send its display to the console of the machine where you were sitting, you should set your DISPLAY environment variable to the console machine. If I were sitting at rosalyn logged in to waashu and wanted to display waashu's netscape on rosalyn, I would type this in my waashu window:

WAASHU joray 202 > setenv DISPLAY rosalyn:0.0

Please remember that the preceding command will only work if your shell is csh or one of its variants. In a rosalyn window, I would type the following:

Rosalyn joray 203 > xhost +waashu

However, if you manually set the DISPLAY environment variable as I have done, you are redirecting the X11 connection over an insecure channel.

When you slogin to a machine, ssh takes care of everything for you! Well, sometimes it does. Take a look at the environment variable setting for DISPLAY directly after I slogin to the machine:

WAASHU joray 201 > echo $DISPLAY

WAASHU:10.0

Funny-looking magical setting! However, that is at least part of the X11 forwarding process with ssh. Sometimes, that is enough to get X11 forwarding to work. In this case, now I can start X-windows applications on waashu and view them on rosalyn. Just typing **xterm** in my waashu window brings up a waashu xterm on rosalyn.

Sometimes, though, you have to edit your /etc/hosts.allow to include an X11 entry that has the machine with the software you would like to display elsewhere as well as the machine where you would like to have it displayed. Sometimes, it is sufficient to add the entry to /etc/hosts.allow as just the following:

```
X11: <host list>
```

Other times, that entry will have to be entered as this:

```
sshdfwd-X11: <host list>
```

If your X11 forwarding fails with a message like the following, you should edit your /etc/hosts.allow:

```
Fwd X11 connection from <hostname> refused by tcp_wrappers.
```

Successfully forwarding your connection is pretty exciting. Figure 16.4 shows Netscape running on a Sun but being displayed to an SGI.

FIGURE 16.4

Here Netscape is running on a Sun and being displayed on an SGI.

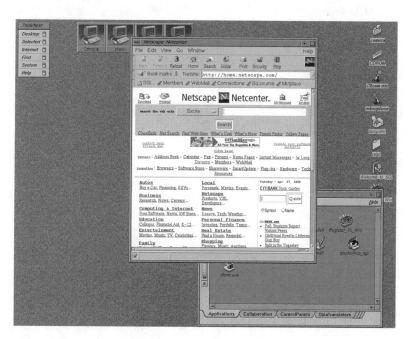

UNIX Box to Mac or PC

As most of your users probably do not have UNIX boxes on their desktops, the more interesting question becomes this: How do you securely forward that connection to a Mac or PC?

On the Mac I have tested eXodus and XTen, which handle the matter in two different ways. I have not had an opportunity to extensively test either one, but I can give you some indication of what to expect initially from each product. For more information and a downloadable demo version of eXodus, visit `http://www.wpine.com`. For more information and a downloadable demo version of XTen, visit `http://www.tenon.com`.

I have not personally tried any X-windows products for the PC, however, Exceed has been recommended to me as a product to try. For more information and a downloadable demo version, visit `http://www.hummingbird.com`.

The trickiest part to securely forwarding an X11 connection for a Mac or PC is again the `/etc/hosts.allow` file on the UNIX machine. It will require an X11 entry for hosts that you want to allow to make X11 connections. As with UNIX box to UNIX box, you might have to include the UNIX machine itself as being allowed X11 forwarded connections.

When you have edited your `/etc/hosts.allow` file, you are ready to try demo versions of the various available products so that you will be able to make recommendations to your users when they ask you.

Forwarding an X11 connection using eXodus is a lot like the port forwarding examples you have already seen with FTP and POP. Start the F-Secure package first. Before you connect anywhere, edit your connection properties so that the Forward X11 box is checked, as shown in Figure 16.5.

FIGURE 16.5

Connection properties dialog box with X11 forwarding checked.

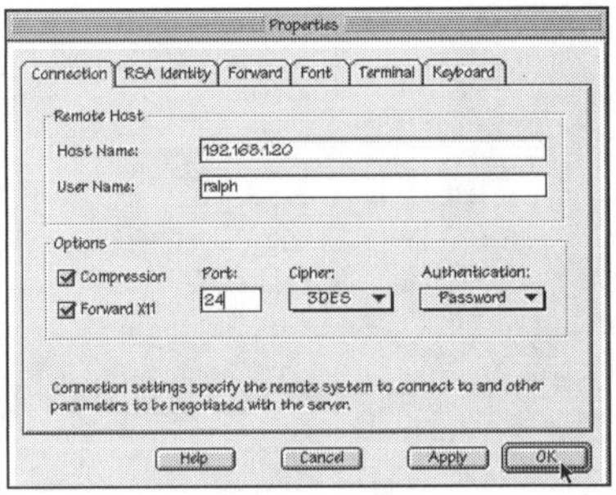

A quick check on the UNIX machine shows the magical forwarding settings are already in place:

```
Barracuda ralph 1 >echo $DISPLAY

Barracuda:10.0
```

If you are doing this for the first time, you will probably see a comment about creating .Xauthority when you log in.

Just as with the FTP and POP programs, you are now ready to start using eXodus. When eXodus is running, you can test how it is working by typing xterm in your SSH client terminal window. You should now see an xterm display in your eXodus window. I will show you a little eXodus display on Day 19, "Optional Software."

Unlike eXodus, XTen does not require that you make a login with the SSH client software. It has its own UNIX and ssh1! Consequently, I have tested it a little more than eXodus. I have used it for displaying xterms as well as the molecular graphics application for which we have an X-windows license.

Because XTen does have its own UNIX, it is a little more difficult to initially set up. You will have to enable ssh, make a user, create a key, and add that key to the ~/.ssh/ authorized_keys file on the UNIX machine. Window manager choices are motif, AfterStep, and OpenLook. A lot of the setup is done through a browser, with Mosaic as the default browser, although it won't reduce your need for vi. What I don't like about XTen is that it only has a rooted window, which means that having XTen on the computer is a lot like having a separate computer on the computer. It takes up the entire screen space. Although you can toggle between it and your Mac desktop, you do not seem to have the capability to integrate it with the rest of the Mac desktop.

Take a look at how you set up XTen. Before you start the program for the first time, set up the XTen control panel. The control panel itself is shown in Figure 16.6.

FIGURE 16.6

XTen control panel.

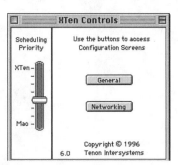

The XTen control panel has a section for general configuration options and networking configuration. Figure 16.7 shows the general configuration panel. This is where you enter the host name and time zone.

FIGURE 16.7

XTen control panel's general configuration panel.

The networking configuration panel is shown in Figure 16.8. Be prepared to provide the usual sorts of settings—name server, subnet mask, gateway, and so on. Make sure the Enable Incoming Connections box is checked.

FIGURE 16.8

XTen control panel's networking configuration panel.

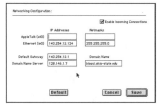

Now, you're ready to start the program! Figure 16.9 shows the default desktop, AfterStep, with the XTen Manager page open in Mosaic.

FIGURE 16.9

The XTen default desktop.

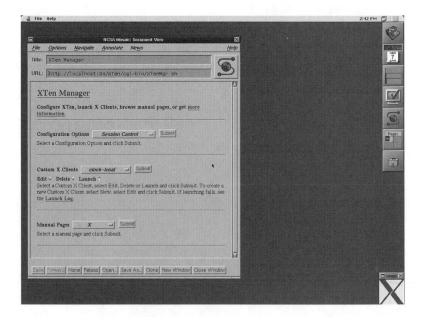

From the XTen Manager shown in Figure 16.9, you can configure just about everything you need for getting set up. From here, you can create a user. You can also set your mouse button settings in the XTen Manager. Even if you don't decide to change your mouse settings, take a moment to look at that panel to see what the default configuration is; this way, you don't waste time guessing or trying to search the accompanying documentation. At the Remote Client Access Control page, you can enter your remote client, as shown in Figure 16.10.

16

FIGURE 16.10

Remote Client Access Control setup.

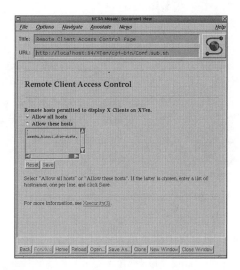

To force the use of ssh connections for all users, uncomment the SECURESHELL line in /usr/X11R6/lib/X11/startX/startXrc. That entry now becomes the following:

```
# Use Secure Shell when launching remote clients
SECURESHELL="/usr/bin/ssh" ; export SECURESHELL
```

Now, you are ready to log out as root and log back in as a user. To log out, select Restart XTen in the XTen Manager.

At this point, you have configured time and networking information about your Mac, created a user, made any customizations that looked interesting to you, set up access for a remote client to access your Mac's X11 server, and forced the use of ssh for any XTen user you make.

Figure 16.11 shows how the login screen looks for my machine after finishing with the initial setup. Notice the Apple menu bar is present and functional, in spite of XTen's monopolizing the screen.

FIGURE 16.11

*XTen is now set up
with XDM login.*

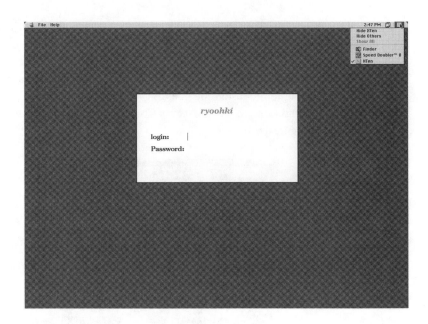

After you are logged back in as the user who wants to have an X11 connection
forwarded, you should run the following:

```
ssh-keygen -N '' -b 1024 -f ~/.ssh/identity
```

This next part is a bit tricky because I haven't determined yet how to copy and paste
between XTen and other applications running on the Mac. Ideally, figure out how to
properly copy and paste. If that is not possible or you do not have the time to figure that
out, it might be easiest to use XTen's copy and paste to get the contents of the identity
file you just made into a mail message that you send to yourself at your UNIX account.

You will have to use `mail`, and at this point, it won't work entirely as you might expect.
As a matter of fact, it might not even work at first. You might see an error from `sendmail`
about `/etc/virtdomains`. For the goal of getting your data to yourself at your UNIX
account, it will be fastest to comment out the `/etc/virthodomains` line in your XTen
`/etc/sendmail.cf` file. You can play later with tweaking your XTen sendmail, if you
feel so inclined. The line would then become the following:

```
# file containing names of hosts for which we receive email
Fw/etc/sendmail.cw
# Fw/etc/virtdomains
```

You can use your regular UNIX account's `mail` to save the message as a file. Yesterday's
Table 15.1 provides everything you need to know for doing that. Then, using the editor

of your choice, put the contents of identity (what you pasted in to your message to yourself) at the end of ~/.ssh/authorized_keys on the UNIX side. Remember, the addition to ~/.ssh/authorized_keys should be one line. If it is not, ssh will not work properly for you.

Make sure that the UNIX machine's /etc/hosts.allow will allow X11 for your Mac.

After you have made the addition to ~/.ssh/authorized_keys on the UNIX side, you are ready to ssh in XTen to the UNIX host. You should be connected to the UNIX host, and if you check the DISPLAY environment variable on the UNIX host, you should see the ssh magic at work again:

```
WAASHU ralph 4 >echo $DISPLAY

WAASHU:10.0
```

Now, you're ready to test X11 forwarding! You might want to start with something basic such as xterm. Figure 16.12 shows Netscape running on an SGI, but being displayed in XTen on the Macintosh.

FIGURE 16.12

Netscape running on an SGI and being displayed in XTen on the Mac.

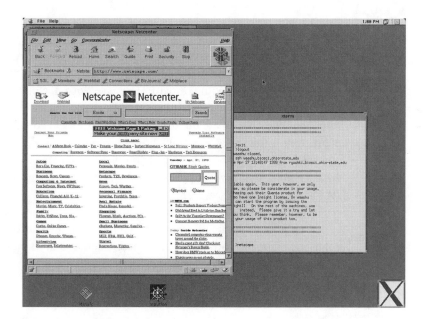

Pretty neat, isn't it?

Summary

In today's lesson you learned how to do the following:

- Set up an anonymous FTP server.
- Set up an alternative FTP server for secure connections for your regular users.
- Install Qpopper.
- Forward FTP and POP connections on the F-Secure Tunnel and Terminal SSH client.
- Forward telnet connections on the SSH client.
- Forward X11 connections between two UNIX machines.
- Forward X11 connections between a UNIX machine and a Mac. You saw two ways that this can be implemented on software available for the Macintosh. The process is similar for the PC.

Q&A

Q What is PASV FTP?

A PASV FTP is server-to-server FTP, also known as passive mode FTP. Technically, the way that FTP normally works is by the creation of two *channels* between the client and the server. With normal FTP connections, the client opens a *command* channel to the server via which the user issues commands and the server issues response codes. When a request for data occurs on the command channel, (such as a directory listing, or a get command), the server opens a *data* channel to the client and sends the requested data. When you're behind a proxy or a firewall or are on a NAT network, the server is prevented from making a connection back to the client. PASV mode tells the server that the client will initiate the data channel, and it requests that it allow this incoming connection. PASV mode is considered server-to-server because it actually can allow a client to request that a server accept a data connection from any arbitrary data source, such as a third-party server, not just from the client. Although this is a security risk, it allows, for example, one client to control the mirroring of an FTP site on one server among a large number of other servers.

Q Why can I even run the `telnet <hostname> 110` popper test? I thought I disabled telnet, as you advised me to.

A You have disabled the telnet daemon and many other connections to your host. However, you have not disabled the capability of other programs to listen at other, or even the same, ports. Telnet is, to put it simply, a communications protocol that is carried over TCP/IP. It is used as the basic communication protocol between many typical Internet services, and the POP3 service is no different. The POP3 daemon listens on port 110 for incoming connections, and because you haven't blocked connections to port 110, or to the POP3 service in your `tcpwrappers` configuration, you can still telnet to it.

Workshop

Exercises

1. Pick an FTP server, install it, and test it. If you decide to upgrade the one you have, be sure to hang on to the current configuration files.

2. Further investigate the POP versus IMAP issue. Which is the larger security risk, and can these risks be mitigated? Is one better suited to your site? Do you even want POP or IMAP, considering that they are currently security risks?

3. Set up the port forwarding for FTP and POP/IMAP, if you installed either one, in your SSH client and try a connection.

4. Play with X11 forwarding. You'll have lots of fun implementing it and watching it actually work.

DAY **17**

WWW Connectivity: Netscape, Apache, and Statistics

Today, you'll connect to the World Wide Web. You will install a browser, Netscape, and the most popular Web server, Apache. In addition, you will take a brief look at some Web site statistics packages.

Installing Netscape

Just as you can get Netscape for your PC or Mac, you can get it for a UNIX machine. Netscape is available at `FTP.netscape.com`.

Probably the most difficult part about installing Netscape is navigating the FTP archives to find the version you need. Your path will likely resemble `pub/communicator/4.51/unix`. Currently, versions ranging from 4.03–4.51 are available. When you're in the `unix` directory, you'll have a choice between supported or unsupported. Check both for a version for your platform. Some of your operating systems might have already come with a vendor-provided version of Netscape.

To install Netscape, you'll need the GNU `gzip` tool. You can either run a script to install Netscape or install it manually. Because the script enables you to specify where you would like Netscape to be installed, the script will probably serve your purposes. As always, read README before you begin.

After unpacking the distribution, go to the source directory and do the following to install Netscape:

1. ./ns-install.
2. Indicate the directory where Netscape should be installed. The default is /usr/local/netscape.
3. If /usr/local/netscape does not already exist, answer yes to the script's question about making the directory.
4. If you don't already have a ~/.netscape and have never used Netscape before, the README suggests using the following:

   ```
   cp /usr/local/netscape/bookmarks.htm ~/.netscape/bookmarks.html
   ```

5. Include the MOZILLA_HOME environment variable in your `.cshrc` or other appropriate file to include the installation directory. This variable should list the installation directory, even if you move the binary file, Netscape, to another location. Your environment variable statement might look like this for `.cshrc`:

   ```
   setenv MOZILLA_HOME /usr/local/netscape
   ```

Now you can finally browse the Web!

Installing Apache

Like Netscape, Apache can be installed either by script or manually. If you use the script, you will specify settings on the `./configure` line. If you do it manually, you will edit a configuration file instead. There is a wealth of documentation on Apache available at `http://www.apache.org`, as well as a list of download sites. As of this writing, Apache is also available for download at `FTP.apache.org`. However, the FTP site indicates that anonymous FTP will go away sometime soon.

Prerequisites for Installation

Before you begin your installation, you will need the following:

- Approximately 12MB of available temporary storage space. After installation, Apache will require at least 3MB, depending on your installation.

- An ANSI C compiler. gcc 2.7.2 or later is recommended.
- If you think you might want to run some Perl support scripts, have Perl 5.003 or later installed.
- Dynamic Shared Object support is optionally available. However, Apache only knows about a limited number of platforms. If your platform is not one of those but your system has the dlopen-style interface and you would like to make the optional support available, you will have to provide appropriate compiler linker flags (CFLAGS_SHLIB, LDFLAGS_SHLIB, and LDFLAGS_SHLIB_EXPORT). If you do not do that, make sure Perl 5 is installed, and Apache might be able to guess options from there.

Installation Overview Using the Installation Script

As always, read the README before the installation procedure. For this one, it would also be a good idea to read src/Configuration. Although you don't have to edit it if you are running the script, it will familiarize you with many of your options and what the defaults are. Then you will do the following:

1. ./configure -prefix=PREFIX.
2. make.
3. make install.
4. Edit the server's configuration files, httpd.conf, access.conf, and srm.conf, in PREFIX/etc/ to suit your needs.
5. Test the server by running PREFIX/bin/apachectl start and viewing a document.
6. If running as a standalone server, edit the appropriate startup file to start the server at boot time.
7. If running out of inetd, edit /etc/inetd.conf. Stop the server with PREFIX/bin/apachectl stop so that it can run out of inetd the next time it is called. Have inetd re-read its configuration file.
8. Make sure you have your system time set properly.

configure supports many options, which are neatly laid out for you in README. Table 17.1 highlights some useful ones.

TABLE 17.1   Useful Options for Apache's Configuration

Option	Function
--help	Provides help.
--prefix	Specifies installation directory for Apache.

continues

TABLE 17.1   continued

Option	Function
--with-perl=FILE	Specifies which version of Perl is available to Apache.
--enable-rule=NAME	Enables a rule. These rules can be specified: SOCKS4, SOCKS5, IRIXNIS, IRIXN32, PARANOID, WANTHSREGEX, SHARED_CORE, SHARED_CHAIN. The PARANOID option prints out code that a module executes as configure runs.
--disable-rule=NAME	Disables a rule.
--add-module=FILE	Incorporates simple third-party modules into Apache's build process. Copies the module source file to the Apache source directory.
--activate-module=FILE	Incorporates complex third-party modules into Apache's build process. Module has to be copied to src/modules/ before running configure.
--enable-module=NAME	Enables the specified module already distributed with the Apache source. Run ./configure -help to get module names. all enables all modules. most enables those usable on all platforms.
--disable-module=NAME	Disables the specified module already distributed with the Apache source. Takes the same special cases as -enable-module.
--enable-shared=NAME	Enables shared object support for the specified module distributed with the Apache source. max enables DSO on all modules except the bootstrapping (mod_so) module. remain enables DSO only for those modules that are still not yet enabled. Some systems might require —enable-rule=SHARED_CORE to be in place for DSO to work.
--disable-shared=NAME	Disables shared object support. Takes same special cases as —enable-shared=NAME.
--permute-module=N1:N2	Switches the module's appearance in the Configuration file, thereby changing the module's priorities. BEGIN: N moves the specified module to the beginning of the list, thereby giving it lowest priority. END: N moves specified module to the end of the list, resulting in the highest priority.

The README neatly tabulates the available modules. They can have many functions, including making content-type decisions, providing scripting support, logging support, server side image map support, and so on.

Manual Installation Overview

Manual installation was the only method available for installing versions of Apache earlier than version 1.3. If you choose to continue this tradition, you will do the following:

1. Unpack your Apache distribution.
2. cd apache-1.x.y/src.

3. `cp Configuration.tmpl Configuration.`

4. Edit `Configuration`. Adjust the various rules to suit your needs. Uncomment optional modules to include them in your configuration. Add lines to include any custom modules. Comment out default modules you might not like.

5. `./Configure.`

6. `make.`

7. `cd ../conf.`

8. `cp httpd.conf-dist httpd.conf.`

9. `cp srm.conf-dist /srm.conf.`

10. `cp access.conf-dist access.conf.`

11. Edit the `.conf` configuration files.

12. Put the Apache binary and related files in the `/usr/local/apache` directory or whatever directory you have specified in your configuration files.

At this point, you have an Apache binary file, a configuration file, and other related files copied to your preferred location for Apache. As you approach the end of the installation, you will do the following:

1. Start the server so that it reads the `httpd.conf` file. Generally, this will be as follows:

   `/usr/local/apache/httpd -f /usr/local/apache/conf/httpd.conf`

2. If running as a standalone server, edit your startup scripts so that the server starts at boot time.

3. If running out of `inetd`, edit `/etc/inetd.conf`, kill the current httpd process, and have `inetd` re-read its configuration file.

4. Make sure you have your system time set properly.

Interesting Modules

When picking modules to include with your build of Apache, you will probably be interested in the default modules. There are a few experimental modules that are not available by default, but the `Configuration` file advises against including them anyway. Some potentially interesting modules not available by default include the following:

- `mime_magic`—Maps file type by examining the contents of a file and comparing that against the `/etc/magic` database.

- `speling`—Attempts to correct URL misspellings by checking capitalization or allowing up to one misspelling. If there is a match, it issues a "spelling corrected" redirection.

- rewrite—A URL rewriting module that provides for URI-to-URI and URI-to-filename mapping.

- cern_meta—A header manipulation module that makes use of CERN Web server's metainformation style.

- expires—Provides expiration information for caching purposes.

- headers—Can set arbitrary http response headers.

> **URI? URL?**   URI is Uniform Resource Identifier. It is a term for the generic set of all names that refer to resources. URL, Uniform Resource Locator, is a subset of URI. A URL specifically provides the instructions necessary to access Internet resources. If you would like more information, try browsing the World Wide Web Consortium at http://www.w3.org.

Editing the Configuration Files

As you might have noticed, the installation overviews for each method for installing Apache refer to three configuration files you ought to edit. When you start to edit the first one, httpd.conf, you'll notice that it is extremely large. More surprisingly, you'll notice that it indicates that the other two files, srm.conf and access.conf, are now empty files with version 1.3, and everything has been consolidated into httpd.conf. If you have inherited a machine that is already running a 1.2 server, hang on to all three configuration files to help you with your edits of the current httpd.conf file. You will find that the information from all three files in version 1.2 is now scattered throughout the httpd.conf file in version 1.3.

With the version 1.2 files, httpd.conf sets up basic server settings, such as port, maximum number of connections, and so on. srm.conf defines default document and directory names and special parsing functions, such as image mapping. access.conf sets up basic access controls. In version 1.3, httpd.conf handles all of this. However, it is divided into three main parts: the server as a whole; the main server, which handles requests not handled through virtual hosts; and virtual hosts.

Because the configuration file is very large, you will not look at the entire file. However, you will look at a number of parts to help you get started editing the directives in yours. Fortunately, the file comes with many guiding comments.

Part 1: General Server Settings

The first part of the httpd.conf file sets directives for the server as a whole. The file begins with a definition for the server type:

```
# ServerType is either inetd, or standalone.  Inetd mode is only
# supported on Unix platforms.
#
ServerType standalone
```

If you expect to have some traffic on your server, you will probably want to set the type as standalone. The standalone version will run as its own process with the controls that you set in this file. If you run it out of `inetd`, `inetd` will start the server each time there is a request and stop it at the end of the request. This option might be all right if your Web server is not expected to be a high traffic server.

Next, the ServerRoot directive is defined. As the comment indicates, this is where the configuration and log files are stored:

```
# ServerRoot: The top of the directory tree under which the server's
# configuration, error, and log files are kept.
#
# NOTE!  If you intend to place this on an NFS (or otherwise network)
# mounted filesystem then please read the LockFile documentation
# (available at <URL:http://www.apache.org/docs/mod/core.html#lockfile>);
# you will save yourself a lot of trouble.
#
# Do NOT add a slash at the end of the directory path.
#
ServerRoot "@@ServerRoot@@"
```

If you chose to install Apache in `/usr/local/apache`, this line would look like the following:

```
ServerRoot /usr/local/apache
```

This section of the file also defines where your various logs will be stored. It is followed by this:

```
# Timeout: The number of seconds before receives and sends time out.
#
Timeout 300

#
# KeepAlive: Whether or not to allow persistent connections (more than
# one request per connection). Set to "Off" to deactivate.
#
KeepAlive On

#
# MaxKeepAliveRequests: The maximum number of requests to allow
# during a persistent connection. Set to 0 to allow an unlimited amount.
# We recommend you leave this number high, for maximum performance.
#
MaxKeepAliveRequests 100

#
```

17

```
# KeepAliveTimeout: Number of seconds to wait for the next request from
# the same client on the same connection.
#
KeepAliveTimeout 15
```

As you can see, this section enables you to specify connection settings as well as a time-out period. The default is 300 seconds, but you might want to decrease that to something like 60 seconds. HTTP connections cost resources, and allowing idle connections to tie up system resources for 300 seconds before requiring that they reconnect can be a big drain on anything but the most lightly used servers. Of course, you have to balance this with the bandwidth reducing benefits of keeping the connection alive. You'll want to strike a happy medium between the resource usage of your machine and the time your Web visitors are likely to take between loading a page and clicking somewhere on it.

Here, you can also specify whether to allow a connection to make more than one request (KeepAlive). The default is to have this directive on. If you keep it on, you can also specify a timeout period for a persistent connection and the maximum number of requests it can make.

Next is a section where you can specify load settings:

```
# Server-pool size regulation.  Rather than making you guess how many
# server processes you need, Apache dynamically adapts to the load it
# sees —- that is, it tries to maintain enough server processes to
# handle the current load, plus a few spare servers to handle transient
# load spikes (e.g., multiple simultaneous requests from a single
# Netscape browser).
#
# It does this by periodically checking how many servers are waiting
# for a request.  If there are fewer than MinSpareServers, it creates
# a new spare.  If there are more than MaxSpareServers, some of the
# spares die off.  The default values are probably OK for most sites.
#
MinSpareServers 5
MaxSpareServers 10


#
# Number of servers to start initially —- should be a reasonable ballpark
# figure.
#
StartServers 5


#
# Limit on total number of servers running, i.e., limit on the number
# of clients who can simultaneously connect —- if this limit is ever
# reached, clients will be LOCKED OUT, so it should NOT BE SET TOO LOW.
# It is intended mainly as a brake to keep a runaway server from taking
# the system with it as it spirals down...
#
```

```
MaxClients 150
#
# MaxRequestsPerChild: the number of requests each child process is
# allowed to process before the child dies.  The child will exit so
# as to avoid problems after prolonged use when Apache (and maybe the
# libraries it uses) leak memory or other resources.  On most systems,
# this isn't really needed, but a few (such as Solaris) do have notable
# leaks in the libraries.
#
MaxRequestsPerChild 30
```

In this section, you can specify how many servers are initially started (StartServers) and how many simultaneous servers can run (MaxClients). The minimum and maximum numbers of spare servers are also defined. The server uses these during periodic peaks in the load. You can also specify the number of requests a process is allowed to handle before terminating it. This setting is available as a precaution against memory leaks after prolonged use.

This first section ends with some Dynamic Shared Object support settings that you can set. All those directives are currently off by default. If you built some modules as shared modules, to be able to use the modules you will have to specify them in this section. httpd.conf advises reading the README.DSO for more details. However, I can't find such a README file in the distribution. Instead, for more details on DSO support, you might want to look at the documentation in your apache-1.x.y/htdocs/manual directory, as well as at the Apache Web site, and check the comp.infosystems.www.servers.unix newsgroup. Because DSO support is currently listed as being platform-dependent, I did not enable it in my build, and I have left these directives off.

Part 2: Main Server Settings

The second section of the file covers main server configuration. That is, it defines directives for a server that does not respond as a virtual host. This portion of the file makes up the bulk of httpd.conf.

This is where the port for a standalone server is set in version 1.3:

```
# Port: The port to which the standalone server listens. For
# ports < 1023, you will need httpd to be run as root initially.
#
Port 80
```

The default is set to the standard port 80. Don't change this unless you have a good reason and know what and why you're doing it.

If the server is running as a standalone server, it must initially run as root if Port < 1023. If the port is set to a greater value, it does not need to initially run as root. If root runs the server, after it has started, it can automatically switch itself to being run by a different user. Specifying the other user/group is done here:

```
# If you wish httpd to run as a different user or group, you must run
# httpd as root initially and it will switch.
#
# User/Group: The name (or #number) of the user/group to run httpd as.
#  . On SCO (ODT 3) use "User nouser" and "Group nogroup".
#  . On HPUX you may not be able to use shared memory as nobody, and the
#    suggested workaround is to create a user www and use that user.
#  NOTE that some kernels refuse to setgid(Group) or semctl(IPC_SET)
#  when the value of (unsigned)Group is above 60000;
#  don't use Group #-1 on these systems!
#
User nobody
Group #-1
```

With the ServerAdmin directive, you will indicate what email address should be used for sending mail about problems with the server. This address will appear on some of the automatically generated error pages.

In the upcoming section, you'll provide the host machine's name and the directory that will serve your pages:

```
# ServerName allows you to set a host name which is sent back to clients
# for your server if it's different than the one the program would get
# (i.e., use "www" instead of the host's real name).
#
# Note: You cannot just invent host names and hope they work. The name you
# define here must be a valid DNS name for your host. If you don't
# understand this, ask your network administrator.
# If your host doesn't have a registered DNS name, enter its IP address
# here. You will have to access it by its address (e.g.,
# http://123.45.67.89/) anyway, and this will make redirections work
# in a sensible way.
#
#ServerName new.host.name


#
# DocumentRoot: The directory out of which you will serve your
# documents. By default, all requests are taken from this directory, but
# symbolic links and aliases may be used to point to other locations.
#
DocumentRoot "@@ServerRoot@@/htdocs"
```

It's in this section where, if your host's real name also has a www alias, you can specify the www alias instead. The DocumentRoot is the directory that will serve your pages. Remember, this is not the ServerRoot. You do not have to specify a directory where the Apache server is also stored, unless you want your main pages to come from there.

Specify whatever directory will store the pages that a person ought to get when she tries to browse www.your.organization.com.

The file then sets some default directory permissions, and it goes on to set specific permissions on your DocumentRoot directory:

```
# This should be changed to whatever you set DocumentRoot to.
#
<Directory "@@ServerRoot@@/htdocs">

#
# This may also be "None", "All", or any combination of "Indexes",
# "Includes", "FollowSymLinks", "ExecCGI", or "MultiViews".
#
# Note that "MultiViews" must be named *explicitly* —- "Options All"
# doesn't give it to you.
#
    Options Indexes FollowSymLinks
```

Note that the default Options are Indexes, which provides a directory listing if there is no DirectoryIndex (index.html, and so on), and FollowSymLinks, which tells the server to follow symbolic links. If you want to allow CGI scripts to be executed in this directory, you will have to include the ExecCGI option.

The file continues with setting permissions on your DocumentRoot directory:

```
#
# This controls which options the .htaccess files in directories can
# override. Can also be "All", or any combination of "Options",
# "FileInfo", "AuthConfig", and "Limit"
#
    AllowOverride None

#
# Controls who can get stuff from this server.
#
    Order allow,deny
    Allow from all
</Directory>
```

Here, you can specify what options .htaccess files can override as well as indicate any special host access controls. Much like what this section does for your DocumentRoot, .htaccess files can be used to control access to pages.

The next section is where you set the standard for how your users' Web sites will be organized:

```
# UserDir: The name of the directory which is appended onto a user's home
# directory if a ~user request is received.
#
```

17

```
UserDir public_html

# DirectoryIndex: Name of the file or files to use as a pre-written HTML
# directory index.  Separate multiple entries with spaces.
#
DirectoryIndex index.html
```

With the `UserDir` directive you set what directory the Web server looks in for user Web pages. `DirectoryIndex` sets what filenames to use as prewritten HTML directory indexes. If a directory does not have a file matching any of the names you list here, a directory listing will appear instead, as I mentioned with the `Options` directive earlier.

A little further in the file, you see where the server looks to determine MIME type and the default setting in cases when it can't determine the MIME type:

```
# TypesConfig describes where the mime.types file (or equivalent) is
# to be found.
#
TypesConfig conf/mime.types


#
# DefaultType is the default MIME type the server will use for a document
# if it cannot otherwise determine one, such as from filename extensions.
# If your server contains mostly text or HTML documents, "text/plain" is
# a good value.  If most of your content is binary, such as applications
# or images, you may want to use "application/octet-stream" instead to
# keep browsers from trying to display binary files as though they are
# text.
#
DefaultType text/plain
```

You should probably look at the `conf/mime.types` file sometime to see what file types the server recognizes. The next default setting in `httpd.conf` checks for whether the `mime_magic` module that makes use of `/etc/magic` (remember `/etc/magic` from the gzip installation on Day 7, "The Most Important Accessory: The C Compiler gcc"?) is included in your build, and if it is, the server also uses it to determine the MIME type.

> **Note**
>
> **Poof! It's Magic**   Haven't you heard about `/etc/magic` before today? Yes, you have. On Day 7, when you were installing `gzip`, you had to add some lines to the `/etc/magic` file. The `mime_magic` module uses UNIX's `file`, which examines the content of a file. `file` uses `/etc/magic` in helping identify a file type.

The next directive, HostnameLookups, is off by default to save time in doing hostname lookups whenever a request arrives. If you turn this on, you run the risk of having your Web server hold up traffic because it is waiting for a response from the name server. This means that with the default, only IP addresses will be logged, but if you need to know the name, you can query the name server yourself:

```
# HostnameLookups: Log the names of clients or just their IP addresses
# e.g., www.apache.org (on) or 204.62.129.132 (off).
# The default is off because it'd be overall better for the net if people
# had to knowingly turn this feature on, since enabling it means that
# each client request will result in AT LEAST one lookup request to the
# nameserver.
#
HostnameLookups Off
```

The httpd.conf file continues with directives for setting your logs and certain aliases and displaying server-generated directory listings. Then, there is a section of AddHandler directives, which enable you to map certain file extensions to certain actions unrelated to file type:

```
# If you want to use server side includes, or CGI outside
# ScriptAliased directories, uncomment the following lines.
#
# To use CGI scripts:
#
#AddHandler cgi-script .cgi

#
# To use server-parsed HTML files
#
#AddType text/html .shtml
#AddHandler server-parsed .shtml

#
# Uncomment the following line to enable Apache's send-asis HTTP file
# feature
#
#AddHandler send-as-is asis

#
# If you wish to use server-parsed imagemap files, use
#
#AddHandler imap-file map

#
# To enable type maps, you might want to use
#
#AddHandler type-map var
```

17

Note, for example, that if you want your users to be able to easily serve CGI scripts, you could uncomment the AddHandler for CGI.

The file then continues with a number of directives relating to meta-information and customizable error responses, which are all turned off by default. The file then specifies some browser-specific directives involving the HTTP protocol. I would trust the defaults and not make any adjustments.

The second part of the httpd.conf file ends with some status and configuration report settings that you could choose to enable, along with some proxy settings.

Part 3: Virtual Hosts Settings

The third and final part to the httpd.conf enables you to set up virtual hosts. The brief section is off by default. However, if you work at an ISP or have users who might need customized hostnames, this section of the configuration file might be useful to you:

```
# VirtualHost: If you want to maintain multiple domains/hostnames on your
# machine you can setup VirtualHost containers for them.
# Please see the documentation at <URL:http://www.apache.org/docs/vhosts/>
# for further details before you try to setup virtual hosts.
# You may use the command line option '-S' to verify your virtual host
# configuration.

#
# If you want to use name-based virtual hosts you need to define at
# least one IP address (and port number) for them.
#
#NameVirtualHost 12.34.56.78:80
#NameVirtualHost 12.34.56.78

#
# VirtualHost example:
# Almost any Apache directive may go into a VirtualHost container.
#
#<VirtualHost ip.address.of.host.some_domain.com>
#    ServerAdmin webmaster@host.some_domain.com
#    DocumentRoot /www/docs/host.some_domain.com
#    ServerName host.some_domain.com
#    ErrorLog logs/host.some_domain.com-error_log
#    CustomLog logs/host.some_domain.com-access_log common
#</VirtualHost>

#<VirtualHost _default_:*>
#</VirtualHost>
```

In this section of the file, you can set up virtual hosts with as many directives as the virtual host might need. A virtual host can be treated a lot like the real host, with an administrator, its own logs, directory settings for its DocumentRoot, and so on.

Web Site Statistics Packages

There are a number of Web site statistics packages available. The applications examine your Web server logs and try to make some sense of them. Some of the packages that might be of interest include the following:

- **Analog**—Analog boasts of being the most popular Web server statistics package in the world. It is freely available at `http://www.statslab.cam.ac.uk/~sret1/analog`. It produces a wide variety of mostly text-based reports, including monthly, weekly, daily, hourly, domain, host, file type, and file size.

- **Wusage**—Wusage is currently a commercial product that was previously available at no cost. It creates graphical reports that include monthly, daily, domain, referring URL, top search keywords, and top user agents. More information is available at `http://www.boutell.com/wusage`.

- **http-analyze**—`http-analyze` is a package that is free for personal use, which is defined as individuals, educational institutions, and nonprofit organizations. However, it has a commercial license for commercial sites. Personal use sites must leave everything about the software intact and receive no support other than what is available online, whereas commercial sites can customize it and are eligible for support. It produces graphical reports, which include yearly, monthly, and most frequently accessed. For more information on this package, see `http://www.netstore.de/Supply/http-analyze`.

- **BrowserCounter**—Although Wusage creates a top user agents report, if you want detailed information on the browsers accessing your site, you might be interested in the Perl script called `BrowserCounter`. It provides a general report and then breaks the browsers down even further by major revision, minor revision, and detailed description. This script is available at `http://www.nihongo.org/snowhare/utilities/browsercounter.html`.

Summary

In today's lesson, you did the following:

- Learned how to install the Netscape Web browser.
- Learned how to install Apache, a Web server, by running a script or by doing it manually.
- Examined highlights of the contents of the configuration file for Apache.
- Learned about some of the available statistics packages for analyzing Web server logs.

Q&A

Q Why is Apache the most popular Web server?

A Well, Apache is free, which means that the price is certainly right. In addition, the source is available, the package works well, and it is regularly maintained.

Q How do I get the machine that I would like to use for hosting the Web site to have a www name?

A Have whoever maintains your name server add an alias that points the www name to the appropriate hostname. When you query the name server for the www name, you'll get output that looks like this:

```
Rosalyn joray 203 > nslookup www.biosci.ohio-state.edu
Server:  ns1.net.ohio-state.edu
Address:  128.146.1.7

Name:    rosalyn.biosci.ohio-state.edu
Address:  140.254.12.151
Aliases:  www.biosci.ohio-state.edu
```

Q I noticed in the configuration file that the default index was `index.html`. However, I have a lot of PC users who are probably making `index.htm` files instead. Is it okay to add `index.htm` to the listing?

A That depends on how close you actually want to stay to the HTML specification. If you want to stay with the specification for the index page, you might want to have your users make a symbolic link in their directories for whatever they want to use as their main page to `index.html`. If you think that is beyond the skills of your users, you might want to consider adding `index.htm` to the `DirectoryIndex` directive.

Q Should I really consider installing a statistics package? I would probably be the only one who would bother to look at the statistics.

A If you have the time and space to install a statistics package, do so. You'll be surprised at the number of users who will use the statistics as feedback on how to organize their Web sites! If you place bandwidth limitations on your users, this is also a way for you to monitor their compliance. Although the results of the statistics could be used to scan for users who are actually conducting questionable activities, I strongly discourage making this a general practice. As you are by now well aware, an ongoing and determined attempt to prevent certain activities can make you legally liable if they should occur. If you should happen to stumble, by virtue of a large increase in consumed bandwidth, across a user using her account to distribute pirated software, by all means, put a stop to it. Do not, however, install and use the statistics packages specifically to scan for this behavior, or you might find yourself a codefendant when the thief is taken to court.

Workshop

Exercise

You and I both know that your system needs Netscape and Apache, so I won't detain you much longer. Get whatever packages you don't already have on your system. Upgrade your Apache if it is an older version, but don't get rid of the old one until you are sure the new one is working. If your have an older Netscape, however, you might want to consider keeping it around as well as installing a new one. Sometimes the old version works better than the new one; it almost always works faster.

17

DAY 18

Multi-OS Connectivity: AppleTalk and Samba

Your machine now has the basic tools it needs for unpacking, building, and compiling downloaded software. Your machine also has the basic tools for sending and receiving mail, browsing the Web, serving Web pages, and serving directories via FTP.

Now, it is time to start to consider other enhancements you might want to add to your system. You might want to consider providing AppleTalk and Samba services, thereby connecting users' Mac or Windows desktops with UNIX machines. Today will be a short day. You will not go into great detail on how to set up either type of service. Your software installation skills are growing, and with all the services that you do have on your machine now, you have all the tools you need to research the details. Even so, you might find a Mac guru and a PC guru helpful as well.

Installing an AppleTalk Server

If you want to support Macintosh file and printer sharing and you plan to install an AppleTalk server, you have essentially two freely available choices: netatalk or Columbia AppleTalk Package (CAP). Netatalk is available at

`http://www.umich.edu/~rsug/netatalk`

CAP is available at

http://www.cs.mu.oz.au/appletalk

Before you start searching for these packages, you might also want to check your vendor's documentation to see if there is an AppleTalk server available. If so, you have an additional choice, and you can decide which among the three, if any, is best for you.

Each freely available package takes a different approach to implementing AppleTalk. Netatalk implements AppleTalk at the kernel level. After you have installed netatalk, the kernel views AppleTalk as just another protocol. Although this might be an interesting and elegant solution, netatalk is not available for all platforms. Be sure to check the FAQ for whether your platform is supported. CAP, on the other hand, runs as an additional server on your machine and can be made to run on a much larger number of platforms.

Whichever package you choose, not only will your Mac users be able to access their directories from their desktops, but you will be able to use the UNIX machine as an AppleTalk router if you need to. If you are not sure whether you need to, check with your Mac guru and whoever set up your Macintosh network.

If you decide to install netatalk, here is an overview of what you will be doing after you unpack the distribution:

- Read the README for your platform.
- If your system is running AFS, Andrew File System, read the README.AFS, for additional instructions on how to build afpd, the daemon that provides Macs with an interface to a UNIX system. AFS was originally developed at Carnegie Mellon University on an andrew.cmu.edu subnet, thereby providing the name for AFS. It is a product similar to NFS and is distributed by Transarc Corporation.
- Set <DESTDIR> in the root makefile. <DESTDIR> is the directory below which binaries will be installed. You might also want to set <MANDIR> for the man pages.
- Run make at the root level of the source directory.
- Run make install, which will install binaries in the directory specified by <DESTDIR>.

- Install the sample configuration files for each daemon in <DESTDIR>/etc. See each daemon's man page for a description of the configuration file and any changes you might need to make.

- If you have a troff or dvi to PostScript filter, you might want to edit <DESTDIR>/etc/etc2ps to use the locally available utilities. The script converts to PostScript anything that psf (PostScript filter) does not recognize.

- Add the contents of services.atalk to /etc/services and update the NIS master's maps.

- Edit your startup script to include <DESTDIR>/etc/rc.atalk, so that netatalk will start at boot time.

- Do whatever the README for your operating system says you should do to install the kernel portions of netatalk.

Unfortunately, the CAP installation requires even more work. Here is some advice to get you started:

- Get the cap60.pl100.tar.Z file as well as all the patch files from 101 on. If you get only cap60.tar.Z, make sure you also get the patches up to 100 as well. CAP is distributed as a base level source installation that's updated once every few years and that has hundreds of updates that each need to be applied to the source. Unpack everything.

- If you think that you will be using the UNIX AppleTalk Router, that package does not come as part of CAP. Get uar.tar.Z via ftp from munnari.oz.au in the mac directory. UNIX AppleTalk Router enables you to use your UNIX machine as an AppleTalk Router. Unless you already have an existing AppleTalk router on your network, you will probably need this package.

- Read README, NOTES, doc/install.ms (also http://www.cs.mu.oz.au/appletalk/manual/install.txt), the online FAQ, the online cookbook installation files, and anything else useful.

- Decide what type of CAP installation you will need: IPTalk, Native EtherTalk/ Kernel AppleTalk, or UAR. Choose IPTalk if you have a majority of Macintoshes on LocalTalk connected to an IPTalk gateway. Use the second if you have a majority of Macintoshes connected via ethernet and you have other EtherTalk gateways. Choose UAR if you have no other gateways, if you need to bridge two EtherTalk networks, or if you want to run CAP with EtherTalk on hosts that don't have native EtherTalk support.

18

- Patch your CAP level distribution in the top level of the `cap60` directory. Specifically, you will run

```
patch -p < cap60.patchNNN
```

where *NNN* is the patch number. To avoid the typing to do this for each of hundreds of patches, the FAQ recommends this in `csh`:

```
foreach i (cap60.patches/cap60.patch*)
patch -p < $i >>& /tmp/patches
end
```

- Follow the instructions from all the CAP resources. The online cookbooks are probably good starting places.

Learning a Little Bit About AppleTalk

AppleTalk is a protocol that Macintoshes use to communicate with each other. AppleTalk can be transported over the basic type of cable that is used to connect Macintoshes and printers. This is LocalTalk. AppleTalk can also be transported over ethernet. This is known as EtherTalk.

A LocalTalk network is a non-extended network. This means that it can only have one network number assigned to it and at most 254 machines attached. An EtherTalk network, on the other hand, is an extended network. This means that network ranges can be assigned. Network numbers are two-byte numbers and can range from 1–65,535. Each network number could have a maximum of 253 machines.

When administrating a network, network numbers are grouped in a zone. When creating a zone, you have to be certain to allow enough numbers for the number of machines on the network to grow. If you don't manage your network with zones, your Macs, which cooperatively network themselves automatically, will pick very widely spaced numbers for themselves. You will be able to manage zones with an AppleTalk router or the UAR software. If you have more than one router on your network, make sure they are configured with the same network ranges, zones, and so on.

The services on each machine open an AppleTalk socket. The address for a machine will be in the form *<network><node><socket>*.

Look at how your network will appear with the two different AppleTalk packages.

Here's a sample of the output from `atlook` on a machine running netatalk. This is by no means the complete output, but it shows some different types of servers and a couple of Macintoshes and printers. The listing contains a column with *<device or service name>:<device or service type>*, and a column with the network address. Software accesses devices and services on the network by looking up the network address based on a device with a particular name and the appropriate service type.

```
                   soyokaze:AFPServer                        23040.5:128
                   soyokaze:netatalk                         23040.5:4
                   soyokaze:Workstation                      23040.5:4
                      HOMER:AFPServer                         23042.80:131
           E159x1@HOMER:Microsoft(Windows NT* Prt 4.00       23041.93:2
Comp Biology Phaser 450:HOMER LaserWriter                    23043.109:128
                    Rosalyn:AFPServer                         23044.249:130
                    ryoohki:AFPServer                         23040.239:248
                    ryoohki:TB2Pro.402 ..M.AIn..cosxtdia.     23040.239:2
                    ryoohki:Timbuktu Host                     23040.239:250
                    ryoohki:ARA - Client-Only                 23040.239:2
                    ryoohki:  Power Macintosh                 23040.239:252
                    ryoohki:Workstation                       23040.239:4
       Comp Biology LW3600:LaserWriter                        23044.233:128
                       CBGA:AFPServer                         23042.174:250
                       CBGA:ARA - Client-Only                 23042.174:2
                       CBGA:  Power Macintosh                 23042.174:252
                       CBGA:Workstation                       23042.174:4
              Rosalyn-le0:UAR                                 23044.250:4
```

A look at the output here shows, along with other information, that soyokaze is running netatalk and rosalyn is running UAR, which means that rosalyn is running CAP instead of netatalk. You see a couple of PowerMacs as well as an NT machine, HOMER, which, like the rest of the machines, is running an AppleShare File Server. You also see two printers.

Take a look at one of the addresses. You see that the entry for ryoohki's AppleShare File Server is 23040.239:248. Assuming the form listed earlier, <network><node><socket>, 23040 is the network number, 239 is the node number, and 248 is the socket number.

> **Note**
>
> Do you notice something odd about the printer called Comp Biology Phaser 450? The other printer you see listed, Comp Biology LW3600, is listed as just being LaserWriter. However, the Phaser is listed as HOMER LaserWriter. HOMER is an NT machine and is providing some AppleTalk services, such as serving printers to the AppleTalk network—a useful utility that NT can provide. The printer Comp Biology Phaser 450, however, is a network-ready printer that serves itself as an AppleTalk/EtherTalk printer. Unfortunately, you don't see the Phaser showing up under its own name because this NT machine seems to be serving the Phaser printer back to the network with a duplicate name, but with a changed device type. This seems to result in printer type HOMER *printer type*.

18

As was mentioned previously, the printer you see here is its own AppleTalk server, and because devices are found by name and type, it doesn't need HOMER's help getting on the network. As a matter of fact, HOMER is confusing the issue because with this setup, there are two devices with LaserWriter as their type that have the same name.

Fortunately, Macintoshes seem to be able to print to this printer so far, even with the confusing network setup. However, that was not the case with the LaserWriter, the other printer listed here. It was also a HOMER LaserWriter for a while and was impossible to print to from some Macs and was almost impossible to print to from other machines. However, from the information that could be obtained from the AppleTalk server software, I was able to diagnose this problem, and the person with the NT machine was eventually able to fix the configuration.

Regardless of whether your users actually use the server for accessing their home directories, you might find AppleTalk server tools to be useful in diagnosing some of your Mac problems.

How does CAP's output look? Here is the output of CAP's `atlook` for the same machines:

```
abInit: [ddp:  90.04, 249] starting
Looking for =:=@goober ...

 26 - CBGA:AFPServer@*                      [Net: 90.2   Node:174 Skt:250]
 29 - HOMER:AFPServer@*                     [Net: 90.2   Node: 80 Skt:131]
 36 - Rosalyn:AFPServer@goober              [Net: 90.4   Node:249 Skt:130]
 42 - ryoohki:AFPServer@*                   [Net: 90.0   Node:239 Skt:248]
 43 - soyokaze:AFPServer@*                  [Net: 90.0   Node:  5 Skt:128]
 64 - Comp Biology Phaser 450:HOMER LaserWriter@goober
```
➥[Net: 90.3   Node:109 Skt:128]

```
 69 - Computational Biology LW3600:LaserWriter@*
```
➥[Net: 90.4   Node:233 Skt:128]

```
 86 - E159x1@HOMER:Microsoft® Windows NT\205 Prt 4.00@*
```
➥[Net: 90.1   Node: 93 Skt: 2]

```
104 - ryoohki:TB2Pro.402 ....M.AIn..cosxtdia..@*
```
➥[Net: 90.0   Node:239 Skt: 2]

```
107 - ryoohki:Timbuktu Host@*              [Net: 90.0   Node:239 Skt:250]
132 - soyokaze:netatalk@*                  [Net: 90.0   Node:  5 Skt:  4]
```

The CAP output definitely looks different. CAP gives you some zone identity with the @goober line. In general, the machines do not take up as many lines as with the netatalk output. You can still see that soyokaze is running netatalk, but you don't see any evidence for what AppleTalk server `rosalyn` is running. Although you don't get much overall feedback on machine type here, you can still see that `HOMER` is an NT machine.

Most noticeably different about the output, however, is the way the network address is written. The entry for `ryoohki`'s AppleShare File Server in CAP shows the address as `[Net: 90.0 Node:239 Skt:248]`. The node number and socket number clearly are the same. What about the network number? Netatalk says that network number is `23040`, but CAP says it is `90.0`. CAP has chosen to express the two-byte number as a decimal instead. If you work out the number that CAP gives you, you get (90*256)+0=23040, which is the same number that netatalk gives you.

If you are interested in learning more about the AppleTalk protocol, check Apple's Technical Information at `http://www.apple.com`.

Installing Samba

If you want your PC users to be able to access their directories from their desktops, you might want to consider installing Samba for them. You can get the latest version of Samba from `http://samba.org`. If you are running Linux, you already have Samba. However, the latest version, 2.0.4 at this writing, includes NT support that the version you already have might not include.

Although Samba will be as overwhelming as AppleTalk, at least there is some friendly documentation available on Samba. There are many Web sites devoted to Samba as well. A couple of sites that you might want to visit include the "Samba Server Step-by-Step Guide," at

`http://www.sfu.ca/~yzhang/linux/samba/`

and "Help on Configuring Samba" (the home page of Benoit Gerrienne) at

`http://www.ping.be/linux-and-samba`

Don't be afraid to get the help you'll need for installing Samba. Two of the Samba team members have even written *SAMS Teach Yourself Samba in 24 Hours*!

Here's a rough idea of what you will be doing after you have unpacked your distribution:

- Read the documentation, especially `UNIX-SMB.txt`, `UNIX_INSTALL.txt`, `UNIX_SECURITY.txt`, and `ENCRYPTION.txt` in `docs/textdocs/`.

- Check the packaging directory to see if anything specific to your platform might already exist. Read any documentation associated with your platform.

- Check `comp.security.ssh` for any comments on the possibility of tunneling Samba connections.

- In the directory source run ./configure. Installation will occur in /usr/local/samba by default, but you can change that if you need to with the appropriate prefix flags attached to configure. In addition to the various directory prefixes, some of the potentially interesting configuration options for Samba are listed in Table 18.1.

TABLE 18.1   Interesting Configuration Options for Samba

Option	Function
--help	Lists all the options
--with-syslog	Enables experimental SYSLOG support
--with-netatalk	Enables experimental netatalk support
--with-quotas	Enables experimental disk-quota support
--with-smbwrapper	Includes SMB wrapper support, which enables the user to navigate a remote SMB share as though it were mounted locally

- Run make.
- Run make install.
- Check sample configuration files in the examples directory. Read the man pages for smb.conf, which are over 120 pages long.
- Consider installing SWAT, Samba Web Administration Tool. Check the man page for instructions on how to do this. SWAT is a Web-based tool that might make configuring smb.conf easier.
- Create the smb.conf file. Put the smb.conf file in the location specified in the makefile.
- Test the smb.conf file you made running testparm.
- Edit /etc/services to include these lines:
  ```
  netbios-ssn        139/tcp
  netbios-ns         137/udp
  ```
- To start smbd, which provides file and print services to SMB clients, and nmbd, which is the NetBIOS name server, add entries to /etc/inetd.conf resembling the following and have inetd re-read its configuration file:
  ```
  netbios-ssn stream tcp nowait root /usr/local/samba/bin/smbd smbd
  netbios-ns dgram udp wait root /usr/local/samba/bin/nmbd nmbd
  ```

  Alternatively, make a startup script like this and add that to the appropriate place in your startup file/directory to start smbd and nmbd as daemons:
  ```
  #!/bin/sh
  /usr/local/samba/bin/smbd -D
  /usr/local/samba/bin/nmbd -D
  ```
- Run more tests to test your setup.

Learning a Little Bit About SMB

SMB, Server Message Block, is a protocol used by PCs to communicate with each other. It is a request-response protocol that can be run over TCP/IP.

NetBIOS, Network Basic Input Output System, provides various services—most notably providing unique names to computers.

SMB is used in conjunction with NetBIOS as a way to allow PCs to share their resources. SMB also includes browsing. That is, servers broadcast their presence and clients develop browse lists based on the server broadcasts. To aid in connecting to a machine outside the subnet, there are browse servers and name servers, with the name servers being either a DNS (Domain Name Server) or a WINS (Windows Internet Name Server) server.

SMB provides two levels of security: share and user. Each shared resource can be password-protected so that a client enters a password to access the entire share. User level protection, however, is based on user access rights assigned to each file.

Microsoft and a group of vendors are working on Internet enhancements to the SMB protocol in an initiative called Common Internet Files System (CIFS).

If you are interested in more details on SMB and CIFS, search Microsoft's site at `http://www.microsoft.com`.

18

Summary

In today's lesson, you saw highlights for installing the following:

- Netatalk or CAP, which are AppleTalk servers
- Samba, a suite that allows Windows users to interact with UNIX from their desktops

Q&A

Q Will I potentially have problems with packet sniffers capturing my users' passwords if I install AppleTalk and Samba?

A Excellent question. I am glad to see that you are thinking about security. Unfortunately, I am not entirely positive.

I have seen some discussion on `comp.security.ssh` on tunneling Samba connections. So you might not have any problems there, other than figuring out exactly how to get it to all work. With the extensive `ssh` experience you have, you probably already have some ideas in mind!

The AppleTalk server software on my network tends to be used more as a way to diagnose problems with the AppleTalk network. However, there is a directory available for use as a drop point for files, if needed. In Samba terms, it could perhaps best be described as a small directory with share-level security.

Workshop

Exercise

Using as many tools as you can think of, investigate whether an AppleTalk server and/or the Samba suite would be useful for your site.

If you find this to be the case, find your Mac or PC guru and install the appropriate package(s). If it is not the case, remember to keep such multi-OS connectivity in mind, should your users ever express the desire to have such connectivity.

DAY 19

Optional Software

Today you will continue your examination of other enhancements you can add to your system by looking at other useful nonservices software. You will install some more useful software, and I will suggest some other optional packages you might want to consider getting for your site.

Installing More Useful Software

To round out your installation of useful utilities, today you will install the following:

- top—Monitors your machine's usage.
- Tcl/Tk—A powerful scripting language and an extension to it that enables you to quickly create graphical user interfaces and attach them to scripts or other programs.
- Expect—Language that enables you to automate interactive applications such as FTP.

Installing top

On Day 4, "A Stroll Through Your System," you got to see some output from top. It is useful as a diagnostic tool for seeing how your machine's resources are being used.

Using Your Investigating Feet

Until now, you have been installing software that you already knew how to find. Now try something you don't know how to find. Being able to find the software you want is as important as deciding what software to get. In this section, I'll walk you through how I'd go about looking for the source for a program that I wanted but did not know where to find.

So far, all the very basic utilities you have installed have been GNU software packages. Maybe top is a GNU package, too. I begin my search with the local GNU mirror site, ftp.cis.ohio-state.edu. As you already know, the GNU software list is immense. Sometimes you end up scrolling past the software you want a few times before you finally notice it. The same happens here: I don't notice top in the listing. Luckily, there are a couple files available in the GNU directory that might help in the search for top: DESCRIPTIONS and ProgramIndex.

So, I get those:

```
ftp> mget DESCRIPTIONS ProgramIndex

mget DESCRIPTIONS? y
200 PORT command successful.
150 Opening BINARY mode data connection for DESCRIPTIONS (84977 bytes).
226 Transfer complete.
84977 bytes received in 0.485 secs (1.7e+02 Kbytes/sec)
mget ProgramIndex? y
200 PORT command successful.
150 Opening BINARY mode data connection for ProgramIndex (29107 bytes).
226 Transfer complete.
29107 bytes received in 0.147 secs (1.9e+02 Kbytes/sec)
```

Now, I can search DESCRIPTIONS and ProgramIndex for top; it can't hide from me that easily—or maybe it can. DESCRIPTIONS definitely doesn't contain what I was looking for:

```
[ray@mother]# grep "top" DESCRIPTIONS
```

```
program runs in to conform with local conventions.  Extended 'getopt'
is built on top of 'libplot'.  Supported devices include X Window System
Many documented Forth libraries are available, e.g. top-down parsing,
GNOME is the GNU GUI desktop project, started by Miguel de Icaza in
```

I decide to try `ProgramIndex` next. That name sounds more promising anyway:

```
[ray@mother]# grep "top" ProgramIndex

autopasswd .......... dejagnu
bdftops ......... ghostscript
gftopk ................. TeX
pfbtops .............. groff
stop-servers ....... metahtml
tftopl ................. TeX
wftopfa ......... ghostscript
```

Oh no! It's not there! It's not a GNU package?!

What to do next? Searching the Web for "top" sounds rather impractical. I would get everything from "Joe's Top 10 To Do List" to "Today's Top News Stories." There must be a better way.

If I had to proceed in this direction, I could run a search on a site that can do a Boolean search, such as AltaVista. This would help me search for the software package and some characteristics that I know about it, such as what it does. If that still doesn't work, I could always ask on an appropriate newsgroup.

Luckily, I have access to another machine that does have `top` installed. I check to see if `top` itself might have any useful information by running `strings`, which attempts to extract any readable textual data from a file:

```
soyokaze bin 203> strings top

qh?en#sdkriI
Copyright (c) 1984, 1992, William LeFebvre
USERNAME
SIbinqus:d:U:
```

This is only the beginning of the output. Unfortunately, no addresses listing where to get a distribution are included, but the author's name, William LeFebvre, makes for a far more distinctive Web search than `top` does.

19

Armed with some useful information, I can now search the Web. Figure 19.1 shows the first page of search results.

FIGURE 19.1

Initial search results on top*'s author.*

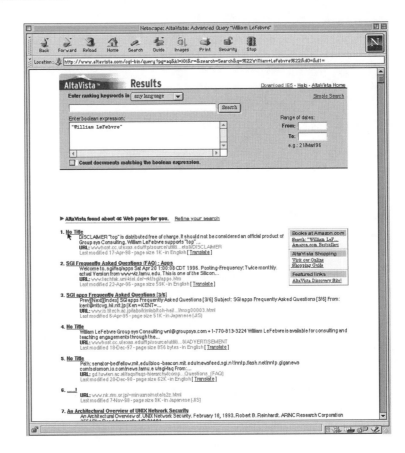

The first item, which has DISCLAIMER included in its description looks like it might be a good start. I click it, and it turns out to be a disclaimer. (Who would have guessed?) If I go up a level, though, I find myself in the following FTP directory, as shown in Figure 19.2.

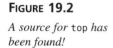

FIGURE 19.2

A source for top *has been found!*

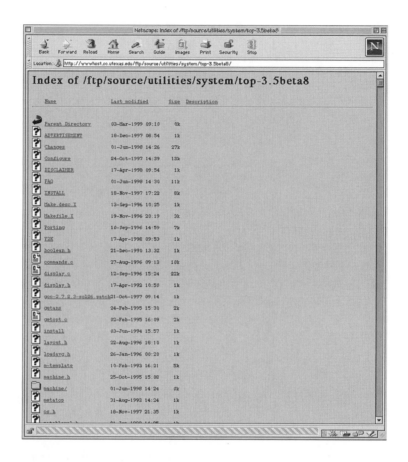

Out of curiosity, I go back to my initial search page to see if there might be anything to indicate whether top has a Web site. To my surprise, in the second half of the list, I find what appears to be a possible candidate: It has information on FTP sources and newsgroups. If you read the FAQ linked to that main page, it is indeed top's Web site, shown in Figure 19.3. Great! I found top.

19

FIGURE 19.3

top's *Web site.*

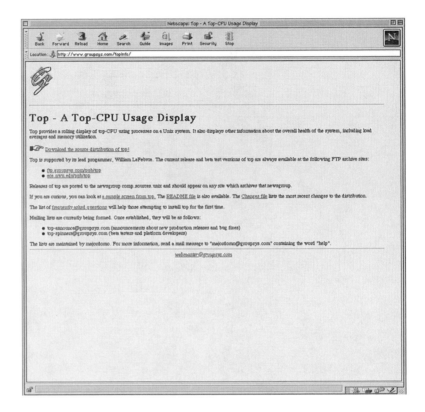

Doing an Installation of top

As usual, after unpacking your distribution, read the README for installation instructions and any hints for your operating system. The README indicates that the procedure should be fairly simple. Expect to run the following:

```
Configure
make
make install
```

You'll find installing top to be a lot like installing Perl, in that top's Configure is interactive.

The README warns that the most common problem with top is that it is very sensitive to a machine's kernel. If you upgrade your operating system and top no longer works, you should recompile top.

Isn't it nice to be back to software that doesn't have a long configuration file or 120+ man pages to describe the configuration file?

Tcl and Tk: Installation Overview

The latest versions of Tcl and Tk are available from `http://www.scriptics.com`.

Binary and source distributions are available for both packages. The README suggests that if a binary version is available for your platform, go ahead and use that. I forgot to look for binary versions, so I will work with source distributions today.

The basic installation procedure is to run the following:

```
./configure
make
make install
make test
```

Table 19.1 outlines the special options available for configuring Tcl/Tk.

TABLE 19.1   Special Configure Options for Tcl/Tk

Option	Function
--enable-gcc	Uses gcc. Do not modify the makefile to use gcc after you have run Configure.
--diable-load	Disallows dynamic loading, even if the system appears to support it.
--enable-share	Builds a shared library if it can figure out how to do so on your platform.

After you have run Configure, check the makefile to be certain that everything will be installed where you want it. The applications and libraries that are installed include the version numbers. Make links without version numbers to the installed items with version numbers.

The README for Tcl warns that you should not run make test as root, or else many tests will fail. Tests that it passes will simply be listed as processed. A failed test will look like the following:

```
acos: DOMAIN error
acos: DOMAIN error
```

Finally, you should install Tcl before Tk. Build both with the same options.

If you want to play with Tcl, you can run tclsh, the application that Tcl installs. You will get a prompt that looks like this:

```
Barracuda source 8 >tclsh
%
```

When you run make test for Tk, remove your .Xdefaults file or delete entries starting with *. The README warns that you might get many errors. However, if the tests don't

19

dump core, everything is probably all right. Don't do anything with your keyboard or display while you are running the tests, unless there is a message on your monitor prompting you for action. At various times, you will have to click a button to complete some of the tests; however, these are the only times you should be interacting with your computer during the testing phase. According to the README, there are also supposedly some special visual tests you can run for Tk in the source's tests directory by running the script visual. However, I couldn't find the script anywhere in the distribution that I got.

To play with your installation of Tk, type wish, the application that Tk installs.

Expect: Installation Overview

Expect can be another interesting application to search for if all you have is an application name. Expect is available at http://expect.nist.gov.

Before you install Expect, make sure you have installed Tcl. If you have installed Tk as well, you will be able to build another package, Expect with Tk.

The basic installation procedure is to unpack the Expect source directory in the same place where the Tcl and Tk source directories have been unpacked. Run this:

```
./configure
make
```

Do some testing, as follows:

```
make install
```

Table 19.2 lists the special configuration options that Expect supports in addition to standard ones.

TABLE 19.2   Special Configuration Options for Expect

Option	Function
--enabled-shared	Compiles a shared library. (Tcl must have been compiled with this option as well).
(--disable-load)	Disallows dynamic loading (option is inherited from the Tcl configuration).
(--enable-gcc)	Enables gcc (option is inherited from the Tcl configuration).
--with-tclconfig=<DIR>	Specifies directory with Tcl's configuration file.
--with-tclinclude=<DIR>	Specifies directory with Tcl's private include files.
--with-tkconfig=<DIR>	Specifies directory with Tk's configuration file.
--with-tkinclude=<DIR>	Specifies directory with Tk's private include files.
--verbose	Causes configure to provide a detailed description of its activities.

If you put your Expect distribution in the same directory as your Tcl and Tk distributions, the only option you really need to worry about is the --enable-shared option. Expect doesn't inherit that option from Tcl's configuration.

The most interesting part of doing this installation is running the testing. Run your tests for Expect and Expect with Tk in the sample directory. If you already have the basic UNIX chess, make sure it's in your path if you want to run the chess.exp test. To run the tests, you will either have to run ../expect <test.exp>, or just <test.exp>, depending on how the test was written. The beer.exp is an interesting test to run multiple times. Just as with a human, its behavior after a few beers varies.

To test Expect with Tk, I ran the tkpasswd test (../expectk tkpasswd). I ran this one through a forwarded X11 connection because I do not yet have a monitor for the machine where Expect is installed. Imagine my amazement when, after a while, I got what you see in Figure 19.4!

Figure 19.4

tkpasswd *test, as seen in eXodus through a forwarded X11 connection.*

If you have problems compiling Expect, it might be because the Tcl/Tk versions have progressed beyond what Expect expects. Check the newsgroups to see if there are any proposed solutions.

Other Useful Optional Software

There are many useful freeware/shareware packages that you might want to consider getting for your machines.

Utilities

More utilities? You can never have too many! The following are some other utilities to consider.

mkisofs

mkisofs can be used to create an ISO 9660 file system of a given directory. This image then provides the content for writing an ISO 9660 CD-ROM with a tool such as cdrecord or whatever your favorite Mac or PC CD-ROM recording software is. mkisofs is available at http://www.andante.org/mkisofs.html. cdrecord is available at http://www.fokus.gmd.de/research/cc/glone/employees/joerg.schilling/private/cdrecord.html.

Emacs

Emacs is a powerful editing package by GNU. Particularly useful is the capability to write macros to automate your editing more. Your users who are programmers will probably find Emacs to be a must. Your users who have Linux at home will want Emacs because that is what they are using at home. Although vi might adequately serve your purposes, Emacs is a package you will likely have to add to the system for your programmer, if not for your users. You can find out more about Emacs at http://www.gnu.org and http://www.emacs.org.

tcsh

tcsh is an enhanced csh. Your users might not care about this one, but you will probably want to get tcsh for yourself. You can readily access previous commands you've issued with the arrow keys. Plus it offers command and filename completion capabilities as you are typing. It is available via anonymous FTP from ftp.astron.com.

less

less is a pager. Unlike more, however, it provides backwards and forwards search capabilities. It can potentially view larger files than vi if your disk space is limited. vi has to make backup copies of a file as it is being edited and therefore uses more disk space, whereas less does not. However, you will probably like it because it gives you the searching capabilities you have in vi without the worry that you might inadvertently change the file. I believe the saying goes something like, "Less is more." less is available at http://www.flash.net/~marknu/less.

Document Preparation

The following are some software packages you might want for your system for preparing documents.

TeX

TeX is a very powerful typesetting language. (No, that's not pronounced as "teks." The "X" stands for the Greek letter "Chi." English speakers pronounce it either as "tek," which is what I most commonly hear, or as "tech," where the "ch" is a softer "k," sort of like "loch.") It takes a while to learn TeX, but any document you create with TeX will look professional. TeX documents have a certain look and feel that you will recognize instantly after you have seen a document made in TeX. TeX outputs to a device-independent file. That file can then be converted to other formats, such as PostScript.

LaTeX

LaTeX is a set of macros for TeX. You must have TeX before you can have LaTeX. (The author of LaTeX has not indicated a preferred pronunciation for this package. You will most commonly hear "laytek" or "lahtek.") LaTeX has layouts for certain types of documents. Some of the journals to which your users submit articles might have LaTeX styles that the submitters must use. For more information on TeX and LaTeX, check the TeX Users Group page at `http://www.tug.org` and the Comprehensive TeX Archive Network at `http://ctan.org`.

Ghostscript

Ghostscript is an interesting package. It comes in two flavors—Aladdin and GNU. The difference between the flavors is the type of public license that comes with each. The Aladdin version does not allow commercial distribution, whereas the GNU one does allow commercial distribution under certain circumstances. It is a package that includes tools for a PostScript and PDF interpreter, and it can be used to display files or print to a non-PostScript printer. Both versions are available at `http://www.cs.wisc.edu/~ghost`. There is also a graphical front end for Ghostscript, Ghostview, available at the same site.

Graphics

There are also many graphics packages available that you might want to consider for your system. This is just a small sampling of what's out there.

GIMP

GIMP is GNU Image Manipulation Program. Yes, that's right: It's a GNU package. Were you beginning to think that all GNU software is useful utilities and programming languages? This one is a fun package. It's a lot like Photoshop for X Windows. You can use it as a paint program or as a photo-retouching program. Like Photoshop, it has many plug-ins available. You can work in layers. Multiple undo/redo times are available. Get the full scoop on this package at `http://www.gimp.org`.

xv

xv is a utility for quickly displaying images. It recognizes a large number of image formats and can generate PostScript files. With it, you can adjust brightness, contrast, gamma, and saturation. Also handy is that it can be used for determining pixel values and (x,y) coordinates for an image. That feature is helpful for creating image maps. Check `http://www.trilon.com/xv` for more information.

ImageMagick

ImageMagick is a collection of tools for displaying and manipulating images. Included in what you can do is combining images, tiling images, displaying images, animating a sequence of images, and converting images. The `convert` tool understands many formats and is very useful for converting an image of an unusual format to a more common format. The `display` tool can display some unusual formats. For more details, visit `http://www.dupont.com/cristy/ImageMagick.html`.

XFIG

XFIG is a drawing tool, similar to Freehand, for X Windows. XFIG is available from `ftp://ftp.x.org/contrib/applications/drawing_tools/xfig`. For links to other XFIG resources, check `http://www.xfig.org`.

POV-Ray

POV-Ray is a package that can be used to create impressive 3D images. Specifically, it is a raytracer. In other words, the method it uses for rendering images involves tracing rays of light. This method generates more photo-realistic images than some other rendering methods. Because computer graphics philosophy is beyond the scope of this book, I will not go into any further detail. More information on POV-Ray can be found at `http://www.povray.org`.

BMRT

Blue Moon Rendering Tools (BMRT) is a collection of RenderMan-compliant rendering tools. These tools provide another way to render 3D images. RenderMan is a language developed by Pixar, the company best known these days for making the films Toy Story and A Bug's Life. For more information on BMRT, check `http://www.bmrt.org`. For more information on RenderMan, check `http://www.pixar.com`.

Summary

In today's lesson, you did the following:

- Learned some strategies for searching for hard-to-search-for items.
- Got an overview on the installation of the following:
    - **top**—A package that monitors your system's activity
    - **Tcl/Tk**—Languages used for developing graphical user interfaces
    - **Expect**—A language used for automating interactive applications

- Got some suggestions for interesting software to consider installing sometime. Suggestions included the following:
    - **Utilities**—`mkisofs`, `emacs`, `tcsh`, and `less`
    - **Document Preparation**—TeX, LaTeX, and Ghostscript
    - **Graphics**—GIMP, `xv`, ImageMagick, XFIG, POV-Ray, and BMRT

Q&A

Q What use would I have for packages like Tcl/Tk?

A To touch just the very tip of the iceberg, you could build graphical machine-monitoring tools for yourself. Tcl/Tk will enable you to build a graphical interface and script control around just about any text-based software you can imagine.

Q Making 3D rendering tools available sounds a bit extreme. Would I really want to consider packages like that?

A That certainly depends on what your users are doing. Remember, these are just suggestions for optional packages. Find out what your users need and like to do. They might wish they had such packages but not know they are out there. Rendering packages might be CPU hogs, but even if they're not useful for your specific mission, if your users enjoy playing with them and aren't interfering with the mission-purposed use of your facility, having them will do more good than harm. Happy users are a good thing.

Workshop

Exercises

1. Tcl/Tk and Expect were pretty easy to install. Visit the Web pages for those sites and find out just what you could do with them. Even if you don't think you'll have a use for them, at least you'll know what to tell your users about them.

2. Visit the Web sites listed for the optional packages in this chapter that you think might be of interest for your site. Get and install whatever might suit your needs.

3. What's listed here is just a drop in the bucket. Starting with sites listed in this lesson, see what else is out there. Some of these sites might eventually lead you to other interesting applications.

4. Find out what your users think they need. It's your job to find some of the generally useful tools. Whether you actually install them at this time or simply learn of their existence, you've at least learned about some applications that could be of general interest. Your users, however, will have a better of idea of what specialized packages they might need for carrying out their work.

DAY 20

How to Be a Good System Administrator

Our three-week whirlwind introduction to system administration is drawing to a close. If you've been following along, you now should have one or more machines up and running. They should be stable, useful, and reasonably secure.

You probably don't yet feel like you're really "in control" of the situation, but don't worry—that will come with time. There is probably not a single person alive who could move from being a normal UNIX user to being a system administrator in the span of three weeks and not feel somewhat overwhelmed by the experience.

To finish out what you need to know, we will spend these final two days going over some things that are rather obvious, but might not come to mind as a new system administrator.

Today is going to be a rather tedious day. You might want to consider taking a break midway through so you can digest the first portion of the information. We will look at some of the things it takes to be a good system administrator, in very general terms. As you have no doubt noticed, both from explicit and implicit statements I've made throughout this book, a reasonably large part of being successful in system administration is your attitude.

Knowledge can make or break you as a system administrator, but so can your attitude. How you apply your knowledge and how you react in situations where you still lack sufficient knowledge can make all the difference between an enjoyable experience and an ongoing nightmare. Today's chapter will give you a taste of habits to get into and things to keep in mind that will help you develop the attitude necessary to be effective and successful as a system administrator.

> **Caution**
>
> **I don't even play a lawyer on TV**   Later in this chapter, I make some comments about legal issues related to how you run your cluster and interact with your users. I am not a lawyer, so do not consider this to be legal advice.
>
> You can consider any statements I make in this chapter regarding legal matters to be the ravings of an addled mind. I would be very surprised if they were even syntactically correct.
>
> Also, I will do my best to make these statements useful to you, regardless of this caveat. These statements are based on my reading of the U.S. Code of Laws and my observation of cases brought against system administrators and users over the years.
>
> My comments are designed to keep your backside out of hot water, rather than to be anything resembling a definitive statement on the law. I obviously can't guarantee that they are sufficient for this purpose, but wherever possible, I've tried to err on the side of caution in presentation. It is possible that in some instances you may be more tightly restricted by the law than what I have portrayed here. However, I have made every effort to write guidelines that are at least as restrictive as the law as I understand it.
>
> That being said, I will caution you that if you have any doubts as to whether something you are doing—or are about to do—is legal for you to do as a system administrator, *go ask a lawyer!*

Get to Know Your Machines

Right now, you probably think of your machines much as you did when you were a normal user, or as you thought of personal computers that you might have encountered. Perhaps you think of them as tools, maybe even slightly confusing tools still, or as "toys" you can use to run fun software. You might be impressed with the complexity and intricacy of the machine and the operating system or pleased with the power that is at your command. In time, you and your UNIX cluster will "bond," and you probably will become much more closely attuned to your UNIX machines than you ever have been to another computer.

If you are like most UNIX administrators, you will in time come to think of your relationship with your machines as though you are the parent and they are your children, or perhaps more as though you are the ruler and they are your subjects. Eventually, you will notice that machines that should be completely identical appear to display distinct "personalities," and if you pay attention, you will be able to tell when your cluster "isn't feeling well." All this probably sounds like so much mumbo-jumbo to you at the moment, but in time you will understand. I did not understand either when I was starting, and I can't truthfully say I am completely attuned to my machines even now. Past my apprenticeship, I have been "master of all I survey" for going on two years now. I find that I finally am beginning to understand how the administrator with whom I apprenticed could walk into the room and instantly know that the Web server was down, or that one of the drives had gone offline. It's all simple, observable physical information, of course, nothing magical, but it's not something you can learn from a book—only by being there and doing things until it all makes sense.

For the time being, suffice it to say that the more you know about your machines, the more in tune you are with their everyday workings, and the better able you will be to keep your machines running smoothly.

Take an Occasional Walk Around

You have a busy schedule and a million-and-one things you need to do or are expected to do. Don't let this keep you from taking the occasional walk through your system directories. Browse around your disks looking for core files. Check the last-modified dates on the files in your mail spool. Look to see what has been left lying around in /tmp, and nose about your anonymous FTP site, if you have one.

Tip

Pitching out the cores Core dumps are both a singularly large nuisance and a real diagnostic benefit. They can eat enormous amounts of your disk space without any real notification to you, which prompts some system administrators to find and delete them in an automatically scheduled cron job. They also are the only way for you (or better yet, your house programmer) to diagnose what went wrong and attempt to fix it.

If you don't have a programmer to dig through the core dump, the automatic pitch routine is probably for you; you probably don't want to learn enough about programming and debugging to effectively use the cores. If you elect to go this route, however, make certain that you get some sort of notification if your auto-delete routine does find and pitch a core. If you don't, you might find that one day you have a broken bit of system software that's dying and dumping core regularly, but that you don't know because it's being cleaned up after automatically. Better to make sure you're notified.

20

> For the same reason, I don't recommend using the shell's capability to prevent core dumps from going to disk—at least not as root. If there's a problem, you want to know about it.

Don't take this suggestion as a license to go digging through your users' files, but as a reason to spend some time getting to know where things are supposed to be. If you take the time to familiarize yourself with where things are, and what sort of "junk" accumulates under normal use, when the inevitably unexpected happens, you'll have something to gauge it against.

Also, this is an opportunity for you to figure out where things are and to ingrain into your memory the pathnames to useful executables and frequently visited directories. Although UNIX still might seem like a huge and confusing place at the moment, you quickly will pick up a real knowledge of where most useful things are, as well as the ability to make reasonably good guesses for those things you don't know.

Pay Attention to Usage Patterns

Get to know the rhythms of your machines. Most of the observable usage statistics follow a regular periodic rhythm. Network traffic ebbs and flows, peaking in the afternoon to early evening and reaching its lowest around dawn. Disk usage likewise rises and falls regularly, though with a somewhat less predictable pattern. CPU usage follows suit.

All these things are indicators to you of the general state of your cluster. If it's the middle of the afternoon and you're not seeing your customary high network load, something's wrong. If your CPU is registering a load of 24 instead of its normal load of .8, something's wrong. If your disks have been oscillating around 75 percent full and suddenly you're getting `Disk Full` kernel messages, something's wrong.

This isn't to say that you won't observe fluctuations in the patterns in the course of everyday life, or that the only time your machines will send up warning flares is when there's an unaccounted-for problem. A drop in network activity could be the result of everybody in your building being invited to a welcoming party for a new department chair, and you'll see `Disk Full` messages much more frequently than you'd like to in the course of everyday life.

You must weigh these factors with everything else you know to determine whether it's time for you to be alarmed, and the only way for you to properly judge their meanings is to know how your machines behave normally.

Learn to Recognize Physical Characteristics

Take the time to sit and listen to your cluster. Learn to take your drive's temperature by feeling the case. Learn to recognize the drive access pattern your drive makes when it's thrashing and the odd quiet that occurs when it's not being accessed at all. Watch the blinking lights on your hub and learn their patterns.

Your hardware displays all sorts of physical characteristics that are clues to how it's performing. With the exception of taste, you can use all your senses as diagnostic tools for your cluster.

Smell

The sense you most want to never have to use for diagnostic purposes is your sense of smell. With the possible exception of "new machine smell" and some printers, you should never be able to smell any of the hardware in your cluster. Pay attention to your sense of smell, nonetheless. Electronic hardware occasionally does have faults, and some of it does occasionally go up in smoke. Before it goes up in smoke, though, it generally spends a very long time being too warm. Also, the plastics used for circuitboards generally aren't particularly happy at elevated temperatures, so they give off some especially noxious odors.

If your equipment smells like it's too hot, chances are it *is* too hot. Hot air doesn't have a smell, so if there's something there to smell, it's something that's coming out of your machine. This usually isn't a good thing. Caught in time, the defective component probably can be replaced, and your hardware should go on to give you its expected service life. Left uncorrected, a component that is running hot eventually will self-destruct—usually with a whimper, but occasionally with a bang. Either way, you're most likely better off repairing or scrapping the hardware before it has a chance to choose which path it will take.

Vision

Although today's machines don't sport nearly the collection of blinking lights that computers from the early days did, you still have a plethora of visual indicators. If you bought smart, you bought a hub with activity, usage, and diagnostic lights. All your hard drives should sport read/write indicators. Many CPU units have diagnostic LEDs as well.

Learn what the patterns are. If you watch your hub usage and diagnostics and learn the patterns, you will see network problems when they occur. You should be able to easily tell when someone in the building is transferring streaming video from a Web site. The pattern of a dump being run should be recognizable, and an operation on a failing NFS mount should be apparent by the fallback pattern it generates.

20

If you are familiar with the normal visual patterns your hub generates, you will be able to quickly discern odd network behavior. A glance at a hub on a shelf takes much less time than running `netstat` or firing up `interman` and can give you an idea of where to look next, if you do have a problem. A machine that indicates abnormally high network use but shows no users and no odd processes with `ps` is a good candidate for having been broken into. A machine with no network activity may have decided to crash.

Your drive's read/write indicators are a good way to observe unbalanced disk use, drives with locked spindles, and yet other out-of-the-ordinary usage patterns.

CPU diagnostic LEDs on the main box can tell you everything from whether the network is functioning to the status of the machine's self-test routines, depending on the hardware and software you use. Software suites are even available that will let you programmatically set the CPU or keyboard LEDs on some systems to produce your own diagnostic readouts.

Hearing

Probably the most useful sense you have for diagnosing your cluster's state of being is your sense of hearing. The human ear is an amazingly sensitive device and can discern patterns the brain cannot describe adequately. Learn to use this asset. Spend a little time on occasion just sitting and listening to your cluster. Listen to the whines and clacks that your drives make and the noise from the fans. On some machines, if you listen closely enough, you can even hear resonances from somewhere on the main board that change with different software usage patterns.

Pay close attention to your normal drive noises. Changes in the pattern can be an early tip-off that something has changed or is wrong with your cluster. Unless you're lucky enough that it never happens to you, learn to recognize the jitterbug performed by the drives that house your swap space just before you hit an `Out of Memory` message.

When you're starting up the system, listen for the clack of the drive heads coming out of locked-down park. As you shut down the system, listen for the difference between the driven and undriven sound of the drive—when the drive is spinning under power versus when the drive motor is momentarily off but the platters are still spinning.

When you lose a drive enclosure, it's likely to be preceded by a period of instability during which the power to the drive motor fails for brief amounts of time, but not long enough to bring down the drive. Your ability to recognize the slight difference between the sound of the platters under power and coasting free can save you the downtime it takes to repair your enclosure.

When a drive's logicboard begins to fail, many drives go through a phase when they work for a while, and after hitting an error, park automatically. Noticing the lack of response from the drive, your system may reset the SCSI bus; on a drive early in the throes of failure, this action may bring the drive back to life. Your ability to recognize that peculiar clack the heads make coming out of park can give you the time to make a full backup before the drive goes completely.

Touch

Touch might not seem like a particularly useful diagnostic tool for electronic hardware, but it still has its uses.

High temperature is an electronics killer, and generally for you to smell it, something has to be very hot. Temperatures that are elevated but not yet "burning up" are still damaging to equipment and still shorten equipment lifetimes. Learn how warm your equipment cases are during normal use. Take the time to go around your cluster and "lay hands on" the hardware at least once a week. A drive enclosure with a failed fan will feel decidedly warmer than you are used to. The drive inside might go on chugging away for months before you notice failures start popping up, and with all the other equipment on, the likelihood that you will audibly notice that the fan has stopped is slim.

Your fingers also have much better positional sensitivity, and sometimes better detection than your hearing. If you detect that a drive is making an odd noise but can't tell which drive out of several in an enclosure, use your fingers. You can feel drive-access patterns that you can't hear, and you easily can tell which drive is active tactilely. Take the time to learn what your drives feel like when they're running smoothly so that you can tell when a drive has picked up an odd vibration or is not spinning at all.

The Big Picture

The lesson you should take home—or to work—from this is basically *the more you know, the better off you are.* Your machines are in many ways like pets or children, and their well-being is your responsibility. A wealth of information about the current state of the machines is available to you, and only some of this is available at the command line or browser window. Much as children or pets usually are incapable of self-diagnosis, your machines are only somewhat aware of their current condition, so you can extract only so much information by talking to the operating system. Paying attention to as many of the other signals your machines give can save you an immense amount of time, as well as make your peers think you have acquired magical powers.

20

Important Things to Remember

The list of things a system administrator has to always remember could fill a book the size of this one. Most of the proselytizing I have done has been an attempt to drive home some of the more important of these points, as well as to encourage a way of thinking that will lead you to develop and remember your own list.

In a final attempt to further my agenda to "bring you up properly," I'll provide a condensed version of what I consider the points most important to keep in mind. Some of these points are for your benefit as a system administrator, some are for the benefit of your users, and some are for the benefit of system administrators as a community. Most items probably indicate a trend toward my particular way of thinking about what makes a good system administrator, but that's what you're here for, right?

Who's in Charge?

Who's the boss—you or the machines? One of the two major errors in attitude you can make is to forget that you are root, and root can do anything. Silly as it may sound, it's important that you develop the confidence to believe in your omnipotence as far as your machines are concerned.

If you don't have confidence in your abilities, you will avoid attempting to fix problems and are likely to end up frustrated and confused when things don't work. If you dread having to meet problems head on, and are essentially afraid of your machines and your responsibility, you will not be effective as a system administrator.

You must develop the attitude that problems are simply opportunities for you to practice your art or annoyances to be brushed aside. When something breaks, you need the confidence to attack the problem as though the machine were in need of discipline.

This anthropomorphizing of your machines, or considering them as children or subjects, may sound like an odd suggestion for the road to success in a technical field. It is an effective way for you to develop the attitude necessary to be successful, however. As root, you do have absolute control over the machines. You quite literally can do anything. When you're just starting out, however, this cold, hard fact does nothing to instill confidence in your ability to use those powers.

A machine that suddenly fails is a mystery, and the thought of trying to determine why, and then make it right can be quite demoralizing. Considering yourself the ruler of your machines, on the other hand, lets you address problems with a different attitude.

In one instance, you are a technician who has experienced a mysterious crash, and you have no useful log entries to diagnose it. In the other case, you are a king faced with a disobedient subject who refuses to talk. It is much easier and much more pleasant to face the reality of needing to take action when you're the king. You hold the subject's life in your hands, and that subject had darned well better obey. If nothing else, it's a confidence builder that you can demonstrate your lordly powers to something, even if that something is a mostly inanimate object.

Eventually, true confidence in your abilities will come. When it does, you can do away with the anthropomorphizing if you like, but why bother? It's the closest you'll probably ever get to being king.

Think About Why You're There

Again, we come back to attitude. The second major way of failing at being a system administrator is to forget *why* you are a system administrator. Too many system administrators forget that their job is essentially a service position. These system administrators may be wonderful machine technicians and do a great job of preventing or fixing problems with their systems. Unfortunately, they universally do an extremely poor job of supporting their users' needs.

Note

The one-man band Obviously, if you're reading this book so that you can administrate your own private cluster for yourself, these comments don't directly apply to you. Keep them in mind, however, as you develop as a system administrator.

There is always a shortage of good system administrators, and the skills you learn at home easily could earn you a good job. An ace up your sleeve at interview time will be your ready understanding of and sensitivity to the needs of the users. Businesses hire as much for compatibility with their existing staff as for knowledge in the field, and it is a rare system administrator who comes to an interview with concern for the user community already on his or her list.

System administrators with this brand of attitude malfunction appear to have forgotten that their primary purpose is to provide an environment that facilitates their users' productivity. They spend money on hardware and software for which their users have no use. They refuse to install hardware or software that their users require to accomplish their jobs, or they disable services that their mission requires. Most of these system administrators run a very tight, neat operation and are quite effective at the technical side of administration. To their users' dismay, however, they seem to develop the attitude that the users are there to appreciate the system administrators for building such a stable system. It completely escapes them that they have built a stable system that doesn't do what the users need, and that they are there to support the users rather than to receive adulation from them.

No matter how tempting it may be, do not fall into this trap. I've seen more than one potentially good system administrator swallowed by the "It's my system, the users will take what I give them and be happy" attitude. On occasion, it's an incredibly appealing

20

way of thinking and an easy path to start to follow. Regardless of how annoying your users might be, how little appreciation they show, or how justified you feel in assuming an attitude of superiority, always remember that your users are your reason for being, and the better you support them, the better you are doing your job.

In light of these comments on the Dark Side, I give you here the top four items on my "respect your users" mantra.

What Is Your Mission?

Know the mission and purpose for your facility. If at all possible, get it in writing. It's imperative that you know why your facility exists so that you can make intelligent decisions. Without a mission statement, it's difficult to justify expenses for hardware and software, and even more difficult to decide which hardware and software you should be considering.

Your mission statement should include both why your facility is there and where it's supposed to be going. Without this statement, your facility will stagnate and is likely to eventually become obsolete.

Always compare purchasing, support, and service plans with what your mission requires. Don't waste money or resources on frivolous hardware or software purchases just because someone asked or because the item is "neat." Invest instead in more of what makes your facility useful.

What Can You Do to Support Your Mission?

Constantly investigate what is current in the field, and look for ways to better the service you provide. Your users will be more than happy to give you suggestions about other hardware or software packages they've heard of or that others in the field are using. Collect their information, but don't act on it blindly. Users generally have very little time to do comparison shopping, so you will end up having to do a bit of legwork to find the best products and the best deals to fit a particular need.

Users also frequently don't keep up with advances in software, so you need to do this for them. If you support a particular software package, keep up with development efforts for it and for its competitors. If you see a distinct reason to upgrade, collect the information and propose it to your users.

Finally, in noncomputational fields that just happen to use computers, you will find that your users frequently don't even know what the machines can really do for them. If you are charged with supporting a facility to run Web services for your organization, your users probably have no idea what is possible with the Web. They may be aware that they could provide database searching via the Web, for example, and they may have even suggested a software package they liked. Chances are, however, they don't know anything about Web databases or the software they've recommended, other than that they like the interface. You need to recognize their need for database services and educate them about the possibilities. You also need to provide some sort of database for their use.

For entirely political reasons, you probably want to start your investigation with the software your users recommend. It may be wonderful database software, or it may be so inefficient that it will drag your machines to their knees. Your users are unlikely to know or even to want to know these sorts of details. It's your job as system administrator to make intelligent decisions for your users or provide them with the information necessary to make the decisions themselves.

Note

> **Micromanagement**   In an ideal world, you would be granted the authority to actually do your job properly—for example, your noncomputational users would ask you, the computational expert, to research and pick the ideal database to suit their needs. Unfortunately, most of us do not live in ideal worlds. You probably will end up having to deal with situations where your users have specified that a product be used that simply will not provide the services they want. In these cases, you have no real option but to provide the software on which they insist (unless you have a truly compelling reason not to, such as a severe security concern), and allow them to come to the realization on their own that it's not working.
>
> It's of little use to anybody for you to become upset about this situation, regardless of how irritating it may be to watch the wrong decisions being made. All that becoming upset does is raise your blood pressure and alienate your users. In time, your users will come back and ask why they can't do what they wanted to do, and you can reiterate your suggestion then.

In short, part of your responsibility as a system administrator is attempting to decipher what your users need based on what they believe they want, and to recognize when those needs would be well served by some new or different way of doing things.

What Can You Do to Extend Your Utility?

Just as your users frequently will not recognize the best way to solve a particular problem, they also frequently will not notice ways in which the facility's functionality can be extended.

If you have the time, attend a computational trade show such as Comdex and spend some time just walking the vendors' floors. You will be amazed at the number of different peripherals you will see interfaced to machines like yours, and the number of uses to which people put these machines. Your user community almost certainly could make good use of any number of these capabilities, but your users aren't very likely to be aware that most of these possibilities even exist.

Recognizing where you can leverage your existing hardware so that you can inexpensively add a completely new function to your facility is also an important system administrator skill.

Keep an eye on what your users do with your facility and what jobs they take elsewhere. Look for ways you can increase the utility of your facility so that your users can keep more of their work in-house and be more productive. As the system administrator, you need to not only be the expert on the current state of your hardware, but on all the options and possibilities for extending and improving on that state.

What Limitations Must You Apply?

In spite of the fact that you're essentially a service provider, you will need to tell your users "no" at times. Even an ideal world needs to have an organizing force and some form of central decision making. The real world in which we all live needs to have not only centralized decision making, but a voice of sanity as well.

Your services, if you are like most system administrators, do not appear to cost anything to the users. Unlike the maintenance shop personnel who bill users for replacement parts, or outside contractors who charge for their time, your time is "free" as far as your users are concerned. They also have no concept of the effort or time required to accomplish any particular task, so they tend to think of everything you do as simply magically happening instantaneously. These misperceptions will combine and conspire to create an impossible workload for you, unless you set some boundaries.

Without boundaries, you eventually will be deluged under requests for various software and services. Unless you set limits on the time and resources you will invest, you eventually will diminish your actual utility to your users as a whole by dividing yourself too thinly among too many frivolous projects. When deciding to take on a new project or to install a new piece of software, you need to weigh the utility to your user community as a whole against the resources it will take to support the new feature. All users believe that their own immediate request should be the most important item on your list of things to do. You need to weigh the actual value of each request against the cost to all the other things you need to do. Don't let your users drown you in a workload that is impossible to maintain; set understandable limits and stick to them.

You also will have to function as the watchdog for security concerns for your facility. Your users don't think about security and don't want to know about security. If they have a piece of software they want to run, they expect that you'll install it for them. At some point, you will need to evaluate the security implications and make a decision as to whether the software is allowable.

For most software, this won't be a problem, because most applications run as the user and have only the user's permissions. Software that provides network services is a different story, however. If your users decide that they want to provide some new network service, you will have to very closely examine the potential for security problems. If the potential exists, it will be exploited. Your users may be willing to take this risk, but are you?

If you run into a situation of this sort, you need to weigh the importance of the security of your cluster against the value of the service the users want to provide. If you've been hired to administrate the cluster that is specifically intended to support this new service, telling your users "No, you can't do that" is probably not a good idea. If it's just a casual interest in trying out a new way of providing data, then telling them "no" might be the smartest thing to do. In either case, you should spend some time examining whether there is a better way to do what the users want, or some way to provide for the need without compromising your machines. Users frequently won't have examined the range of possibilities, and you may be able to steer them onto a better track by providing helpful suggestions.

Note

Your users will think nothing of asking you to set up an insecure service and then asking you to sit there and baby-sit it to maintain its security. In this case, you have two reasons to say "no": the unreasonable security risk and the unreasonable workload. Be aware that users don't take well to being told "no," however. I've actually had users call for my head on a platter because I refused to bring a just-compromised machine right back online without spending the time to make it secure.

Because of conflicts such as this, it's important for you to have a good relationship with and the support of your supervisor. Even if your supervisor is not directly involved with system administration, you need to keep him or her "in the loop." A large portion of a supervisor's job is to act as an interface and to handle political situations for workers so that they can do their jobs effectively. Make sure that your supervisor knows what you're doing and what your limits are. Your supervisor is the person who should be stepping up to defend you and your decisions when irate users take exception to the fact that you doing your job properly prevents them from having their way. That's your supervisor's job, and you need to give your supervisor sufficient information so that he or she can do it properly.

20

Keep the Users You Have, Attract the Ones You Don't

Your users depend on you to keep the system running and provide the services they need. Frequently, however, you will find that a large segment of your user population is not aware of all the services you provide. Many potential users may not even know that your facility exists.

The facility I administrate started its life as a computational graphics and molecular modeling facility brainchild of one particular faculty member. This faculty member wasn't really a UNIX person, but he knew that he needed the power of workstation-class machines to do what he wanted, and he lobbied the college for funding to put in a centralized, high-powered computing environment.

After that initial investment and the hiring of the first system administrator, the facility languished largely in obscurity for several years. The faculty member who secured the funding retired, and the new faculty members who took over the computer facility were not particularly inclined to advertise its presence to the rest of the college, even though the college had provided the money.

It eventually came to pass that the facility was almost disbanded because, in a college with more than 100 faculty members and thousands of students, roughly two dozen people actually knew the machines existed. This in spite of the fact that every last person walked past the unmarked door to the machine room every day on their way into the building. The college was not particularly interested in continued funding for a facility that served so few people, and several faculty members had gone out and purchased their own UNIX machines to run exactly the same software the college already was providing for free.

All this is in the past now, but only as a result of an ongoing user-education program. We now distribute "About the Facility" brochures to incoming students, we hold periodic usergroup meetings, and we even got permission to put a sign on the door. Usage is booming, and the faculty and students who didn't know the facility existed are quite pleased at the power that appeared at their fingertips.

The moral of this story is that I have intimate knowledge of what I'm talking about when I say that you have a large potential user base that doesn't even know you exist. Your users are your justification for being there. More users equal more justification.

Do you really want more users? Of course you do! Without users, you'd have no reason to be a system administrator, so the more users you have, the more reason you have for being. More users also make supporting purchasing and upgrading decisions easier and aid considerably when you're lobbying for more funding.

You would not be wasting your time to create quality fliers advertising your facility and the services it provides. A hanging variety posted on announcement boards and a trifold brochure stuffed in mail or left in literature bins might be appropriate.

You also should consider printing facility business cards with quick-reference email addresses for computing emergencies (pointing to an email address that is forwarded automatically to your entire staff, of course) and any other email and phone contact information you feel is appropriate.

Holding monthly usergroup meetings with varied topics is also a good idea. Offer regularly scheduled "Know Your Facility" open-house meetings, as well as meetings dedicated to specific programs or topics your users might want to discuss. It's not out of line to have your facility pay for the pizza and soda, either. This is a small price to pay for the goodwill you will generate at these meetings.

The more your users think that you're providing a valuable service, the easier your life will be, and the more support—both monetary and in vocal and moral varieties—you will get. The more users you have, the more will be around to give that support. Take every opportunity to grow your user base with any potential users you find.

Random Stuff You Mustn't Forget

As with most things in life, you need to remember certain things about system administration. Here are a few of them:

- **Make backups**—The more regular your backup schedule, the better. Whether you do backups as a daily or weekly thing will have to be a decision you make for yourself. Weigh the importance of having access to yesterday's files instead of files from a week ago against the time you would need to spend to do daily backups. For some people, the cost of not having backups is too high, and they opt for daily backups. Smaller operations with only one or two system administrators, however, might need to forego daily backups simply because there aren't enough hours in the day to do them. Don't neglect to make your backups regularly. A regular backup schedule also makes it much easier to figure out what's on tape 17 when you forget to label it.

- **Keep an on-paper database**—Keep records of your backups on paper. There is the online dumplog entry, if you choose to make it, and the /etc/dumpdates entry to keep track of what you have dumped and when. If the system isn't working, however, you won't be able to access this information, and spinning through multiple tapes looking for where you put a particular file can be very tedious.

- **Disperse backup copies off site**—Keep your backups far away from the machine they backed up. If a fire or another disaster occurs, you don't want to lose the tapes as well as the machine you left them sitting next to. If your organization's policy allows, you may simply be able to send your backup tapes home with one of your trustworthy administration staff members.

- **Make copies of configuration files**—Back up things before you change them. Simply making a copy of a configuration file with a .back suffix will frequently

20

save you hours of wasted time. Few things are more annoying than spending hours fighting to update the configuration on a properly working server, eventually giving up, and then finding that you have no idea how to get the configuration file back to its previously working condition.

- **Keep written records**—Written records of changes you make, where you've installed things, and any customization you have made to the system are an absolute must. Your memory may be fantastic, but three years down the road when you are trying to update a program, chances are you aren't going to remember every one of the configuration options you used for the first installation. Print out listings of anything you do that doesn't follow the defaults. Print out listings of most things that do follow the defaults.

- **Comment changes and settings in files**—When you make a change in a configuration file, put a comment in the file. Include the date of the change and an identifier— usually your initials or username. Also log the change and your reasons for it in your written record. This way, when people need to know why something was changed or to find everywhere changes were made, they can simply use a `grep` command instead of going through a lot of manual checking and digging through notes.

- **Post-it notes are your friend**—Keep a pad of Post-its handy wherever you are. The uses for Post-its are simply innumerable.

- **Check your logs**—Check your logs, check your logs, check your logs. This should have a little tune written to go with it, and you should be humming it all the time. You can't rely completely on your logs for all information about your machines, but your logs are your "Headline News" telling you the major happenings as they happen. You can waste a significant amount of time chasing problems without checking your logs when a simple look in the log files would have led to a simple solution.

- **Use `alias rm rm -i`**—Nothing is more depressing than to discover you've just deleted your entire file system accidentally.

- **Use `fsck` frequently**—Only accidentally deleting your entire file system yourself is more depressing than allowing it to self-destruct by not occasionally checking for consistency.

- **Check the password file regularly**—Make certain that locked accounts remain in their properly locked state, and that no accounts have mysteriously changed their numeric user ID. Be especially watchful of `userid 0` for root.

You also need to keep a number of other things in mind (yes, your mind will become a virtual file-o-facts). Remember, for example, that unless your machine has hot swappable bays, you always should turn off the system and drive before adding or removing a device. You can zap delicate electronics by unplugging a SCSI cable while any device along the cable still is powered up. You might not even immediately notice that you've zapped it, because you might only suffer increased SCSI errors and crashes. No matter how well you think you believe in this rule, there will come a time when you're rushing to move things around, and you think to yourself, "just this once." Don't do it!

A few more things you shouldn't forget:

- If you make a configuration change and you're not certain what effect it will have on the system, consider rebooting the machine at the time of the change to see whether there are any noticeable side effects. It's easier to figure out that you broke something now than to try to remember what changes you made over the last three months.

- Randomly test your backup tapes to be certain there really is data on them. You never know when you'll meet a defective tape or when your tape drive might die. Considering the regularity with which most system administrators actually use their tapes, you could go for six months before finding out that your tape drive has died if you don't check regularly.

- When you are doing your random tests, remember that `mt erase` is not the same as `mt rewind`. (OK, this one goes up there with `rm -rf *` for depressing.)

- When you are having a lot of trouble compiling a program, turn the problem over to your programmer. You have better things to do, and it irritates your programmer to see you fiddling with code just as much as it irritates you to see your marketing person fiddling with online policy.

- When you've successfully compiled a program, but it doesn't seem to work right, check the newsgroups to see whether the problem has been discussed before you spend a lot of time on it. Don't spend time reinventing the wheel.

- Check your supplies regularly. It's not a very system administrator–like task, but when you don't have toner and can't print the man page you need to reference, you'll wish you had done the menial labor anyway.

- Know what file systems are mounted where. Keep a map of your cluster. It's amazing how quickly you can forget and how difficult it is to figure out the complete arrangement of a large group of machines. Of course, this does argue for simplicity in file-sharing design, but who can maintain simplicity?

- Make sure the `unmount` command you have issued really does take before you remove that entire file system. If you don't, learn to press that Ctrl+C key combination really quickly when you hear a protracted grinding coming from the wrong drive.

20

- Always su to root. Never log in directly as root. Accountability is good. As a matter of fact, if you can disable root logins entirely (except in single-user mode), you're probably smart to do it.

- Make users who want to have their passwords reset come in with ID before you complete the request. Not only does this precaution remove the possibility that someone might hijack another user's account, but it convinces people to pay close attention to their password the next time.

- Disable services you don't need. Services you don't need are just problems waiting to happen.

- Attend security group meetings, if there are any. If there aren't, consider making that one of your facility user topics. If you advertise, you're almost certain to get many people who wanted a group but didn't know what to do.

- Learn to use the find command effectively. It can save you a lot of manual digging time. The find command can be cryptic and difficult to figure out initially, but force yourself to use it until it becomes second nature. It's a highly useful command.

- Take the time to keep up on computer matters in general. You're only as good as what you know, and keeping on top of current events in the wide world of the Internet is an important part of being able to do your job well. Over time, you will get much more of your useful information from the online community than you ever will from printed reference manuals or program man pages.

Caution

> **Abrupt Turn Ahead!** Up to this point in the chapter, I've been discussing general good habits and good mindset issues for root—practical day-to-day good behavior stuff. Now, I'll take a sharp turn to a completely philosophical discussion of the ethical and legal considerations root must take into account. Both these widely divergent areas will be important to you as root, and both revolve around how you, as root, must behave to be a good system administrator. These topics may be a bit difficult to digest in a single sitting, however. You might want to take a break here, and let the first portion of this chapter sink in a bit before tackling the rest—I don't want you to forget the contents of either of these important sections because of information overload.

Ethics

No proper introduction to system administration could be complete without a discussion of ethics. The situational ethics in your particular environment may be slightly different from those discussed here, but the concepts are similar, and this should make a good starting place.

Basically, you must consider what is *appropriate* behavior as compared to what is *possible* behavior. As root, you have been given the power and capability, and probably even the authority, to do just about anything you can think of to the system. This means that you also wield an incredible amount of power over your users.

The fact that you have this power does not mean that you always should feel free to use this power, however. There are intangible limitations on the use of root powers and invisible lines across which use becomes abuse. Sometimes, these limitations and lines fall in obvious places, and in other instances they may be difficult to predict. In either case, crossing the boundary and acting outside "good taste" as a system administrator can have serious repercussions, both politically and legally. It therefore is important for you to think seriously about the appropriate use and limitation of root's powers before a potentially volatile situation arises.

The Godlike Powers of Root

Obviously, as root, you are in complete control of the machine. Regardless of whether your job description actually specifies that you have complete command, when you are at the keyboard, what you type is the law of the land.

As overused as the quotation "Power corrupts, and absolute power corrupts absolutely" may be, it is still a valid caution. When you are root, you have absolute power, and it is important that you be aware of the potentially corrupting influence of that power.

You might think of being root in much the same way you should think of owning a deadly weapon. Just as owning a deadly weapon gives you a terrible power, so does being root. Owning a deadly weapon thrusts upon you the enormous burden of responsibility in use, of just and appropriate application only in the preservation of life and limb, and the need to prevent that weapon from falling into the wrong hands. Being root requires you to assume the responsibility for the unbiased and even application of root's powers for the good of your user community, as well as the prevention of unauthorized use of that power.

Some may argue that this comparison is invalid because it would be almost impossible to actually take a life with the power of root. However, the inappropriate use of root power could drastically affect people's lives, destroy their families, or ruin them professionally (I'll explain how later in this chapter), so I don't think these comparisons are as disparate as they may appear.

Being root really does place on you an immense burden to use root's power responsibly. When you become root on a machine, you enter into a small fraternity of administrators who, at least for the moment, are assumed to be absolutely trustworthy, absolutely incorruptible, and absolutely selfless in their application of power. Please do your best not to violate the trust and faith of this fraternity. The knowledge that when you contact the root

20

operator at a site you are speaking with someone with the same level of responsibility and trustworthiness as yourself is one of the few things that keeps the Internet from descending into complete disarray.

Root, the Enlightened Dictator

As has been mentioned, as root, you are in absolute control. It is incumbent upon you, in your capacity as root, to use your power wisely and fairly. Thankfully, it is fairly well agreed upon that the most efficient form of government that poses the least burden on its subjects is that of enlightened dictatorship. As root, you certainly have all the powers of a dictator. It only remains for you to behave as magnanimously as possible in furthering the work and goals of your subjects/users.

Of course, you should keep in mind that in your particular form of dictatorship, you probably actually answer to a higher power (your boss). Outside of mandates that come down to you from this higher power, however, you need to keep in mind that the highest goal toward which you can use your root power is in the furthering of your users' needs.

If You're Going to Be Root, Be a Good Root

As enlightened dictator of your computer cluster, one of the personal acts of hubris against which you must constantly guard is government for the sake of government. It seems that some people find it very tempting to legislate other's behavior for no reason other than that they can.

Do not fall into this trap as root. You run your cluster for the good of your users. Do not impose unnecessary restrictions on your users, and fight for the removal of restrictions that others have imposed. As long as your facility supports the mission that it is chartered to support, there is no reason users should not be allowed to use the facility for other tasks. Of course, you should never allow nonmission computing uses to interfere with the mission-directed computing uses of your cluster, but if there are uses that do not interfere, there is no reason you should prohibit them.

Here's an example from the earlier days of the facility I administrate. We initially had a no-printing policy. The people who took over the facility from its originator believed that if users were given the capability to print, they'd spend all the facility's resources writing term papers. Therefore, a printer was not purchased for the facility, and anything more powerful than vi was banned from the system for text editing.

The fact of the matter, of course, is that the workstations are so completely overpowered for word processing that even if dozens of users were running TeX or FrameMaker simultaneously, it wouldn't affect the molecular modeling calculations in the slightest. The lack of a printer also made system administration tasks much more difficult than they needed to be, and it made producing output for both term and research papers almost impossible.

Eventually a printer was purchased when one of the powers-that-be discovered that he wanted to print pages from the World Wide Web. The rest of the users got to print when the system administrator at the time "forgot" how to limit printing to only a privileged few. Now we have several printers, including one for output to slides, one for black-and-white PostScript, and one for photo-quality color prints. We're considering a wide-format printer for posters as well. None of this affects the utility of the facility for its main purpose (molecular modeling), but it makes the facility much more useful for other purposes as well.

You already may have similar silly restrictions in place that really could be removed. It might be something like a prohibition against using the system for personal email, or against browsing the Web (perhaps specifically the Dilbert Web page—several companies supposedly ban that one).

In any case, examine whether the restrictions actually contribute to furthering the computing mission or only to annoying and inconveniencing the users. If the only point of the restriction is to limit the user, chances are it's a bad restriction. Removing it probably will make your users happier, and they'll enjoy using the machines more. Happy users are more productive.

The moral of the story? Rules and regulations for the sake of having rules and regulations is a bad idea. Don't do it.

It's Good to Be Root

With the powers of root come certain privileges. Again, as root, you have the capability to do just about anything. Outside the bounds of what you need to do to support your users' computing goals, you can do whatever pleases you:

- You can create, delete, read, or modify any file or parameter on the system.
- If you want more disk space, you can rearrange or delete things until you have enough disk space.
- If you want to know what's in a file, there's nothing stopping you from accessing it.
- If providing a new sort of Web service amuses you, all you need to do is install the software.
- If you feel like granting certain users the capability to control certain system functions, it's just keystrokes away.
- If archiving recipes for home-brewed beer turns you on, you have the entire resources of your cluster at your disposal to scour the net and collect recipes.
- The list goes on. For root, if it can be done, you can do it.

Of course, just because you have the capability to do all these things doesn't mean your organization would be particularly supportive of some of these uses of its resources. On the other hand, you really should lobby for and support a policy that allows any

20

nonmission computing use, as long as it does not interfere with any of your mission computing uses.

It's Lonely at the Top

With the job of root comes a certain amount of isolation. This is an unfortunate but necessary side effect of the responsibility you have. With the exception of other system administrators with whom you work, there is no one with whom you can really share your responsibilities. None of your users is more informed or more able to make the hard decisions than you. You're the top dog, the head honcho, the big cheese. Users expect you to have all the answers, all the time, and to always be right. They also will challenge almost any decision you make. Unless you handle them very gently, they will attempt to fillet you alive if they catch you in an error.

Who do you turn to for help and support? You turn to your administrator peers. If you don't have a system support staff to turn to, you turn to the body of administrators on the net. Many Web pages, newsgroups, and IRC chats are devoted to system administration. I list some general system administrator help and support pages in Appendix E, "Useful Resources," but I also will mention the two most appealing pages here.

First, there is the Usenet newsgroup `alt.sysadmin.recovery`. As the title suggests, this newsgroup is sort of the system administrator version of the corner bar, where sysadmins go to unwind after work. You'll see everything from tirades against idiot *lusers* (the `alt.sysadmin.recovery` spelling for what usually is pronounced "users"—the "l" is silent) to system administrators nearly in tears because of problems. These are good (well, mostly, anyway) people in tough jobs. If you have a problem and nowhere to turn, take it to `alt.sysadmin.recovery`—they'll help, lend a shoulder, or teach you to laugh about it. There's also a chance that they'll mock you until you're more upset about that than your original problem, but that doesn't happen too frequently to people who aren't in desperate need of it in the first place. (In a self-referential attempt at the explanation of a term you will meet on ASR, a *LART* is a thing that you will have applied to you if you ask what it is. At least according to some, it stands for *Luser Attitude Readjustment Tool.*)

The other resource I will mention specifically is a Web page devoted to the escapades of a system administrator named Simon. Simon is the *BOFH*. That's the *Benign Operator from Heaven,* only it's not really "Benign" or "Heaven". Simon is the system administrator we all occasionally wish we could be. His job is keeping his system running smoothly; he knows his job, and he does his job. With no ifs, no ands, no buts, and no mercy. I don't recommend that you actually take after most of the leads that Simon sets, though on occasion they'd be good practice for us all. I do recommend reading about Simon as a great way to reduce tension and to vicariously take out some of the frustrations you might be feeling if you are having problems with your equipment, your users, or your boss. Currently, `http://www.networkweek.com/bofh/story/topStory` points to the BOFH page, but it has moved around occasionally. There has been a link to it from the top Network Week site for several years now, so if this one doesn't work, try starting there. Be sure to navigate your way to the 1995 archives and start at the beginning, because Simon's personality develops over the first few episodes.

The Pantheon of Roots

Never make the mistake of thinking that you and your machines live in a vacuum. If you are connected to the Internet, you and your machines are part of a sort of worldwide microorganism. Each of the clusters attached to the Internet is capable of functioning independently as an isolated set of machines, but because of the benefits worldwide connectivity confers, they are all linked. This setup requires an extreme amount of trust in the administrators of the machines, and an extreme amount of responsibility on the parts of those administrators.

There are two main avenues for errors in judgement when dealing with the Internet community as a whole. The primary one is allowing an untrustworthy user trusted access. Do not, I repeat, *do not ever* allow a user in whom you lack complete and total trust access to any form of root capability. This is simply not acceptable practice. By giving a user access to any sort of root powers, you allow that user to affect not only your machines but the entire Internet community. You cannot allow this. It is a serious breach of your integrity as a system administrator and a serious breach of the trust given to you by the system administrators around the world.

Occasionally, you might be pressured to allow some form of privileged access to some users, with the expectation that they're unlikely to cause any harm. That is not acceptable. Say "NO." You have a responsibility above and beyond that to your users to protect the rest of the Internet community from bad decisions made by your users. The power to affect that community cannot be given out on a whim, and giving that power to a user in whom you do not have complete trust betrays the trust you have been given. There is simply no acceptable reason for users who aren't completely trustworthy system administrators to have any form of root access. If they have machines that "need" access to protected (for example, NFS) services on your machines, then they can have you administrate their machines. If they don't want your staff to administrate their machines, how can you possibly think of giving them administrative access to yours?

20

> **Note**
>
> If you follow this policy, it only stands to reason that if you give users root privileges, you consider them to be completely trustworthy. I mention this because I have noticed a tendency for some facilities to have the oddest restrictions on the actions of their system administrators. These facilities place all the responsibility for the consequences of decisions and all the power to implement those decisions on the system administrator, yet they place the authority to make the decisions in the hands of others. This type of setup seems to me to be completely bizarre, and it definitely causes the administrators in these situations great stress.

The second largest error in judgement when dealing with the Internet community is assuming that because you can, you should. This doesn't apply to your use of the local machines and resources, and it certainly doesn't apply to the Internet. You may be ruler of all you survey, but the Internet is a very big place, and there are thousands of rulers just like you all around the world. Each expects a certain amount of civility and requires a certain amount of trust from you.

The Internet functions largely as a giant anarchy, and it is a fascinating demonstration that in certain environments, anarchy is a wonderful thing. Each cluster attached to the Internet has its own priorities, its own goals, and its own agenda. Each cluster cooperates in forming the larger functional collective known as the Internet. In this collective, many of the witty quotes you've undoubtedly heard can be applied quite aptly. "Don't Tread on Me," "All for One, and One for All," and "Speak Softly and Carry a Big Stick" all are quite appropriate. Most clusters don't concern themselves with the affairs of other clusters unless some other cluster becomes a bother. Most clusters band together in times of need to solve collective problems, and most clusters usually are mild-mannered and civilized but have quite large teeth when necessary.

As an example of the sort of thing you shouldn't do even though you can, you shouldn't allow or support *spamming*. Spamming is the practice of sending out a multitude of unsolicited email messages—the electronic equivalent of junk mail. The name comes from a British comedy sketch in which an individual whirls around in circles with a can of Spam (the brand name for a particular potted meat product) flinging its contents indiscriminately at bystanders. Email spam has much the same effect—it annoys the bystanders and usually gets the point of origin trounced.

A Wonderful Day in History

As an illustration of the spam and inverse spam phenomenon, I give you one of the last truly fine examples of the Internet reacting as a single huge beast, terrible in its power and splendor.

Prior to the full commercialization of the Internet, the net was a kinder, gentler place. There were no fly-by-night ISPs, no dialed-in loonies, and no mega-ISPs pandering to the lowest common denominator. The net was populated by government sites, educational sites, the occasional business (providing services, not sales), and the occasional nonprofit organization. Usenet newsgroup discussions were on topic, and the signal-to-noise ratio was very high. There was an unwritten agreement that people would adhere to basic "golden rule" courtesy. "Do unto others as you would have them do unto you" was the law of the land. People who broke the unwritten rules were reprimanded, not by any organized force, but by "concerned citizens of the net," and largely the Internet was an idyllic place. Work was done, information was exchanged, friendships were made, the occasional flame war broke out, and mostly people just got along. On the rare occasions when it had to be pointed out that a person's postings to a newsgroup weren't appropriate, people were strict but courteous and fair. "Newbies" learned the ropes quickly and took to the unwritten "do unto others" rule with ease and a certain sense of pride in the responsibility they were allowed.

Then everything changed. The Internet went commercial. Businesses run by people with no interest other than in capitalizing on the success of the Internet—even if it meant the destruction of a good thing—appeared overnight.

In the early days of this tragic happening, one such business made a mistake that has not to my knowledge been repeated. An unrepentant commercial spammer appeared. This was unheard of, because it had previously been illegal to use the Internet for commercial applications. Occasionally someone would send a commercial message, be reprimanded, apologize, and everyone was happy. This time things were different.

The spammer was contacted and informed that it costs people money to download their spam and that this was not appreciated. (Remember, this was in the days of dollar-a-minute dial-in connections with 2400 and 9600 baud modems.) The spammer was asked to please stop. The spammer, a small business that had purchased an account at a fledgling ISP and had sent thousands of messages to hundreds of completely unrelated newsgroups and mailing lists, said "no." Not only did it say "no," but it had the unmitigated gall to send the same spam again, and again, and again to the thousands of places it didn't belong. The spammer said, "We paid for our access, we'll do anything with it that we damned well please."

The spammer's ISP was contacted and informed that not only was this sort of thing against *netiquette* (that's *net etiquette),* but that in some parts of the Usenet newsgroup hierarchy these messages were illegal, and they were obligating other people to pay for their illegal messages to boot. "Please explain that this is inappropriate, and see that it is stopped." At this point, the ISP made a critical error. Being new to the Internet, and not bothering to take the time to learn about the net, the net culture, and the unwritten but strictly adhered-to laws of the net, the ISP made the mistake of thinking that because it could, it should. Instead of considering the consequences of the spammer's actions to others and why the unwritten rules were good and just rules, the ISP said "no." As a matter of fact, it said "No, they paid for their access, they can do anything they damned well please."

20

The great sleeping beast that is the collective consciousness of every user on the Internet awoke that day. It was a terrible and wonderful thing to behold. The beast awoke and smote the ISP with such fury that three days later this message was posted to the newsgroups:

```
Please, please, please stop. We've learned our lesson, their account is
terminated, we will never ever do that again. Please stop sending email as our
servers have gone down from the load and we cannot delete the mail fast enough
to bring them back. We are sorry.
```

It was a magical moment. Untold thousands upon thousands of users on the Internet rose in unison and with a single voice cried "Enough!" The memory still brings a tear of joy to my eye, even today. Not since that time has the Internet moved with such purity of purpose and unity, but I believe that even through the signal degraded by so much off-topic traffic, the beast still slumbers. It would be both terrifying and wonderful to see it awaken again.

Today, unlike in the true spam story, the trouncing of the source usually is handled by smaller groups. ISPs have become smarter as well, as they actively attempt to prevent spammers from operating from their sites. Still, the lesson stands—you may be ruler of your own cluster, but the Internet is an army only waiting for a cause against which to rally.

When deciding whether it's appropriate to provide some service or allow your users to use some protocol, ask yourself how this will affect the rest of the Internet community. If you wouldn't appreciate it happening if you were outside your site, chances are nobody else will either. Don't risk raising the ire of the Internet community.

Privacy Issues

The single largest place where your absolute power as root can be in ethical conflict with both the desires and the legal rights of others is in the area of privacy. As root, you have the capability to access any file on the system. This does not in any way mean that you have the legal right to access any file on the system. Nor does it mean that even if you do have the legal right, you have an ethical right to do so.

The issues involved in privacy ethics are many and varied, and your individual situation and policies may bring additional factors into play. Regardless of the circumstances that might affect your individual situation, certain privacy-related ground rules and ethics apply almost anywhere.

The general rule to apply is *when in doubt, presume that you shouldn't.* The consequences of overestimating your legal authority or overstepping your ethical boundaries can be severe for both you and your users.

Your users are not angels, they are normal people. Their personal, private email may contain all manner of damaging information that could completely destroy their lives. They, as well as your supervisors, trust you to do your job—keeping the machines alive—and to not pry into things that are not your business.

Given the statistics of the behavior of average human beings, if you have more than a few users, you probably have more than one user who is being unfaithful to his or her spouse. There's even a reasonable chance that there is evidence of this in the mail spool. If your reading of a user's mail somehow allows this information to get out, you could destroy a marriage, a family, and several lives.

If your users are anything resembling normal, a reasonable fraction of them will be "closet" homosexuals. It's not your position to comment, judge, or in any way "out" them. Your users' sexual proclivities in no way affect their professional life, and you have no right to know—let alone allow it to affect your interaction—what they do behind closed doors.

Don't even dream of looking through users' Web browser cache files. If you ever are obliged to do this, you will discover just how varied your users really are. Unless you have a particularly strong stomach and a particularly strong belief in your users' privacy and constitutional rights, you will have a very difficult time dealing with what you probably will find. If it turns out that you *cannot* deal with what you find, and you use this information for anything or tell anyone, your users will have a very good case against you for unjustified invasion of privacy. You probably are going to land your backside in court, and you probably will lose. As a matter of fact, it doesn't even matter if what you find is of questionable legality. What you did in observing and divulging that information is very probably illegal, and you will be the one on the wrong side of the law.

Your Users' Rights

Surprising as it may seem, and as frequently as you might hear people speak of their "right to privacy," there is actually no such guarantee in the Constitution or Bill of Rights. The right to privacy certainly is perceived to be a right by the vast majority of citizens of the United States, but there is no specific wording to support this perception.

Instead, the rights an individual has with regard to privacy are largely determined by case law, which means by juries' perceptions of what those rights should be. Unfortunately, this makes definitive statements regarding what rights your users have—or would be held to have by a court of law—to be impossible.

Juries have decided that citizens of this country have "a reasonable expectation of privacy" in certain situations. They also have placed restrictions on when and where

20

this expectation of privacy applies, and on when it may be violated. This is the section of the U.S. Code that appears to be most relevant:

```
Title 18, Crimes and Criminal Procedure
PART I - CRIMES
CHAPTER 119 - WIRE AND ELECTRONIC COMMUNICATIONS INTERCEPTION AND
INTERCEPTION OF ORAL COMMUNICATIONS
```

Consider these excerpted portions of this section of the code:

```
(1) Except as otherwise specifically provided in this chapter any person
who -
    (a)  intentionally intercepts, endeavors to intercept, or procures any
         other person to intercept or endeavor to intercept, any wire,
         oral, or electronic communication;
...
    (c)  intentionally discloses, or endeavors to disclose, to any other
         person the contents of any wire, oral, or electronic
         communication, knowing or having reason to know that the
         information was obtained through the interception of a wire,
         oral, or electronic communication in violation of this
         subsection;
...
shall be punished as provided in subsection (4) or shall be subject to
suit as provided in subsection (5).
```

Translated, this says that if you intercept an electronic communication (such as email), you're breaking the law. It also says that if you tell anyone what you saw while intercepting the communication, you're breaking the law again, so when your coworker tells you about the amusing email he sniffed from one of your colleagues, he's not only breaking the law, but probably making you an accomplice.

Thankfully for your ability to do your job as a system administrator, the section also says this:

```
(2)
  (a)
    (i)  It shall not be unlawful under this chapter for an operator of a
         switchboard, or an officer, employee, or agent of a provider of
         wire or electronic communication service, whose facilities are
         used in the transmission of a wire or electronic communication,
         to intercept, disclose, or use that communication in the normal
         course of his employment while engaged in any activity which is
         a necessary incident to the rendition of his service or to the
         protection of the rights or property of the provider of that
         service, except that a provider of wire communication service to
         the public shall not utilize service observing or random
         monitoring except for mechanical or service quality control
         checks.
```

This language at least allows you to intercept traffic if it's necessary to do your job. It also qualifies that concept of "necessary," making it clear that regular or random monitoring is acceptable only in the capacity of mechanical or quality-control checks. No sniffing all the traffic, all the time, and calling it "necessary." Just how much would be considered "necessary" in a court of law would probably be a thing of considerable legal contention. Legal contention costs lots of money, so you want to keep interception to a minimum if it does occur. My feeling is that less is probably better if you want to prove that interception occurred only when necessary.

The U.S. Code also states the following:

```
(ii)    Notwithstanding any other law, providers of wire or electronic
        communication service, their officers, employees, and agents,
        landlords, custodians, or other persons, are authorized to
        provide information, facilities, or technical assistance to
        persons authorized by law to intercept wire, oral, or electronic
        communications or to conduct electronic surveillance...
```

This section of the U.S. Code says that you may sniff traffic and provide this information to persons with legal permission to intercept the data. The section goes on to provide specifics as to who is authorized and under what circumstances, and also covers other crimes and specific exceptions. I have included relevant sections of this chapter of the U.S. Code in Appendix D, "Legal Stuff."

Another document you might want to be aware of is the American Library Association's Library Bill of Rights, which states the following:

```
                    Library Bill of Rights

The American Library Association affirms that all libraries are forums
        for information and ideas, and that the following basic policies
        should guide their services.

I.Books and other library resources should be provided for the interest,
        information, and enlightenment of all people of the community
        the library serves. Materials should not be excluded because of
        the origin, background, or views of those contributing to their
        creation.

II.Libraries should provide materials and information presenting all
        points of view on current and historical issues. Materials should
        not be proscribed or removed because of partisan or doctrinal
        disapproval.

III.Libraries should challenge censorship in the fulfillment of their
        responsibility to provide information and enlightenment.

IV.Libraries should cooperate with all persons and groups concerned with
        resisting abridgment of free expression and free access to ideas.
```

20

V.A person's right to use a library should not be denied or abridged
      because of origin, age, background, or views.

VI.Libraries which make exhibit spaces and meeting rooms available to the
      public they serve should make such facilities available on an
      equitable basis, regardless of the beliefs or affiliations of
      individuals or groups requesting their use.

Adopted June 18, 1948.
Amended February 2, 1961, and January 23, 1980,
inclusion of "age" reaffirmed January 23, 1996,
by the ALA Council.

This data comes from the American Library Association's Web site, `www.ala.org`, where you can find many more useful resources for data providers.

Note

> Of course, you probably aren't a library, and your business may have goal-directed usage policies that forbid certain material or allow only certain material. There is nothing wrong with this environment, but you should be aware that unless you have an acceptable-use policy that specifically forbids or allows certain content, there may be a legal assumption that everything is allowed. If that is the case, imposition of censorship that isn't supported by your acceptable-use policy may open you up to legal action.
>
> On the other hand, if you provide data, allow your users to do so, or support something like a public ftp server, you very well may want to consider yourself to be a library. The guidelines for library policy have been very well thought out over a long period of time. You probably will find these guidelines applicable to your situation and a good base set of rules from which to work.

Beyond attempting to follow the law as laid down by previous decisions, you should follow certain guidelines; the foremost of these is caution. Users' rights to privacy are governed by the decisions of juries. Jury decisions frequently are controlled by jury perceptions of appropriateness or abuse of power. If you are ever put in a situation where a jury has to make a decision as to whether you've violated a person's right to privacy, that jury's perception of you and your actions as reasonable is important. If you are perceived as having a cavalier attitude, the chances of the jury finding in that person's favor are much greater.

Reciprocity

One good thing to keep in mind when deciding what sort of policy to make "acceptable use" is the idea of reciprocity. Given the cautions against any form of censorship or control that is not predetermined by the acceptable-use policy, it's tempting to write a draconian acceptable-use policy.

Your initial impression might be that this type of policy would give you tighter control over your users and make your facility more productive. This isn't likely to be the case in actual practice, though. It will definitely give you greater control, but it most likely will reduce productivity. The World Wide Web, Usenet news, and mailing lists are such wonderfully useful and powerful tools because of the wealth of information and experience accessible through them.

Your users will be using these tools, so let them give something back. The vast majority of truly useful content on the Web is provided free of charge by users who do it because they want to. Allow your users this freedom. If you're going to use the resources of the Internet community, you owe it to your users and the community to allow them to reciprocate.

Will this eat up server resources and network bandwidth? It can't help but do so. Is it worth it? If everyone with a Web server based the decision of whether to carry a particular piece of data on whether they received a direct benefit from it, the majority of the data on the Web would disappear overnight. The benefits of allowing your users to read, create, and distribute almost any sort of data conceivable are mostly intangible, but they're the backbone on which the Internet community is built. The health and well-being of the WWW and the Internet community as a whole depend on system administrators like yourself seeing past the immediate question of direct benefit to their mission and on to the benefits of the thousands of other sites around the world.

Plain Old Common Sense

Outside the strictly legal concerns you should have with staying on the right side of the law, you should keep some common-sense rules and simple facts of human nature in mind:

20

- People don't respond well to threats. Policies need to be worded strictly, but fairly. Policies that appear to be overly threatening only invite user disdain.
- People have an innate curiosity about things and sometimes poke their noses in places they don't belong. This doesn't make them bad people or even necessarily untrustworthy people.
- People come from all walks of life and all backgrounds, lifestyles, and personalities. Attempting to proscribe or prescribe any of these at your site will only cause you trouble.
- People tend to react poorly to rules for the sake of rules. Rules that appear to have been written only as an exercise of authority (whether or not this is the case) tend to be looked on as rules to be skirted, perverted, or outright broken.

- People display a built-in mistrust for authority. Users try to hide files from root and each other. They also are guarded in responses to queries about issues or behaviors. This behavior does not automatically mean that they have done something wrong.

There's no legal reason for you to be concerned with these items, but there are big practical and political reasons to be concerned. Your relationships with your users will be governed largely by their perception of how concerned you are for their needs. If you aren't sensitive to the needs and perceived boundaries of your users, your relationship will end up being hostile. Hostile users are not something you want to have to deal with and are not something you will survive trying to work for.

When It's Better Not to Know

Finally, there are times when it's simply in your best interests not to know. If your users are normal human beings, they do strange and interesting things. You are likely to have users with wildly differing political views, social views, and lifestyles. Unless these views are illegal (and in this country, it is not yet illegal to have any views a user chooses), they are none of your business, and you're best off not trying to make them your business.

If your system allows any form of personal use, expect that your users will use it for personal purposes. You have no right to know about, access, or investigate those personal uses without cause.

You probably will find that some of your users hold views you find personally, politically, or philosophically repulsive. This is perfectly normal and acceptable in a civilized society. People hold differing views, they disagree civilly, and life goes on. Your personal or professional differences with users give you no right to use your powers as root to violate those users' privacy or to discriminate against them in any way.

When functioning as a system administrator, it is your obligation to remove any personal philosophical concerns from your decision-making process. You need to make any decisions with respect to acceptable use on an entirely level playing field, and with no concern for whether you find the user's actions to be personally offensive. Your only concern should be whether the actions of your users are within the law and your organization's acceptable-use policies. Consider these examples:

- Regardless of your sexual preferences, you have no right to restrict your users' personal Web pages to views that you find acceptable.

- Your personal fear of firearms gives you no right to prevent your users from reading pro-gun mailing lists.

- Your religious views can have no effect on your decisions with respect to what newsgroups your users can read.

- Your feelings regarding obscenity or perversion cannot be made policy for governing which Web sites your users are allowed to browse.

Consider the earlier example of a user who is being unfaithful to his or her spouse. If, while browsing around the system, you happen to read this user's mail or a file in the user's directory where the mail is hidden, what do you do? If a co-worker is looking over your shoulder as you do this and then starts telling jokes about the user in the lunchroom, who is responsible? If the user's spouse is one of your close friends, what is your response? It's better just to not know.

I'll cover some specific instances, and the correct decisions to make in each, in detail in the "Q&A" section later in this chapter. For the time being, observe that these statements are simply different ways of saying *Keep your nose out of your users' business.* Your users can and will do things that are legal but that will inevitably upset you if you know about them. You don't need the headaches, and there's nothing legal that you can do about it. It's simply better for you to not know.

Note

> **Ignorance *is* an excuse** Contrary to what you may have heard in the movies, in some cases, ignorance is an acceptable legal defense. Above and beyond the simple reasoning that you'll only upset yourself by knowing too much about what your users do, you also create legal problems for yourself if they are doing something illegal. The less you claim to know, and the less you in practice do know about what your users are doing, the less legally responsible for them you are.
>
> If you set the precedent that you routinely dig through your users' files looking for things that are illegal, this can be used against you legally. If one of your users is found to be doing something illegal, an argument can be made that you must have known about it due to your routine probings, and that you therefore are implicated as well.
>
> Don't put yourself in this position. As mentioned in the discussion of policy, a reactive legal policy is a safer one than a proactive policy.

20

Security Issues

The one area where you do have some level of carte blanche in accessing or modifying anything on the system is when reacting to a security concern. As root, you have (or should have—if your organization has intelligent policies defined) police powers in the case of security emergencies. These powers include the right to access anything necessary to secure the system and to prevent a recurrence of the problem. These powers do not include the right to access files outside that need or to make changes that are not related directly to the security threat.

Note

> Very specifically, be very, very aware that you do not have the right to access a user's private information without a clear indication that there is a current threat to system security, and that the user's information is directly involved.
>
> This means that it is not appropriate for you to routinely check the processes your users run or the files they create, or to routinely sniff and examine your traffic "just in case."
>
> If you do routinely sniff your traffic and actually find something that is illegal, you probably will end up paying large sums of money to the user for violating that person's privacy.
>
> Although many system administrators seem to be oblivious to this, there are laws against "wire tapping" to listen in on a person's communications. Most of these laws apply to a user's email as well as Web-browsing traffic. The only time you are legally allowed to monitor your users' communications without their permission is when under a court order, and under a very specifically defined additional set of circumstances. You are allowed to access this type of information without permission when actively attempting to eliminate a current security threat. Other than in this case, and if you've been ordered by a court to monitor a user's communications, unless you feel like being the person on trial, don't even dream of trying to "catch" your users doing something "wrong." React to problems and legal concerns; do not search for them.

You looked at specific security measures and policies earlier in this book. Here, I'll just cover the legal and ethical topics involved when you are dealing with a security problem.

What to Do

Find out who's doing what, and from where. Getting this information may involve rooting through system logs, carefully scrutinizing user processes, and running a packet sniffer on your network. The following is a look at things you should keep in mind.

- Be aware that when you're doing this digging around, you're likely to come across information that your users usually would consider private. Resist with all your might the desire to look through this for interesting tidbits. If you're lucky, you won't find any. If you're unlucky, you'll discover that one of your favorite users leads a lifestyle that you find offensive, and your relationship with that person will be forever changed.

- Be certain that any information you access is absolutely necessary for the tracing of the security problems, because accessing this information without permission or a court order is likely to land you in hot water.

- Examine processes that are running on your machines for connections that are being made to or from outside machines.

- Run `strings` on interesting-looking commands to see what sort of textual information they might contain. This will help you determine the purpose of the command.

- Be aware that the `ps` command can miss short-duration processes that run between invocations.

- Be aware that connections to back-door servers will not show up in your listings of online users and can hide the true identity or origin of the attack.

- Keep in mind that after a machine is compromised, the source of the break-in can make it appear as though it is coming from anywhere and anyone. In general, you should expect multiple levels of indirection, pointing at many innocent targets. These innocent targets might be on your local machine or on remote sites. It appears that a reasonable number of break-ins actually are attempts at indirectly sabotaging a remote site. Instead of breaking into the target site directly, they break into a number of different sites and modify logs and plant evidence that leads back to the intended target. Unless they are very careful, system administrators at the sites that were actually broken into mistake the source of the attack and point fingers. As a result, the target ends up spending days of downtime while attempting to diagnose a security problem they never actually had. Others leave misleading evidence in attempts to incriminate users at your site and to cover their tracks.

Once you believe you know the source of the problem, do what you can to eliminate it. Your primary concern, as always, is the safety and stability of the system, and the productivity of your users. Tracing the attack to its source and notifying the administration of that source is usually your final step.

Who to Do It To

Obviously, you're interested in finding the origin of your security problem. Once you know, you need to eliminate the problem.

If your search leads you to believe that it is an attack from an outside site, this means contacting the site administrators and asking them to further the search at their end. Don't have illusions of system administrator vigilante grandeur—generally all that's required is that you contact the site administrator and ask. On the rare occasions when this is not sufficient, it is time for you to contact the Internic and find out who is paying for the site and who is its upstream provider. Armed with that information, you can have the site physically removed from the Internet if it persists in such antisocial behavior.

Only on rare occasions should you ever have any reason to attempt to raise old-style Internet vigilante justice against an intrusion. This is not a suggestion that you should

20

ever really take this route but a caution as to why you shouldn't. There are very close to absolutely zero good reasons to ever violate good netiquette yourself in an attempt to solve a security problem. You will find the occasional system administrator who thinks it's acceptable to break into a remote system to stop a break-in in progress when its administration will not respond. This is not a view that generally is held to be acceptable, and frequently you will find these system administrators paying legally imposed fines for taking the law into their own hands. On that one-in-a-million chance that you'll ever encounter a problem where more force is required than comes from a simple check of Internic and a call to the offending site or its upstream provider, I suggest that you contact `alt.sysadmin.recovery` for suggestions before taking any action. You will, almost without exception, get so completely roasted for such a suggestion that you will be obliged to learn to think twice. If it should happen that your cause is just, you can be sure that the fraternity of UNIX system administrators takes care of its own.

If you trace your problem to one of your local users, you have a bigger problem. You are going to have to deal with the problem, but without extremely good proof that you know which user it is, you are not going to be able to take any action against the user. Once a system is broken, it is very easy for the actual perpetrator to make it appear as though the source is any other user on the system. Remember that the person who has broken into your system now has exactly the same access and control over the system that you do. This gives the person the capability to lead you in false directions and to frame other users as being the source of the problem.

If you can document that a particular user is the problem, you need some way of guaranteeing that it will not happen again. This is most easily accomplished by terminating the user's account and closing the hole that user exploited. If you work for a large corporation, you may be pressured to simply reprimand the user and to continue to allow use of the system. That person's perceived contribution to the good of the rest of the country may, in the eyes of the powers that be, outweigh the potential damage. You need to make it clear to whoever holds this opinion that you as an administrator cannot in any way be responsible for the actions of a user who cannot be trusted to respect the other users and policies of the system. You need to document this in writing. If management insists that the user be granted access, you should do everything possible to limit that user's capability to affect other users. Remove that user's network access, limit access to one particular terminal, do what you can to prevent further potential for damage, but ultimately, start looking for a new job. A business that is so irresponsible as to allow its employees free access to damage its own machines, and by implication affect the entire Internet community, does not deserve good system administrators. Find a company that knows your value and treats you with the respect you deserve.

When to Stop

Sometimes, in the heat of trying to track down the source of a security problem, it's hard to determine when you've passed the point of diminishing returns.

After you have secured your system and prevented the same problem from being exploited in the future, is it really necessary for you to find the actual source? In the heat of the chase, it certainly feels like this is a necessity, but that is also when you need to stop and ask yourself whether what you are doing is the best use of your time and resources. If you spend a week of your time trying to pinpoint a break-in, to the exclusion of all else, that's a week's worth of patches and security fixes that you haven't taken the time to install; a week's worth of user assistance and problem-fixing that you haven't taken the time to do.

You must keep in mind that your primary concern is the usefulness of your facility and the productivity of your users. After you have secured the system and the threat is no longer present, it is frequently not in the best interests of your facility for you to continue the pursuit.

You and the Law

You might think it's a silly thing to remind you of, but it's important that you know and follow the law. It's not really quite as silly a thing as it may seem. In everyday life, you're mostly prevented from doing illegal things by common sense and the constant concern that someone will catch you. That you ought not steal someone else's property seems pretty obvious, and the fact that they probably would physically prevent you if caught is a constant reminder. Crimes that you or your users might commit using a computer are frequently neither as obvious nor anywhere near as observable. This doesn't mean that you can't or won't be held liable if caught. Instead you need to pay extra attention to make certain that you know and don't accidentally break the law.

As dry reading as it is, I suggest that you spend some time looking over the U.S. Code (presuming you're located in the United States) and learning what the law actually says. This shouldn't be taken as a definitive statement of everything that is and would be considered to be the law, but is a good base from which to start. I've included some applicable parts of the U.S. Code in Appendix D, "Legal Stuff," for your reference, but you can access the entire text at the following URL: http://www4.law.cornell.edu/uscode/.

You also should be aware that the law governing computing use and legalities is in a constant state of flux. There is considerable confusion in the courts as to the right and wrong of computing. Unlike laws governing physical property, which have been revised and improved for as long as laws have existed, laws governing computing technology are in their infancy.

20

Property laws are an area in which most members of legislative bodies or juries have some experience. In comparison, computer laws cover a subject in which most of these people are not experts, or even particularly experienced. They may not even understand all the terms about which they're making laws; instead, they may rely on the testimony of expert witnesses or base their decisions on the political influence that some companies may buy.

This leads to sometimes confusing laws, and sometimes amazingly nonintuitive things being declared illegal. The illegality of the export of encryption technology as a piece of software, but the legality of the export of the same software as a printed work is just one example of this oddity.

Know Your Rights

Beyond the rights that you are guaranteed by the Constitution and Bill of Rights (or the equivalent documents from your country—I'll be rather nationality-centric in this section), there are rights you are given by the legal code, and others that stem from the public's perception of common sense. Your adherence to, and your insistence upon, these rights will make your job easier and more enjoyable.

You have certain rights as an employee, as well as your rights as a system administrator. Among the most important that should concern you more than the average employee is the right to not be asked to be responsible for something you don't have the authority to affect. This applies to both your immediate job responsibilities and your responsibilities in the eyes of the law.

Do not accept responsibility for the successful completion of administrative tasks that you do not have the authority to complete. Also, you should not accept responsibility for things that you legally have no authority to enforce.

What Are You Allowed to Do as a System Administrator?

"Assume as little as possible" is actually guaranteed to you as a right. It's safer this way. You have the right and responsibility to do your job, the right and responsibility to maintain your machines. The law may guarantee you other specific rights, but don't count on any particular item being within your purview unless you have that in writing. Also, be cautious that a business will not always know the law when defining job responsibilities. It's entirely possible that you may be put in a position where one of your job directives requires you to violate the law. My recommendation, should this occur, is that you follow the law.

Also, the range of things you are allowed to do will somewhat depend on user agreements you may have in place. For example, you can apparently (this is still being argued in the courts) reduce your users' reasonable expectations of privacy by sufficient notification that they have no privacy. This includes clear notification that their files and communications can be accessed at any time. This notification must be present prominently in the user agreement. It appears to help your position, should you choose to take this route, if this information also is presented to the user at every login and every time any connection is made to the system.

I personally don't recommend this way of working with your users. It is less productive than trusting your users and can lead to legal problems of other sorts. Still, some companies require this sort of tight reign on the users' activities. If you should work for such a company, be aware that you are safer in your activities if your users are regularly notified of the limitations placed on their privacy.

What Are You Required to Do?

You have obligations placed on you by your users and your facility. You are required to execute those obligations within the boundaries of the law.

If a court orders you to access a user's files, you are obliged to follow the dictates of that court. If you receive a request to access a user's files without a court order, be aware that to do so may be considered illegal search and seizure. You cannot be "ordered" to access a user's files by law enforcement without a warrant.

You do have the obligation to report illegal activities carried out on your system if you should happen to discover them. As I have cautioned repeatedly, it is a bad idea to make any proactive attempts to discover illegal activities. Make it clear to your users that illegal activities will not be tolerated, but do not make yourself responsible for the activities of your users by attempting to watch their every move.

Unfortunately, chances are your users will occasionally do illegal things. Usually, these will be victimless crimes that nobody will ever notice, you will never know about, and nobody will be affected. Occasionally, someone else may notice their activity and report it to you. Then, you must act. On very rare occasions, you may stumble across the illegal activity yourself. In these cases, you are obliged to follow whatever protocol your organization dictates.

It is not, by the way, generally acceptable to "look the other way." The laws that your users are most likely to violate are primarily copyright laws (U.S. Code Title 17). Many people do not consider the copying of software without permission to be a "real" crime. Don't believe them. If you have people using your system for copying and illegally trading software, you are opening yourself up to a very large lawsuit by the copyright owners, or by one of the watchdog organizations that works for the owners.

20

The next most likely laws your users may break are ones that make the possession of certain types of data illegal. Many places outside the United States post things on the Internet that are illegal in the U.S., and many places in the U.S. simply ignore the laws. Users may be under the impression that because this information is just a click away, it really is acceptable for them to access. It is unfortunate that this is not always the case.

As an example of the type of data it might be illegal for your users to possess, consider the case of pornographic images of minors. Your immediate reaction to the idea of someone taking, distributing, or possessing nude images of children probably is repulsion. This is a healthy reaction, but you should be aware that your reaction is not necessarily the best possible. The law is specifically against pornographic images of minors. "Pornographic" is a loosely defined legal term, making the determination of whether an image is pornographic difficult at best.

If you stumble across a nude picture of a child in a user's directory (why you would have been looking, after the cautions I've given you, is beyond me), how would you determine whether it is pornographic? Simple nudity does not constitute pornography (in most jurisdictions). If you blow the whistle and are right, you've done a good thing. If you blow the whistle and are wrong, you might have just ruined the life of a user who took an innocent picture of one of his children.

When No Means No

Sometimes, as a system administrator, you just have to say "no." In this case, I am talking particularly about when you must be clear regarding your rights and your users' rights, and where they end. If you are asked to do something that you know is a violation of your users' rights or of your rights, say "no." If this means that you need to go looking for a new job, so be it. If you do not do this, you will be directly violating or assisting in the violation of the law. You will be legally responsible, and if someone ever brings this to the attention of the courts, you will be held responsible for your actions. You do not need an employer with this level of irresponsibility toward its employees. Again, there are plenty of responsible employers out there and a shortage of good system administrators. If your employer is going to ask you to break the law, you do not need that employer.

Along the same line of reasoning, if your employer places you in a situation where you are expected to take responsibility for actions that you do not have the authority to control, it's time to get new business cards.

Working and Playing Well Together

Beyond the technical knowledge required to do the job, a large portion of what is necessary to be a system administrator can be summed up simply as "working and playing well with others." You need to interact with the rest of your administrative staff, your online administrative peers, and your user community, all in a professional and helpful manner.

As I've mentioned before, power is a corrupting influence, and you have a lot of power. You also have a very difficult job and a customer base that expects more from you than a normal human can give. You, of course, have every right to be treated professionally by your users as well, but don't allow yourself to slip into the trap of thinking of your users as second-class citizens.

Mutual Respect

To survive and succeed as a system administrator, you and your users will have to develop mutual respect. You need to keep in mind, as I've repeatedly pointed out, that you are there in a service position to your users. Taking the attitude that your users aren't deserving of your time is a sure path to stress and poor user relations. Your users need to know your boundaries and that the time commitments to your job prevent you from investing time in problems outside that job.

Coming to this mutual respect will not be easy, and you will have to take the first steps. You are a system administrator, so you already have a thick skin. You will need to bear the load of insensitive users until you can convince them that you're not an adversary. The easiest way to convince them of this is to be helpful. Pay attention to what they're doing and the problems they're having. Be ready with ways to help before they come to you with a complaint. After your users are convinced that you're actively working to further their interests, your interactions with them will be much more pleasant.

Initially, when users come to you with a problem and you say "There's the pile, you're number 127," their first impression is going to be that you've just said "Go away, I don't have time for your piddly problem." Although this might in fact not be that far from what you're thinking, that's not the image you want the users to have. You want users to come away with the impression that you're up to your ears but striving mightily to solve problems for them and 126 of their colleagues. You want them to go away with the thought that you're expending superhuman effort on their behalf, and that maybe they shouldn't add to your workload with a trivial problem the next time.

The ideal goal state is one in which your users respect you as the system administration and computational expert, and they allow you the authority and time to do your job. Most reasonable people will come to you with a problem only when they have no other choice, or when they think you aren't doing enough for them. After you've convinced them that you are doing more than enough for them, they'll come to you with only the real problems. The path to this environment may take a considerable amount of work on your part, and a considerable amount of trying to educate your users, but it's the only survivable environment for a system administrator.

20

Implicit Assumptions About Users

In an entirely self-serving note, I'll take this time to tell you about one of my other pet peeves about system administrator behavior. That is, some of them seem to immediately start distrusting users after they've given them accounts. This usually is evidenced by things like administrators canceling user accounts on the mere suspicion or accusation of wrongdoing.

I understand and have preached about the need for security and control throughout this book, but this seems to be utter silliness. You make the implicit assumption that users are trustworthy, and that they can be trusted at their word when you give them an account. If you don't trust them, you shouldn't be giving them the account in the first place. Because you implicitly do trust them, there is no reason for that level of trust to change simply because of an accusation of security violations or wrongdoing.

As a system administrator, you are aware of the amazing power of root and that a successful cracker can modify log entries and processes to misdirect you. You therefore have no reason to assume that a previously trusted user suddenly has become untrustworthy. Unless you have direct evidence to the contrary, you have no more reason to mistrust his "No, I didn't do it" response than you did his "Yes, I will abide by the rules" response on his application.

Avoiding Legal Problems

The key to avoiding most legal problems as a system administrator is to be aware of the legal implications of your actions. Too many system administrators, and too many supervisors in charge of system administrators, assume that just because something can be done, they have the right to do it. This is not and should not be any more true for system administrators than it is for normal users.

As a system administrator, you need to be held to a higher standard of accountability and a higher standard of trustworthiness than the average user. If you'd like to avoid the vast majority of legal problems without having to consult a lawyer regarding every decision you make, live by the following rules:

- **Don't invent trouble**—If there isn't a problem with a situation, don't invent a rule just to create a problem. Some people seem to feel a need to continuously create and enforce new rules. The fewer rules you have and the more freedoms you give your users, the happier they'll be, the less problems they'll cause, and the less likely you will be to invent a rule that violates someone's rights. Also, don't go looking for trouble. Trouble will find you all on its own with no problem. If you go looking for trouble, you're more than likely going to find it, and in ways that you might not have expected.

- **Don't assume problems that aren't yours**—Your job is keeping your machines up and running for your users. Don't assume the role of "fixer of problems" for problems that don't relate to this job. If someone complains that one of your users has a Web page that they find offensive, for example, unless the content is illegal, you should take absolutely no action. Your job isn't to act as a censor or to invent arbitrary standards for Web content. If you decide to dabble in this area, you again risk violating someone's rights.

- **Never practice any form of censorship**—Especially never practice any sort of proactive censorship. If your organization has standards for your users' personal Web pages, enforcing those standards is acceptable. Do this only in a reactive fashion, though. If you attempt to proactively check the appropriateness of content, you open yourself up to being held legally accountable for anything that's on the site.

- **Define policy**—Define your policies clearly, and make certain that users are aware of them. If you have a policy that allows you some level of random access to user files, make certain that you notify the users of this regularly. Your users need to know exactly what their boundaries are and exactly what behavior they can expect from your administrative staff.

- **Adhere to policy**—Strictly adhere to the policy you have written. If the policy says that a certain action is grounds for termination of an account, terminate the account. Do this even if the person with the account is your best friend. If you do not apply your policies consistently, you open yourself up to charges of discrimination when you actually do enforce your policies.

Summary

This lesson gave you a large summary of most of the advice I've tried to impress upon you throughout the book. Additionally, I covered some of the legal issues you will want to consider when making decisions.

Q&A

For this question-and-answer section, I will take advantage of a wonderful resource provided by the Electronic Frontier Foundation (www.eff.org). This organization provides support and direction regarding user privacy and use of information issued. Among other projects it supports is the Computers and Academic Freedom Project. Karl M. Kadie of EFF has done a wonderful service by cataloging a number of real instances of system administrators having to make tough decisions about content. Some or all of these scenarios are likely to be applicable to your cluster at some time. Excerpted and slightly edited

20

for paper presentation, the situations here are presented in even greater detail at `http://www.eff.org/CAF/cafuiuc.html`.

Question 1:

The Case of NYX

The Scenario

March 12, 1994 (Saturday)

> You are a CS professor at Denver U. and creator of NYX, a free public access computer service affiliated with the University. The *Sunday Denver Post* reports that NYX carries `alt.sex.intergen`.
>
> `alt.sex.intergen` is a newsgroup about intergenerational sexual relations.
>
> The newspaper suggests the newsgroup carries illegal material.
>
> In fact, the newsgroup discusses "is pedophilia OK/evil."

Do you kill the newsgroup?

Answer:

The Library Bill of Rights says

> Materials should not be proscribed or removed because of partisan or doctrinal disapproval.

So,

> Don't remove something just because it is offensive to many or even to yourself.
>
> If you believe that the principles of intellectual freedom developed for libraries apply to public-access computer sites, you should not remove the newsgroup.

The Rest of the Story:

> Sys Op Andrew Burt declined to kill the newsgroup.
>
> Last I checked, NYX is still online.
>
> The *Denver Post* has received faxes critical of its one-sided reporting.

Question 2:

The Case of CICA (Center for Innovative Computer Applications)

The Scenario

January 2, 1994 - February 6, 1994

> You're a computer staffer at Indiana University and creator of the CICA online archive.

> The archive is the most popular Microsoft Windows software archive in the world.

> You work on the archive on your own time.

> The university provides significant computer and network resources.

> Someone submits a Windows hypertext version of *Fanny Hill,* the 18th-century sexual novel.

> Someone else says that having *Fanny Hill* on the net violates New Zealand law.

> You fear the university considers sexual subject matter unacceptable.

How should you decide whether to include *Fanny Hill* in your collection?

Answer:

The American Library Association's statement on "Challenged Materials" says

> [I]t is the responsibility of every library to have a clearly defined materials selection policy in written form which reflects the

> LIBRARY BILL OF RIGHTS, and which is approved by the appropriate governing authority.

The American Library Association's *Workbook for Selection Policy Writing* lists "legitimate" selection criteria (with respect to intellectual freedom). Some of these follow:

> Contribution the subject matter makes to the curriculum and to the interests of the students.

> Contribution the material makes to breadth of representative viewpoints on controversial issues.

> High degree of potential user appeal.

> Value commensurate with cost and/or need.

"Offensiveness" is not considered a legitimate selection criterion.

20

The "Freedom to Read" statement of the ALA and others says

> There is no place in our society for efforts [...] to confine adults to the reading matter deemed suitable for adolescents [...].

You, the CICA archivist, should

> Clarify your authority.

> Create a selection policy consistent with intellectual freedom.

> Apply it fairly.

The Rest of the Story:

The CICA archivist created this selection policy:

> As is a standard practice with most anonymous ftp sites (that are supported with funds from an independent host institution), certain programs, files, and software are outside the general scope of archive operations, and therefore will NOT be accepted.

> These files include (but are not limited to) any software: containing political, religious, racist, ethnic, or other prejudiced or discriminatory messages therein; that is adult or sexually explicit in nature; otherwise considered unsuitable by the site moderator.

Critique:

> Does not clarify authority.

> Violates intellectual freedom standards.

> Is not applied fairly (e.g., the Bible).

Question 3:

The Case of the Greek List

The Scenario

July 1993

> You are a system administrator at Brown University, American University, or the University of Georgia.

> Your site is a node for the Hellas (Greek) mailing list.

> You have just received email from Dr. Georgious, the system administrator at the Democritus National Research Center (DNRC) in Athens, Greece.

He says he is suing your university because people on Hellas "libel, slander, defame his character" and cause him "great emotional stress, and problems with his family and friends."

What do you do?

Answer:

The American Library Association's "Intellectual Freedom Statement" says

We need not endorse every idea contained in the materials we produce and make available.

The statement on "Challenged Materials" says

Freedom of expression is protected by the Constitution of the United States, but constitutionally protected expression is often separated from unprotected expression only by a dim and uncertain line.

The Constitution requires a procedure designed to focus searchingly on challenged expression before it can be suppressed. An adversary hearing is a part of this procedure.

You should

Get advice from the university legal counsel.

Take no action because of a one-sided legal threat.

The Rest of the Story:

Within a day, all three system administrators shut down their Hellas node.

Then, shutout forum participants spoke up. They said Hellas did talk about the censorship, privacy violations, and arbitrary punishment at the DNRC.

They said this was legitimate and should not be censored.

As of July 13, 1993, two of the sites restored their nodes.

Question 4:

The Case of the Free-Net

The Scenario

Pre-1991

You are on the organizing committee of the Cleveland Free-Net.

20

The Free-Net mission: to provide free computer and network resources to the community.

Some parents may not want their kids to access some of the more "adult" resources.

Ohio may have a "harmful to minors law."

What do you do?

Answer:

The ALA "Library Bill of Rights" says

A person's right to use a library should not be denied or abridged because of origin, age, background, or views.

The ALA's "Free Access to Libraries for Minors" says

…[P]arents — and only parents — have the right and the responsibility to restrict the access of their children — and only their children — to library resources. […] Librarians and governing bodies cannot assume the role of parents or the functions of parental authority in the private relationship between parent and child.

The ALA's "Access for Children and Young People to Videotapes and Other Nonprint Formats" says

ALA acknowledges and supports the exercise by parents of their responsibility to guide their own children's reading and viewing.

The "Freedom to Read" statement says

There is no place in our society for efforts to coerce the taste of others, to confine adults to the reading matter deemed suitable for adolescents, or to inhibit the efforts of writers to achieve artistic expression.

The "Intellectual Freedom Statement" says

With every available legal means, we will challenge laws or governmental action restricting or prohibiting the publication of certain materials or limiting free access to such materials.

So,

Don't ban so-called adult material.

Don't stop access by minors unless your competent legal advisor says you must.

Lobby to repeal so-called "harmful to minor" laws (especially as applied to not-for-profit information providers).

The Rest of the Story:

As of 1991, the Cleveland Free-Net

Segregates adult material.

Stipulates that users who want access must certify that they are 18 years old or have their parent's permission.

I believe other Free-Nets ban all adult material.

Question 5:

The Case of Iowa State University

The Scenario

February 1992 - present

You are a professor at Iowa State University.

Your computer administrators have changed the Netnews facilities.

Users now can access sex-related newsgroups (e.g., alt.sex) only from a computer account on a special computer and after "acknowledg[ing] their responsibility in access, using, and distributing material from it" (by signing a statement).

Some people say the university's action is OK because anyone who wants access can get it. What do you think?

Answer:

ALA's "Books/Materials Challenge Terminology" statement says "censorship" is

The change in the access status of material, made by a governing authority or its representatives. Such changes include: exclusion, restriction, removal, or age/grade level changes.

The ALA "Restricted Access to Library Materials" statement says

Attempts to restrict access to library materials violate the basic tenets of the LIBRARY BILL OF RIGHTS. [...] In any situation which restricts access to certain materials, a barrier is placed between the patron and those materials. [...] Because restricted collections often are composed of materials which some library patrons consider objectionable, the potential users may be predisposed to think of the materials as objectionable and, therefore, are reluctant to ask for them.

20

The Rest of the Story:

The restrictions at Iowa State University continue.

Question 6:

The Case of the V-Chip

The Scenario

May 1993 - present

You are a United States Congressperson.

Congressman Markey has introduced the "V-Chip" bill.

Under this bill, broadcasters must send a violence signal whenever they depict "violence."

New TVs must have a violence-signal detection chip.

When the chip is enabled, say, by a parent, the TV blanks the screen.

Do you support the bill?

Answer:

The American Library Association's "Statements on Labeling" say

Labeling is the practice of describing or designating materials by affixing a prejudicial label and/or segregating them by a prejudicial system. The American Library Association opposes these means of predisposing people's attitudes toward library materials for the following reasons: Labeling is an attempt to prejudice attitudes and as such, it is a censor's tool.[...]

You should oppose the bill.

The Rest of the Story:

The bill is in committee.

Question 7:

The Case of CERT

The Scenario

December 1992 - present

You are a university computer system administrator.

CERT (the Computer Emergency Response Team) suggests a sign-in message that says (in part)

Individuals using this computer ... in excess of their authority are subject to having all of their activities on this system monitored and recorded [...] In the course of monitoring individuals improperly using this system, or in the course of system maintenance, the activities of authorized users may also be monitored. ... Anyone using this system expressly consents to such monitoring and is advised that if such monitoring reveals possible evidence of criminal activity, system personnel may provide the evidence of such monitoring to law enforcement officials.

Do you put a sign-in message on your system?

Answer:

The ALA's "Statement Concerning Confidentiality of Personally Identifiable Information about Library Users" says

The First Amendment [...] requires [... that] the corresponding rights to hear what is spoken and read what is written be preserved, free from fear of government intrusion, intimidation or reprisal. [...] If there is a reasonable basis to believe such records are necessary to the progress of an investigation or prosecution, our judicial system provides the mechanism for seeking release of such confidential records: the issuance of a court order, following a showing of good cause based on specific facts, by a court of competent jurisdiction.

So,

Reject the CERT suggested message. Users should not lose all their privacy based on your personal determination about "in excess of their authority."

Work with the university legal counsel and university policymakers to determine whether any statement is necessary and to make it as specific as necessary.

The Rest of the Story:

At least the following schools have adopted a variant of the CERT banner:

Salt Lake Community College

Northwestern University

An anonymous state university

Weber State University

20

Stevens Institute of Technology

University of Michigan

Arizona State University

Worcester Polytechnic Institute

University of South Florida

Northern Arizona University

Question 8:

The Case of K-12

The Scenario

January 1993

You are a system administrator at the University of Kentucky.

Goal: Provide a Netnews newsfeed to high schools.

You and the teachers have decided:

—Not to provide `alt.sex`.

—If possible, to provide the newsgroup `news.answers`.

Problem: The `alt.sex` frequently asked questions (FAQ) file appears in `news.answers`.

Should you filter out the `alt.sex` FAQ from `news.answers` before passing it on?

Answer:

The ALA statement "Expurgation of Library Materials" says

Expurgating library materials is a violation of the LIBRARY BILL OF RIGHTS. Expurgation [...] includes any deletion [or] excision [...] of any part(s) of books or other library resources by the library. [...] By such expurgation, the library is in effect denying access to the complete work and the entire spectrum of ideas that the work intended to express.

You should

Not remove the FAQ. (And if you do, you should at least change the name of the resulting newsgroup so that readers know that it is being censored.)

The Rest of the Story:

As of January 1993, the University of Kentucky was providing an expurgated feed with no notice to its readers.

Quiz

1. Your co-worker has just told you a great joke. Then, he claims to have seen it in one of the user's mailboxes as he looked through users' mail when he was bored. What action should you take?

2. You start getting an increasing number of complaints from users on the Internet that they are receiving unsolicited mail, and that the mail is being routed through your mail server. What should you do about it?

3. What should you do once you are finished with this book?

20

DAY **21**

Troubleshooting

Troubleshooting is the bane of all system administrators, but we all end up doing it occasionally. In an ideal world, everything would work, and it would work all the time. You'd spend your time installing new hardware and software, patching bits that needed to be patched, and helping the occasional user.

If the computer gods are smiling on you, chances are that things will function in a surprisingly close to ideal way for extended periods of time. Machines will stay up for months at a time, only being rebooted when you reboot them yourself. Software will install properly the first time and won't develop bit-rot and slowly consume itself. Your network won't be plagued by gremlins, and your users will actually read the manuals.

If you've offended the computer gods somehow (forgot to issue the correct `fsck` incantation, ignored a CERT call to arms, or otherwise misbehaved), you will eventually be faced with tracking and eliminating problems, rather than proactively preventing them. In this chapter, I will cover some of the most prevalent directions from which trouble will come. I am not going to cover security problems or diagnosing break-ins here, only the annoying "spontaneously occurring" sort of problem.

Hardware

First, start with the problems you're least likely to regularly encounter and the ones you're least able to do anything about. Problems with your main CPU unit or with your peripheral hardware are exceedingly difficult to diagnose, frequently fall into the "no user serviceable parts" category, and are thankfully rather rare. Your usual procedure for dealing with most of these will be to notice that something stopped working, toggle the power on it a few times, perhaps try built-in diagnostics (if they're available), and then give up and send it off for repairs. This is a much easier process than diagnosis and repair of problems that you are actually going to have to take care of yourself.

Tip

Things fall apart   Nothing is a perfect system that is 100 percent bug-free. Everything has minor problems, and if left running long enough, everything eventually fails though the cumulative effect of many small problems, even in the absence of any one large problem.

Once upon a time, there was a computer line that was legendary for the fact that nobody could keep a machine up for more than a day or two at a time. I've intentionally left the name out, to protect the guilty. People used these machines because they were very fast while they were running, making them appropriate for computationally intensive short jobs, but not for server-type applications.

Many years after this machine line was a thing of the past, there was a small group of hobbyists still playing with the hardware and fixing bugs in the software. It was eventually reported on the Usenet Newsgroups that they had fixed enough bugs to get a cluster of these machines to run stably. Shortly thereafter, they reported yet another unexpected and mysterious crash. After a considerable amount of diagnostic work, they determined that this one was the biggie and that it was not going to be repairable. All these machines would crash, always, at somewhat under a month of uptime due to a bug in the machine's clock that kept track of how long the machine had been up. There was simply nothing more to be done.

The moral of this somewhat longwinded story? Sometimes, the solution is simply to reboot. If you have a machine or piece of hardware that has problems after it's been on a while, arrange for it to reboot itself periodically or for the power to be cycled on the device. It's not an ideal solution to the problem, but it's a solution that has kept some servers around this campus running for years on hardware and software that refuses to stay up continuously.

The Box

First on the list of potential trouble spots is your CPU. In general use in the UNIX world, this doesn't literally mean the central processing unit Integrated Circuit (IC), as it does in the personal computing world. Generally, when you hear a person talk about his CPU, he is speaking of the entire main "box"—the motherboard, processor, memory, and anything else that's in there.

Problems with the CPU are few and far between, and there's little you can do when they occur, so this section will be short and sweet.

Spotting Trouble

Your first sign of a problem with the CPU will usually be an entry in one of your log files. It might say

```
iobus interrupt not serviced: reset
```

or

```
parity error detected at 0x098fa45b3
```

or

```
panic: watchdog reset
```

It might say any number of other odd things as well. Usually, it will only say it once, and your machine might follow this with an automatic reboot.

This message is an indication that something odd happened and that some part of the OS or hardware recognized that it was odd. What with all the cosmic rays flying around, it's quite possible that it was simply the interaction of some sub-atomic particle buzzing a bit too close to the wrong circuit. It might never happen again.

On the other hand, it might be an indication of some bit of circuitry that is starting to fail. Sometimes, these things die quickly and spectacularly, and other times they die slowly over the course of years. If it's the slow failure variety that you've got on your hands, chances are that your machine will reboot and will run just fine—maybe for days, or even weeks, before another indication is seen. If it's the spectacular variety, your machine might do anything from simply becoming power-off dead to complaining of power-on self-test errors and refusing to boot to going up in flames.

Built-In Diagnostics

Your machine almost certainly has some built-in diagnostic routines. Most will run a set of these automatically at startup. There might be others available from your hardware maintenance and control menus. On Suns, for example, the probe-scsi diagnostic is very

21

useful for determining the functionality of your SCSI controllers, as well as checking your peripherals.

Always go first to your built-in diagnostics and record any information that they might give. It might look like cryptic gobbledygook to you, but the error codes and responses that the machine gives during its built-in diagnostics are key to having it fixed by a repair center. Be certain to record this information as soon as possible after the fault. You might experience temperature-sensitive faults that go away after time, or your machine might be in the process of toasting some component to death, and you will want to capture the diagnostic information before it becomes a doorstop.

Diagnosing the Hardware Problem

In addition to the built-in diagnostics, there are other diagnostics that you can do for yourself. Even if you're going to be sending the machine in for repair, it's a good idea to check these things yourself (after your machine is out of warranty, that is).

Repair people charge money for time, and if they have the opportunity, they'll start with the least likely components and work up to the most likely, thereby raising your repair bill. For this reason, you want to strip machines down to the smallest set of malfunctioning components possible before sending them off for diagnosis and repair. In the process, of course, you're going to need to check the status of the machine to make sure that you haven't just removed the component causing the problem and diagnosed it yourself. Follow these steps:

1. Start by grounding yourself adequately to the chassis. I recommend that you spend the $10 on a real grounding wrist strap. Ground it to the power-supply cage, slip it on your wrist, and get to work.

2. Disconnect any external devices and retest the machine.

3. Pull any peripheral cards that your machine might have and retest for the error. This might mean hooking your machine up to a serial terminal so that you can boot over the serial port if you don't have on-motherboard video.

4. Pull all the memory and retest. Some machines won't power up with no memory, so you might have to put base memory back in. If possible, use fresh memory or borrow some from a machine that's known to be working. Leave base memory in the machine for the next test.

5. Pull any internal drives and retest. At this point, you obviously won't be able to boot, but if the machine should pass, try reconnecting external drives and test again. I've encountered more than one machine that had problems with the internal SCSI bus but on which the external bus worked okay.

6. If you've got a machine with a removable processor (ZIF socketed, or card-edge connected), try swapping it for the processor from a working machine. If you have a multiprocessor machine, pull the second processor and retest. Swap the second for the primary and retest.

7. Pull the motherboard battery and check it for the correct voltage. Many computers do strange things when the motherboard battery dies.

8. Try letting the machine cool down for a day or two, and see whether the problem is still there. If the problem is gone, it might be a temperature-dependent fault. Depending on the severity, you might be able to live with the machine just by keeping it cooler.

 Caution   **Danger, high voltages present!**   Be careful while digging around in your machine's guts. It is an electronic appliance, and it does have the potential to electrocute you. If all is working properly, you shouldn't meet any lethal voltages on the motherboard, but by now you should know that you should never expect everything to be working properly.

Fixing the Hardware Problem

The easy part of hardware problems! Send it off to be fixed! Fixing real, live hardware problems is a job best left to professional computer repair persons. This is not a productive way for you to spend your time. Box up whatever you found to be the smallest collection of parts that displayed the problem (hopefully just a bare motherboard in a case), and send it off to be fixed. If you determined that one particular plug-in card causes the problem to manifest itself, you have to decide whether it's better to send the whole thing back or to just replace the card. If you just replace the card, you might find out that it's really part of the motherboard logic for talking to that card that's the problem. If you send the whole thing back, you might find out that it's just the card.

If it turns out to be a memory-related problem, you might be able to completely diagnose it by swapping memory around with other machines until you isolate it to a particular SIMM or DIMM or to a particular socket on the motherboard. If you can live without the defective piece of memory or without the use of that socket, you can probably just start using your machine again as it is.

In the event that it's a SCSI bus problem, you might be able to work around it by moving your internal devices outside the case. (They stay cooler that way and contribute less to the internal case temperature as well.)

21

If the problem appears to be temperature-related, you might be able to make the machine stable by simply making certain that the internal temperature stays lower. The first thing I would recommend is that you move any internal drives out of the case. Most high-performance drives give off a tremendous amount of heat, and you can decrease your internal temperature significantly by simply removing them. Also, increase your internal forced-air cooling. Many people mount external fans on the case's ventilation slots to move more air into the machine. Some machines have internal space for additional fans. There is also at least one product that will mount in a PCI slot opening and give you two small internal fans that you can aim as you like.

The Peripherals

Next on the list of difficult-to-diagnose sources of problems come your peripherals. Obviously, there are too many types of peripherals to discuss completely here, but I'll mention the important things to check with all of them, as well as a few points about the most common sources.

Spotting Peripheral Trouble

Your signs of peripheral trouble will range from the peripheral simply ceasing to function to the occasional mysterious entry in your log. Some problems come swiftly, whereas others develop over time. It's important to keep an eye on your logs for just this reason. A failing disk drive usually gives an indication that it's going to die by reporting incrementally more and more errors over some period of time. This period of time might be a few minutes, or it might be a few years, depending on the device and its personality.

Drive Errors   One type of noncritical peripheral error you will probably meet with some frequency is corrupted disk information. If, on reboot, your machine stops at a prompt saying that there were errors checking a drive and that you need to run `fsck` manually, don't be overly alarmed. This is an indication that the automatic `fsck` has detected errors on your drive, but chances are that they are not severe. If the machine was improperly shut down, you will almost always end up with this message. Even if the machine wasn't shut down improperly, if your uptime is measured in months, there's a lot of time for minor errors to collect in the drive's structure tables.

To diagnose a drive error, first make sure the drive is really up and spinning and that it's being recognized by the SCSI controller. Some drives don't take to being shut off very well, and they're sticky and refuse to start, or they start very slowly. Sticky drives can usually be cured by a sharp rap on the corner with the handle of a screwdriver (tap them so that the case would try to rotate around the platters in the normal axis of rotation). Slow drives are frequently a sign of a marginal or failing power supply. They'll usually run okay when they're up, but getting them spinning after a power-off can be a bit of a challenge.

You should also make sure that the drive is connected properly and that the SCSI cable is okay. Using a spare SCSI cable or swapping in one from a working system while doing diagnostics is probably a good idea, just to eliminate this possible failure point.

Then, boot into single-user mode and fsck the drives manually. The syntax for each version of UNIX seems slightly different, so this is one man page that you'll probably want to have on paper.

Answer yes to anything you don't have a better answer for.

When fsck completes, run it again to make sure that the changes have actually taken and that there are no other observable problems.

Reboot the machine. It should pass its startup fsck and come back online as normal. You probably won't have any further problems.

You should only be really concerned about startup complaints about disk errors if this is a persistent problem. If it's a transient problem that doesn't occur on every reboot, your machine is probably fine, and you're probably just seeing minor directory glitches. If it happens every time you reboot your machine, even if the machine has only been on for a few weeks, then you should be concerned that the drive might be starting to die. It's time to consider retiring it and installing one that won't be risking your data.

Old Disk Drives Never Die; They Just Spin Slower   Although you might be inclined to try to keep your machines running the fastest, most up-to-date drive hardware available, I've found that this isn't always the best strategy.

Hard drive technology today is simply amazing, with projected MTBF (Mean Time Between Failure) times measured in the hundreds of thousands of hours. These figures would lead you to have supreme confidence in the belief that the drive would far outlive its usefulness.

Unfortunately, I haven't found this to be the case. I have a sneaking suspicion it's a temperature tolerance thing, but our facility burns up top-of-the-line SCSI drives in about three years of use. I'm betting that it has something to do with the fact that our building coordinator's response to the complaint that it was 92 degrees Fahrenheit in the machine bay was "The product specs say 'operating range 25 to 95 degrees Farenheit. It's 92. What's the problem?"

In any case, I've found that at least some older drives just keep going, and going, and going. The drives in my personal SPARCstation were all manufactured prior to 1991,

21

with the oldest two being from 1987. These drives have been running constantly, in the same conditions as our self-toasting Seagate Barracudas for almost six years now without a fault. They're slower, they're bigger, they hold less data, but *they're stable*. The biggest factor to which I can attribute this is that they're also considerably cooler running. In normal operation, a Seagate Barracuda mechanism will be almost hot enough to cause burns to the skin—certainly hot enough that you don't want to touch it for more than a second or two. A Digital Equipment Corp. RZ57-E runs so cool that you can't usually tell it's on by touching it.

Stuff to Check Before the Logs

Normally, I tell you to always check your logs immediately when trying to diagnose a problem. When troubleshooting hardware, there are a few things to check before the logs. I know it sounds silly to suggest these, but the number of support calls I get from people who can't access their printer because they turned it off, who can't use their modem because they unplugged it, and who can't telnet to their machine because it has crashed, is simply amazing.

Before bothering to check the logs when a piece of hardware doesn't seem to be working, check the hardware itself. Ask yourself the following questions:

- Is it on? Is the power cord plugged in to both the device and the wall? Is the power switch in the on position? Does the power light indicate that the power is on? Is the fan spinning? Has the fuse blown?

- Is it hooked up? Is the interface cable plugged in? At both ends? Are the locking latches or screws tightened down? Is it actually plugged in to the socket it's supposed to be plugged in to?

- Is it running? Does it look like it's running? Does it feel like it's running? Does it sound like it's running? If it's a disk, is it spinning? If it's a printer, will it print its test page? If it has LEDs, does it have a startup diagnostic, and what does it say?

You'll save yourself an amazing amount of time digging around in log files looking for error messages and staring at configuration settings if you ask these three sets of questions first.

Note

> **Brain damage, it's not just for users any more!**   As a system administrator, you'll see plenty of users do plenty of silly things. The frequency with which "Help! I can't print!" is solved by walking to the user's office and either turning on or reconnecting the printer might lead you to believe that all users suffer from brain damage.

Unfortunately, either brain damage is universal or we're all users some of the time. Being a system administrator doesn't seem to be any cure or provide any immunity against making plain old brain-was-switched-off mistakes.

You should take this as both a suggestion to check the "simplest explanation" first when diagnosing problems and as a caution to not poke too much fun at users when they display less-than-rootly powers of observation. You'll do the same thing yourself frequently enough, and brain damage is much more of a liability in your position.

Software Diagnostics

If everything about the device appears to be correct, your next step is to try whatever software diagnostics are available. Frequently, you will get diagnostic software when you purchase a device—at least if you purchase the device from a reputable dealer. Find it, run it, record whatever information it gives, and call the technical support number. That's usually about the end of your involvement. Problem solved.

If you don't have diagnostic software, contact the technical support department for the hardware manufacturer or vendor. These people will either be able to provide you with diagnostic software or walk you through doing the diagnostics with software that you do have.

Tip

Service is worth paying for When purchasing peripherals, it is usually worth the extra cost to buy from a dealer who specializes in peripherals for your hardware. This does not necessarily mean to buy only directly from your CPU vendor, but it does mean to buy from a reputable dealer with a good track record in the UNIX peripheral market. I've included contact information for several vendors that I've had good luck with in Appendix E, "Useful Resources."

When purchasing from a good vendor, you get good technical support. Instead of having to fight your way through fixing built-in problems with a product with a "Did it install without giving you an error? Good, that's all we can help with. Goodbye," response from technical support, you get real help.

For some peripherals, a good vendor will give you a support contract that guarantees things such as the following:

- If you have a problem, they will configure a machine to be identical to yours and sit an engineer down in front of it to walk you through the fix.

- If you determine it's a hardware fault, you'll have a replacement on your doorstep by FedEx within 48 hours of your call (frequently even by the next morning!), and a return-box for the broken unit will follow.

21

- Availability of at-your-site repair or diagnostic service.
- You'll get the ability to talk to engineers who actually know something about the product, rather than help-desk personnel who can't help beyond the answers in their menu-driven answer database. You'll get access to technicians who will sit down and go over board-level diagnostics with you if you're comfortable with an Oscilloscope and a logic probe.

If stability is a concern for your site, don't short-change yourself by shopping for the cheapest provider. You can find hardware for much cheaper than the high-service dealers provide, but if it has a problem, you'll be on your own.

Do-It-Yourself Diagnostics

If you're stuck diagnosing a problem on your own, all is not lost. You'll have a lot more work to do than if you have the right software or professional help, but with sufficient time and effort, you can frequently work around these deficiencies.

The first thing to try is to see what the machine's own diagnostic routines say about the problem. On an SGI, you'd start with `hinv` and check to see if the peripheral showed up in the inventory. If the peripheral isn't one that the OS needs to be in constant communication with, you might have to reboot to see an inventory change. On a Sun, rebooting the machine and watching as it itemizes its devices would be the first step. Also, checking `dmesg` to see what it had to say at the last boot and any more recent diagnostics would be in order.

If the hardware shows up correctly in these itemizations, it's reasonable to expect that the hardware is at least still communicating properly with the CPU. Next, you will want to try using whatever OS-level software there is to talk to the device. If it's a printer, you'll want to remove any printer filter software and try dumping data straight to the printer port. If it's a disk drive, try using the disk check facilities of your drive-formatting software.

Finally, look for ways to use other hardware in your diagnosis. Frequently, Macintosh and PC diagnostic tools are more powerful and more convenient than UNIX diagnostic tools.

If you seem to have a dead drive, plug it in to a Mac and fire up something like FWB's HardDisk Toolkit. If this software can't diagnose and fix the problem with your SCSI drive, nothing can.

Likewise, if your problem seems to be with a printer or a PCI card, a PC with Windows-* might be your best friend. Diagnostic software and configuration software for most PCI devices and printers is much more easily available for the Windows world than anywhere else.

Fixing the Peripheral Problem

After you've diagnosed the problem, you have to fix it. Fortunately or unfortunately, depending on your point of view, there's not much to be done to fix most peripheral problems.

If you have a failure with a disk drive, there is probably nothing you can do. Even if it's something like the appearance of some new bad blocks, there's a reasonable chance that you're looking at the beginning of the end for the device. If you want to keep using it, make sure that it's not being used for mission-critical data because you'll have no way of knowing when it will decide to completely die.

If you have a failure with a mechanical device, there's at least a possibility that it's something simple, such as removing some offending object from the paper path in a printer. (It's always like a little treasure hunt, looking to see what users have dropped inside their printers.)

Usually though, your fix for most peripheral problems will be to either send it off to be fixed or to retire it and replace it with something newer, faster, and cheaper.

The Network

Your network can be one of your biggest sources of migraine headaches. Count yourself as unbelievably lucky if you have a network administrator who takes care of diagnosing and repairing network faults. If, on the other hand, you're stuck diagnosing your network yourself, be prepared to spend as much as 50 percent of your time just fighting with elusive network errors. In this section, I'll cover some of the things you can do to attempt to diagnose your network problems the "wrong way." The "right way" involves buying a several–thousand-dollar piece of hardware that's specially designed for diagnosing network hardware. Unless you're rich or your organization is feeling unusually generous, you probably won't have access to one of these.

Before you even get started, I must warn you that network diagnostics without proper network testing hardware is slow, laborious, and full of guesswork. You probably have only a 50 percent chance of finding and fixing a problem, and you are not going to have fun doing it. If there is any way to get a network test set or to convince someone else to do the job, you want to take that route instead of trying to do it yourself. If that simply isn't an option and you have a network that's giving you trouble, you don't have a lot of choices. Time to find a "Family Size" bottle of aspirin and a 24-pack of Mountain Dew, and get to work.

21

The first thing you need to know is that network problems come from several different sources. For the purposes of this book, I'll divide the causes of networking problems into the following categories:

- User error
- Software configuration
- Software errors
- Network cabling problems
- Network hardware (other than cabling) problems

I won't be discussing the first three of these in depth here because these aren't really system administrator topics. Your users will come to you with these problems on a regular basis, but these are relatively easy to fix and won't cause you much lost sleep for the most part. Network cabling and network hardware problems, on the other hand, are human-effort black holes. They'll suck you in and never let you go.

User and Software Network Problems

User network errors are almost always typing error problems, such as the following:

Users will call you and say, "The FTP server isn't working." This could mean, "I typed the FTP server address wrong," or maybe "I didn't type my username and password correctly."

Users will complain, "I just uploaded pages to my Web site, and I can't access them." This could mean, "I uploaded them from a Mac or PC, and I left spaces in the filenames," or "I forgot that UNIX filenames are case sensitive". On occasion, it might mean, "I FTPed my files to my account, and I forgot that the Web server doesn't run on the same machine I FTPed them to."

Users will complain, "There's something wrong with your Web server. I uploaded my files, and I can list them in my directory and read them from the shell, but the Web server keeps saying I don't have permission to view them." This probably means, "I have my `public_html` directory set so that only I can read it." Oddly, when this is pointed out to most users who have made this mistake, they say "But I want it set that way. I don't want anyone looking at my files!"

Users will spend hours poring over a CGI script that they've tried to use on their Web page and will finally come to you confused as to why the server keeps telling them "Forbidden. You don't have permission to access *some file* on this server." This means, "I'm very careful about security and have the file permissions set so that only I can execute the CGI script."

Users will ask why their images take so long to download from your server. The normal answer is, "Because you uploaded a 4MB 1152×870 24-bit image and are displaying it as a 100×100 thumbnail on your page."

On rare occasions, users will have network-related problems that aren't due to simple typing errors, but these are mostly software configuration errors. For the most part, these will be things such as specifying incorrect IP addresses or gateway information on a personal computer. Generally, you should avoid getting into the business of configuring personal computers. The closest you should approach this, if you want to have any time for doing your actual job, is to provide standardized configuration information in a helpful format. It's never a bad idea to have a neatly presented set of instructions for accessing your corporate FTP site, for example. Beyond constructing this document, making certain that the procedure outlined is clear and complete, and putting it in the user's hands, you should avoid personal computer issues.

Spotting Network Hardware Trouble

One of the reasons that users rarely come to you with anything other than typographical or configuration errors is the fact that they don't really have the tools to notice any other type of errors. You, on the other hand, have access to a decent suite of programs that can tell you that you have trouble.

Unfortunately, although these tools are good at indicating the presence of problems, they can't tell you where or what the trouble is. Later in this chapter, I'll go over how you can use the results of some of these tests to start making guesses about the source of the trouble. For now, you get the tools that can tell you when you have a problem. After all, they do say, "Knowing you have a problem is the first step to overcoming it," right? For some reason, whenever I'm faced with trying to diagnose network problems without the appropriate test set, the saying, "Ignorance is bliss," comes more readily to mind.

Note

Reality is stranger than fiction The network results I'll be showing you are real, live results from a real, live, sick network. This network has been a constant source of headaches for the past seven years and shows no sign of ever being repaired. It's cobbled together out of random lengths of coaxial cable and the occasional twisted-pair segment.

Spanning nine floors in a college teaching and laboratory building, the network loops over ceilings and dangles down service access shafts. It picks up RF noise from running too near to power cables and light fixtures. On the one occasion that I know of that a network test set was attached to it, the test set's response was something very close to "I am a very expensive piece of precision equipment. Please disconnect me from your TV antenna."

21

I don't think it expressed this in quite so many words, but it definitely was under the impression that it wasn't hooked to a legitimate piece of network cable.

Surprisingly, some days, this haphazard collection of cabling actually works mostly correctly. Other days, the users aren't so lucky. The diagnostics you'll see here are indicative of the sort of confusing and conflicting responses that you will see when trying to diagnose a network of this magnitude without the proper tools.

Before you get started looking for problems, it's important to know what sort of hardware problems you might meet. With a network, surprisingly few things can usually go wrong. Either the data gets from its origin to its destination or it doesn't, and it gets there either damaged or intact. Things that prevent traffic from getting from Point A to Point B tend to fall into the badly broken hardware or badly broken software category.

Harder to diagnose are things that damage traffic en route. These range from buggy software to malfunctioning hardware, such as routers or repeaters, to things that cause noise in the wire or that attenuate the signal. Just on the noise-causing front alone, you have problems such as machines with improper grounding, network cables running too close to florescent lighting, missing network terminators, and sharp bends in the wire.

Who Would Have Thought?

It certainly would seem like wire is wire is wire, right? Unfortunately, the signals that you're pushing around your network are rather sensitive to the slightest disturbances. Using slightly different types of wire in different parts of your network can cause what are known as "impedance mismatches." An impedance mismatch in a piece of wire causes a reflected signal in the wire, and to your machines, that reflection is noise.

Time for a silly science lesson. It's not necessary that you actually do the following, but either doing or imagining the following should give you a very clear understanding of what's happening on a much smaller and much faster scale in your network cable.

As an example of the phenomenon, find yourself a piece of heavy string about eight feet long, and tie one end of it to your doorknob or some other stationary point. Stand back about seven feet from the door and hold the other end in your hand. The string should be just slightly slack. Holding your hand in front of you, raise and lower your hand sharply one time only—a bit of a flick of the wrist helps. You should see a "pulse" travel down your string until it hits the doorknob.

When it hits the doorknob, what happens? It reflects back towards you. This is what happens when a signal on your network reaches the end of an unterminated piece of wire. If you could make a doorknob that moved up and down with the pulse as it got there but, other than following the pulse, did nothing more, you would be able to see what a terminator does. On your network, a terminator "swallows" the signals as they get to it so that they aren't bounced back into the network as noise.

Your unterminated string is an example of a severe impedance mismatch, none to infinite. See what happens if you have an impedance "bump" somewhere along the wire. Find a friend who won't think you're crazy for tying strings to doors and waving them about. Repeat the preceding experiment, but this time have your friend hold a finger out near the middle of the string so that the peak of the "pulse" will hit the finger as it travels. Ideally, you want to put the finger at about half the peak height.

What happens this time? If everything worked and you managed to keep your friend from just laughing at you and leaving, you should have seen a diminished pulse continue past the finger and a reflected pulse bounce back to you. This is exactly what happens when a signal in your wire hits an "impedance bump," such as a sharp bend in a wire. (Yes, a sharp bend in a wire causes what is known as "work hardening" of the wire. This changes the crystalline structure of the wire and thereby its electrical properties).

You can have yet more fun and see more interesting science in action if you feel like it by adding a section of string of different stiffness or weight to your string network. This would simulate the use of differing types of wire.

The thing to remember here is that every modification you make to your string causes small reflected signals and attenuation of the signal that is passed. The only way to have a perfectly clean signal with no interruptions is to have a perfectly clean string with no fingers (no knots) that goes on to infinity. Your network would be fairly useless if it was a single piece of wire not hooked up to anything, but that's the only way to prevent it from experiencing any generation of noise. Because you have to have junctions to install machines, you don't have any choice about some small impedance mismatch problems, but every little reflected signal adds up. You need to avoid doing anything that will unnecessarily introduce any new reflections.

Your first sign of network trouble is likely to be a sense that the network is slow. This isn't easy to quantify, but it is easy to observe when it happens. Web sites are slow to respond, file copies take forever, and you might even experience a delay in characters being echoed back to your screen in a terminal window. When this happens, your first sane step is to hope that it's just a transient spike in your local network load and that it will go away in a few minutes. If you're lucky, this will be the case, and you can go back to more enjoyable tasks. If you're not lucky, something is amiss, and you're going to have to intervene to fix it.

The first place to look for confirmation is the front panel on your twisted-pair hub. You did buy a twisted-pair hub with traffic diagnostics on the front panel, didn't you? Watch for high bandwidth utilization and high collisions. A healthy network will run in the 2 to 5 percent utilization range normally. The occasional spike into higher utilization is also

21

normal. Be worried if you're seeing continuous traffic in the 10 percent utilization range, and be especially worried if it's above that. Above 10 percent utilization, your network drops off rapidly into collisions and retransmissions, and utilization increases rapidly. It's generally accepted that by 30 percent utilization, your network is almost completely useless, being bogged down almost entirely with retransmissions of collided packets, with very little useful data getting through.

If your network shows continuous high traffic, this is almost certainly the cause of your slowdown. Chances are that you're seeing a high number of collisions, which isn't helping either.

If your network doesn't show high traffic, pay close attention to the collision indicator. If you see lower traffic but a collision on almost every packet, that indicates a different variety of problem.

Your next step is to check a few software diagnostics. Start off with the ping command. ping any nearby host, and note the results. Here, you see the results of a ping from a SunOS machine. On other flavors of UNIX, you will need to determine the flag to use for "keep going until stopped" instead of -s:

Note   Keep in mind that due to per-line character limitations related to the printing of this book, the following screen listings (and throughout the previous sections of the book as well) will not necessarily match those that your machine produces.

```
soyokaze ray 95> ping -s rosalyn
PING rosalyn.biosci.ohio-state.edu: 56 data bytes
64bytes from rosalyn.biosci.ohio (140.254.12.151):icmp_seq=0. time=1. ms
64bytes from rosalyn.biosci.ohio (140.254.12.151):icmp_seq=1. time=1. ms
64bytes from rosalyn.biosci.ohio (140.254.12.151):icmp_seq=2. time=1. ms
64bytes from rosalyn.biosci.ohio (140.254.12.151):icmp_seq=3. time=1. ms
64bytes from rosalyn.biosci.ohio (140.254.12.151):icmp_seq=4. time=1. ms
64bytes from rosalyn.biosci.ohio (140.254.12.151):icmp_seq=5. time=1. ms
64bytes from rosalyn.biosci.ohio (140.254.12.151):icmp_seq=6. time=1. ms
64bytes from rosalyn.biosci.ohio (140.254.12.151):icmp_seq=7. time=1. ms
64bytes from rosalyn.biosci.ohio (140.254.12.151):icmp_seq=8. time=1. ms
64bytes from rosalyn.biosci.ohio (140.254.12.151):icmp_seq=9. time=1. ms
64bytes from rosalyn.biosci.ohio (140.254.12.151):icmp_seq=10. time=1. ms
^C
——rosalyn.biosci.ohio-state.edu PING Statistics——
11 packets transmitted, 11 packets received, 0% packet loss
round-trip (ms)  min/avg/max = 1/1/1
```

Notice that there are several interesting fields in the data returned. First, there is the `time=` field. This field indicates that the packets each took one millisecond (thousandth of a second) to make the trip from `soyokaze` to `rosalyn` and back. That's not bad at all, but the machines are on the same local area network, so it's not unexpected either. See what happens if I `ping` a machine that's halfway across the country.

```
soyokaze ray 92> ping -s wuarchive.wustl.edu
PING wuarchive.wustl.edu: 56 data bytes
64 bytes from wuarchive.wustl (128.252.135.4): icmp_seq=0. time=101. ms
64 bytes from wuarchive.wustl (128.252.135.4): icmp_seq=1. time=82. ms
64 bytes from wuarchive.wustl (128.252.135.4): icmp_seq=2. time=89. ms
64 bytes from wuarchive.wustl (128.252.135.4): icmp_seq=3. time=92. ms
64 bytes from wuarchive.wustl (128.252.135.4): icmp_seq=4. time=83. ms
64 bytes from wuarchive.wustl (128.252.135.4): icmp_seq=5. time=80. ms
64 bytes from wuarchive.wustl (128.252.135.4): icmp_seq=6. time=82. ms
64 bytes from wuarchive.wustl (128.252.135.4): icmp_seq=7. time=101. ms
64 bytes from wuarchive.wustl (128.252.135.4): icmp_seq=8. time=80. ms
64 bytes from wuarchive.wustl (128.252.135.4): icmp_seq=9. time=97. ms
64 bytes from wuarchive.wustl (128.252.135.4): icmp_seq=10. time=88. ms
^C
— —wuarchive.wustl.edu PING Statistics— —
11 packets transmitted, 11 packets received, 0% packet loss
round-trip (ms)  min/avg/max = 80/88/101
```

Now, the times have gone up into the range of 80–100ms. That's still not bad for connecting from the middle of Ohio to a machine at Washington University in Missouri.

Now note the `icmp seq=` field. This field starts at zero and increases by one for each packet sent. If there are missing sequence numbers in the listing that `ping` returns, this is an indication that packets are missing. As you can see, for each `ping` attempt, I got back all the packets in the range 0–10. The statistics that `ping` outputs at the end agree with this, and note that there was 0 percent packet loss. On occasion, you will lose a single packet at the very end when you press Control+C, but any more than the final packet lost indicates a problem somewhere roughly between you and the host you have `ping`ed.

Next, you should look at the results from your `netstat` command:

```
soyokaze ray 93> netstat -i
Name  Mtu  Net/Dest  Address      Ipkts    Ierrs Opkts    Oerrs Collis Queue
le0   1500 default   soyokaze.bio 2577282  114   1854982  0     16996  0
lo0   1536 loopback  localhost    1607565  0     1607565  0     0      0
```

As you can see, the `netstat` command returns responses for network behavior on each of my network interfaces. The `lo0` interface is the loopback interface, which is used to enable the machine to talk to itself internally instead of hitting the physical network when it wants to talk to `localhost`. The `le0` interface is the actual physical Ethernet interface on this machine.

21

Note the Ipkts field for packets that this interface has read and the Opkts field for packets that it has written.

The Queue field would be nonzero only if there were packets backed up waiting to get onto the network.

The Collis field indicates how many of the written packets resulted in collisions. In this case, the collisions amount to .9 percent of the total output traffic. This number is quite encouraging. Collision rates and network usage generally run fairly close to each other, so you might expect that the network is seeing roughly 1 percent bandwidth utilization.

The final two interesting fields for this listing, Ierrs and Oerrs, are not as promising. Having 0 Oerrs is a good thing, but having 114 Ierrs is much too high. It does not matter that this is only a fraction of a percent of the traffic. In a properly configured, properly maintained network, you would have 0 actual errors, ever. This number indicates that there is something wrong with the network—something wrong to such an extent that it is destroying packets beyond recognition. That's not many, to be sure, but any is a sign of trouble. You shouldn't see Ierrs or Oerrs greater than single-digit values for machines that have been on for months at a time, and this machine has only been on for six days since the last reboot.

Take a look at another machine on a better-maintained network, just for comparison:

```
Name  Mtu  Net/Dest  Address       Ipkts      Ierrs Opkts       Oerrs Collis Queue
le0   1500 128.146.  pacific.mps   344747707  9     294347793   7     9076383 0
lo0   1536 loop      loopback.mps  99861051   0     99861051    0     0       0
```

That's more like it! This machine, by the way, has been up for 54 days on a much more heavily loaded network than soyokaze. The collision rate indicates that it's running at about a 3 percent network load, which is in the healthy range. soyokaze has seen 2.6 million packets and has seen 114 of them damaged in 6 days (that's 430,000 packets a day and 6 errors a day). pacific, on the other hand, has seen 344 million packets, with 9 of them damaged in 54 days (that's 6.4 million packets a day, with one packet damaged every 6 days). This is much more like what a healthy network should look like.

Next, look at the spray program and the diagnostics that it can provide. To use the spray program, you need to have the sprayd daemon enabled on the target machine. It does not seem to pose much of a security threat, so leaving it turned on is probably safe. It is possible to exploit it in a denial of service attack, however, so if you do leave it perpetually enabled, be aware of that as a potential source of occasional trouble.

First, check the network statistics for the target machine, and note the Ipkts value:

```
Rosalyn ray 12 > netstat -i
Name Mtu  Net/Dest   Address     Ipkts    Ierrs Opkts    Oerrs Collis Queue
lo0  8232 loopback   localhost   287885   0     287885   0     0      0
le0  1500 140.254.12. rosalyn.bio 6894652  3     6923834  2     554607 0
```

Overall, rosalyn looks relatively healthy. The one warning sign is that the collision rate is a bit high, at 8 percent. This doesn't break the "stay below 10 percent" rule for a healthy network, but it's a bit odd for a machine with such low utilization to have such a high collision rate. One possible cause would be if this was a machine that didn't get much use on a network full of more active machines. Another possibility is that there's a somewhat "nearby" network error and that this machine is frequently colliding with itself. (Remember the string and the reflected wave?) With no other information, it's impossible to determine the cause at this time.

For a machine that's only been on for 6 days, the Ierrs and Oerrs are high as well, but it's not too uncommon for a machine to pick up a few initial errors when it and the hardware around it are powering up. If those numbers doubled again next week, I'd start to worry.

Now, use the spray program. The spray command literally sprays packets at the remote host as fast as the local machine can get them on the wire:

```
soyokaze ray 107> spray rosalyn
sending 1162 packets of lnth 86 to rosalyn ...
        in 10.4 seconds elapsed time,
        355 packets (30.55%) dropped
Sent:   112 packets/sec, 9.4K bytes/sec
Rcvd:   77 packets/sec, 6.5K bytes/sec
```

The output from the spray command is relatively easy to understand. It tells you what it did and how fast. It also tells you what the statistics were. Two pieces of data should set off immediate alarm bells here. The first frightening number is that 30.55 percent dropped packets figure. Somewhere along the line, 355 packets, out of the total 1162 that were sent, got lost. This isn't exactly the sort of thing you'd want out of a stable network.

Your immediate supposition might be that rosalyn just isn't fast enough to receive all that data as quickly as soyokaze sent it out. If you knew the actual hardware involved, that possibility wouldn't be too high on your list. If you do use spray as a diagnostic, you should be aware that an overloaded machine, or one that can't read data from the network fast enough, can give false impressions. To make absolutely certain this isn't the case here, I check the netstat data for rosalyn again:

```
Rosalyn ray 13 > netstat -i
Name Mtu  Net/Dest    Address     Ipkts    Ierrs Opkts   Oerrs Collis Queue
lo0  8232 loopback    localhost   287895   0     287895  0     0      0
le0  1500 140.254.12. rosalyn.bio 6895841  3     6923851 2     554607 0
```

Notice that rosalyn's Ipkts value has gone from 6894652 to 6895841. 6,895,841–6,894,652=1,189. It certainly seems likely that rosalyn got all 1,162 of the packets from soyokaze, and that it picked up a few from somewhere else, as well.

21

The packets that it echoes back to soyokaze unfortunately don't get added to the Opkts count, but you can see from this that rosalyn accepted all the packets.

The other numbers that should alarm you are the data rates. 9.4KB/second sent, and 6.5KB/second received? A good modem can almost beat those speeds! For a pair of machines separated by five floors and a couple hundred feet of network cable, this is quite poor performance. For those machines on an almost unloaded network at midnight, that performance is so abysmally bad that it's laughable.

To further the diagnostic a bit, try the same thing from a different machine:

```
pacific:  31>> spray rosalyn.biosci.ohio-state.edu
sending 1162 packets of lnth 86 to rosalyn.biosci.ohio-state.edu ...
        in 0.5 seconds elapsed time,
        1 packets (0.09%) dropped
Sent:   2387 packets/sec, 200.5K bytes/sec
Rcvd:   2385 packets/sec, 200.3K bytes/sec
```

Okay! That's more like it. One packet dropped isn't a horrible amount of loss (although I'd like 0 better), and the transfer rates are running at about 1/5 the theoretical bandwidth and 1/3 the practical bandwidth. This isn't too bad at all! Unfortunately, whereas soyokaze is located five floors away from rosalyn, the new machine, pacific, is located in a different building on a different network that is about a mile across campus from soyokaze and rosalyn. Something is very wrong here.

See what else you can find out:

```
pacific: 32>> spray soyokaze.biosci.ohio-state.edu
sending 1162 packets of lnth 86 to soyokaze.biosci.ohio-state.edu ...
        in 0.5 seconds elapsed time,
        1 packets (0.09%) dropped
Sent:   2470 packets/sec, 207.5K bytes/sec
Rcvd:   2468 packets/sec, 207.3K bytes/sec
```

You can find out that for the same remote machine, soyokaze is just as quick and just as stable a connection as rosalyn. Commence to scratching your head harder. There doesn't seem to be anything wrong with the connection between the world and either machine. Something must be wrong between them.

Just to confirm this, I'll spray soyokaze from rosalyn:

```
Rosalyn ray 19 > spray soyokaze
sending 1162 packets of length 86 to soyokaze ...
        906 packets (77.969%) dropped by soyokaze
        16 packets/sec, 1437 bytes/sec
```

Yikes! I get data in a slightly different format because rosalyn is a Solaris machine instead of the SunOS machines I've been using spray on, but that's even worse than the other way around! The packet loss is up so high that one can consider the network between these machines to be essentially dead. The transmission rate, a mighty 1.4KB per second, confirms this. If I need to move a file between these machines, I might as well write it down on paper, walk upstairs, and type it back in! (Just so you know, no, the answer isn't that soyokaze can't keep up with rosalyn's data rate, either. This can also be verified by netstat.)

Finally, you can run a check using the nfsstat program. The nfsstat command gives you statistics on the behavior of your NFS server and client mounts. It also turns out to be one of the most useful network diagnostic tools at your disposal. It keeps track of when it has to duplicate requests because it never got a response, as well as when it got duplicate responses out of order, presumably as a result of it timing out and asking for the same data twice. I have one of rosalyn's drives NFS-mounted on soyokaze, so I'll copy a file from it to my directory on soyokaze to generate some NFS traffic.

First, look at the client machine and see what the statistics currently look like:

```
soyokaze mnt2 124> nfsstat -c
```

```
Client rpc:
calls     badcalls retrans  badxid    timeout  wait      newcred  timers
72        0        0        0         0        0         0        0

Client nfs:
calls     badcalls  nclget    nclsleep
72        0         72        0
null      getattr   setattr   root      lookup    readlink  read
0   0%    17 23%    0   0%    0   0%    40 55%    0   0%    5   6%
wrcache   write     create    remove    rename    link      symlink
0   0%    0   0%    0   0%    0   0%    0   0%    0   0%    0   0%
mkdir     rmdir     readdir   fsstat
0   0%    0   0%    5   6%    5   6%
```

The interesting data is all on the first line, and you can see that not much has happened with NFS on soyokaze since it was rebooted. Next, I'll copy a relatively large file from the directory mounted from rosalyn to my home directory:

```
soyokaze mnt2 125> cp installed/ssh-1.2.26.tar ~/
```

One of the symptoms of this particular building's sick network is exceptionally slow NFS traffic, so this copy takes minutes instead of the seconds that it should take.

After it finally returns a prompt, it's time to take another look at soyokaze's nfsstat output:

```
soyokaze mnt2 126> nfsstat -c
```

```
Client rpc:
calls     badcalls retrans  badxid    timeout  wait      newcred  timers
1703      19       0        0         19       0         0        0
```

21

```
Client nfs:
calls      badcalls    nclget      nclsleep
1684       0           1684        0
null       getattr     setattr     root       lookup     readlink   read
0  0%      19  1%      0  0%       0  0%      40  2%     0  0%      1615 95%
wrcache    write       create      remove     rename     link       symlink
0  0%      0  0%       0  0%       0  0%      0  0%      0  0%      0  0%
mkdir      rmdir       readdir     fsstat
0  0%      0  0%       5  0%       5  0%
```

As you can see, just this one cp command generated considerably more traffic than the machine had seen in the previous week. The important fields to note again are all in the first line of data. Specifically, the badcalls and timeout fields have jumped to 19 each. The badcalls field is an indication of how many times the client has gotten information that it could not interpret and that it needed to throw away. This matches nicely with the timeout field, which is the number of packets that the client was waiting for and that never arrived.

You might not think that 19 packets out of 1,700 is a significant amount of traffic loss, and overall, you'd be right. It's nowhere near the 30 percent or greater loss that you see with spray. These numbers alone don't tell the whole story. The problem is not just the number of lost packets, but how this network is losing them. NFS uses a timer fallback routine to deal with lost data. When it gets a timeout on expected data, it doubles the previous timeout value, asks again, and waits again. Repeated several times, the 10 millisecond default wait for the next packet turns into a 10 second wait for the next packet.

Although I hate to personify to the extent of assigning malicious intent to a piece of wire, this network seems to selectively damage packets in such a way as to maximize NFS timeout delays. If I rearrange machines on the same wire, I can produce differences in these numbers and in this behavior. This is theoretically impossible. Theory, at least here, doesn't work.

Interpretation

Now that you've seen how to detect that there is a problem, you're probably wondering how that data can be used to diagnose what it is and how to fix it. The short answer to the question is that with only these tools, you can at best determine whether the problem is still there. You have no way to localize it to a particular piece of wire or to a particular device without exhaustively going through your network and removing and substituting bits until the problem goes away.

There are some hints that the software diagnostics gives you that might be useful in determining where to look, however:

- Check the `Ierrs` and `Oerrs` fields for your machine's interfaces. If there's something wrong with the cabling connection to an interface or with an interface itself, you might expect that the `Ierrs` and `Oerrs` values would be relatively close. In soyokaze's case, the `Ierrs` value that is significantly higher than the `Oerrs` value is likely to indicate something relatively far away from the machine is corrupting the data.

- If the `netstat` data for the machine receiving a `spray` doesn't show that all the packets are showing up, consider whether the receiving machine is fast enough to capture all the data. If you're relatively certain that it is, check to see, for example, whether 30 percent of the packets you send don't get to the `sprayd` machine and whether 30 percent of the remaining 70 percent don't get back to the machine that sent the `spray`. Network problems in cabling should be symmetric. If a cable is going to corrupt data, it doesn't matter what end the data came from, it's still going to corrupt data. Hardware such as repeaters or switches, on the other hand, can selectively corrupt data based on content, origin, or any number of other factors.

- If the `nfsstat` data shows `badxid` values that increase rapidly, expect that something is delaying network traffic somewhere, rather than completely losing it. The `badxid` value shouldn't increase unless the client resends a request due to a timeout and then gets back a response to both the original and the duplicate request.

- If sprays between certain machines cause packet loss but both machines show clean network connections to a third machine, suspect some piece of hardware such as a repeater or switch.

- If `netstat` shows a higher collision rate than your average network load, chances are that you're seeing the results of the machine producing collisions with itself. Because the length of your network cable is so short compared to the speed of light, data that your machine writes is essentially everywhere on the cable simultaneously. Reflections then bounce back and are seen by the writing interface while it's still in the process of writing. This results in a collision and a resend. If you have a thinnet network, suspect a faulty or missing terminator somewhere between the machine and any repeaters, switches, or routers. Collisions that happen on the other side of a repeater or other packet-forwarding hardware won't be seen by your machine's interface, so they won't be logged by `netstat`.

- Try playing with your NFS send and receive buffer sizes (see your man pages for details), and watch the changes in the `nfsstat` data. If your network behaves better the smaller you make your transmission buffers, you almost certainly have a buggy piece of hardware on your network.

- Remember that "between" in the network sense means everything that's directly attached to your network and not on the other side of a router. Just because the

21

machines you're using for diagnosis are next to each other in an office, that doesn't mean that the problems you're seeing regarding transferring data between them isn't at the end of their network segment two floors down. Unless your network uses switches everywhere, instead of hubs, a given machine's signal is more or less "everywhere" on a network simultaneously, so a problematic length of wire or defective piece of hardware doesn't have to be "line of wire" between the machines to affect the signal.

Note

> I have a sneaking suspicion that the source of the sick network's problems I've presented to you are with an antique (pre-1991) repeater somewhere in the building. Unfortunately for the users in this building, it's not my network to take care of. Older repeaters are known to have trouble dealing with back-to-back strings of packets, and both NFS and spray generate exactly this sort of behavior. This supposition is further supported by the results of the ping; remember the results from the ping, back when things looked encouraging? If the network were really losing 30 to 70 percent of the traffic between soyokaze and rosalyn, it would have lost 30 to 70 percent of the ping traffic as well. Because it didn't, I can fairly safely rule out cabling problems, which would leave me with only hardware to check.

Network Hardware Diagnostics

Hardware diagnostics are the way that you should be tracking and fixing these problems, especially if you want to maintain your sanity and your pleasant personality.

The prime piece of hardware for network testing is a network fault tester. This wonderful little object can be plugged into your network and will tell you, frequently to the nearest inch, where any sources of impedance problems are. It can literally walk you right to a defective Tee connector or faulty length of wire. If you're going to be doing network diagnostics, this is one piece of hardware that you really should not be without.

The second piece of hardware that you will want for network testing is a protocol tester. The protocol tester usually comes in two parts: a signal injection unit and a monitoring unit. The signal injection unit can be taken anywhere in your network and can be used to generate different types of network traffic. The monitor then listens to the different types of traffic and produces a diagnostic that indicates the behavior of your network for "real situation" type loads.

I can't say this frequently enough. If you have to diagnose and fix problems with your network, beg, borrow, or steal network testing hardware. The capability to use one of these devices can make the difference between a network that is fixed and running in a day and a network that goes for years without the source of an ongoing problem ever being identified.

Fixing the Network Problem

Without a network tester to bring you straight to the source of a problem, the solution becomes a game of guesswork. You will have to isolate the portion of your network that seems to cause the problem to manifest, and then go through this segment removing or replacing hardware until the problem goes away. Unfortunately, you will sometimes find that the problem is some compound problem that requires some collection of machines and hardware to be present to manifest itself. These are the most annoying and the most difficult to find.

Your repair procedure then becomes replace, diagnose, and repeat as necessary. Tedious, troublesome, and prone to miss problems with large pieces of hardware that you can't afford to simply swap out multiple instances of, this is really your only solution, unless you can find a network tester.

Software

What can you, as the system administrator, do about software errors? That's a good question. There is only so much that you can do because you are the system administrator rather than the programmer. Document what you are doing so that if you have to, you can give the software author something to work with.

Defining the Software Problem

The most useful capacity in which you can usually serve as a system administrator fighting with a software problem is in the definition of the problem. First of all, check the logs. Do the logs provide any helpful clues? If they do, try to fix whatever the logs indicate could be a problem. This could be simple, or even with the help of the logs, this could take a while to track down.

You have to be able to reproduce the error. Take down as much information as you can about the circumstances of the error. What software is also running? What commands were you trying to execute at the time? Is there a certain time of day connected with the problem? Does it only happen for certain users? If so, are they close to their quota? What about their account might be different from a user who doesn't have the problem?

Try to reproduce the error on another machine. Can you reproduce the error? Does it have the same type of entry in the logs? Is the problem reproducible on only one machine?

21

Diagnosing the Software Problem

Check and recheck your configuration files. Sometimes, the use of tabs rather than spaces, or having or not having a space at the end of the line or the end of the file, makes the difference between software that works and software that doesn't work.

Check the newsgroups. Are others experiencing the same trouble? Would their solution work for you? If so, implement it.

Are you having a problem with software for which you have a support contract? If so, make use of that contract.

Does the problem still persist after you've tried everything you can think of to solve it? Contact the software author. No one knows the code better than the author does. Because most UNIX software authors are genuinely interested in producing quality code, you might volunteer access to your system so that they can address the bug directly.

Don't bother the author more than necessary. She might have a solution for you after a while, or if the author says that even she doesn't know what the problem is, that's as good as it gets.

Did you contact the author but he didn't have time to try to deal with the problem directly on your site? Give him as much information as you have been able to document on the problem, but don't be a pest. The more information he already has, the more likely he will be to try to find time to examine the problem.

Were you lucky enough to narrow down the cause of the problem and actually fix it? If so, send to the author the fix you made as well as everything about the circumstances of the problem so that she can examine the problem even further at her end. Try bribing your local programmer with the notion of the fame and adulation he will receive if he fixes the problem for the author. Buy him a 12-pack of Mountain Dew as thanks.

Human Error

Although it might seem like your job should deal exclusively with the machines, you wouldn't be needed if there weren't users who had to use those machines. Like it or not, you will have to help the users with their problems. The human errors will be annoyingly the most frequent and frequently the most annoying problems you will have to deal with. Do not fall into the trap of thinking of your users as some sort of second-class computer users, however. They will make many mistakes that to you seem completely idiotic, but they aren't system administrators and don't have your level of familiarity with the operating system and the machines. This is completely normal and something that you should be pleased about, not an excuse for you to belittle them. After all, if they knew as much about the machines as you do, what would they need you for? And if you knew as much about their jobs as they do, you might be in danger of being a pointy-haired manager! Yikes!

In any case, you need to deal with your users fairly and kindly, but frequently firmly. Holding users' hands will turn out to be a bigger part of your job than you would probably like it to be, but it is something you need to practice in moderation. Make yourself available enough that you don't alienate yourself from your users, but make certain that you don't overextend your helpfulness and decrease your actual productivity in maintaining your cluster.

What Did You Change?

The wonderful 90-percent perfect LART—this solution to users' problems won't always work, but it will work more often than you might imagine. To get it to work, it usually has to be applied several times—sometimes to the point of pain. Be strong: It's for their own good. Just as you can make stupid mistakes with what you're doing, so can your users with what they are doing. Sometimes they need to be reminded of this.

This solution is usually a good place to start when you get the questions like "The Web server stopped working; when will it be fixed?" or "Why can't I access the FTP server today?" Whether you get the question when you first arrive in the morning or later in the day, do whatever you can to double-check that the service that you already know has been working for a while is still working. After all, you have to make the users feel like you're doing the most that you can.

After you have quickly verified that it's not your machine or cluster, apply the "What did you change?" LART. When the question posed to you only involves the user's machine, skip the verification step and go directly to the application step. The response, of course, will be "nothing." After a few more applications, the response will still be "nothing." Eventually, if you are persistent, you will finally get what you need to hear. This is when you will discover that he tried to change a setting somewhere in the software package or in his PC's OS. Or he upgraded his software but forgot to change that one little setting that makes a difference. Or he upgraded his operating system last week, but this is the first time since then that he has tried to access this service. Or he got a new machine.

I think you get the picture.

Read the Fine Manual

Sometimes it's necessary to tell your users that they should "RTFM," which means "Read the Fine Manual" (at least it's usually better if you tell them it's a "Fine" manual, anyway). They should be able to read the manual just as well as you can, or better,

21

actually, if they are trying to use software that makes use of their areas of expertise. Your time, in that it belongs to all your users, is as valuable as theirs, and there is no way for you to know how to run every piece of software on the system or on the user's machine. So, don't be afraid to tell your users to read the manual.

When the users are trying to do something for which you have already written instructions, be especially sure to ask that very important question, "Have you read the instructions?" You'll be surprised to find out how many people are just calling you to avoid reading those instructions that you wrote so that they wouldn't have to call you!

Walking Through a Problem

Yes, sometimes, it will be completely unavoidable. Sometimes, you will have to try to walk a user through a problem. Sometimes, when you've asked if she has read the manual, she will actually say "yes" and point to what she believes is the pertinent section of the manual.

So, you're wondering, how am I supposed to help someone use software that involves areas I know nothing about? Sometimes, that is when you can be more helpful than you realize. Sometimes, you can just somehow flip through the manual and find what the user needs to know.

Other times, you read the manual with the user, have the user do exactly what he is supposed to be doing, and personally see that it doesn't work for him. It might surprise you, but you can frequently see his problem coming a mile away. It usually has nothing at all to do with the software and usually does have something to do with a lack of understanding of UNIX or a lack of ability to follow direction. I've taken to carrying around a red pen so that I can underline the step in the procedure that a user's ignored now for the 54th time in a row, rather than having to actually tell him out loud. If what he's doing actually resembles what the instructions say to do, try doing it once yourself. Your users might have more of a science or math (or whatever) background than you do, but actually holding down the mouse button while dragging is probably more intuitive to you.

Sometimes, the users can be so caught up in the science behind what they are doing that using what appears to be an obvious tool to you doesn't cross their minds. Likewise, few users probably realize that the numeric keypad usually doesn't produce numbers, or they don't know any number of other perfectly natural UNIX quirks that are second nature to you but are completely foreign to them.

You'll be quite amazed at what you can figure out about your users' software without knowing anything in their areas of expertise. It's frightening too. Especially when they suddenly ask you about the science that they are supposed to know!

When to Give Up

As helpful as you might want to be, you have too much to do. You aren't going to be able to help all your users with all their problems all the time. When you start to do that, you will start getting calls for every little problem. After that, you spend more time away from your office than in it, and you get further and further behind in your job of keeping your machines stable and secure.

Sometimes, you will just have to say up front that you don't have the time. Your users won't like that, but you do have to get some of your job done too. Try to suggest some Web sites, manuals, or other users who might be able to help. Where possible, send them to a co-worker after they've tried the other suggestions you've made.

Common Problems or Error Messages

In this lesson, I covered both the approach to problem solving and some specific methods that you might use for solving general problems with your machines. The information that follows is a list of the top problems I have encountered. Some of these are problems that you will encounter yourself as a system administrator, and some are problems that your users will bring to you. Listed here are problems or error messages you might see, followed by probable reasons or things to check to find the likely cause.

Note

> I'm trying to keep these answers short and to the point. Because of this, some of the ones that deal with users are going to verge on brutality. As previously mentioned, don't take this as justification for user abuse. When I say that the complaint "Machine <some UNIX machine> isn't working" is almost always due to a user who can't type, you should read this to mean "Out of the hundreds of times that I've seen this complaint, it's almost universally from a user who mistyped something, who insists that she didn't mistype it, and who probably didn't bother to try again because when I hike across campus to her office and make her try again in front of me, it all works just fine." No offense to the users is intended, but I don't feel like having to repeat that over and over for each of the user-oriented problems below.

NIS domain shipsahoy not responding.

Is ypbind running on the client machine? Have you properly configured any configuration files that might be required on the client? Is the NIS master running? Is the network up and functional? Is shipsahoy actually your NIS domain?

21

NFS server mother not responding.

Is mother up? Does this happen so regularly that it could be problems with your network? Did mother reboot and forget to export the drives?

Network traffic to remote machines works, but to local machines, it does not. Sometimes, this comes worded as "When is the Web server going to be fixed? I can access the WWW, but I can't access our server."

This is almost certainly a `netmask` problem. Is it `255.255.0.0` when it is supposed to be `255.255.255.0`?

Network traffic to local machines works, but to remote machines, it does not.

This is almost certainly a machine without a default route or, on a personal computer, without a "gateway" configured. A few UNIX implementations used to come with no provision for setting a default route in the `rc` files, and you had to add a `route` statement by hand. If `netstat -r` or `route` (depending on your OS) doesn't show a "default" route as one of your choices, read your `route` man page for how to set the default.

Machine `<some UNIX machine>` isn't working.

What about it isn't working? Don't you just love specific error reports? This is a typical user complaint. It usually means that the user mistyped something, and rather than try again, she's calling you.

I can't log in.

Assuming that you haven't actually locked them out on purpose, you say, "Have you tried again? Did you type your password correctly? Do you remember your password?" On the off chance that it's not one of those, you might also check whether the drive with the user's directory is up and mounted. Some UNIX flavors won't let you log in when your home directory is missing. After you've hiked to the user's office, remind him that passwords are case-sensitive, and everything will work.

I get "permission denied" when I try to execute a script.

Have you added execution permission to your script?

I get "Command not found" when I try to execute a script.

Ahh! A tricky one. This could be the standard error output of the script or of any command in the script. Make sure that all the commands in the script (including the shell startup command on the first line) actually use findable executable commands.

NFS traffic is slow.

You're losing data somewhere. Use nfsstat -c on the client and nfsstat -s on the server. Move a few big files over the network and try to correlate the error statistics you see. The short answer is generally "your network is broken," and you should remember my thoughts on that.

Ping indicates high packet loss.

Your network is broken. There's a good possibility that it's cabling- or termination-related. Try to isolate what portions of the network show the high packet loss, and see if you can whittle it down to a straight wire between two machines.

Host not found.

This is either a typo, or you aren't getting name service for some reason. Netscape in particular seems to have a problem finding hosts that actually do exist. If it's a user complaint and he's using Netscape, tell him to click the link again. Usually, the Netscape-specific problem goes away on the second try. On rare occasions, Netscape seems determined to not find a particular, legitimate host. In this case, you might try pinging the host because just talking to it with ping seems to be enough to coax Netscape back to reality. Alternatively, you're seeing a nameserver problem. Use nslookup and see if you can find a host that you know exists.

Fatal error while compiling—symbol not found.

You're missing a library that should be being linked, or a library you have is missing a routine that the programmer expected. After you learn everything else about system administration, you can tackle this one by a clever application of the nm command. Until then, consider the software broken and find a programmer.

Fatal error while compiling—syntax error.

Unless you've been mucking about in the code, this isn't an error you should see frequently as a system administrator. If you do, it might be a difference in the version of the programming language that was used. You might try using a different C compiler (gcc accepts many things that cc finds offensive in its usual mode and rejects many things that cc accepts when you turn on -pedantic mode). If that doesn't work, again, don't waste your time. Find a programmer and move on to more productive things.

Fatal error while compiling—unexpected EOF.

Your makefile is broken. This happens occasionally in transport or when a programmer doesn't notice that something is wrong because in her development environment it never takes that path to the product. Usually, the problem that causes this is that there are

21

spaces instead of tabs in the makefile. Find all the makefiles associated with the software you're compiling, edit them, delete any leading spaces on lines, and replace them all with a single tab. If that doesn't work, see the preceding two problems.

Perfect-looking configuration file produces errors or fails silently.

Check the logs for any useful hints. Frequently, this is another manifestation of the "spaces look like tabs" problem. It often comes from copying a configuration file entry from a Web page.

Printer not responsive, processing light blinking, not printing.

What's in the queue? Is someone printing a job that will take a long time to process? Some printers don't communicate with some UNIX flavors very well—especially if you're stuck on a System V printing environment with an unsupported printer that you've tricked into working with another printer's description. These printers frequently get "stuck" waiting for data from the computer when a job is canceled and the computer doesn't terminate the job correctly. When the next job comes along, the computer checks with the printer, sees that it's in the process of receiving data, and waits for the printer to finish. If you're serving an AppleTalk printer network, it might be that someone impolite has registered a printer with a duplicate name; it seems that Windows NT is capable of doing this incredibly useless thing and creating considerable confusion among the AppleTalk printer users.

Terminal hangs on exit.

You're using `ssh2` on a Sun, right? Open another window on the client and kill the `ssh2` or `slogin` process.

Login very slow.

Quotas are turned on, your NFS system is dragging, or both. Quotas being turned on in addition to NFS running slowly can cause logins to take seemingly forever.

High CPU usage.

Too much stuff is running! If you see continual usage values much over the low single digits, your machine is being over-utilized. Usually, this only happens when something is wrong, unless you have an older machine that is providing legacy services for a growing user base. Frequently the cause, if you should happen to see high CPU usage, is either an errant process that's gone and forked a gadzillion copies of itself or a denial of service attack in progress.

Process table full.

This comes along with the high CPU usage when something breaks and goes forking away. This can also be the *result* of a denial of service attack in progress. Usually, it's almost impossible to get a command in edgewise when this happens, but if you can manage, kill off some parented process that creates lots of children, such as your Web server. If you can kill a parent that will take out 20 children with it, you might have the few seconds you need to get in a few syncs and a clean halt, rather than having to power-off.

The FTP server won't let me store files.

You say, "Let me guess, either you're trying to store into a directory that doesn't have write permission, or you're using a Mac or a PC and have spaces or strange characters in your filenames."

<command> not found.

Is the directory containing *<command>* in your path? Did you type the command correctly?

Couldn't find lib<somelib>.so.

Does lib*<somelib>*.so exist? If it does, is the path to the directory containing it in your LD_LIBRARY_PATH?

Can't open display.

You probably didn't set your DISPLAY environment variable, or possibly it's pointing at a machine on which you haven't enabled the client access to display. Use xhost +*<machinename>* or the xauth program (if you feel brave) on the server (to be displayed to machine) to add permission. Use setenv DISPLAY *<hostname>*:0.0 to point the client's display somewhere in particular.

Disk filled overnight.

Crackers or illegal software traders found your open anonymous FTP site. Something went wrong and your logs are growing at 10MB/min. You've got a server that's core-dumping and an OS that's kind enough to keep all your spare cores.

Network is slow.

Your network is broken. Find someone qualified to fix it before you go insane.

Drive is difficult to get online after power off.

It's in a case with a failing power supply, or you're having "stiction" problems. The solution is to not shut it off. UNIX isn't designed to have the machines or drives shut off ever anyway. Get yourself a UPS and leave everything humming away happily ever after. By the way, have you made a full backup recently?

21

Traffic is low but collisions are high.

You're on a coaxial network, and you're missing a terminator. Your machine's traffic collides with itself every time it tries to talk.

Program doesn't behave as expected.

Coming from a system administrator, this usually means that you misconfigured something. Reread the documentation, find the appropriate Usenet newsgroup, read the FAQ, then politely ask, and then try again. Coming from a user, this generally means that she expected the wrong thing.

NFS mounts stopped working.

You're using an OS that uses that horrid automounter. Your previous mounts are all now neatly stored where you don't want them in the /net directory (most likely). Search out and destroy the automounter.

Machine crashes frequently and randomly.

OS bugs, disk errors on the swap space, and problems with your SCSI chain are the first place to look. Memory problems are another possibility.

My email all disappeared.

The user reads his email with a popmail client, doesn't he? It's probably on whatever machine he last read email on, dutifully downloaded and deleted from the server. There's also the possibility that he's using a mail-reading client that moves the mail out of the system mailbox into $HOME/mbox after it has been read.

Can't write to an NFS mounted drive.

You probably don't have root access set properly. Something else to check is that some NFS servers are picky about whether you specify the clients by name or IP and will "almost" work with the option they don't prefer, but they won't quite work right.

The Web server says "Forbidden."

Check the permissions on the file you are trying to access and the directory it's in. Are group and world allowed to access the file and complete path? Is it a restricted access site? Does the site know about your machine?

My X11 display is nonresponsive.

You've hit an annoying X11 bug. You have either just stopped, killed, or exited a process and then sent a key click or mouse event to it before it unregistered with the X11 server. The server is waiting for the software to accept your action before talking to you again, and the software is either dead or in limbo and isn't taking any callers. The only solution I've found is to access the machine remotely and kill off the X11 server.

I try to save files that I've edited but the changes don't show up.

You say, "Did you pay any attention when you logged in and it said, 'You're 40MB over your allowed disk quota. You will not be able to write any files until you have reduced your allocation and are under the quota limit again?'"

I wrote a Perl script to do something, but it seems to just hang.

It's not actually hanging (probably). Perl outputs through an output buffer and won't write its data to the screen or output stream until it has accumulated a certain amount of data. If you've written a program that outputs periodic diagnostics just so that you know it's working and you don't see them, expect that this is what you're seeing. It is left as an exercise for the reader to figure out how to flush `stdout` in Perl.

The network load and Web or FTP usage just went through the roof.

Either you've just been cracked, you've just been discovered as an open anonymous FTP site, or one of your users just posted a nudie picture of herself to her Web page and announced it to the world.

On Bogons, Cosmic Rays, and Other Sources of Random Failure

Sometimes, it seems like the gods of computers are just against you. Things crash for no apparent reason, software that once worked perfectly decides to contract "bit rot" and suddenly becomes buggy, things just go wrong. You might blame some of this on the occasional passing cosmic ray that grazes a bit too close to your CPU, but other times the "cosmic ray" theory would have you believe you'd suddenly moved to somewhere uncomfortably close to a quasar.

System administrators the world over have come to the conclusion that there is an additional, as yet undiscovered elementary particle in the universe. This particle is known as a "bogon" and is theorized to be the elementary particle of which stupidity is made. Certain users, certain computers, and certain software in some situations seem to spontaneously emit bogons. This generally wreaks havoc with any nearby equipment or software and is theorized to be the cause of much suffering in the computing world.

Whether the occasional outbreak of random failures is related to cosmic rays, bogons, or just plain old bad luck, sometimes it happens, and when it does, there's nothing you can do about it. On these days, it's best to just find a good book, walk outside, ponder the

21

meaning of that big burning thing in the sky, and take a break. Read something other than a technical manual. Go out and get a meal that's not fast food or twinkies. Get a good night's sleep for a change; tomorrow, it's back to chasing dragons and tilting at windmills.

Summary

In finishing out the topics for your three week introduction to system administration, you covered troubleshooting hardware, software, and human errors. Hopefully, you won't need the information contained in this chapter for quite a while, but if you do, always keep in mind that the more you know and the better you document it, the better off you will be.

In today's lesson, you covered the following:

- Spotting and diagnosing problems with your CPU
- Spotting and diagnosing problems with your peripherals
- Network diagnostics on the cheap and not easy
- Software errors
- Human errors

Q&A

Q My *device* stopped working; what's wrong?

A AAARRRGH!!! You're a system administrator! Don't act like a user! If you're going to ask someone to help you with a problem, give her complete information. Quantify "stopped working." How did it stop? What did it do normally? What did it do last? What does it do now? What diagnostics are available? Do you have a manual? What does it say? What have you tried? How would you know if it started working again?

Q I think I'm having network problems. Whenever I copy a file...

A Don't even continue with the question. If you have network problems, you're in for a long process of guesswork and hair-pulling if you don't have a network test set. If you do have a test set, don't spend any time on software diagnostics; plug it in and follow the instructions. If you don't have a test set and you have a network with more than a handful of computers, consign yourself to *at least* several hundred hours of nerve-wracking attempts to diagnose the problem and the knowledge that even after all that, you've got at best a 50 percent chance of fixing it. The best I can offer are the diagnostic hints in this chapter and my condolences.

Q A user is having a problem with *something*. For everyone else, it seems to work fine. Where do I start?

A It's almost certainly human error of some sort. I've only run into one situation where a piece of software genuinely didn't work properly for one particular user, and that was because the NIS server username was too long for the OS that the NIS client was running. In your case, you're almost certainly looking at a user who ran the software once, set some personal preferences in some dialog box, and has (inconveniently) forgotten what he did. You'll have the most luck searching around in the user's directory for a configuration file for the program and deleting it. Beware—the user will immediately complain that he desperately needed the settings in the configuration file he didn't remember creating. If that approach doesn't yield rapid results, save yourself the headaches and just create a new account for him and let him move his old files over to the new account.

Workshop

Quiz

1. What things should you check even before the logs when you have problems with peripheral hardware?

2. My disk drive found a bunch of new "bad blocks" recently. Is it safe to keep using it?

3. My disk drives are new, supposedly super-reliable mechanisms, but they keep dying. Why might that be?

4. What does the author recommend as the right way to find network problems?

Exercises

I'm tempted to tell you to find a friend and have her create a network error for you—such as loosening a connection slightly or swapping in a mismatched terminator—and have you try to track it down. That, however, would be cruel and unusual treatment and probably not a realistic exercise because your friend, assuming she's really your friend, will eventually take pity on you and fix it for you.

Instead, I'll point out that no system is ever perfect or error-free. If you've followed along, you should have a rather solid installation with few software or hardware errors. There's not much I can do to suggest ways to get practice diagnosing hardware, but I'll forward the notion that your software installation undoubtedly could use tweaking. You're a system administrator now, and your entire system is your responsibility—and your testing grounds. Finding and fixing problems is now what you do, hopefully for fun. Find a problem, and fix it. Repeat as necessary. This exercise should take you, roughly, the rest of your career. Good luck!

21

APPENDIXES

At a Glance

You can use the appendixes to gain more information about topics discussed in this book, as well as supplemental forms to help get you on your way as a system administrator—and don't forget the answers to all of those quiz questions you've been asked!

- Appendix A, "Useful UNIX Commands for the System Administrator"
- Appendix B, "Sample Operating System Installations"
- Appendix C, "Useful Files"
- Appendix D, "Legal Stuff"
- Appendix E, "Useful Resources"
- Appendix F, "Useful Sample Forms"
- Appendix G, "Quiz Answers"

A

B

C

D

E

F

G

APPENDIX A

Useful UNIX Commands for the System Administrator

This appendix contains brief information about commands that the system administrator will find useful. The commands described here are fairly common commands. This appendix does not describe commands specific to a particular operating system. Not all available options to a command are listed, because not every operating system supports every option. Only potentially interesting options are listed.

This listing is only intended to give you a quick overview of what a command may be able to do for you. As always, consult the man pages for your operating system for more specific details.

df—Lists amount of free disk space

Use

df [-iklm] [-F FSType] [filesystem]

df [-t FSType] [filesystem]

Description

df summarizes disk block use of a filesystem. It provides information on total blocks, amount used, and amount available.

Depending on your operating system, there can be a lot of options with df.

Options

- i—Reports number of used and free inodes.
- k—Reports in 1024-byte units (KB). This is the default on some systems. On others, 512-byte units are the default.
- l—Reports on local filesystems.
- m—Reports in 1,048,576-byte units (MB).
- F FSType—Reports on the specified filesystem type.
- t type—Reports on the specified filesystem type.

Examples

df -t 4.2 (Reports for filesystems of type 4.2 on SunOS system.)

```
Filesystem            kbytes       used      avail   capacity    Mounted on
/dev/sd0a              47575       6804      36014      16%       /
/dev/sd0g             311975     172435     108343      61%       /usr
/dev/sd2a            1155517     537638     502328      52%       /usr/local
/dev/sd2d             606463          9     545808       0%       /archive
/dev/sd2e             900158        232     809911       0%       /home
```

df -lm (Reports in MB for local filesystems on IRIX system.)

```
Filesystem           Type  MB-blocks    use     avail  %use Mounted on
/dev/root            xfs        4014    2790     1224   70  /
```

df -k -F efs (Reports in KB for efs filesystems on IRIX system.)

```
Filesystem           Type  blocks      use      avail  %use Mounted on
/dev/dsk/dks1d3s6    efs   7822720    6972307    850413  90  /old_local_share
```

du—Summarizes disk use

Use

du [-askx] [name]

Description

du summarizes the number of blocks used in a directory (recursively) or file. If no argument is given, the default is the current directory.

Options

- a—Generates output for each file. The default is to only generate output for a directory.
- s—Generates a grand total.
- k—Summarizes in 1024-byte (KB) blocks. This is the default on some systems. On others, 512-byte blocks are the default.
- x—Excludes calculating disk use for files not located in the same filesystem as the argument.

Examples

du -a misc-logs (Summarizes disk use of file misc-logs.)

6   misc-logs

du -sk work (Provides a grand total summary of directory work.)

1630   work

du -a 2drp (Generates output listing for each file in 2drp directory.)

453   2drp/2drp.pdb
454   2drp

dump—Incremental filesystem backup

Use

dump [options] [arguments] filesystem

Description

dump backs up all files in a filesystem or all files in a filesystem that have changed since the last dump. Backed up files can then be retrieved later using command restore which we will address later in this appendix.

[options] is a string of options.

[arguments] is a list of the arguments that appear in the order of the *[options]*.

It is recommended that full dumps be done in single-user mode. Be sure to clean your tape heads as recommended by your manufacturer. Also, check your man pages for any recommendations on blocking factor, size, density, and other options.

In Solaris, ufsdump is equivalent to dump. Other operating systems may use a streaming dump instead, which will likely be quite different from this dump.

Options

0-9 specifies the dump level. 0 denotes a full dump, which is a backup of all the files in the filesystem.

- f—Specifies a dump output location other than the default tape device. If the output location is of the form machine:device, the dump is being sent to a remote device. Because dump normally is run by root, the local machine must appear in root's .rhosts on the remote machine. If the output location is -, dump is written to standard out.
- u—Updates the dump record in /etc/dumpdates.
- b—Specifies a blocking factor (1KB blocks) for dumps to tape. Check your man pages for any specific blocking factor recommendations.
- d—Tape density, expressed in *bytes per inch* (bpi).
- s—Size of the tape in feet.
- n—Notifies all operators belonging to the operator, sys, or other appropriate group that dump needs attention.
- c—Sets defaults for cartridge tape instead of half-inch reel.
- W—Warns the operator of which filesystems need to be dumped based on information in /etc/dumpdates.
- C—An option in IRIX's dump for efs filesystems. Replaces c, s, and d. Specifies total tape capacity.

Examples

```
dump 0bdsfu 128 48000 6000 casper:/dev/rmt/0n /
```

(Specifies a full dump of / to remote machine casper's tape drive. Blocking factor, density, and size have been put together from various man pages. This setup seems to work well for DDS1 90m DAT.)

```
dump 0bCfu 128 1800k casper:/dev/rmt/0n /
```

(Specifies the same dump on the same type of tape using the total tape capacity option available in IRIX's dump for efs filesystems.)

exportfs—Exports and unexports directories to NFS clients

Use

```
exportfs [-aiuv] [-o options] [directory]
```

Description

exportfs makes a local directory available for NFS clients. Invoked with no arguments, it lists information on directories currently exported. The options list is a comma-separated list of options that also can be applied in /etc/exports. Your operating system may have a different command for doing this. Solaris uses share.

Options

- a—Exports all directories listed in /etc/exports. Combined with u, it unexports all currently exported directories.

- i—Ignores the options in /etc/exports.

- v—Verbose. Prints each directory as it is exported or unexported.

- u—Unexports the specified directories.

- o <*options*>—Comma-separated list of optional characteristics for the directory being exported. See Day 11, "Making Your Machines Communicate with Each Other," Table 11.1, for some of the common options.

find—Finds files

Use

```
find pathname-list [expression]
```

Description

find recursively searches each pathname in the pathname list for the files matching the specified criteria. If the expression does not include -print, -exec, or -ok, it is assumed to be -print in some operating systems.

Expressions

- name <*file*>—True if a file matches <*file*>. Normal shell argument syntax can be used if escaped. Especially watch out for [, ?, and *.

- user <*username*>—True if file belongs to <*username*>. If <*username*> is numeric and does not appear as a login name in /etc/password, it is assumed to be a user ID.

- group *<groupname>*—True if file belongs to *<groupname>*. If *<groupname>* is numeric and does not appear as a login name in /etc/group, it is assumed to be a group ID.

- size *n[c]*—True if file is *n* blocks long (512-byte blocks). If *n* is followed by *c*, the size is in characters or bytes.

- atime [+-]*n*—True if file was accessed *n* days ago. The access time of directories in the path is changed by find itself. The + prefix means more than *n* days ago; - means less than *n* days ago.

- mtime [+-]*n*—True if file was modified *n* days ago.

- ctime [+-]*n* True if file was changed *n* days ago.

- exec cmd—True if executed command returns a 0 value. The end of a command must be punctuated by an escaped semicolon (e.g. `\;'). The current pathname replaces a command argument `{}'.

- ok cmd—Like -exec, except that the command is written to standard output, reads standard input, and is executed if the response is y.

- print—Always true for many operating systems. Check the behavior with your operating system. This option may not always be true in spite of what your man pages may say.

- fstype *<fstype>*—True if the filesystem type is *<fstype>*.

Complex expressions

\(expression \) True if parenthesized expression is true. The parentheses are special to the shell and must be escaped.

! expression True if not expression.

expression1 [-a] expression2 True if expression1 and expression2 are true The -a is not required.

expression1 -o expression2 True if expression1 or expression2 is true.

Examples

find ./ -name *ps* -print (Finds files in the current directory whose names contain ps.)

```
./teaching_lab/proposal.later.nofoot3.ps
./teaching_lab/proposal.later.ps
./teaching_lab/proposal.nofoot3.ps
./teaching_lab/proposal.ps
```

find ./ -name core -exec rm {} \; (Finds files in the current directory named core and removes them. Space before \; is important!)

format—Disk partitioning and maintenance utility

Find the man page for your operating system's version of format, print it out, and keep it handy!

fsck—Checks and repairs filesystems

fsck options seem to vary from operating system to operating system. Find the man page for your operating system's version of fsck, print it out, and keep it handy! If your operating system supports more than one filesystem type for itself, such as IRIX's efs and xfs, find the man pages for each fsck program.

grep—Searches for a specified pattern

Use

grep [-cilnv] [-e <pattern_list>] [-f <pattern_file>] [file]

Description

grep searches for specified patterns. It often is safest to place your pattern in quotes. You will find more uses for grep than you may be able to imagine at the moment.

Options

- c—Lists a count of the number of lines in the file containing the matching pattern.
- i—Ignores case.
- l—Lists the names of the files with the matching pattern.
- n—Lists the line numbers of the lines containing the matching pattern in the file.
- v—Lists the lines that do not contain the matching pattern.
- e *<pattern_list>*—Specifies one or more patterns to be used during the search. The pattern in the list must be separated by a newline character.
- f *<pattern_file>*—Reads one or more patterns from *<pattern_file>*. Each pattern in *<pattern_file>* must be on a separate line.

Examples

grep -li proj * */* (Searches for a pattern containing proj in all files in the current directory and in all files in directories below the current directory. Prints a list of the files containing the pattern and ignores case.)

```
COPYING
ChangeLog
acconfig.h
config.h
config.h.in
configure
```

A

```
configure.in
libdes-COPYING
libdes-README
sshd.c
gmp-2.0.2-ssh-2/Makefile
gmp-2.0.2-ssh-2/Makefile.am
gmp-2.0.2-ssh-2/Makefile.in
gmp-2.0.2-ssh-2/gmp.info-2
gmp-2.0.2-ssh-2/gmp.texi
zlib-1.0.4/Makefile.riscos
zlib-1.0.4/README
```

grep -in micro proposal.tex (Searches for a pattern containing micro in
proposal.tex. Ignores case and displays line numbers with the lines containing the
patterns.)

```
65:relationships and analysis.  Microbiology is also addressing some
67:bioinformatics and with the recently approved Microbiology
111:directed specifically at a need by the Department of Microbiology for
191:                        \item Web pages for Microbiology 509, 520, 521,
```

kill—Sends a signal to a process

Use kill [-signal] <pid>

kill -l

Description

kill sends a signal to a process. By default, it sends a terminate signal, 15, if no other
signals are specified. Signal 9 is a sure way to kill a process.

Check your man pages for more details, especially man pages on kill and signal. Here
is a listing of some common signals:

SIGHUP	1	Exit	Hangup
SIGINT	2	Exit	Interrupt
SIGQUIT	3	Core	Quit
SIGILL	4	Core	Illegal Instruction
SIGTRAP	5	Core	Trace/Breakpoint Trap
SIGABRT	6	Core	Abort
SIGEMT	7	Core	Emulation Trap
SIGFPE	8	Core	Arithmetic Exception
SIGKILL	9	Exit	Killed
SIGBUS	10	Core	Bus Error
SIGSEGV	11	Core	Segmentation Fault

SIGSYS	12	Core	Bad System Call
SIGPIPE	13	Exit	Broken Pipe
SIGALRM	14	Exit	Alarm Clock
SIGTERM	15	Exit	Terminated

Examples

kill -9 150 (Kills process number 150.)

kill -HUP 250 (Sends hang-up signal to process number 250.)

kill -l (Lists signals that can be sent to a process.)

HUP INT QUIT ILL TRAP ABRT EMT FPE KILL BUS SEGV SYS PIPE ALRM TERM URG
STOP TSTP CONT CHLD TTIN TTOU IO XCPU XFSZ VTALRM PROF WINCH LOST USR1
➥USR2

last—Displays last logins of users and terminals

Use

last [-number] [-f file] [name] [tty]

Description

last reads the default accounting file with login/logout information. If called with no arguments, last displays the contents of the accounting file in this general format:

username terminal from date with beginning and end time duration

Options

- [-number]—Limits display to *<number>* of lines.
- [-f file]—Reads a file other than the default file.
- [name]—Displays the information for the username specified.
- [tty]—Displays the information for the terminal specified. Check the man pages for your operating system for any special terminal naming conventions that should be used.

Examples

last -5 (Displays five lines of last report.)

```
joray     ttyp2    rosalyn.biosci.o Mon May 10 11:59 - 12:04  (00:05)
joray     ttyp2    rosalyn.biosci.o Mon May 10 10:15 - 10:21  (00:06)
joray     ttyp1    ryoohki.biosci.o Mon May 10 09:19   still logged in
joray     ttyp1    rosalyn.biosci.o Fri May  7 10:56 - 10:57  (00:00)
joray     ttyp0    rosalyn.biosci.o Thu May  6 15:54   still logged in
```

```
last -5 -f /var/adm/OLDwtmp (Displays five lines of the old accounting file.)
```

```
joray     ttyq0                         Fri Apr 23 18:22 - 18:35  (00:13)
joray     ttyq0                         Fri Apr 23 17:48 - 17:51  (00:03)
joray     ttyq0                         Thu Apr 22 11:47 - 11:52  (00:05)
mpickle   ttyq0                         Thu Apr 22 11:41 - 11:42  (00:00)
mpickle   ttyq0                         Thu Apr 22 11:38 - 11:38  (00:00)
```

```
last -4 joray (Displays four lines of the report on user joray's logins.)
```

```
joray     pts/10    ryoohki.biosci.o Mon May 10 10:10   still logged in
joray     console                    Thu May  6 16:43   still logged in
joray     pts/10    ryoohki.biosci.o Thu May  6 14:54 - 17:18  (02:24)
joray     pts/10    ryoohki.biosci.o Thu May  6 13:33 - 13:34  (00:00)
```

```
last -3 q0 (Displays three lines of the report on logins on terminal ttyq0.)
```

```
joray     ttyq0     140.254.12.98    Mon May 10 13:56   still logged in
joray     ttyq0     140.254.12.191   Thu May  6 10:36 - 10:52  (00:16)
joray     ttyq0     140.254.12.151   Wed May  5 13:00 - 14:07  (01:06)
```

mount/umount—Mounts and unmounts filesystems

mount/umount options also seem to vary from operating system to operating system. Find the man page for your operating system's version of mount/umount, print it out, and keep it handy!

mt—Magnetic tape control

Use

```
mt [-f tapename] command [count]
```

Description

mt communicates with a magnetic tape device. Check the man pages for your operating system to identify the default tape device for mt.

Options

- fsf—Forward space over EOF marks. Positions tape at first block of the file.
- fsr—Forward space over count records (blocks).
- bsf—Back space over EOF marks. Positions tape at the beginning-of-tape side of EOF mark.
- bsr—Back space over count records (blocks).

The following do not take a count:

- erase—Erases the entire tape.
- offline—Rewinds the tape and takes unit offline by unloading the tape.
- status—Prints status information about tape unit.

A

Examples

`mt status` (Provides status of default tape device. In this case, nothing is in the tape drive.)

`/dev/rmt/0: no tape loaded or drive offline`

`mt rewind` (Rewinds default tape device.)

`mt -f /dev/rmt/0n fsf 10`

(Fast forwards tape to end of file 10, at the beginning block of file 11.)

`mt -f /dev/rmt/0n bsf 4`

(Backs up tape four EOF marks and positions tape at BOT side of EOF mark. If issued directly after the `fsf` statement, backs up tape to file 7's EOF mark and positions tape at BOT side of the EOF, which is the beginning of file 8.)

newfs—Constructs a filesystem

Find the man page for your operating system's version of `newfs`, print it out, and keep it handy! Or if `newfs` does not exist on your operating system, use `mkfs` command instead.

ps—Displays process status report

Use

`ps [options]`

Description

`ps` displays information about the current active processes. Without any options, `ps` displays only processes associated with your user ID and attached to a controlling terminal.

This is one of those commands that greatly varies between the flavors of UNIX. In some flavors of UNIX, the - is not used with the options. Check your man pages for more details.

Options—System V

- a—Prints information about all processes most frequently requested, except those with process group leaders and those not associated with a terminal.
- A—Prints information for all processes.
- c—Prints information in a format that reflects scheduler properties. Use of the `-c` option affects the output of the `-f` and `-l` options.
- e—Prints information about every process now running.
- f—Generates a full listing.

- j—Prints session ID and process group ID.
- l—Generates a long listing.

Options—BSD

- a—Includes information about processes owned by others.
- g—Displays all processes.
- l—Displays a long listing.
- u—Displays user-oriented output.
- w—Wraps output that is longer then one line (80 characters). -ww wraps output the second time in case output is longer then 2 lines, and so on.
- x—Includes processes with no controlling terminal.

Common fields displayed

Not all of the fields listed here are used in the different flavors of UNIX.

- USER—Name of the owner of the process.
- UID—User ID of the owner of the process. (Login name is printed instead when -f option is invoked.)
- PID—Process ID. This is needed to kill a process.
- PPID—Parent process ID.
- PRI Process priority—Without -c option, higher numbers mean lower priority. With -c option, higher numbers mean higher priority.
- NI—Nice value. Used in calculating priority.
- WCHAN—Address of an event for which the process is sleeping. If blank, the process is running.
- STIME—Starting time of the process. If started more than 24 hours ago, given in months and days.
- START—Starting time of the process. If started more than 24 hours ago, given in months and days.
- %CPU—CPU use of the process.
- %MEM—Percentage of real memory used by a process.
- TTY—Process's controlling terminal. If ? defines the field, there is no controlling terminal.
- TIME—Cumulative execution time for a process.
- CMD—Command name. (Full command name and its argument—up to 80 characters—are printed under -f option.)

- COMMAND—Command name. (Full command name and its argument—up to 80 characters—are printed under -f option.)

Examples

```
ps -elf ¦ more

UID         PID      PPID  C   STIME TTY      TIME CMD
root          1         0  0   Apr 29 ?       0:25 /etc/init
  lp        312         1  0   Apr 29 ?       0:00 /usr/lib/lpsched
root        320         1  0   Apr 29 ?       0:48 /sbin/cron
root         88         1  0   Apr 29 ?       0:05 /usr/etc/syslogd
root        451         1  0   Apr 29 ?       0:00 /usr/etc/rtmond -a
➥localhost
root        164         1  0   Apr 29 ?       0:00 /usr/etc/rpcbind
root        461         1  0   Apr 29 ?       0:00 /usr/bin/X11/xdm

ps -A ¦ more

PID TTY      TIME CMD
  1 ?        0:25 init
312 ?        0:00 lpsched
320 ?        0:48 cron
 88 ?        0:05 syslogd
451 ?        0:00 rtmond
164 ?        0:00 rpcbind
461 ?        0:00 xdm

ps -auxww ¦ more

USER        PID %CPU %MEM    SZ  RSS TT STAT START   TIME COMMAND
root          0  0.0  0.0     0    0 ?  D    Apr  8  0:30 swapper
root          1  0.0  0.0    52    0 ?  IW   Apr  8  0:00 /sbin/init -
root          2  0.0  0.0     0    0 ?  D    Apr  8  0:00 pagedaemon
root        111  0.0  0.0    28    0 ?  I    Apr  8  0:00 (nfsd)
root         61  0.0  0.0   128    0 ?  IW   Apr  8 11:23 ypserv -i

ps ¦ grep inetd

ray       22695  0.0  0.0   124    8 p0 R    00:37  0:00 grep inetd
root        293  0.0  2.7   780  396 ?  S    May  4  0:00 inetd
```

restore—Incremental filesystem restore

Use

```
restore rRtxi [bfsvyhm]
```

Description

restore reads data written to tape by dump and restores it relative to the current directory. The format of restore is restore *[function]* *[function modifier]*. There may be only one function.

The Solaris equivalent to restore is `ufsrestore`. The operating systems with streaming `dump` commands will have `restore` commands that complement their `dump` commands.

Options—Functions

- `r`—Restores the entire tape.
- `R`—Resumes restoring.
- `t`—Table of contents. Lists each specified `<filename>` if it occurs on the tape. If no argument is given, the root directory is listed, which results in a listing of the entire tape's contents.
- `x`—Extracts the named files. If the name file is a directory name and the `h` modifier has not been specified, the directory is recursively extracted. If no argument is given, the root directory is extracted, resulting in extraction of the entire tape's contents.
- `i`—Invokes interactive restore. Commands available in interactive restore follow:
    - `ls [directory]`—Lists current or specified directory. Directory listings end with `/`. Items to be extracted have `*` prepended. If the `verbose` option is in effect, inode numbers also are listed.
    - `cd <dir>`—Changes directory.
    - `pwd`—Prints current working directory.
    - `add [filename]`—Adds the current directory or specified file to the list of files to be extracted. If a directory is specified, it and its files are recursively added, unless the `h` modifier has been specified.
    - `delete [filename]`—Deletes the current directory or specified file from the list of files to be extracted. If a directory is specified, it and its files are recursively deleted, unless the `h` modifier has been specified.
    - `extract`—Extracts all files from the extraction list. `restore` then asks which volume to mount. The fastest way to extract a few files is to start with the last volume and work forward.
    - `verbose`—Toggles the `v` modifier. When in effect, `verbose` causes `ls` to print inode numbers by listed entries and `restore` to print information about each file as it is extracted.
    - `help`—Lists a summary of available commands.
    - `quit` Exits `restore` immediately, even if there are still files to be extracted.

Options—Function modifiers

When more than one function modifier is used, the arguments to the modifiers must appear in the same order as the function modifiers.

- b—Specifies a blocking factor.
- f—Specifies the device to be used if it is not the default tape device. If the device is -, `restore` restores from standard input. Because `restore` normally is run by root, if the device is a remote tape device, the local machine name must appear in `.rhosts` on the remote device.
- s—Skips to the file number specified.
- v—Verbose. Causes `restore` to print a line for each file that contains file type and the filename.
- y—Causes `restore` to not ask whether it should abort when tape errors are encountered. `restore` tries to skip over the bad tape block(s) and continue.
- h—Extracts the actual directory, rather than the files it references, to prevent hierarchical restoration of the directory.
- m—Extracts by inode number rather than filename.

Examples

```
restore ibf 128 barracuda:/dev/rmt/0n
```

(Sets `restore` to interactive mode. `restore` will use a blocking factor of 128 and will use a tape device on a remote machine.)

```
dump 0f - / ¦ (cd /new1; restore rf -)
```

(Does a full-level dump of / to standard out, changes directory to /new1, and restores everything to standard out. This is convenient to use when replacing a drive. Your /etc/fstab entry then is changed to mount /new1 as /.)

`unlink`/`link`—Unlinks and links files and directories

Use

```
unlink file
link file1 file2
```

Description

`link` creates a filename that points to another file. `unlink` removes a link to a file. `link` makes the link system call, and `unlink` makes the unlink system call. No error checking is performed by either.

It is recommended that `ln`, `rm`, and `rmdir` be used instead. However, it may be useful to know that `link` and `unlink` exist on most operating system, should you ever have the need for them.

who—Displays who is on the system

Use

who [-bmHr] [file]

who [file]

who -qn x [file]

whoami

who am i

Description

who can display a variety of information from the default who file. Check your operating system's man pages to see what the default file is. who also can read another specified file. With some operating systems, no additional options may be available.

Options

- b—Displays date and time of the last reboot.
- m—Displays information about the current terminal.
- H—Prints column headings.
- r—Indicates the current run level of the init process.
- q—Quick display—only displays usernames and the total number of users currently logged on. Using this option causes the other options to be ignored.
- n x—For use with the -q option. Specifies that x number of users per line be displayed.

whoami Displays who you currently are. As system administrator, you easily can lose track of this information.

who am i Displays who you logged in as and some additional information, including terminal and date.

Examples

who -bH (Displays reboot information with column labels.)

```
NAME        LINE        TIME
   .        system boot  Apr 22 09:01
```

who -rH (Displays information on run level of the init process with column labels.)

```
NAME        LINE        TIME        IDLE   PID  COMMENTS
   .        run-level 3  Apr 22 09:01    3     0  S
```

whoami (This example was run after doing su - ralph.)

ralph

who am i (Displays who you logged in as.)

```
joray        pts/10        May 10 10:10      (ryoohki.biosci.ohio-state.edu)
```

who

```
joray     ttyp0    May  6 15:54    (rosalyn.biosci.o)
joray     ttyp1    May 10 09:19    (ryoohki.biosci.o)
joray     ttyp2    May 10 14:45    (rosalyn.biosci.o)
```

APPENDIX B

Sample Operating System Installations

In the main part of the book, you saw a sample installation of a BSD-flavor operating system, SunOS 4.1.4. In this appendix, you will see a few System V samples: Solaris 7 and IRIX 6.5. Although these samples will not prepare you for every possible operating system variant, they should provide some insight into what you can expect. If you are installing Linux, be prepared to answer questions about your hardware.

As always, read the documentation before you begin. As you saw in Day 2, "Designing Your Cluster: From Planning to Policy," sometimes that documentation is only a small booklet, but read it anyway.

Solaris 7

This is a transcript of an installation of Solaris 7 on a Sun system. Two installation methods are available: Solaris Web Start and Solaris Interactive Installation, which works a lot like `suninstall` for SunOS 4.1.4.

If your machine is a new out-of-the-box machine, decide which program you would like to use, turn on the system, and follow the online instructions.

If your system is an existing system, get your system to the ok prompt. If you plan to use Solaris Web start, enter

```
boot cdrom - browser
```

If you plan to use Solaris Interactive Installation, enter

```
boot cdrom
```

If you have an older SPARC system, use this instead:

```
boot sd(0,6,2)
```

> **Note**
>
> If you have a new, out-of-the-box machine, don't let anyone touch it before you do. If there are any other Solaris machines on your network, you run the risk of the curious enthusiast inadvertently causing your new machine to boot off another machine on the network, thereby putting yourself in the existing system category. Cleaning up after that mess can be unpleasant. Let the enthusiast look once the operating system is installed.

This installation uses the Solaris Interactive Installation program on a terminal to the machine.

```
Can't open input device.
Keyboard not present.  Using ttya for input and output.


Sun (TM) Enterprise 250 (2 X UltraSPARC-II 296MHz), No Keyboard
OpenBoot 3.12, 512 MB memory installed, Serial #11112294.
Ethernet address 8:0:20:a9:8f:66, Host ID: 80a98f66.


{0} ok boot cdrom
Boot device: /pci@1f,4000/scsi@3/disk@6,0:f  File and args:
SunOS Release 5.7 Version Generic_106541-02 UNIX(R) System V Release 4.0
Copyright (c) 1983-1998, Sun Microsystems, Inc.
Configuring devices...
The system is coming up.  Please wait.


Select a Language

  0) English
  1) German
  2) Spanish
  3) French
```

```
4) Italian
5) Swedish

?0


Select a Locale

The locale you select on this screen becomes the default displayed
on your desktop after you reboot the system.  Selecting a locale
determines how online information is displayed for a specific
locale or region (for example, time, date, spelling, and monetary value.)

NOTE: The ASCII only option gives you the default 128-character set that
was available in previous releases.  If you do not need to send/receive
international correspondence where you need locale-specific alphabetic
characters (like accented or umlaut characters) the ASCII only set
is sufficient. Otherwise, you can select an ISO locale which contains
a 256-character set.  Selecting an ISO locale can cause a minor
performance degradation (in many cases, less than 5%).

 0) USA (ASCII)                      22) Macedonia (ISO8859-5)
 1) Bulgaria (ISO8859-5)             23) Netherlands (ISO8859-1)
 2) Czech Republic (ISO8859-2)       24) Belgium (ISO8859-1)
 3) Denmark (ISO8859-1)              25) Belgium (ISO8859-15 - Euro)
 4) Denmark (ISO8859-15 - Euro)      26) Netherlands (ISO8859-15 - Euro)
 5) Greece (ISO8859-7)               27) Norway (ISO8859-1)
 6) Greece (ISO8859-7 + Euro glyph)  28) Norway (ISO8859-1 - Nynorsk)
 7) Australia (ISO8859-1)            29) Bosnia (ISO8859-2)
 8) Canada (ISO8859-1)               30) Poland (ISO8859-2)
 9) Great Britain (ISO8859-1)        31) Portugal (ISO8859-1)
10) Great Britain (ISO8859-15 - Euro) 32) Brazil (ISO8859-1)
11) Ireland (ISO8859-1)              33) Portugal (ISO8859-15 - Euro)
12) Ireland (ISO8859-15 - Euro)      34) Romania (ISO8859-2)
13) New Zealand (ISO8859-1)          35) Russia (ISO8859-5)
14) USA (ISO8859-1)                  36) Russia (KOI8-R)
15) Estonia (ISO8859-1)              37) Slovakia (ISO8859-2)
16) Finland (ISO8859-1)              38) Slovenia (ISO8859-2)
17) Finland (ISO8859-15 - Euro)      39) Albania (ISO8859-2)
18) Croatia (ISO8859-2)              40) Serbia (ISO8859-5)
19) Hungary (ISO8859-2)              41) Turkey (ISO8859-9)
20) Lithuania (ISO8859-13)           42) Go Back to Previous Screen
21) Latvia (ISO8859-13)


Type a number and press Return or Enter [0]: 0


What type of terminal are you using?
 1) ANSI Standard CRT
 2) DEC VT52
 3) DEC VT100
```

B

```
   4) Heathkit 19
   5) Lear Siegler ADM31
   6) PC Console
   7) Sun Command Tool
   8) Sun Workstation
   9) Televideo 910
  10) Televideo 925
  11) Wyse Model 50
  12) X Terminal Emulator (xterms)
  13) Other
Type the number of your choice and press Return: 3


- The Solaris Installation Program ---------------------------------------

  The Solaris installation program is divided into a series of short
➡sections
  where you'll be prompted to provide information for the installation.
  At the end of each section, you'll be able to change the selections
  you've made before continuing.

  About navigation...
             - The mouse cannot be used
             - If your keyboard does not have function keys, or they do not
               respond, press ESC; the legend at the bottom of the screen
               will change to show the ESC keys to use for navigation.




-------------------------------------------------------------------------
     F2_Continue      F6_Help

- Identify This System ------------------------------------------------

  On the next screens, you must identify this system as networked or
  non-networked, and set the default time zone and date/time.

  If this system is networked, the software will try to find the
  information it needs to identify your system; you will be prompted
  to supply any information it cannot find.




-------------------------------------------------------------------------
     Esc-2_Continue     Esc-6_Help

- Host Name --------------------------------------------------------------
```

On this screen you must enter your host name, which identifies this
system on the network. The name must be unique within your domain;
creating a duplicate host name will cause problems on the network
after you install Solaris.

A host name must be at least two characters; it can contain letters,
digits, and minus signs (-).

B

  Host name: ryoko

- -
     Esc-2_Continue   Esc-6_Help

- Network Connectivity -

  Specify Yes if the system is connected to the network by one of the
  Solaris or vendor network/communication Ethernet cards that are
  supported on the Solaris CD. See your hardware documentation for the
  current list of supported cards.
  Specify No if the system is connected to a network/communication card
  that is not supported on the Solaris CD, and follow the instructions
  listed under Help.

     Networked
     - - - - - - - - -
     [X] Yes
     [ ] No

- -
     Esc-2_Continue   Esc-6_Help

- IP Address -

On this screen you must enter the Internet Protocol (IP) address for
this system. It must be unique and follow your site's address
conventions, or a system/network failure could result.

IP addresses contain four sets of numbers separated by periods (for
example 129.200.9.1).

  IP address: 140.254.12.240

```
- - - - - - - - - - - - - - - - - - - - - - - - - - - - - - - - - - - - - - - - - - - -
     Esc-2_Continue     Esc-6_Help

- Confirm Information - - - - - - - - - - - - - - - - - - - - - - - - - - - - - - - - - -

  > Confirm the following information.  If it is correct, press F2;
    to change any information, press F4.


                     Host name: ryoko
                     Networked: Yes
                     IP address: 140.254.12.240




- - - - - - - - - - - - - - - - - - - - - - - - - - - - - - - - - - - - - - - - - - - -
     Esc-2_Continue     Esc-4_Change     Esc-6_Help
```

All the questions on name service are asking for NIS/NIS+ information.

```
- Name Service - - - - - - - - - - - - - - - - - - - - - - - - - - - - - - - - - - - - -

  On this screen you must provide name service information. Select NIS+
  or NIS if this system is known to the name server; select Other if your
  site is using another name service (for example, DCE or DNS); select
  None if your site is not using a name service, or if it is not yet
  established.

  > To make a selection, use the arrow keys to highlight the option
    and press Return to mark it [X].


     Name service
     - - - - - - - - - - - - - - - -
     [ ] NIS+
     [X] NIS (formerly yp)
     [ ] Other
     [ ] None



- - - - - - - - - - - - - - - - - - - - - - - - - - - - - - - - - - - - - - - - - - - -
     Esc-2_Continue     Esc-6_Help

- Domain Name - - - - - - - - - - - - - - - - - - - - - - - - - - - - - - - - - - - - -
```

On this screen you must specify the domain where this system resides.
Make sure you enter the name correctly including capitalization and
punctuation.

    Domain name: mickeymouse

    Esc-2_Continue   Esc-6_Help

- Name Server --

On this screen you must specify how to find a name server for this
system. You can let the software try to find one, or you can specify
one. The software can find a name server only if it is on your local
subnet.

> To make a selection, use the arrow keys to highlight the option and
  press Return to mark it [X].

    Name server

    [ ] Find one
    [X] Specify one

    Esc-2_Continue   Esc-6_Help

- Name Server Information --

On this screen you must enter the host name and IP address of your name
server. Host names must be at least two characters, and may contain
letters, digits, and minus signs (-). IP addresses must contain four
sets of numbers separated by periods (for example 129.200.9.1).

    Server's host name: critter.biosci.ohio-state.edu
    Server's IP address: 140.254.12.10

```
-----------------------------------------------------------------------
      Esc-2_Continue     Esc-6_Help

- Subnets ------------------------------------------------------------
```

On this screen you must specify whether this system is part of a
subnet. If you specify incorrectly, the system will have problems
communicating on the network after you reboot.

> To make a selection, use the arrow keys to highlight the option and
  press Return to mark it [X].


```
      System part of a subnet
      -----------------------
      [X] Yes
      [ ] No
```


```
-----------------------------------------------------------------------
      Esc-2_Continue     Esc-6_Help

- Netmask ------------------------------------------------------------
```

On this screen you must specify the netmask of your subnet. A default
netmask is shown; do not accept the default unless you are sure it is
correct for your subnet. A netmask must contain four sets of numbers
separated by periods (for example 255.255.255.0).


```
      Netmask: 255.255.255.0
```


```
-----------------------------------------------------------------------
      Esc-2_Continue     Esc-6_Help

- Confirm Information ------------------------------------------------
```

> Confirm the following information. If it is correct, press F2;
  to change any information, press F4.

```
            Name service: NIS (formerly yp)
            Domain name: mickeymouse
            Name server: Specify one
     Server's host name: critter.biosci.ohio-state.edu
     Server's IP address: 140.254.12.10
 System part of a subnet: Yes
                Netmask: 255.255.255.0
```

B

```
- - - - - - - - - - - - - - - - - - - - - - - - - - - - - - - - - - - - - - - -
     Esc-2_Continue      Esc-4_Change      Esc-6_Help
```

done.

You will experience a brief pause after done before continuing with time-zone questions.

```
- Time Zone - - - - - - - - - - - - - - - - - - - - - - - - - - - - - - - - - - -

  On this screen you must specify your default time zone. You can specify
  a time zone in three ways:  select one of the geographic regions from
  the list, select other - offset from GMT, or other - specify time zone
  file.

  > To make a selection, use the arrow keys to highlight the option and
    press Return to mark it [X].


      Regions
      - - - - - - - - - - - - - - - - - - - - - - - - -
    ¦  [ ] Asia, Western
    ¦  [ ] Australia / New Zealand
    ¦  [ ] Canada
    ¦  [ ] Europe
    ¦  [ ] Mexico
    ¦  [ ] South America
    ¦  [X] United States
    ¦  [ ] other - offset from GMT
    ¦  [ ] other - specify time zone file

- - - - - - - - - - - - - - - - - - - - - - - - - - - - - - - - - - - - - - - -
     Esc-2_Continue      Esc-6_Help

- Time Zone - - - - - - - - - - - - - - - - - - - - - - - - - - - - - - - - - - -
```

> To make a selection, use the arrow keys to highlight the option and
  press Return to mark it [X].

      Time zones

      [X] Eastern
      [ ] Central
      [ ] Mountain
      [ ] Pacific
      [ ] East-Indiana
      [ ] Arizona
      [ ] Michigan
      [ ] Samoa
      [ ] Alaska
      [ ] Aleutian
      [ ] Hawaii

      Esc-2_Continue   Esc-5_Cancel   Esc-6_Help

- Date and Time ---

  > Accept the default date and time or enter
    new values.

  Date and time: 1999-05-11 10:39

      Year   (4 digits) : 1999
      Month (1-12)   : 05
      Day   (1-31)   : 11
      Hour   (0-23)   : 10
      Minute (0-59)   : 45

      Esc-2_Continue   Esc-6_Help

- Confirm Information --

  > Confirm the following information. If it is correct, press F2;
    to change any information, press F4.

```
        Time zone: US/Eastern
   Date and time: 1999-05-11 10:45:00
```

```
--------------------------------------------------------------------
      Esc-2_Continue     Esc-4_Change     Esc-6_Help
```

System identification is completed.

You will experience a much longer pause here. If the pause continues abnormally long, though, something may have gone wrong and you should power-cycle the computer, and start from the beginning, double-checking your selections and input.

```
- Solaris Interactive Installation -------------------------------------

   You'll be using the initial option for installing Solaris software on
   the system. The initial option overwrites the system disks when the new
   Solaris software is installed.

   On the following screens, you can accept the defaults or you can
   customize how Solaris software will be installed by:

           - Allocating space for diskless clients or AutoClient systems
           - Selecting the type of Solaris software to install
           - Selecting disks to hold software you've selected
           - Specifying how file systems are laid out on the disks

   After completing these tasks, a summary of your selections (called a
   profile) will be displayed.
```

```
--------------------------------------------------------------------
      F2_Continue     F5_Exit     F6_Help
```

```
- Allocate Client Services? --------------------------------------------

   Do you want to allocate space for diskless clients and/or AutoClient
   systems?
```

```
       - - - - - - - - - - - - - - - - - - - - - - - - - - - - - - - - - - - - - - - - - - -
       Esc-2_Continue   Esc-3_Go Back   Esc-4_Allocate   Esc-5_Exit   Esc-6_Help
```

Although I did not allocate any client services on my machine, here is a look at the platforms you would choose from:

```
- Select Platforms - - - - - - - - - - - - - - - - - - - - - - - - - - - - - - - - - - - - - - - - -

  On this screen you must specify all platforms for clients that this
  server will need to support. The server's platform is selected by
  default and cannot be deselected.

                    [X]   sparc.sun4u
                    [ ]   sparc.sun4m
                    [ ]   sparc.sun4us
                    [ ]   sparc.sun4c
                    [ ]   sparc.sun4d
```

```
       - - - - - - - - - - - - - - - - - - - - - - - - - - - - - - - - - - - - - - - - - - -
       Esc-2_Continue    Esc-3_Go Back    Esc-5_Exit    Esc-6_Help
```

```
- Select Languages - - - - - - - - - - - - - - - - - - - - - - - - - - - - - - - - - - - - - - - -

  Select the languages you want for displaying the user interface after
  Solaris software is installed. English is automatically installed by
  default.

                    [ ]   French
                    [ ]   German
                    [ ]   Italian
                    [ ]   Spanish
                    [ ]   Swedish
```

```
       - - - - - - - - - - - - - - - - - - - - - - - - - - - - - - - - - - - - - - - - - - -
       Esc-2_Continue    Esc-3_Go Back    Esc-5_Exit    Esc-6_Help
```

The installation guide lists no drawbacks to choosing 64-bit in this menu:

```
- Select 64 Bit - - - - - - - - - - - - - - - - - - - - - - - - - - - - - - - - - - - - - - - - - -

  Select 64-bit if you want to install the Solaris 64-bit packages on this
  system.
```

```
        [X]  Select To Include Solaris 64-bit Support
```

B

```
- - - - - - - - - - - - - - - - - - - - - - - - - - - - - - - - - - - - - - - - - - -
      Esc-2_Continue     Esc-3_Go Back     Esc-5_Exit
```

If you want to be able to compile things, make sure you choose the developer option or a higher option in the Select Software menu. If you are curious to see precisely which packages will be installed, choose Customize.

```
- Select Software - - - - - - - - - - - - - - - - - - - - - - - - - - - - - - - - - - - - - - - - - - - - - - - - - - -

Select the Solaris software to install on the system.

NOTE: After selecting a software group, you can add or remove software
by customizing it. However, this requires understanding of software
dependencies and how Solaris software is packaged. The software groups
displaying 64-bit contain 64-bit support.

      [X]  Entire Distribution plus OEM support 64-bit  1126.00 MB (F4 to
➤ Customize)
      [ ]  Entire Distribution 64-bit ................. 1105.00 MB
      [ ]  Developer System Support 64-bit ............ 1047.00 MB
      [ ]  End User System Support 64-bit ............. 687.00 MB
      [ ]  Core System Support ....................... 333.00 MB
```

```
- - - - - - - - - - - - - - - - - - - - - - - - - - - - - - - - - - - - - - - - - - - - - - - - - - - - - - - - - - - - - - -
Esc-2_Continue    Esc-3_Go Back   Esc-4_Customize    Esc-5_Exit    Esc-6_Help
```

If you discover in the Select Disks menu that the boot disk is not the one you thought it would be, you can quit the installation program and move your drives around. You will start from the beginning again, but you'll be better at answering the questions, and everything will go relatively quickly.

```
- Select Disks - - - - - - - - - - - - - - - - - - - - - - - - - - - - - - - - - - - - - - - - - - - - - - - - - - - - -

  On this screen you must select the disks for installing Solaris
  software. Start by looking at the Suggested Minimum field; this value
  is the approximate space needed to install the software you've
  selected. Keep selecting disks until the Total Selected value exceeds
  the Suggested Minimum value.
```

```
        Disk Device (Size)         Available Space
        ===========================================
   [X] c0t0d0   (8633 MB) boot disk     8633 MB  (F4 to edit)
   [ ] c0t8d0   (8633 MB)               8633 MB
   [ ] c0t9d0   (4092 MB)               4092 MB

                     Total Selected:    8633 MB
                 Suggested Minimum:      740 MB
```

Esc-2_Continue   Esc-3_Go Back   Esc-4_Edit   Esc-5_Exit   Esc-6_Help

After moving my disks around, I now have the boot disk I wanted:

- Select Disks ---

On this screen you must select the disks for installing Solaris
software. Start by looking at the Suggested Minimum field; this value
is the approximate space needed to install the software you've
selected. Keep selecting disks until the Total Selected value exceeds
the Suggested Minimum value.

```
        Disk Device (Size)         Available Space
        ===========================================
   [X] c0t0d0   (4092 MB) boot disk     4092 MB  (F4 to edit)
   [ ] c0t8d0   (8633 MB)               8633 MB
   [ ] c0t9d0   (8633 MB)               8633 MB

                     Total Selected:    4092 MB
                 Suggested Minimum:      740 MB
```

Esc-2_Continue   Esc-3_Go Back   Esc-4_Edit   Esc-5_Exit   Esc-6_Help

- Select Boot Disk ---

On this screen you can select the disk for installing the root (/) file
system of the Solaris software.

Original Boot Device : c0t0d0

```
           Disk
        ===============================
   [X] c0t0d0    (F4 to select boot device)
```

```
     Please wait ...
--------------------------------------------------------------------
     Esc-2_OK     Esc-4_Edit     Esc-5_Cancel     Esc-6_Help


- Select Disks ----------------------------------------------------

  On this screen you must select the disks for installing Solaris
  software. Start by looking at the Suggested Minimum field; this value
  is the approximate space needed to install the software you've
  selected. Keep selecting disks until the Total Selected value exceeds
  the Suggested Minimum value.

            Disk Device (Size)          Available Space
      ==========================================
      [X] c0t0d0   (4092 MB) boot disk      4092 MB   (F4 to edit)
      [ ] c0t8d0   (8633 MB)                8633 MB
      [ ] c0t9d0   (8633 MB)                8633 MB

                    Total Selected:   4092 MB
                 Suggested Minimum:    740 MB



--------------------------------------------------------------------
Esc-2_Continue     Esc-3_Go Back   Esc-4_Edit     Esc-5_Exit     Esc-6_Help


- Preserve Data? -------------------------------------------------

  Do you want to preserve existing data? At least one of the disks you've
  selected for installing Solaris software has file systems or unnamed
  slices that you may want to save.




--------------------------------------------------------------------
Esc-2_Continue   Esc-3_Go Back   Esc-4_Preserve   Esc-5_Exit   Esc-6_Help


- Automatically Layout File Systems? -----------------------------

  Do you want to use auto-layout to automatically layout file systems?
Manually laying out file systems requires advanced system administration
  skills.
```

```
. . . . . . . . . . . . . . . . . . . . . . . . . . . . . . . . . . . . . . . . . . . . . . . . . .
Esc-2_Auto Layout Esc-3_Go Back Esc-4_Manual Layout Esc-5_Exit Esc-6_Help


- File System and Disk Layout ---------------------------------------------

  The summary below is your current file system and disk layout, based on
  the information you've supplied.

  NOTE: If you choose to customize, you should understand file systems,
  their intended purpose on the disk, and how changing them may affect
  the operation of the system.

          File system/Mount point        Disk/Slice           Size
          =========================================================
          overlap                        c0t0d0s2           4092 MB




. . . . . . . . . . . . . . . . . . . . . . . . . . . . . . . . . . . . . . . . . . . . . . . . . .
Esc-2_Continue    Esc-3_Go Back    Esc-4_Customize  Esc-5_Exit   Esc-6_Help
```

If you choose to customize your disk, the program gives you the opportunity to change
your mind until you have the layout you are happiest with. A lot of the supplemental
software that comes on the other Solaris CDs will install in /opt, so you might want to
consider an /opt partition, or linking /opt to a partition with some space.

```
- Customize Disk: c0t0d0 -------------------------------------------------
  Boot Device: c0t0d0s0


  Entry: /var                    Recommended:   15 MB    Minimum:   13 MB
  ==========================================================================
  Slice  Mount Point            Size (MB)
    0    /                          248
    1    swap                      1024
    2                                 0
    3                                 0
    4                                 0
    5    /var                       512
    6    /usr                       776
    7    /usr/local                1531
  ==========================================================================
                    Capacity:      4092 MB
                   Allocated:      3579 MB
              Rounding Error:         2 MB
                        Free:       511 MB
```

```
--------------------------------------------------------------
      Esc-2_OK    Esc-4_Options    Esc-5_Cancel    Esc-6_Help
```

```
- File System and Disk Layout --------------------------------------

The summary below is your current file system and disk layout, based on
the information you've supplied.

NOTE: If you choose to customize, you should understand file systems,
their intended purpose on the disk, and how changing them may affect
the operation of the system.

          File system/Mount point        Disk/Slice           Size
          ==================================================================
          /                              c0t0d0s0            248  MB
          swap                           c0t0d0s1           1024  MB
          /var                           c0t0d0s5            511  MB
          /usr                           c0t0d0s6            776  MB
          /usr/local                     c0t0d0s7           1531  MB
```

```
--------------------------------------------------------------
Esc-2_Continue   Esc-3_Go Back   Esc-4_Customize  Esc-5_Exit   Esc-6_Help
```

```
- Profile ----------------------------------------------------------

The information shown below is your profile for installing Solaris
software. It reflects the choices you've made on previous screens.

==========================================================================

          Installation Option: Initial
                   Boot Device: c0t0d0s0
                Client Services: None
                      Software: Solaris 2.7, Entire Distribution plus OEM s

     File System and Disk Layout: /                c0t0d0s0  248 MB
                                  swap             c0t0d0s1 1024 MB
                                  /var             c0t0d0s5  511 MB
                                  /usr             c0t0d0s6  776 MB
                                  /usr/local       c0t0d0s7 1531 MB
```

B

```
------------------------------------------------------------------

      Esc-2_Continue    Esc-4_Change    Esc-5_Exit    Esc-6_Help
```

```
- Reboot After Installation? ----------------------------------------

  After Solaris software is installed, the system must be rebooted. You
  can choose to have the system automatically reboot, or you can choose
  to manually reboot the system if you want to run scripts or do other
  customizations before the reboot.  You can manually reboot a system by
  using the reboot(1M) command.


          [X] Auto Reboot
          [ ] Manual Reboot
```

```
------------------------------------------------------------------

      Esc-2_Begin Installation    Esc-5_Cancel
```

```
Preparing system for Solaris install

Configuring disk (c0t0d0)
        - Creating Solaris disk label (VTOC)

Creating and checking UFS file systems
        - Creating / (c0t0d0s0)
        - Creating /var (c0t0d0s5)
        - Creating /usr (c0t0d0s6)
        - Creating /usr/local (c0t0d0s7)

Beginning Solaris software installation
```

As the software is installing, you will see real-time updates here:

```
    Solaris Initial Install


        MBytes Installed:    28.66
        MBytes Remaining:    589.3

          Installing: Core Solaris, (Usr)

    ####
    I         I         I         I         I         I
    0        20        40        60        80       100
```

```
Solaris 2.7 software installation succeeded

Customizing system files
        - Mount points table (/etc/vfstab)
        - Unselected disk mount points (/var/sadm/system/data/vfstab.
➥unselected)
        - Network host addresses (/etc/hosts)

Customizing system devices
        - Physical devices (/devices)
        - Logical devices (/dev)

Installing boot information
        - Installing boot blocks (c0t0d0s0)

Installation log location
        - /a/var/sadm/system/logs/install_log (before reboot)
        - /var/sadm/system/logs/install_log (after reboot)


Installation complete
Executing SolStart postinstall phase...
Executing finish script "patch_finish"...


Finish script patch_finish execution completed.
Executing JumpStart postinstall phase...

The begin script log 'begin.log'
is located in /var/sadm/system/logs after reboot.

The finish script log 'finish.log'
is located in /var/sadm/system/logs after reboot.

May 11 15:03:48 rpcbind: rpcbind terminating on signal.
syncing file systems... done
rebooting...
Resetting ...


Can't open input device.
Keyboard not present.  Using ttya for input and output.


Sun (TM) Enterprise 250 (2 X UltraSPARC-II 296MHz), No Keyboard
OpenBoot 3.12, 512 MB memory installed, Serial #11112294.
Ethernet address 8:0:20:a9:8f:66, Host ID: 80a98f66.
```

B

```
Rebooting with command: boot
Boot device: disk  File and args:
SunOS Release 5.7 Version Generic_106541-02 64-bit [UNIX(R) System V
➥Release 4.0]
Copyright (c) 1983-1998, Sun Microsystems, Inc.
configuring network interfaces: hme0.
Hostname: ryoko
Configuring the /devices directory
Configuring the /dev directory
Configuring the /dev directory (compatibility devices)
The system is coming up.  Please wait.
checking ufs filesystems
/dev/rdsk/c0t0d0s7: is clean.
Configuring network interface addresses: hme0.
RPC: Timed out
NIS domainname is mickeymouse
starting routing daemon.
starting rpc services: rpcbind keyserv ypbind done.

On this screen you can create a root password.

A root password can contain any number of characters, but only the first
eight characters in the password are significant. (For example, if you
create 'a1b2c3d4e5f6' as your root password, you can use 'a1b2c3d4' to
gain root access.)

You will be prompted to type the root password twice; for security, the
password will not be displayed on the screen as you type it.

> If you do not want a root password, press RETURN twice.

Root password:


Re-enter your root password.


Press Return to continue.



System identification is completed.
Setting netmask of hme0 to 255.255.255.0
Setting default interface for multicast: add net 224.0.0.0: gateway ryoko
syslog service starting.
Print services started.
volume management starting.
The system is ready.

ryoko console login:
```

When you are done installing Solaris, you can continue with installing supplemental software. Three options are available for installing supplemental software: Solaris Web Start, Admintool, and pkgadd. Because this installation was done on a terminal, pkgadd was the most convenient tool to use.

Here's a sample of what results to expect when using pkgadd to install a product (be sure to read the man page on pkgadd before you use it for the first time!):

```
Installation of <SUNWffbgl> was successful.

Processing package instance <SUNWafbgl> from </cdrom/solaris7_399_suppcd/
➥Product>

Sun OpenGL for Solaris Elite3D Support
(sparc) 1.1.2,REV=1998.08.26
Copyright 1998 Sun Microsystems, Inc. All rights reserved.
Using </usr> as the package base directory.
## Processing package information.
## Processing system information.
   4 package pathnames are already properly installed.
## Verifying package dependencies.
## Verifying disk space requirements.
## Checking for conflicts with packages already installed.
## Checking for setuid/setgid programs.

Installing Sun OpenGL for Solaris Elite3D Support as <SUNWafbgl>

## Installing part 1 of 1.
/usr/openwin/lib/GL/devhandlers/oglSUNWafb.so.3
[ verifying class <none> ]

Installation of <SUNWafbgl> was successful.

Processing package instance <SUNWglrtx> from </cdrom/solaris7_399_suppcd/
➥Product>

Sun OpenGL for Solaris 64-bit Runtime Libraries
(sparc) 1.1.2,REV=1998.08.26
Copyright 1998 Sun Microsystems, Inc. All rights reserved.
Using </usr> as the package base directory.
## Processing package information.
## Processing system information.
   10 package pathnames are already properly installed.
## Verifying package dependencies.
## Verifying disk space requirements.
## Checking for conflicts with packages already installed.
## Checking for setuid/setgid programs.

Installing Sun OpenGL for Solaris 64-bit Runtime Libraries as <SUNWglrtx>
```

B

```
## Installing part 1 of 1.
/usr/lib/sparcv9/libGL.so <symbolic link>
/usr/lib/sparcv9/libGL.so.1 <symbolic link>
/usr/lib/sparcv9/libGLU.so <symbolic link>
/usr/lib/sparcv9/libGLU.so.1 <symbolic link>
/usr/lib/sparcv9/libGLw.so <symbolic link>
/usr/lib/sparcv9/libGLw.so.1 <symbolic link>
/usr/openwin/demo/GL/sparcv9/ogl_install_check
/usr/openwin/lib/sparcv9/GL/devhandlers/oglSUNWmmap.so.3
/usr/openwin/lib/sparcv9/libGL.so <symbolic link>
/usr/openwin/lib/sparcv9/libGL.so.1
/usr/openwin/lib/sparcv9/libGLU.so <symbolic link>
/usr/openwin/lib/sparcv9/libGLU.so.1
/usr/openwin/lib/sparcv9/libGLw.so <symbolic link>
/usr/openwin/lib/sparcv9/libGLw.so.1
/usr/openwin/platform/sun4u/lib/sparcv9/GL/libvis.so.1
/usr/openwin/platform/sun4u/lib/sparcv9/GL/oglSUNWcore.so.3
/usr/openwin/platform/sun4u/lib/sparcv9/GL/oglSUNWsr.so.3
/usr/openwin/platform/sun4u/lib/sparcv9/GL/oglSUNWsrz.so.3
[ verifying class <none> ]

Installation of <SUNWglrtx> was successful.

Processing package instance <SUNWafbgx> from </cdrom/solaris7_399_suppcd/
➥Product>

Sun OpenGL for Solaris 64-bit Elite3D Support
(sparc) 1.1.2,REV=1998.08.26
Copyright 1998 Sun Microsystems, Inc. All rights reserved.
Using </usr> as the package base directory.
## Processing package information.
## Processing system information.
   5 package pathnames are already properly installed.
## Verifying package dependencies.
## Verifying disk space requirements.
## Checking for conflicts with packages already installed.
## Checking for setuid/setgid programs.

Installing Sun OpenGL for Solaris 64-bit Elite3D Support as <SUNWafbgx>

## Installing part 1 of 1.
/usr/openwin/lib/sparcv9/GL/devhandlers/oglSUNWafb.so.3
[ verifying class <none> ]

Installation of <SUNWafbgx> was successful.

Processing package instance <SUNWffbgx> from </cdrom/solaris7_399_suppcd/
➥Product>
```

```
Sun OpenGL for Solaris 64-bit Creator Graphics (FFB) Support
(sparc) 1.1.2,REV=1998.08.26
Copyright 1998 Sun Microsystems, Inc. All rights reserved.
Using </usr> as the package base directory.
## Processing package information.
## Processing system information.
   5 package pathnames are already properly installed.
## Verifying package dependencies.
## Verifying disk space requirements.
## Checking for conflicts with packages already installed.
## Checking for setuid/setgid programs.

Installing Sun OpenGL for Solaris 64-bit Creator Graphics (FFB) Support
➥as <SUNWffbgx>

## Installing part 1 of 1.
/usr/openwin/lib/sparcv9/GL/devhandlers/oglSUNWffb.so.3
[ verifying class <none> ]

Installation of <SUNWffbgx> was successful.
```

IRIX 6.5

The sample here is not a complete installation of IRIX 6.5. However, the highlights of an IRIX installation are shown.

As of this writing, IRIX 6.5.4 is shipping with machines. When our machine arrived, IRIX was between major releases. The machine came with one version of IRIX installed and the latest version to be installed. Because I am not sure how much of IRIX you will have to install, I am providing samples to try to meet as many of the possibilities as I can.

Remember to read that little booklet for Silicon Graphics, Inc.'s recommendations on how to proceed. It may be small, but it provides the commands you will need. You may have to install IRIX or an update to the version of IRIX already installed, or you just may have to install potentially useful applications from some of the other CDs that come with the IRIX distribution.

We will start with the assumption that you have to install IRIX for the first time.

Figure B.1 shows what the screen looks like when the machine is starting up. Click the Stop for Maintenance button.

FIGURE B.1

*The SGI startup
screen.*

Clicking the Stop for Maintenance button brings up the menu shown in Figure B.2.

FIGURE B.2

*The IRIX maintenance
menu.*

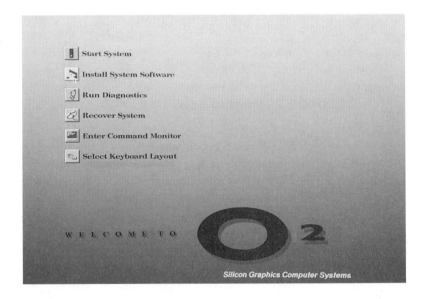

Pick the appropriate device in the Install System Software menu—most likely, the local
CD-ROM drive (see Figure B.3).

FIGURE B.3

The Install System Software menu.

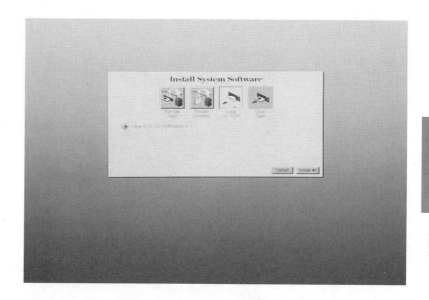

After you select the appropriate device, you are prompted to insert a CD-ROM. Insert the Installation Tools CD-ROM. Next, the machine copies the installation tools to disk, as Figure B.4 shows.

FIGURE B.4

Copying installation tools to disk.

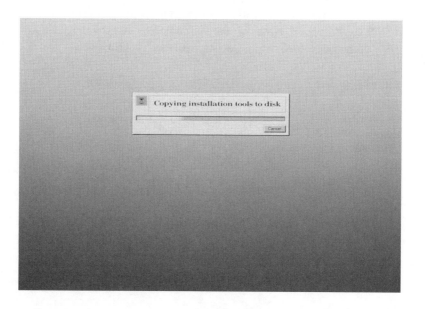

After the tools are copied, the Inst menu appears (see Figure B.5).

FIGURE B.5

The Inst menu.

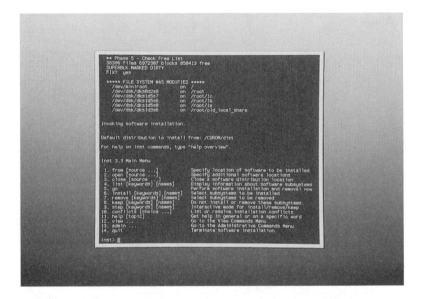

Look at that Inst menu carefully. The commands you will be using are listed on the initial screen. Figure B.6 shows the start of the software listing you see by entering the list command. Note that the listing begins by providing definitions to the codes listed in the left column of the software listing.

FIGURE B.6

The beginning of the software listing on the first IRIX 6.5 CD-ROM.

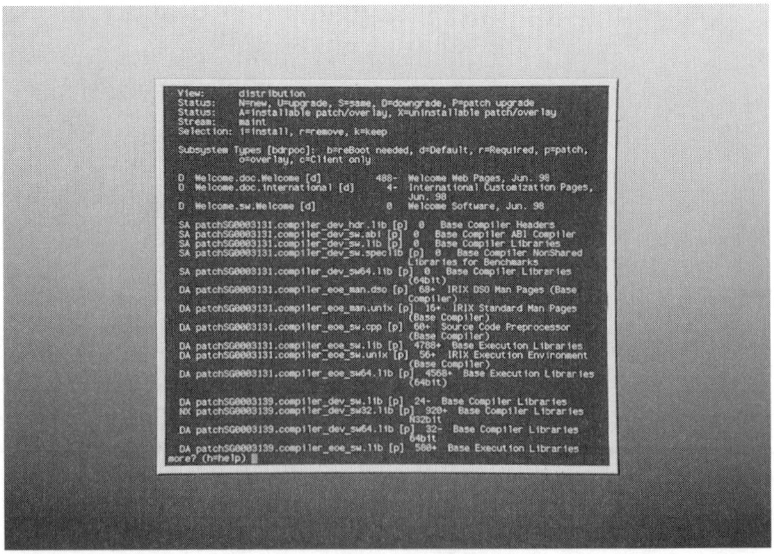

Figure B.7 shows the end of the listing. You get a tally of your disk space.

FIGURE B.7

The end of the soft-ware listing on the first IRIX 6.5 CD-ROM.

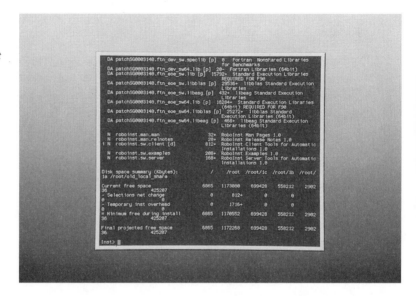

Insert your CD-ROMs from lowest to highest sequence number. Read any recommendations the booklet has on how many CD-ROMs you can start off with. The system reads the contents of each CD-ROM; you then make your selections, check for any conflicts, and start the process. You are prompted to insert CD-ROMs as necessary. Read which CD-ROM the system asks for, because it does not necessarily ask for them in the same order in which you inserted them.

I have found it safe to start with the first four CD-ROMs of the IRIX 6.5 distribution. Currently, those CD-ROMs are Installation Tools, Foundation 1, Foundation 2, and Applications. Note that NFS is a separate product located on the ONC3/NFS CD-ROM. A nondefault package you might want to consider adding is eoe.sw.svr4net, which provides additional networking tools. Additionally, you will be able to install headers for various programming languages from the main CD-ROMs; however, the languages themselves are separate products.

Instead of issuing patches, SGI is releasing maintenance streams (available to everyone) and feature streams (available to those with support contracts). If you do not have a support contract, at least sign up for a membership in Supportfolio/SurfZone, the area where you can download the updates. This area also has instructions on installing IRIX and brief descriptions of the contents of the CD-ROMs. The URL for Supportfolio is in Appendix E, "Useful Resources."

What we have shown here is how to begin a miniroot installation of IRIX. When you download an update from SGI, a patch may be available for you to install so that you can do a live installation of the update. Live installations do not require rebooting the machine into maintenance mode.

Because the product descriptions are rather difficult to decipher, you may learn over time that you do not have something installed that you need. As long as you keep your CD-ROMs in a safe place, even if you already have installed an update, you still can add products. Start by selecting your product in the update distribution. When you run `conflicts`, `inst` asks for a CD-ROM with the base distribution, and you can easily continue.

What follows now is a transcript of adding a product to a machine that has the IRIX 6.5.3 update. This will give you an idea of what some of the `inst` commands that you follow from the booklet do.

```
inst -f 653m

Default distribution to install from: 653m

For help on inst commands, type "help overview".


Inst 3.6 Main Menu

    1. from [source ...]          Specify location of software to be
  installed
    2. open [source ...]          Specify additional software locations
    3. close [source ...]         Close a software distribution location
    4. list [keywords] [names]    Display information about software
  subsystems
    5. go                         Perform software installation and
  removal now
    6. install [keywords] [names] Select subsystems to be installed
    7. remove [keywords] [names]  Select subsystems to be removed
    8. keep [keywords] [names]    Do not install or remove these
  subsystems
    9. step [keywords] [names]    Interactive mode for install/remove/keep
   10. conflicts [choice ...]     List or resolve installation conflicts
   11. help [topic]               Get help in general or on a specific
  word
   12. view ...                   Go to the View Commands Menu
   13. admin ...                  Go to the Administrative Commands Menu
   14. quit                       Terminate software installation
```

Running `list` gives a listing of the software in this distribution:

```
Inst> list
```

```
IRIX 6.5.3 Installation Tools and Overlays, February 1999 README
Silicon Graphics, Inc.
--------------------------------------------------------------------------
```

This CD contains the miniroot and other components necessary to boot
the system into the basic installation environment for operating
system installs and upgrades. It also contains documentation called
"Customer Welcome", which includes Start Here pages that provide important
information you should read before you install this release of IRIX.

To view the Start Here pages:
1. Insert the Installation Tools and Overlays CD 1-of-2 February 1999
   into the CD-ROM drive.
2. Open a Web browser and enter the following address:
   file:/CDROM/WhatsNew/yourSystem.html

        NOTE: Literally type yourSystem.html; do not
              type your actual system name.

3. Click the "Start Here" link.

You may also access the Start Here pages from SupportFolio at the
following URL:
              http://support.sgi.com/6.5/installing.html

and on the IRIX 6.5.3 Base Documentation, February 1999 CD.

Important

Carefully follow the instructions in the CD booklet that came packaged
with the 6.5.3 CDs. It is especially important to follow the
instructions when upgrading from a release prior to IRIX 6.5. Among
other things, these instructions tell you how to insert all
applicable IRIX 6.5 CDROMs (or open all network distribution
directories) as well as the 6.5.3 CDROMs, before issuing any "keep"
or "install" commands. If this is not done, your installation will
not be successful (you will get unresolvable conflicts). Refer to the
CD installation booklet for a list of applicable and necessary CDs.

6.5.3 Unbundled directory on Overlays CD 2-of-2 February 1999

The Overlays CD 2-of-2 February 1999 contains overlays for the following
unbundled products.

        ATM Software, 2.3.2
        DIVO Video Execution Environment, 1.2 for IRIX 6.5
        OCTANE Personal Video Execution Environment, 6.5.3m
        Galileo Video Execution Environment, 6.5.3m
        ImageVision Library, 3.2.1
        IMPACT Indigo2 Video Execution Environ, 6.5.3m
        IMPACT Compression Execution Environment 6.5.3m
        IMPACT Video Execution Environment, 6.5.3m
        InSight Developer Book Building Tools, 4.0
        Sirius Video Execution Environment, 6.5.3m

These updates can be found in the following directory:

        /CDROM/dist/unbundled

If you use these products, you should install these updates.

Reading product descriptions .. 100%

This software distribution contains overlay products. In order to
complete the installation, you may need to insert additional CDs
(or specify additional network distribution directories) that contain the
base software for these overlays.

If additional CDs are required, "Conflict" messages later in the
installation will prompt you to load any other necessary CDs.
(See the "overlay" help topic for more information.)
    View: distribution
    Status: N=new, U=upgrade, S=same, D=downgrade
    Stream: maint
    Selection: i=install, r=remove, k=keep

    Subsystem Types [bdrpoc]: b=reBoot needed, d=Default, r=Required,
               p=patch, o=overlay, c=Client only

    N FDDIXPress.sw.FDDIXPress [o]   204+   FDDIXPress Software

    S Register.sw.Register [do]   0   On-Line Registration, 1.6

    S ViewKit_dev.books.ViewKit_PG [do] 0   ViewKit Programming Guide
    S ViewKit_dev.man.pages [do]   0   ViewKit man pages, 1.5.3
    S ViewKit_dev.man.relnotes [do]   0   ViewKit Release notes, 1.5.3
    S ViewKit_dev.sw.base [do]   16+   ViewKit header files, 1.5.3
    N ViewKit_dev.sw.debug [o]   12232+   ViewKit debugging libraries,
➥1.5.3
    S ViewKit_dev.sw.demo [do]   0   ViewKit demo and example
➥programs, 1.5.3
    S ViewKit_dev.sw.lib [do]   0   ViewKit archive libraries,
➥1.5.3
    N ViewKit_dev.sw64.debug [o]   5352+   ViewKit 64-bit debugging
➥libraries, 1.5.3
    N ViewKit_dev.sw64.lib [o]   3588+   ViewKit archive 64-bit
➥libraries, 1.5.3

    S ViewKit_eoe.man.relnotes [do]   0   ViewKit Release notes, 1.5.3
➥and 2.1.0
    S ViewKit_eoe.sw.base [do]   0   ViewKit Execution Environment,
➥1.5.3 and 2.1.0
    N ViewKit_eoe.sw64.base [o]   4136+   ViewKit 64-bit Execution
➥Environment, 1.5.3 and 2.1.0

```
    S  Welcome.doc.Welcome [d]           0    Welcome Web Pages, February 99
    S  Welcome.doc.international [d]      0    International Customization
➥Pages, February 99
    S  Welcome.sw.Welcome [d]            0    Welcome Software, February 99

    S  compiler_eoe.man.dso [do]         0    IRIX DSO Man Pages (Base
➥Compiler)
    S  compiler_eoe.man.relnotes [do]    0    Standard Execution Libraries
➥Release Notes (Base

                                              Compiler)
    S  compiler_eoe.man.unix [do]        0    IRIX Standard Man Pages (Base
➥Compiler)
    S  compiler_eoe.sw.cpp [dor]         0    Source Code Preprocessor (Base
➥Compiler)
    S  compiler_eoe.sw.lib [dor]         0    Base Execution Libraries
    S  compiler_eoe.sw.unix [dor]        0    IRIX Execution Environment
➥(Base Compiler)
    S  compiler_eoe.sw64.lib [o]         0    Base Execution Libraries
➥(64bit)
    S  compiler_eoe.sw64.unix [o]        0    IRIX Execution Environment
➥(Base Compiler) (64bit)

<… some material deleted here in the interest of space…>

    S  ftn_eoe.man.relnotes [do]         0    Standard Execution Libraries
➥Release Notes
    S  ftn_eoe.sw.lib [do]               0    Standard Execution Libraries
➥(N32bit)
    S  ftn_eoe.sw.libblas [o]            0    libblas Standard Execution
➥Libraries (N32bit)
    S  ftn_eoe.sw.libeag [o]             0    libeag Standard Execution
➥Libraries (N32bit)
    S  ftn_eoe.sw64.lib [o]              0    Standard Execution Libraries
➥(64bit)
    S  ftn_eoe.sw64.libblas [o]          0    libblas Standard Execution
➥Libraries (64bit)
    S  ftn_eoe.sw64.libeag [o]           0    libeag Standard Execution
➥Libraries (64bit)

    N  gl_dev.man.fortran [o]          20+    GL and OpenGL Fortran Manual
➥Pages
    S  gl_dev.man.gldev [do]             0    GL Development Manual Pages
    N  gl_dev.man.ogldebug [o]          8+    OpenGL Debugger Manual Page
    S  gl_dev.man.relnotes [do]          0    GL Development Release Notes
    N  gl_dev.man.widget [o]           12+    OpenGL Widget
    N  gl_dev.sw.fortran [o]          408+    Fortran headers and libraries
    S  gl_dev.sw.gldev [do]              0    GL Development Environment
    N  gl_dev.sw.ogldebug [o]        6348+    OpenGL Debugger Execution
➥Environment
    N  gl_dev.sw.samples [o]           64+    OpenGL Sample Code
    S  gl_dev.sw.widget [do]             0    OpenGL Widget Development
```

B

```
➥Environment
  N  gl_dev.sw64.fortran [o]          268+  OpenGL Fortran 64bit libraries
  N  gl_dev.sw64.ogldebug [o]        3700+  OpenGL Debugger 64bit
➥Execution Environment
  N  gl_dev.sw64.widget [o]            80+  OpenGL Widget 64bit
➥Development Environment

  <…some material deleted here in the interest of space…>

  S  nfs.books.NIS_AG [do]              0   NIS Administration Guide
  S  nfs.books.ONC3NFS_AG [do]         0   ONC3NFS Administrator's Guide
  S  nfs.man.nfs [do]                   0   NFS Support Manual Pages
i N  nfs.sw.autofs [bdo]              256+  AutoFS Support
  N  nfs.sw.cachefs [bo]              376+  CacheFS Support
  N  nfs.sw.dskless_client [oc]      1160+  Diskless Client Support
  N  nfs.sw.dskless_server [o]         32+  Diskless Server Support
  S  nfs.sw.nfs [bdo]                   0   NFS Support
  S  nfs.sw.nis [bdo]                   0   NIS (formerly Yellow Pages)
➥Support

  N  pcp_eoe.man.pages [o]             96+  PCP EOE Manual Pages, 2.0
i N  pcp_eoe.man.relnotes [do]         32+  PCP EOE Release Notes, 2.0
i N  pcp_eoe.sw.eoe [do]             2544+  PCP EOE, 2.0
  N  pcp_eoe.sw.monitor [o]           484+  PCP EOE Monitor, 2.0
  N  pcp_eoe.sw64.eoe [o]             464+  PCP EOE Optional N64 developer
➥libraries, 2.0

i N  performer_demo.man.demo [do]      16+  Performer2.2.4 Demo Man Pages
  N  performer_demo.sw32.igl_demo [o]  492+  Performer2.2.4 IRIS GL
➥Demos (n32)
i N  performer_demo.sw32.ogl_demo [do]  768+  Performer2.2.4 OpenGL
➥Demos (n32)
  N  performer_demo.sw64.demo [o]      816+  Performer2.2.4 Demos (n64)
  N  performer_demo.swO32.igl_demo [o]  488+  Performer2.2.4 IRIS GL
➥Demos (o32)
  N  performer_demo.swO32.ogl_demo [o]  764+  Performer2.2.4 OpenGL
➥Demos (o32)

  <…some material deleted here in the interest of space>

Disk space summary (Kbytes):              /
Current free space                  1170864
- Selections net change                3008+
- Temporary inst overhead              7924+
= Minimum free during install       1159932

Free space after reboot             1167856
```

The results of list show that some products already are selected for installation (they have an "i" in front of them). The next section shows what happens when you tell inst to keep * and then run list again. Only the tail end of list is shown.

```
Inst> keep *

Inst> list

Disk space summary (Kbytes):            /

Current free space            1170836
- Selections net change             0
- Temporary inst overhead           0
= Minimum free during install  1170836

Final projected free space    1170836
```

keep * tells inst not to select anything. install tells the inst program which products to install. Running list again shows that the products have been selected for installation and an update on the disk space summary. Again, only the tail end of list is shown.

```
Inst> install gl_dev.man.fortran gl_dev.man.ogldebug gl_dev.man.widget gl
➥dev.sw.fortran

Inst> install gl_dev.sw.ogldebug gl_dev.sw.samples

Inst> list

Disk space summary (Kbytes):            /

Current free space            1170836
- Selections net change          6860+
- Temporary inst overhead        1716+
= Minimum free during install  1162260

Final projected free space    1163976
```

Run conflicts before you actually install anything, and make decisions to solve the conflicts. Inst prompts you on how to indicate your decisions. Note that it is all right to solve the ones you can see onscreen and keep running conflicts until you run out of conflicts.

```
Inst>> conflicts

Overlay product gl_dev.sw.samples (1275309320) cannot be installed because
of missing prerequisites: base product gl_dev.sw.samples (1274627335)
  1a. Do not install gl_dev.sw.samples (1275309320)
  1b. Also install base product gl_dev.sw.samples (1274627335) from an
      additional distribution -- insert another CD or specify another
      software distribution

Overlay product gl_dev.sw.ogldebug (1275309320) cannot be installed because
of missing prerequisites: base product gl_dev.sw.ogldebug (1274627335)
  2a. Do not install gl_dev.sw.ogldebug (1275309320)
```

2b. Also install base product gl_dev.sw.ogldebug (1274627335) from an
    additional distribution -- insert another CD or specify another
    software distribution

Overlay product gl_dev.sw.fortran (1275309320) cannot be installed because
of missing prerequisites: base product gl_dev.sw.fortran (1274627335)
  3a. Do not install gl_dev.sw.fortran (1275309320)
  3b. Also install base product gl_dev.sw.fortran (1274627335) from an
      additional distribution -- insert another CD or specify another
      software distribution

Overlay product gl_dev.man.widget (1275309320) cannot be installed because
of missing prerequisites: base product gl_dev.man.widget (1274627335)
  4a. Do not install gl_dev.man.widget (1275309320)
  4b. Also install base product gl_dev.man.widget (1274627335) from an
      additional distribution -- insert another CD or specify another
      software distribution

Overlay product gl_dev.man.ogldebug (1275309320) cannot be installed
because of missing prerequisites: base product gl_dev.man.ogldebug
(1274627335)
  5a. Do not install gl_dev.man.ogldebug (1275309320)
  5b. Also install base product gl_dev.man.ogldebug (1274627335) from an
      additional distribution -- insert another CD or specify another
      software distribution

Overlay product gl_dev.man.fortran (1275309320) cannot be installed
➥because
of missing prerequisites: base product gl_dev.man.fortran (1274627335)
  6a. Do not install gl_dev.man.fortran (1275309320)
  6b. Also install base product gl_dev.man.fortran (1274627335) from an
      additional distribution -- insert another CD or specify another
      software distribution

Resolve conflicts by typing "conflicts choice choice ..."
or try "help conflicts"

Inst> conflicts 1b 2b 3b 4b 5b 6b
Note: this operation opens a distribution and selects all
of its default or upgrade products for install. If you
wish to open just a single product, append the product
name to the distribution name, as in /CDROM/dist/eoe.
See the "distribution" help topic for more information.
Enter new distribution from list:

 1 irix653m
 2 /CDROM/dist
 3 /var/tmp/tardista01QTM
 4 /tmp/M037135895009A6E3.tardist

```
 5 /old_local_share/patch-65-2
 6 /old_local_share/patch-65/patch3413
 7 /old_local_share/patch-65
 8 /CDROM/dist/dist6.5
 9 /usr/local/testing/libjpeg-6b
10 /usr/local/testing/rasmol-26b2
11 quit (no additional distributions, return to inst prompt)

Install software from: [irix653m]  2
Reading product descriptions ..  100%

Inst> conflicts
No conflicts
```

After all the conflicts are solved, run go. If appropriate, continue with more CD-ROMs, or quit inst. You are prompted if a reboot is required.

```
Inst> go
Pre-installation check ..   8%
Checking space requirements ..  16%
Installing/removing files ..  16%
Installing new versions of selected gl_dev.sw subsystems
Installing/removing files ..  37%
Installing new versions of selected gl_dev.man subsystems
Installing/removing files ..  92%
Installing new versions of selected gl_dev.sw subsystems
Installing/removing files ..  93%
Installing new versions of selected gl_dev.man subsystems
Installing/removing files ..  94%
Running exit-commands ..  99%
Checking dependencies .. 100% Done.
Calculating sizes .. 100% Done.
Installations and removals were successful.
You may continue with installations or quit now.

To install from another CD, change the CD in the drive and enter
command "from".

Inst> quit
Requickstarting ELF files (see rqsall(1)) .. 100% Done.
```

Again, when you are installing IRIX, follow the instructions in the booklet. Hopefully this look at a brief IRIX product installation gives you a better understanding of what the booklet instructions indicate. The booklet doesn't leave a whole lot of room for explanation.

If you are upgrading a machine from IRIX 5.3 to 6.5, check the online IRIX Administrative books, available at http://techpubs.sgi.com/library, for details. Those instructions are very thorough.

Next, we will take a look at a unique way for setting up a machine. We will do what we can to feel the experience, given that we only have paper to work with. The O2 comes with an exciting experience, called the OutOfBox Experience, for configuring it. You get sound and movies, and you get to navigate your way through a three-dimensional world!

Figure B.8 shows the beginning of the tour. At this point, there is also background music.

FIGURE B.8

Starting the OutOfBox Experience.

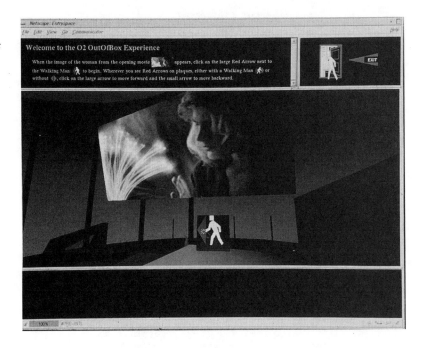

In Figure B.9, you have just entered and are going down the stairs. The earth is spinning here.

By Figure B.10, you are at the Language and Time Zone station. The woman in the movie provides some brief instructions.

Figure B.11 shows the System Setup station. Here, the woman tells you that you will configure your machine and make some user accounts.

Your final official stop is the EndUser Registration station, shown in Figure B.12. Here, you provide registration information for the machine.

FIGURE B.9

Going down the stairs.

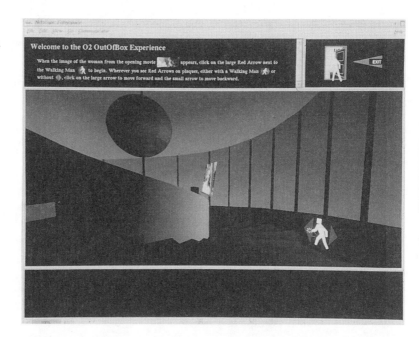

FIGURE B.10

The Language and Time Zone station.

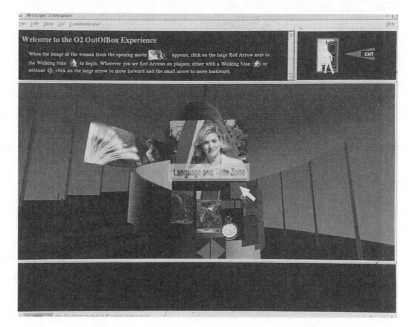

FIGURE B.11

The System Setup station.

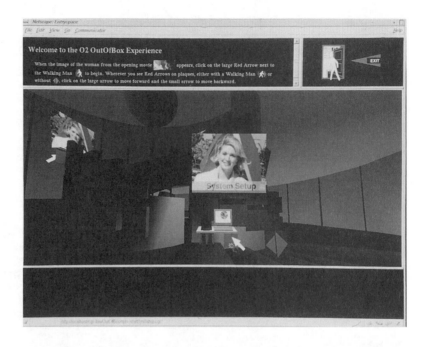

FIGURE B.12

The EndUser Registration station.

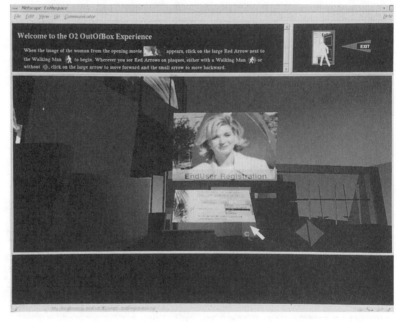

But that's not all. There is a whole *Virtual Reality Modeling Language (VRML)* world available for you to explore! Figure B.13 shows part of the virtual O2 tour, which shows you a bit about your new O2.

FIGURE B.13

Living O2 VRML world.

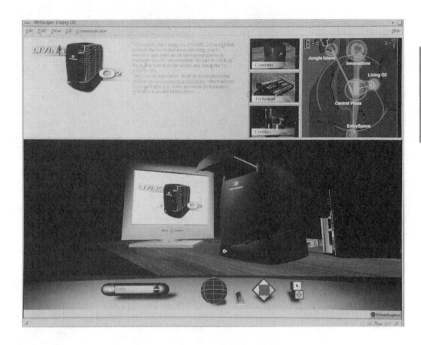

In Figure B.14, you are outside in your VRML world, standing at the foot of an O2.

By Figure B.15, you have gone investigating and can look up at the powerful O2s.

Figure B.16 shows even more of your virtual world, with some walkways and water. In the distance, you can see a gate to Jungle Island.

As you can only just start to see here, SGI's O2 provides a most unique way to configure it. Even if you don't choose to configure your machine using the OutOfBox Experience, you should take some time to play in your special VRML world.

FIGURE B.14

At the foot of an O2.

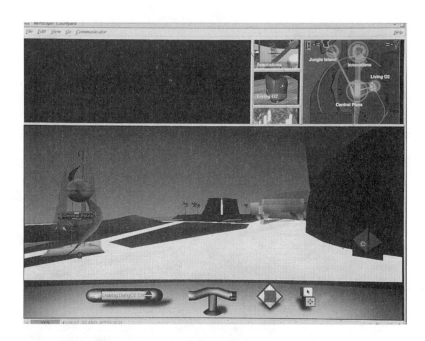

FIGURE B.15

The Central Plaza area.

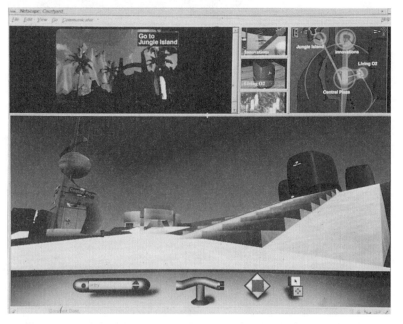

FIGURE B.16

An overview of the world.

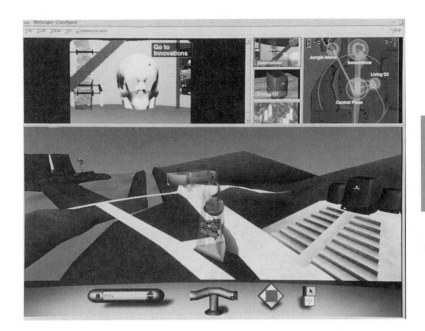

APPENDIX C

Useful Files

Here are some sample configuration files you can use as a starting place for configuring your machines or your user accounts. Obviously, some parts of these are system specific, but you should be able to figure out where corresponding paths on your machines are without difficulty.

Configuring Paths and Aliases

Configuration file for csh and tcsh. Configures paths and aliases that I like and use frequently. Note that it picks up the /usr/local/extras/ cshrc_extensions after adding its own material. Goes in user's home directory.

.cshrc

```
if($?prompt) then
#
# A nifty little routine that sets X11 titlebars
# to your current full path, and prompts to your
# current host and directory
#
set cdcmd=''
set cdcmd='echo -n "_]0;$cwd_"'
```

```
set norm_suf='\!''> '
set root_suf='\!''# '
if ( ($SHELL == /bin/cshe) ¦¦ ($SHELL =~ *tcsh)) then
    alias _normal    'set prompt="$HOST $cwd:t $norm_suf"'
    alias _root      'set prompt="%S$HOST%s $cwd:t $root_suf"'
    if ( 'whoami' =~ *root* ) then
        alias prmpt_s _root
    else
        alias prmpt_s _normal
    endif
endif


if ($term == xterm) then
    alias win_s 'eval "$cdcmd"'
    alias cd 'chdir \!*;prmpt_s;win_s'
else
    alias win_s 'echo $cwd'
    alias cd 'chdir \!*;prmpt_s'
endif

prmpt_s;win_s
set history=200 savehist=200


# Preferred editor for mail/news purposes
setenv VISUAL emacs

# Set up some variables that I use frequently
setenv OPENWINHOME /usr/openwin
setenv TCL_LIBRARY /usr/local/lib/tcl
setenv TK_LIBRARY /usr/local/lib/tk
setenv XENVIRONMENT ~/.Xenv
setenv X11HOME /usr/local/X11R5
setenv X11PATH '/usr/local/X11R5/bin'
setenv LIBPATH /usr/local/X11R5/lib

# Some versions of dump/restore and mt will use the
# device specified by the TAPE variable if you don't
# override it with a commandline switch.
setenv TAPE /dev/nrst0

# Note that the current directory comes _last_!
set STDPATH=(/usr/bin $X11PATH /usr/ucb /etc /usr/etc /usr/local/bin
➥$HOME/bin .)

set path=($STDPATH)
source /usr/local/extras/cshrc_extensions

limit coredumpsize 0

umask 0022
```

```
# I dislike /usr/bin/mail, but like /usr/ucb/Mail
alias mail Mail
alias lo exit
# Interactive ftp mode is a drag
alias ftp ftp -i
alias h history
# Always use rm in interactive mode!
alias rm rm -i
# Everything, all the time
alias ps "ps -auxww ¦ more"
# Show line numbers in the files
alias grep grep -n
# Trick to keep our window names correct even when moving via push
alias pushd 'pushd \!*; cd .'
alias popd 'popd; cd .'
# Quick look at who was last on the system
alias whodunit "/usr/lib/acct/fwtmp < /var/adm/wtmp ¦ tail -30"
# Emacs starting a new window for itself is annoying.  If I wanted
#  it in a window, I'd start one for it.
alias emacs 'emacs -nw'
# Look for files more recent than...
alias recent 'find ./ -mtime -\!* -exec ls -ld {} \;'
alias xlock 'xscreensaver-command -activate'
# Alias to copy in my blank TeX starter document
alias startletter 'cp ~ray/miscdata/myltr.tex \!*.tex'
# Start xv up with corrected gamma, and my old 8-bit screen
alias xv 'xv -gamma 2 -8 -owncmap '

endif
```

Login Shells

Configuration file for login shell. This file performs a similar function to the .cshrc, except that it is used only for login shells, not for other shells that are spawned. Goes in user's home directory.

.login

```
#
echo "An Acceptable Solution"
#


# in case we got here somehow without setting these, and I need them
# for anything I might decide to do here.
setenv X11HOME /usr/local/X11R5
setenv X11PATH /usr/local/X11R5/bin
setenv X11LIBPATH /usr/local/X11R5/lib
```

```
set STDPATH=(/usr/bin $X11PATH /usr/ucb /etc /usr/etc /usr/local/bin .)
set path=($path $STDPATH)


# Spit out a blank line
echo ''

# If we're on the console, record this login in .loginfile - for
#  my own login/logout tracking
# Then let me choose between X11, a standard console prompt, or Sun's
#  OpenWindows environment.  Copy in a few configuration files
#  as appropriate for the choice.  Openwin software sometimes confuses
#  things if OPENWIN* variables are set, even if OPENWIN is not being
#  run, so don't set them unless I have to
if ('tty' == "/dev/console") then
    echo "login  -> " 'date' >> .loginfile
    echo "...Console login..."; echo ''
    ask:
    echo "a. Xwindows"
    echo "b. Nothing"
    echo "c. OpenWin"; echo ''
    echo -n "Choice: "
    set choice=$<
    if ($choice == "a") then
        set path=($path $X11PATH)
        setenv LD_LIBRARY_PATH {$X11LIBPATH}:/usr/lib:/usr/local/lib
        cp .xinitrc-X11 .xinitrc
        xinit
    else if ($choice == "b") then
        tcsh
    else if ($choice == "c") then
        setenv OPENWINHOME /usr/openwin
        setenv OPENWINBIN /usr/openwin/bin
        setenv LD_LIBRARY_PATH {$OPENWINHOME}/lib:/usr/lib:/usr/local/lib
        set path=($OPENWINBIN $path)
        cp .xinitrc-openwin .xinitrc
        openwin
    else
        echo "Please choose a, b, or c."
        goto ask
    endif

# Fall through to here after exiting X11, or whatever
    goto exit

else
# If we're not on the console, presume that X11 will do, record the
#  login in the .loginfile, set the terminal's erase to work with my
#  normal terminal delete key, and get on with the connection
    setenv LD_LIBRARY_PATH {$X11LIBPATH}:/usr/lib:/usr/local/lib
    echo "remotelogin  -> " 'date' >> .loginfile
```

```
        echo "...Remote login..."; echo ''
        stty erase '^?'
        tcsh
        goto exit2


exit:
# Do some cutsie stuff like load an image on the console, record the
#  logout, and fall on out to the logout
        echo "Logout"
        screenload -b -i plum3 $HOME/junk/AMG-ld5.ras
        echo "logout -> " 'date' >> .loginfile
        goto done


exit2:
# Same as exit, only we're on from remote, so we don't diddle the
#  local display
        echo "... Remote logout..."; echo ''
        echo "remotelogout  -> " 'date' >> .loginfile
        goto done


done:
# Echo something, just so we know we got here in the script,
#  Then bail
        echo "Offline"
        logout
```

Configuring csh

More csh configuration files. I use this as a system-wide global configuration file to supplement users' individual .cshrc files.

/usr/local/extras/cshrc_extensions

```
# include configuration and paths that all users might want to have
# I use this file to configure paths and environment variables that
# will be generally useful so that I don't have to edit each user's
# .cshrc individually (obviously these won't all be directly
# applicable to your system as the paths are installation-dependent)

# set up fsp client aliases
source /usr/local/extras/fsp_setup

# add some generally useful paths that everyone might like
set path=($path /usr/local/atalk/bin /usr/local/testbin /usr/openwin/bin
/usr/openwin/demo /usr/local/webmaker/bin /usr/local/bin/pbmplus
/usr/local/Acrobat3/Reader/bin/ /usr/local/mysql/bin)
```

C

```
# set the LD_LIBRARY_PATH so that silly programs can find their shared
# libraries
setenv LD_LIBRARY_PATH /usr/local/X11R5/lib

# tell X programs where to find their application default settings
setenv XAPPLRESDIR /usr/local/X11R5/lib/X11/app-defaults

# LIBWWW_PERL for some reason needs to know where it is
setenv LIBWWW_PERL /usr/local/lib/libwww-perl-0.40

# Mesa OpenGL emulation setup stuff
setenv MESA_NO_DITHER TRUE
setenv MESA_BACK_BUFFER 2
setenv GL_LIGHT_MODEL_LOCAL_VIEWER FALSE
setenv GL_COLOR_MATERIAL FALSE
# setenv MESA_DEBUG TRUE

# set a good default for where to look for man pages
setenv MANPATH {/usr/openwin/man:/usr/man:/usr/local/man}
```

Configuring X Environments

Configure and place X11 windows and widgets in each of the X environments that I use.
Because the window managers are slightly different, there are some different arguments
in these, but it is more of an example that you can have different X configurations in
your login.

.xinitrc-X11

```
#!/bin/sh
xrdb -load $HOME/.X11defaults
xset m 2 5 s off
xset fp+ /usr/local/fonts
xscreensaver -timeout 10 -lock &

echo  "XTerm*ttyModes:erase ^?" | xrdb -merge
/usr/local/X11R5/bin/twm &
xset bc
xclock -bg "slategrey" -fg "lightgrey" -geometry 60x60+220+1 -padding 4 &
xterm -rw  -si -sl 2000 -fn 6x10 -geometry 83x50+1+300 &
xterm -rw  -si -sl 2000 -fn 6x10 -geometry 80x52+1+280 &
xterm -rw  -si -sl 2000 -fn 6x10 -geometry 83x15+1+100 &
xterm -fn 6x10 -geometry 99x86+525+1 -e emacs -nw &
xterm -rw -sf -si -sl 2000  -fn 6x10 -geometry 83x4+1+828 &
xterm -title "CONSOLE" -C -geometry 80x24+1+1 -T Console -iconic
```

.xinitrc-openwin

```
#!/bin/sh
xrdb -load $HOME/.X11defaults
```

```
xmodmap -e 'keysym BackSpace = Delete'
echo  "XTerm*ttyModes:erase ^?" ¦ xrdb -merge

# xset settings don't work here, so don't use them here
xclock -bg "slategrey" -fg "lightgrey" -geometry 60x60+220+1 -padding 4 &

# olwm is OpenWindows' windows manager.  I could run twm here, but that
# would be kind of weird with openwindows
olwm &
xterm -rw  -si -sl 2000 -fn 6x10 -geometry 83x50+1+300 &
xterm -rw  -si -sl 2000 -fn 6x10 -geometry 80x52+1+280 &
xterm -rw  -si -sl 2000 -fn 6x10 -geometry 83x15+1+100 &
xterm -fn 6x10 -geometry 99x86+525+1 -e emacs -nw &

xterm -rw -sf -si -sl 2000 -fn 6x10 -geometry 83x4+1+828 &
xterm -title "CONSOLE" -C -geometry 80x24+1+1 -T Console -iconic
```

Mail Processing

Define mail processing recipes for procmail. Each of these recipes matches a set of mail header fields and performs rearrangements and processing of the mail as appropriate. Procmail can be used to implement quite sophisticated automated mail handling by the addition of simple rules. Place in user's home directory.

.procmailrc

```
PATH=$HOME/bin:/usr/local/bin:/usr/ucb:/bin:.
MAILDIR=/usr/spool/mail      # You'd better make sure it exists
DEFAULT=lists
LOGFILE=$HOME/.procmail_log
# VERBOSE=yes
LOCKFILE=$HOME/.lockmail
SHELL=/bin/sh

# First, a testing routine - this one should junk mail
# that appears to come from ray@banana.biosci.ohio-state.edu
# and is To ray (at the local machine)
:0
          * !^FROM_DAEMON
          * ^From: ray@banana.biosci.ohio-state.edu
          * ^TOray
          ¦ cat >> /dev/null

# Next another testing routine - this one should catch mail
# to test@banana.biosci.ohio-state.edu and twiddle the headers so
# that replies go back to test@banana.biosci.ohio-state.edu, but
# the From field keeps the original sender.  Subject and
# other fields are carried over as appropriate, and an X-loop
# field is created, which this routine checks to prevent it
```

```
# from getting stuck in loops mailing itself.
# The mail is finally disposed of by sending it to the
# apparent user "test-outgoing", which in this case is
# handled by an entry in /etc/aliases
:0
          * !^FROM_DAEMON
          * !^X-Loop: test@banana.biosci.ohio-state.edu
          * ^TOtest
          ¦ formail -f -k -r -b \
              -A "X-Loop: test@banana.biosci.ohio-state.edu"  \
              -i "Reply-To: test@banana.biosci.ohio-state.edu" \
              -I "To: test@banana.biosci.ohio-state.edu" \
              -i "From:" -i "Subject:" \
              ¦ formail -u "Subject" -I "References" \
              ¦ $SENDMAIL -oi test-outgoing

# A real processing routine.  An entry in /etc/aliases forwards
# mail to mboy-trans@banana.biosci.ohio-state.edu to this account.
# This routine catches the mail, makes sure it's not talking to
# itself, tweaks the headers and sends it back out.
# mboy-trans-outgoing is also an alias handled by /etc/aliases
# that forwards to a group of email addresses contained in a
# file.  This processing routine is different than the previous
# in that it also pushes the data forward to the next routine.
:0 cE
          * !^FROM_DAEMON
          * !^X-Loop: mboy-trans@banana.biosci.ohio-state.edu
          ¦ formail -f -k -r -b \
              -A "X-Loop: mboy-trans@banana.biosci.ohio-state.edu"  \
              -i "Reply-To: mboy-trans@banana.biosci.ohio-state.edu" \
              -I "To: mboy-trans@banana.biosci.ohio-state.edu" \
              -i "From:" -i "Subject:" \
              ¦ formail -u "Subject" -I "References" \
              ¦ $SENDMAIL -oi mboy-trans-outgoing

# And this one saves it in a file.  This is actually a
# quick and dirty implementation of a mailing list for a
# cooperative translation project.  Mailings to the list are
# forwarded to all the list members, and are simultaneously
# archived.  A crontab job then moves this archive file off
# to the translation project ftp site daily.
:0 a
          /home/lists/mboytrans_today
```

Mail Aliases

You also can configure system-wide mail aliases. Aliases are of the form *Incoming_name: outgoing_name*, where *incoming_name* is the name for which mail is received by the system and *outgoing_name* is the name or action to which the mail actually is sent.

/etc/aliases

```
##
#  Aliases can have any mix of upper- and lowercase on the left-hand
#     side, but the right-hand side should be proper case
#     (usually lower) whenever the aliases is redirected to a file or
#     a program.
#
#  - >>>>>>>>>>    The program "newaliases" will need to be run after
#    >> NOTE >>    this file is updated for any changes to
#    >>>>>>>>>>    show through to sendmail.
#
##


# Following alias is required by the mail protocol, RFC 822
# Set it to the address of a HUMAN who deals with this system's mail
# problems.
Postmaster: root

# Alias for mailer daemon; returned messages from our MAILER-DAEMON
# should be routed to our local Postmaster.
MAILER-DAEMON: postmaster

nobody: /dev/null

#######################
# Local aliases below #
#######################
# When mail for "access" is received, forward it to "adam" and "ray"
access: adam,ray
# Mail to "ippon" goes to all addresses in the file
#            /home/adam/ippon/ippon.list
ippon: :include:/home/adam/ippon/ippon.list
# Mail to mboy-trans gets forwarded to user "lists"
#    This is the user that has the .procmailrc file that
#    processes mail for this addressee
mboy-trans: lists
# Mail to mboy-trans-request gets forwarded to a real
#    user to deal with administration
mboy-trans-request: ray
# After procmail processes the mail to mboy-trans for user lists,
#    it's sent back to mboy-trans-outgoing.  This address, like
#    the ippon address above, sends to all email addresses contained
#    in a file, in this case, /home/lists/mboytrans.list
mboy-trans-outgoing: :include:/home/lists/mboytrans.list
# A forwarding address for one of the test routines
test-outgoing: ray@apple.biosci.ohio-state.edu
```

C

Configuring `twm`

Sample configuration file for `twm`. Configures interface colors, pop-up menus, custom actions to be performed for mouse clicks in windows on menus, etc. Place in user's home directory.

`.twmrc`

```
# Set up color preferences for twm
Color
{
    BorderColor "maroon4"

    BorderTileForeground "bisque4"
    BorderTileBackground "darkorchid4"

    TitleForeground "darkslategray"
    TitleBackground "bisque3"

    DefaultBackground "bisque"
    DefaultForeground "slategrey"

    MenuForeground "slategrey"
    MenuBackground "moccasin"

    MenuTitleForeground "slategrey"
    MenuTitleBackground "bisque3"
    MenuShadowColor "bisque4"
    IconForeground "lightgrey"
    IconBackground "slategray"
    IconBorderColor "darkslategray"
    IconManagerForeground "darkslategrey"
    IconManagerBackground "bisque"
    IconManagerHighlight  "maroon4"

}

# Set up preferences if our screen is monochrome
Monochrome
{
    BorderColor "black"
    BorderTileForeground "black"
    BorderTileBackground "white"
    TitleForeground "black"
    TitleBackground "white"
}

# Set many behavioral characteristics, window
# border sizes, fonts, where to put icons, how
# much movement constitutes a "drag", etc.
NoGrabServer
```

```
BorderWidth     4
FramePadding    2
TitleFont      "8x13"
MenuFont       "8x13"
IconFont       "6x10"
ResizeFont     "fixed"
NoTitleFocus
Zoom # 20
IconBorderWidth  4
IconRegion "=60x60" South West 80 80
MoveDelta       5
RestartPreviousState
IconManagerGeometry    "=200x10+290+1"
ShowIconManager
IconManagerFont        "variable"

# Programs that I don't want to see in the
# iconmanager view
IconManagerDontShow
{
    "xclock"
    "xbiff++"
    "perfmeter"
}

IconDirectory    "/usr/local/X11R5/include/X11/bitmaps"
ForceIcons
Icons
{
    "xterm"     "terminal"
}

# Programs that I don't want to show me titles
# on their icons
NoTitle
{
  "TWM"
  "xload"
  "xclock"
  "xckmail"
  "perfmeter"
  "Perfmeter V3"
  "dclock"
  "xbiff++"
  "xeyes"
  "oclock"
}

# Programs that I shouldn't highlight when I select them
NoHighlight
{
```

C

```
      "xclock"
      "perfmeter"
      "Perfmeter V3"
      "xckmail"
      "dclock"
      "xload"
      "xbiff++"
   }


   # Autoraise is just plain confusing!
   AutoRaise
   {
      "nothing"
   }


   DefaultFunction f.menu "default-menu"


   # Functions to perform when the user clicks a mouse button,
   # and what part of the screen the cursor needs to be on to
   # invoke them.
   #Button = KEYS : CONTEXT : FUNCTION
   #————————————————————
   Button1 =        : root   : f.menu "button1"
   Button2 =        : root   : f.menu "button2"
   Button3 =        : root   : f.menu "button3"

   Button1 =        : title  : f.function "blob"
   Button2 =        : title  : f.lower

   Button1 =        : frame  : f.raiselower
   Button2 =        : frame  : f.move
   Button3 =        : frame  : f.lower

   Button1 =        : icon   : f.function "blob"
   Button2 =        : icon   : f.iconify
   Button3 =        : icon   : f.menu "default-menu"
   Button1 = m      : icon   : f.iconify
   Button2 = m      : icon   : f.iconify
   Button3 = m      : icon   : f.iconify
   Button3 = c      : root   : f.function "beep-beep"

   "L5"    =        : window : f.raiselower
   "L5"    =        : title  : f.raiselower

   "L6"    =        : window : f.lower
   "L6"    =        : title  : f.lower

   "L7"    =        : window : f.iconify
   "L7"    =        : icon   : f.iconify
```

```
# Function definitions as used in the above map
Function "beep-beep"
{
    f.beep
    f.beep
    f.beep
    f.beep
    f.beep
}

Function "de-raise-n-focus"
{
    f.deiconify
    f.raise
    f.focus
}

Function "raise-n-focus"
{
    f.raise
    f.focus
}

Function "blob"
{
    f.raise
    f.move
}

# Menus to display, and what actions to take for
# each choice.
menu "exitmenu"
{
"Exit"          f.exec "exit"
}

menu "Feel"
{
"Behavior"      f.menu "Behavior"
"Bell Loud"     ! "xset b 7 &"
"Bell Normal"     ! "xset b 3 &"
"Bell Off"      ! "xset b off &"
"Click Loud"      ! "xset c 8 &"
"Click Soft"      ! "xset c on &"
"Click Off"       ! "xset c off &"
"Lock On"       ! "xset l on &"
"Lock Off"        ! "xset l off &"
"Mouse Fast"      ! "xset m 4 2 &"
"Mouse Normal"      ! "xset m 2 5 &"
"Mouse Slow"        ! "xset m 1 1 &"
}
```

C

```
menu "Behavior"
{
"Auto Raise"      f.autoraise
"Frame Focus"     f.focus
}

menu "button1"
{
"Window Ops"      f.title
"(De)Iconify"     f.iconify
"Move"         f.move
"Resize"      f.resize
"Lower"          f.lower
"Raise"          f.raise
"Redraw Window"   f.winrefresh
"Focus Input"     f.focus
"Unfocus Input"     f.unfocus
"Window Info"     f.identify
}

menu "button2"
{
"Window Mgr"     f.title
"Circle Up"      f.circleup
"Circle Down"     f.circledown
"Refresh All"     f.refresh
"Reload Resource"    ! "echo -n '__' >/dev/console;\
                         xrdb -D$X11VERSION -load $HOME/.X11defaults;\
                         echo -n '_' > /dev/console"
"Source .twmrc"     f.twmrc
"Beep"          f.beep
"Show Icon Mgr"     f.showiconmgr
"Hide Icon Mgr"     f.hideiconmgr
"Feel"          f.menu "Feel"
}


menu "button3"
{
"Clients"         f.title
"Xterm"             ! "xterm &"
"Lock Screen"       ! "xnlock &"
"Xman"            ! "xman &"
"Calculator"        ! "xcalc &"
}

menu "default-menu"
{
"Default Menu"       f.title
"Refresh"         f.refresh
"Refresh Window"     f.winrefresh
```

```
"twm Version"        f.version
"Focus on Root"        f.unfocus
"Source .twmrc"        f.twmrc
"Cut File"        f.cutfile
"(De)Iconify"        f.iconify
"DeIconify"        f.deiconify
"Move Window"        f.move
"ForceMove Window"    f.forcemove
"Resize Window"        f.resize
"Raise Window"        f.raise
"Lower Window"        f.lower
"Focus on Window"    f.focus
"Raise-n-Focus"        f.function "raise-n-focus"
"Zoom Window"        f.zoom
"FullZoom Window"    f.fullzoom
"Kill twm"        f.quit
"Destroy Window"    f.destroy
}

RightTitleButton "icon" = f.zoom
LeftTitleButton "icon" = f.destroy
```

Reconfiguring Kernels for SunOS

Here is BARRACUDA_SMALL, the configuration file from Day 3, "Other Useful Software:
Useful Utilities," used for reconfiguring the kernel on the SunOS machine.

/sys/sun4c/conf/BARRACUDA_SMALL

```
#
# @(#) GENERIC_SMALL from master 1.75 94/10/13 SMI
#
# This config file describes a generic Sun-4/60 kernel,
# including software options and support for the following hardware:
#     8 SCSI disks, 4 SCSI tapes, 2 CD-ROM drives
#
# Some software options are commented out to generate a smaller kernel.
#
machine          "sun4c"
cpu              "SUN4C_60"      # Sun-4/60

#
# Name this kernel GENERIC_SMALL.
#
ident            "BARRACUDA_SMALL"

#
# This kernel supports about 4 users.  Count one user for each
# timesharing user, one for each window that you typically use, and one
```

```
# for each diskless client you serve.  This is only an approximation used
# to control the size of various kernel data structures, not a hard limit
#
maxusers        15


#
# Include all possible software options.
#
# The INET option is not really optional; every kernel must include it.
#
options INET                # basic networking support - mandatory


#
# The following options are all filesystem related.  You only need
# QUOTA if you have UFS.  You only need UFS if you have a disk.
# Diskless machines can remove QUOTA, UFS, and NFSSERVER.  LOFS and TFS
# are only needed if you're using the Sun Network Software Environment.
# HSFS is only needed if you have a CD-ROM drive and want to access
# ISO-9660, High Sierra, or Rock Ridge format CD discs.
#
#options         QUOTA           # disk quotas for local disks
options UFS                 # filesystem code for local disks
options NFSCLIENT           # NFS client side code
options NFSSERVER           # NFS server side code
#options         TMPFS           # tmp (anonymous memory) file system
options HSFS                # High Sierra (ISO 9660) with Rock Ridge extensions
options PCFS                # Unix access to MS-DOS file system


#
# The following options are for accounting and auditing.  SYSAUDIT
# should be removed unless you are using the C2 security features.
#
#options         SYSACCT         # process accounting, see acct(2) & sa(8)
#options         SYSAUDIT        # C2 auditing for security


#
# The following options are for various System V IPC facilities.
# Most standard software does not need them, although they are
# used by SunGKS and some third-party software.
#
#options         IPCMESSAGE      # System V IPC message facility
#options         IPCSEMAPHORE    # System V IPC semaphore facility
#options         IPCSHMEM        # System V IPC shared-memory facility


#
# The following option is only needed if you want to use the trpt
# command to debug TCP problems.
#
options TCPDEBUG        # TCP debugging, see trpt(8)


#
```

```
# The following option includes the software DES support, needed if
# you're using secure NFS or secure RPC.
#
options CRYPT            # software encryption


#
# The following two options are needed for asynchronous I/O.
#
#options     LWP              # kernel threads
#options     ASYNCHIO         # asynch I/O (requires LWP)


#
# The following option adds support for loadable kernel modules.
#
options VDDRV            # loadable modules


#
# The following option adds support for SunView 1 journaling.
#
#options     WINSVJ           # SunView 1 journaling support


#
# Build one kernel based on this basic configuration.
# It will use the generic swap code so that you can have
# your root filesystem and swap space on any supported device.
# Put the kernel configured this way in a file named "vmunix".
#
config  vmunix_small    swap generic


#
# Include support for all possible pseudo-devices.
#
# The first few are mostly concerned with networking.
# You should probably always leave these in.
#
pseudo-device   pty              # pseudo-tty's, also needed for SunView
pseudo-device   ether            # basic Ethernet support
pseudo-device   loop             # loopback network - mandatory


#
# The next few are for SunWindows support, needed to run SunView 1.
#
pseudo-device   win128           # window devices, allow 128 windows
pseudo-device   dtop4            # desktops (screens), allow 4
pseudo-device   ms               # mouse support


#
# The following is needed to support the Sun keyboard, with or
# without the window system.
#
pseudo-device   kb               # keyboard support
```

C

```
#
# The "open EEPROM" pseudo-device is required to support the
# eeprom command.
#
pseudo-device   openeepr         # onboard configuration NVRAM


#
# The following is needed to support the Sun dialbox.
#
#pseudo-device  db        # dialbox support


#
# The following are for streams NIT support.  NIT is used by
# etherfind, traffic, rarpd, and ndbootd.  As a rule of thumb,
# NIT is almost always needed on a server and almost never
# needed on a diskless client.
#
pseudo-device   snit             # streams NIT
pseudo-device   pf               # packet filter
pseudo-device   nbuf             # NIT buffering module


#
# The following is for the "clone" device, used with streams devices.
# This is required if you include streams NIT support, RFS, or an audio
# device.
#
pseudo-device   clone            # clone device


#
# The following section describes which standard device drivers this
# kernel supports.
#
device-driver   sbus             # 'driver' for sbus interface
# device-driver bwtwo            # monochrome frame buffer
# device-driver cgthree          # 8-bit color frame buffer
device-driver   cgsix            # 8-bit accelerated color frame buffer
device-driver   cgtwelve         # 24-bit accelerated color frame buffer
device-driver   gt               # double-buffered 24-bit graphics
device-driver   dma              # 'driver' for dma engine on sbus
device-driver   esp              # Emulex SCSI interface
device-driver   fd               . # Floppy disk
device-driver   audioamd         # AMD79C30A sound chip
device-driver   lebuf            # ethernet buffer
device-driver   le               # LANCE ethernet
device-driver   zs               # UARTs


#
# The following section describes SCSI device unit assignments.
#
scsibus0 at esp                            # declare first scsi bus
disk sd0 at scsibus0 target 3 lun 0        # first hard SCSI disk
disk sd1 at scsibus0 target 1 lun 0        # second hard SCSI disk
```

```
disk sd2 at scsibus0 target 2 lun 0       # third hard SCSI disk
disk sd3 at scsibus0 target 0 lun 0       # fourth hard SCSI disk
disk sd5 at scsibus0 target 5 lun 0       # fifth hard SCSI disk
tape st0 at scsibus0 target 4 lun 0       # first SCSI tape
# tape st1 at scsibus0 target 5 lun 0     # second SCSI tape
disk sr0 at scsibus0 target 6 lun 0       # CD-ROM device

# scsibus1 at esp                               # declare second scsi bus
# disk sd4 at scsibus1 target 3 lun 0     # fifth hard SCSI disk
# disk sd5 at scsibus1 target 1 lun 0     # sixth hard SCSI disk
# disk sd6 at scsibus1 target 2 lun 0     # seventh hard SCSI disk
# disk sd7 at scsibus1 target 0 lun 0     # eighth hard SCSI disk
# tape st2 at scsibus1 target 4 lun 0     # third SCSI tape
# tape st3 at scsibus1 target 5 lun 0     # fourth SCSI tape
# disk sr1 at scsibus1 target 6 lun 0     # 2nd CD-ROM device
```

MySql Definitions

From Day 14, "Other Useful Software: Useful Utilities," here are the MySQL definitions and adduser.pl script for you to work with.

mysql.personinfo.def

```
create table personinfo (
userid CHAR(20),
firstname CHAR(20),
lastname CHAR(20),
address1 CHAR(40),
address2 CHAR(40),
city CHAR(40),
state CHAR(40),
zip CHAR(10),
phone CHAR(14))
;
```

mysql.projectinfo.def

```
create table projectinfo (
supervisorfirstname CHAR(20),
supervisorlastname CHAR(20),
projectname CHAR(40) NOT NULL PRIMARY KEY,
termination DATE,
description TEXT)
;
```

mysql.projectmembers.def

```
create table projectmembers (
projectname CHAR(40),
userid CHAR(20))
;
```

mysql.userinfo.def

```
create table userinfo (
userid CHAR(20) NOT NULL PRIMARY KEY,
usernum MEDIUMINT,
defaultgroup MEDIUMINT,
homedir CHAR(120),
shell CHAR(40))
;
```

adduser.pl

```perl
#!/usr/local/bin/perl
require DBD::mysql;
$|=1;                    # set Perl for non-buffered output

$databaseuser="demo";         # bad form to put passwords in here
$databasepass="demopassword";    # but this is just a demo


$databasename=$ARGV[0];         # arguments from the command line
                 # come in the ARGV[] array
                 # Remember that UNIX and Perl
# are zero based.

# be good, check our arguments
if(@ARGV != 1) {print "usage is adduser.pl <databasename>\n"; exit 1};

# establish a connection to the database
$dbh=DBI->connect("DBI:mysql:$databasename",
                  "$databaseuser",
                  "$databasepass")
                 || die "Couldn't open the database you specified\n";

# get some responses from the user
# <STDIN> is the standard input stream
print "Enter user's first name: ";
$firstname = <STDIN>;
print "Enter user's last name : ";
$lastname = <STDIN>;

print "Enter user's street address - use the form\n";
print "address line 1\n";
print "address line 2\n";
print "City, State Zipcode\n";
$addressline1 = <STDIN>;
$addressline2 = <STDIN>;
$citystatezip = <STDIN>;

print "Enter the user's phone number : ";
$phoneno = <STDIN>;
```

```perl
# chomp deletes the return off the end of the values that
# the user supplied.  Perl is very literal
chomp($firstname); chomp($lastname);
chomp($addressline1); chomp($addressline2);
chomp($citystatezip); chomp($phoneno);

# split splits things up into arrays based on the first
# argument.  The comma between the city, state zip
# lets us pull the city off by splitting into an array
# containing [city][ state zip]
@splitaddress = split(/\,/,$citystatezip);
$city = $splitaddress[0];

# Now we need to separate the state and zip - use the
# space.  Note that it comes in with a leading space, so
# the result is [][state][zip]
@moresplitaddress = split(/ /,$splitaddress[1]);
$state = $moresplitaddress[1]; $zip = $moresplitaddress[2];

# Split the first name up on nothing, to make it an array
# of letters.  Build the potential username from the first
# character of the first name, and the entirety of the last
# name.  In Perl, the period is a concatenation operator.
@nameletters = split(//,$firstname);
$userid = $nameletters[0].$lastname;

# Translate the userid into all lowercase
$userid=~tr/[A-Z]/[a-z]/;

# Make sure that the derived userid is OK with the user
# entering data
print "Built userid ",$userid,"\n";
print "Is this OK?  (Y/N) : ";
$getok = <STDIN>;
chomp($getok);
if ($getok ne "Y")
{

# ne is one of the Perl ways of saying "not equal"
# for numeric values you use the more "C" like != syntax
  print "Enter an acceptable userid : ";
  $userid = <STDIN>;
  chomp($userid);
  print "You entered ",$userid,"\n";
  print "Is this OK?  (Y/N) : ";
  $getok = <STDIN>;
  chomp($getok);
  if ($getok ne "Y") {print "Sorry, please try again\n"; exit 2};
}


# Do the SQL database insert
$dbh->do("INSERT INTO personinfo
```

C

```
                    SET firstname='$firstname', lastname='$lastname',
                    address1='$addressline1', address2='$addressline2',
                    city='$city', state='$state', zip='$zip',
                    phone='$phoneno',userid='$userid'");


print "Is this user attached to a project? (Y/N) : ";
$getok = <STDIN>;
chomp($getok);
if($getok eq "Y")
{
  # eq is the Perl way of saying "equal" character strings
  # == is the syntax for numeric values.
  # NOTE  if you mistakenly use "=" instead of "==" in an
  # if statement, you're actually making an assignment between
  # the "compared" values and evaluating the if based on the
  # success or failure of the assignment!


  # Build the SQL query
  $sql=$dbh->prepare("SELECT projectname, supervisorfirstname,
                       supervisorlastname FROM projectinfo");
  $sql->execute;

  # Get the results back in a multidimensional array
  $allproj=$sql->fetchall_arrayref;

  # Clean up after ourselves
  $sql->finish;

  # One of several Perl "for" syntaxes - for each entry returned
  for $i (0..$#{$allproj})
  {
      print "Project ",$i," ",$allproj->[$i][0],
            "\n   Supervised by ",$allproj->[$i][1],
            " ",$allproj->[$i][2],"\n";
  }
  print "Please pick a project (0-",$#{$allproj},") : ";
  $getproj=<STDIN>;
  chomp($getproj);

  # Based on the number we pick, insert the userid and the
  # corresponding project name into the project member
  # table
  $dbh->do("INSERT INTO projectmembers
            SET projectname='$allproj->[$getproj][0]',
            userid='$userid'");
}

# And we're out of here!
print "User Added.  Exiting\n\n";
```

APPENDIX D

Legal Stuff

In this appendix, you will find excerpted portions of the U.S. Code. These were selected as examples of the legal standards and requirements to which you may be held. They are not the sole source of laws that apply, however, so you should consider them as only representative, not definitive. For the sake of brevity, certain sections of limited applicability have been omitted. Also, some formatting changes were necessary so that the text would fit on these pages. Otherwise, every effort has been made to include these excerpts exactly as they appeared May 5 and 6, 1999, on the Web pages of the legal information institute at http://www4.law.cornell.edu/uscode/.

You might find that some of the sections quoted here do not directly apply to your situation, and some seem unlikely to apply to any computing facilities at all. I have quoted the entire text of several relevant portions of the code, however, both to prevent misstatements by omission, and because some readers may find that the principles embodied in these sections are applicable to their computational environment. For example, you may find that the rights in the Sound Recordings section are relevant to you when your facility begins to support Web-based services and Web-page authors begin to attach sound files to their pages.

You might find it useful to read some sections of the online version of the U.S. Code that were removed from this text. Although some sections may seem entirely irrelevant at first glance, they provide a useful foundation you can use to interpret the law in certain cases that are not specifically addressed.

As an example, you might consider it unlikely that the copyright discussion in the Architectural Works section will have any application to you as a system administrator. However, the text deals with the implications of a work as an "artistic installation" and the limitations to the control the copyright holder has over modifications to that installation. It is not difficult to imagine that a less-than-scrupulous provider of monolithic custom hardware and software solutions might attempt to use copyright law injunctions against the creation of derivative works to prevent the end user from modifying the system. Understanding how copyright law actually treats other instances of monolithic installation works might give you some insight into what your actual legal options would be.

Of course, you should consider this information only as a reference for your own understanding; always consult a lawyer before making decisions regarding the law.

After the information excerpted from the U.S. Code, you will find the full text of the GNU public license, which you should find useful in determining your legal rights and restrictions with respect to much of the UNIX freeware and open-source software available on the Internet.

United States Code

TITLE 18 - CRIMES AND CRIMINAL PROCEDURE

PART I - CRIMES

CHAPTER 119 - WIRE AND ELECTRONIC COMMUNICATIONS INTERCEPTION AND INTERCEPTION OF ORAL COMMUNICATIONS

§ 2510. Definitions.

§ 2511. Interception and disclosure of wire, oral, or electronic communications prohibited.

§ 2512. Manufacture, distribution, possession, and advertising of wire, oral, or electronic communication intercepting devices prohibited.

§ 2513. Confiscation of wire, oral, or electronic communication intercepting devices.

(2514 . Repealed.)

§ 2515. Prohibition of use as evidence of intercepted wire or oral communications.

§ 2516. Authorization for interception of wire, oral, or electronic communications.

§ 2517. Authorization for disclosure and use of intercepted wire, oral, or electronic communications.

§ 2518. Procedure for interception of wire, oral, or electronic communications.

§ 2519. Reports concerning intercepted wire, oral, or electronic communications.

§ 2520. Recovery of civil damages authorized.

§ 2521. Injunction against illegal interception.

§ 2522. Enforcement of the Communications Assistance for Law Enforcement Act.

Sec. 2510. Definitions

As used in this chapter —

(1) "wire communication" means any aural transfer made in whole or in part through the use of facilities for the transmission of communications by the aid of wire, cable, or other like connection between the point of origin and the point of reception (including the use of such connection in a switching station) furnished or operated by any person engaged in providing or operating such facilities for the transmission of interstate or foreign communications or communications affecting interstate or foreign commerce and such term includes any electronic storage of such communication;

(2) "oral communication" means any oral communication uttered by a person exhibiting an expectation that such communication is not subject to interception under circumstances justifying such expectation, but such term does not include any electronic communication;

(3) "State" means any State of the United States, the District of Columbia, the Commonwealth of Puerto Rico, and any territory or possession of the United States;

(4) "intercept" means the aural or other acquisition of the contents of any wire, electronic, or oral communication through the use of any electronic, mechanical, or other device.

(5) "electronic, mechanical, or other device" means any device or apparatus which can be used to intercept a wire, oral, or electronic communication other than —

(a) any telephone or telegraph instrument, equipment or facility, or any component thereof, (i) furnished to the subscriber or user by a provider of wire or electronic communication service in the ordinary course of its business and being used by the subscriber or user in the ordinary course of its business or furnished by such subscriber or user for connection to the facilities of such service and used in the ordinary course of its business; or (ii) being used by a provider of wire or electronic communication service in the ordinary course of its business, or by an investigative or law enforcement officer in the ordinary course of his duties;

(b) a hearing aid or similar device being used to correct subnormal hearing to not better than normal;

(6) "person" means any employee, or agent of the United States or any State or political subdivision thereof, and any individual, partnership, association, joint stock company, trust, or corporation;

(7) "Investigative or law enforcement officer" means any officer of the United States or of a State or political subdivision thereof, who is empowered by law to conduct investigations of or to make arrests for offenses enumerated in this chapter, and any attorney authorized by law to prosecute or participate in the
prosecution of such offenses;

(8) "contents," when used with respect to any wire, oral, or electronic communication, includes any information concerning the substance, purport, or meaning of that communication;

(9) "Judge of competent jurisdiction" means —

(a) a judge of a United States district court or a United States court of appeals; and

(b) a judge of any court of general criminal jurisdiction of a State who is authorized by a statute of that State to enter orders authorizing interceptions of wire, oral, or electronic communications;

(10) "communication common carrier" shall have the same meaning which is given the term "common carrier" by section 153(h) [1] of title 47 of the United States Code;

(11) "aggrieved person" means a person who was a party to any intercepted wire, oral, or electronic communication or a person against whom the interception was directed;

(12) "electronic communication" means any transfer of signs, signals, writing, images, sounds, data, or intelligence of any nature transmitted in whole or in part by a wire, radio, electromagnetic, photoelectronic or photooptical system that affects interstate or foreign commerce, but does not include —

    (A) any wire or oral communication;

    (B) any communication made through a tone-only paging device;

    (C) any communication from a tracking device (as defined in section 3117 of this title); or

    (D) electronic funds transfer information stored by a financial institution in a communications system used for the electronic storage and transfer of funds;

(13) "user" means any person or entity who —

    (A) uses an electronic communication service; and

    (B) is duly authorized by the provider of such service to engage in such use;

(14) "electronic communications system" means any wire, radio, electromagnetic, photooptical or photoelectronic facilities for the transmission of electronic communications, and any computer facilities or related electronic equipment for the electronic storage of such communications;

(15) "electronic communication service" means any service which provides to users thereof the ability to send or receive wire or electronic communications;

(16) "readily accessible to the general public" means, with respect to a radio communication, that such communication is not —

    (A) scrambled or encrypted;

    (B) transmitted using modulation techniques whose essential parameters have been withheld from the public with the intention of preserving the privacy of such communication;

    (C) carried on a subcarrier or other signal subsidiary to a radio transmission;

    (D) transmitted over a communication system provided by a common carrier, unless the communication is a tone-only paging system communication; or

    (E) transmitted on frequencies allocated under part 25, subpart D, E, or F of part 74, or part 94 of the Rules of the Federal Communications Commission, unless, in the case of a communication transmitted on a frequency allocated under part 74 that is not exclusively allocated to broadcast auxiliary services, the communication is a two-way voice communication by radio;

(17) "electronic storage" means —

    (A) any temporary, intermediate storage of a wire or electronic communication incidental to the electronic transmission thereof; and

    (B) any storage of such communication by an electronic communication service for purposes of backup protection of such communication; and

(18) "aural transfer" means a transfer containing the human voice at any point between and including the point of origin and the point of reception.

Sec. 2511. Interception and disclosure of wire, oral, or electronic communications prohibited

(1) Except as otherwise specifically provided in this chapter any person who —

(a) intentionally intercepts, endeavors to intercept, or procures any other person to intercept or endeavor to intercept, any wire, oral, or electronic communication;

(b) intentionally uses, endeavors to use, or procures any other person to use or endeavor to use any electronic, mechanical, or other device to intercept any oral communication when —

(i) such device is affixed to, or otherwise transmits a signal through, a wire, cable, or other like connection used in wire communication; or

(ii) such device transmits communications by radio, or interferes with the transmission of such communication; or

(iii) such person knows, or has reason to know, that such device or any component thereof has been sent through the mail or transported in interstate or foreign commerce; or

(iv) such use or endeavor to use (A) takes place on the premises of any business or other commercial establishment the operations of which affect interstate or foreign commerce; or (B) obtains or is for the purpose of obtaining information relating to the operations of any business or other commercial establishment the operations of which affect interstate or foreign commerce; or

(v) such person acts in the District of Columbia, the Commonwealth of Puerto Rico, or any territory or possession of the United States;

(c) intentionally discloses, or endeavors to disclose, to any other person the contents of any wire, oral, or electronic communication, knowing or having reason to know that the information was obtained through the interception of a wire, oral, or electronic communication in violation of this subsection;

(d) intentionally uses, or endeavors to use, the contents of any wire, oral, or electronic communication, knowing or having reason to know that the information was obtained through the interception of a wire, oral, or electronic communication in violation of this subsection; or

(e)

(i) intentionally discloses, or endeavors to disclose, to any other person the contents of any wire, oral, or electronic communication, intercepted by means authorized by sections 2511(2)(a)(ii), 2511(2)(b)-(c), 2511(2)(e), 2516, and 2518 of this chapter, (ii) knowing or having reason to know that the information was obtained through the interception of such a communication in connection with a criminal investigation, (iii) having obtained or received the information in connection with a criminal investigation, and (iv) with intent to improperly obstruct, impede, or interfere with a duly authorized criminal investigation, shall be punished as provided in subsection (4) or shall be subject to suit as provided in subsection (5).

(2)

(a)

(i) It shall not be unlawful under this chapter for an operator of a switchboard, or an officer, employee, or agent of a provider of wire or electronic communication service, whose facilities are used in the transmission of a wire or electronic communication, to intercept, disclose, or use that communication in the normal course of his employment while engaged in any activity which is a necessary incident to the rendition of his service or to the protection of the rights or property of the provider of that service, except that a provider of wire communication service to the public shall not utilize service observing or random monitoring except for mechanical or service quality control checks.

(ii) Notwithstanding any other law, providers of wire or electronic communication service, their officers, employees, and agents, landlords, custodians, or other persons, are authorized to provide information, facilities, or technical assistance to persons authorized by law to intercept wire, oral, or electronic communications or to conduct electronic surveillance, as defined in section 101 of the Foreign Intelligence Surveillance Act of 1978, if such provider, its officers, employees, or agents, landlord, custodian, or other specified person, has been provided with —

(A) a court order directing such assistance signed by the authorizing judge, or

(B) a certification in writing by a person specified in section 2518(7) of this title or the Attorney General of the United States that no warrant or court order is required by law, that all statutory requirements have been met, and that the specified assistance is required, setting forth the period of time during which the provision of the information, facilities, or technical assistance is authorized and specifying the information, facilities, or technical assistance required. No provider of wire or electronic communication service, officer, employee, or agent thereof, or landlord, custodian, or other specified person shall disclose the existence of any interception or surveillance or the device used to accomplish the interception or surveillance with respect to which the person has been furnished a court order or certification under this chapter, except as may otherwise be required by legal process and then only after prior notification to the Attorney General or to the principal prosecuting attorney of a State or any political subdivision of a State, as may be appropriate. Any such disclosure shall render such person liable for the civil damages provided for in section 2520. No cause of action shall lie in any court against any provider of wire or electronic communication service, its officers, employees, or agents, landlord, custodian, or other specified person for providing information, facilities, or assistance in accordance with the terms of a court order or certification under this chapter.

(b) It shall not be unlawful under this chapter for an officer, employee, or agent of the Federal Communications Commission, in the normal course of his employment and in discharge of the monitoring responsibilities exercised by the Commission in the enforcement of chapter 5 of title 47 of the United States Code, to intercept a wire or electronic communication, or oral communication transmitted by radio, or to disclose or use the information thereby obtained.

(c) It shall not be unlawful under this chapter for a person acting under color of law to intercept a wire, oral, or electronic communication, where such person is a party to the communication or one of the parties to the communication has given prior consent to such interception.

(d) It shall not be unlawful under this chapter for a person not acting under color of law to intercept a wire, oral, or electronic communication where such person is a party to the communication or where one of the parties to the communication has given prior consent to such interception unless such communication is intercepted for the purpose of committing any criminal or tortious act in violation of the Constitution or laws of the United States or of any State.

(e) Notwithstanding any other provision of this title or section 705 or 706 of the Communications Act of 1934, it shall not be unlawful for an officer, employee, or agent of the United States in the normal course of his official duty to conduct electronic surveillance, as defined in section 101 of the Foreign Intelligence Surveillance Act of 1978, as authorized by that Act.

(f) Nothing contained in this chapter or chapter 121, or section 705 of the Communications Act of 1934, shall be deemed to affect the acquisition by the United States Government of foreign intelligence information from international or foreign communications, or foreign intelligence activities conducted in accordance with otherwise applicable Federal law involving a foreign electronic communications system, utilizing a means other than electronic surveillance as defined in section 101 of the Foreign Intelligence Surveillance Act of 1978, and procedures in this chapter or chapter 121 and the Foreign Intelligence Surveillance Act of 1978 shall be the exclusive means by which electronic surveillance, as defined in section 101 of such Act, and the interception of domestic wire and oral communications may be conducted.

(g) It shall not be unlawful under this chapter or chapter 121 of this title for any person —

(i) to intercept or access an electronic communication made through an electronic communication system that is configured so that such electronic communication is readily accessible to the general public;

(ii) to intercept any radio communication which is transmitted —

(I) by any station for the use of the general public, or that relates to ships, aircraft, vehicles, or persons in distress;

(II) by any governmental, law enforcement, civil defense, private land mobile, or public safety communications system, including police and fire, readily accessible to the general public;

(III) by a station operating on an authorized frequency within the bands allocated to the amateur, citizens band, or general mobile radio services; or

(IV) by any marine or aeronautical communications system;

(iii) to engage in any conduct which —

(I) is prohibited by section 633 of the Communications Act of 1934; or

(II) is excepted from the application of section 705(a) of the Communications Act of 1934 by section 705(b) of that Act;

(iv) to intercept any wire or electronic communication the transmission of which is causing harmful interference to any lawfully operating station or consumer electronic equipment, to the extent necessary to identify the source of such interference; or

(v) for other users of the same frequency to intercept any radio communication made through a system that utilizes frequencies monitored by individuals engaged in the provision or the use of such system, if such communication is not scrambled or encrypted.

(h) It shall not be unlawful under this chapter —

(i) to use a pen register or a trap and trace device (as those terms are defined for the purposes of chapter 206 (relating to pen registers and trap and trace devices) of this title); or

(ii) for a provider of electronic communication service to record the fact that a wire or electronic communication was initiated or completed in order to protect such provider, another provider furnishing service toward the completion of the wire or electronic communication, or a user of that service, from fraudulent, unlawful or abusive use of such service.

(3)

(a) Except as provided in paragraph (b) of this subsection, a person or entity providing an electronic communication service to the public shall not intentionally divulge the contents of any communication (other than one to such person or entity, or an agent thereof) while in transmission on that service to any person or entity other than an addressee or intended recipient of such communication or an agent of such addressee or intended recipient.

(b) A person or entity providing electronic communication service to the public may divulge the contents of any such communication —

   (i) as otherwise authorized in section 2511(2)(a) or 2517 of this title;

   (ii) with the lawful consent of the originator or any addressee or intended recipient of such communication;

   (iii) to a person employed or authorized, or whose facilities are used, to forward such communication to its destination; or

   (iv) which were inadvertently obtained by the service provider and which appear to pertain to the commission of a crime, if such divulgence is made to a law enforcement agency.

(4)

   (a) Except as provided in paragraph (b) of this subsection or in subsection (5), whoever violates subsection (1) of this section shall be fined under this title or imprisoned not more than five years, or both.

   (b) If the offense is a first offense under paragraph (a) of this subsection and is not for a tortious or illegal purpose or for purposes of direct or indirect commercial advantage or private commercial gain, and the wire or electronic communication with respect to which the offense under paragraph (a) is a radio communication that is not scrambled, encrypted, or transmitted using modulation techniques the essential parameters of which have been withheld from the public with the intention of preserving the privacy of such communication, then —

      (i) if the communication is not the radio portion of a cellular telephone communication, a cordless telephone communication that is transmitted between the cordless telephone handset and the base unit, a public land mobile radio service communication or a paging service communication, and the conduct is not that described in subsection (5), the offender shall be fined under this title or imprisoned not more than one year, or both; and

      (ii) if the communication is the radio portion of a cellular telephone communication, a cordless telephone communication that is transmitted between the cordless telephone handset and the base unit, a public land mobile radio service communication or a paging service communication, the offender shall be fined under this title.

   (c) Conduct otherwise an offense under this subsection that consists of or relates to the interception of a satellite transmission that is not encrypted or scrambled and that is transmitted —

      (i) to a broadcasting station for purposes of retransmission to the general public; or

      (ii) as an audio subcarrier intended for redistribution to facilities open to the public, but not including data transmissions or telephone calls, is not an offense under this subsection unless the conduct is for the purposes of direct or indirect commercial advantage or private financial gain.

(5)

   (a)

      (i) If the communication is —

         (A) a private satellite video communication that is not scrambled or encrypted and the conduct in violation of this chapter is the private viewing of that communication and is not for a tortious or illegal purpose or for purposes of direct or indirect commercial advantage or private commercial gain; or

(B) a radio communication that is transmitted on frequencies allocated under subpart D of part 74 of the rules of the Federal Communications Commission that is not scrambled or encrypted and the conduct in violation of this chapter is not for a tortious or illegal purpose or for purposes of direct or indirect commercial advantage or private commercial gain, then the person who engages in such conduct shall be subject to suit by the Federal Government in a court of competent jurisdiction.

(ii) In an action under this subsection —

(A) if the violation of this chapter is a first offense for the person under paragraph (a) of subsection (4) and such person has not been found liable in a civil action under section 2520 of this title, the Federal Government shall be entitled to appropriate injunctive relief; and

(B) if the violation of this chapter is a second or subsequent offense under paragraph (a) of subsection (4) or such person has been found liable in any prior civil action under section 2520, the person shall be subject to a mandatory $500 civil fine.

(b) The court may use any means within its authority to enforce an injunction issued under paragraph (ii)(A), and shall impose a civil fine of not less than $500 for each violation of such an injunction.

Sec. 2512. Manufacture, distribution, possession, and advertising of wire, oral, or electronic communication intercepting devices prohibited

(1) Except as otherwise specifically provided in this chapter, any person who intentionally —

(a) sends through the mail, or sends or carries in interstate or foreign commerce, any electronic, mechanical, or other device, knowing or having reason to know that the design of such device renders it primarily useful for the purpose of the surreptitious interception of wire, oral, or electronic communications;

(b) manufactures, assembles, possesses, or sells any electronic, mechanical, or other device, knowing or having reason to know that the design of such device renders it primarily useful for the purpose of the surreptitious interception of wire, oral, or electronic communications, and that such device or any component thereof has been or will be sent through the mail or transported in interstate or foreign commerce; or

(c) places in any newspaper, magazine, handbill, or other publication any advertisement of —

(i) any electronic, mechanical, or other device knowing or having reason to know that the design of such device renders it primarily useful for the purpose of the surreptitious interception of wire, oral, or electronic communications; or

(ii) any other electronic, mechanical, or other device, where such advertisement promotes the use of such device for the purpose of the surreptitious interception of wire, oral, or electronic communications, knowing or having reason to know that such advertisement will be sent through the mail or transported in interstate or foreign commerce, shall be fined under this title or imprisoned not more than five years, or both.

(2) It shall not be unlawful under this section for —

(a) a provider of wire or electronic communication service or an officer, agent, or employee of, or a person under contract with, such a provider, in the normal course of the business of providing that wire or electronic communication service, or

(b) an officer, agent, or employee of, or a person under contract with, the United States, a State, or a political subdivision thereof, in the normal course of the activities of the United States, a State, or a political subdivision thereof, to send through the mail, send or carry in interstate or foreign commerce, or manufacture, assemble, possess, or sell any electronic, mechanical, or other device knowing or having reason to know that the design of such device renders it primarily useful for the purpose of the surreptitious interception of wire, oral, or electronic communications.

(3) It shall not be unlawful under this section to advertise for sale a device described in subsection (1) of this section if the advertisement is mailed, sent, or carried in interstate or foreign commerce solely to a domestic provider of wire or electronic communication service or to an agency of the United States, a State, or a political subdivision thereof which is duly authorized to use such device.

Sec. 2513. Confiscation of wire, oral, or electronic communication intercepting devices

Any electronic, mechanical, or other device used, sent, carried, manufactured, assembled, possessed, sold, or advertised in violation of section 2511 or section 2512 of this chapter may be seized and forfeited to the United States. All provisions of law relating to (1) the seizure, summary and judicial forfeiture, and condemnation of vessels, vehicles, merchandise, and baggage for violations of the customs laws contained in title 19 of the United States Code, (2) the disposition of such vessels, vehicles, merchandise, and baggage or the proceeds from the sale thereof, (3) the remission or mitigation of such forfeiture, (4) the compromise of claims, and (5) the award of compensation to informers in respect of such forfeitures, shall apply to seizures and forfeitures incurred, or alleged to have been incurred, under the provisions of this section, insofar as applicable and not inconsistent with the provisions of this section; except that such duties as are imposed upon the collector of customs or any other person with respect to the seizure and forfeiture of vessels, vehicles, merchandise, and baggage under the provisions of the customs laws contained in title 19 of the United States Code shall be performed with respect to seizure and forfeiture of electronic, mechanical, or other intercepting devices under this section by such officers, agents, or other persons as may be authorized or designated for that purpose by the Attorney General.

Sec. 2515. Prohibition of use as evidence of intercepted wire or oral communications

Whenever any wire or oral communication has been intercepted, no part of the contents of such communication and no evidence derived therefrom may be received in evidence in any trial, hearing, or other proceeding in or before any court, grand jury, department, officer, agency, regulatory body, legislative committee, or other authority of the United States, a State, or a political subdivision thereof if the disclosure of that information would be in violation of this chapter.

Sec. 2516. Authorization for interception of wire, oral, or electronic communications

(1) The Attorney General, Deputy Attorney General, Associate Attorney General, [1] or any Assistant Attorney General, any acting Assistant Attorney General, or any Deputy Assistant Attorney General or acting Deputy Assistant Attorney General in the Criminal Division specially designated by the Attorney General, may authorize an application to a Federal judge of competent jurisdiction for, and such judge may grant in conformity with section 2518 of this chapter an order authorizing or approving the interception of wire or oral communications by the Federal Bureau of Investigation, or a Federal agency having responsibility for the investigation of the offense as to which the application is made, when such interception may provide or has provided evidence of —

(a) any offense punishable by death or by imprisonment for more than one year under sections 2274 through 2277 of title 42 of the United States Code (relating to the enforcement of the Atomic Energy Act of 1954), section 2284 of title 42 of the United States Code (relating to sabotage of nuclear facilities or fuel), or under the following chapters of this title: chapter 37 (relating to espionage), chapter 90 (relating to protection of trade secrets), chapter 105 (relating to sabotage), chapter 115 (relating to treason), chapter 102 (relating to riots), chapter 65 (relating to malicious mischief), chapter 111 (relating to destruction of vessels), or chapter 81 (relating to piracy);

(b) a violation of section 186 or section 501(c) of title 29, United States Code (dealing with restrictions on payments and loans to labor organizations), or any offense which involves murder, kidnapping, robbery, or extortion, and which is punishable under this title;

(c) any offense which is punishable under the following sections of this title: section 201 (bribery of public officials and witnesses), section 215 (relating to bribery of bank officials), section 224 (bribery in sporting contests), subsection (d), (e), (f), (g), (h), or (i) of section 844 (unlawful use of explosives), section 1032 (relating to concealment of assets), section 1084 (transmission of wagering information), section 751 (relating to escape), section 1014 (relating to loans and credit applications generally; renewals and discounts), sections 1503, 1512, and 1513 (influencing or injuring an officer, juror, or witness generally), section 1510 (obstruction of criminal investigations), section 1511 (obstruction of State or local law enforcement), section 1751 (Presidential and Presidential staff assassination, kidnapping, and assault), section 1951 (interference with commerce by threats or violence), section 1952 (interstate and foreign travel or transportation in aid of racketeering enterprises), section 1958 (relating to use of interstate commerce facilities in the commission of murder for hire), section 1959 (relating to violent crimes in aid of racketeering activity), section 1954 (offer, acceptance, or solicitation to influence operations of employee benefit plan), section 1955 (prohibition of business enterprises of gambling), section 1956 (laundering of monetary instruments), section 1957 (relating to engaging in monetary transactions in property derived from specified unlawful activity), section 659 (theft from interstate shipment), section 664 (embezzlement from pension and welfare funds), section 1343 (fraud by wire, radio, or television), section 1344 (relating to bank fraud), sections 2251 and 2252 (sexual exploitation of children), sections 2312, 2313, 2314, and 2315 (interstate transportation of stolen property), section 2321 (relating to trafficking in certain motor vehicles or motor vehicle parts), section 1203 (relating to hostage taking), section 1029 (relating to fraud and related activity in connection with access devices), section 3146 (relating to penalty for failure to appear), section 3521(b)(3) (relating to witness relocation and assistance), section 32 (relating to destruction of aircraft or aircraft facilities), section 1963 (violations with respect to racketeer influenced and corrupt organizations), section 115 (relating to threatening or retaliating against a Federal official), and section 1341 (relating to mail fraud), section 351 (violations with respect to congressional, Cabinet, or Supreme Court assassinations, kidnapping, and assault), section 831 (relating to prohibited transactions involving nuclear materials), section 33 (relating to destruction of motor vehicles or motor vehicle facilities), section 175 (relating to biological weapons), section 1992 (relating to wrecking trains), a felony violation of section 1028 (relating to production of false identification documentation), section 1425 (relating to the procurement of citizenship or nationalization unlawfully), section 1426 (relating to the reproduction of naturalization or citizenship papers), section 1427 (relating to the sale of naturalization or citizenship papers), section 1541 (relating to passport issuance without authority), section 1542 (relating to false statements in passport applications), section 1543 (relating to forgery or false use of passports), section 1544 (relating to misuse of passports), or section 1546 (relating to fraud and misuse of visas, permits, and other documents);

(d) any offense involving counterfeiting punishable under section 471, 472, or 473 of this title;

(e) any offense involving fraud connected with a case under title 11 or the manufacture, importation, receiving, concealment, buying, selling, or otherwise dealing in narcotic drugs, marihuana, or other dangerous drugs, punishable under any law of the United States;

(f) any offense including extortionate credit transactions under sections 892, 893, or 894 of this title;

(g) a violation of section 5322 of title 31, United States Code (dealing with the reporting of currency transactions);

(h) any felony violation of sections 2511 and 2512 (relating to interception and disclosure of certain communications and to certain intercepting devices) of this title;

(i) any felony violation of chapter 71 (relating to obscenity) of this title;

D

(j) any violation of section 60123(b) (relating to destruction of a natural gas pipeline) or section 46502 (relating to aircraft piracy) of title 49;

(k) any criminal violation of section 2778 of title 22 (relating to the Arms Export Control Act);

(l) the location of any fugitive from justice from an offense described in this section;

(m) a violation of section 274, 277, or 278 of the Immigration and Nationality Act (8 U.S.C. 1324, 1327, or 1328) (relating to the smuggling of aliens);

(n) any felony violation of sections 922 and 924 of title 18, United States Code (relating to firearms);

(o) any violation of section 5861 of the Internal Revenue Code of 1986 (relating to firearms);

(p) [2] a felony violation of section 1028 (relating to production of false identification documents), section 1542 (relating to false statements in passport applications), section 1546 (relating to fraud and misuse of visas, permits, and other documents) of this title or a violation of section 274, 277, or 278 of the Immigration and Nationality Act (relating to the smuggling of aliens); or

[2] So in original. Two subpars. (p) have been enacted.

(p) [2] any conspiracy to commit any offense described in any subparagraph of this paragraph.

(2) The principal prosecuting attorney of any State, or the principal prosecuting attorney of any political subdivision thereof, if such attorney is authorized by a statute of that State to make application to a State court judge of competent jurisdiction for an order authorizing or approving the interception of wire, oral, or electronic communications, may apply to such judge for, and such judge may grant in conformity with section 2518 of this chapter and with the applicable State statute an order authorizing, or approving the interception of wire, oral, or electronic communications by investigative or law enforcement officers having responsibility for the investigation of the offense as to which the application is made, when such interception may provide or has provided evidence of the commission of the offense of murder, kidnapping, gambling, robbery, bribery, extortion, or dealing in narcotic drugs, marihuana or other dangerous drugs, or other crime dangerous to life, limb, or property, and punishable by imprisonment for more than one year, designated in any applicable State statute authorizing such interception, or any conspiracy to commit any of the foregoing offenses.

(3) Any attorney for the Government (as such term is defined for the purposes of the Federal Rules of Criminal Procedure) may authorize an application to a Federal judge of competent jurisdiction for, and such judge may grant, in conformity with section 2518 of this title, an order authorizing or approving the interception of electronic communications by an investigative or law enforcement officer having responsibility for the investigation of the offense as to which the application is made, when such interception may provide or has provided evidence of any Federal felony.

Sec. 2517. Authorization for disclosure and use of intercepted wire, oral, or electronic communications

(1) Any investigative or law enforcement officer who, by any means authorized by this chapter, has obtained knowledge of the contents of any wire, oral, or electronic communication, or evidence derived therefrom, may disclose such contents to another investigative or law enforcement officer to the extent that such disclosure is appropriate to the proper performance of the official duties of the officer making or receiving the disclosure.

(2) Any investigative or law enforcement officer who, by any means authorized by this chapter, has obtained knowledge of the contents of any wire, oral, or electronic communication or evidence derived therefrom may use such contents to the extent such use is appropriate to the proper performance of his official duties.

(3) Any person who has received, by any means authorized by this chapter, any information concerning a wire, oral, or electronic communication, or evidence derived therefrom intercepted in accordance with the provisions of this chapter may disclose the contents of that communication or such derivative evidence while giving testimony under oath or affirmation in any proceeding held under the authority of the United States or of any State or political subdivision thereof.

(4) No otherwise privileged wire, oral, or electronic communication intercepted in accordance with, or in violation of, the provisions of this chapter shall lose its privileged character.

(5) When an investigative or law enforcement officer, while engaged in intercepting wire, oral, or electronic communications in the manner authorized herein, intercepts wire, oral, or electronic communications relating to offenses other than those specified in the order of authorization or approval, the contents thereof, and evidence derived therefrom, may be disclosed or used as provided in subsections (1) and (2) of this section. Such contents and any evidence derived therefrom may be used under subsection (3) of this section when authorized or approved by a judge of competent jurisdiction where such judge finds on subsequent application that the contents were otherwise intercepted in accordance with the provisions of this chapter. Such application shall be made as soon as practicable.

Sec. 2518. Procedure for interception of wire, oral, or electronic communications

(1) Each application for an order authorizing or approving the interception of a wire, oral, or electronic communication under this chapter shall be made in writing upon oath or affirmation to a judge of competent jurisdiction and shall state the applicant's authority to make such application. Each application shall include the following information:

(a) the identity of the investigative or law enforcement officer making the application, and the officer authorizing the application;

(b) a full and complete statement of the facts and circumstances relied upon by the applicant, to justify his belief that an order should be issued, including (i) details as to the particular offense that has been, is being, or is about to be committed, (ii) except as provided in subsection (11), a particular description of the nature and location of the facilities from which or the place where the communication is to be intercepted, (iii) a particular description of the type of communications sought to be intercepted, (iv) the identity of the person, if known, committing the offense and whose communications are to be intercepted;

(c) a full and complete statement as to whether or not other investigative procedures have been tried and failed or why they reasonably appear to be unlikely to succeed if tried or to be too dangerous;

(d) a statement of the period of time for which the interception is required to be maintained. If the nature of the investigation is such that the authorization for interception should not automatically terminate when the described type of communication has been first obtained, a particular description of facts establishing probable cause to believe that additional communications of the same type will occur thereafter;

(e) a full and complete statement of the facts concerning all previous applications known to the individual authorizing and making the application, made to any judge for authorization to intercept, or for approval of interceptions of, wire, oral, or electronic communications involving any of the same persons, facilities or places specified in the application, and the action taken by the judge on each such application; and

(f) where the application is for the extension of an order, a statement setting forth the results thus far obtained from the interception, or a reasonable explanation of the failure to obtain such results.

(2) The judge may require the applicant to furnish additional testimony or documentary evidence in support of the application.

(3) Upon such application the judge may enter an ex parte order, as requested or as modified, authorizing or approving interception of wire, oral, or electronic communications within the territorial jurisdiction of the court in which the judge is sitting (and outside that jurisdiction but within the United States in the case of a mobile interception device authorized by a Federal court within such jurisdiction), if the judge determines on the basis of the facts submitted by the applicant that —

    (a) there is probable cause for belief that an individual is committing, has committed, or is about to commit a particular offense enumerated in section 2516 of this chapter;

    (b) there is probable cause for belief that particular communications concerning that offense will be obtained through such interception;

    (c) normal investigative procedures have been tried and have failed or reasonably appear to be unlikely to succeed if tried or to be too dangerous;

    (d) except as provided in subsection (11), there is probable cause for belief that the facilities from which, or the place where, the wire, oral, or electronic communications are to be intercepted are being used, or are about to be used, in connection with the commission of such offense, or are leased to, listed in the name of, or commonly used by such person.

(4) Each order authorizing or approving the interception of any wire, oral, or electronic communication under this chapter shall specify —

    (a) the identity of the person, if known, whose communications are to be intercepted;

    (b) the nature and location of the communications facilities as to which, or the place where, authority to intercept is granted;

    (c) a particular description of the type of communication sought to be intercepted, and a statement of the particular offense to which it relates;

    (d) the identity of the agency authorized to intercept the communications, and of the person authorizing the application;

and

    (e) the period of time during which such interception is authorized, including a statement as to whether or not the interception shall automatically terminate when the described communication has been first obtained. An order authorizing the interception of a wire, oral, or electronic communication under this chapter shall, upon request of the applicant, direct that a provider of wire or electronic communication service, landlord, custodian or other person shall furnish the applicant forthwith all information, facilities, and technical assistance necessary to accomplish the interception unobtrusively and with a minimum of interference with the services that such service provider, landlord, custodian, or person is according the person whose communications are to be intercepted. Any provider of wire or electronic communication service, landlord, custodian or other person furnishing such facilities or technical assistance shall be compensated therefor by the applicant for reasonable expenses incurred in providing such facilities or assistance. Pursuant to section 2522 of this chapter, an order may also be issued to enforce the assistance capability and capacity requirements under the Communications Assistance for Law Enforcement Act.

(5) No order entered under this section may authorize or approve the interception of any wire, oral, or electronic communication for any period longer than is necessary to achieve the objective of the authorization, nor in any event longer than thirty days. Such thirty-day period begins on the earlier of the day on

which the investigative or law enforcement officer first begins to conduct an interception under the order or ten days after the order is entered. Extensions of an order may be granted, but only upon application for an extension made in accordance with subsection (1) of this section and the court making the findings required by subsection (3) of this section. The period of extension shall be no longer than the authorizing judge deems necessary to achieve the purposes for which it was granted and in no event for longer than thirty days. Every order and extension thereof shall contain a provision that the authorization to intercept shall be executed as soon as practicable, shall be conducted in such a way as to minimize the interception of communications not otherwise subject to interception under this chapter, and must terminate upon attainment of the authorized objective, or in any event in thirty days. In the event the intercepted communication is in a code or foreign language, and an expert in that foreign language or code is not reasonably available during the interception period, minimization may be accomplished as soon as practicable after such interception. An interception under this chapter may be conducted in whole or in part by Government personnel, or by an individual operating under a contract with the Government, acting under the supervision of an investigative or law enforcement officer authorized to conduct the interception.

(6) Whenever an order authorizing interception is entered pursuant to this chapter, the order may require reports to be made to the judge who issued the order showing what progress has been made toward achievement of the authorized objective and the need for continued interception. Such reports shall be made at such intervals as the judge may require.

(7) Notwithstanding any other provision of this chapter, any investigative or law enforcement officer, specially designated by the Attorney General, the Deputy Attorney General, the Associate Attorney General, or by the principal prosecuting attorney of any State or subdivision thereof acting pursuant to a statute of that State, who reasonably determines that —

(a) an emergency situation exists that involves —

(i) immediate danger of death or serious physical injury to any person,

(ii) conspiratorial activities threatening the national security interest, or

(iii) conspiratorial activities characteristic of organized crime, that requires a wire, oral, or electronic communication to be intercepted before an order authorizing such interception can, with due diligence, be obtained, and

(b) there are grounds upon which an order could be entered under this chapter to authorize such interception, may intercept such wire, oral, or electronic communication if an application for an order approving the interception is made in accordance with this section within forty-eight hours after the interception has occurred, or begins to occur. In the absence of an order, such interception shall immediately terminate when the communication sought is obtained or when the application for the order is denied, whichever is earlier. In the event such application for approval is denied, or in any other case where the interception is terminated without an order having been issued, the contents of any wire, oral, or electronic communication intercepted shall be treated as having been obtained in violation of this chapter, and an inventory shall be served as provided for in subsection (d) of this section on the person named in the application.

(8)

(a) The contents of any wire, oral, or electronic communication intercepted by any means authorized by this chapter shall, if possible, be recorded on tape or wire or other comparable device. The recording of the contents of any wire, oral, or electronic communication under this subsection shall be done in such a way as will protect the recording from editing or other alterations. Immediately upon the expiration of the period of the order, or extensions thereof, such recordings shall be made available to the judge issuing such order and sealed under his directions. Custody of the recordings shall be wherever the judge orders. They shall not be destroyed except upon an order of the issuing or denying judge and in any event shall be kept for ten years. Duplicate recordings may be made for use or disclosure pursuant to the provisions of subsections (1) and (2) of section 2517 of this chapter for investigations. The presence of the seal provided for by this subsection, or a satisfactory explanation for the absence thereof, shall be a prerequisite for the use or disclosure of the contents of any wire, oral, or electronic communication or evidence derived therefrom under subsection (3) of section 2517.

(b) Applications made and orders granted under this chapter shall be sealed by the judge. Custody of the applications and orders shall be wherever the judge directs. Such applications and orders shall be disclosed only upon a showing of good cause before a judge of competent jurisdiction and shall not be destroyed except on order of the issuing or denying judge, and in any event shall be kept for ten years.

(c) Any violation of the provisions of this subsection may be punished as contempt of the issuing or denying judge.

(d) Within a reasonable time but not later than ninety days after the filing of an application for an order of approval under section 2518(7)(b) which is denied or the termination of the period of an order or extensions thereof, the issuing or denying judge shall cause to be served, on the persons named in the order or the application, and such other parties to intercepted communications as the judge may determine in his discretion that is in the interest of justice, an inventory which shall include notice of —

(1) the fact of the entry of the order or the application;

(2) the date of the entry and the period of authorized, approved or disapproved interception, or the denial of the application; and

(3) the fact that during the period wire, oral, or electronic communications were or were not intercepted. The judge, upon the filing of a motion, may in his discretion make available to such person or his counsel for inspection such portions of the intercepted communications, applications and orders as the judge determines to be in the interest of justice. On an ex parte showing of good cause to a judge of competent jurisdiction the serving of the inventory required by this subsection may be postponed.

(9) The contents of any wire, oral, or electronic communication intercepted pursuant to this chapter or evidence derived therefrom shall not be received in evidence or otherwise disclosed in any trial, hearing, or other proceeding in a Federal or State court unless each party, not less than ten days before the trial, hearing, or proceeding, has been furnished with a copy of the court order, and accompanying application, under which the interception was authorized or approved. This ten-day period may be waived by the judge if he finds that it was not possible to furnish the party with the above information ten days before the trial, hearing, or proceeding and that the party will not be prejudiced by the delay in receiving such information.

(10)

(a) Any aggrieved person in any trial, hearing, or proceeding in or before any court, department, officer, agency, regulatory body, or other authority of the United States, a State, or a political subdivision thereof, may move to suppress the contents of any wire or oral communication intercepted pursuant to this chapter, or evidence derived therefrom, on the grounds that —

(i) the communication was unlawfully intercepted;

(ii) the order of authorization or approval under which it was intercepted is insufficient on its face; or

(iii) the interception was not made in conformity with the order of authorization or approval. Such motion shall be made before the trial, hearing, or proceeding unless there was no opportunity to make such motion or the person was not aware of the grounds of the motion. If the motion is granted, the contents of the intercepted wire or oral communication, or evidence derived therefrom, shall be treated as having been obtained in violation of this chapter. The judge, upon the filing of such motion by the aggrieved person, may in his discretion make available to the aggrieved person or his counsel for inspection such portions of the intercepted communication or evidence derived therefrom as the judge determines to be in the interests of justice.

(b) In addition to any other right to appeal, the United States shall have the right to appeal from an order granting a motion to suppress made under paragraph (a) of this subsection, or the denial of an application for an order of approval, if the United States attorney shall certify to the judge or other official granting such motion or denying such application that the appeal is not taken for purposes of delay. Such appeal shall be taken within thirty days after the date the order was entered and shall be diligently prosecuted.

(c) The remedies and sanctions described in this chapter with respect to the interception of electronic communications are the only judicial remedies and sanctions for nonconstitutional violations of this chapter involving such communications.

(11) The requirements of subsections (1)(b)(ii) and (3)(d) of this section relating to the specification of the facilities from which, or the place where, the communication is to be intercepted do not apply if —

(a) in the case of an application with respect to the interception of an oral communication —

(i) the application is by a Federal investigative or law enforcement officer and is approved by the Attorney General, the Deputy Attorney General, the Associate Attorney General, an Assistant Attorney General, or an acting Assistant Attorney General;

(ii) the application contains a full and complete statement as to why such specification is not practical and identifies the person committing the offense and whose communications are to be intercepted; and

(iii) the judge finds that such specification is not practical; and

(b) in the case of an application with respect to a wire or electronic communication —

(i) the application is by a Federal investigative or law enforcement officer and is approved by the Attorney General, the Deputy Attorney General, the Associate Attorney General, an Assistant Attorney General, or an acting Assistant Attorney General;

(ii) the application identifies the person believed to be committing the offense and whose communications are to be intercepted and the applicant makes a showing of a purpose, on the part of that person, to thwart interception by changing facilities; and

(iii) the judge finds that such purpose has been adequately shown.

(12) An interception of a communication under an order with respect to which the requirements of subsections (1)(b)(ii) and (3) (d) of this section do not apply by reason of subsection (11) shall not begin until the facilities from which, or the place where, the communication is to be intercepted is ascertained by the person implementing the interception order. A provider of wire or electronic communications service that has received an order as provided for in subsection (11)(b) may move the court to modify or quash the order on the ground that its assistance with respect to the interception cannot be performed in

a timely or reasonable fashion. The court, upon notice to the government, shall decide such a motion expeditiously.

Sec. 2520. Recovery of civil damages authorized

(a) In General. — Except as provided in section 2511(2)(a)(ii), any person whose wire, oral, or electronic communication is intercepted, disclosed, or intentionally used in violation of this chapter may in a civil action recover from the person or entity which engaged in that violation such relief as may be appropriate.

(b) Relief. — In an action under this section, appropriate relief includes —

(1) such preliminary and other equitable or declaratory relief as may be appropriate;

(2) damages under subsection (c) and punitive damages in appropriate cases; and

(3) a reasonable attorney's fee and other litigation costs reasonably incurred.

(c) Computation of Damages. — (1) In an action under this section, if the conduct in violation of this chapter is the private viewing of a private satellite video communication that is not scrambled or encrypted or if the communication is a radio communication that is transmitted on frequencies allocated under subpart D of part 74 of the rules of the Federal Communications Commission that is not scrambled or encrypted and the conduct is not for a tortious or illegal purpose or for purposes of direct or indirect commercial advantage or private commercial gain, then the court shall assess damages as follows:

(A) If the person who engaged in that conduct has not previously been enjoined under section 2511(5) and has not been found liable in a prior civil action under this section, the court shall assess the greater of the sum of actual damages suffered by the plaintiff, or statutory damages of not less than $50 and not more than $500.

(B) If, on one prior occasion, the person who engaged in that conduct has been enjoined under section 2511(5) or has been found liable in a civil action under this section, the court shall assess the greater of the sum of actual damages suffered by the plaintiff, or statutory damages of not less than $100 and not more than $1000.

(2) In any other action under this section, the court may assess as damages whichever is the greater of —

(A) the sum of the actual damages suffered by the plaintiff and any profits made by the violator as a result of the violation; or

(B) statutory damages of whichever is the greater of $100 a day for each day of violation or $10,000.

(d) Defense. — A good faith reliance on —

(1) a court warrant or order, a grand jury subpoena, a legislative authorization, or a statutory authorization;

(2) a request of an investigative or law enforcement officer under section 2518(7) of this title; or

(3) a good faith determination that section 2511(3) of this title permitted the conduct complained of; is a complete defense against any civil or criminal action brought under this chapter or any other law.

(e) Limitation. — A civil action under this section may not be commenced later than two years after the date upon which the claimant first has a reasonable opportunity to discover the violation.

Sec. 2521. Injunction against illegal interception

Whenever it shall appear that any person is engaged or is about to engage in any act which constitutes or will constitute a felony violation of this chapter, the Attorney General may initiate a civil action in a district court of the United States to enjoin such violation. The court shall proceed as soon as practicable to the hearing and determination of such an action, and may, at any time before final determination, enter such a restraining order or prohibition, or take such other action, as is warranted to prevent a continuing and substantial injury to the United States or to any person or class of persons for whose protection the action is brought. A proceeding under this section is governed by the Federal Rules of Civil Procedure, except that, if an indictment has been returned against the respondent, discovery is governed by the Federal Rules of Criminal Procedure._____United States Code

TITLE 17 — COPYRIGHTCHAPTER 1 — SUBJECT MATTER AND SCOPE OF COPYRIGHT

§ 101. Definitions.

§ 102. Subject matter of copyright: In general.

§ 103. Subject matter of copyright: Compilations and derivative works.

§ 104. Subject matter of copyright: National origin.

§ 104A. Copyright in restored works.

§ 105. Subject matter of copyright: United States Government works.

§ 106. Exclusive rights in copyrighted works.

§ 106A. Rights of certain authors to attribution and integrity.

§ 107. Limitations on exclusive rights: Fair use.

§ 108. Limitations on exclusive rights: Reproduction by libraries and archives.

§ 109. Limitations on exclusive rights: Effect of transfer of particular copy or phonorecord.

§ 110. Limitations on exclusive rights: Exemption of certain performances and displays.

§ 111. Limitations on exclusive rights: Secondary transmissions.

§ 112. Limitations on exclusive rights: Ephemeral recordings.

§ 113. Scope of exclusive rights in pictorial, graphic, and sculptural works.

§ 114. Scope of exclusive rights in sound recordings.

§ 115. Scope of exclusive rights in nondramatic musical works: Compulsory license for making and distributing phonorecords.

§ 116. Negotiated licenses for public performances by means of coin-operated phonorecord players.

(116A . Renumbered.)

§ 117. Limitations on exclusive rights: Computer programs.

§ 118. Scope of exclusive rights: Use of certain works in connection with noncommercial broadcasting.

§ 119. Limitations on exclusive rights: Secondary transmissions of superstations and network stations for private home viewing.

§ 120. Scope of exclusive rights in architectural works.

§ 121. Limitations on exclusive rights: reproduction for blind or other people with disabilities.

Sec. 101. Definitions Except as otherwise provided in this title, as used in this title, the following terms and their variant forms mean the following: An "anonymous work" is a work on the copies or phonorecords of which no natural person is identified as author.

An "architectural work" is the design of a building as embodied in any tangible medium of expression, including a building, architectural plans, or drawings. The work includes the overall form as well as the arrangement and composition of spaces and elements in the design, but does not include individual standard features. "Audiovisual works" are works that consist of a series of related images which are intrinsically intended to be shown by the use of machines, or devices such as projectors, viewers, or electronic equipment, together with accompanying sounds, if any, regardless of the nature of the material objects, such as films or tapes, in which the works are embodied. The "Berne Convention" is the Convention for the Protection of Literary and Artistic Works, signed at Berne, Switzerland, on September 9, 1886, and all acts, protocols, and revisions thereto. A work is a "Berne Convention work" if —

(1) in the case of an unpublished work, one or more of the authors is a national of a nation adhering to the Berne Convention, or in the case of a published work, one or more of the authors is a national of a nation adhering to the Berne Convention on the date of first publication;

(2) the work was first published in a nation adhering to the Berne Convention, or was simultaneously first published in a nation adhering to the Berne Convention and in a foreign nation that does not adhere to the Berne Convention;

(3) in the case of an audiovisual work —

(A) if one or more of the authors is a legal entity, that author has its headquarters in a nation adhering to the Berne Convention; or

(B) if one or more of the authors is an individual, that author is domiciled, or has his or her habitual residence in, a nation adhering to the Berne Convention;

(4) in the case of a pictorial, graphic, or sculptural work that is incorporated in a building or other structure, the building or structure is located in a nation adhering to the Berne Convention; or

(5) in the case of an architectural work embodied in a building, such building is erected in a country adhering to the Berne Convention. For purposes of paragraph (1), an author who is domiciled in or has his or her habitual residence in, a nation adhering to the Berne Convention is considered to be a national of that nation. For purposes of paragraph (2), a work is considered to have been simultaneously published in two or more nations if its dates of publication are within 30 days of one another.

The "best edition" of a work is the edition, published in the United States at any time before the date of deposit, that the Library of Congress determines to be most suitable for its purposes.

A person's "children" are that person's immediate offspring, whether legitimate or not, and any children legally adopted by that person.

A "collective work" is a work, such as a periodical issue, anthology, or encyclopedia, in which a number of contributions, constituting separate and independent works in themselves, are assembled into a collective whole.

A "compilation" is a work formed by the collection and assembling of preexisting materials or of data that are selected, coordinated, or arranged in such a way that the resulting work as a whole constitutes an original work of authorship. The term "compilation" includes collective works.

"Copies" are material objects, other than phonorecords, in which a work is fixed by any method now known or later developed, and from which the work can be perceived, reproduced, or otherwise communicated, either directly or with the aid of a machine or device. The term "copies" includes the material object, other than a phonorecord, in which the work is first fixed.

"Copyright owner," with respect to any one of the exclusive rights comprised in a copyright, refers to the owner of that particular right.

The "country of origin" of a Berne Convention work, for purposes of section 411, is the United States if —

(1) in the case of a published work, the work is first published —

   (A) in the United States;

   (B) simultaneously in the United States and another nation or nations adhering to the Berne Convention, whose law grants a term of copyright protection that is the same as or longer than the term provided in the United States;

   (C) simultaneously in the United States and a foreign nation that does not adhere to the Berne Convention; or

   (D) in a foreign nation that does not adhere to the Berne Convention, and all of the authors of the work are nationals, domiciliaries, or habitual residents of, or in the case of an audiovisual work legal entities with headquarters in, the United States;

(2) in the case of an unpublished work, all the authors of the work are nationals, domiciliaries, or habitual residents of the United States, or, in the case of an unpublished audiovisual work, all the authors are legal entities with headquarters in the United States; or

(3) in the case of a pictorial, graphic, or sculptural work incorporated in a building or structure, the building or structure is located in the United States. For the purposes of section 411, the "country of origin" of any other Berne Convention work is not the United States.

A work is "created" when it is fixed in a copy or phonorecord for the first time; where a work is prepared over a period of time, the portion of it that has been fixed at any particular time constitutes the work as of that time, and where the work has been prepared in different versions, each version constitutes a separate work.

A "derivative work" is a work based upon one or more preexisting works, such as a translation, musical arrangement, dramatization, fictionalization, motion picture version, sound recording, art reproduction, abridgment, condensation, or any other form in which a work may be recast, transformed, or adapted. A work consisting of editorial revisions, annotations, elaborations, or other modifications which, as a whole, represent an original work of authorship, is a "derivative work."

A "device," "machine," or "process" is one now known or later developed.

A "digital transmission" is a transmission in whole or in part in a digital or other non-analog format.

To "display" a work means to show a copy of it, either directly or by means of a film, slide, television image, or any other device or process or, in the case of a motion picture or other audiovisual work, to show individual images nonsequentially.

The term "financial gain" includes receipt, or expectation of receipt, of anything of value, including the receipt of other copyrighted works.

A work is "fixed" in a tangible medium of expression when its embodiment in a copy or phonorecord, by or under the authority of the author, is sufficiently permanent or stable to permit it to be perceived, reproduced, or otherwise communicated for a period of more than transitory duration. A work consisting of sounds, images, or both, that are being transmitted, is "fixed" for purposes of this title if a fixation of the work is being made simultaneously with its transmission.

The terms "including" and "such as" are illustrative and not limitative.

A "joint work" is a work prepared by two or more authors with the intention that their contributions be merged into inseparable or interdependent parts of a unitary whole.

"Literary works" are works, other than audiovisual works, expressed in words, numbers, or other verbal or numerical symbols or indicia, regardless of the nature of the material objects, such as books, periodicals, manuscripts, phonorecords, film, tapes, disks, or cards, in which they are embodied.

"Motion pictures" are audiovisual works consisting of a series of related images which, when shown in succession, impart an impression of motion, together with accompanying sounds, if any.

To "perform" a work means to recite, render, play, dance, or act it, either directly or by means of any device or process or, in the case of a motion picture or other audiovisual work, to show its images in any sequence or to make the sounds accompanying it audible.

"Phonorecords" are material objects in which sounds, other than those accompanying a motion picture or other audiovisual work, are fixed by any method now known or later developed, and from which the sounds can be perceived, reproduced, or otherwise communicated, either directly or with the aid of a machine or device. The term "phonorecords" includes the material object in which the sounds are first fixed.

"Pictorial, graphic, and sculptural works" include two-dimensional and three-dimensional works of fine, graphic, and applied art, photographs, prints and art reproductions, maps, globes, charts, diagrams, models, and technical drawings, including architectural plans. Such works shall include works of artistic craftsmanship insofar as their form but not their mechanical or utilitarian aspects are concerned; the design of a useful article, as defined in this section, shall be considered a pictorial, graphic, or sculptural work only if, and only to the extent that, such design incorporates pictorial, graphic, or sculptural features that can be identified separately from, and are capable of existing independently of, the utilitarian aspects of the article.

A "pseudonymous work" is a work on the copies or phonorecords of which the author is identified under a fictitious name.

"Publication" is the distribution of copies or phonorecords of a work to the public by sale or other transfer of ownership, or by rental, lease, or lending. The offering to distribute copies or phonorecords to a group of persons for purposes of further distribution, public performance, or public display, constitutes publication. A public performance or display of a work does not of itself constitute publication.

"Registration," for purposes of sections 205(c)(2), 405, 406, 410(d), 411, 412, and 506(e), means a registration of a claim in the original or the renewed and extended term of copyright.

To perform or display a work "publicly" means —

(1) to perform or display it at a place open to the public or at any place where a substantial number of persons outside of a normal circle of a family and its social acquaintances is gathered; or

(2) to transmit or otherwise communicate a performance or display of the work to a place specified by clause (1) or to the public, by means of any device or process, whether the members of the public capable of receiving the performance or display receive it in the same place or in separate places and at the same time or at different times.

"Sound recordings" are works that result from the fixation of a series of musical, spoken, or other sounds, but not including the sounds accompanying a motion picture or other audiovisual work, regardless of the nature of the material objects, such as disks, tapes, or other phonorecords, in which they are embodied.

"State" includes the District of Columbia and the Commonwealth of Puerto Rico, and any territories to which this title is made applicable by an Act of Congress.

A "transfer of copyright ownership" is an assignment, mortgage, exclusive license, or any other conveyance, alienation, or hypothecation of a copyright or of any of the exclusive rights comprised in a copyright, whether or not it is limited in time or place of effect, but not including a nonexclusive license.

A "transmission program" is a body of material that, as an aggregate, has been produced for the sole purpose of transmission to the public in sequence and as a unit.

To "transmit" a performance or display is to communicate it by any device or process whereby images or sounds are received beyond the place from which they are sent.

The "United States," when used in a geographical sense, comprises the several States, the District of Columbia and the Commonwealth of Puerto Rico, and the organized territories under the jurisdiction of the United States Government.

A "useful article" is an article having an intrinsic utilitarian function that is not merely to portray the appearance of the article or to convey information. An article that is normally a part of a useful article is considered a "useful article."

The author's "widow" or "widower" is the author's surviving spouse under the law of the author's domicile at the time of his or her death, whether or not the spouse has later remarried.

A "work of visual art" is —

(1) a painting, drawing, print, or sculpture, existing in a single copy, in a limited edition of 200 copies or fewer that are signed and consecutively numbered by the author, or, in the case of a sculpture, in multiple cast, carved, or fabricated sculptures of 200 or fewer that are consecutively numbered by author and bear the signature or other identifying mark of the author; or

(2) a still photographic image produced for exhibition purposes only, existing in a single copy that is signed by the author, or in a limited edition of 200 copies or fewer that are signed and consecutively numbered by the author. A work of visual art does not include —

(A)

    (i) any poster, map, globe, chart, technical drawing, diagram, model, applied art, motion picture or other audiovisual work, book, magazine, newspaper, periodical, data base, electronic information service, electronic publication, or similar publication;

    (ii) any merchandising item or advertising, promotional, descriptive, covering, or packaging material or container;

    (iii) any portion or part of any item described in clause (i) or (ii);

(B) any work made for hire; or

(C) any work not subject to copyright protection under this title.

A "work of the United States Government" is a work prepared by an officer or employee of the United States Government as part of that person's official duties.

D

A "work made for hire" is —

(1) a work prepared by an employee within the scope of his or her employment; or

(2) a work specially ordered or commissioned for use as a contribution to a collective work, as a part of a motion picture or other audiovisual work, as a translation, as a supplementary work, as a compilation, as an instructional text, as a test, as answer material for a test, or as an atlas, if the parties expressly agree in a written instrument signed by them that the work shall be considered a work made for hire.

For the purpose of the foregoing sentence, a "supplementary work" is a work prepared for publication as a secondary adjunct to a work by another author for the purpose of introducing, concluding, illustrating, explaining, revising, commenting upon, or assisting in the use of the other work, such as forewords, afterwords, pictorial illustrations, maps, charts, tables, editorial notes, musical arrangements, answer material for tests, bibliographies, appendixes, and indexes, and an "instructional text" is a literary, pictorial, or graphic work prepared for publication and with the purpose of use in systematic instructional activities.

A "computer program" is a set of statements or instructions to be used directly or indirectly in a computer in order to bring about a certain result.

Sec. 102. Subject matter of copyright: In general

(a) Copyright protection subsists, in accordance with this title, in original works of authorship fixed in any tangible medium of expression, now known or later developed, from which they can be perceived, reproduced, or otherwise communicated, either directly or with the aid of a machine or device. Works of authorship include the following categories:

(1) literary works;

(2) musical works, including any accompanying words;

(3) dramatic works, including any accompanying music;

(4) pantomimes and choreographic works;

(5) pictorial, graphic, and sculptural works;

(6) motion pictures and other audiovisual works;

(7) sound recordings; and

(8) architectural works.

(b) In no case does copyright protection for an original work of authorship extend to any idea, procedure, process, system, method of operation, concept, principle, or discovery, regardless of the form in which it is described, explained, illustrated, or embodied in such work.

Sec. 103. Subject matter of copyright: Compilations and derivative works

(a) The subject matter of copyright as specified by section 102 includes compilations and derivative works, but protection for a work employing preexisting material in which copyright subsists does not extend to any part of the work in which such material has been used unlawfully.

(b) The copyright in a compilation or derivative work extends only to the material contributed by the author of such work, as distinguished from the preexisting material employed in the work, and does not imply any exclusive right in the preexisting material. The copyright in such work is independent of, and does not affect or enlarge the scope, duration, ownership, or subsistence of, any copyright protection in the preexisting material.

Sec. 104. Subject matter of copyright: National origin

(a) Unpublished Works. — The works specified by sections 102 and 103, while unpublished, are subject to protection under this title without regard to the nationality or domicile of the author.

(b) Published Works. — The works specified by sections 102 and 103, when published, are subject to protection under this title if —

(1) on the date of first publication, one or more of the authors is a national or domiciliary of the United States, or is a national, domiciliary, or sovereign authority of a foreign nation that is a party to a copyright treaty to which the United States is also a party, or is a stateless person, wherever that person may be domiciled; or

(2) the work is first published in the United States or in a foreign nation that, on the date of first publication, is a party to the Universal Copyright Convention; or

(3) the work is first published by the United Nations or any of its specialized agencies, or by the Organization of American States; or

(4) the work is a Berne Convention work; or

(5) the work comes within the scope of a Presidential proclamation. Whenever the President finds that a particular foreign nation extends, to works by authors who are nationals or domiciliaries of the United States or to works that are first published in the United States, copyright protection on substantially the same basis as that on which the foreign nation extends protection to works of its own nationals and domiciliaries and works first published in that nation, the President may by proclamation extend protection under this title to works of which one or more of the authors is, on the date of first publication, a national, domiciliary, or sovereign authority of that nation, or which was first published in that nation. The President may revise, suspend, or revoke any such proclamation or impose any conditions or limitations on protection under a proclamation.

(c) Effect of Berne Convention. — No right or interest in a work eligible for protection under this title may be claimed by virtue of, or in reliance upon, the provisions of the Berne Convention, or the adherence of the United States thereto. Any rights in a work eligible for protection under this title that derive from this title, other Federal or State statutes, or the common law, shall not be expanded or reduced by virtue of, or in reliance upon, the provisions of the Berne Convention, or the adherence of the United States thereto._____

Sec. 106. Exclusive rights in copyrighted worksSubject to sections 107 through 120, the owner of copyright under this title has the exclusive rights to do and to authorize any of the following:

(1) to reproduce the copyrighted work in copies or phonorecords;

(2) to prepare derivative works based upon the copyrighted work;

(3) to distribute copies or phonorecords of the copyrighted work to the public by sale or other transfer of ownership, or by rental, lease, or lending;

(4) in the case of literary, musical, dramatic, and choreographic works, pantomimes, and motion pictures and other audiovisual works, to perform the copyrighted work publicly;

(5) in the case of literary, musical, dramatic, and choreographic works, pantomimes, and pictorial, graphic, or sculptural works, including the individual images of a motion picture or other audiovisual work, to display the copyrighted work publicly; and

(6) in the case of sound recordings, to perform the copyrighted work publicly by means of a digital audio transmission._____

Sec. 107. Limitations on exclusive rights: Fair useNotwithstanding the provisions of sections 106 and 106A, the fair use of a copyrighted work, including such use by reproduction in copies or phonorecords or by any other means specified by that section, for purposes such as criticism, comment, news reporting, teaching (including multiple copies for classroom use), scholarship, or research, is not an infringement of copyright. In determining whether the use made of a work in any particular case is a fair use the factors to be considered shall include —

(1) the purpose and character of the use, including whether such use is of a commercial nature or is for nonprofit educational purposes;

(2) the nature of the copyrighted work;

(3) the amount and substantiality of the portion used in relation to the copyrighted work as a whole; and

(4) the effect of the use upon the potential market for or value of the copyrighted work. The fact that a work is unpublished shall not itself bar a finding of fair use if such finding is made upon consideration of all the above factors.

Sec. 108. Limitations on exclusive rights: Reproduction by libraries and archives

(a) Notwithstanding the provisions of section 106, it is not an infringement of copyright for a library or archives, or any of its employees acting within the scope of their employment, to reproduce no more than one copy or phonorecord of a work, or to distribute such copy or phonorecord, under the conditions specified by this section,

if —

(1) the reproduction or distribution is made without any purpose of direct or indirect commercial advantage;

(2) the collections of the library or archives are (i) open to the public, or (ii) available not only to researchers affiliated with the library or archives or with the institution of which it is a part, but also to other persons doing research in a specialized field; and

(3) the reproduction or distribution of the work includes a notice of copyright.

(b) The rights of reproduction and distribution under this section apply to a copy or phonorecord of an unpublished work duplicated in facsimile form solely for purposes of preservation and security or for deposit for research use in another library or archives of the type described by clause (2) of subsection (a), if the copy or phonorecord reproduced is currently in the collections of the library or archives.

(c) The right of reproduction under this section applies to a copy or phonorecord of a published work duplicated in facsimile form solely for the purpose of replacement of a copy or phonorecord that is damaged, deteriorating, lost, or stolen, if the library or archives has, after a reasonable effort, determined that an unused replacement cannot be obtained at a fair price.

(d) The rights of reproduction and distribution under this section apply to a copy, made from the collection of a library or archives where the user makes his or her request or from that of another library or archives, of no more than one article or other contribution to a copyrighted collection or periodical issue, or to a copy or phonorecord of a small part of any other copyrighted work, if —

(1) the copy or phonorecord becomes the property of the user, and the library or archives has had no notice that the copy or phonorecord would be used for any purpose other than private study, scholarship, or research; and

(2) the library or archives displays prominently, at the place where orders are accepted, and includes on its order form, a warning of copyright in accordance with requirements that the Register of Copyrights shall prescribe by regulation.

(e) The rights of reproduction and distribution under this section apply to the entire work, or to a substantial part of it, made from the collection of a library or archives where the user makes his or her request or from that of another library or archives, if the library or archives has first determined, on the basis of a reasonable investigation, that a copy or phonorecord of the copyrighted work cannot be obtained at a fair price, if —

> (1) the copy or phonorecord becomes the property of the user, and the library or archives has had no notice that the copy or phonorecord would be used for any purpose other than private study, scholarship, or research; and

> (2) the library or archives displays prominently, at the place where orders are accepted, and includes on its order form, a warning of copyright in accordance with requirements that the Register of Copyrights shall prescribe by regulation.

(f) Nothing in this section —

> (1) shall be construed to impose liability for copyright infringement upon a library or archives or its employees for the unsupervised use of reproducing equipment located on its premises: Provided, That such equipment displays a notice that the making of a copy may be subject to the copyright law;

> (2) excuses a person who uses such reproducing equipment or who requests a copy or phonorecord under subsection (d) from liability for copyright infringement for any such act, or for any later use of such copy or phonorecord, if it exceeds fair use as provided by section 107;

> (3) shall be construed to limit the reproduction and distribution by lending of a limited number of copies and excerpts by a library or archives of an audiovisual news program, subject to clauses (1), (2), and (3) of subsection (a); or

> (4) in any way affects the right of fair use as provided by section 107, or any contractual obligations assumed at any time by the library or archives when it obtained a copy or phonorecord of a work in its collections.

(g) The rights of reproduction and distribution under this section extend to the isolated and unrelated reproduction or distribution of a single copy or phonorecord of the same material on separate occasions, but do not extend to cases where the library or archives, or its employee —

> (1) is aware or has substantial reason to believe that it is engaging in the related or concerted reproduction or distribution of multiple copies or phonorecords of the same material, whether made on one occasion or over a period of time, and whether intended for aggregate use by one or more individuals or for separate use by the individual members of a group; or

> (2) engages in the systematic reproduction or distribution of single or multiple copies or phonorecords of material described in subsection (d): Provided, That nothing in this clause prevents a library or archives from participating in interlibrary arrangements that do not have, as their purpose or effect, that the library or archives receiving such copies or phonorecords for distribution does so in such aggregate quantities as to substitute for a subscription to or purchase of such work.

(h) The rights of reproduction and distribution under this section do not apply to a musical work, a pictorial, graphic or sculptural work, or a motion picture or other audiovisual work other than an audiovisual work dealing with news, except that no such limitation shall apply with respect to rights granted by subsections (b) and (c), or with respect to pictorial or graphic works published as illustrations, diagrams, or similar adjuncts to works of which copies are reproduced or distributed in accordance with subsections (d) and (e).

D

Sec. 109. Limitations on exclusive rights: Effect of transfer of particular copy or phonorecord

(a) Notwithstanding the provisions of section 106(3), the owner of a particular copy or phonorecord lawfully made under this title, or any person authorized by such owner, is entitled, without the authority of the copyright owner, to sell or otherwise dispose of the possession of that copy or phonorecord. Notwithstanding the preceding sentence, copies or phonorecords of works subject to restored copyright under section 104A that are manufactured before the date of restoration of copyright or, with respect to reliance parties, before publication or service of notice under section 104A(e), may be sold or otherwise disposed of without the authorization of the owner of the restored copyright for purposes of direct or indirect commercial advantage only during the 12-month period beginning on —

(1) the date of the publication in the Federal Register of the notice of intent filed with the Copyright Office under section 104A(d)(2)(A), or

(2) the date of the receipt of actual notice served under section 104A(d)(2)(B), whichever occurs first.

(b)

(1)

(A) Notwithstanding the provisions of subsection (a), unless authorized by the owners of copyright in the sound recording or the owner of copyright in a computer program (including any tape, disk, or other medium embodying such program), and in the case of a sound recording in the musical works embodied therein, neither the owner of a particular phonorecord nor any person in possession of a particular copy of a computer program (including any tape, disk, or other medium embodying such program), may, for the purposes of direct or indirect commercial advantage, dispose of, or authorize the disposal of, the possession of that phonorecord or computer program (including any tape, disk, or other medium embodying such program) by rental, lease, or lending, or by any other act or practice in the nature of rental, lease, or lending. Nothing in the preceding sentence shall apply to the rental, lease, or lending of a phonorecord for nonprofit purposes by a nonprofit library or nonprofit educational institution. The transfer of possession of a lawfully made copy of a computer program by a nonprofit educational institution to another nonprofit educational institution or to faculty, staff, and students does not constitute rental, lease, or lending for direct or indirect commercial purposes under this subsection.

(B) This subsection does not apply to —

(i) a computer program which is embodied in a machine or product and which cannot be copied during the ordinary operation or use of the machine or product; or

(ii) a computer program embodied in or used in conjunction with a limited purpose computer that is designed for playing video games and may be designed for other purposes.

(C) Nothing in this subsection affects any provision of chapter 9 of this title.

(2)

(A) Nothing in this subsection shall apply to the lending of a computer program for nonprofit purposes by a nonprofit library, if each copy of a computer program which is lent by such library has affixed to the packaging containing the program a warning of copyright in accordance with requirements that the Register of Copyrights shall prescribe by regulation.

(B) Not later than three years after the date of the enactment of the Computer Software Rental Amendments Act of 1990, and at such times thereafter as the Register of Copyrights considers appropriate, the Register of Copyrights, after consultation with representatives of copyright owners and librarians, shall submit to the Congress a report stating whether this paragraph has achieved its intended purpose of maintaining the integrity of the copyright system while providing nonprofit libraries the capability to fulfill their function. Such report shall advise the Congress as to any information or recommendations that the Register of Copyrights considers necessary to carry out the purposes of this subsection.

(3) Nothing in this subsection shall affect any provision of the antitrust laws. For purposes of the preceding sentence, "antitrust laws" has the meaning given that term in the first section of the Clayton Act and includes section 5 of the Federal Trade Commission Act to the extent that section relates to unfair methods of competition.

(4) Any person who distributes a phonorecord or a copy of a computer program (including any tape, disk, or other medium embodying such program) in violation of paragraph (1) is an infringer of copyright under section 501 of this title and is subject to the remedies set forth in sections 502, 503, 504, 505, and 509. Such violation shall not be a criminal offense under section 506 or cause such person to be subject to the criminal penalties set forth in section 2319 of title 18.

(c) Notwithstanding the provisions of section 106(5), the owner of a particular copy lawfully made under this title, or any person authorized by such owner, is entitled, without the authority of the copyright owner, to display that copy publicly, either directly or by the projection of no more than one image at a time, to viewers present at the place where the copy is located.

(d) The privileges prescribed by subsections (a) and (c) do not, unless authorized by the copyright owner, extend to any person who has acquired possession of the copy or phonorecord from the copyright owner, by rental, lease, loan, or otherwise, without acquiring ownership of it.

(e) Notwithstanding the provisions of sections 106(4) and 106(5), in the case of an electronic audiovisual game intended for use in coin-operated equipment, the owner of a particular copy of such a game lawfully made under this title, is entitled, without the authority of the copyright owner of the game, to publicly perform or display that game in coin-operated equipment, except that this subsection shall not apply to any work of authorship embodied in the audiovisual game if the copyright owner of the electronic audiovisual game is not also the copyright owner of the work of authorship.

Sec. 110. Limitations on exclusive rights: Exemption of certain performances and displaysNotwithstanding the provisions of section 106, the following are not infringements of copyright:

(1) performance or display of a work by instructors or pupils in the course of face-to-face teaching activities of a nonprofit educational institution, in a classroom or similar place devoted to instruction, unless, in the case of a motion picture or other audiovisual work, the performance, or the display of individual images, is given by means of a copy that was not lawfully made under this title, and that the person responsible for the performance knew or had reason to believe was not lawfully made;

(2) performance of a nondramatic literary or musical work or display of a work, by or in the course of a transmission, if —

(A) the performance or display is a regular part of the systematic instructional activities of a governmental body or a nonprofit educational institution; and

(B) the performance or display is directly related and of material assistance to the teaching content of the transmission; and

(C) the transmission is made primarily for —

(i) reception in classrooms or similar places normally devoted to instruction, or

    (ii) reception by persons to whom the transmission is directed because their disabilities or other special circumstances prevent their attendance in classrooms or similar places normally devoted to instruction, or

    (iii) reception by officers or employees of governmental bodies as a part of their official duties or employment;

(3) performance of a nondramatic literary or musical work or of a dramatico-musical work of a religious nature, or display of a work, in the course of services at a place of worship or other religious assembly;

(4) performance of a nondramatic literary or musical work otherwise than in a transmission to the public, without any purpose of direct or indirect commercial advantage and without payment of any fee or other compensation for the performance to any of its performers, promoters, or organizers, if —

    (A) there is no direct or indirect admission charge; or

    (B) the proceeds, after deducting the reasonable costs of producing the performance, are used exclusively for educational, religious, or charitable purposes and not for private financial gain, except where the copyright owner has served notice of objection to the performance under the following conditions;

        (i) the notice shall be in writing and signed by the copyright owner or such owner's duly authorized agent; and

        (ii) the notice shall be served on the person responsible for the performance at least seven days before the date of the performance, and shall state the reasons for the objection; and

        (iii) the notice shall comply, in form, content, and manner of service, with requirements that the Register of Copyrights shall prescribe by regulation;

(5) communication of a transmission embodying a performance or display of a work by the public reception of the transmission on a single receiving apparatus of a kind commonly used in private homes, unless —

    (A) a direct charge is made to see or hear the transmission;

    or

    (B) the transmission thus received is further transmitted to the public;

(6) performance of a nondramatic musical work by a governmental body or a nonprofit agricultural or horticultural organization, in the course of an annual agricultural or horticultural fair or exhibition conducted by such body or organization; the exemption provided by this clause shall extend to any liability for copyright infringement that would otherwise be imposed on such body or organization, under doctrines of vicarious liability or related infringement, for a performance by a concessionaire, business establishment, or other person at such fair or exhibition, but shall not excuse any such person from liability for the performance;

(7) performance of a nondramatic musical work by a vending establishment open to the public at large without any direct or indirect admission charge, where the sole purpose of the performance is to promote the retail sale of copies or phonorecords of the work, and the performance is not transmitted beyond the place where the establishment is located and is within the immediate area where the sale is occurring;

(8) performance of a nondramatic literary work, by or in the course of a transmission specifically designed for and primarily directed to blind or other handicapped persons who are unable to read normal printed material as a result of their handicap, or deaf or other handicapped persons who are unable to hear the

aural signals accompanying a transmission of visual signals, if the performance is made without any purpose of direct or indirect commercial advantage and its transmission is made through the facilities of: (i) a governmental body; or (ii) a noncommercial educational broadcast station (as defined in section 397 of title 47); or (iii) a radio subcarrier authorization (as defined in 47 CFR 73.293-73.295 and 73.593-73.595); or (iv) a cable system (as defined in section 111(f));

(9) performance on a single occasion of a dramatic literary work published at least ten years before the date of the performance, by or in the course of a transmission specifically designed for and primarily directed to blind or other handicapped persons who are unable to read normal printed material as a result of their handicap, if the performance is made without any purpose of direct or indirect commercial advantage and its transmission is made through the facilities of a radio subcarrier authorization referred to in clause (8)(iii), Provided, That the provisions of this clause shall not be applicable to more than one performance of the same work by the same performers or under the auspices of the same organization; and

(10) notwithstanding paragraph (4), the following is not an infringement of copyright: performance of a nondramatic literary or musical work in the course of a social function which is organized and promoted by a nonprofit veterans' organization or a nonprofit fraternal organization to which the general public is not invited, but not including the invitees of the organizations, if the proceeds from the performance, after deducting the reasonable costs of producing the performance, are used exclusively for charitable purposes and not for financial gain. For purposes of this section the social functions of any college or university fraternity or sorority shall not be included unless the social function is held solely to raise funds for a specific charitable purpose._____

Sec. 113. Scope of exclusive rights in pictorial, graphic, and sculptural works

(a) Subject to the provisions of subsections (b) and (c) of this section, the exclusive right to reproduce a copyrighted pictorial, graphic, or sculptural work in copies under section 106 includes the right to reproduce the work in or on any kind of article, whether useful or otherwise.

(b) This title does not afford, to the owner of copyright in a work that portrays a useful article as such, any greater or lesser rights with respect to the making, distribution, or display of the useful article so portrayed than those afforded to such works under the law, whether title 17 or the common law or statutes of a State, in effect on December 31, 1977, as held applicable and construed by a court in an action brought under this title.

(c) In the case of a work lawfully reproduced in useful articles that have been offered for sale or other distribution to the public, copyright does not include any right to prevent the making, distribution, or display of pictures or photographs of such articles in connection with advertisements or commentaries related to the distribution or display of such articles, or in connection with news reports.

(d)

(1) In a case in which —

(A) a work of visual art has been incorporated in or made part of a building in such a way that removing the work from the building will cause the destruction, distortion, mutilation, or other modification of the work as described in section 106A(a)(3), and

(B) the author consented to the installation of the work in the building either before the effective date set forth in section 610(a) of the Visual Artists Rights Act of 1990, or in a written instrument executed on or after such effective date that is signed by the owner of the building and the author and that specifies that installation of the work may subject the work to destruction, distortion, mutilation, or other modification, by reason of its removal, then the rights conferred by paragraphs (2) and (3) of section 106A(a) shall not apply.

(2) If the owner of a building wishes to remove a work of visual art which is a part of such building and which can be removed from the building without the destruction, distortion, mutilation, or other modification of the work as described in section 106A(a)(3), the author's rights under paragraphs (2) and (3) of section 106A(a) shall apply unless —

(A) the owner has made a diligent, good faith attempt without success to notify the author of the owner's intended action affecting the work of visual art, or

(B) the owner did provide such notice in writing and the person so notified failed, within 90 days after receiving such notice, either to remove the work or to pay for its removal. For purposes of subparagraph (A), an owner shall be presumed to have made a diligent, good faith attempt to send notice if the owner sent such notice by registered mail to the author at the most recent address of the author that was recorded with the Register of Copyrights pursuant to paragraph (3). If the work is removed at the expense of the author, title to that copy of the work shall be deemed to be in the author.

(3) The Register of Copyrights shall establish a system of records whereby any author of a work of visual art that has been incorporated in or made part of a building, may record his or her identity and address with the Copyright Office. The Register shall also establish procedures under which any such author may update the information so recorded, and procedures under which owners of buildings may record with the Copyright Office evidence of their efforts to comply with this subsection._____

Sec. 114. Scope of exclusive rights in sound recordings

(a) The exclusive rights of the owner of copyright in a sound recording are limited to the rights specified by clauses (1), (2), (3) and (6) of section 106, and do not include any right of performance under section 106(4).

(b) The exclusive right of the owner of copyright in a sound recording under clause (1) of section 106 is limited to the right to duplicate the sound recording in the form of phonorecords or copies that directly or indirectly recapture the actual sounds fixed in the recording. The exclusive right of the owner of copyright in a sound recording under clause (2) of section 106 is limited to the right to prepare a derivative work in which the actual sounds fixed in the sound recording are rearranged, remixed, or otherwise altered in sequence or quality. The exclusive rights of the owner of copyright in a sound recording under clauses (1) and (2) of section 106 do not extend to the making or duplication of another sound recording that consists entirely of an independent fixation of other sounds, even though such sounds imitate or simulate those in the copyrighted sound recording. The exclusive rights of the owner of copyright in a sound recording under clauses included in educational television and radio programs (as defined in section 397 of title 47) distributed or transmitted by or through public broadcasting entities (as defined by section 118(g)): Provided, That copies or phonorecords of said programs are not commercially distributed by or through public broadcasting entities to the general public.

(c) This section does not limit or impair the exclusive right to perform publicly, by means of a phonorecord, any of the works specified by section 106(4).

(d) Limitations on Exclusive Right. — Notwithstanding the provisions of section 106(6) —

(1) Exempt transmissions and retransmissions. — The performance of a sound recording publicly by means of a digital audio transmission, other than as a part of an interactive service, is not an infringement of section 106(6) if the performance is part of —

(i) (A)a nonsubscription transmission other than a retransmission;

(ii) an initial nonsubscription retransmission made for direct reception by members of the public of a prior or simultaneous incidental transmission that is not made for direct reception by members of the public; or

(iii) a nonsubscription broadcast transmission;

(B) a retransmission of a nonsubscription broadcast transmission: Provided, That, in the case of a retransmission of a radio station's broadcast transmission –

(1) the radio station's broadcast transmission is not willfully or repeatedly retransmitted more than a radius of 150 miles from the site of the radio broadcast transmitter, however -

(I) the 150 mile limitation under this clause shall not apply when a nonsubscription broadcast transmission by a radio station licensed by the Federal Communications Commission is retransmitted on a nonsubscription basis by a terrestrial broadcast station, terrestrial translator, or terrestrial repeater licensed by the Federal Communications Commission; and

(II) in the case of a subscription retransmission of a nonsubscription broadcast retransmission covered by subclause (I), the 150 mile radius shall be measured from the transmitter site of such broadcast retransmitter;

(ii) the retransmission is of radio station broadcast transmissions that are —

(I) obtained by the retransmitter over the air;

(II) not electronically processed by the retransmitter to deliver separate and discrete signals; and

(III) retransmitted only within the local communities served by the retransmitter;

(iii) the radio station's broadcast transmission was being retransmitted to cable systems (as defined in section 111(f)) by a satellite carrier on January 1, 1995, and that retransmission was being retransmitted by cable systems as a separate and discrete signal, and the satellite carrier obtains the radio station's broadcast transmission in an analog format: Provided, That the broadcast transmission being retransmitted may embody the programming of no more than one radio station; or

(iv) the radio station's broadcast transmission is made by a noncommercial educational broadcast station funded on or after January 1, 1995, under section 396(k) of the Communications Act of 1934 (47 U.S.C. 396(k)), consists solely of noncommercial educational and cultural radio programs, and the retransmission, whether or not simultaneous, is a nonsubscription terrestrial broadcast retransmission; or

(C) a transmission that comes within any of the following categories —

(i) a prior or simultaneous transmission incidental to an exempt transmission, such as a feed received by and then retransmitted by an exempt transmitter: Provided, That such incidental transmissions do not include any subscription transmission directly for reception by members of the public;

(ii) a transmission within a business establishment, confined to its premises or the immediately surrounding vicinity;

(iii) a retransmission by any retransmitter, including a multichannel video programming distributor as defined in section 602(12) [1] of the Communications Act of 1934 (47 U.S.C. 522(12)), of a transmission by a transmitter licensed to publicly perform the sound recording as a part of that transmission, if the retransmission is simultaneous with the licensed transmission and authorized by the transmitter; or

(iv) a transmission to a business establishment for use in the ordinary course of its business: Provided, That the business recipient does not retransmit the transmission outside of its premises or the immediately surrounding vicinity, and that the transmission does not exceed the sound recording performance complement. Nothing in this clause shall limit the scope of the exemption in clause (ii).

(2) Subscription transmissions. — In the case of a subscription transmission not exempt under subsection (d)(1), the performance of a sound recording publicly by means of a digital audio transmission shall be subject to statutory licensing, in accordance with subsection (f) of this section, if —

(A) the transmission is not part of an interactive service;

(B) the transmission does not exceed the sound recording performance complement;

(C) the transmitting entity does not cause to be published by means of an advance program schedule or prior announcement the titles of the specific sound recordings or phonorecords embodying such sound recordings to be transmitted;

(D) except in the case of transmission to a business establishment, the transmitting entity does not automatically and intentionally cause any device receiving the transmission to switch from one program channel to another; and

(E) except as provided in section 1002(e) of this title, the transmission of the sound recording is accompanied by the information encoded in that sound recording, if any, by or under the authority of the copyright owner of that sound recording, that identifies the title of the sound recording, the featured recording artist who performs on the sound recording, and related information, including information concerning the underlying musical work and its writer.

(3) Licenses for transmissions by interactive services. —

(A) No interactive service shall be granted an exclusive license under section 106(6) for the performance of a sound recording publicly by means of digital audio transmission for a period in excess of 12 months, except that with respect to an exclusive license granted to an interactive service by a licensor that holds the copyright to 1,000 or fewer sound recordings, the period of such license shall not exceed 24 months: Provided, however, That the grantee of such exclusive license shall be ineligible to receive another exclusive license for the performance of that sound recording for a period of 13 months from the expiration of the prior exclusive license.

(B) The limitation set forth in subparagraph (A) of this paragraph shall not apply if —

(i) the licensor has granted and there remain in effect licenses under section 106(6) for the public performance of sound recordings by means of digital audio transmission by at least 5 different interactive services: Provided, however, That each such license must be for a minimum of 10 percent of the copyrighted sound recordings owned by the licensor that have been licensed to interactive services, but in no event less than 50 sound recordings; or

(ii) the exclusive license is granted to perform publicly up to 45 seconds of a sound recording and the sole purpose of the performance is to promote the distribution or performance of that sound recording.

(C) Notwithstanding the grant of an exclusive or nonexclusive license of the right of public performance under section 106(6), an interactive service may not publicly perform a sound recording unless a license has been granted for the public performance of any copyrighted musical work contained in the sound recording: Provided, That such license to publicly perform the copyrighted musical work may be granted either by a performing rights society representing the copyright owner or by the copyright owner.

(D) The performance of a sound recording by means of a retransmission of a digital audio transmission is not an infringement of section 106(6) if —

(i) the retransmission is of a transmission by an interactive service licensed to publicly perform the sound recording to a particular member of the public as part of that transmission; and

(ii) the retransmission is simultaneous with the licensed transmission, authorized by the transmitter, and limited to that particular member of the public intended by the interactive service to be the recipient of the transmission.

(E) For the purposes of this paragraph —

(i) a "licensor" shall include the licensing entity and any other entity under any material degree of common ownership, management, or control that owns copyrights in sound recordings; and

(ii) a "performing rights society" is an association or corporation that licenses the public performance of nondramatic musical works on behalf of the copyright owner, such as the American Society of Composers, Authors and Publishers, Broadcast Music, Inc., and SESAC, Inc.

(4) Rights not otherwise limited. —

(A) Except as expressly provided in this section, this section does not limit or impair the exclusive right to perform a sound recording publicly by means of a digital audio transmission under section 106(6).

(B) Nothing in this section annuls or limits in any way —

(i) the exclusive right to publicly perform a musical work, including by means of a digital audio transmission, under section 106(4);

(ii) the exclusive rights in a sound recording or the musical work embodied therein under sections 106(1), 106(2) and 106(3); or

(iii) any other rights under any other clause of section 106, or remedies available under this title, as such rights or remedies exist either before or after the date of enactment of the Digital Performance Right in Sound Recordings Act of 1995.

(C) Any limitations in this section on the exclusive right under section 106(6) apply only to the exclusive right under section 106(6) and not to any other exclusive rights under section 106. Nothing in this section shall be construed to annul, limit, impair or otherwise affect in any way the ability of the owner of a copyright in a sound recording to exercise the rights under sections 106(1), 106(2) and 106(3), or to obtain the remedies available under this title pursuant to such rights, as such rights and remedies exist either before or after the date of enactment of the Digital Performance Right in Sound Recordings Act of 1995.

(e) Authority for Negotiations. —

(1) Notwithstanding any provision of the antitrust laws, in negotiating statutory licenses in accordance with subsection (f), any copyright owners of sound recordings and any entities performing sound recordings affected by this section may negotiate and agree upon the royalty rates and license terms and conditions for the performance of such sound recordings and the proportionate division of fees paid among copyright owners, and may designate common agents on a nonexclusive basis to negotiate, agree to, pay, or receive payments.

(2) For licenses granted under section 106(6), other than statutory licenses, such as for performances by interactive services or performances that exceed the sound recording performance complement —

    (A) copyright owners of sound recordings affected by this section may designate common agents to act on their behalf to grant licenses and receive and remit royalty payments:

        Provided, That each copyright owner shall establish the royalty rates and material license terms and conditions unilaterally, that is, not in agreement, combination, or concert with other copyright owners of sound recordings; and

    (B) entities performing sound recordings affected by this section may designate common agents to act on their behalf to obtain licenses and collect and pay royalty fees: Provided, That each entity performing sound recordings shall determine the royalty rates and material license terms and conditions unilaterally, that is, not in agreement, combination, or concert with other entities performing sound recordings.

(f) Licenses for Nonexempt Subscription Transmissions. —

    (1) No later than 30 days after the enactment of the Digital Performance Right in Sound Recordings Act of 1995, the Librarian of Congress shall cause notice to be published in the Federal Register of the initiation of voluntary negotiation proceedings for the purpose of determining reasonable terms and rates of royalty payments for the activities specified by subsection (d)(2) of this section during the period beginning on the effective date of such Act and ending on December 31, 2000, or, if a copyright arbitration royalty panel is convened, ending 30 days after the Librarian issues and publishes in the Federal Register an order adopting the determination of the copyright arbitration royalty panel or an order setting the terms and rates (if the Librarian rejects the panel's determination). Such terms and rates shall distinguish among the different types of digital audio transmission services then in operation. Any copyright owners of sound recordings or any entities performing sound recordings affected by this section may submit to the Librarian of Congress licenses covering such activities with respect to such sound recordings. The parties to each negotiation proceeding shall bear their own costs.

    (2) In the absence of license agreements negotiated under paragraph (1), during the 60-day period commencing 6 months after publication of the notice specified in paragraph (1), and upon the filing of a petition in accordance with section 803(a)(1), the Librarian of Congress shall, pursuant to chapter 8, convene a copyright arbitration royalty panel to determine a schedule of rates and terms which, subject to paragraph (3), shall be binding on all copyright owners of sound recordings and entities performing sound recordings. In addition to the objectives set forth in section 801(b)(1), in establishing such rates and terms, the copyright arbitration royalty panel may consider the rates and terms for comparable types of digital audio transmission services and comparable circumstances under voluntary license agreements negotiated as provided in paragraph (1). The Librarian of Congress shall also establish requirements by which copyright owners may receive reasonable notice of the use of their sound recordings under this section, and under which records of such use shall be kept and made available by entities performing sound recordings.

    (3) License agreements voluntarily negotiated at any time between one or more copyright owners of sound recordings and one or more entities performing sound recordings shall be given effect in lieu of any determination by a copyright arbitration royalty panel or decision by the Librarian of Congress.

    (4)

        (A) Publication of a notice of the initiation of voluntary negotiation proceedings as specified in paragraph (1) shall be repeated, in accordance with regulations that the Librarian of Congress shall prescribe —

(i) no later than 30 days after a petition is filed by any copyright owners of sound recordings or any entities performing sound recordings affected by this section indicating that a new type of digital audio transmission service on which sound recordings are performed is or is about to become operational; and

(ii) in the first week of January, 2000 and at 5-year intervals thereafter.

(B)

(i) The procedures specified in paragraph (2) shall be repeated, in accordance with regulations that the Librarian of Congress shall prescribe, upon the filing of a petition in accordance with section 803(a)(1) during a 60-day period commencing —

(I) six months after publication of a notice of the initiation of voluntary negotiation proceedings under paragraph

(1) pursuant to a petition under paragraph (4)(A)(i); or

(II) on July 1, 2000 and at 5-year intervals thereafter.

(ii) The procedures specified in paragraph (2) shall be concluded in accordance with section 802.

(5)

(A) Any person who wishes to perform a sound recording publicly by means of a nonexempt subscription transmission under this subsection may do so without infringing the exclusive right of the copyright owner of the sound recording —

(i) by complying with such notice requirements as the Librarian of Congress shall prescribe by regulation and by paying royalty fees in accordance with this subsection; or

(ii) if such royalty fees have not been set, by agreeing to pay such royalty fees as shall be determined in accordance with this subsection.

(B) Any royalty payments in arrears shall be made on or before the twentieth day of the month next succeeding the month in which the royalty fees are set.

(g) Proceeds From Licensing of Subscription Transmissions. —

(1) Except in the case of a subscription transmission licensed in accordance with subsection (f) of this section —

(A) a featured recording artist who performs on a sound recording that has been licensed for a subscription transmission shall be entitled to receive payments from the copyright owner of the sound recording in accordance with the terms of the artist's contract; and

(B) a nonfeatured recording artist who performs on a sound recording that has been licensed for a subscription transmission shall be entitled to receive payments from the copyright owner of the sound recording in accordance with the terms of the nonfeatured recording artist's applicable contract or other applicable agreement.

(2) The copyright owner of the exclusive right under section 106(6) of this title to publicly perform a sound recording by means of a digital audio transmission shall allocate to recording artists in the following manner its receipts from the statutory licensing of subscription transmission performances of the sound recording in accordance with subsection (f) of this section:

(A) 2 1/2 percent of the receipts shall be deposited in an escrow account managed by an independent administrator jointly appointed by copyright owners of sound recordings and the American Federation of Musicians (or any successor entity) to be distributed to nonfeatured musicians (whether or not members of the American Federation of Musicians) who have performed on sound recordings.

(B) 2 1/2 percent of the receipts shall be deposited in an escrow account managed by an independent administrator jointly appointed by copyright owners of sound recordings and the American Federation of Television and Radio Artists (or any successor entity) to be distributed to nonfeatured vocalists (whether or not members of the American Federation of Television and Radio Artists) who have performed on sound recordings.

(C) 45 percent of the receipts shall be allocated, on a per sound recording basis, to the recording artist or artists featured on such sound recording (or the persons conveying rights in the artists' performance in the sound recordings).

(h) Licensing to Affiliates. —

(1) If the copyright owner of a sound recording licenses an affiliated entity the right to publicly perform a sound recording by means of a digital audio transmission under section 106(6), the copyright owner shall make the licensed sound recording available under section 106(6) on no less favorable terms and conditions to all bona fide entities that offer similar services, except that, if there are material differences in the scope of the requested license with respect to the type of service, the particular sound recordings licensed, the frequency of use, the number of subscribers served, or the duration, then the copyright owner may establish different terms and conditions for such other services.

(2) The limitation set forth in paragraph (1) of this subsection shall not apply in the case where the copyright owner of a sound recording licenses —

(A) an interactive service; or

(B) an entity to perform publicly up to 45 seconds of the sound recording and the sole purpose of the performance is to promote the distribution or performance of that sound recording.

(i) No Effect on Royalties for Underlying Works. — License fees payable for the public performance of sound recordings under section 106(6) shall not be taken into account in any administrative, judicial, or other governmental proceeding to set or adjust the royalties payable to copyright owners of musical works for the public performance of their works. It is the intent of Congress that royalties payable to copyright owners of musical works for the public performance of their works shall not be diminished in any respect as a result of the rights granted by section 106(6).

(j) Definitions. — As used in this section, the following terms have the following meanings:

(1) An "affiliated entity" is an entity engaging in digital audio transmissions covered by section 106(6), other than an interactive service, in which the licensor has any direct or indirect partnership or any ownership interest amounting to 5 percent or more of the outstanding voting or non-voting stock.

(2) A "broadcast" transmission is a transmission made by a terrestrial broadcast station licensed as such by the Federal Communications Commission.

(3) A "digital audio transmission" is a digital transmission as defined in section 101, that embodies the transmission of a sound recording. This term does not include the transmission of any audiovisual work.

(4) An "interactive service" is one that enables a member of the public to receive, on request, a transmission of a particular sound recording chosen by or on behalf of the recipient. The

ability of individuals to request that particular sound recordings be performed for reception by the public at large does not make a service interactive. If an entity offers both interactive and non-interactive services (either concurrently or at different times), the non-interactive component shall not be treated as part of an interactive service.

(5) A "nonsubscription" transmission is any transmission that is not a subscription transmission.

(6) A "retransmission" is a further transmission of an initial transmission, and includes any further retransmission of the same transmission. Except as provided in this section, a transmission qualifies as a "retransmission" only if it is simultaneous with the initial transmission. Nothing in this definition shall be construed to exempt a transmission that fails to satisfy a separate element required to qualify for an exemption under section 114(d)(1).

(7) The "sound recording performance complement" is the transmission during any 3-hour period, on a particular channel used by a transmitting entity, of no more than —

(A) 3 different selections of sound recordings from any one phonorecord lawfully distributed for public performance or sale in the United States, if no more than 2 such selections are transmitted consecutively; or

(B) 4 different selections of sound recordings —

(i) by the same featured recording artist; or

(ii) from any set or compilation of phonorecords lawfully distributed together as a unit for public performance or sale in the United States, if no more than three such selections are transmitted consecutively:

Provided, That the transmission of selections in excess of the numerical limits provided for in clauses (A) and (B) from multiple phonorecords shall nonetheless qualify as a sound recording performance complement if the programming of the multiple phonorecords was not willfully intended to avoid the numerical limitations prescribed in such clauses.

(8) A "subscription" transmission is a transmission that is controlled and limited to particular recipients, and for which consideration is required to be paid or otherwise given by or on behalf of the recipient to receive the transmission or a package of transmissions including the transmission.

(9) A "transmission" includes both an initial transmission and a retransmission._____

Sec. 117. Limitations on exclusive rights: Computer programsNotwithstanding the provisions of section 106, it is not an infringement for the owner of a copy of a computer program to make or authorize the making of another copy or adaptation of that computer program provided:

(1) that such a new copy or adaptation is created as an essential step in the utilization of the computer program in conjunction with a machine and that it is used in no other manner, or

(2) that such new copy or adaptation is for archival purposes only and that all archival copies are destroyed in the event that continued possession of the computer program should cease to be rightful. Any exact copies prepared in accordance with the provisions of this section may be leased, sold, or otherwise transferred, along with the copy from which such copies were prepared, only as part of the lease, sale, or other transfer of all rights in the program. Adaptations so prepared may be transferred only with the authorization of the copyright owner.

D

The GNU General Public License

The GNU General Public License, as extracted from `http://www.gnu.org/`.

GNU GENERAL PUBLIC LICENSE

Version 2, June 1991

Copyright (C) 1989, 1991 Free Software Foundation, Inc., 59 Temple Place, Suite 330, Boston, MA 02111-1307 USA

Everyone is permitted to copy and distribute verbatim copies of this license document, but changing it is not allowed.

Preamble

The licenses for most software are designed to take away your freedom to share and change it. By contrast, the GNU General Public License is intended to guarantee your freedom to share and change free software— to make sure the software is free for all its users. This General Public License applies to most of the Free Software Foundation's software and to any other program whose authors commit to using it. (Some other Free Software Foundation software is covered by the GNU Library General Public License instead.) You can apply it to your programs, too.

When we speak of free software, we are referring to freedom, not price. Our General Public Licenses are designed to make sure that you have the freedom to distribute copies of free software (and charge for this service if you wish), that you receive source code or can get it if you want it, that you can change the software or use pieces of it in new free programs; and that you know you can do these things.

To protect your rights, we need to make restrictions that forbid anyone to deny you these rights or to ask you to surrender the rights. These restrictions translate to certain responsibilities for you if you distribute copies of the software, or if you modify it.

For example, if you distribute copies of such a program, whether gratis or for a fee, you must give the recipients all the rights that you have. You must make sure that they, too, receive or can get the source code. And you must show them these terms so they know their rights.

We protect your rights with two steps: (1) copyright the software, and (2) offer you this license which gives you legal permission to copy, distribute and/or modify the software.

Also, for each author's protection and ours, we want to make certain that everyone understands that there is no warranty for this free software. If the software is modified by someone else and passed on, we want its recipients to know that what they have is not the original, so that any problems introduced by others will not reflect on the original authors' reputations.

Finally, any free program is threatened constantly by software patents. We wish to avoid the danger that redistributors of a free program will individually obtain patent licenses, in effect making the program proprietary. To prevent this, we have made it clear that any patent must be licensed for everyone's free use or not licensed at all.

The precise terms and conditions for copying, distribution, and modification follow.

GNU GENERAL PUBLIC LICENSE TERMS AND CONDITIONS FOR COPYING, DISTRIBUTION, AND MODIFICATION

    0. This License applies to any program or other work which contains a notice placed by the copyright holder saying it may be distributed under the terms of this General Public License. The "Program," below, refers to any such program or work, and a "work based on the Program" means either the

Program or any derivative work under copyright law: that is to say, a work containing the Program or a portion of it, either verbatim or with modifications and/or translated into another language. (Hereinafter, translation is included without limitation in the term "modification.") Each licensee is addressed as "you."

Activities other than copying, distribution and modification are not covered by this License; they are outside its scope. The act of running the Program is not restricted, and the output from the Program is covered only if its contents constitute a work based on the Program (independent of having been made by running the Program). Whether that is true depends on what the Program does.

1. You may copy and distribute verbatim copies of the Program's source code as you receive it, in any medium, provided that you conspicuously and appropriately publish on each copy an appropriate copyright notice and disclaimer of warranty; keep intact all the notices that refer to this License and to the absence of any warranty; and give any other recipients of the Program a copy of this License along with the Program.

   You may charge a fee for the physical act of transferring a copy, and you may at your option offer warranty protection in exchange for a fee.

2. You may modify your copy or copies of the Program or any portion of it, thus forming a work based on the Program, and copy and distribute such modifications or work under the terms of Section 1 above, provided that you also meet all of these conditions:

   a. You must cause the modified files to carry prominent notices stating that you changed the files and the date of any change.

   b. You must cause any work that you distribute or publish, that in whole or in part contains or is derived from the Program or any part thereof, to be licensed as a whole at no charge to all third parties under the terms of this License.

   c. If the modified program normally reads commands interactively when run, you must cause it, when started running for such interactive use in the most ordinary way, to print or display an announcement including an appropriate copyright notice and a notice that there is no warranty (or else, saying that you provide a warranty) and that users may redistribute the program under these conditions, and telling the user how to view a copy of this License. (Exception: if the Program itself is interactive but does not normally print such an announcement, your work based on the Program is not required to print an announcement.)

   These requirements apply to the modified work as a whole. If identifiable sections of that work are not derived from the Program, and can be reasonably considered independent and separate works in themselves, then this License, and its terms, do not apply to those sections when you distribute them as separate works. But when you distribute the same sections as part of a whole which is a work based on the Program, the distribution of the whole must be on the terms of this License, whose permissions for other licensees extend to the entire whole, and thus to each and every part regardless of who wrote it.

   Thus, it is not the intent of this section to claim rights or contest your rights to work written entirely by you; rather, the intent is to exercise the right to control the distribution of derivative or collective works based on the Program.

   In addition, mere aggregation of another work not based on the Program with the Program (or with a work based on the Program) on a volume of a storage or distribution medium does not bring the other work under the scope of this License.

3. You may copy and distribute the Program (or a work based on it, under Section 2) in object code or executable form under the terms of Sections 1 and 2 above provided that you also do one of the following:

   a. Accompany it with the complete corresponding machine-readable source code, which must be distributed under the terms of Sections 1 and 2 above on a medium customarily used for software interchange; or,

    b. Accompany it with a written offer, valid for at least three years, to give any third party, for a charge no more than your cost of physically performing source distribution, a complete machine-readable copy of the corresponding source code, to be distributed under the terms of Sections 1 and 2 above on a medium customarily used for software interchange; or,

    c. Accompany it with the information you received as to the offer to distribute corresponding source code. (This alternative is allowed only for noncommercial distribution and only if you received the

    program in object code or executable form with such an offer, in accord with Subsection b above.)

The source code for a work means the preferred form of the work for making modifications to it. For an executable work, complete source code means all the source code for all modules it contains, plus any associated interface definition files, plus the scripts used to control compilation and installation of the executable. However, as a special exception, the source code distributed need not include anything that is normally distributed (in either source or binary form) with the major components (compiler, kernel, and so on) of the operating system on which the executable runs, unless that component itself accompanies the executable.

If distribution of executable or object code is made by offering access to copy from a designated place, then offering equivalent access to copy the source code from the same place counts as distribution of the source code, even though third parties are not compelled to copy the source along with the object code.

4. You may not copy, modify, sublicense, or distribute the Program except as expressly provided under this License. Any attempt otherwise to copy, modify, sublicense or distribute the Program is void, and will automatically terminate your rights under this License. However, parties who have received copies, or rights, from you under this License will not have their licenses terminated so long as such parties remain in full compliance.

5. You are not required to accept this License, since you have not signed it. However, nothing else grants you permission to modify or distribute the Program or its derivative works. These actions are prohibited by law if you do not accept this License. Therefore, by modifying or distributing the Program (or any work based on the Program), you indicate your acceptance of this License to do so, and all its terms and conditions for copying, distributing or modifying the Program or works based on it.

6. Each time you redistribute the Program (or any work based on the Program), the recipient automatically receives a license from the original licensor to copy, distribute or modify the Program subject to these terms and conditions. You may not impose any further restrictions on the recipients' exercise of the rights granted herein. You are not responsible for enforcing compliance by third parties to this License.

7. If, as a consequence of a court judgment or allegation of patent infringement or for any other reason (not limited to patent issues), conditions are imposed on you (whether by court order, agreement or otherwise) that contradict the conditions of this License, they do not excuse you from the conditions of this License. If you cannot distribute so as to satisfy simultaneously your obligations under this License and any other pertinent obligations, then as a consequence you may not distribute the Program at all. For example, if a patent license would not permit royalty-free redistribution of the Program by all those who receive copies directly or indirectly through you, then the only way you could satisfy both it and this License would be to refrain entirely from distribution of the Program.

If any portion of this section is held invalid or unenforceable under any particular circumstance, the balance of the section is intended to apply and the section as a whole is intended to apply in other circumstances.

It is not the purpose of this section to induce you to infringe any patents or other property right claims or to contest validity of any such claims; this section has the sole purpose of protecting the integrity of the free software distribution system, which is implemented by public license practices. Many people have made generous contributions to the wide range of software distributed through that system in reliance on consistent application of that system; it is up to the author/donor to decide if he or she is willing to distribute software through any other system and a licensee cannot impose that choice.

This section is intended to make thoroughly clear what is believed to be a consequence of the rest of this License.

8. If the distribution and/or use of the Program is restricted in certain countries either by patents or by copyrighted interfaces, the original copyright holder who places the Program under this License may add an explicit geographical distribution limitation excluding those countries, so that distribution is permitted only in or among countries not thus excluded. In such case, this License incorporates the limitation as if written in the body of this License.

9. The Free Software Foundation may publish revised and/or new versions of the General Public License from time to time. Such new versions will be similar in spirit to the present version, but may differ in detail to address new problems or concerns.

   Each version is given a distinguishing version number. If the Program specifies a version number of this License which applies to it and "any later version," you have the option of following the terms and conditions either of that version or of any later version published by the Free Software Foundation. If the Program does not specify a version number of this License, you may choose any version ever published by the Free Software Foundation.

10. If you wish to incorporate parts of the Program into other free programs whose distribution conditions are different, write to the author to ask for permission. For software which is copyrighted by the Free Software Foundation, write to the Free Software Foundation; we sometimes make exceptions for this. Our decision will be guided by the two goals of preserving the free status of all derivatives of our free software and of promoting the sharing and reuse of software generally.

NO WARRANTY

11. BECAUSE THE PROGRAM IS LICENSED FREE OF CHARGE, THERE IS NO WARRANTY FOR THE PROGRAM, TO THE EXTENT PERMITTED BY APPLICABLE LAW. EXCEPT WHEN OTHERWISE STATED IN WRITING THE COPYRIGHT HOLDERS AND/OR OTHER PARTIES PROVIDE THE PROGRAM "AS IS" WITHOUT WARRANTY OF ANY KIND, EITHER EXPRESSED OR IMPLIED, INCLUDING, BUT NOT LIMITED TO, THE IMPLIED WARRANTIES OF MERCHANTABILITY AND FITNESS FOR A PARTICULAR PURPOSE. THE ENTIRE RISK AS TO THE QUALITY AND PERFORMANCE OF THE PROGRAM IS WITH YOU. SHOULD THE PROGRAM PROVE DEFECTIVE, YOU ASSUME THE COST OF ALL NECESSARY SERVICING, REPAIR OR CORRECTION.

12. IN NO EVENT UNLESS REQUIRED BY APPLICABLE LAW OR AGREED TO IN WRITING WILL ANY COPYRIGHT HOLDER, OR ANY OTHER PARTY WHO MAY MODIFY AND/OR REDISTRIBUTE THE PROGRAM AS PERMITTED ABOVE, BE LIABLE TO YOU FOR DAMAGES, INCLUDING ANY GENERAL, SPECIAL, INCIDENTAL OR CONSEQUENTIAL DAMAGES ARISING OUT OF THE USE OR INABILITY TO USE THE PROGRAM (INCLUDING BUT NOT LIMITED TO LOSS OF DATA OR DATA BEING RENDERED INACCURATE OR LOSSES SUSTAINED BY YOU OR THIRD PARTIES OR A FAILURE OF THE PROGRAM TO OPERATE WITH ANY OTHER PROGRAMS), EVEN IF SUCH HOLDER OR OTHER PARTY HAS BEEN ADVISED OF THE POSSIBILITY OF SUCH DAMAGES.

How to Apply These Terms to Your New Programs

If you develop a new program, and you want it to be of the greatest possible use to the public, the best way to achieve this is to make it free software which everyone can redistribute and change under these terms.

To do so, attach the following notices to the program. It is safest to attach them to the start of each source file to most effectively convey the exclusion of warranty; and each

D

file should have at least the "copyright" line and a pointer to where the full notice is found.

```
<one line to give the program's name and a brief idea of what it does.>
Copyright (C) <year> <name of author>
```

This program is free software; you can redistribute it and/or modify it under the terms of the GNU General Public License as published by the Free Software Foundation; either version 2 of the License, or (at your option) any later version.

This program is distributed in the hope that it will be useful, but WITHOUT ANY WARRANTY; without even the implied warranty of MERCHANTABILITY or FITNESS FOR A PARTICULAR PURPOSE. See the GNU General Public License for more details.

You should have received a copy of the GNU General Public License along with this program; if not, write to the Free Software Foundation, Inc., 59 Temple Place, Suite 330, Boston, MA 02111-1307 USA

Also add information on how to contact you by electronic and paper mail.

If the program is interactive, make it output a short notice like this when it starts in an interactive mode:

Gnomovision version 69, Copyright (C) year name of author
Gnomovision comes with ABSOLUTELY NO WARRANTY; for details type 'show w'.
This is free software, and you are welcome to redistribute it under certain conditions;
type `show c' for details.

The hypothetical commands 'show w' and 'show c' should show the appropriate parts of the General Public License. Of course, the commands you use may be called something other than 'show w' and 'show c'; they could even be mouse-clicks or menu items—whatever suits your program.

You should also get your employer (if you work as a programmer) or your school, if any, to sign a "copyright disclaimer" for the program, if necessary. Here is a sample; alter the names:

```
Yoyodyne, Inc., hereby disclaims all copyright interest in the program
➡'Gnomovision' (which makes passes at compilers) written by James Hacker.
<signature of Ty Coon>, 1 April 1989
Ty Coon, President of Vice
```

This General Public License does not permit incorporating your program into proprietary programs. If your program is a subroutine library, you may consider it more useful to permit linking proprietary applications with the library. If this is what you want to do, use the GNU Library General Public License instead of this License.

APPENDIX E

Useful Resources

World Wide Web

Information

`http://www.altavista.com`

AltaVista, one of the better WWW search engines. Proper Boolean queries are very powerful tools.

`http://www.deja.com`

Deja, archive of Usenet News postings.

Vendors/Operating Systems

`http://www.bsdi.com`

Berkely Software Design, Inc.

`http://www.calderasystems.com`

Caldera Systems, Inc.

`http://www.debian.org`

Debian GNU/Linux

```
http://www.dec.com
```
Compaq Digital products

```
http://www.freebsd.org
```
The FreeBSD Project

```
http://www.hp.com
```
Hewlett-Packard Company

```
http://www.ibm.com
```
IBM

```
http://www.linux.org
```
Linux Online

```
http://www.openbsd.org
```
OpenBSD

```
http://www.redhat.com
```
Red Hat Software

```
http://www.sco.com
```
SCO

```
http://www.sgi.com
```
SGI

```
http://www.sun.com
```
Sun Microsystems, Inc.

System Administrator Self-Help and Information

```
http://www.networkweek.com/bofh/story/topStory
```
The adventures of Simon, the Benign Operator we all wish we could be.

```
http://www.unitedmedia.com/comics/dilbert
```
The Dilbert Zone. Everyone needs Dilbert.

```
http://www.cauce.org/
```
The Coalition against Unsolicited Commercial Email. Good people to toss spammers to.

```
http://www2.misnet.com/~wfugitt/unix_ref.html
```
A whacking big categorized list of UNIX-related links.

`http://www.firebringer.net/spam/index.html`

Some more useful anti-spam links.

`alt.sysadmin.recovery`

(Newsgroup) Your world-wide local hotspot for system administration advice, commentary, and commiseration.

Patches

`ftp://ftp.bsdi.com/bsdi/patches`

Patches archive for BSD/OS.

`ftp://ftp.calderasystems.com/pub/openlinux/updates`

`ftp://ftp.calderasystems.com/pub/openlinux/patches`

Updates and patches to OpenLinux are available from these two sites.

`ftp://ftp.us.debian.org/debian/dists/proposed-updates`

FTP archive for security updates to Debian Linux.

`http://www.service.digital.com/patches`

Digital Services Online. You can download publicly available DEC patches from this site.

`http://www.freebsd.org/ports`

FreeBSD Ports page. Upgrade kits for FreeBSD are available here.

`http://us-support.external.hp.com`

HP Electronic Support Center. Patches for HP-UX and other support are available at this site.

`ftp://updates.redhat.com`

An archive of fixes for Red Hat Linux. If you have trouble connecting to this site, check `http://www.redhat.com/mirrors.html` for the mirrors listing.

`http://service.software.ibm.com/support/rs6000`

RS/6000 TechSupport. The latest general and Y2K AIX fixes are available here.

`http://www.openbsd.org/errata.html`

OpenBSD release errata. Patches for OpenBSD are available here.

`ftp://ftp.sco.com/pub/patches`

Recommended and Y2K patches for SCO are available at this site.

E

`ftp://ftp.sco.com/SSE`

System Security Enhancement Area. Download security patches for SCO from this site.

`http://support.sgi.com/member/profile.cgi/Supportfolio/SurfZone`

Apply at this site for your SupportFolio/SurfZone membership. This allows you to access the recommended security and Y2K patches and maintenance stream releases for IRIX.

`http://support.sgi.com/surfzone/patches`

SupportFolio/SurfZone. The site where you can actually download maintenance stream releases and security and Y2K recommended patches.

`http://sunsolve.sun.com`

SunSolve Online. Security, Y2K, and recommended patches are available for SunOS 4.1.3 and later and Solaris 2.3 and later.

Precompiled software

`http://aixpdslib.seas.ucla.edu`

Public Domain Software Library for AIX. An archive of public domain software for AIX.

`ftp://ftp.calderasystems.com/pub/openlinux/contrib`

Site where users contribute freeware packages for Caldera OpenLinux.

`http://www.debian.org/distrib/packages`

Debian GNU/Linux Packages. A variety of software packages is available at this site, free and for a fee, for Debian Linux.

`ftp://ftp.digital.com/rom/freeware-bin`

The online copy of the freeware CD-ROM that comes with the Digital UNIX distribution.

`ftp://ftp.freebsd.org/pub/FreeBSD/ports/ports`

The online copy of the FreeBSD ports available on the FreeBSD CD-ROM.

Check `http://www.freebsd.org/handbook/ports-getting.html` for instructions on installing the ported software. For general information on the FreeBSD ports collection, check `http://www.freebsd.org/handbook/ports.html`.

`http://hpux.ee.ualberta.ca`

The HP-UX Porting and Archive Centre. Archive of precompiled public domain packages to run under HP-UX.

```
http://www.openbsd.org/ports.html
```

OpenBSD Ports Mechanism. Start here to learn about getting ports of third-party software for OpenBSD. This page also contains instructions for installing them.

```
ftp://contrib.redhat.com
```

Archive of user-contributed RPMs (The Red Hat Package Manager) for Red Hat Linux.

```
ftp://developer.redhat.com
```

More RPMs for Red Hat Linux.

```
http://freeware.sgi.com
```

SGI freeware. The online copy of the freeware CD-ROM distributed with IRIX 6.5. Houses precompiled versions of freeware packages to run under IRIX 6.2 and later. Check it every few months.

```
http://www.sunfreeware.com
```

Freeware for Solaris. Home of the Solaris Freeware Project and an archive of precompiled freeware packages to run under Solaris 2.5 through Solaris 7.

Security

```
http://www.cert.org
```

CERT Coordination Center.

```
http://www.cs.purdue.edu/coast
```

Computer Operations, Audit, and Security Technology. A repository of security information and research.

```
http://www.first.org
```

Forum of Incident Response and Security Teams (FIRST). FIRST is an international organization that sponsors the FIRST Conference on Computer Security Incident Handling and Response.

```
http://www.nipc.gov
```

National Infrastructure Protection Center. Especially interesting for the *CyberNotes* publication it produces every two weeks in PDF format. *CyberNotes* includes sections on bugs, holes, patches, recent Exploit scripts, and viruses.

```
http://www.8lgm.org
```

Network ICE's Security Resources page. Also can be accessed through `http://www.netice.com/Advice`. Many security-related links.

E

`http://www.sans.org`

SANS Institute. Sponsors the Conference on *System Administration, Networking and Security* and the Conference on UNIX and NT Network Security. Also provides a wealth of security information, including a glossary of security terms.

`http://www.ssh.fi`

SSH Communications Security. Includes information on the SSH (Secure Shell) protocol and obtaining SSH.

`http://www.deter.com/~unix/`

Assorted software and some philosophical treatises regarding UNIX security and the right or wrong ways of doing things.

Censorship/Intellectual Freedom

`http://www.ala.org`

American Library Association. Of particular interest at this site is the Library Bill of Rights, specifically available at `http://www.ala.org/work/freedom/lbr.html`.

`http://www.eff.org`

Electronic Frontier Foundation. One of the largest shakers and movers in the worlds of UNIX freeware/open source software and online legal rights lobbying.

`http://www.eff.org/CAF/cafuiuc.html`

Computers and Academic Freedom: Sex, Censorship, and the Internet. Good reading on the topic of censorship and why you shouldn't do it.

`http://www.law.cornell.edu`

Legal Information Institute. A vast repository of legal information.

`http://www.mit.edu:8001/activities/safe/notsee.html`

The censor bait site. A site hosted as an experiment to see just how many people really don't believe in the First Amendment to the U.S. Constitution.

UNIX freeware/shareware mentioned in the book

`http://www.gnu.org`

The GNU Project and Free Software Foundation. Home of a vast amount of free useful software.

`http://egcs.cygnus.com`

egcs project home page. Home of the experimental development of GCC (GNU Compiler Collection).

`http://www.mysql.com`

MySQL by T.c.X DataKonsultAB.

`http://www.cpan.org`

Comprehensive Perl Archive Network. The latest version of Perl and other information are available at this site.

`ftp://ftp.porcupine.org/pub/security`

Wietse Venema's FTP archive. Archive of security tools, mostly written by Wietse Venama, author of TCP Wrapper, and his papers.

`http://www.sendmail.org`

Sendmail home page. The latest version of sendmail is available from this site. Includes a lot of information on compiling and configuring sendmail.

`http://www.washington.edu/pine`

Pine Information Center. The latest version of Pine, *Program for Internet News and Email,* is available here.

`http://www.math.fu-berlin.de/~guckes/elm`

The Elm Mail System.The source for the latest version of Elm and Elm information.

`http://www.procmail.org`

Procmail home page. The source for the latest version of procmail, a powerful mail filter.

`http://eudora.qualcomm.com/freeware/qpop.html`

Qpopper home page. The latest version of qpopper, a POP mail server, is available here.

`http://www.washington.edu/imap`

IMAP Information Center. The University of Washington *Internet Message Access Protocol* (IMAP) server is available at this site.

`http://www.imap.org`

The IMAP Connection. A source of information on IMAP.

`ftp://ftp.vr.net/pub/wu-ftpd/wu-ftpd`

WU-FTPD Server Software. The latest version of wu-ftpd is available here.

`http://home.netscape.com/download`

Netscape products. The latest version of the Netscape Web browser is available here or at `ftp.netscape.com`.

`http://www.apache.org`

Apache Server Project. Home of the Apache Web server. The latest version and a lot of information on Apache are available at this site.

`http://www.slcc.edu/lynx`

SLCC Lynx pages. The latest version of Lynx, a nongraphical Web browser, is available here.

`http://www.statslab.cam.ac.uk/~sret1/analog`

Analog: WWW logfile analysis. The home of Analog, a popular Web statistics package.

`http://www.netstore.de/Supply/http-analyze`

http-analyze—Log analyzer for Web servers. The source for another Web statistics package, http-analyze. Free for personal or educational use.

`http://www.nihongo.org/snowhare/utilities/browsercounter.html`

BrowserCounter, a Perl script that produces summaries of what browsers people used to view your site, is available here.

`http://www.umich.edu/~rsug/netatalk`

The latest version of netatalk, an AppleTalk server, is ava.

`http://www.cs.mu.oz.au/appletalk/cap.html`

Information on where to get Columbia AppleTalk Package (CAP), an AppleTalk server, and how to install it.

`ftp://munnari.oz.au/mac`

UAR, *Unix AppleTalk Router,* is available for download here. UAR can be used in conjunction with CAP.

`http://samba.org`

From here you can pick the closest mirror site to view the Samba Web pages, where you can find the latest version of Samba, documentation, and other information.

`http://www.groupsys.com/topinfo`

Home of top, the utility that produces displays of the CPU usage of your machine.

`http://www.scriptics.com`

Scriptics: The Tcl Platform Company. The latest open source Tcl/Tk packages are available from this site, as well as other Tcl/Tk information.

```
http://expect.nist.gov
```

The Expect home page. The latest version of Expect and information on Expect is available at this site.

```
http://www.andante.org/mkisofs.html
```

The latest version of mkisofs, a tool that makes an ISO9660 file system to be used for recording a CD-ROM, is available here.

```
http://www.fokus.gmd.de/research/cc/glone/employees/joerg.schillig/
➥private/cdrecord.html
```

Cdrecord release information. Get the latest version of cdrecord, a utility for recording CD-ROMs.

```
http://www.emacs.org
```

Welcome to emacs.org. Houses a wealth of information on emacs.

```
ftp://ftp.astron.com/pub/tcsh
```

The latest version of tcsh, an enhanced csh, is available from this archive.

```
http://www.flash.net/~marknu/less
```

The less home page. Offers the latest version of less, a more robust pager than more.

```
http://www.tug.org
```

TeX Users Group home page. Information on TeX and LaTeX is available here.

```
http://ctan.org
```

Comprehensive TeX Archive Network. A vast repository of TeX information.

```
http://www.cs.wisc.edu/~ghost
```

Ghostscript, Ghostview, and Gsview. Ghostscript and Ghostview, a PostScript and PDF interpreter package and its X11 user interface, are available here. There are two versions of each: Aladdin and GNU. The difference between them is in licensing. GSview is for OS/2 and Windows.

```
http://www.gimp.org
```

The GIMP home page. Download the latest version of the GNU image-manipulation program, freely available photo retouching, and imagemaking software from this site.

```
http://www.trilon.com/xv
```

John's World of XV'n'Stuff. The latest version of xv, an image-display program, is available here.

E

`http://www.wizards.dupont.com/cristy/ImageMagick.html`

ImageMagick - X11 Image Processing and Display Package. The home of the ImageMagick suite.

`ftp://ftp.x.org/contrib/applications/drawing_tools/xfig`

The drawing tool XFIG is available for download from this archive.

`http://www.xfig.org`

XFIG drawing program for X Window System. A repository of information on the XFIG program.

`http://www.povray.org`

POV-Ray—the Persistence of Vision Raytracer. Home of the POV-Ray raytracer.

`http://www.bmrt.org`

Blue Moon Rendering Tools home page. The latest version of BMRT, a collection of RenderMan compliant tools, is available at this site.

Commercial software mentioned in the book

`http://www.easysw.com`

ESP Software sells a program called ESP print, which makes configuring printers for IRIX, Solaris, and HP-UX a more pleasant experience.

`http://www.datafellows.com`

Data Fellows makes F-Secure Tunnel and Terminal client software for the Mac and PC to access machines running the SSH server. Data Fellows also sells the commercial version of the SSH server.

`http://www.tenon.com`

Tenon Intersystems sells XTen, an X Windows server for the Mac.

`http://www.wpine.com`

White Pine Software sells another X Windows server for the Mac, eXodus.

`http://www.hummingbird.com`

Hummingbird Communications sells Exceed, an X Windows server for the PC.

`http://www.boutell.com/wusage`

Wusage home page. The commercial Web server statistics package, Wusage, is available from this site.

`http://www.netstore.de/Supply/http-analyze`

http-analyze—Log analyzer for Web servers. This Web server statistics package, http-analyze, free for personal and education use, is available commercially for other uses.

```
http://www.pixar.com
```

Pixar Animation Studios offers RenderMan products.

Macintosh

```
http://www.apple.com
```

Apple Computer, Inc. Macintosh product information and a searchable Tech Library.

```
http://www.macintouch.com
```

MacInTouch home page. Check this site regularly for the latest Macintosh news.

```
http://www.macfixit.com
```

MacFixIt. Check this site for Mac troubleshooting information when your Macintosh is sick.

```
http://www.mklinux.apple.com
```

MkLinux: Linux for the Power Macintosh. Provides some information on the Linux variant for the Macintosh.

PC

```
http://www.microsoft.com
```

Microsoft Corporation. Windows product information. Also enables you to search for technical information such as the SMB/CIFS specs.

Web

```
http://www.patents.com/weblaw.sht
```

Web Law FAQ. Addresses issues such as whether you can use images from other Web sites; whether you can copy material from other Web sites; whether MIDI, WAV, and MP3 files violate copyright law; and so on.

```
http://www.ncsa.uiuc.edu/General/Internet/WWW/HTMLPrimer.html
```

A Beginner's Guide to HTML. NCSA's HTML primer provides a good beginning to understanding HTML.

```
http://info.med.yale.edu/caim/manual/contents.html
```

Yale Style Manual. A site devoted to the basics of Web site design.

```
http://www.iumj.indiana.edu/texonweb.html
```

TeX on the Web provides information on publishing your TeX documents on the Web.

```
http://java.sun.com
```

Java Technology home page. Sun's Java information site.

E

`http://www.gamelan.com`

The Official Java Directory. A repository of Java information.

`http://www.acm.org/sigweb`

SIGWEB. Home of the ACM (Association for Computing Machinery) Special Interest Group on Hypertext, Hypermedia, and Web. Includes information on various conferences and workshops, as well as links to other resources.

`http://www.siggraph.org`

ACM SIGGRAPH. Home of the ACM Special Interest Group on Computer Graphics. Although this interest group is concerned with the technical details of computer graphics, it does sponsor an annual conference that will give you a memorable, visual experience. You may have an interest in graphics only as they relate to the Web, or you may only have an interest in finding a good deal on computing power. In any case, this conference can be fun, even if you don't know a thing about computer graphics.

Miscellaneous

`http://www.acm.org`

Association for Computing Machinery. Home of the organization with the SIGWEB and SIGGRAPH groups.

`http://www.zdevents.com`

ZD Events, Inc. Check this site for news on various conferences, such as COMDEX, NetWorld+Interop, and Seybold. Many are likely to have vendors selling their wares.

Miscellaneous vendors

`http://www.bestpower.com`

Best Power Uninterruptible Power Systems. The manufacturer to consider if you decide to buy a UPS.

`http://www.thechipmerchant.com`

The Chip Merchant, Inc. A source for reasonably-priced Mac and PC memory.

`http://www.memoryx.com`

MemoryX. A source of memory for Sun Microsystems and other computers.

```
http://www.mti.com
```

MTI Technology Corporation. A reputable supplier of storage devices. You aren't going to get the cheapest deal, because you also pay for the guarantee that if it breaks, MTI will replace it immediately.

References

Lynch, Patrick J., and Sarah Horton. *Web Style Guide: Basic Design Principles for Creating Web Sites.* Yale University Press, 1999.

Nemeth, Evi, Garth Snyder, Scott Seebass, and Trent R. Hein. *UNIX System Administration Handbook.* Prentice Hall, 1995.

Frisch, Aeleen. *Essential System Administration: Help for UNIX System Administrators.* O'Reilly & Associates, 1996.

Hunt, Craig. *TCP/IP Network Administration.* Edited by Gigi Estrabrook. O'Reilly & Associates, 1998.

Costales, Bryan, and Eric Allman. *Sendmail.* Edited by Gigi Estabrook. O'Reilly & Associates, 1997.

Ray, William. *Sams Teach Yourself UNIX in 10 Minutes.* Sams Publishing, 1999.

Ray, John. *Special Edition Using TCP/IP.* Que Corporation, 1999.

Chapman, D. Brent, and Elizabeth D. Zwicky. *Building Internet Firewalls.* Edited by Deborah Russell. O'Reilly & Associates, 1995.

Cheswick, William R., and Steven M. Bellovin. *Firewalls and Internet Security: Repelling the Wily Hacker.* Addison-Wesley, 1994.

E

APPENDIX F

Useful Sample Forms

You may copy the samples provided in this appendix and modify them to suit your needs. Space has been left at the top of the Policy and Account forms so that you can copy them onto your letterhead or add information as needed.

Guidelines for System Security Requirements

Security Policy

Users who want to use corporate computing resources or network resources agree that they have read and understand the following:

A breach of system or network security is any attempt to connect to, view data on, or otherwise access computing resources without authorization. This includes, but is not limited to, use of computer facilities or network facilities without an account or authorization, accessing files belonging to other users without the written consent of said user, and authorized use of facilities for purposes outside the intent of the authorization. An action that causes a breach of system or network security constitutes a direct violation of corporate computing security policy. Employees found to have willfully violated corporate computing security policies will be remanded to corporate disciplinary affairs.

Account security on the facility UNIX machines is the responsibility of the account holder. Passwords are not to be shared. Passwords are not to be written down or otherwise recorded. Loaning passwords to other users is considered a direct breach of system security and is grounds for immediate revocation of your account. Discovery of recorded copies of passwords also indicates a direct breach of system security and will be dealt with in the same manner.

Non-UNIX machines attached to the building network:

Execution of system-crashing or system-compromising software such as (but not limited to) "Win-nuke," "Bitch-slap," and "Nestea" is grounds for removal of a system from the building network. This constitutes electronic vandalism and/or theft of service and subjects the person executing the software to potential legal liability. The facility staff will provide any assistance necessary to track and prosecute anyone found to be conducting such attacks.

Collection of network traffic that is not destined for the user and the machine in use (via, but not limited to, such methods as packet sniffers and ARP (Address Resolution Protocol) spoofing) constitutes grounds for removal of a system from the building network. Collection of network traffic without court authorization or without a direct and immediate need to diagnose network problems constitutes execution of an illegal wire tap. Users should be comfortable that their data and electronic transactions are secure against eavesdropping.

Additionally, users can be assured that the facility staff will not intercept network traffic without legal authorization or an immediate need to diagnose an existing network problem.

Execution of port-scanning software or other software that attempts to discern or determine vulnerabilities in UNIX or non-UNIX hardware without facility staff approval will not be tolerated. Execution of such software is considered an attempt to breach system security and will be dealt with as such.

Users will not run FTP, HTTP, or other data servers that provide illegal data (commercial software or other illegal data types). The facility staff cannot and will not attempt to police the building network for such behavior, but reports of copyright infringement or other illegal behavior will be forwarded to the appropriate authorities.

Users will not run software designed to provide unintended gateways into services that are intended to have a limited scope. Depending on the service and the manner in which the service is gatewayed to unintended users, execution of such software may constitute theft of service. The facility staff cannot and will not attempt to police the network for the execution of such software but will cooperate fully in any investigation brought by users whose services have been compromised.

UNIX machines:

Execution of software similar in purpose to any of the software detailed in the "Non-UNIX" section will be dealt with in the same manner as detailed above, and/or a user's account will be terminated without recourse.

Execution of password-cracking software against the computational facility password database is considered an attempt to breach system security and will be dealt with as such.

The use of .rhosts files or other methods of circumventing connection-authentication procedures is a direct violation of security policy. Users with a documented need for .rhosts connection capabilities may apply to the facility administration for a written exception.

Users who want to install UNIX machines on the building network can do this in two ways:

i. Machines that are considered by the computational facility System Manager to be of general use and interest to the facility at large may, at the discretion of the System Manager, be set up as part of the facility. Machines handled in this fashion

F

will be administered by the facility staff as full peers in the facility UNIX cluster, and system security will be handled through the facility staff. Machines administered in this fashion remain the property of their respective owners and are to be considered primarily intended for the use of their owners. As full peers of the facility UNIX cluster, these machines may be used by other facility users (at least remotely) when they are not fully used by their owners.

Security for these machines will be handled in the same manner as security for all computational facility UNIX cluster machines. Users can be assured that all reasonable security precautions have been taken and that known potential security problems will be dealt with in a timely fashion.

If a security violation occurs involving one of these machines, it will be dealt with by the computational facility staff and should not require significant time or effort from the owner of the machine.

ii.   Machines that are to be administered by their owners or their owners' assignees will be maintained at a level of security at a minimum in compliance with the requirements in this document and with security guidelines as defined by the computational facility staff.

Violations of policy laid down in this document are to be dealt with as defined in this document. Requirements for account maintenance and termination will be strictly enforced.

Administration security guidelines will be based on current security problems as reported by corporate network security and the online security community. These guidelines will be provided by the computational facility staff on a set of Web pages dedicated to building network security. It is expected that administrators will bring their machines into compliance with the guidelines within seven (7) days of the guidelines being posted.

Computational Facility staff will keep a database of independently administrated UNIX hardware and administrators, and the administrators will be notified immediately when guidelines are updated.

Periodic scans of the building network for known security problems will be conducted by computational facility staff. Results will be made available to administrators of self-administrated machines as soon as the data is available. Facility machines will be protected against any vulnerabilities found by facility staff. Independently administered machines will be brought into compliance by their respective administrators. Failure to bring a machine into compliance will result in the machine being removed from the building network.

Due to the usual speed at which security problems occur and their potential for rapid damage, plus the fact they mostly occur during off hours:

- Computational facility staff may require physical access to any computing or network hardware in the building at any time. To facilitate such, master keys for access will be provided in a sealed package in the facility safe. Access to these keys will be logged, justification given, and the party whose area requires access will be notified immediately upon opening this sealed package.

- Computational facility staff may require administrative access to any computing hardware in the building at any time. To facilitate such, administrators of independent machines will provide to the computational facility staff root or other appropriate administrative passwords, which must be kept sealed unless needed in a crisis. Independent administrators will keep these passwords up to date at all times. Access to these passwords will be logged, justification given, and appropriate administrators notified immediately if use of these sealed passwords is required.

- Responsibility and authority for the maintenance of security guidelines and for the definition of and action upon network security threats lie with the computational facility System Manager. If the System Manager is not, or is unavailable to be, administrating the facility UNIX cluster, the responsibility and authority pass to the facility UNIX cluster Lead System Administrator. Facility assistant administration staff have the authority to deal with immediate crisis situations as necessary until the Lead System Administrator can be contacted.

Effective Date:

F

Application for UNIX account

Name: _____ ID#: _____
        First   (Please print)   Last

Department: _____

Position: _____

Supervisor: _____

Office address: _____

_____

Office phone: _____

Home address: _____

_____

_____

Home phone: _____

Most frequently used email address: _____

Intended use of system: _____

_____

Projected duration of need: _____

Read and sign below:

The computational support cluster on which you are applying for an account is a facility operated to support the corporate mission. Your account on the system is made available for work-related purposes. Because system resources are limited, users must work in a cooperative manner. Excessive use of the system for storage of personal files, or for non-authorized computing purposes will be frowned upon both by the administration and users. You account security is your personal responsibility -- choose a secure password and do not loan it or use of your account to anybody.

Abuse of the system will not be tolerated and is grounds for revocation of your account.

Signature: _____ Date: _____

Supervisor's signature: _____ Date: _____

Please return this form to:

Failure to complete all portions of this form is grounds for rejection of request.

Office Use Only:	Date Recd: _____	Date Filled: _____	ADM: _____
User Name _____		UID # _____	GID # _____
Home Path _____			
Initial Pass _____			

Drive Partioning Sheet

General Information

Host name: _____

Drive and Manufacturer Model: _____

Cylinders _____ Tracks _____ Sectors _____ Heads _____

Location: ___ Internal ___ External

SCSI ID: ___ SCSI controller: ___ Capacity: _____

Partitions

part	type/tag	flag	cylinders	blocks	size	mount pt

F

Host Information Sheet

General Information

Host name: _____

Manufacturer and Model: _____

Architecture: _____

Operating System: _____

Serial number: _____

System number: _____

Location: _____

Network Information

IP Address: _____

Default Route: _____

Netmask: _____

Domain Name: _____

NIS Information

Function: ___ Server   ___ Slave   ___ Client   ___ None

NIS domain name: _____

APPENDIX G

Quiz Answers

Day 1, "What Is System Administration?"

1. **Why does a UNIX system need a system administrator?**

   A UNIX system is a very complex and powerful system that usually is connected to the Internet. The power available makes UNIX a popular system for high-end server systems, but the complexity makes it unlikely that the normal user will completely understand the system. The additional factors of connectivity and multiple simultaneous users make competent administration a must for the smooth operation of the machine and the protection of users both local and worldwide.

2. **Why does root access carry more responsibility on a UNIX machine than on your own personal computer?**

   UNIX root access carries significantly more responsibility because root users have access to—and are believed to be trustworthy with—the account contents of potentially hundreds of users. The fact that system administrators expect a certain level of accountability and trustworthiness from other system administrators adds weight to this responsibility.

3. **Assuming that you have settled into your new office space a bit, and that you have inherited a UNIX cluster already in place, what are some of the things you might do on your first day on the job?**

   Investigate your system's hardware and software configuration. Take a walk around your business and try to get to know your users. Try to find all of the documentation for the programs that are on your machines.

4. **You have just become root to take care of a certain task, and the phone rings. What do you do?**

   Log off, or at least lock the screen. Never leave yourself logged in as root. An open terminal with a running root login is a recipe for disaster. Even if you lock the terminal, you run the risk of forgetting you're root in that window when you next use it and entering a command as root that could be unfortunate.

5. **It turns out that the call was from a user who has forgotten her password and would like to know if you can tell her what it is so that she can log in again. How do you respond?**

   Have her come to your office with identification. After you verify her identification, change her password to a known value and immediately expire it. The password data is encrypted so that even you cannot decrypt it to learn the password (and this is a good thing). The best you can do for the user is to set the password to a new value and have her change it to a value of her choice immediately.

Day 2, "Designing Your Cluster: From Planning to Policy"

1. **Why do you need written policy documents?**

   Without a written policy, you are obliged to make decisions on a case-by-case basis, using only your judgement. Your judgement may be very good, but unless you put your policy in writing, you will be accused of applying it inconsistently, and of preferential treatment or discrimination. Written policy gives you a stable and consistent platform from which to make administrative decisions.

2. **True or false: A good policy document provides the opportunity for administrator judgement in its enforcement.**

   False. A good policy document should provide relatively complete coverage of situations and enforcement decisions. You may feel that giving yourself leeway to make personal calls regarding enforcement is a good idea, but it can lead to considerable political trouble in your office.

3. **A good administrator always takes what into consideration when making policies and decisions?**

   The worst possible case scenario. If you're prepared for the worst, you can handle anything else. Some version of "the worst" almost inevitably happens to every administrator, and if you don't plan for it, you can't be prepared.

4. **What is your first action in the case of a system security breach?**

   Usually, secure your machines to prevent damage. Your responsibility, except in special situations, is to keep your machines up and running for your users. Searching out and destroying whoever had the gall to attack your system will be high on your list of personal responses when this happens, but if you're not specifically on a cracker hunt, simply securing your machines is a wiser course of action.

Day 3, "Setting Up a Machine: From the Box to the Desktop"

No quiz.

Day 4, "A Stroll Through Your System"

1. **What's the root of the filesystem?**

   The top-level directory for that filesystem. For an entire machine, the root-level directory is the directory /, but each physical partition has a root directory that is the root of that filesystem as well. If any given drive were mounted as the only drive, its root level directory would be the system root directory. Mounted as a subdirectory somewhere in the overall filesystem, the root-level directory for a particular partition is the directory at which it is mounted.

2. **How do you find out what processes are running?**

   Use the `ps` command. Depending on the operating system you are running, `ps -augxww`, `ps -auxww`, or `ps -elf` should give you the complete listing of all the processes your machine is running.

3. **How do you find out what users are using your machine?**

   The `w` or `who` command is a good place to start. The `last` command gives information on who was on when, and the `ps` command showing all processes can give you information on running processes that don't show a user connected to any normal service.

G

4. **How do you get rid of a process that you want stopped?**

   Use the `kill` command. `kill -9 <process id>` should do the trick. If a process is stuck waiting for certain types of system activity, even a `kill -9` will not stop the process immediately. This is normal behavior—the process will go away when the activity it's waiting for finishes. On some systems, `kill -9 -1` kills all processes belonging to the current user—a great way to remove a user's presence from a system, and a very bad thing to do as root.

5. **Where are your executables coming from?**

   Try `echo $path` to find the answer. Also, `which <command>` gives you information on the location of `<command>` in particular.

Day 5, "On Root's Best Behavior"

No quiz.

Day 6, "Deciding What Kind of Software to Install: Free Versus Commercial"

1. **How is UNIX "freeware" different from freeware in the personal computer world?**

   UNIX "freeware," for all intents and purposes in this book, means the many completely free programs. You should keep in mind that you won't find this to be a universal naming convention. To most UNIX users, regular software is generally free, and the exceptional few pieces that cost money are thought of as "commercial software."

2. **Say that you wrote a useful utility script to scan backup tape inventories to determine what filesystem they belong to. What should you do with it after you get it working?**

   The UNIX community is unique in that it has an extremely strong spirit of cooperation among its user base. Traditionally, when UNIX users write a useful piece of software, they make it available to other users in the community. Large pieces of software are frequently adopted by entire groups of volunteer developers who spend their own free time and resources keeping the software up-to-date. So, share your scripts with your fellow users!

Day 7, "The Most Important Accessory: The C Compiler gcc"

1. **What command do you use to compile a program?**

   Use cc if you're stuck with your system's C compiler; use gcc after you install the GNU compiler.

2. **What is the first thing you do when you have a new package to install?**

   Read the README file!

3. **What do you do if a compile results in a "Fatal Error"?**

   Examine the error. If it's a missing library routine, see whether you can find the appropriate library to link in. You can use the nm *<library name>* command to list the names of all routines contained in the library *<library name>*. When you're more comfortable with UNIX and installing software, this won't be as intimidating as it may sound. If it's not a missing library, you're probably looking at a syntax error in the code—not something you want to try to fix—or a problem with the makefile. You can try using GNU's version of make, making sure all leading white space in the makefile is tabs, and switching your C compiler from or to gcc. If the program is distributed on the Internet, chances are some combination of these changes will be helpful.

4. **True or False: A "Segmentation Fault" is a bad thing.**

   A trick question! A segmentation fault indicates that the operating system decided that your program tried to step outside the memory that had been allocated to it. This kills the program, so from the point of view of running the program, a segmentation fault is a bad thing. However, segmentation faults are caused to prevent the program from twiddling bits of memory that don't belong to it, causing potentially unpredictable behavior. From the point of view of system stability, a segmentation fault is a good thing.

Day 8, "Adding Basic Devices"

1. **What does the author think of System V's general way of doing things?**

   Not too highly, and thank you for asking! System V has some nice features and tries very hard to make some things as convenient as possible for the system administrator and users. Unfortunately, other things in most System V implementations seem to have been done not for the good of the users or the stability of the system, but because it was a good "marketing" decision. Unfortunately, what sells machines to nonuser corporate higher-ups frequently isn't related to anything that makes machines more useful for your users or more stable for you.

G

2. **If your drive has 12 platters, how many heads is it likely to have?**

   It probably has 23 usable heads. The 24th head will be reserved for tracking and timing data. Some older drives might have 21 or 22 heads because some older mechanisms didn't use the far outside platter surfaces or used them only for tracking information.

3. **If you have a network printer already installed and want to configure BSD printing, the following is true:**

   a. **Life is good.**

   b. **It's time for a change of career.**

   c. **Be prepared for long nights and learn to like coffee.**

   a. Life is good. All you need to do is install a `printcap` entry with an `rm` (remote machine) defined printer, and chances are everything will work just fine.

4. **If you have a band printer (you do remember band-printers, don't you? The "antique" impact line-printers that printed at rates in the pages-per-second on fanfold paper?) and want to configure System V printing to use it, the following is true:**

   a. **Life is good.**

   b. **It's time for a change of career.**

   c. **Be prepared for long nights and learn to like coffee.**

   b. It's time for a change of career. Band printers are great tools if you need very fast text printing, but most of these available today are legacy hardware or are found only with mainframes. Attempting to configure System V's `lp` printing system to work with a printer that doesn't come with from-the-manufacturer drivers for your operating system is nearly impossible.

5. **If you have an HPGL printer (an alternative graphics language to PostScript for printer page imaging) and want to make it available in a BSD environment, the following is true:**

   a. **Life is good.**

   b. **It's time for a change of career.**

   c. **Be prepared for long nights and learn to like coffee.**

c. Be prepared for long nights and learn to like coffee. If the device can be printed to, it can be used from BSD. You might need to get the technical specs and write your own driver that sends whatever hexadecimal codes configure the printer and that translates PostScript into HPGL, but after you've written these, you can configure the `lpd` system to use what you've written.

Day 9, "What About Security?"

No quiz.

Day 10, "Defending Your Machines and Encrypting Traffic"

1. Where do you look to turn off services on your machine?

Look in `/etc/inetd.conf` and in whatever serves as your `rc` file or files—`/etc/rc.local`, `/etc/rc.*`, `/etc/init.d/rc*.d/*`, and `/etc/rc*.d` seem to be popular places.

2. Is it a good idea to leave on a service that provides support of a networked multiplayer game?

Is it a mission priority for your cluster? If not, you're providing a potential security hole as well as a multiplayer game server. Finding a personal computer to use to run your game server is a smarter choice.

3. What do you always do with configuration files before you make changes to them?

Save a backup copy. Don't risk making an edit that you can't figure out how to undo at some future date.

4. Why is it important to turn off Telnet?

Telnet data is carried in clear text. If you don't turn off Telnet, everything your users type, including their logins and passwords, is transmitted across the network in a format that can be sniffed by anyone with a personal computer or another UNIX box.

5. Why don't you put `sshd` in `/etc/inetd.conf`?

The `/etc/inetd.conf` file is used to start services that start each time a connection comes in. The `sshd` daemon runs continuously, accepting connections and spawning children as necessary, so it doesn't need to be put in `inetd.conf`. As a matter of fact, if you want to make a very tightly protected machine, after `sshd` is

G

installed, you can even remove your `inetd.conf` file completely. You still will be able to access the machine by `ssh`, but all `inetd` services will be disabled.

Day 11, "Making Your Machines Communicate with Each Other: NIS and NFS"

1. Where do you specify disk export information?

`/etc/exports` or `/etc/dfs/dfstab`

2. As a paranoid system administrator, do you think NFS is secure?

No! No way, no how! Unfortunately, a secure, widely available way of sharing files over the network is not available, so you're sort of stuck with NFS for now. Thankfully, NFS doesn't seem to be one of the highly popular points of sniffing attack, although the mounting daemon has had vulnerabilities.

3. If your drive doesn't mount, what's the first thing you should do?

Check to see whether it's turned on and spinning. Next check your log entries, and make sure you have all the correct permissions set for which machines can access the drive.

4. Given its obvious security implications, why do we put up with NIS?

Because if we don't, we relegate our wonderful UNIX machines to being little more than glorified personal computers. The cluster-wide integration and cohesion of account information is one of the things that makes UNIX such a useful system. Replacing NIS with something more secure would be a great idea, but there are so many more easily broken services that it doesn't seem to be high on the cracker's lists, leaving us to continue using it until the next great thing comes along.

5. A user has changed their password, but can't use the new password to log on. What's wrong?

They can't type? (Seriously, I had a user spend two weeks fuming that something was wrong with her account because she couldn't log in using her new password, and I had left town for a conference and vacation. When I returned, she was completely irate at the fact that I had given her an incorrect password, but on attempting to demonstrate that it was incorrect, she logged in with no problem. It turns out she hadn't bothered to try retyping it after the initial failure.) If that's not the problem, your NIS maps may not have been pushed yet. This should be handled automatically by your root crontab, but you can do it manually as well by `cd`-ing to your NIS/YP directory and issuing the `make` command.

Day 12, "The Basics of Making User Accounts"

1. **How do you lock a user account so that he can't log in?**

   Place an asterisk (*) in the password field in /etc/password and push the NIS maps. For good record-keeping practices, you might consider putting an asterisk in the field, along with a note explaining when and why you locked the account.

2. **What's the first thing you should do after assigning a password to a new account?**

   Expire the password so that the user is forced to change it on his next login.

3. **Why do you need to create the passwd file entry before taking care of the user directory?**

   So that you can change ownership of the directory to belong to the correct user after you've created it. Additionally, this procedure gives you the opportunity to make certain that you aren't duplicating a username or home directory name.

4. **A user who is over quota can or cannot log in to the machine?**

   The user can log in but cannot write anything to disk if her grace period has expired or if she's attempted to exceed her hard limit. Don't let users or managers put roadblocks in the way of quotas by claiming that quotas prevent logins. Quotas only prevent the unfair overuse of resources by some users.

Day 13, "Saving Your World: Making Backups to Tape"

1. **Say it's now Friday of Week 3. Also, say that Friday's daily dump was done early in the morning. As soon as you get in, one of your users tells you that he was logged in Thursday evening to do some work, he accidentally deleted the contents of one of his directories, and he wants to know if you might be able to restore his data for him. To what state can you restore his account?**

   You can restore the directory to the state it was in when you did your Thursday daily dump. Your Friday dump was done after the damage, so it will be of no help.

2. **You've completely confused your dump schedule and can't figure out what's going to go on any dump you make. You can easily create a known state for your world by doing what?**

   Do a level-zero dump. A full dump of the system will back up everything, and the next dump you do will be based on changes since this one. Remember to keep better track of what you've done and when in the future!

G

3. **A user needs a directory restored to the condition it was in on a particular date in the past. Without knowing the details of your dump schedule, what tapes do you need to pull?**

   You must pull the full, monthly, weekly, and daily (if you have each of those levels) tapes that most closely precede the date in question. Remember that each dump level builds on the previous, so if there are files in the directory that haven't been changed at all since the full dump, you'll need to get those from there, but files that were changed just before the deletion will require you to go to the daily. Restore each tape in order, from oldest to newest, to rebuild the directory to the condition it was in at the time of the most recent daily dump before the date needed.

4. **Are you going to need as many tapes for each of the higher-level dumps as you do for the full dumps?**

   You won't need as much space on the tapes because the full dumps save everything, and the others only save things that have changed. It's your choice, however, whether you use separate tapes for each partition's daily dumps; or one tape for all dailies for a month; or one tape per machine for monthlies, weeklies, and dailies, or...the list could go on and on.

Day 14, "Other Useful Software: Useful Utilities"

1. Suppose it has been decided that your new machine will become the Web server. You have installed the latest Perl in /usr/local/bin/perl, and the latest version of Apache, a Web server, on the machine. (As a matter of fact, you will look at installing a Web server on Day 17, "WWW Connectivity: Netscape, Apache, Statistics.") After you are finished with your installations, but before you make the new machine the official Web server machine for your facility, you decide that it might be a good idea to verify that some of the main pages that rely on some Perl code working properly still work. So you start Netscape on your PC and try to load one of the pages, but you get an error page instead. Fortunately the error page suggests that you might want to look at the error_log for more details. On looking at the log, you see the following:

```
[Wed Jun 30 10:01:40 1999] [error] (2)No such file or
➥directory: exec of
/net/suzie/usr/people/kyoko/public_html/diagnostic.cgi
➥failed
[Wed Jun 30 10:01:40 1999] [error] [client 140.254.12.124]
➥Premature end
of script headers: /net/suzie/usr/people/kyoko/public_html/
➥diagnostic.cgi
```

You don't really understand the error messages, but you understand enough to suspect that there must be something wrong with the Perl script that Web server is trying to access. Here are the first few lines of that script:

```
#!/opt/bin/perl

if (-f "/usr/local/apache/cgi-bin/johnclient.pl") { require
➥'/usr/local/apache/cgi-bin/johnclient.pl';
 }
```

What should you check?

The very first line of the Perl script (`#!/opt/bin/perl`) tells the system that it should look for the Perl interpreter in `/opt/bin/perl`. But the question indicates that you've just installed Perl in `usr/local/bin/perl`!

The CGI program will fail. You must either change all the Perl scripts to correct for the location of the Perl interpreter (for example, change `#!/opt/bin/perl` to `#!/usr/local/bin/perl`) or create a symbolic link to point from `/opt/bin/perl` to `/usr/local/bin/perl`. (Creating the link would help you avoid the headache of worrying whether you've successfully located all the scripts and pondering whether all the users have been alerted to the new location of Perl.) To create a symbolic link, first make sure that the directory `/opt/bin` exists (you might have to first create `/opt` and then `/opt/bin`). Next, you must execute `ln -s /usr/local/bin/perl /opt/bin/perl`. No more worries!

While you are creating symbolic links, you might want to make a link from `/usr/bin/perl` as well. A lot of preconfigured scripts that users can find on the Internet have that as the location of Perl, as in the following:

```
ln -s /usr/local/bin/perl /usr/bin/perl
```

2. **For what reasons is the MySQL package recommended to be installed as a precompiled binary?**

The installation of MySQL is a rather unfriendly task—nothing at all like that of Perl. There are dozens of manual pages discussing the MySQL installation alone. If you don't plan to modify the C and C++ code for MySQL, installing a binary distribution should be sufficient. Many platforms are supported, and it's a lot easier to put together than trying to work from a source distribution. If there is a binary already available for your platform, definitely install that!

3. **What is required to use Perl to access a MySQL database?**

To access MySQL using Perl, you'll need to get the following Perl modules (all available at `ftp.cpan.org`):

- Data-Dumper (if you have Perl 5.004_71 or later, it is part of the standard distribution)
- DBI

G

- Data-ShowTable
- Msql-Mysql

Days 15–19

No quizzes.

Day 20, "How to Be a Good System Administrator"

1. **Your co-worker has just told you a great joke. Then he claims to have seen it in one of the user's mailboxes as he looked through users' mail when he was bored. What action should you take?**

   You should immediately inform your superior and let him make the appropriate decision(s); if you are it, you need to take any and all action(s) required of you and mandated in rules and regulations for your facility. (You do have rules and regulations, right?) Failing to do either of those two actions makes you an accomplice to a crime! Remember, I talked about how law enables you to intercept and view users' mail if, and only if, your duties require you to—not because it amuses you!

2. **You start getting an increasing number of complaints from users on the Internet that they are receiving unsolicited mail, and that the mail is being routed through your mail server. What should you do about it?**

   First, let me say what you should not do! You should not simply ignore these complaints. If you do, your mail server is likely to become blacklisted by an increasing number of mail servers around the Internet. This would result in your own users being unable to send messages to their peers around the globe. In turn, that would mean that because of your own actions (or lack thereof) you've failed your user community. Wouldn't that be just the opposite of what your goals should be?

   Now, what you should do is take action! Start with identifying the source of mail: Is it local or remote? If local, take actions set forth in your rules and regulations. Otherwise, inform your counterpart at the remote source. If complaining users request a response or if you deem it would be appropriate to do so, let them know what actions you've taken. Finally, as a service to the Internet community and your users (and because it is your job), you should do what you can to prevent similar abuse in the future.

3. **What should you do once you are finished with this book?**

Make sure to read Chapter 20 again. It will help you avoid potentially dangerous pitfalls you might encounter at your new job as a UNIX system administrator.

Day 21, "Troubleshooting"

1. **What things should you check even before the logs when you have problems with peripheral hardware?**

Diagnosing hardware problems can be a somewhat arduous task. Before reading through log after log, you should always ask yourself a few questions:

- Is the hardware on? Is the power cord plugged in to both the device and the wall? Is the power switch in the "on" position? Does the power light indicate that the power is on? Is the fan spinning? Has the fuse blown?

- Is the hardware hooked up? Is the interface cable plugged in? At both ends? Are the locking latches or screws tightened down? Is it actually plugged in to the socket it's supposed to be plugged in to?

- Is the hardware running? Does it look like it's running? Does it feel like it's running? Does it sound like it's running? If it's a disk, is it spinning? If it's a printer, will it print its test page? If it has LEDs, does it have a startup diagnostic, and what does it say?

2. **My disk drive found a bunch of new "bad blocks" recently. Is it safe to keep using it?**

If bad blocks are appearing, chances are good that you're seeing the beginning of the end for the drive. Be certain that mission-critical data isn't being stored on it. You never know when it will take the opportunity to die.

3. **My disk drives are new, supposedly super-reliable mechanisms, but they keep dying. Why might that be?**

Get out your thermometer! The problem could be temperature-related. High-performance drives are notorious for giving off a tremendous amount of heat, and you can decrease your machine's internal temperature significantly by externally relocating the drives. Another approach is to increases the amount of air moving internally and around the machine.

4. **What does the author recommend as the right way to find network problems?**

The right way to identify network problems involves buying a several–thousand-dollar piece of hardware that's specially designed for diagnosing network hardware. Unfortunately, unless you're rich or your organization is feeling unusually generous, you probably won't have access to one of these—but it still is the right way to go about things, in this author's opinion at least!

G

INDEX

Symbols

 # (pound sign)
    inetd daemon, 111
    mini-roots, 93
%CPU field (ps command), 610
%MEM field (ps command), 610
' (single quotes) shortcut, 119
. (dot), paths, 149
\ (backslash), commands, 147
/ (forward slash), root directories, 13-15, 125
100BASE-T cabling, 44
10BASE-2 cabling (thinnet), 43, 73
10BASE-T (twisted pair),
    cabling, 44-46
    hubs (networks), 573-574

3D images, 502-503
64-bit support (installing Solaris 7), 628
81gm Web site, 263

A

-a option (exportfs command), 329
abstraction, 13-15
acceptable-use guidelines
    common-sense rules, 535
    networks, 54
    reciprocity, 534-535
    UNIX system, 52-53
access
    court orders, 543
    denial of service attacks, 256

    guest access policies, 59
    hardware administrative access policy example, 68, 743
    hardware physical access policy example, 67, 743
    normal users, 148
    sudo, 312
        download site, 313
        installation, 313-314
        security issues, 315
        sudoers files, 313-314
        visudo editor, 314
    superuser, 24
        granting, 527-528
        legal issues, 541
        privacy issues, 530-537, 554-556
        security emergencies, 537-541
        sharing, 148
        traffic sniffing, 532-533, 538

S

SAMS Teach Yourself in **21** Days

Sams Teach Yourself in 21 Days *teaches you all the skills you need to master the basics and then moves on to the more advanced features and concepts. This series is designed for the way you learn. Go chapter by chapter through the step-by-step lessons or just choose those lessons that interest you the most.*

Microsoft SQL Server 7.0

*Richard Waymire,
Rick Sawtell*
ISBN: 0-672-31290-5
$39.99 US/$59.95 CAN

Other Sams Teach Yourself in 21 Days Titles

Java 1.2
*Laura Lemay,
Rogers Cadenhead*
ISBN: 1-57521-390-7
$29.99 US/$42.95 CAN

Internet Programming with Visual Basic
Peter Aitken
ISBN: 0-672-31459-2
$29.99 US/$42.95 CAN

Visual Basic 6
Greg Perry
ISBN: 0-672-31310-3
$29.99 US/$42.95 CAN

More Visual Basic 6
Lowell Mauer
ISBN: 0-672-31307-3
$29.99 US/$42.95 CAN

Microsoft Small Business Server 4.5
Harry Brelsford
ISBN: 0-672-31513-0
$29.99 US/$42.95 CAN

DB2 Universal Database
Susan Visser
ISBN: 0-672-31278-6
$49.99 US/$71.95 CAN

Active Server Pages 2.0
Sanjaya Hettihewa
ISBN: 0-672-31333-2
$34.99 US/$46.99 CAN

TCP/IP Network Administration
Brian Komar
ISBN: 0-672-31250-6
$29.99 US/$42.95 CAN

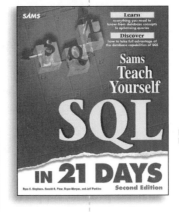

SQL

Bryan Morgan
ISBN: 0-672-31110-0
$39.99 US/$59.95 CAN

Web Publishing with HTML 4

*Laura Lemay,
Denise Tyler*
ISBN: 0-672-31345-6
$29.99 US/$42.95 CAN

SAMS

All prices are subject to change.

Get **FREE** books and more...when you register this book online for our Personal Bookshelf Program

http://register.samspublishing.com/

SAMS

Register online and you can sign up for our *FREE Personal Bookshelf Program*...unlimited access to the electronic version of more than 200 complete computer books—immediately! That means you'll h̶ ̶ ̶ ̶ ̶ ̶ ̶ ̶ ̶es of valuable information onscreen, at your fingertips!

including complimentary downloads, technical ̶anion Web sites, author sites, and more!

̶ceive a *FREE subscription to a weekly email* ̶s, announcements, sample book chapters, and ̶s, and various product giveaways!

̶e registration process takes only a few minutes ̶lue going—absolutely FREE!

̶ ̶ ̶his Great Opportunity!

Sams is a brand of Macmillan Computer Publishing USA.

For more information, please visit *www.mcp.com*